Egerton Ryerson

The loyalists of America and their times : from 1620 to 1816

Vol II

Egerton Ryerson

The loyalists of America and their times : from 1620 to 1816
Vol II

ISBN/EAN: 9783742858474

Manufactured in Europe, USA, Canada, Australia, Japa

Cover: Foto ©ninafisch / pixelio.de

Manufactured and distributed by brebook publishing software (www.brebook.com)

Egerton Ryerson

The loyalists of America and their times : from 1620 to 1816

THE
LOYALISTS OF AMERICA

AND

THEIR TIMES:

FROM 1620 TO 1816.

BY EGERTON RYERSON, D.D., LL.D.

*Chief Superintendent of Education for Upper Canada
from 1844 to 1876.*

IN TWO VOLUMES.

VOL. II.

TORONTO:
WILLIAM BRIGGS, 80 KING STREET EAST;
JAMES CAMPBELL & SON, AND
WILLING & WILLIAMSON.
MONTREAL: DAWSON BROTHERS.

1880.

CONTENTS.

CHAPTER XXVII.

ALLIANCE BETWEEN CONGRESS AND FRANCE NOT PRODUCTIVE OF THE EFFECT ANTICIPATED; EFFORTS OF THE BRITISH GOVERNMENT FOR RECONCILIATION WITH THE COLONIES 1-16

	PAGE
Alliance deferred twelve months by France after it was applied for by Congress, until the King of France was assured that no reconciliation would take place between England and the Colonies........................	1
Lord Admiral Howe and his brother, General Howe, Commissioners to confer with Congress with a view to reconciliation; their power limited; Congress refuses all conference with them, but the vast majority of the Colonists in favour of reconciliation.......................................	2
Reasons of the failure of the two Commissioners..........................	4
New penal laws against the Loyalists.....................................	5
Three Acts of Parliament passed to remove all grounds of complaint on the part of the Colonists, and the appointment of five Commissioners; Lord North's conciliatory speech; excitement and opposition in the Commons, but the bills were passed and received the royal assent................	6
Lord North's proposed resignation, and preparations for it..................	8
Opinions of Lords Macaulay and Mahon as to the success of a commission; proposed terms of reconciliation if appointed and proposed by the Earl of Chatham	8
The large powers and most liberal propositions of the five Royal Commissioners for reconciliation between the Colonies and the Mother Country.........	11
The refusal of all negotiation on the part of Congress; bound by treaty to the King of France to make no peace with England without the consent of the French Court	12
The three Acts of Parliament, and proposals of the five Commissioners of all that the Colonists had desired before the Declaration of Independence; but Congress had transferred allegiance from England to France, without even consulting their constituents.......................................	12
Appeal of the representative of France to the Canadians to detach Canada from England (in a note)...	12

iv   CONTENTS.

                                                                              PAGE
Sycophancy of the leaders of Congress to France against England............ 13
The feeling of the people in both England and America different from that of
    the leaders of Congress.... 14
The war more acrimonious after the alliance between Congress and the King
    of France and the failure of the British Commissioners to promote recon-
    ciliation between Great Britain and the Colonies........................ 16

CHAPTER XXVIII.

COMPLETE FAILURE OF THE FRENCH FLEET AND ARMY, UNDER COUNT D'ESTAING, TO ASSIST THE CONGRESS 17-32

Count D'Estaing arrives in America with a powerful fleet and several thousand
    soldiers... 17
Anchors off Sandy Hook for eleven days; goes to Long Island by Washington's
    advice, and sails up Newport River, whither he is pursued by the Lord
    Admiral Howe with a less powerful fleet; the ships, with 4,000 French
    soldiers and 10,000 Americans, to land and attack the British on Long
    Island, who were only 5,000 strong 17
The two fleets separated by a storm; only fighting between individual ships.. 18
Count D'Estaing, against the remonstrances and protests of American officers,
    determines to sail for Boston Harbour for the repair of his ships 18
Bitter feeling and riot between the American sailors and citizens and French
    seamen and soldiers in the streets of Boston.......................... 19
Raids in New England by British expeditions (in a note)................... 19
Differences between Count D'Estaing and the American officers as to the mode
    of attacking the British on Long Island............................. 19
Early in November Count D'Estaing with his fleet quitted the port of Boston
    and sailed for the West Indies, thus disappointing the hopes of the
    Americans from the French alliance.................................. 20
Count D'Estaing, though strengthened by the fleet of Count De Grasse, could
    not be induced to come to close fight with Admiral Byron.............. 21
The French take St. Vincent.. 21
Count D'Estaing complained of by the Americans to the French Court, which
    orders him to return to the American coasts and assist the Colonists..... 22
D'Estaing arrives suddenly on the American coasts with twenty-two sail-of-the-
    line and eleven frigates and six thousand soldiers; his magnificent plans
    and expectations... 22
D'Estaing arranges with General Lincoln to attack Savannah and rescue the
    province of Georgia, and afterwards other Southern provinces, from the
    British.. 23
Account of the Siege of Savannah, and the defeat of the French and their
    American allies; result of the contest............................... 24
Mutual recriminations and jealousies between the French and American
    officers; Count D'Estaing sails with his fleet for France............... 25
Why this minute account of Count D'Estaing's abortive expeditions to
    America; the barren results of the first two years' alliance between Con-
    gress and the King of France, by Dr. Ramsay........................ 27
Spain joins France against England in 1779 28

	PAGE
Low state of the American army and finances; discouragement and despondency of the Americans in 1780	28
The degeneracy of Congress in 1778, as stated by General Washington	29
Depreciation of public credit; sale of the confiscated property of "Tories"	30

CHAPTER XXIX.

1780—A YEAR OF WEAKNESS AND DISASTER TO THE AMERICAN CAUSE, AND OF SUCCESS TO THE BRITISH............32-41

Depression of American finances	32
Weakness of Washington's army	32
La Fayette returns from France with a loan of money and reinforcements of naval and land forces	33
The British receive naval reinforcement of war ships, and become superior to the French	33
Failure of the French reinforcements	33
Sir Henry Clinton goes South; besieges and takes Charleston	34
Conditions of the surrender and treatment of the inhabitants, as stated by Dr. Ramsay and misrepresented by Mr. Bancroft	35
Sir Henry Clinton's bad administration and bad proclamation in South Carolina; his exaggerated statements of his success; re-embarks at Charleston for New York	36
Expeditions to secure the universal submission of the people; but they weakened the cause of the British in the hearts of the people	36
The military power of Congress reduced and crushed in the Southern States	37
Lord Cornwallis's antecedents, and those of Lord Rawdon (afterwards Marquis of Hastings); but their severe policy unjustifiable and injurious to the British cause	38
Military proceedings in the North also unfavourable to the Congress; its confessed weakness and gloomy prospects	40
Appeal of Congress to France for men and money as their only hope	40
Washington's despondency without French aid (in a note)	41
Mr. Hildreth, the historian, on the gloomy state of American affairs at the close of the year 1780, though the English victories and rule did not attract the hearts of the people to the British cause	41

CHAPTER XXX.

THE FRENCH AND CONGRESS ALLIES RECOVER VIRGINIA; SURRENDER OF LORD CORNWALLIS; RESULTS 42-52

General Washington and the French Commander plan an expedition to the South	42
Sir Henry Clinton deceived as to their design	43
Count De Grasse sails for the Chesapeake with a fleet of 28 ships and 7,000 French troops	43
Remarkable march of the allied army, five hundred miles from New York to Virginia, without committing any depredations whatever upon the inhabitants, even in the season of fruits	43

	PAGE
Plan of the siege of York Town.....................................	44
Earl Cornwallis's measures of defence...............................	44
Position and strength of the allied forces, and their process of operations......	45
Lord Cornwallis's courageous and protracted defence ; is disappointed of promised reinforcements from New York	45
Lord Cornwallis capitulates to superior forces	45
Conditions of capitulation...	46
Circumstances of the Loyalists.......................................	46
Groundless boastings of American orators and writers over the surrender of Lord Cornwallis, commanding but a small part of the British forces.....	47
The unrivalled skill and courage of Washington undoubted, as well as the bravery and endurance of his soldiers ; but the success of the siege of York Town chiefly owing to the French, but for whose ships, artillery and land forces, Lord Cornwallis would have been the conqueror, rather than conquered, in this famous siege and battle	47
The resources of England ; the peace party opposed to the continuance of the American War irrespective of the Battle of York Town................	48
The war party and corrupt administration at length defeated in the House of Commons, after repeated and protracted debates and various intrigues..	50
Change of Government, and end of Lord North's twelve years' administration	51
Seven years' war and bloodshed, and an unnatural alliance would have been prevented, liberty secured, and the united life of the Anglo-Saxon race saved, had Congress, in 1776, adhered to its previous professions (in a note)..	52

CHAPTER XXXI.

CHANGE OF ADMINISTRATION IN ENGLAND ; CHANGE OF POLICY FOR BOTH ENGLAND AND THE COLONIES ; PEACE NEGOTIATIONS AT PARIS ; CAUSE OF THE UNITED EMPIRE LOYALISTS ; CHANGE OF MINISTRY ; THE KING COMPELLED TO YIELD.................... 53-65

Names of the new Ministers; death of the Marquis of Rockingham, the Premier, succeeded by the Earl of Shelburne, in consequence of which several Ministers resign, and are succeeded by others, among whom was Pitt, as Chancellor of the Exchequer (in a note)......................	53
Correspondence between Dr. Franklin, at Paris, and the Earl of Shelburne, which led to negotiations for peace..................................	54
Parliament does not pass an Act to authorize peace with America until three months after the accession of the new Ministry........................	54
Dr. Franklin proposes to include *Canada* in the United States.............	54
English and American Commissioners meet at Paris and hold protracted negotiations, with many delays, in regard to terms of peace............... .	56
Two most difficult questions of the treaty—The fishing grounds of Newfoundland and the Loyalists..	56
It was agreed that the Americans should have the right to take fish on the Banks of Newfoundland, but not to dry or cure them on any of the King's settled dominions..,.........	56
Preamble and articles of the treaty (in a note).............................	56
The most important question of the Loyalists............................	57

	PAGE
They constituted the majority of the population of the Colonies at the beginning of the contest	57
It was at length agreed that the Congress should recommend to the several States to compensate the Loyalists ; but Dr. Franklin anticipated no success from it, as of course he did not desire it	58
Dr. Franklin's counter-scheme to defeat the proposition of the English Commissioners, who gave way	58
Dr. Ramsay on the Loyalists being "sacrificed" to their sufferings	59
Mr. Hildreth on the same subject	61
What was demanded for the Loyalists had been sanctioned by all modern civilized nations in like circumstances	61
How honourable to the United States to have imitated such examples	62
The fallacy of the plea or pretext that Congress had no power to grant an amnesty and compensation to the Loyalists	62
Severe censure of the royal historian, Dr. Andrews, upon the English Commissioners for having agreed to sacrifice the Loyalists (in a note)	62
"All parties in the Commons unanimously demand amnesty and indemnity for the Loyalists." (Bancroft, in a note)	62
Dr. Franklin and his colleagues outwitted the English Commissioners not only in regard to the Loyalists but also in regard to immense territories	63
Deplorable condition of the Loyalists during the war ; utter abandonment by the English Commissioners	64

CHAPTER XXXII.

ORIGIN OF REPUBLICANISM AND HATRED OF MONARCHY IN AMERICA ; THOS. PAINE, SKETCH OF HIS LIFE, CHARACTER, AND WRITINGS, AND THEIR EFFECTS..66-71

CHAPTER XXXIII.

THE HIRING OF FOREIGN SOLDIERS AND EMPLOYMENT OF INDIANS IN THE CIVIL WAR 72-84

The policy of the British Ministry in employing foreign soldiers and Indians in the war with the Colonies deprecated by all classes in England and America and throughout Europe	72
Violent opposition in Parliament to the hiring of foreign troops ; exasperation in the Colonies (in a note)	73
Unreliable and bad character of the Hessian mercenaries	74
Remarks upon the bad policy of employing them, and their bad conduct, by the royal historian (in a note)	74
The employment of Indians still more condemned and denounced than the hiring of foreign troops	74
Employment of Indians by both the French and English during the war of 1755-63, between France and England	75
At the close of the war the French authorities recommended the Indians to cultivate the friendship of England	75
Both Congress and the English sought the alliance and co-operation of the Indians ; misstatements of the Declaration of Independence on this	

	PAGE
subject (in a note); the advantages of the latter over the former in conciliating the Indians	75
The employment of the Indians in every respect disadvantageous to England	76
English Generals in America individually opposed to the employment of the Indians in the military campaigns	76
Failure, if not defeat, of General Burgoyne's army by the bad conduct, and desertion, of his Indian allies	76
But Washington and Congress, as well as the English Government, sanctioned the employment of the Indians in the war, and the first idea of thus employing them originated with the first promoters of revolution in Massachusetts	77
Omissions of American writers to state that the aggressions and retaliations of the Congress soldiers and their coadjutors far exceeded in severity and destruction the aggressions and retaliations of the Indians on the white inhabitants	77
Many letters and biographies of actors in the Revolution show that very much of what was written or reported during the Revolution against the English Loyalists and Indians was fictitious or exaggerated	78
Proceedings of the Provincial Congress of Massachusetts (before the affairs of Concord and Lexington) to enlist and employ the Indians against the British	79
General Washington, under date of July 27th, 1776, recommends the employment of Indians in the revolutionary cause	80
The Americans have no ground of boasting over the English in regard to the employment of Indians and their acts during the war	81
Efforts of General Burgoyne to restrain the Indians, who were an incumbrance to his army, and whose conduct alienated great numbers of Loyalists from the British cause	82
The conduct and dread of the Indians roused great numbers to become recruits in General Gates' army, and thus rendered it far more numerous than the army of General Burgoyne (in a note)	83
American invasion and depredations in the Indian country the latter part of 1776, as stated by Dr. Ramsay	84
The invasion unprovoked, but professedly as a "precaution" to "prevent all future co-operation between the Indians and British in that quarter" bordering in Virginia, North and South Carolina, and Georgia	84
Complete destruction of Indian settlements; their country a desolation	84

CHAPTER XXXIV.

THE MASSACRE OF WYOMING; FOUR VERSIONS OF IT BY ACCREDITED AMERICAN HISTORIANS, ALL DIFFERING FROM EACH OTHER; THE FACTS INVESTIGATED AND FALSE STATEMENTS CORRECTED.....................85-98

The original inflated and imaginary accounts of the "Massacre of Wyoming"	85
Four versions of it by accredited historians	85
The account given by Dr. Ramsay	87
Remarks upon Dr. Ramsay's account	88
Description of Wyoming	88
Mr. Bancroft's account of the "Massacre"	88

	PAGE
Mr. Tucker's brief account of the "Massacre"	90
Mr. Hildreth's more intelligible and consistent account of the "Massacre"	90
Remarks on the discrepancies in four essential particulars of these four accounts	94
Supplementary remarks, founded on Colonel Stone's refutation of the original fabulous statements of the "Massacre," in his "*Life of Joseph Brant, including the Border Wars of the American Revolution*"	98

CHAPTER XXXV.

AMERICAN RETALIATION FOR THE ALLEGED "MASSACRE OF WYOMING," AS NARRATED BY AMERICAN HISTORIANS 99-122

Destruction of Indian villages and settlements for several miles on both sides of the Susquehanna by the Americans	99
Attack in retaliation "by Indians and Tories" on Cherry Valley, but more than revenged by Colonel G. Van Shaick on the settlements	99
The destruction of Indian villages and other settlements to the extent of "several miles on both sides of the Susquehanna," more than an equivalent revenge for the destruction of Wyoming (in a note)	100
This only the beginning of vengeance upon the Indian settlements on the part of the "Continentals;" cruelties compared	100
General Sullivan's expedition, and destruction of the towns, settlements, crops, and orchards of the Six Nations of Indians, as stated by Dr. Andrews	100
The same expedition, as stated by Mr. Bancroft, Mr. Hildreth, Mr. Holmes, and Dr. Ramsay	102
Further examples of "retaliation," so-called, inflicted upon the Indians and their settlements (in a note)	106
The "Tories," driven among the Indians as their only refuge, treated as traitors; their conduct and duty	108
Colonel Stone's account in detail of General Sullivan's expedition of extermination against the Six Nations of Indians	108
Dr. Franklin's fictions on the massacre and scalping of the whites by Indians, in order to inflame the American mind against England; his fictions recorded as history	115
Injustice done to the Indians in American accounts of them; their conduct compared with that of their white enemies	119

CHAPTER XXXVI.

SITUATION AND TREATMENT OF THE LOYALISTS DURING THE WAR....123-138

Summary of the condition and treatment of the Loyalists	123
The relation of both parties before the Declaration of Independence	123
How the Declaration of Independence changed the relations of parties both in England and America	123
At the Declaration of Independence the adherents to England the largest part of the population of the Colonies	124
Elements of their affectionate attachment to England	125
Their claims to have their rights and liberties respected	125

x   CONTENTS.

                                                                        PAGE
Their position and character stated by Mr. Hildreth; abused by mobs and
    oppressed by new Acts and authorities................................ 125
John Adams the prompter and adviser for hanging "Tories;" his letter to
    the Governor of Massachusetts on the subject......................... 127
First scene of severity against Loyalists at Boston; new American maxim of
    morals for not forgiving "Tories".................................... 127
Treatment of Loyalists in New York, Philadelphia, Virginia, and other places 128
Kindness of the French officers and soldiers after the defeat of Lord Cornwallis 129

APPENDIX TO CHAPTER XXXVI.

State Legislative and Executive acts against the Loyalists............... 130
Rhode Island; Connecticut.. 130
Massachusetts.. 131
New Hampshire; Virginia; New York.. 131
New Jersey; Pennsylvania; Delaware....................................... 132
Maryland; North Carolina; Georgia.. 132
South Carolina... 134
Remarks on the Confiscation Acts and policy of the several States mentioned. 136

CHAPTER XXXVII.

TREATMENT OF THE LOYALISTS ON THEIR APPLICATIONS FOR REDRESS AFTER
    THE REVOLUTION 139-144
Impolicy of such persecuting proceedings on the part of the States, by an
    American writer.. 141

APPENDIX "A" TO CHAPTER XXXVII.

Review of the principal characteristics of the American Revolution, and re-
    marks on the feelings which should now be cultivated by both of the
    former contending parties, by Mr. J. M. Ludlow....................... 145

APPENDIX "B" TO CHAPTER XXXVII.

Reflections of Lord Mahon on the American contest; apology for George III.;
    unhappiness of Americans since the Revolution; unity of the Anglo-
    Saxon Race... 154

CHAPTER XXXVIII.

TREATMENT OF THE LOYALISTS BY THE BRITISH GOVERNMENT AND PAR-
    LIAMENT AFTER THE REVOLUTION 159-182

PART FIRST.

Proceedings in Parliament; refusal of the States to compensate the Loyalists,
    as proposed in the Treaty of Peace, and contrary to the example and prac-
    tice of civilized nations... 159

CONTENTS. xi

PAGE

In the House of Commons, Mr. Wilberforce, Lord North, Lord Mulgrave, Secretary Townsend, Mr. Burke, Mr. Sheridan, Mr. Norton, Sir Peter Burrell, Sir William Bootle, and other members of Parliament, spoke on the subject 160
In the House of Lords, Lords Walsingham, Townsend, Stormont, Sackville, Loughborough and Shelburne, also advocated the claims of the Loyalists. 163
Grounds of the responsibility of Parliament to the Loyalists for compensation 164
Unpopular and unprecedented omissions in the terms of Peace 164
Fallacy of the argument of advocates of the Treaty........................ 165

PART SECOND.

Agents in England of the Loyalists ; proceedings of the Parliamentary Commission ; results 166-182

CHAPTER XXXIX.

THE LOYALISTS DRIVEN FROM THE UNITED STATES TO THE BRITISH PROVINCES 183-190

CHAPTER XL.

BRIEF SKETCHES OF SOME INDIVIDUAL LOYALISTS IN THE BRITISH PROVINCES; FIRST SETTLERS IN CANADA, AND HOW THEY TRAVELLED HITHER 190-208

1. Samuel Anderson ; 2. Rev. John Bethune ; 3. Doanes—five brothers ; 4. Stephen Jarvis ; 5. Wm. Jarvis ; 6. David Jones ; 7. Jonathan Jones ; 8. Captain Richard Lippincott ; 9. The McDonalds ; 10. John McGill ; 11. Donald McGillis ; 12. Thomas Merritt ; 13. Beverley Robinson ; 14. Beverley Robinson, jun.; 15. Christopher Robinson ; 16. Sir John Beverley Robinson ; 17. Sir Charles Frederick Phillipse Robinson ; 18. Morris Robinson; 19. John Robinson ; 20. Roger Morris ; 21. Allen McNab ; 22. Luke Carscallian ; 23. John Diamond ; 24. Ephraim Tisdale; 25. Lemuel Wilmot ....
Dr. Canniff's account of the migration of the first Loyalists from Lower Canada, and settlement on the North Shore of the St. Lawrence, and in the country round and west of Kingston 204

CHAPTER XLI.

FIRST SETTLEMENT OF LOYALISTS IN THE BRITISH PROVINCES—ESPECIALLY OF UPPER CANADA,—THEIR ADVENTURES AND HARDSHIPS, AS WRITTEN BY THEMSELVES OR THEIR DESCENDANTS....................208-270

First settlement of the first company of Loyalists at the close of the Revolutionary War, in and near Kingston, Upper Canada, by the late Bishop Richardson, D.D. 208
First settlement of Loyalists in Nova Scotia, by a gentleman of that Province 211

CONTENTS

	PAGE
Colonel Joseph Robinson, his adventures and settlement, by the late Hon. R. Hodgson, Chief Justice of Prince Edward Island	213
Robert Clark, his sufferings in the Revolutionary War, and settlement in the Midland District, U. C.; by his son, late Colonel John C. Clark	216
Captain William B. Hutchinson, his sufferings and settlement in Walsingham, County of Norfolk, U. C.; by his grandson, J. B. Hutchinson, Esq.	218
Patriotic feeling and early settlement of Prince Edward County and neighboring Townships; by Canniff Haight, Esq.	219
Colonel Samuel Ryerse, his adventures, settlement, and character, in the County of Norfolk; in letters by his son, the late Rev. George J. Ryerse; and in a memorandum, including a history of the early settlement of the County of Norfolk, and recollections of the war of 1812-1815; by Mrs. Amelia Harris, of Eldon House, London, U. C.	226
Colonel Joseph Ryerson, his adventures, sufferings, and settlement in the County of Norfolk, U. C.; by an intimate friend of the family	257
NOTE.—Colonel Samuel Ryerse and Colonel Joseph Ryerson were brothers, and both officers in the British army during the Revolutionary War; but in the commission of the former, his name was spelled Ryerse; and it being difficult at that time to correct such an error, he and his descendants have always spelt their name Ryerse, though the original name of the family, in the records of New Jersey, in Holland, and previously in the history of Denmark, is Ryerson.	
Interesting piece of local history; by the Rev. Dr. Scadding	259
Loyalty and sufferings of the Hon. John Monroe; by his son	261
Sufferings of the U. E. Loyalists during the Revolutionary War; vindication of their character—including that of Butler's Rangers—their privations and settlement in Canada; by the late Mrs. Elizabeth Bowman Spohn, of Ancaster, in the County of Wentworth, U.C., together with an introductory letter by the writer of this history	264

CHAPTER XLII.

ORIGIN AND CHARACTER OF THE GOVERNMENTS OF BRITISH NORTH AMERICA—NOVA SCOTIA	271-276

CHAPTER XLIII.

NEW BRUNSWICK	277-280

CHAPTER XLIV.

PRINCE EDWARD ISLAND	280

CHAPTER XLV.

GOVERNMENT OF LOWER CANADA	281-306
The famous Quebec Act, 14th Geo. III.; its provisions; why and by whom opposed; opposed in the Lords and Commons, and in the Colonies; supposed to have promoted the American Declaration of Independence	281

CONTENTS.

	PAGE
Constitutional Act of 1791—Act 31st George III., chapter 31	285

Mr. Pitt explains the principal provisions of the Bill; provided against the imposition of taxes in the colonies by the Imperial Parliament; opposed by some members in the Commons; rupture between Burke and Fox (in a note); Pitt's defence of the Bill... 285

The Bill becomes an Act; separates Upper from Lower Canada; constitutes a legislature for each province; how the two branches of the legislature were constituted; the *representative* form of government obtained by the United Empire Loyalists... 286

The Administration of the Government and Legislation in Lower Canada under the new constitution.. 288

Lord Dorchester Governor-General; first session of the Legislature; Speakers of the two Houses; a Speaker elected in the House of Assembly who could speak both the French and English language......................... 289

The Governor's first speech to the Legislature 290

The cordial and loyal response of the House of Assembly................... 290

Useful and harmonious legislation; a noble example and illustration of loyalty by the House of Assembly before the close of the session............... 292

The Governor's speech at the close of the session.............................. 294

Unjust statements against the French corrected (in a note)................. 294

Second session of the Legislature called by Lord Dorchester on his arrival from England; his cordial reception; beneficial legislation; Canadians recoil from the horrors of the French Revolution 295

French Republican agents endeavour to incite Canadians to revolt, and to excite hostilities against England in the United States 297

Mutual cordiality between the Governor-General and the House of Assembly.. 297

Visit of the Duke of Kent to Lower Canada as Commander of the Forces; his wise and patriotic counsels; beneficial influence of his visit and residence. 297

Lord Dorchester lays the public accounts before the Assembly; their contents; this proceeding highly satisfactory to the Assembly; bills passed and assented to 298

Interval of quiet between the second and third Sessions of the Legislature; Lord Dorchester's practical and noble speech at the opening of the third Session; Mr. Christie's remarks upon it; cordial answer of the House of Assembly, to whom the public accounts were transmitted, even more comprehensive and complete than those sent down the previous Session.. 299

Commissioners first appointed to adjust the revenues between Upper and Lower Canada; their courteous and fair proceedings on both sides...... 301

Gratifying close of the third Session... 302

Auspicious opening, useful legislation, and happy conclusion of the fourth and last Session of the first Parliament of Lower Canada..................... 302

Termination of Lord Dorchester's thirty-six years connection with Canada; review of his conduct and character by the historian Bancroft; cordial addresses to him, and his affectionate answers....................................... 303

Meritorious conduct of the French Canadians................................... 305

CHAPTER XLVI.

GOVERNMENT OF UPPER CANADA 307-315

PAGE

How governed and divided by Lord Dorchester before the Constitutional Act of 1791.. 307
The Constitutional Act of 1791, 31 George III., chapter 31, and construction of governments under it 307
General John Graves Simcoe the first Governor; character of his government; arrives at Kingston 8th July, 1792, where the members of the Executive Legislative Councils were sworn into office, and writs issued for the election of members of the House of Assembly............................. 308
The seat of government first established at Newark, now Niagara, where a small frame house was built for the Governor, and in which also the first Session of the Legislature was held.. 308
Number of members of the Legislative Council and House of Assembly present at the opening of the Session; their character............................. 309
Number and character of the population of the country, including the Mohawk Indians, headed by Joseph Brant 309
First Session of the first Parliament and its work........................... 309
Remarkable speech of Governor Simcoe at the close of the Session, explanatory of our constitution of government................................... 310
Change of the seat of government and reasons for it......................... 311
Governor Simcoe's work and policy; removal to the West Indies, and abandonment of his wise policy 311
Parliament meets at Niagara until 1797; its legislation; Governor Simcoe's successor, the Hon. Peter Russell and General Hunter; population of Upper Canada in 1800 312
Legislation, progress, trade, custom-houses.................................. 313
Provision for one Grammar School Master in each of the eight districts...... 314
Emigration; legislation; experience of the country during sixteen years under the new constitution 314
State of the country in 1809. 314
Anticipated hostilities between Great Britain and the United States; concluding remarks on this period of Canadian history............................. 315

CHAPTER XLVII.

WAR OF THE UNITED STATES AGAINST GREAT BRITAIN, FROM 1812 TO 1815 316-317

Introductory and general remarks; illustrations of true loyalty; war struggles of England for human liberty when the United States joined the tyrant of Europe in war and invaded Canada; comparative population of Canada and the United States; Canada, almost unaided, successfully resists the eleven invasions of the United States against her; phases of the war against her 316

CHAPTER XLVIII.

DECLARATION OF WAR BY THE UNITED STATES AGAINST BRITAIN, AND PRE-
PARATIONS FOR THE INVASION OF CANADA 318-330

PAGE

The alleged and real causes of the war; the Democratic party in the United
States always hostile to England and her colonies, and sympathisers with
every raid against Canada 318
Two alleged causes for the war by the United States; Berlin decrees, and
answers to them by British Orders in Council—results............... 319
Collusion between Napoleon and the President of the United States against
England; seduction and desertion of British sailors (nearly 10,000) besides soldiers; the justice and acknowledged right of the British claims,
and injustice and unreasonableness of the Madison Government's proceedings 319
The event between the war-ships' *Leopard* and *Chesapeake*; American misrepresentations of it; dishonest conduct of President Madison in respect
to it; noble and generous proposal of the British Government, disclaim-
ing the conduct of the captain of the *Leopard*, and offering to compensate
all parties for injuries done them by the *Leopard*................. 323
The "Henry Plot" affair; conduct of President Madison in respect to it;
declaration of war by the United States........................... 327

CHAPTER XLIX.

DECLARATION OF WAR BY THE UNITED STATES.................... 331-336

Declaration of war, June 18, 1812; votes in the House of Representatives for
and against it 331
Character of the war party and its Generals 333
Opposition to the war, and reasons against it, by a State Convention of New
York.. 333
Address of the House of Representatives of Massachusetts against the war... 334
The Orders in Council, as administered, beneficial to American merchants... 335

CHAPTER L.

PREPARATIONS MADE BY THE CANADIANS FOR THEIR DEFENCE....... 337-351

War against the Canadas being contemplated in the United States......... 337
Preparations by Lower Canada; Sir George Prevost succeeds Sir James Craig
as Governor-General; his character and first speech to the Legislature.. 338
The loyal answer of the Assembly, and liberal provisions for the defence of the
Province 338
Organization of militia 339
American residents allowed twenty days to leave the Province............. 340
Second Session of the War Legislature, 16th July, 1812; the Governor's
speech, relying upon the Province, and noble reply, and further various
and liberal supplies and measures of the Legislative Assembly to meet the
emergency 340

CONTENTS.

	PAGE
Preparations in Upper Canada for self-defence	341

General Brock calls a meeting of the Legislature, July 27, 1812; his stirring speech at the opening of the session; hearty response and liberal supplies of the House of Assembly...... 342

Patriotic address of the Assembly to the people of Upper Canada, and remarks upon it...... 342

CHAPTER LI.

FIRST INVASION OF UPPER CANADA, IN THE WESTERN DISTRICT, BY GENERAL HULL, AND HIS PROCLAMATION TO THE INHABITANTS OF UPPER CANADA, GIVEN ENTIRE IN A NOTE...... 346-351

General Brock's manly and overwhelming reply to General Hull's proclamation, in an address to the people of Canada 349

CHAPTER LII.

GENERAL BROCK TAKES DETROIT, GENERAL HULL'S ARMY, THE TERRITORY OF MICHIGAN, AND IMMENSE MILITARY STORES...... 352-364

INCIDENTS OF THIS GREAT ACHIEVEMENT.

1. Smallness of General Brock's army, and the manner in which he collected it 353

Preparations at Windsor for the attack upon Detroit before General Brock's arrival there...... 353

Crossing the river, and the surrender of Fort Detroit, &c...... 354

2. General Brock's council with the Indians at Sandwich before crossing the river at Detroit; his conversation with the great chief Tecumseh; and after the taking of Detroit, takes off his sash and places it around Tecumseh, who next day placed it around the Wyandot chief, Round Head; reasons for it given to General Brock...... 355

General Brock's estimate of Tecumseh, and the latter's watching and opinion on the conduct of the former...... 356

Particulars of Tecumseh's personal history and death (in a note) 357

Surprise and taking of Michillimackinack, and other defeats, discouraging to General Hull, before his surrender of Detroit 358

Particulars of the surrender...... 361

General Brock's proclamation to the people of Michigan...... 362

Remarks on the difference in sentiment and style between this proclamation to the inhabitants of Michigan and that of General Hull to the inhabitants of Canada...... 363

General Brock's return to York; having in 19 days settled public legislative business, raised a little army, taken a territory nearly as large as Upper Canada, and an army three times as numerous as his own...... 364

CONTENTS. xvii

CHAPTER LIII.

SECOND INVASION OF UPPER CANADA AT QUEENSTON 365-371

PAGE

Crossing of the river from Lewiston to Queenston of 1,500 regular troops, who, by a private path, gain Queenston Heights ; death of General Brock ; the invaders dislodged from the Heights and driven down the banks of the river ; American militia refuse to cross the river ; American soldiers surrender to General Sheaffe to the number of 900 men, besides officers, including General Wadsworth and Colonel Winfield Scott................ 365
Armistice.. 368
Incidents on the Niagara frontier after the death of General Brock, by Lieutenant Driscoll, of the 100th Regiment 368

CHAPTER LIV.

THIRD AMERICAN INVASION OF CANADA 372-379

A large American army assembled ; confidence of its success................ 372
No reinforcements from England ; but the sacrifice and zeal of the Canadians for the defence of their country against this third and most formidable invasion of the year 373
The Commander-in-Chief's (General Smyth) address to his army, given entire in a note... 373
Its effect to bring 2,000 volunteers from the State of Pennsylvania 374
The troops embark ; General Smyth does not appear ; failure of the attempted invasion ; General Smyth's flight from his own soldiers, who shoot off their guns in disgust and indignation.................................. 375
Three armies, altogether of 10,000 men, defeated by less than 1,000 Canadian volunteers and soldiers... 378

CHAPTER LV.

AN INVADING ARMY OF 10,000 MEN, UNDER GENERAL DEARBORN, DEFEATED BY COLONEL DE SALABERRY, WITH 300 CANADIANS, AT CHATEAUGUAY; DESCRIPTION OF THE BATTLE 380-382

The Canadian militia put in readiness to repel a second apprehended invasion, but General Dearborn does not venture it, and retires with his hosts into winter quarters 381
The Canadian militia allowed to retire for the winter...................... 382
The armistice between Generals Sheaffe and Smyth injurious to Upper Canada (in a note)... 382

CHAPTER LVI.

CAMPAIGNS OF 1813 383-425

Americans determined to conquer Canada this year...................... 383
Disadvantage of the Governor-General of Canada from the fewness of his troops, regulars and militia, compared with those of the invading armies........ 383

xviii CONTENTS.

PAGE

Three American invading armies—one consisting of 18,000 men, the second of 7,000 men, and the third of 8,000 men 384
General Proctor's slender force at Detroit 384
Battle of Frenchtown ; victory of Colonel Proctor ; American misrepresentations respecting it corrected.................................. 385
Colonel Proctor promoted to be General 388
Several American plundering raids on Brockville and neighbourhood ; retaliatory raid of the British on Ogdensburg ; town ordnance, arms, &c., taken, and vessels destroyed 388
Canadian preparations in the winter of 1813 for the season's campaign ; U. E. Loyalist regiment comes from Fredericton, New Brunswick, to Quebec, on snow shoes.................................. 390
The American plan of campaign to invade and take Canada in 1813 390
The American fleet on Lake Ontario superior to the British fleet ; attack upon York with 1,700 men, commanded by Generals Dearborn and Pike ; battle, explosion of a magazine; many of both armies killed ; Canadians defeated and York taken.................................. 391
Americans evacuate York and return to Sackett's Harbour, after having destroyed public buildings, and taken much booty.................................. 393
Americans attack Fort George, Newark (Niagara), by land and water, and after a hard fight take the town and fort, the British retiring to Queenston 393
General Vincent, having destroyed the fortifications on the frontier, retreats to Burlington Heights, pursued by Generals Chandler and Winder, with an army of 3,500 infantry and 300 cavalry 394
Colonel Harvey, with 700 men, surprises the whole American army at Stoney Creek, captures their two generals and 150 men, &c.................................. 395
American army retreats in great disorder towards Fort George.................................. 396
The affair at the Beaver Dams; the capture of 700 American soldiers, with their officers, by a small party of soldiers and Indians—the captured prisoners being five to one of their captors.................................. 397
The American army confined to Fort George and its neighbourhood.................................. 397
A small party of the British retaliate the marauding game of the Americans by crossing the river at Chippewa, attacking and dismantling Fort Schlosser and bringing off military stores ; and seven days afterwards, 11th July, crossing from Fort Erie to Black Rock, and burning the enemy's blockhouses, stores, barracks, dockyards, &c 397
The two armies almost within gunshot of each other at Fort George ; but the Americans could not be drawn out to a battle, though their numbers were two to one to the British.................................. 398
General Harrison prepares to prosecute the war for recovering the Territories of Michigan ; General Proctor raises the siege of Lower Sandusky, and retires to Amherstburg.................................. 399
Unsuccessful expedition of Governor-General Prevost and Sir James L. Yeo against Sackett's Harbour ; Sir George Prevost orders the withdrawment of the troops, at the very crisis of victory, to the great disappointment and dissatisfaction of his officers and men.................................. 399

OCCURRENCES ON LAKE ONTARIO.

	PAGE
Second unsuccessful attempt of Commodore Sir James Yeo on Sackett's Harbour	401
Commodore Chauncey's expedition to the head of the lake to take Burlington Heights is deferred by the preparations of Colonels Harvey and Battersby to receive him	402
Commodore Chauncey makes a second raid upon York (Toronto), plunders, burns, and departs; singular coincidence	402
The British fleet, sailing from Kingston the last day of July, with supplies for the army at the head of the lake, encounters the American fleet at Niagara, and after two days' manœuvring, a partial engagement ensues, in which the British capture two small vessels—the *Julia* and *Growler*	402
A graphic account of the naval manœuvring and battle by the American historian of the war, Breckenridge (in a note)	402
Encounters and tactics of the British and American fleets on Lake Ontario for the rest of the season	404

OCCURRENCES ON LAKE ERIE AND IN THE WEST.

Fleet fitting out by Commodore Perry at Presqu' Isle (Erie) blockaded by Commodore Barclay, who, neglecting his duty and absenting himself from Presqu' Isle, allowed the American fleet to get over the bar at the mouth of the harbour, and getting into the lake with their cannon reshipped and completely equipped	405
Commodore Barclay, the enemy too well manned and too powerful for him, sails for Amherstburg; is pursued by Commodore Perry and compelled to fight, in which he lost his fleet, though he fought bravely	406
In consequence of the loss of the fleet on Lake Erie, the British army in possession of the territory of Michigan, left without resources, evacuate the territory and Fort Detroit, before an American army of 7,000 men and 1,000 dragoons, under General Harrison	407
General Proctor retreats up the Thames; is pursued by General Harrison, with a force of 3,000 men, including 1,000 Kentucky dragoons, and overtaken near Moravian Town, where a battle ensues, in which General Proctor is defeated with heavy loss—the Indians remaining loyal, fighting longest, suffering most, with the loss of their chief, Tecumseh	408
Shameful burning of Moravian Town by the Americans	410
Americans accept Indian alliance; Americans intoxicated by these successes, but driven from every inch of Canadian territory before the end of the year	410

AMERICAN INVASION OF LOWER CANADA.

Defeat of an American advance invading division, and capture of two vessels, the *Growler* and *Eagle*, of eleven guns each, at the Isle-aux-Noix, by 108 men, under the command of Lieut.-Col. George Taylor	411
Attacks upon and capture and destruction of the American war materials, hospitals, barracks, &c., at Plattsburg, under Colonel Murray (General Moore retreating with 1,500 men), at Burlington (where was encamped General Hampton with 4,000 men), capturing and destroying four vessels, and	

CONTENTS.

afterwards at the towns of Champlain and Swanton, destroying the blockhouses and barracks 412
These successes but preliminary to the Canadian victories of Chateauguay, and Chrysler's Farm.. 413

BATTLE OF CHATEAUGUAY.

General Hampton, with 5,000 men, defeated by the skill and courage of Colonel DeSalaberry with 300 Canadians; the battle described, and the close of it witnessed, by the Governor-General Prevost and Major-General DeWatteville 413
General Hampton with his demoralized army retires into winter quarters at Plattsburg.. 417
Next expedition against Montreal by the St. Lawrence, under command of General Wilkinson, with a force of 10,000 men; the American soldiers promised grand winter quarters at Montreal.. 417
American army descends the St. Lawrence from near Kingston in 300 boats; is followed by a detachment of the British from Kingston, under the command of Lieutenant-Colonel Morrison, who overtakes and skirmishes with divisions of the American army on the way; at the American post, at the town of Hamilton, takes a considerable quantity of provisions and stores, and two pieces of ordnance.. 418

BATTLE OF CHRYSLER'S FARM.

American force engaged between 3,000 and 4,000 men; the British forces were about 800 rank and file; preliminaries and description of the battle, said to be the most squarely and scientifically fought battle of the war....... 419
Losses; General Wilkinson's testimony as to the loyalty and courage of the Canadians 420
General Wilkinson proceeds down the St. Lawrence with his flotilla; disappointment and mortification at General Hampton's disobedience and failure to meet him at St. Regis; crosses the St. Lawrence and retires into winter quarters at Salmon River 420
The campaign of the season terminated in Lower Canada; the Canadian militia dismissed to their homes with thanks and applause.. 421

BRITISH VICTORIES IN UPPER CANADA.

In December, 1813, Lieutenant-General Drummond supersedes Major-General DeRottenburgh in command of Upper Canada, and proceeds to York and the head of the Lake at Burlington Heights; despatches Colonel Murray to arrest the predatory incursions of General McClure in the neighbourhood of Fort George, of which he was then in possession.. 422
McClure's plundering the inhabitants; his barbarous act in burning the town of Newark (Niagara), and flight to the American side of the river 423
The British, under command of Colonel Murray, take Fort Niagara, the whole garrison, and much warlike supplies 423
Lewiston, Manchester, Black Rock and Buffalo destroyed in retaliation for the burning of Newark (Niagara), and exposure of 400 women and children, by McClure 424

Proclamation issued by General Drummond, deprecating this savage mode of warfare, and declaring his purpose not to pursue it, unless compelled by the measures of the American Government.................................... 425

CHAPTER LVII.

MOVEMENTS AND CAMPAIGNS IN 1814—THE THIRD AND LAST YEAR OF THE WAR 426-434

Two years' expensive failures of American invasions against Canada; preparations on both sides for the third year's campaigns................... 426
Volunteers, soldiers and sailors, march through the woods from New Brunswick to Canada... 426
Expression of Royal satisfaction and admiration of the loyalty and courage of the Canadians during the war, making special mention of the affair of Chateauguay and Colonel De Salaberry 427
First American invasion of Lower Canada in 1814; the American soldiers, crossing Lake Champlain on the ice, attack LeColle Mill (Block-house), and are driven back by a small but heroic force of Canadians.......... 427
General Wilkinson returns with his army to Plattsburg; and, disappointed and mortified at his failures, retires from the army................... 428
Prairie du Chien, on the Mississippi, taken by the British, and Fort Michillimackinack triumphantly defended against a large American force; and Sir John C. Sherbrook, Lieutenant-Governor of Nova Scotia, reduces an extensive portion of American territory adjoining New Brunswick, and adds it to that Province.. 428
Peace in Europe; reinforcements of 16,000 veteran soldiers from England to Canada 430
Sir George Prevost's abortive expedition against Plattsburg censured; recalled to England to be tried by court-martial; dies a week before the day of trial 330
The estimate of Mr. Christie, the Canadian historian, of the character and policy of Sir George Prevost.. 431
Opening of the campaign in Upper Canada; expedition from Kingston against Oswego, which is dismantled, its fortifications destroyed, military stores, &c., seized.. 432
British fleet, supreme on Lake Ontario, blockades Sackett's Harbour; intercepts supplies being sent from Oswego to Sackett's Harbour, but is unsuccessful in pursuing American supply boats up the Sandy Creek; the pursuers taken prisoners and well treated by the Americans................. 433

CHAPTER LVIII.

LAST INVASIONS AND LAST BATTLES OF THE WAR 435-460

Americans, in two divisions, under command of Brigadier-Generals Scott and Ripley, cross the river and land on the Canadian side above and below Fort Erie, which is commanded by Major Buck, and surrendered without firing a shot, to the great loss of the British, and to the great advantage of the Americans.. 435
General Brown, with a force of over 4,000 troops, advances down the river from Fort Erie, with a view of taking Chippewa; is encountered by

General Riall, who is compelled to retire to the rear of his works at Chippewa; heroism of the Lincoln Militia.................................. 436
General Riall retires to Fort George, pursued by General Brown; pillage of the American soldiers and officers in the neighbourhood of Fort George.. 437
Both armies reinforced; General Brown in difficulties; retreats towards Chippewa; is pursued by General Riall; burns the village of St. David's; makes a stand at Lundy's Lane called Bridgewater by the Americans.. 437
Battle of Lundy's Lane; preliminaries to it..................................... 438
The battle itself; protracted and bloody struggle; Americans retreat to beyond Chippewa... 439
Forces engaged; losses on both sides; victory absurdly claimed on the American side 441
American army retreats to Fort Erie, pursued by General Drummond, who invests the fort.. 443
Storming the fort; terrible conflict; on the point of victory a magazine blown up, destroying all the British soldiers who had entered the fort—including Colonels Drummond and Scott—compelling the retirement of the assailants; British losses severe... 444
The enemy shut up for a month in the fort by the British investment....... 445
At the expiration of a month the enemy makes a sortie, with his whole force; surprises and destroys the batteries; a bloody conflict; the enemy compelled to return to the fort with a loss of 600 men.................. 445
Incessant rains prevent General Drummond repairing his batteries; he raises the siege and tries in vain to bring General Brown to a general engagement, but he evades it and evacuates Fort Erie 446
Thus terminates the last American invasion of Canada, without acquiring possession of an inch of Canadian territory.................. 446
Summary review of Canadian loyalty, and the causes, characteristics, and the results of the war, in an address delivered at Queenston Heights, near Brock's Monument, by the author, at the anniversary of the Battle of Lundy's Lane, July, 1875 447

CHAPTER LIX.

MISCELLANEOUS DOCUMENTS AND PAPERS EXTRACTED FROM UNITED EMPIRE LOYALIST MANUSCRIPTS IN THE DOMINION LIBRARY AT OTTAWA..461-464

Character of the Canadian Militia 461
American invasions of Canada and their military forces.................... 462
Notice of Colonel John Clarke and his manuscript contributions............ 462
The treatment of Canadians by the American invaders 463
The Royal Patriotic Society of Upper Canada and its doings in raising and distributing upwards of £20,000 to relieve Canadian sufferers by the war 466

CHAPTER LX.

STATE OF CANADA AFTER THE CLOSE OF THE WAR; CONCLUSION........469

THE
LOYALISTS OF AMERICA

AND

THEIR TIMES,

FROM 1620 TO 1816.

CHAPTER XXVII.

THE WAR OF THE AMERICAN REVOLUTION AFTER THE DECLARATION OF INDEPENDENCE—THE ALLIANCE BETWEEN THE CONGRESS AND KING OF FRANCE—THE ALLIANCE NOT PRODUCTIVE OF THE EFFECTS ANTICIPATED—EFFORTS OF THE BRITISH GOVERNMENT FOR RECONCILIATION WITH THE COLONIES NOT SUCCESSFUL.

IT was supposed, both in America and France, that when the alliance between the King of France and Congress, referred to in the last chapter of the previous volume, became known in England, though it was not publicly avowed until February, 1778, England would be weakened and discouraged from further warlike effort, and immediately offer terms of peace, upon the ground of American independence ; but the reverse was the case.

The alliance between Congress and the King of France was kept in abeyance by the latter during more than a twelve-month after it was applied for by the agents of Congress, until after the defeat and capture of General Burgoyne and the refusal of Congress to confer with Lord and General Howe, as British Commissioners, without the previous acknowledgment by the Commissioners of the independence of the United States.*

* "While the American Commissioners were urging the Ministers of the King of France to accept the treaty proposed by Congress, they received

VOL. II.—1

Lord Admiral Howe, having spent some months with his fleet at Halifax, did not arrive at Sandy Hook until the 12th of July, eight days after the Declaration of Independence. "Besides the troops, Lord Howe had brought with him a document which it was hoped might render them unnecessary—the Royal warrant appointing himself and General Howe Commissioners under the Act of Parliament for the pacification of America. No doubt the selection of such men was most wisely made. The memory of their elder brother, who had fallen gloriously in the wars against the French in Canada, was endeared to the colonists, who had fought by his side. Both Lord Howe and the General, but Lord Howe especially, had ever since cultivated a friendly intercourse with Americans, and now entertained a most earnest wish to conclude the strife against them. But judicious as was the choice of the Commissioners, the restricted terms of the Commission were certainly in the highest degree impolitic. Lord Howe had laboured, but vainly, to obtain its enlargement; it amounted, in fact, to little

assurances of the good wishes of the Court of France; but were from time to time informed that the important transactions required further consideration, and were enjoined to observe the most profound secrecy. Matters remained in this fluctuating state from December, 1776, till December, 1777. Private encouragement and public discountenance were alternated; but both varied according to the complexion of news from America. The defeat on Long Island, the reduction of New York, and the train of disastrous events in 1776, which have already been mentioned, sunk the credit of the Americans very low, and abated much of the national ardour for their support. Their subsequent successes at Trenton and Princeton effaced these impressions, and rekindled active zeal in their behalf. The capture of Burgoyne (October, 1777) fixed these wavering politics. The successes of the American campaign of 1777 placed them on high ground. Their enmity proved itself formidable to Britain, and their friendship became desirable to France. It was therefore determined to take them by the hand and publicly espouse their cause. The Commissioners of Congress, on the 16th of December, 1777, were informed by M. Gerard, one of the Secretaries of the King's Council of State, 'that it was decided to acknowledge the independence of the United States, and to make a treaty with them; that in the treaty no advantage would be taken of their situation to obtain terms which otherwise it would not be convenient for them to agree to; that his Most Christian Majesty desired the treaty, once made, should be durable, and their amity to subsist for ever, which could not be expected if each nation did not find an interest in its continuance as well as in its commencement.'" (Dr. Ramsay's History of the United States, Vol. II., Chap. xv., pp. 246, 247.)

more than the power, first, of receiving submissions, and then, but not till then, of granting pardons and inquiring into grievances.* Yet, still, since these terms had not been divulged, and were much magnified by common rumour, the name of the Commission was not ill adapted for popular effect. Had Lord Howe arrived with it a few weeks before, as he might and should have done, we are assured by American writers that an impression might have been produced by it, in some at least of the thirteen colonies, to an extent which they 'cannot calculate,' or rather, perhaps, which they do not like to own. But these few months had been decisive in another direction. During these months both the feeling and the position of the insurgents had most materially changed."†

"The two Royal Commissioners," says Dr. Ramsay, "Admiral and General Howe, thought proper, before they commenced their

---

* "MS. Instructions, May, 6th, 1776, State Paper Office.—It is therein required as a preliminary condition, before any province shall be declared in the King's peace, that its Convention, or Committee, or Association 'which have usurped powers,' shall be dissolved."

† Lord Mahon's History of England, Vol. VI., Chap. liii., pp. 137, 138.

Lord Mahon adds: "At the beginning of the troubles, as I have already shown, and for a long time afterwards, the vast majority of the Americans had no wish nor thought of separation from the mother country. Their object was substantially, and with some new safeguards for their rights, to revert to the same state in which they had been before the Administration of George Grenville. But the further the conflict proceeded, the less and less easy of attainment did that object seem. How hard, after what had passed, to restore harmonious action between the powers now at strife, for the people to trust the Governors appointed by the King, and for the King to trust the Assembly elected by the people. Even where the actual wrong might have departed, it would still leave its fatal legacy, rancour and suspicion, behind. Under the influence of these feelings a great number of persons in all the colonies were gradually turning their minds to the idea of final separation from the parent State. Still, in all these colonies, except only in New England, there were many lingering regrets, many deep-rooted doubts and misgivings. John Adams writes as follows: 'My dear friend Gates, all our misfortunes arise from a single source—the reluctance of the Southern colonies to republican government' (March, 1776, American Archives, Vol. V., p. 472). Here are the words of another popular leader: 'Notwithstanding the Act of Parliament for seizing our property, there is a strange reluctance in the minds of many to cut the knot which ties us to Great Britain'" (Letter of Reed to Washington, March 3rd, 1776).—*Ib.*, pp. 139, 140.

military operations, to try what might be done in their civil capacity towards effecting a reunion between Great Britain and the colonies. It was one of the first acts of Lord Howe to send on shore a circular letter to several of the Royal Governors in America, informing them of the late Act of Parliament 'for restoring peace to the colonies, and granting pardon to such as should deserve mercy,' and desiring them to publish a declaration which accompanied the same. In this, he informed the colonists of the power with which his brother and he were entrusted 'of granting general or particular pardons to all those who, though they had deviated from their allegiance, were willing to return to their duty:' and of declaring 'any colony, province, county or town, port, district or place, to be in the peace of his Majesty.' Congress, impressed with the belief that the proposals of the Commissioners, instead of disuniting the people, would have a contrary effect, ordered them to be speedily published in the several American newspapers. Had a *redress of grievances* been at this late hour offered, though the honour of the States was involved in supporting their late Declaration of Independence, yet the love of peace, and the bias of great numbers to their parent State, would, in all probability, have made a powerful party for rescinding the Act of Separation, and for re-uniting with Great Britain; but when it appeared that the power of the Royal Commissioners was little more than to grant pardons, Congress appealed to the good sense of the people for the necessity of adhering to the Act of Independence."*

It was a diplomatic blunder and an unwise policy for the English Commissioners to make known to the public the restricted authority of their commission, instead of simply stating in general terms their commission under the authority of the Act of Parliament "for restoring peace to the colonies." On such grounds and for such an object the Congress could have offered no justifiable excuse for refusing a conference with the Royal Commissioners; and when, in the course of the discussion, it should have been found that the Commissioners could not agree with, and did not feel themselves authorized to accede to,

* Dr. Ramsay's History of the United States, Vol. II., Chap. xi., pp. 121, 122.

all the demands of the agents of Congress, the Royal Commissioners (both of whom were known to be friends of the colonies, and opposed to the high-handed measures of the Parliament) could have noted the points of difference, and agreed to recommend the demands made upon them to the most favourable consideration of the King's Government: at all events, friendly intercourse and negotiations would have been opened which would have been probably followed by a suspension of hostilities, if not complete reconciliation. But this was what Congress, led by John Adams and Dr. Franklin—bitter enemies to reconciliation—dreaded; and they very shrewdly saw and improved the imprudent exposure of the Royal Commissioners, by directing the publication of their circular letter and declaration in all the provincial newspapers, "that the good people of the United States may be informed of what nature are the Commissioners, and what the terms, with expectation of which the insidious Court of Great Britain had endeavoured to amuse and disarm them; and that the few who still remain suspended by a hope, founded either on the justice or moderation of their late King, might now at length be convinced that the valour alone of their country is to save its liberties."

Thus all conference with the Royal Commissioners was refused on the part of the leaders in Congress; war and bloodshed followed, and a year of disastrous defeats to the Revolutionists; but the position of the Loyalists may be inferred from the resolution of the New York Revolutionary Convention, adopted a few days after the Declaration of Independence, and before the actual commencement of hostilities, and which was as follows: "That all persons residing within the State of New York, and claiming protection from its laws, owed it allegiance; and that any person owing it allegiance, and levying war against the State, *or being an adherent to the King of Great Britain, should be deemed guilty of treason and suffer death.*" The Convention also resolved: "That as the inhabitants of King's County had determined not to oppose the enemy, a Committee should be appointed to inquire into the authenticity of these reports, and to *disarm and secure the disaffected, to remove or destroy the stock of grain, and, if necessary, to lay the whole country waste.*" Such treatment of adherents to the unity of the empire, and of even neutrals, at the very commencement of the war, goes far to account for the warfare of extermination in many places between the two parties in subsequent years. This mode of warfare was first instituted against the Loyalists, who acted on the defensive, and who have been loudly complained of by American historians for having afterwards, and on some occasions cruelly retaliated upon those who had driven them to desperation.

A little more than eighteen months after the Declaration of Independence, 17th of February, 1778, three Bills were introduced into and passed by the British Parliament, which entirely removed all the grounds of complaint made by the colonists in previous years, and provided for the appointment of Commissioners to settle all differences between the colonies and the mother country. The first of these Bills was entitled, "For removing Doubts and Apprehensions concerning Taxation by the Parliament of Great Britain in any of the Colonies." It expressly repealed by name the tea duty in America, and declared: "That from and after the passing of this Act the King and Parliament of Great Britain will not impose any duty, tax, or assessment whatever in any of his Majesty's (American) colonies, except only such duties as it may be expedient to impose for the regulation of commerce; the net produce of such duties to be always paid and applied to and for the use of the colony in which the same shall be levied." "Thus," says Lord Mahon, "was the claim of parliamentary taxation fully, at last, renounced."

The second Bill was "To enable his Majesty to appoint Commissioners with sufficient power to treat, consult, and agree upon the means of quieting the disorders now subsisting in certain of the colonies, plantations, and provinces of North America." The Commissioners were to be five in number, and were invested with extensive powers; they were to raise no difficulties as to the rank or title of the leaders on either side, but were left at liberty to treat, consult, and agree with any body or bodies politic, or any person or persons whatsoever; they might proclaim a cessation of hostilities on the part of the King's forces by sea or land, for any time, or under any conditions or restrictions; they might suspend any Act of Parliament relating to America passed since the 10th of February, 1763. In short, it was intimated that the Commissioners might accept almost any terms of reconciliation short of independence, and subject to be confirmed by a vote of Parliament.

Lord North introduced his Bills in an able and eloquent speech of two hours, in which he reviewed his own career and the several questions of dispute with the colonies.*

But though taunted from all sides, his Bills passed speedily through both Houses of Parliament. Lord Mahon remarks: "In spite of such taunts and far from friendly feelings on all sides, the Conciliatory Bills, as they have been termed, were not in reality opposed from any quarter. There was only one division on a clause moved by Mr. Powys, to repeal expressly by name the Massachusetts Charter Act. Lord North induced a large majority to vote against that clause, but agreed that the object in view should be attained by a separate measure. A Bill for that purpose was therefore introduced by Mr. Powys, and passed through Parliament concurrently with the other two. In the House of Lords the same arguments were, with little change, renewed. Lord Shelburne took occasion to declare his

* " The impression on the House that night, while Lord North was speaking, and after he sat down, is well described by the pen of a contemporary—no other, in all probability, than Burke : 'A dull, melancholy silence for some time succeeded to this speech. It had been heard with profound attention, but without a single mark of approbation to any part, from any description of men, or any particular man in the House. Astonishment, dejection, and fear overclouded the whole assembly. Although the Minister had declared that the sentiments he expressed that day had been those which he always entertained, it is certain that few or none had understood him in that manner; and he had been represented to the nation at large as the person in it the most tenacious of those parliamentary rights which he now proposed to resign, and the most remote from the submissions which he now proposed to make.'

" It may be said, indeed, that there was not a single class or section within the walls of Parliament to which the plan of Lord North gave pleasure. The Ministerial party were confounded and abashed at finding themselves thus requested to acknowledge their past errors and retrace their former steps. Some among them called out that they had been deceived and betrayed. In general, however, the majority acquiesced in sullen silence. On the other part, the Opposition were by no means gratified to see the wind, according to the common phrase, taken from their sails. They could not, indeed, offer any resistance to proposals so consonant to their own expressed opinions, but they took care to make their support as disagreeable and damaging as possible." (Lord Mahon's History of England, etc., Vol. VI., Chap. lvii., pp. 327—329.)

full concurrence in the sentiments of Lord Chatham, expressing 'the strongest disapprobation of every idea tending to admit the independence of America,' although acknowledging that future circumstances might create a necessity for such a submission. Lord Chatham himself was ill with gout at Hayes, and did not appear. There was no division; and on the 11th of March (1778), the King, seated on his throne, gave to all three measures the royal assent.*

Lord North and other members of his Administration were convinced that the American problem could not be solved by their own party; that such a work could be accomplished by the Earl of Chatham alone, as he had a few years before, by his skill and energy, when the affairs of America were in a desperate state after five years' unsuccessful war with France, dispossessed France, in the short space of two years, of every inch of American territory. The Duke of Richmond advocated immediate surrender of independence to the Americans, and peace with them, in order to avoid a war with France; he doubted the possibility of even Lord Chatham being able to effect a reconciliation between the American colonies and Great Britain. Three-fourths of a century afterwards, Lord Macaulay expressed the same opinion; but Lord Mahon, in his History, has expressed a contrary opinion, and given his reasons in the following words, well worthy of being carefully read and pondered:

"In the first place, let it be remembered with what great and what singular advantages Lord Chatham would have set his hand to the work. He had from the outset most ably and most warmly supported the claims of the colonists. Some of his eloquent sentences had become watchwords in their mouths.

---

* History of England, etc., Vol. VI., Chap. lvii., pp. 329, 330.

Lord Mahon adds: "Only two days previously, Lord North, who had opened his Budget on the 6th, had carried through his financial resolutions in the House of Commons, involving a new loan of £6,000,000, which was contracted on advantageous terms. Thus were funds provided to pursue the war, should that be requisite. Thus was an opening made for negotiations, should they be practicable. In either case the path was cleared for a new Administration. Here then was the moment which Lord North had for some time past desired—the moment when, with most honour to himself and with most advantage to his country, he could fulfil his intentions of resigning." (Lord Mahon's History of England, Vol. VI., Chap. lvii., pp. 330, 331.)

His statue had been erected in their streets; his portrait was hanging in their Council Chambers. For his great name they felt a love and reverence higher as yet than for any one of their own chiefs and leaders, not even at that early period excepting Washington himself. Thus, if even it could be said that overtures of reconciliation had failed in every other British hand, it would afford no proof that in Chatham's they might not have thriven and borne fruit.

"But what at the same period was the position of Congress? Had that assembly shown of late an enlightened zeal for the public interests, and did it then stand high in the confidence and affection of its countrymen? Far otherwise. The factions and divisions prevailing at their town of York (in Virginia, where they removed from Baltimore), the vindictive rigour to political opponents, the neglect of Washington's army, and the cabals against Washington's powers, combined to create disgust, with other less avoidable causes, as the growing depreciation of the paper-money, the ruinous loss of trade, and the augmented burdens of the war. Is the truth of this picture denied? Hear then, as witnesses, the members of Congress themselves. We find in this very month of March (1778), one of them write to another on the necessity of joint exertions to "revive the expiring reputation of Congress." (Letter from William Duer, of New York, to Robert Morris, dated March 6th, 1778, and printed in the Life of Reed, Vol. I., p. 365.) We find another lamenting that 'even good Whigs begin to think peace, at some expense, desirable.' (General Reed to President Wharton, February 1, 1778.)

"When such was the feeling in America, both as regarded Lord Chatham and as regarded the Congress, it would not certainly follow that any overture from the former would be rejected on account of the disapprobation of the latter. The provinces might, perhaps, have not been inclined to the deliberations, or even cast off the sway of the central body, and make terms of peace for themselves. At any rate, all such hope was not precluded; at least some such trial might be made.

"Nor does it appear to me, as to Mr. Macaulay, that there was any, even the slightest, inconsistency in Lord Chatham having first pronounced against the conquest of America, and yet refusing to allow her independence. After the declaration in her behalf of France, Lord Chatham had said, no doubt, that America could not be conquered. Had he ever said she could not be reconciled? It was on conciliation, and not on conquest, that he built his later hopes. He thought the declaration of France no obstacle to his views, but rather an instrument for their support. He conceived that the treaty of alliance concluded by the envoys of the Congress with the Court of Versailles might tend beyond any other cause to rekindle British feelings in the hearts of the Americans. Were the glories of Wolfe and Amherst, in which they had partaken, altogether blotted from their minds? Would the soldier-yeomen of the colonies be willing to fight side by side with those French whom, till within fifteen years, they had found in Canada their bitter hereditary foes? That consequences like to these—that some such revulsion of popular feeling in America might, perhaps, ensue from an open French alliance, is an apprehension which, during the first years of the contest, we find several times expressed in the secret letters of the Revolution chiefs; it was a possibility which we see called forth their fears; why then might it not be allowed to animate the hopes of Chatham?"*

But Lord Chatham was not destined even to try the experiment of giving America a second time to England; in a few days he fell in the House of Lords, to rise no more, with the protest on his lips against the separation of the American colonies from England. The Americans had no confidence in the professions of a Parliament and Ministry which had oppressed and sought to deceive them for twelve years. As low as the Congress had fallen in the estimation of a large part of the colonists, the English Ministry was regarded with universal distrust and aversion. The Congress refused even to confer with the Royal Commissioners, and had sufficent influence to prevent any province from entering into negotiations with them. All the former grounds of complaint had been removed by the three Acts of Parliament above referred to, and all the concessions demanded had been granted. The Royal Commissioners requested General Washington, on the 9th of June (1778), to furnish a passport for their Secretary, Dr. Ferguson,

---

* Lord Mahon's History of England, Vol. VI., Chap. lvii., pp. 344—347.

with a letter from them to Congress; but this was refused, and the refusal was approved by Congress. They then forwarded, in the usual channel of communication, a letter addressed "To his Excellency Henry Laurens, the President, and other Members of Congress," in which they enclosed a copy of their commission and the Acts of Parliament on which it was founded; and they offered to concur in every satisfactory and just arrangement towards the following among other purposes:

"To consent to a cessation of hostilities both by sea and land;

"To restore free intercourse, to revive mutual affection, and renew the common benefits of naturalization through the several parts of this empire;

"To extend every freedom to trade that our respective interests can require;

"To agree that no military forces shall be kept up in the different States of North America without the consent of the General Congress, or particular Assemblies;

"To concur in measures calculated to discharge the debts of America, and to raise the credit and value of the paper circulation;

"To perpetuate our union by a reciprocal deputation of an agent or agents from the different States, who shall have the privilege of a seat and voice in the Parliament of Great Britain; or if sent from Great Britain, in that case to have a seat or voice in the Assemblies of the different States to which they may be deputed respectively, in order to attend to the several interests of those by whom they are deputed;

"In short, to establish the power of the respective Legislatures in each particular State; to settle its revenue, its civil and military establishment, and to exercise a perfect freedom of legislation and internal government; so that the British States throughout North America, acting with us in peace and war under one common sovereign, may have the irrevocable enjoyment of every privilege that is short of total separation of interests, or consistent with that union of force on which the safety of our common religion and liberty depends."*

The three Acts of Parliament and the proposals of the five

* Dr. Ramsay's History of the United States, Vol. II., Chap. xv., pp. 254, 255.

English Commissioners were far in advance of any wishes which the colonists had expressed before the Declaration of Independence, and placed the colonists on the footing of Englishmen—all that the Earl of Chatham and Mr. Burke had ever advocated—all that the free, loyal, and happy Dominion of Canada enjoys at this day—all and nothing more than was required for the unity of the empire and of the Anglo-Saxon race ; but the leaders of Congress had determined upon the dismemberment of the empire—had determined to sever all connection with the elder European branch of the Anglo-Saxon family—had determined, and that without even consulting the constituents whom they professed to represent, to transfer their allegiance from England to France, to bind themselves hand and foot to France—that they would make no peace with England, upon any terms, without the consent of the French Court.

It may be easily conceived what an effect would be produced upon the truly national mind of both England and America by such a transition on the part of the leaders of Congress and their representatives abroad—a transition which might be called a revolution, involving new issues and new relations of parties; for the question was no longer one of mere separation from England, much less the question of Stamp Acts, or taxation without representation, or suspension of charters—all acts and pretensions of this kind having been repealed and renounced; but the question was now one of union with the hereditary foe of England and her colonies ; and the unnatural alliance contemplated the invasion of England by the French, the destruction of British commerce, the wresting from England of the West Indies as well as Canada,* and the possession

---

* While Count D'Estaing was at Boston repairing his shattered fleet, he was not unmindful of an essential part of his commission—to detach Canada from England. "In pursuance of this design, a Declaration was published (dated the 28th of October, 1778), addressed in the name of the King of France to the French inhabitants of Canada, and of every other part of America formerly subject to that Crown. This Declaration contained the highest praises of the valour of the Americans; it laid before the inhabitants of Canada the mortification they must endure in bearing arms against the allies of their parent State; it represented to them, in the strongest terms, the ties formed by origin, language, manners, government, and religion, between the Canadians and the French, and lamented the misfortune which had

by France of whatever islands or territory her navy and army should conquer.

All this was a different thing from mere independence of the mother country. The United Empire Loyalists and advocates of colonial rights were now subject to a new allegiance, and punished as rebels and their property confiscated if they would not unite with the French against their English forefathers and brethren. So enamoured were the leaders of Congress with their new allies, that they interrupted the reading of the official letter from the British Commissioners on account of a passage which reflected upon France, and debated three days whether they should allow the remaining part of the letter to be read.*

But the feelings of all classes in England, and of a large part,

---

occasioned a disjunction of that colony from France; it recalled to their remembrance the brave resistance they had made during the many wars they had been engaged in against England, especialy the last; it reminded them of their favourite warriors and generals, particularly the valiant Montcalm, who fell at their head, in defence of their country; it earnestly entreated them to reflect seriously on their disagreeable subjection to strangers living in another hemisphere, differing from them in every possible respect, who could consider them no otherwise than as a conquered people, and would always, of course, treat them accordingly. It concluded by formally notifying, that the Count D'Estaing was authorized and commanded by the King of France to declare, in his name, that all his former subjects in North America who should renounce their allegiance to Great Britain might depend on his protection and support." (Dr. Andrews' History of the American War, Vol. III., Chap. xxxviii., p. 171.)

* The conciliatory acts of the British Parliament and the letter of the Commissioners were referred by the Congress to a Committee of three—all known to be opposed to any reconciliation with England. This Committee made, the next day after its appointment, a report which was adopted by Congress, that the British acts were merely intended to operate upon the hopes and fears of the American people, and to produce divisions among them; " that those who made any partial convention or agreement with the Commissioners of Great Britain would be regarded as enemies; and that the United States could hold no conference with such Commissioners until the British Government *first withdrew its fleets and armies, or acknowledged the independence of the United States.*"

" This *rejection* of terms which they not long before would have cordially welcomed, *was, no doubt, caused by the confident expectation they then had of the support and alliance of France;* and accordingly the news of that alliance soon after reached them, and diffused a general joy throughout the land." (Tucker's History of the United States, Vol. I., Chap. iii., pp. 221, 222.)

if not the great majority, of the colonists, were different from those of the leaders of Congress, now depleted of many distinguished men who attended its previous year's sittings.*

* "The Declaration of Independence effected an alteration of sentiments in England. It was esteemed by many of the most judicious persons in this country, a measure wholly unnecessary, and without recurring to which America might have compassed every point proposed by continuing its resistance to Britain on the same footing it had begun. This measure occasioned an alienation from its interests in the minds of many of its former adherents. It was looked upon as a wanton abuse of the success with which it had opposed the efforts of the British Ministry to bring them to submission, and as an ungrateful return for the warmth with which their cause had been espoused in Parliament, and by such multitudes as in the idea of many amounted to a plurality."

"The Declaration of France completed the revolution that had been gradually taking place in the opinions of men on their being repeatedly apprised of the determination of Congress to break asunder all the bonds of former amity, and to unite themselves in the closest manner with that kingdom." (Dr. Andrews' History of the American War, Vol. III., Chap. xxxiv., pp. 82—84.)

The Declaration of France in favour of the independence of the American colonies, and of alliance with them, was officially communicated to the British Government the 13th of March, 1778, a few days after which the French fleet under the command of Count D'Estaing sailed from Toulon, and arrived off the coast of America in July—after a long voyage of eighty-seven days. On learning the departure of the French fleet for America, the British Government sent out, in the same ships with the Peace Commissioners, orders to Sir Henry Clinton to concentrate his forces on Long Island and at New York. "The successor of Howe, Sir Henry Clinton, was," says Lord Mahon, "in character, as upright and amiable; in skill and enterprise, much superior. Had the earlier stages of the war been under his direction, his ability might not have been without influence upon them. But it was his misfortune to be appointed only at a time when other foes had leagued against us, when the path was beset with thorns and briars, when scarce any laurels rose in view. In consequence of the impending war with France, and in conformity with the advice of Lord Amherst to the King, instructions had been addressed to Sir Henry, on the 23rd of March, to retire from the hard-won city of Philadelphia, and concentrate his forces at New York. This order reached him at Philadelphia, in the month of May, only a few days after he had assumed the chief command; only a few days before, there came on shore the British Commissioners of Peace. These Commissioners might well complain with some warmth, in a secret letter to Lord George Germaine, that an order so important, so directly bearing on the success of their mission, should have been studiously concealed from them until they landed in America, and beheld it in progress of execution. Thus to a private friend wrote Lord Carlisle (one of the

By this alliance with France the allied colonies became, as it were, a part of France, bound up in oneness with it—refusing all overtures or negotiations with the representatives of England without the approval of the French Court. The coasts, cities, towns, etc., of the American allies of France therefore became liable to the same treatment on the part of the British army and navy as the coasts, cities, and towns of France. Of this the British Commissioners informed the Congress, after the latter had declared its identity with France, and refused any further intercourse with them.*

Commissioners): 'We arrived at this place, after a voyage of six weeks, on Saturday last, and found everything here in great confusion—the army upon the point of leaving the town, and about three thousand of the miserable inhabitants embarked on board of our ships, to convey them from a place where *they think they would receive no mercy from those who will take possession after us.*'"

"Thus from the first," says Lord Mahon, "the Commissioners had against them the news of a retreat from Philadelphia, and the news of the treaty of Paris; further, they had against them, as the Opposition in England had long foreseen and foretold, the fact of their connection with Lord North. Even at the outset, before their affairs could be known (June 14, 1778), one of the leaders in America, General Joseph Reed, answered a private note from one of them as follows: 'I shall only say that after the unparalleled injuries and insults this country has received from the men who now direct the affairs of Great Britain, a negotiation under their auspices has much to struggle with.'" "How different," remarks Lord Mahon, "might have been his feelings, had they brought their Commission from Lord Chatham." (History of England, Vol. VI., Chap. lviii., pp. 372—374.)

Lord Mahon adds: "Not any, even the smallest opening, was afforded to these messengers of peace. They desired to despatch to the seat of Congress their Secretary, Dr. Adam Ferguson, the well-known Professor of Edinburgh, and they applied to Washington for a passport, but Washington refused it until the pleasure of Congress should be known. The Congress, on their part, had put forth a resolution declining even to hold any conference with the Commissioners unless, as a preliminary, they should either withdraw the fleets and armies, or else, in express terms, acknowledge the independence of the United States. In vain did the Commissioners address the President of the Congress, and entreat some consideration of their terms. (For the terms, see page 11.) To none of these terms, so tempting heretofore, would the Congress hearken; and after their first letter, they decided in a summary manner that no further reply should be returned."—*Ib.*, pp. 374, 375.

* "Finding it impossible to proceed with their negotiations, the Commissioners prepared to re-embark for England. First, however, they issued

The war for a short time after this period became more acrimonious and destructive on both sides than before, as between the French and English. But this policy of devastation and retaliation was disapproved of by the British Government—was confined mostly to some certain coast towns in New England, while in the South the conduct of Col. Campbell, on the subjugation of Georgia, was marked by lenity and generosity.

a manifesto, or proclamation, to the American people, appealing to them against the decisions of the Congress, and offering to the colonies at large, or singly, a general or separate peace. This proclamation was in most parts both ably and temperately argued. But there was one passage liable to just exceptions. The Commissioners observed, that hitherto the hopes of a reunion had checked the extremes of war. Henceforth the contest would be changed. If the British colonies were to become an accession to France, the law of self-preservation must direct Great Britain to render the accession of as little avail as possible to her enemy. Mr. Fox and others in the House of Commons inveighed with great plausibility against this passage, as threatening a war of savage desolation. Others again, as friends of Lord Carlisle and Mr. Eden (afterwards Lord Auckland), asserted that no such meaning was implied. The error, whatever it might be, lay with the Commissioners, and in no degree with the Government at home; for Lord North denied, in the most express terms, that his Ministers had intended to give the least encouragement to the introduction of any new kind of war in North America." (Debate in the House of Commons, Dec. 4, 1778.)

Lord Mahon's History of England, etc., Vol. VI., Chap. lviii., pp. 376, 377.

CHAPTER XXVIII.

COMPLETE FAILURE OF THE FRENCH FLEET AND ARMY, UNDER COUNT D'ESTAING, TO ASSIST THE CONGRESS.

THE leaders of Congress were disappointed in the high expectations which they had entertained from their unnatural alliance with France. Count D'Estaing left France with a much more powerful fleet than Lord Howe commanded in America, besides bringing an army of several thousand soldiers. He had expected to surprise and capture the British ships in the River Delaware; but Lord Howe had sailed for New York several days before his arrival. Count D'Estaing pursued, and lay eleven days at anchor off Sandy Hook, not being able to get his large ships over the bar into New York harbour. He at length directed his course, by Washington's advice, to Long Island, and sailed up the Newport river, whither he was followed by Lord Howe. "An attack against the British in that quarter had been projected between the new allies. The French promised to land from their ships four thousand troops, and the Americans actually sent a detachment of ten thousand under General Sullivan. The British troops, only five thousand strong, retired within their lines at Newport.

"At these tidings, Lord Howe, whose intended successor, Admiral Byron, had not yet arrived, issued forth from the Hudson and sailed in pursuit of D'Estaing. The two fleets were on the point of engaging when separated by a violent storm; there were conflicts between individual ships only, in which the honour of the British flag was worthily maintained. D'Estaing now declared his fleet so far damaged by the storm as to compel him to put into Boston harbour and refit. In this resolution he persisted, though Sullivan, Greene, and other American officers altogether denied the necessity, and even transmitted to him a written protest against it, couched in the most acrimonious terms."*

Certain it is, that the course which D'Estaing pursued on this occasion not only forced the Americans to relinquish their enterprise upon Long Island, but roused up among them a bitter feeling against the French. To such an extent was this

---

* "They urged D'Estaing to return with his fleet into the harbour; but his principal officers were opposed to the measure, and protested against it. He had been instructed to go into Boston if his fleet met with any misfortune. His officers insisted on his ceasing to prosecute the expedition against Rhode Island, that he might conform to the orders of their common superiors. A protest was drawn up and sent to him, which was signed by John Sullivan, Nathaniel Greene, John Hancock, I. Glover, Ezekiel Cornel, William Whipple, John Tyler, Solomon Lovell, John Fitconnel. They protested against the Count's taking the fleet to Boston, as derogatory to the honour of France, contrary to the intention of his Christian Majesty and the interests of his nation, destructive in the highest degree to the welfare of the United States, and highly injurious to the alliance formed between the two nations. Had D'Estaing prosecuted his original plan within the harbour, either before or immediately after the pursuit of Lord Howe, the reduction of the British post on Rhode Island (which had been in the possession of the British since 1776) would have been probable; but his departure in the first instance to engage the English fleet, and in the second from Rhode Island to Boston, frustrated the whole." (Dr. Ramsay's History of the United States, Vol. II., Chap. xvi., p. 272.)

"Whatever were the reasons which induced Count D'Estaing to adopt that measure (of sailing with his fleet direct for Boston), the Americans were greatly dissatisfied. They complained that they had incurred great expense and danger, under the prospect of the most effective co-operation; that, depending thereon, they had risked their lives on an island, where, without naval protection, they were exposed to particular dangers; that in this situation they were first deserted, and afterwards totally abandoned, at a time when, by persevering in the original plan, they had well-grounded hopes of speedy success. Under these apprehensions the discontented militia went home in such crowds that the regular army, which remained, was in danger of being cut off from a retreat. In these embarrassing circumstances, General Sullivan extricated himself with judgment and ability. He began to send off his heavy artillery and baggage on the 26th, and retreated from the lines on the night of the 28th." (Lord Mahon's History of England, etc., Vol. VI., Chap. lviii., p. 173.)

animosity carried that riots ensued in the streets of Boston*
between the American seamen and their new allies.†
Even in regard to the mode of attacking the British on
Long Island, differences arose between Count D'Estaing and his
new American friends on questions of etiquette. Mr. Tucker
says: "D'Estaing's fastidiousness on points of etiquette, and
his refusal to aid in what would have given so serious a blow
to the British power in America, is calculated to raise a doubt
whether he was really anxious to bring the war to an immediate conclusion."‡ Early in November, Count D'Estaing, with
the French squadron, quitted the port of Boston and sailed for

---

* "The inveteracy to the French, traditionally inherent in the lower classes of the New England people, could not be restrained from breaking out in Boston, in a manner that might have been attended with the most serious consequences to the interests of both France and America, had not the prudence of the magistracy interposed on the one hand, and the sagacity of Count D'Estaing co-operated on the other. A desperate fray happened in that city between the populace and the French sailors, in which these were roughly handled, and had much the worse. A number of them were hurt and wounded, and some, it was reported, were killed."

"Precisely at the same time, a disturbance of a like nature happened at Charleston, in South Carolina, between the French and American seamen, but it was carried to much greater extremities; they engaged on both sides with small arms, and even with cannon. A number of people were killed and wounded." (Dr. Andrews' History of the American War, Vol. III., Chap. xxxviii., pp. 172, 173.

† Lord Mahon's History of England, etc., Vol. VI., Chap. lviii., pp. 380, 381.

"During this time Sir Henry Clinton sent out several expeditions in various quarters. Near Tappan, a body of American horsemen under Colonel Baylor were surprised and routed, or put to the sword. In Egg-Harbour, great part of Count Pulaski's foreign legion was cut to pieces. At Buzzard's Bay, and on the island called Martha's Vineyard, many American ships were taken or destroyed, storehouses burned, and contributions of sheep and oxen levied. In these expeditions the principal commander was General Charles Grey, an officer of great zeal and ardour, whom the Americans sometimes surnamed the 'No-flint General,' from his common practice of ordering the men to take the flints out of their muskets, and trust to their bayonets alone. After some twenty years of further service, the veteran was raised, by the favour of his Sovereign, to the peerage as Lord Grey of Howick, and afterwards Earl Grey. His son became Prime Minister (father of the present Earl Grey), and the greatest orator who, since the death of Chatham, had appeared in the House of Lords."—*Ib.*, pp. 382, 383.

‡ Tucker's History of the United States, Vol. I., Chap. iii., p. 231.

the West Indies, there to pursue exclusively French objects. "Deep was the disappointment and loud the animadversion of the Americans in the Northern provinces. They had formed the most sanguine hopes from the French alliance. They had found that alliance as yet little better than a name."*

The results of Count D'Estaing's expedition, and of the French alliance thus far, are well summed up by Dr. Ramsay in the following words: "With the abortive expedition to Rhode Island there was an end to the plans which were in this first campaign projected by the allies of Congress for co-operation. The Americans had been intoxicated with hopes of the most decisive advantages; but in every instance they were disappointed. Lord Howe, with an inferiority of force, not only preserved his own fleet, but counteracted and defeated all the views and attempts of Count D'Estaing. The French fleet gained no direct advantages for the Americans; yet their arrival was of great service to their cause. Besides deranging the plans of the British, it carried conviction to their minds that his Most Christian Majesty was seriously disposed to support them. The good-will of their new allies was manifested to the Americans; and though it had failed in producing the effects expected from it, the failure was charged to winds, weather, and unavoidable incidents. Some censured Count D'Estaing; but while they attempted to console themselves by throwing blame on him, they felt and acknowledged their obligation to the French nation, and were encouraged to persevere in the war, from the hope that better fortune would attend their future co-operation."† Count D'Estaing proceeded with his fleet to the West Indies, where he did nothing worthy of the large fleet, reinforced by that of Count de Grasse with several thousand troops, against the English fleet under the command

---

* Lord Mahon's History of England, Vol. VI., Chap. lviii., p. 384.

Mr. Tucker remarks on this subject: "On the 3rd of November D'Estaing sailed for the West Indies, and thus ended the costly and fruitless expedition which bade fair to be decisive of the contest; and which failed first by disasters from the elements, and then from misunderstandings in which the interests of the common cause seem to have been sacrificed to paltry personal feelings on both sides." (History of the United States, Vol. I., Chap. iii., p. 234.)

† Dr. Ramsay's History of the United States, Vol. II., Chap. xvi., p. 275.

of Admiral Byron—much inferior in both men and metal; but the French admiral declined and evaded any general engagement, though repeatedly provoked to it. "The British fleet endeavoured in vain to compel the enemy to come to close fight; they avoided it with the utmost circumspection and dexterity."*

It became indispensably necessary for Admiral Byron to provide a powerful convoy to the merchant shipping now on the eve of their departure for England, and whose cargoes were of immense value. Under all the circumstances, Admiral Byron determined to convoy the homeward trade with his whole fleet, till it was out of danger of being followed by Count D'Estaing or of falling in with M. de la Motte, who was on his way from France to the French islands with a strong squadron. During Admiral Byron's absence, Count D'Estaing directed an attack to be made on the island of St. Vincent, the garrison of which was very inconsiderable, and soon surrendered to the superior strength of the French, assisted by a great multitude of the Caribbee Indians, and who seized this opportunity of revenging themselves for injuries inflicted upon them by the English during the last French war.

In the meantime Count D'Estaing was still further reinforced by the arrival of the squadron commanded by M. de la Motte. His fleet now consisted of twenty-six ships of the line and twelve frigates, and his land force amounted to ten thousand men. With this powerful armament he sailed for the island of Grenada, the strength of which consisted of about one hundred and fifty regulars and three or four hundred armed inhabitants. The garrison was compelled to yield to the prodigious superiority of force against them, after a most heroic defence, in

---

* "Early in January, 1779, reinforcements under Admiral Byron transferred maritime superiority to the British; and D'Estaing for six months sheltered his fleet in the bay of Port Royal. At the end of June, Byron having left St. Lucia to convoy a company of British merchant ships through the passage, D'Estaing detached a force against St. Vincent, which, with the aid of the oppressed and enslaved Caribs, was easily taken. At the same time the French admiral made an attack on the island of Grenada, whose garrison surrendered on the 4th of July, at discretion." (Bancroft, Vol. X., Chap. xiii., p. 295.)

which no less than three hundred of the French were killed and wounded.*

The complaints of the Americans of the failure of Count D'Estaing's expedition to America, of his abandoning the expedition against Long Island, of his leaving the coasts of the Southern colonies unprotected and exposed, and proceeding to the West Indies, reached the French Court, which sent instructions to Count D'Estaing enjoining him to return with all speed to the assistance of the colonies. For this purpose he left the West Indies on the 1st of September. Mr. Tucker remarks: "General Lincoln (commander of the colonial forces in Carolina) having informed Count D'Estaing that the British ships had gone into port to repair the damages sustained in the late engagement with his fleet in the West Indies, and that a fair opportunity was presented of destroying the British army in Georgia, with the co-operation of the French fleet, the Count immediately left the West Indies, with twenty-two sail of the line and eleven frigates. He had on board six thousand land forces, and arrived so unexpectedly on the coast that a British fifty-gun ship and three frigates fell into his hands. He then, in conjunction with General Lincoln, planned an attack on the town of Savannah."†

The arrangements for the attack having been made, the whole French fleet came to anchor at the mouth of the Savannah river on the 1st day of September. He was occupied ten days

---

* "Two days after the taking of Grenada," says Mr. Bancroft, "the fleet of Byron arrived within sight of the French, and, though reduced in number, sought a general close action, which his adversary knew how to avoid." (History of the United States, Vol. X., Chap. xiii., p. 295.)

† History of the United States, Vol. I., Chap. iii., p. 249.
"Count D'Estaing's intentions and his hopes were, as before, directed to objects of the first magnitude. The first measure of the plan and contemplation was to expel the British forces out of Georgia, and to place that province and the contiguous province of South Carolina, and in short all the Southern colonies, on a footing of perfect security from any future invasions by the British troops. After the accomplishment of this object, he next proposed no less than a total deliverance of America from the terror of the British arms. This was to be effected by the destruction of the British fleet at New York. The latter part of the plan he doubted not to accomplish through the co-operation of the American army under Washington." (Dr. Andrews' History of the Late War, Vol. III., Chap. xlv., pp. 308, 309.)

in landing his troops and artillery; on the 15th of September a junction was formed between the French and General Lincoln,* and with the utmost confidence of success.†

They determined to take the town by siege rather than by storm in the first instance.‡

On the 16th of September they demanded, in a very confident and haughty tone, the surrender of the town to the arms of the King of France; but General Prevost declined surrendering on a general summons, and requested a specific statement of the terms of it. The Count replied that it was for the besieged to propose the terms. General Prevost requested and obtained twenty-four hours' suspension of hostilities to prepare his answer. Before the twenty-four hours

* " A junction being formed by the French and American forces, they amounted together to between nine and ten thousand men. Count D'Estaing had five thousand regulars, and near one thousand stout mulattos and free negroes, well armed. The body of Americans that joined him under the command of General Lincoln consisted of about two thousand at first, but were soon augmented to twice that number.

" To oppose this formidable strength, General Prevost (the commander of Savannah) had no more, altogether, than three thousand men; but they were such as continual experience had shown he could place the utmost dependence on. Numbers were refugees (loyalists), *whom resentment for the usage they had received* exasperated to a degree that rendered them desperate."—*Ib.*, p. 312.

† " As soon as the arrival of Count D'Estaing on the coast was known, General Lincoln, with the army under his command, marched for the vicinity of Savannah; and orders were given for the militia of Georgia and South Carolina to rendezvous near the same place. The British were equally diligent in preparing for their defence. The American militia, flushed with the hope of speedily expelling the British from their southern possessions, turned out with an alacrity which far surpassed their exertions in the previous campaign." (Dr. Ramsay's History of the United States, Vol. II., Chap. xvii., p. 302.)

‡ " The French and the Americans encamped separately. Count D'Estaing thought it most prudent to keep them apart. He knew by experience how apt they were to disagree; and he hoped that, by acting asunder from each other, a reciprocal emulation would be excited. It was agreed, accordingly, that each of them should carry on their respective approaches without interference from the other side. This method was particularly agreeable to the French, who, looking upon themselves as incomparably superior to the Americans, did not choose to divide any honour with these, to which they imagined that they alone were entitled." (Dr. Andrews' History of the Late War, Vol. III., Chap. xlv., pp. 312, 313.)

had elapsed, Lieutenant-Colonel Maitland, with several hundred men who had been stationed at Beaufort, made their way through inland channels and swamps, and joined the royal standard at Savannah; and General Prevost gave his answer of no surrender. The French and Americans, who formed a junction the evening after, resolved to besiege the town, and consumed several days in preparing for it, while the works of the garrison were hourly strengthened by great labour and skill. From the 24th of September to the 4th of October a heavy cannonade on both sides was kept up; but the allied army, finding that they could make little or no impression on the works of the besieged, resolved on a bombardment, with a stronger cannonading than ever. On the 4th of October the besiegers opened on the town three batteries, with nine mortars, thirty-seven pieces of cannon from the land side, and fifteen from the water. The firing from these batteries lasted, with little intermission, during five days; but the damage they did was confined mostly to the town, where some houses were destroyed and some women and children killed. Soon after the commencement of the cannonade, General Prevost requested permission to remove the women and children out of the town to a place of safety; but this request was refused in offensive terms on the part of Count D'Estaing, by the advice of General Lincoln, on the pretext that a desire of secreting the plunder lately taken from the South Carolinas was covered under the veil of humanity, but the real reason was that the surrender of the town would be expedited by keeping the women and children in it.*

* Count D'Estaing was afterwards so ashamed of this inhuman refusal, that after the repulse of his assault upon the garrison he apologized for it, and offered the permission requested, but which was no longer needed, and therefore refused.

General Stedman, referring to this circumstance, says: "On the morning of the 4th of October, the batteries of the besiegers having opened with a discharge from fifty-three pieces of heavy cannon and fourteen mortars, a request was made by General Prevost that the women and children might be permitted to leave the town and embark on board vessels in the river, which should be placed under the protection of Count D'Estaing, and wait the issue of the siege. But this proposal, dictated by humanity, was rejected with insult. Fortunately, however, for the inhabitants as well as the garrison, although an incessant cannonade from so many pieces of artillery was continued from the

Count D'Estaing, finding that his five days' cannonading made no impression on the defensive works of the city, and his officers remonstrating against his continuing to risk so valuable a fleet on a dangerous coast, in the hurricane season, and at so great a distance from shore that it might be surprised by a British fleet, now completely repaired in the West Indies and fully manned, he decided to assault the town. The attack was commenced in three columns on the 9th, an hour before sunrise.

"Though the besieged were prepared for the assault, and their fire was very destructive, the assailants pressed on and planted (for a few minutes) the standard of both nations on the walls; but the contest being still obstinately continued, the assailants were brought to a pause by the fall of Count Pulaski (commanding an American corps), who received a mortal wound; and Major Glaziers, who commanded the garrison, rushing at the head of a body of grenadiers and marines, drove back the allied troops, who were ordered to retreat. The French lost seven hundred men; the Americans, two hundred and thirty-four. The British garrison lost only fifty-five in killed and wounded. On the 16th of October the siege was raised by the Count, who thus for the third time failed in his co-operation with the Americans, after the fairest prospects of success."*

4th to the 9th of October, less injury was done to the houses in the town than might have been expected; few lives were lost, and the defences were in no respect materially damaged." (Stedman's History of the American War, Vol. II., Chap. xxx., p. 127.)

* Tucker's History of the United States, Vol. I., Chap. iii., p. 250.

This disastrous attack upon Savannah was followed by mutual recriminations between the French and American officers and soldiers.

"No good agreement, it has been said, subsisted between the French and Americans from the commencement of the siege, and their mutual dislike was now increased by disappointment. After the assault, the French could no longer conceal their contempt for their new allies; they styled them 'insurgents' in common conversation and even in written memorials." (General Stedman's History of the American War, Vol. II., Chap. xxx., p. 132.)

"While the British troops were enjoying the satisfaction resulting from the success that was due to their conduct and valour, the enemy was in a condition of discontent and sullenness which had like to have terminated fatally. The Americans could not conceal their disapprobation of the whole proceedings of Count D'Estaing, nor he the contemptuous light in which he

Mr. Bancroft states the final struggle of this eventful contest, and the results and effects of it on the Southern colonies, in the following words :—" After an obstinate struggle of fifty-five minutes to carry the redoubt, the assailants retreated before a charge of grenadiers and marines, led gallantly by Maitland. The injury sustained by the British was trifling; the loss of the Americans was about two hundred; of the French, thrice as many. The French withdrew their ships, and sailed for France; the patriots of Georgia who had joined them fled to the backwoods or across the river.

" Lincoln repaired to Charleston, and was followed by what remained of his army; the militia of South Carolina returned to their homes; its continental regiments were melting away: and its paper money became so nearly worthless, that a bounty of twenty-five hundred dollars for twenty-one months' service had no attraction. The dwellers near the sea between Charleston and Savannah were shaken in their allegiance, not knowing

held them. Reciprocal taunts and reproaches came to such a height between both the officers and soldiers of either party, that it was once thought they would have proceeded to actual violence.

" A motive which strongly influenced the Americans was the jealousy they had conceived against the French commander, on account of his having summoned General Prevost to *surrender to the arms of France*, without including those of the United States of America. They inferred from thence, that either he considered them as unworthy of the honour of being mentioned conjointly with the King of France, or that he meant to retain the province of Georgia for that Crown in case of reduction. Whichever of the two was the meaning of the French commander, it exposed him equally to the indignation of the Americans.

" To this it may be added, that the inhuman refusal of the request of General Prevost for a permission to the women and children to depart from the town of Savannah during the siege, was now by the French attributed to the Americans, whom they accused of brutality, and whose general, a French officer of rank, was loaded with the coarsest and most injurious appellations, in common with his other countrymen.

" From the day of their repulse, both the French and Americans abandoned all further prosecution of the siege.

" In this manner was the province of Georgia cleared a third time of the enemy, after the most sanguine expectations had been entertained by all America that the reduction of this province would have been a preparatory step to the expulsion of the British fleets and armies from every part of the continent." (Dr. Andrews' History of the War, etc., Vol. III., Chap. xlv., pp. 316—318.)

where to find protection. Throughout the State the people were disheartened, and foreboded desolation."*

I have given a more minute account of Count D'Estaing and his abortive expeditions to America, and of his final attack upon Savanah and its results; how completely disappointed were the American revolutionists thus far in their unnatural alliance with France against England; how little mutual respect or good-will, and what quarrels occurred, whenever they came or attempted to act together, whether at Boston, or Long Island, or Charleston, or Savannah; and how much feebler the army and more gloomy the prospects of the Congress party were at the end of 1779 than they were two years before, when the alliance with France was formed. Dr. Ramsay well sums up these events as follows:

"The campaign of 1779 is remarkable for the feeble exertions of the Americans. Accidental causes, which had previously excited their activity, had in a great measure ceased to have influence. An enthusiasm for liberty made them comparatively disregard property and brave all dangers in the first years of the war. The successes of their arms near the beginning of 1777, and the hope of capturing Burgoyne's army in the close of it, together with the brisk circulation of a large quantity of paper-money, in good credit, made that year both active and decisive. The flattering prospects inspired by the alliance with France in 1778 banished all fears of the success of the revolution, but the failure of every scheme of co-operation produced a despondency of mind unfavourable to great exertions. Instead of driving the British out of the country, as the Americans vainly presumed, the campaigns of 1778 and 1779 terminated without any direct advantage from the French fleet sent to their aid. Expecting too much from their allies, and then failing in these expectations, they were less prepared to prosecute the war with their own resources than they would have been if D'Estaing had not touched on their coast. Their army was reduced in its numbers and badly clothed.

"In the first years of the war, the mercantile character was lost in the military spirit of the times; but in the progress of it the inhabitants, cooling in their enthusiasm, gradually returned

* Bancroft's History of the United States, Vol. X., Chap. xiii., pp. 297, 298.

to their former habits of lucrative business. This made distinctions between the army and citizens, and was unfriendly to military exertions. While several foreign events tended to the embarrassment of Great Britain,* and indirectly to the establishment of independence, a variety of internal causes relaxed the exertions of the Americans, and for a time made it doubtful whether they would ultimately be independent citizens or conquered subjects."†

Even a year later—"The military force," says Mr. Tucker, "embarked in the beginning of 1781, to maintain the cause of independence, is thus stated in (Chief Justice) Marshall's Life of Washington: 'The Southern troops, from Pennsylvania to Georgia, did not exceed three thousand men. Of the Northern troops, twelve hundred had been detached to Virginia, under La Fayette; with these they amounted only to three thousand effective men in April. The cavalry and artillery was less than one thousand. With some small additions, the whole reached four thousand men in May. They were ill supplied with clothing, and were seriously threatened with a want of provisions. The quartermaster's department was without means of transport," (Marshall, Vol. IV., p. 446).‡

Such was the character and such the fruits of the alliance with France during the first two years of its existence; and such was the state of the revolutionary army in 1780, and which seems to have been largely owing to the incapacity and ill conduct of the Congress itself, which had become degenerate and corrupt—equal to that of any British Parliament, or of any Provincial Legislature, under any Royal Governor.§

---

* "In the latter part of this year (1779), Spain decided on joining France in the war, anxious as she was to take the chance of recovering Gibraltar, Jamaica, and the Floridas." (Tucker's History of the United States, Vol. I., Chap. iii., p. 251.)

Thus England had arrayed against her two of the most powerful Governments, with the two most powerful fleets in Europe, besides the war in America.

† Dr. Ramsay's History of the United States, Vol. II., Chap. xvii., pp. 305, 306.)

‡ Tucker's History of the United States, Vol. I., Chap. iii., p. 282.

§ "There were never more than forty members present—often no more than twenty. These small numbers, however, by no means insured harmony, nor precluded violent and unseemly quarrels, rumours of which were not

Abundant evidence can be adduced in proof and illustration of this statement from the warmest partizans of Congress; but the testimony of Washington himself is ample and indisputable. In the winter of 1778-9 he had to concert his measures with Congress at Philadelphia, and he writes from thence as follows to his friend Benjamin Harrison:

"If I were to be called upon to draw a picture of the times and of men from what I have seen, heard, and in part known, I should in one word say that idleness, dissipation, and extravagance seem to have laid fast hold of them; that speculation, peculation, and an insatiable thirst for riches seem to have got the better of every other consideration and of every order of men; that party disputes and personal quarrels are the great business of the day; whilst the momentous concerns of an empire, a great and accumulating debt, ruined finances, depreciated money, and want of credit, which in its consequence is the want of everything, are but secondary considerations, and postponed from day to day, and from week to week, as if our affairs wore the most promising aspect. * * Our money is now sinking fifty per cent. a day in this city, and I shall not be surprised if in the course of a few months a total stop is put to the currency of it; and yet an assembly, a concert, a dinner, a supper, that will cost three or four hundred pounds, will not only take men from acting in this business, but from thinking of it; while a great part of the officers of our army, from absolute necessity, are quitting the service. * * I have no resentments, nor do I mean to point at particular characters. This I can declare upon my honour, for I have every attention paid me by Congress that I could possibly expect. * * But

---

slow in passing the Atlantic. 'For God's sake,' thus writes La Fayette from France, 'For God's sake prevent the Congress from disputing loudly together. Nothing so much hurts the interest and reputation of America.' (Letter of La Fayette to Washington, June 12th, 1779.) Thus the object of concealment, unless, perhaps, for private purposes, was most imperfectly attained, although, in name at least, the deliberations of Congress at this time were secret. Historically, even the Journal which they kept gives little light as to their true proceedings. An American gentleman, who has studied that document with care, laments that it is painfully meagre, the object being apparently to record as little as possible." (Life of President Reed, by Mr. William Reed, Vol. II., p. 18.)

Lord Mahon's History of England, etc., Vol. VI., Chap. lviii., pp. 420, 421.

such is the picture which from my inmost soul I believe to be true; and I confess to you that I feel more real distress on account of the present appearances of things, than I have done at any time since the commencement of the dispute."*

Such is General Washington's own account of the character and occupation of the Congress of the United States in the third year of the revolutionary war, and in the second year of their alliance with France—idleness, dissipation, extravagance, speculation, peculation, avarice, party and personal quarrels, dancing, feasting; while the credit was reduced almost to nothing, and the army neglected and suffering.†

---

* Letter to Benjamin Harrison, December 30th, 1778. Washington's Writings, Vol. VI., p. 151, quoted in Lord Mahon's History, Vol. VI., Chap. lviii., pp. 419, 420.

† Dr. Ramsay, referring to this depreciation of the currency, says: "The confiscation and sale of the property of Tories, for the most part, brought but very little into the public treasury. The sales were generally made on credit, and by the progressive depreciation, what was dear at the time of the purchase, was very cheap at the time of payment. When this measure was first adopted, little or no injustice resulted from it, for at that time the paper bills were equal, or nearly equal, to gold or silver of the same nominal sum. In the progress of the war, when depreciation took place, the case was materially altered.

"The aged, who had retired from the scenes of active business to enjoy the fruits of their industry, found their substance melting away to a mere pittance, insufficient for their support. The widow who lived comfortably on the bequests of a deceased husband, experienced a frustration of all his well-meant tenderness. The laws of the country interposed and compelled her to receive a shilling, where a pound was her due. The hapless orphan, instead of receiving from the hands of an executor a competency to set out in business, was obliged to give a final discharge on the payment of sixpence in the pound." (Dr. Ramsay's History of the United States, Vol. II., Chap. xviii., pp. 315, 316.)

"The paper-money," says Lord Mahon, "had gradually fallen to one-twentieth, to one-thirtieth, nay, in some cases to not less than one-hundredth of its nominal value! But perhaps one practical instance may make this case clearer. In December of this year (1779), and in the State of Maryland, an English officer received an innkeeper's bill, which in his Travels he has printed at full length, amounting in paper-money to £732 and some shillings; and this bill he paid in gold with four guineas and a half." (Aubury's Travels, Vol. II., p. 492.) (Lord Mahon's History, etc., Vol. VI., Chap. lviii., p. 416.)

General Washington thus describes this state of things in regard to every man in the public service: "What officers can bear the weight of prices that

Such was the progress of the war; such the failure of the expeditions of the French alliance; such the state of the revolutionary army, and of the public credit; and such the degenerate character and proceedings of Congress and its surroundings in the beginning of 1780—the fifth year of the civil war.

every necessary article is now got to ? A rat, in the shape of a horse, is not to be bought at this time for less than two hundred pounds, nor a saddle under thirty or forty pounds; boots twenty, and shoes and other articles in like proportion. How is it possible, therefore, for officers to stand this without an increase of pay? And how is it possible to advance their pay when flour is selling at different places from five to fifteen pounds per hundredweight, hay from ten to thirty pounds, and beef and other essentials in like proportion?" The depreciation still proceeding, Washington a few months afterwards says that "a waggon load of money will now scarcely purchase a waggon load of provisions." (Letters to Governor Morris, October 4th, 1778; and to the President of the Congress, April 23rd, 1779.)

CHAPTER XXIX.

1780—A YEAR OF WEAKNESS AND DISASTER TO THE AMERICAN CAUSE, AND OF SUCCESS TO THE BRITISH ARMS.

THE year 1780 was inauspicious for the revolutionary cause, but auspicious for the English. The financial embarrassments arising from the depreciation of the paper-money engaged the anxious deliberations of Congress,* and Washington's army was by no means able to cope with the northern division of the English army.†

---

* " The commissaries, greatly in debt, had neither money nor credit, and starvation began to stare the soldiers in the face. To support his army, Washington was again obliged to resort to the harsh expedient of levying contributions on the surrounding country. Each county was called upon for a certain quantity of flour and meat ; but as the civil authorities took the matter of supply in hand, for which certificates were given by the commissaries on the appraisement of two magistrates, the use of force did not become necessary." (Hildreth's History of the United States, Vol. III., Chap. xi., p. 301.)

† " Washington's entire force scarcely exceeded ten thousand men, a number not equal to the (British) garrison of New York ; and even of these a considerable number were militia drafts, whose terms of service were fast expiring."—*Ib.*, p. 303.

But though New York was in possession of the British, and strongly garrisoned, apprehensions were entertained of attacks upon the several English garrison posts in the State from invasions of marauding parties of the revolutionary army, from facilities of approach on account of the freezing over of all the rivers from the extreme severity of this winter. It is singular that while Benjamin Franklin was leader of the Revolutionists, and now United States Minister to France, his son was one of the leaders of the Loyalists. "It was now," says Mr. Hildreth, "that the ' Board of Associated Loyalists' was formed, of which Franklin, late Royal Governor of New

But La Fayette, now returned from a recent visit to France, during which he had obtained from the French Court a loan of money and reinforcements of naval and land forces, Washington contemplated the recovery of New York, which had long been a favourite object with him. The French squadron of seven sail of the line, and five frigates and transports, under the command of Chevalier de Ternay, arrived at Newport harbour, Long Island, on the 10th July, having on board six thousand troops, under the command of Count de Rochambeau, who, in order to prevent the repetition of previous disputes, was directed to put himself under Washington's orders; and on all points of precedence and etiquette—this was the first division of the promised reinforcements from France—the French officers were to give place to the Americans. Washington and Count de Rochambeau agreed upon an attack on New York. The British had in New York only four ships of the line and a few frigates; but three days after the arrival of the French squadron, Admiral Graves reached New York with six ships of the line. Having now the naval superiority, the British, instead of waiting to be attacked, proposed to attack the French at Newport, and for which purpose Sir Henry Clinton embarked with six thousand men; but as Sir Henry Clinton and Admiral Arbuthnot could not agree on a plan of operations, the British troops were disembarked. The fleet proceeded to blockade the French ships, and the revolutionary army was obliged to remain at Newport for their protection. "News presently arrived that the French second division was detained at Brest, blockaded there by another British squadron. Instead of being an assistance, the French auxiliaries threatened to be a burden; three thousand troops and five hundred militia were kept under arms at Newport to assist in guarding the French ships. Thus a third time—as it seemed, almost a sort of fatality—the attempt at French co-operation proved a failure."*

Sir Henry Clinton, on leaving the Count D'Estaing after his defeat at Savannah, had left the coast of Georgia with his fleet

---

Jersey, released by exchange from his tedious confinement in Connecticut, was made president. Washington, however, was in no condition to undertake an attack, and the winter passed off with few skirmishes." (Hildreth's History of the United States, Vol. III., Chap. xi., p. 303.)

* *Ib.*, pp. 311, 312.

for France, determined to extend his military operations south, with a view of completing the submission of the Southern States. Leaving the garrison of New York under the command of General Knyphausen, he proceeded in person on an expedition against South Carolina, and besieged Charleston, the capital. Information had been obtained at Charleston of Sir Henry Clinton's intention two months before the arrival of his fleet and troops, and the city was fortified on all sides, and on its redoubts, lines, and batteries were mounted eighty pieces of cannon and mortars. The commander, General Lincoln, had a force of 7,000 men of all denominations under arms, and was expecting large reinforcements. The army of Sir Henry Clinton was increased by a reinforcement of 3,000 men—making in the whole about 9,000 men under his command.

At the commencement of the siege, the Governor of the State, by the extraordinary powers conferred upon him by the Legislature, issued a proclamation requiring such of the militia as were regularly drafted, and all the inhabitants and *owners of property in the town, to repair to the American standard and join the garrison immediately, under pain of confiscation.*

The siege commenced the 3rd of April, and was protracted to the 11th of May. The terms of capitulation proposed by each party in the earlier part of the siege were mutually declined. Cannonading continued on each side until the British opened batteries on the third parallel, played upon the American garrison with cannon and mortars at a distance of less than a hundred yards, advanced within twenty-five yards of the American works, and were ready for making a general assault by land and water when, on the 11th of May, "a great number of citizens addressed General Lincoln in a petition, expressing their acquiescence in the terms which Sir Henry Clinton had offered, and requested his acceptance of them. On the reception of this petition, General Lincoln wrote to Sir Henry, and offered to accept the terms before proposed. The royal commanders, wishing to avoid the extremity of storming the city, and unwilling to press to unconditional submission an enemy whose friendship they wished to conciliate, returned a favourable answer. A capitulation was signed on the 12th of May, and Major General Leslie took possession of the town the next day. Upwards of 400 pieces of artillery were surrendered.* By the articles of capitulation, the garrison was to march out of town and deposit their arms in front of the works, but the drums were not to beat a British march, nor the colours to be uncased. The continental troops and seamen were to keep their baggage and remain prisoners of war till exchanged. The militia were to be permitted to return to their respective homes, as prisoners on parole; and while they adhered to their parole, were not to be molested by the British troops in person or property. The inhabitants, of all conditions, were to be considered as prisoners on parole, and to hold their property on the same terms with the militia. The officers of the army and navy were to retain their servants, swords, pistols, and baggage unsearched. They were permitted to sell their horses, but not to remove them. A vessel was allowed to proceed to Philadelphia with General Lincoln's despatches unopened."†

Shortly after the capture of Charleston, Sir Henry Clinton embarked for New York with the principal part of his army ;‡

---

* "In the siege, the British lost seventy-six killed and one hundred and eighty-nine wounded; the Americans about an equal number. The prisoners, exclusive of sailors, amounted to five thousand six hundred and eighteen, counting all the adult males of the town." (Tucker's History of the United States, Vol. I., Chap. lii., p. 253.)

† Dr. Ramsay's History of the United States, Vol. II., Chap. xx., pp. 337, 338.

Yet in the face of the facts above stated by Dr. Ramsay, who was an officer on General Washington's staff, and afterwards member of Congress, where he had access to the official documents and letters from which he compiled his history, Mr. Bancroft makes the following statements and remarks: "The value of the spoil, which was distributed by English and Hessian commissaries of captures, amounted to about £300,000 sterling, so that the dividend of a major-general exceeded 4,000 guineas. There was no restraint on private rapine; the silver plate of the planters was carried off; all negroes that had belonged to the rebels were seized, even though they had themselves sought an asylum within the British lines; and at one embarkation 2,000 were shipped to a market in the West Indies. British officers thought more of amassing fortunes than of reuniting the empire. The patriots were not allowed to appoint attorneys to manage or sell their estates, a sentence of confiscation hung over the whole land, and British protection was granted only in return for the unconditional promise of loyalty." (Bancroft's History of the United States, Vol. X., Chap. xiv., pp. 305, 306.)

‡ "Sir Henry Clinton, having left about 4,000 men for Southern service,

but before his departure he performed several important acts both as Royal Commissioner and as Commander-in-Chief of the army.

After the surrender of the capital, it was proposed to awe the disaffected and secure the universal submission of the people by sending out three expeditions.

"One expedition was sent by Clinton up the Savannah, to encourage the loyal and reduce the disaffected in the neighbourhood of Augusta; another proceeded for like purpose to the district of Ninety-Six, where Williamson surrendered his post and accepted British protection. A third and larger party, under Cornwallis, moved across the Santee towards Camden."*

These expeditions rather weakened than strengthened the influence of the British cause, as compulsion rather than conciliation was employed to re-establish British supremacy; and

embarked early in June with the main army for New York. On his departure the command devolved on Lieutenant-General Cornwallis." (Dr. Ramsay's History of the United States, Vol. II., Chap. xx., p. 341.)

"They saw South Carolina apparently won back to the royal cause, and with some probability that North Carolina would follow the example. But at this crisis intelligence reached Sir Henry Clinton that the Americans upon the Hudson (under the command of General Washington) were on the point of receiving considerable succours; that a French fleet sent to their aid, with several French regiments on board, might soon be expected off the New England coasts. Sir Henry deemed it his duty to provide in person for the safety of his principal charge. In the first days of June he accordingly re-embarked for New York, with a portion of his army; leaving, however, about 4,000 men under Lord Cornwallis's command. The instructions given to Lord Cornwallis were to consider the maintenance of Charleston, and in general of South Carolina, as his main and indispensable objects; but consistently with these, he was left at liberty to make 'a solid move,' as it was termed, into North Carolina, if he judged it proper or found it possible." (Lord Mahon's History, etc., Vol. VII., Chap. lxii., p. 70.)

On the eve of leaving Charleston for New York, Sir Henry reported to the British Colonial Minister, Lord Germaine: "The inhabitants from every quarter declare their allegiance to the King, and offer their services in arms. There are few men in South Carolina who are not either our prisoners or in arms with us."

* Bancroft's History of the United States, Vol. X., Chap. xiv., p. 306.

"The universal panic consequent on the capture of Charleston had suspended all resistance to the British army. The men of Beaufort, of Ninety-Six, and of Camden, had capitulated under the promise of security. They believed that they were to be treated as neutrals or as prisoners on parole. There remained to them no possibility of flight with their families; and if the proclamations and orders issued by Sir Henry Clinton before his departure for New York, defeated rather than promoted the objects intended by them.*

After issuing his proclamation (for the purport of which see previous note), Sir Henry Clinton took his departure, with the major part of his army, for New York, leaving Lord Cornwallis in command with four thousand troops.†

---

they were inclined to take up arms, there was no American army around which they could rally." (Bancroft's History of the United States, Vol. X., Chap. xiv., p. 307.)

"No organized American force was now left in either of the Carolinas. The three most Southern States had not a battalion in the field, nor were the next three much better provided. The Virginia line had been mostly captured at Charleston, or dispersed in subsequent engagements. The same was the case with the North Carolina regiments. The recent battle of Camden had reduced the Maryland line to a single regiment—the Delaware line to a single company." (Hildreth's History of the United States, Vol. III., Chap. xi., p. 316.)

* "On the 22nd of May, confiscation of property and other punishments were denounced against all who should thereafter oppose the King in arms, or hinder any one from joining his forces. On the 1st of June, a proclamation by the Commissioners Clinton and Arbuthnot, offered pardon to the penitent on their immediate return to allegiance ; to the loyal, the promise of their former political immunities, including freedom from taxation, except by their own Legislature. This policy of moderation might have familiarized the Carolinians once more to the British Government ; but the proclamation was not communicated to Cornwallis—so that when, three weeks later, two leading men, one of whom had been in a high station, and both principally concerned in the rebellion, went to that officer to surrender themselves under its provisions, he could only answer that he had no knowledge of its existence.

"On the 3rd of June (the day of his departure from Charleston), Clinton, by a proclamation which he alone signed, cut up British authority in Carolina by the roots. He required all the inhabitants of the province, even those outside of Charleston, 'who were now prisoners on parole,' to take an active part in securing the royal government. 'Should they neglect to return to their allegiance,' so ran the proclamation, 'they will be treated as rebels to the government of the King.' He never reflected that many who accepted protection from fear or convenience, did so in the expectation of living in a state of neutrality, and that they might say, 'If we *must fight*, let us fight on the side of our friends, of our countrymen of America.'" (Bancroft's History of the United States, Vol. X., Chap. xiv., pp. 307, 308.)

† "Earl (afterwards Marquis) Cornwallis was born in 1738. Early in life he had embraced the military profession, which he pursued with undeviating honour, though variable success. In him the want of any shining talents

"Lord Cornwallis, considering South Carolina as entirely re-annexed to Great Britain, would admit of no neutrality among the inhabitants; but insisted on their taking the oath of allegiance, which, however, was generally taken with reluctance by the people of the lower country. This part of the State was still further alienated by the licentious and plundering habits of the British soldiers over a conquered country, and by the seduction of many of the slaves from their masters."*

There can be no justification of Lord Cornwallis's policy; but there were some mitigating circumstances that palliate the severities which he inflicted. Among those who had been taken prisoners at the capture of Charleston, and professed loyalty, was, as Lord Mahon says, "One Lisle, who had not only taken the oath of allegiance, but accepted military rank as a King's officer; waited just long enough to supply his battalion with clothes, arms, and ammunition from the royal stores, and then quietly led them back to his old friends. Highly incensed at such signal acts of treachery as Lisle's, Lord Cornwallis had recourse to some severe orders in return. The penalty of death was denounced against all militiamen

---

was in a great measure supplied by probity, by punctuality, by steady courage, by vigilant attention to his duties. In 1776, on the Declaratory Bill, he had shown his conciliatory temper to the colonies; denying, with Lord Camden and only three Peers besides, any right we had to tax them while they remained unrepresented in the House of Commons. When, however, the war broke forth, he acted solely as became a soldier. Under Lord Cornwallis was now serving a young officer of no common spirit and daring, destined, like himself, to attain, at another period, the highest office that an Englishman out of England can fill—the office of Governor-General of India. This was Francis Lord Rawdon, subsequently better known, first as Earl of Moira, and then as Marquis of Hastings. In the ensuing battle of Camden, where he held a second rank, he played a distinguished part; he was not yet twenty-six years of age, and he had already gained renown five years before, in the battle of Bunker's Hill." (Lord Mahon's History, etc., Vol. VII., Chap. lxii., p. 71.)

* Tucker's History of the United States, Vol. I., Chap. iii., p. 254.

"There was no longer any armed American force in South Carolina; and Lord Cornwallis resorted to energetic means of preventing disaffection. All those who were found in arms after they had submitted to British protection were considered as having forfeited their lives, and several of them were hung on the spot. But these severities, instead of their intended effect, produced a strong reaction."—*Ib.*, p. 256.

who, after serving with the English, went off to the insurgents. Several of the prisoners in the battle of Camden, men taken with arms in their hands and British protections in their pockets, were hanged. Other such examples were made at Augusta and elsewhere. Some who had been living on their parole at Charleston, and who, in spite of that parole, carried on a secret correspondence with their insurgent countrymen, were shipped off to St. Augustine. A proclamation was issued, sequestering the estates of those who had been the most forward to oppose the establishment of the royal authority within the province. Perhaps these measures exceeded the bounds of justice; certainly they did the bounds of policy. This was shown by the fatal event, when, on the overthrow of the royalist cause in South Carolina, the measures of Lord Cornwallis became the plea for other executions and for every act of oppression that resentment could devise."

"Within the more limited sphere of his own command, Lord Rawdon had recourse to, or at the very least announced, some measures still more severe, and far less to be justified. In a letter to one of his officers, which was intercepted, we find, for example, what follows: 'I will give the inhabitants ten guineas for the head of every deserter belonging to the volunteers of Ireland; and five guineas only if they bring him in alive.' No amount of provocation or of precedent in his enemies, no degree of youthful ardour in himself, are at all adequate to excuse these most blamable words. When, however, he was called upon to vindicate them, Lord Rawdon declared that many of his threats were meant only 'to act on the fears and prejudices of the vulgar,' and by no means to be carried into practical effect."*

During the latter part of the year there were various skirmishes and battles between volunteer parties of Independents, under such leaders as Sumpter and Clarke, and detachments of the British army, with various success, but nothing which affected the supremacy of the royal cause, though the moral influence of it was widely weakened by the arbitrary policy of the British commanders and the conduct of the British troops. The prospects of the revolution were very gloomy,†

---

* Lord Mahon's History, etc., Vol. VII., Chap. lxii., pp. 75, 76.
† "While the war raged in South Carolina, the campaign of 1780, in the

and its leaders were much disheartened. In these circumstances of depression and despondency, an earnest appeal was made to France for men and money,* and the transactions following show that the appeal was not made in vain, and that French ships and troops were the main instruments in deciding the battle which was followed by the acknowledgment of American Independence.†

Mr. Hildreth, referring to the close of this year, says: "So far, indeed, as related to America, Great Britain had good reason to be satisfied with the late campaign. Georgia was entirely subdued, and the royal government re-established. The Northern States, was barren of important events. The campaign of 1780 passed away in the Northern States, as has been related, in successive disappointments and reiterated distresses. The country was exhausted; the continental currency expiring. The army, for want of subsistence, was kept inactive and brooding over its calamities. While these disasters were openly menacing the ruin of the American cause, treachery was silently undermining it. A distinguished officer (General Arnold) engaged, for a stipulated sum of money, to betray into the hands of the British an important post committed to his care," etc. (Dr. Ramsay's History of the United States, Vol. II., Chap. xxiv., pp. 364—377.)

* "Congress could do nothing, and confessed that it could do nothing. 'We have required,' thus they wrote to the States on the 15th of January, 1781, 'aids of men, provisions and money; the States alone have authority to execute.' Since Congress itself made a public confession of its powerlessness, nothing remained but *to appeal to France* for rescue, not from a foreign enemy, but from the evils consequent on its own want of government. 'If France lends not a speedy aid,' wrote General Greene from the South to her Minister in Philadelphia, 'I fear the country will be for ever lost.' It was therefore resolved for the moment to despatch to Versailles, as a special minister, one who had lived in the midst of the ever-increasing distresses of the army, to set them before the Government of France in the most striking light. The choice fell on the younger Laurens, of South Carolina. To this agent Washington confided a statement of the condition of the country; and with dignity and candour avowed that it had reached a crisis out of which it could not rise by its own unassisted strength. To Franklin he wrote in the same strain; and La Fayette addressed a like memorial of ripe wisdom to Vergennes" (the French Minister for Foreign Affairs). (Bancroft's History of the United States, Vol. X., Chap., xix., pp. 417, 418.)

"Scarce any one of the States had as yet sent an eighth part of its quota into the field; and there was no prospect of a glorious offensive campaign, unless their generous allies should help them with money, and with a fleet strong enough to secure the superiority at sea."—*Ib.*, p. 425.

† It was in the latter part of this year, 1780, that the treachery of General Arnold and the melancholy tragedy of Major André's execution took place.

possession of Charleston, Augusta, Ninety-Six, and Camden, supported by an army in the field, secured entire control over all the wealthy parts of South Carolina. North Carolina was full of Tories, anxiously awaiting the approach of Cornwallis. The three Southern States were incapable of helping themselves, and those further north, exhausted and penniless, were little able to send assistance. It seemed as if the promises so often made by Lord George Germaine's American correspondents were now about to be fulfilled, and the rebel colonies to sink beneath the accumulated pressure of this long-protracted struggle.*

Thus, at the close of 1780, the military conflicts were almost invariably successful on the side of the British; the resources of the revolutionists in both money and men were exhausted, and their hopes of success utterly extinguished without foreign aid. But though the British were successful on the fields of battle, they everywhere lost in the confidence, esteem, and affections of the people, even of the Loyalists. Yet the prospects of the war party of independence were gloomy indeed. General Washington felt that some great achievement was necessary to revive the hopes of his fellow-countrymen, and save from dissolution his daily decreasing army. His only hope was in aid from France. His words were:

"Without an immediate, ample, and efficacious succour in money, we may make a feeble and expiring effort in our next campaign, *in all probability the period of our opposition. Next to a loan in money, a constant naval superiority on these coasts* is the object the most interesting."

* Hildreth's History of the United States, Vol. III., Chap. xli., p. 331.
"Though British conquests had rapidly succeeded each other, yet no advantages accrued to the victors. The minds of the people were unsubdued, or rather were alienated from every idea of returning to their former allegiance. Such was their temper, that the expense of retaining them in subjection would have exceeded all the profits of the conquest. British garrisons kept down open resistance, in the vicinity of the places where they were established; but as soon as they were withdrawn and the people left to themselves, a spirit of revolt hostile to Great Britain always displayed itself; and the standard of independence, whenever it was prudently raised, never wanted followers among the active and spirited part of the community." (Dr. Ramsay's History of the United States, Vol. II., Chap. xx., p. 363.)

CHAPTER XXX.

THE FRENCH AND CONGRESS ALLIES IN 1781 RECOVER VIRGINIA—SURRENDER OF LORD CORNWALLIS—RESULTS.

UNDER the adverse circumstances and gloom which attended and closed the year 1780, as stated in the preceding chapter, Washington felt the necessity of doing something bold and great to revive the confidence of his countrymen and arrest the decline of his army.

Under these circumstances, a campaign of operations was devised and agreed upon by Washington and the commander of the French troops. The centres of British power in America were the army of about ten thousand men in New York, under the immediate command of Sir Henry Clinton, who was, indeed, Commander-in-Chief of the British forces in North America; and secondly, the army of Virginia, about seven thousand men, under the command of Earl Cornwallis; and thirdly, the garrison of Charleston, South Carolina, under the command of Lord Rawdon; Savannah, the capital of Georgia, was also occupied by a British garrison. Washington's plan was to pretend an attack upon New York, but to make a real attack upon the army of Virginia, with the view of extinguishing British power in the Southern States. So well was the appearance of an intended attack upon New York kept up, that Sir Henry Clinton made all needful preparations for its defence, and actually ordered Lord Cornwallis to send a detachment of his men to New York to strengthen its defence; but after their embarkation for that purpose the order was countermanded, and Lord Cornwallis was allowed to retain them. Nothing could be more complete than the deception practised upon Sir

Henry Clinton; nor did he suspect the real intention of the allied armies until they had crossed the Hudson and were on their way, through the Jerseys, Pennyslvania, and Maryland, to Virginia.*

"In the latter end of August," says Dr. Ramsay, "the American army began their march to Virginia from the neighbourhood of New York. Washington had advanced as far as Chester before he received information of the arrival of De Grasse. The French troops marched at the same time, for the same place. In the course of this summer they passed through all the extensive settlements which lie between Newport and Yorktown. It seldom if ever happened before, that an army led through a foreign country at so great a distance from their own, among a people of different principles, customs, language, and religion, behaved with so much regularity. In their march to Yorktown they had to pass through five hundred miles of a country abounding in fruit, and at a time when the most delicious productions of nature, growing on and near the public highways, presented both opportunity and temptation to gratify

* It appears, however, that in the first consultation, which "took place at Weathersfield, between Generals Washington, Knox, and Du Portail on the part of the Americans, and Count de Rochambeau and the Chevalier Chastellux on the part of the French, it was agreed to lay siege to New York in concert with the French fleet, which was to arrive on the coast in the month of August. Washington addressed letters to the executive officers of New Hampshire, Massachusetts, Connecticut, and New Jersey, requiring them to fill up their battalions, and to have their quotas of six thousand two hundred militia in readiness within a week after the time they might be called for. But all these States not adding five hundred men to Washington's army, Sir Henry Clinton having received a reinforcement of three thousand Germans, and intelligence having been received that Count de Grasse, with a French fleet of twenty-eight ships and seven thousand troops (besides seamen), had sailed for the Chesapeake, Washington and Count de Rochambeau changed their plan of operations and determined to proceed to Virginia, and, in combination with the French fleet and soldiers, to capture the army under the command of Earl Cornwallis in Virginia. The appearance of an intention to attack New York was nevertheless kept up. While this deception was played off, the allied army crossed the North River on August 24th, and passed on by the way of Philadelphia through the intermediate country to Yorktown, Virginia. An attempt to reduce the British force in Virginia promised success with more expedition, and to secure an object of nearly equal importance to the reduction of New York." (Ramsay's History of the United States, Vol. II., Chap. xxv., pp. 448—451.)

their appetites, yet so complete was their discipline, that in this long march scarce an instance could be produced of a peach or an apple being taken without the consent of the inhabitants."*

On the 14th of September, Washington and De Rochambeau, in advance of their armies and with their respective staffs of officers, arrived at Williamsburg; and with Generals Chastellux, Du Portail, and Knox, visited Count de Grasse on board his famous ship, the *Ville de Paris*, and agreed on the plan of operations against Earl Cornwallis at Yorktown, on York river, to which the allied armies at once proceeded, for the purpose of besieging it. On the 1st day of October, General Washington was able to report to the President of Congress that the investment of the place was completed. "Gloucester (on the opposite side of the river, not a mile wide there), which was held by Colonel Dundas, was beleaguered by some Virginian troops, and by the French legion of the Duke de Lauzun. Yorktown, where Cornwallis in person, and with his main force, commanded, saw to his left the division of La Fayette, and to his right the division of St. Simon. Other bodies of troops filled the space between them, while Washington and Rochambeau fixed their posts near together, towards the centre. They brought up fifty pieces of cannon, for the most part heavy, by aid from the French ships, as also sixteen mortars, and they lost no time in commencing their first parallel against the town.† By the 9th the first parallel was completed, when the town and its defences were cannonaded and shelled. Within another week a second parallel was completed within

---

* Dr. Ramsay's History of the United States, Vol. II., Chap. xxv., pp. 450, 451.

† Lord Mahon's History of England, etc., Vol. VII., Chap. lxiv., p. 172.

"On the other hand, Lord Cornwallis is admitted to have shown most undaunted resolution. The officers under him, and the troops, German and English, all did their duty well. For some weeks they had laboured hard, and unremittingly, in raising their defences; and they were now prepared with equal spirit to maintain their half-completed works. But besides the enemy without, they had another within—an epidemic sickness, that stretched many hundreds helpless in their pallet-beds. Nor could they hinder Washington from completing his first parallel and opening his fire upon them in the evening of the 9th of October. For two days the fire was incessant from heavy cannon, and from mortars and howitzers, throwing

three hundred yards of the defences, two redoubts stormed and taken—one by the French and the other by the Americans—and the further defence of the town rendered impossible.

Down to this time, the 15th of October, Lord Cornwallis had expected reinforcements of ships and troops from New York ;* but he now despaired of aid from that quarter, and attempted to escape with his army in the night across the river, which was prevented by a storm, when the only alternative left him was to surrender on the best terms he could obtain. On the morning of the 17th he sent a flag of truce to Washington, proposing a cessation of arms, and a treaty for the capitulation of his post. Hostilities ceased; the terms of surrender were discussed and agreed upon on the 18th by four commissioners, two field officers being named on each side. The army, and all that belonged to it, was surrendered to Washington; and the ships and seamen to Count de Grasse " (Tucker).

"All the artillery and public stores in the two forts, together with the shipping and boats in the two harbours, were to be surrendered by the English. On the other hand, private pro-

---

shells in showers on the town, until, says Cornwallis, all our guns on the left were silenced, our works much damaged, and our loss of men considerable. By these shells, also, the *Charon*, a ship of forty-four guns, together with three British transports in the river, were set in flames and consumed."—*Ib.*, p. 173.

* Before the investment of Yorktown, Lord Cornwallis sent a despatch to Sir Henry Clinton, informing him of the delicacy and danger of his situation, and requesting reinforcements. On the evening of the 29th of September, Lord Cornwallis was cheered by the arrival of an express, bringing despatches from Sir Henry Clinton, dated the 24th, informing him that by the 5th of October a fleet of twenty-three sail of the line, three of which were three-deckers, with 5,000 men, rank and file, would start for his assistance. The auxiliary forces at New York were ready and eager to depart by the 5th of October; but the ships were delayed by the slowness and obstinacy of Admiral Arbuthnot. Sir Henry Clinton writes : " We had the misfortune to see almost every succeeding day produce some naval obstruction or other to protract our departure ; and I am sorry to add, that it was the afternoon of the 19th before the fleet was fairly at sea. This was the day of Lord Cornwallis's capitulation. Five days afterwards the fleet with the 5,000 troops arrived off the Chesapeake, when they received the news of the surrender of Lord Cornwallis, and sailed back to New York. Had these auxiliary forces started from New York at the time promised, the siege of Yorktown would have been raised, the allied army defeated, and Lord Cornwallis and his little army would have been victors instead of prisoners."

perty of every kind was to be respected by the Americans and French. The garrisons of York and Gloucester were to march out with the same honours of war as had been granted by Sir Henry Clinton at Charleston; the land forces to remain prisoners of the United States, and the naval forces prisoners of France. The soldiers were to be kept in Virginia, Maryland, or Pennsylvania, and as much by regiments as possible. The general staff and other officers not left with the troops to be permitted to go to New York, or to Europe, on parole."*

The battle of Yorktown, and the surrender of Lord Cornwallis to the arms of the French and the Americans, may be regarded as the last battle of importance of the civil war in America. American writers and orators are fond of saying that here was brought face to face on the battle-field the strength of Old England and Young America, and the latter prevailed. No statement can be more unfounded, and no boast more groundless than this. England, without an ally, was at war with three kingdoms—France, Spain, and Holland—the most potent naval and military powers of Europe; while were also arrayed against her, by an "armed neutrality," Russia,

---

* Lord Mahon's History of England, etc., Vol. VII., Chap. lxiv., pp. 177, 178.

"The officers were to retain their side arms and private property of every kind, but all property obviously belonging to inhabitants of the United States to be subject to be reclaimed; the soldiers to be supplied with the same rations as were allowed to soldiers in the service of Congress. Cornwallis endeavoured to obtain permission for the British and German troops to return to their respective countries, under no other restrictions than an engagement not to serve against France or America. He also tried to obtain an indemnity for those of the inhabitants who had joined him; but he was obliged to recede from the former, and also to consent that the loyalists in his camp should be given up to the unconditional mercy of their countrymen. His lordship, nevertheless, obtained (from Washington) permission for the *Bonetta* sloop of war to pass unexamined to New York. This gave an opportunity of screening such of the loyalists as were most obnoxious to the Americans." (Dr. Ramsay's History of the United States, Vol. II., Chap. xxv., pp. 454, 455.)

"The regular troops of France and America, employed in this siege, consisted of about 7,000 of the former (besides ships and seamen), and 5,500 of the latter; and they were assisted by about 4,000 militia. The troops of every kind that surrendered prisoners of war were about 7,000; but so great was the number of the sick and wounded, that there were only 3,800 capable of bearing arms."—*Ib.*, p. 455.

Prussia, Denmark, and Sweden. England was armed to the teeth for the defence of her own shores against threatened invasion, while her navies were maintaining in sundry battles the honour of the British flag on three seas.

A small part only of the British land and naval forces was on the coast of America; yet there were garrisons at Savannah and Charleston, and a much larger military force at New York, under the command of Sir Henry Clinton, than that of Yorktown, under Lord Cornwallis. In the following campaign the English fleet was victorious over the French fleet in the West Indies, capturing the great ship *Ville de Paris*, and taking Count de Grasse himself prisoner. In the siege of Yorktown there were about 18,000 of the allied army of French and Americans, besides ships of the line and sailors, while the effective men under command of Lord Cornwallis amounted to less than 4,000. It was a marvel of skill and courage that with an army so small, and in a town so exposed and so incapable of being strongly fortified, and against an allied force so overwhelming, Lord Cornwallis was able to sustain a siege for a fortnight, until he despaired of reinforcements from New York.

Be it also observed, that the greater part of the forces besieging Yorktown were not Americans, but French, who supplied the shipping and artillery; in short, all the attacking forces by water, and a duplicate land enemy—the one part under the command of Count de Rochambeau, and the other part under the command of the Marquis de La Fayette. Had it not been for the French fleet and the French land forces, Washington would not have attempted an attack upon Yorktown. The success of the siege was, therefore, more French than American, though Washington had the nominal command of the allied army.

No one can doubt the undaunted courage and matchless skill of Washington, and his great superiority over any English general ever sent against him; nor can the bravery and endurance of his army be justly questioned; nor the dash and boldness and gallantry of the French army. But it is idle to speak of the siege of Yorktown as a trial of strength between Young America and Old England. And it is equally incorrect to say that the resources of England, in men or money, in ships or land forces, were exhausted, or that England was compelled to make peace in consequence of the disaster of Lord Cornwallis. There had been a peace party, both in and out of Parliament, opposed to the American war from the beginning. That party included some of the ablest statesmen in England, and increased in strength and influence from year to year, by exposing the incompetence, extravagance, and corruption of the Administration, the failure of all their plans, and the non-fulfilment of any of their promises in regard to America; that although they could defeat the Americans in the field of battle, they had not conquered and they could not conquer the hearts of the people, who became more and more alienated from England by the very example and depredations of the British officers and soldiers. The surrender of Lord Cornwallis, the importance of which was greatly magnified, increased the intensity of English feeling against the continuance of the American war, until the peace party actually gained a majority in the House of Commons, compelled the retirement of the old and corrupt Ministry, which had been the cause of all the oppressions in the American colonies and all the miseries of the war. Session after session, the leaders of the Opposition in both the Lords and Commons moved resolutions condemning the American war and the manner of conducting it; the Duke of Richmond, the Marquis of Rockingham, the Earl of Shelburne in the Lords; and General Conway, Mr. Fox, Mr. Burke, Lord John Cavendish, Mr. Hartley, Mr. Dunning (afterwards Lord Ashburton), and Sir James Lowther in the Commons. Several resolutions were introduced into the Commons condemnatory of the war in America, with a view of reducing the colonies to submission, and were defeated by small majorities—in one a majority of ten, and in another a majority of only *one*. At length they were censured and rejected by the Commons without a division.

On the 22nd of February, General Conway moved "That an address should be presented to his Majesty, to implore his Majesty to listen to the advice of his Commons, that the war in America might no longer be pursued for the impracticable purpose of reducing the inhabitants of that country to obedience by force, and to express their hopes that his Majesty's desire to restore the public tranquillity might be forwarded and made effectual by a happy reconciliation with the revolted colonies."

After a lengthened debate, this resolution was negatived—one hundred and ninety-three for the resolution, against it one hundred and ninety-four—a majority of one for the continuance of the war.

The motion having been objected to as vague in its terms, General Conway, on the 27th of February, introduced another motion, the same in substance with the previous one, but varied in phraseology, so as to meet the rules of the House, and more explicit in its terms. This resolution was strongly opposed by the Ministry; and after a long debate the Attorney-General moved the adjournment of the House: For the adjournment voted two hundred and fifteen; against it, two hundred and thirty-four—majority of nineteen against the Ministry—so that the original question, and an address to the King, framed upon the resolution, were then carried without a division.* The King returned a gracious but vague answer.

General Conway, after moving a vote of thanks to the King for his gracious answer, followed by moving a resolution: "That this House would consider as enemies to his Majesty and the country all those who should advise or by any means attempt the further prosecution of offensive war, on the continent of North America, for the purpose of reducing the revolted colonies to obedience by force." This motion, after a feeble opposition from the Ministry, was allowed to pass without a division.

It might be supposed, under these circumstances, that the Ministry would forthwith resign; but they continued to hold on to office, which they had held for twelve years, to the great injury of England and her colonies.

---

* During the discussion on this question, it had been argued that the Americans are fed, clothed, and paid by France; they are led on by French officers; the French and the American armies are incorporated into one; it was merely a locality that should give name to a war. France had formerly been fought with success in Germany, and there could be no solid objection to fighting her in America. General Conway argued that French troops did not cost more than £40 per man a year, while the expense of the English troops cost £100 per man a year. General Conway reminded the House that though seventy-three thousand men were voted and paid for, we had never above half that number in actual service. Government had, therefore, only to complete the regiments, and they would have more men in America than ever they had before." (Annual Register of Parliament for 1782, pp. 158—161.)

To bring the matter to an issue, the following resolution was moved on the 8th of March by Lord John Cavendish, seconded by Mr. Powys:

"That it appears to this House, that since the year 1775 upwards of one hundred millions of money have been expended on the army and navy in a fruitless war.

"That it appears to this House, that during the above period we have lost the thirteen colonies of America, which anciently belonged to the Crown of Great Britain (except the ports of New York, Charleston, and Savannah), the newly acquired colony of Florida, many of our valuable West India and other islands, and those that remain are in the utmost danger.

"That it appears to this House, that Great Britain is at present engaged in an expensive war with America, France, Spain, and Holland, without a single ally.

"That it appears to this House, that the chief cause of all these misfortunes has been the want of foresight and ability in his Majesty's Ministers.*"

The facts stated in the first three of these resolutions were admitted on all sides; the discussion, therefore, turned upon the conclusion drawn in the last resolution, the justice of which was patent to all from the uniform failure and disgrace of the policy and all the separate measures of Ministers during the whole of their administration. It was attempted to be argued, in defence of Ministers, that misfortune did not always prove misconduct; that the failure of execution of measures might depend, not on those who planned them, but on the fault of those who were to execute them. But "this ground," says the Parliamentary Register, "appeared so weak, even to the friends of the Administration, that it was almost entirely deserted, except by the Ministers themselves; and the question was taken up with great art and ingenuity on other topics, as to who would succeed the Administration they were endeavouring to remove, and the diversity of opinions among them. But the efforts on the part of Ministers and their friends to create jealousies and discords among the members of the Opposition proved fruitless; and when the final vote was proposed, the Secretary of War evaded it by moving the order of the day, which was carried by a majority of ten."

* Annual Register of Parliament for 1782, Vol. XXIX., p. 173.

In the interval between the 8th and 14th, every intrigue was employed to create discord among the members of the Opposition, and to bring about a coalition under the presidency of Lord North, and a resolution was moved to that effect, which was lost by a majority of only nine.

The Earl of Surrey gave notice that on the morning of the 20th inst. he would move, in substance, Lord John Cavendish's resolution directly condemnatory of the Ministry. On that morning Lord North and the Earl of Surrey rose at the same moment, and neither would give way to the other. The general cry was " Lord Surrey, and no adjournment." As soon as the House could be reduced to order, it was moved " That the Earl of Surrey be now heard," when Lord North, having obtained the right to speak, said, " I rise to speak to the motion before the House." He observed that had he been suffered to proceed before, he believed much unnecessary heat and disorder would have been prevented. He meant no disrespect to the noble earl; but as notice had been given that the object of the intended motion was the removal of his Majesty's Ministers, he meant to have acquainted the House that such a motion had become unnecessary. He could assure the House with authority that *the present Administration was no more*, and that his Majesty had come to a full determination of changing his Ministers; and that it was for the purpose of giving necessary time for new arrangements that he meant to have moved an adjournment.

The noble lord then took leave of the House as a Minister of the Crown, and with many kind and courteous words thanked them for the honourable support they had given him during so long a course of years.*

* Abridged from the Parliamentary Register for 1782, Vol. XXV., Chap. vii. See also Lord Mahon's History of England, etc., Vol. VII., Chap. lxv.

Lord Mahon concludes his account of this Administration as follows :

" Thus ended Lord North's Administration of twelve years. It is certainly strange, on contemplating these twelve years, to find so many harsh and rigorous measures proceed from the most gentle and good-humoured of Prime Ministers. Happy, had but greater firmness in maintaining his own opinions been joined to so much ability in defending opinions even when not his own.

" Even as to the disasters and miscarriages, however, which could not be denied in his Administration, the friends of Lord North contended that in

By such blows following each other in the Commons, in rapid succession and with accelerated force, was driven from power an Administration which had inflicted greater evils upon the Crown, the constitution, the people of England and of the colonies, than any Administration since the Revolution of 1688.*

truth he was not answerable for them. The points in his favour were argued a few days before his fall by Mr. George Onslow in the House of Commons. 'Why,' said Mr. Onslow, 'have we in this war with America such ill success? Mainly,' he continued, 'from the support and countenance given in that House to American rebellion. The army of Washington had been called by the Opposition "our army;" the cause of the Americans had been called "the cause of liberty;" and one gentleman (this was Mr. Burke), while lavishing his praises on Dr. Franklin and Mr. Laurens, had declared he would prefer a prison with them to freedom in company with those who were supporting the cause of England.' But this vindication, though spirited, nay, though true, is faulty; because, though true, it is not the whole truth; because it overlooks what no statesman should—the certainty that when free principles are at stake, dissensions will always arise in a free country."—*Ib.*, pp. 209, 210.

* I have not a shadow of doubt, that had the leaders in Congress adhered to their pretensions of contending and fighting for British constitutional rights, as aforetime, instead of renouncing those rights and declaring Independence in 1776, the changes which took place in the Administration in England in 1783 would have taken place in 1777; for the corrupt Administration showed as strong symptoms of decline, and was as manifestly "tottering to its fall" in the parliamentary session which commenced in 1776, as it did in the session which commenced in 1782. In both cases its predictions and assured successes had been completely falsified; in both cases the indignation of the nation was aroused against the Administration, and the confidence of Parliament was on the point of being withdrawn in 1776-77, as it was withdrawn in the session of 1782-83; but in 1776, the Congress, instead of adhering to its heretofore professed principles, was induced by its leaders, as related in Chapter xxvi., to renounce its former principles; to falsify all its former professions to its advocates in England and fellow-subjects in America; to renounce the maintenance of the constitutional rights of British subjects; to adopt a Declaration of Independence, of eternal separation from England; to extinguish the national life of the British empire and the unity of the Anglo-Saxon race, and seek an alliance with their own and Great Britain's hereditary enemies for a war upon their mother country, which had protected them for a hundred years against the French and Spaniards, who had also employed and rewarded the Indians to destroy them.

CHAPTER XXXI.

CHANGE OF ADMINISTRATION IN ENGLAND—CHANGE OF POLICY FOR BOTH ENGLAND AND THE COLONIES—PEACE NEGOTIATIONS AT PARIS—THE CAUSE OF THE UNITED EMPIRE LOYALISTS.

DURING the adjournment of Parliament from the 24th to the 28th of March, the new Administration was formed, and announced in the Commons on the 28th, when the House adjourned over the Easter holidays, to give time for the re-election of such members as had accepted office. The King first sent for the Earl of Shelburne to form a new Administration, naming some members of it; but the Earl of Shelburne declined, as unable to form an Administration upon such conditions, and recommended the King to send for the Marquis of Rockingham. The King refused to see Rockingham face to face, but requested Shelburne to be the bearer of a message to him; but Shelburne only consented on the condition of "full power and full confidence." "Necessity," relates the King, "made me yield to the advice of Lord Shelburne." Before accepting the offer of First Lord of the Treasury, the Marquis of Rockingham, without neglecting some minor matters, stipulated that there should be no veto to the independence of America.* But it was nearly three months before an Act passed

---

* The new Cabinet was composed as follows: The Marquis of Rockingham, First Commissioner of the Treasury; the Earl of Shelburne and Mr. Fox, Secretaries of State; Lord Camden, President of the Council; Duke of Grafton, Privy Seal; Lord John Cavendish, Chancellor of the Exchequer; Admiral Keppel, raised to be a Viscount, First Commissioner of the Admiralty; General Conway, Commander of the Forces; Duke of Richmond, Master General of the Ordnance. Lord Thurlow was continued in the office of

the Commons authorizing peace with America, and the acknowledgment of American Independence, and it was nearly a year before the treaty for that purpose was agreed upon.

In the meantime, "Immediately before the fall of Lord North's Ministry, in anticipation of that event, Dr. Franklin had written from Paris to Lord Shelburne with general expressions of his pacific views. On receiving that letter, Lord Shelburne, then Secretary of State, sent to Paris, as agent, Mr. Richard Oswald, a London merchant well versed in American affairs. Dr. Franklin readily conferred with Mr. Oswald, and put into his hands a paper drawn up by himself, suggesting that, in order to produce a thorough reconciliation, and to prevent any future quarrel on the North American continent, England should not only acknowledge the thirteen united States, but concede to them the Province of Canada. Such a project was not likely to find favour in the eyes of any British statesman. Mr. Oswald, however, undertook to return to England and lay it before his chief, Dr. Franklin, at his departure, expressing an earnest hope that all future communications to himself might pass through the same hands.

"Under these circumstances, the Cabinet determined that Mr. Oswald should go back to France and carry on the treaty with Franklin, though by no means with such concessions as the American philosopher desired."*

Lord High Chancellor, and Mr. Dunning raised to the peerage under the title of Lord Ashburton, as Chancellor of the Duchy of Lancaster. Mr. Burke was not made a member of the Cabinet, but was appointed to the lucrative office of Paymaster of the Forces, and was further gratified by the appointment of his son to a small office.

About six months after the formation of the new Cabinet the Marquis of Rockingham died, and the Earl of Shelburne was appointed to succeed him, when the Duke of Richmond, Mr. Fox, and Lord John Cavendish seceded from the Cabinet, and were succeeded by Mr. Thomas Townsend and Lord Graham as Secretaries of State, while the place of Lord John Cavendish, as Chancellor of the Exchequer, was more than filled by Mr. Pitt.

* Lord Mahon's History of England, etc., Vol. VII., Chap. lxvi., pp. 265, 266.

"At Paris, the negotiations had been much impeded by the resignation of Mr. Fox and the return of Grenville. These events had, in many minds, cast a shade of doubt over the true intentions of the British Government. Lord Shelburne, however, renewed the most pacific assurances, sending to Paris, in place of Mr. Grenville and conjointly with Mr. Oswald, Mr. Alleyne

After the termination of hostilities between Great Britain and the colonies, the American Commissioners evinced a desire to treat with England alone. Mr. Oswald, as early as July, 1782, wrote privately to Lord Shelburne, " The Commissioners

Fitzherbert, well known in after years as Lord St. Helens. These gentlemen acted in amity and concert with each other, although, strictly speaking, negotiation with America was, as before, the province of Mr. Oswald, and negotiation with the European Powers the province of Mr. Fitzherbert. Dr. Franklin, on the other hand, had associated with him three other American Commissioners, arriving in succession—first, Mr. Jay, from Spain ; then Mr. Adams, from Holland ; and finally, Mr. Laurens, from London.

" It became, ere long, apparent to the British agents that the Courts of France and Spain were by no means earnest and sincere in the wish for an immediate close of the war. With the hope of soon reducing Gibraltar, or of otherwise depressing England, they put forward at this time either inadmissible pretensions, or vague and ambiguous words. It therefore became an object of great importance to negotiate, if possible, a separate pacification with America. At first sight there appeared almost insuperable difficulties in the way of such a scheme. The treaty of alliance of February, 1778, between France and the United States, stipulated in the most positive terms that neither party should conclude a peace or truce with England, unless with the consent of the other party first obtained. Since that time the French, far from falling short of their engagement, had gone much beyond it. To say nothing of their despatch of a fleet and army, and besides their annual loans and advances to the United States, they had made, in 1781, a free gift of six millions of livres, and in the spring of 1782 granted another to the same amount.

" On the other hand, however, there was a strong temptation to treat without delay. War, if still waged, would be mainly for French and Spanish purposes. It could be made clear that when the independence of the Americans was fully established and secured, they had no interest any more than England in continuing an unprofitable contest."—*Ib.*, pp. 291—293.

" Moreover, there had sprung up in the minds of the American Commissioners at Paris a strong feeling of distrust and suspicion against their new allies. That feeling we find most plainly expressed by Mr. Adams in relating his own conversations with Mr. Oswald. ' You are afraid,' said Mr. Oswald to-day, ' of being made the tools of the Powers of Europe ?' ' Indeed I am,' said I. ' What Powers ?' said he. ' All of them,' said I.

" But in the minds of the American Commissioners, the distrust against France was more vehement than against any other State. The best American writers of the present day acknowledge that all surmises thence arising were, in truth, ill-founded ; that the conduct of France towards the United States had been marked throughout not only by good faith and honour, but by generosity." (Lord Mahon's History of England, etc., Vol. VII., Chap. lxvi., pp. 293, 294.)

of the colonies have shown a desire to treat and to end with us on a separate footing from the other Powers." "The separate negotiation thus arising was delayed," says Lord Mahon, "first by the severe illness of Dr. Franklin, and next by some points of form in the commission of Mr. Oswald. When at length the more solid part of the negotiation was commenced, the hints of Franklin for the cession of Canada were quietly dropped, with greater ease from their having been transmitted in a confidential form. It is also worthy of note that Lord Shelburne prevailed, in his desire of acknowledging the independence of the United States, by an article of the treaty, and not, as Mr. Fox had wished, by a previous declaration."

The two most difficult questions of the treaty related to the fishing grounds of Newfoundland, and the Loyalists or "Tories," as they were called. The English were unwilling to concede the use of the fishing grounds, but the Americans were firm; the result was, that by the provisions of the treaty it was agreed that the Americans should have the right to take fish on the banks of Newfoundland, but not to dry or cure them on any of the King's settled dominions.*

---

* In the preamble of the treaty, it was provided that "The treaty was not to be concluded until terms of peace shall be agreed upon between Great Britain and France." By this limitation (which was a mere form, as the provisional articles were to be meanwhile binding and effective), the Americans were in hopes of avoiding, at least of softening, their French allies. "The first Article acknowledged in the fullest terms the independence of the United States. The second fixed their boundaries, and certainly to their advantage. The third gave their people the right to take fish on all the banks of Newfoundland, but not to dry or cure them on any of the King's settled dominions in America. By the fourth, fifth, and sixth Articles, it was engaged that Congress should earnestly recommend to the several Legislatures to provide for the restitution of all estates belonging to real British subjects who had not borne arms against them. All other persons were to be at liberty to go to any of the provinces and remain there for twelve months to wind up their affairs, the Congress also recommending the restitution of their confiscated property, on their repayment of the sums for which they had been sold. No impediment was to be put in the way of recovering *bona fide* debts; no further prosecutions were to be commenced, no further confiscations made. It was likewise stipulated in the seventh and eighth Articles, that the English should at once withdraw their fleets and armies from every port or place which they still possessed within the limits of the United States; and that the navigation of the Mississippi, from its source to the ocean,

But the question which transcended all others in importance, with which this work has chiefly to do, was that of the Loyalists—a class which, by the testimony of American historians themselves, constituted, at the beginning of the war, a majority of the population of the colonies. Their numbers had been greatly reduced from various causes during the war; they had been plundered and scattered by the alternate ascendancy of opposite parties; they had all of them suffered in their property and liberty; many of them had suffered imprisonment, and not a few of them had been executed as criminals for preferring their oath of allegiance and connection with the mother country to a renunciation of their former profession of faith, and absolute submission to a nearly self-created authority of rule and a new political creed. At the conclusion of the war, and in the treaty of peace, "the question of Loyalists or Tories," says Lord Mahon, "was, as it ought to be, a main object with the British Government to obtain, if possible, some restitution to the men who, in punishment for their continued allegiance to the King, had found their property confiscated and

should be for ever free and open to both parties." (Lord Mahon's History, etc., Vol. VII., Chap. lxvi., pp. 297, 298.)

"It is not to be supposed that the French Government could view with unconcern the studied secrecy of this negotiation. The appearances of amity were, indeed, for the sake of mutual interest, kept up on either side. But thus did the Comte de Vergennes (the French Minister of Foreign Affairs) unbosom himself in writing to the French Minister at Philadelphia: 'You will surely be gratified, as well as myself, with the very extensive advantages which our allies, the Americans, are to receive from the peace; but you certainly will not be less surprised than I have been with the conduct of the commissioners. * * They have cautiously kept themselves at a distance from me. Whenever I have had occasion to see any one of them, and enquire of them briefly respecting the progress of the negotiation, they have constantly clothed their speech in generalities, giving me to understand that it did not go forward, and that they had no confidence in the sincerity of the British Ministry. Judge of my surprise when, on the 30th of November, Dr. Franklin informed me that Articles were signed. The reservation retained on our account does not save the infraction of the promise which we have made to each other, not to sign except conjointly. * * This negotiation has not yet so far advanced in regard to ourselves as that of the United States; not but what the King, if he had shown as little delicacy in his proceedings as the American Commissioners, might have signed articles with England long before them.'"—*Ib.*, pp. 298, 299.

their persons banished. But from the first Dr. Franklin held out no hopes of any satisfaction on that point. 'The Commissioners,' he said, 'had no such power, nor had even Congress.'* They were willing that Congress should, with certain modifications, recommend those indemnities to the several States; and, as one of the negotiators from England tells us, they to the last 'continued to assert that the recommendation of Congress would have the effect we proposed.' The British diplomatists persevered in their original demand, and at one time there seemed a probability that the negotiations might break off, chiefly on this ground. Twice was Mr. Strachey, the Under-Secretary of State, an able and experienced man, dispatched to Paris to aid Mr. Oswald with his counsel and co-operation. But at last the mind of Franklin, ever ingenious and fertile of resources, devised a counter scheme. He said that he would allow the losses which the Loyalists had suffered, provided another account were opened of the mischief they had done, as of slaves carried off, or houses burned; new Commissioners to be appointed to strike a balance between the two computations. At this formidable proposal, involving an endless train of discussions and disputes, the negotiators from England finally gave way."†

This account of the negotiation in regard to the United Empire Loyalists, taken from Lord Mahon's impartial history, is corroborated in all essential particulars by American historians. Mr. Bancroft says that "Franklin having already explained that nothing could be done for the Loyalists by the United States, as their estates had been confiscated by laws of particular States, which Congress had no power to repeal, he further demonstrates that Great Britain had forfeited every right to intercede for them by its conduct and example, to which end he read to Oswald the orders of the British in Carolina for confiscating and selling the lands and property of all patriots under the direction of the military; and he declared definitely that, though the separate governments might show compassion where it was deserved, the American Commissioners

---

* It was self-contradictory to say that Congress had power to confiscate property, and yet had no power to restore it when confiscated.

† Lord Mahon's History of England, etc., Vol. VII., Chap. lxvi., pp. 295, 296.

for Peace could not make compensation of refugees a part of the treaty."

"This last demand (adequate indemnity for the confiscated property of loyal refugees) touched alike the sympathy and the sense of honour of England. The previous answer, that the Commissioners had no power to treat on the business of the Loyalists, was regarded as an allegation that though they claimed to have full power, they were not plenipotentiaries; that they were acting under thirteen separate sovereignties, which had no common head. To meet the exigence, Shelburne proposed either an extension of Nova Scotia to the Penobscot, or Kennebec, or the Saco, so that a province might be formed for the reception of Loyalists; or that a part of the money to be received from sales of the Ohio lands might be applied to their subsistence."

"On the 29th of November, 1782, Strachey, Oswald, and Fitzherbert, on the one side, and Jay, Franklin, Adams, and for the first time Laurens, on the other, came together for their last word at the apartments of Jay. The American Commissioners agreed that there should be no future confiscations nor prosecutions of Loyalists, that all pending prosecutions should be discontinued, and that Congress should recommend to the several States and their Legislatures, on behalf of refugees, amnesty and the restitution of their confiscated property." "On the 30th, the Commissioners of both countries signed and sealed fair copies of the Convention." "The treaty was not a compromise, nor a compact imposed by force, but a free and perfect solution and perpetual settlement of all that had been called in question."*

Dr. Ramsay observes: "From the necessity of the case, the Loyalists were sacrificed, nothing further than a simple recommendation for restitution being stipulated in their favour. * * The case of the Loyalists was undoubtedly a hard one, but unavoidable from the complex Constitution of the United States. The American Ministers engaged, as far as they were authorized, and Congress did all they constitutionally could; but this was no more than simply to recommend their case to

---

* History of the United States, Vol. X., Chap. xxix., pp. 555, 583, 589, 590, 591.

the several States, for the purpose of making them restitution. To have insisted on more, under such circumstances, would have been equivalent to saying that there should be no peace. It is true, much more was expected from the recommendations of Congress than resulted from them; but this was not the consequence of deception, but of misunderstanding the principles of the confederation. In conformity to the letter and spirit of the treaty, Congress urged, in strong terms, the propriety of making restitution to the Loyalists, but to procure it was beyond their power. * * There were doubtless among the Loyalists many worthy characters, friends of peace and lovers of justice. To such restitution was undoubtedly due, and to many such it was made; but it is one of the many calamities incident to war, that the innocent, from the impossibility of discrimination, are often involved in the same distress with the guilty.

"The return of the Loyalists to their former places of residence was as much disrelished by the Whig citizens of America as the proposal for reimbursing their confiscated property. In sundry places Committees were formed, who, in an arbitrary manner, opposed their peaceable residence. The sober and dispassionate citizens exerted themselves in checking these irregular measures; but such was the violence of party spirit, and so relaxed were the sinews of government, that, in opposition to legal authority and the private interference of the judicious and moderate, many indecent outrages were committed on the persons and property of the returning Loyalists.

"Nor were these all the sufferings of those Americans who had attached themselves to the royal cause. Being compelled to depart from their native country, many of them were obliged to take up their abodes in the inhospitable wilds of Nova Scotia, or on the barren shores of the Bahama Islands. Parliamentary relief was extended to them; but this was obtained with difficulty, and distributed with a partial hand. Some, who invented plausible tales of loyalty and distress, received much more than they ever possessed; while others, less artful, were not half reimbursed for their actual losses."*

---

* Dr. Ramsay's History of the United States, Vol. II., Chap. xxvii., pp. 489, 490, 491.

Mr. Hildreth remarks, under date of September, 1783, "that at New York a general release of prisoners had taken place on both sides; but the necessity of finding transports for the numerous Loyalists assembled there protracted the evacuation of New York. In consequence of laws still in force against them, several thousand American Loyalists found it necessary to abandon their country. A considerable portion of these exiles belonged to the wealthier classes; they had been officials, merchants, large landholders, conspicuous members of the colonial aristocracy. Those from the North settled principally in Nova Scotia or Canada, provinces the politics of which their descendants continued to control until quite recently. Those from the South found refuge in the Bahamas and other West India islands. Still objects of great popular odium, the Loyalists had little to expect from the stipulated recommendations of Congress in their favour. Some of the States, whose territory had been longest and most recently occupied by the enemy, were even inclined to enact new confiscations."*

In each and all of these historical statements it is clearly admitted that the claim of the Loyalists to compensation for loss of property was founded in equity, as well as in national policy. This is sanctioned by the admission of the American Commissioners and the recommendation of Congress. The want of power in Congress to do what is admitted to be an act of justice to the Loyalists is the plea for not restoring them the property which had gone into the hands of their opponents, who were proportionally enriched thereby. It was left to local avarice and local resentment to deal with the property of banished exiles.

What was claimed by and in behalf of the Loyalists accorded with the practice of even modern nations, as well as with the sentiments of humanity. When the Dutch provinces asserted their independence of Spain, and after a long and bloody war obtained the recognition of it, they cordially agreed to an act of oblivion, and even restored to those who had adhered to the cause of Spain, their property of every denomination that had been confiscated, or the full value of it. Even Spain herself had twice thus acted towards the province of Catalonia—first, on its

---

* Hildreth's History of the United States, Vol. III., Chap. xlv., p. 439.

revolting from that Crown, and calling in the assistance of France; and secondly, on its refusing to acknowledge the Bourbon family, at the beginning of the last century. Though the inhabitants had forfeited life and property, yet, on their return to obedience, life, possessions, laws and immunities remained inviolate. England had conducted herself in the same spirit towards that party in Ireland which had taken up arms in support of James the Second. No proscriptions took place, and every man, on submitting to Government, was admitted to the undisturbed enjoyment of his property. Had this spirit actuated, and these examples, with many others of like character, influenced the Americans, how much more honourable to them, and more consistent with sound policy, to efface at once all remembrance of internal discords, than to pursue, in the execrable spirit of revenge and avarice, those of their countrymen who differed from them in opinion in the late contest, and sided with Great Britain.* That the plea that Congress had no power in granting amnesty and compensation to the Loyalists was a mere pretext, is manifest from the fact that the Commissioners agreed that there should be no more confisca-

---

* The royal historian, Dr. Andrews, remarks strongly on this subject as follows:

"The demands of restitution to the Loyalists of their property confiscated during the war, for their attachment to our cause, had been refused by the American Commissioners, on pretence that neither they, nor Congress itself, could comply with it, any farther than by recommendation of it to the different States. The demand was in itself so just, and founded on so many historical precedents, that Congress could not possibly plead a want of foresight that it would be made. It had been usual in all ages, on the cessation of civil war, to grant a general amnesty. No other motive but that of the basest and most barbarous revenge could induce men to express an averseness to so humane and necessary a measure. Next to the cruelty of such a refusal was the meanness of those who submitted to it.

"Circumstances empowered this nation to have acted with such firmness as to compel the Americans to relax their obstinacy in this particular. Until they had consented to a generous treatment of the Loyalists, we ought to have withheld the restitution of the many strong places still remaining in our hands, and made the surrender of them the price of their acquiescence in our demands in favour of the brave and faithful people who had suffered so much on our account." (Dr. Andrews' History of the Late War, Vol. IV., pp. 401, 402.)

"All parties in the Commons unanimously demanded amnesty and indemnity for the Loyalists." (Bancroft, Vol. X., Chap. xxix., p. 586.)

tions or proscriptions against the Loyalists; for if the laws under which these prosecutions were instituted and confiscations made were State laws, with which Congress had no power to interfere, how could the Congress Commissioners stipulate that there should be no more confiscations or proscriptions?

Dr. Franklin, the most experienced and ablest of the American diplomatists, was the most crafty and overbearing against England. At the beginning of the negotiations for peace, he demurely proposed, and half converted Mr. Oswald to his proposition, to concede Canada (which at that time meant all British North America) to the United States, though his commission related simply to the independency of the thirteen colonies; and when the British Cabinet vetoed this extra-official and extravagant proposition, Dr. Franklin and his colleagues overreached the ignorance and weakness of the British diplomatists by carefully constructed maps for the purpose of making the boundary lines between the proposed possessions of Great Britain and the United States on their northern and northwestern frontiers. These lines were so ingeniously drawn as to take from Great Britain and include in the United States the immense and valuable territories, back settlements, and the whole country between the Alleghany Mountains and the Mississippi, and which have since become the States of Ohio, Indiana, Illinois, Iowa, Wisconsin, Missouri, Michigan, Minnesota, etc.—to not one foot of which the thirteen American colonies had the slightest claim—territories ample to compensate Loyalists for their losses and banishment, but whose interests, together with these most valuable possessions, were lost to Great Britain by the subserviency of the British Commissioner, Oswald (a London and American merchant), who looked to his own interests, and was the subservient tool and echo of Dr. Franklin. The above territories were a part of the domain of Congress, irrespective of any State, and therefore at the absolute disposal of Congress. Yet, with these immense accessions of resources, the American Commissioners professed that the Congress had no power or means to compensate the United Empire Loyalists for the confiscation and destruction of their property! One knows not at which most to marvel—the boldness, skill, and success of the American Commissioners, or the cowardice, ignorance, and recklessness of the British diplomatists.

The result of these negotiations was, that the adherents to Great Britain during the civil war were deprived of the amnesty and restoration of property upon any ground of right, as had been granted at the termination of civil strife by all civilized nations—to the restoration of what had been taken from them during the war—and turned over as suppliant culprits to the several States by whose laws their property had been confiscated, and themselves declared guilty of treason, and condemned to the death of traitors. Dr. Franklin, in the beginning of his negotiations, had proposed to give all that now constitutes British North America to the United States, and thus leave to the British Loyalists not an inch of ground on which to place their feet; but all that was now left to them, as far as America was concerned, was to prostrate themselves as suppliants before the Legislatures of the several States, each of which was for the most part a seething cauldron of passion and resentment against them.*

---

* Dr. Ramsay justly remarks: "The operation of treason laws added to the calamities of the war. Individuals on both sides, while they were doing no more than they supposed to be their duty, were involved in the penal consequences of capital crimes. The Americans, in conformity to the usual policy of nations, demanded the allegiance of all who resided among them; but many preferred the late royal government, and were disposed, when opportunity offered, to support it. While they acted in conformity to these sentiments, the laws enacted for the security of the new government condemned them to death. Of all wars, civil are most to be dreaded. They are attended with the bitterest of resentments, and produce the greatest quantity of human woes. In the American war the distresses of the country were greatly aggravated from the circumstance that every man was obliged, some way or other, to be in the public service. In Europe, where the military operations are carried on by armies hired and paid for the purpose, the common people partake but little of the calamities of the war; but in America, where the whole people were enrolled as a militia, and where both sides endeavoured to strengthen themselves by oaths and by laws, denouncing the penalties of treason on those who aided or abetted the opposite party, the sufferings of individuals were renewed as often as fortune varied her standard. Each side claimed the co-operation of the inhabitants, and was ready to punish them when it was withheld.

"In the first institution of the American governments the boundaries of authority were not properly fixed. Committees exercised legislative, executive, and judicial powers. It is not to be doubted that in many instances these were improperly used, and that private resentments were often covered under the specious veil of patriotism. The sufferers, in passing over to the

Loyalists, carried with them a keen remembrance of the vengeance of Committees, and when opportunity presented were tempted to retaliate. From the nature of the case, the original offenders were less frequently the objects of retaliation than those who were entirely innocent. One instance of severity begat another, and they continued to increase in a proportion that doubled the evils of common war. * * The Royalists raised the cry of persecution, and loudly complained that, merely for supporting the Government under which they were born, and to which they owed a natural alleigance, they were doomed to suffer all the penalties of capital offenders. Those of them who acted from principle felt no consciousness of guilt, and could not but look with abhorrence upon a Government which could inflict such severe punishments for what they deemed a laudable line of conduct. Humanity would shudder at a particular recital of the calamities which the Whigs inflicted on the Tories and the Tories on the Whigs. It is particularly remarkable, that many on both sides consoled themselves with the belief that they were acting and suffering in a good cause." (History of the United States, Vol. II., Chap. xxvi., pp. 467, 468, 469.)

CHAPTER XXXII.

ORIGIN OF REPUBLICANISM AND HATRED OF MONARCHY IN AMERICA—
THOMAS PAINE: A SKETCH OF HIS LIFE, CHARACTER, AND WRITINGS,
AND THEIR EFFECTS.

No social or political phenomenon in the history of nations has been more remarkable than the sudden transition of the great body of the American colonists, in 1776, from a reverence and love of monarchical institutions and of England, in which they had been trained from their forefathers, to a renunciation of those institutions and a hatred of England. Whatever influence the oppressive policy of the British Administration may have had in producing this change, was confined to comparatively few in America, was little known to the masses, and had little influence over them. This sudden and marvellous revolution in the American mind was produced chiefly by a pamphlet of forty pages, written at the suggestion of two or three leaders of the American revolutionists, over the signature of "An Englishman." This Englishman was no other than Thomas Paine, better known in after years as Tom Paine, "the blasphemous infidel and beastly drunkard," as the New York *Observer*, in answer to a challenge, proved him to be beyond the possibility of successful contradiction. Tom Paine was of a Quaker family; was a staymaker by trade, but an agitator by occupation. He had obtained an appointment as exciseman, but was dismissed from his office, and emigrated to America in 1774. He somehow obtained an introduction to Dr. Franklin in London, who gave him a letter of introduction to a gentleman in Philadelphia, through whom he procured employment in the service of a bookseller. Beginning forthwith to write for a leading newspaper on the agitated questions of the day, his articles attracted attention and procured him the acquaintance of some influential persons, and he at length became editor of the "Pennsylvania Magazine." He was the master of a singularly attractive, lucid, and vituperative style, scarcely inferior to that of *Junius* himself. At the suggestion of Franklin and one or two other leaders of the revolution, he wrote a pamphlet of forty pages in favour of Independence, entitled "Common Sense," and over the signature of "An Englishman," yet bitter against England and English institutions. It was addressed to the inhabitants of America, and was arranged under four heads: first, "Of the origin and design of government in general, with concise remarks on the English Constitution ;" secondly, "Of monarchy and hereditary succession ;" thirdly, "Thoughts on the present state of military affairs ;" fourth, "Of the present ability of America, with some miscellaneous reflections." Mr. Frothingham says: "The portion on Government has little of permanent value; the glance at the English Constitution is superficial; and the attack on Monarchy is coarse. The treatment of the American question under the two last heads gave the pamphlet its celebrity."*

Mr. Gordon says that "No publication so much promoted

---

* Frothingham's Rise of the Republic of the United States, Chap. xi., p. 472.

The pamphlet was called "Common Sense," and was written by Thomas Paine, an Englishman, who held and expressed extreme opinions upon the "Rights of Man." He had been a staymaker in England, and was ruined ; when, in the winter of 1774, by Franklin's advice, he came to America and rapidly grasped and comprehended the position of affairs. (Elliott's History of New England, Vol. II., Chap. xxviii., p. 383.)

Referring to this demagogue of the American and French Revolution, his American biographer, Cheetham, says : "All sects have had their disgraceful members and offspring. Paine's father, a peaceful and industrious Quaker, connects him with the exemplary sect of the Friends. He received his education at the Grammar School of his native place, Thetford, in Norfolk, but attained to little beyond the rudiments of Latin. His first application to business was in the trade of his father, that of staymaker, which he followed in London, Dover, and Sandwich, where he married ; afterwards he became a grocer and an exciseman, at Lewes, in Sussex. This situation he lost through some misdemeanor. After this, however, so well were the public authorities of his native country disposed to serve him, that one of the Commissioners of Excise gave him a letter of recommendation to Dr. Franklin, then a colonial agent in London, who recommended him to go to

the cause of Independence as that. The statements which are now adopted were then strange, and Paine found difficulty in procuring a publisher to undertake it."

Dr. Ramsay says: "The style, manner, and language of Thomas Paine's performance were calculated to interest the America. At this period he had first exercised his talents as a writer by drawing up a pamphlet recommending the advance of the salaries of excisemen.

"His age at this time was thirty-seven. His first engagement in Philadelphia was with Mr. Aitkin, a respectable bookseller, who, in January, 1775, commenced the 'Pennsylvania Magazine,' the editorship of which work became the business of Mr. Paine, who had a salary of £50 currency a year. When Dr. Rush, of Philadelphia, suggested to Paine the propriety of preparing the Americans for a separation from England, it seems that he seized with avidity the idea, and immediately commenced his famous pamphlet on that subject, which being shown in MS. to Doctors Franklin and Rush and Mr. Samuel Adams, was, after some discussion, entitled, at the suggestion of Dr. Rush, 'Common Sense.' For this production the Legislature of Pennsylvania voted him £500. Shortly afterwards Paine was appointed Secretary to the Committee of the United States on Foreign Affairs. His business was merely to copy papers, number and file them, and generally do the duty of what is now called a clerk in the Foreign Department. But in the title-page of his 'Rights of Man,' he styles himself 'Secretary for Foreign Affairs to the Congress of the United States in the Late War.' While in this office, he published a series of appeals on the struggle between Great Britain and the colonies. In 1777 he was obliged to resign his secretaryship on account of a quarrel with Silas Deane, American agent in France. The next year, however, he obtained the appointment of Clerk to the Assembly of Pennsylvania; and in 1785, on the rejection of a motion to appoint him historiographer to the United States, the Congress granted him three thousand dollars, and the Legislature of New York granted him an estate of 500 acres of highly cultivated land, the confiscated property of a Loyalist. Having no more revolutionary occupation in the United States, he embarked for France in 1787, with a letter of recommendation from Dr. Franklin to the Duke de la Rochefoucault. From Paris he went to London, where, the following year, he was arrested for debt, but was bailed by some American merchants. He went to Paris in 1791 to publish, under the name of 'Achilles Du Chatellet,' a tract *recommending the abolition of royalty*. He again returned to London and wrote the first part of his 'Rights of Man,' in answer to Mr. Burke's 'Reflections on the French Revolution.' The second part was published early in 1792. He was ordered to be arrested and prosecuted for his seditious and blasphemous writings, but escaped to France, and was elected a member of the French National Convention—grateful for the honour which the bloody anarchists had conferred upon him by electing him a member of their order. His conduct, however, offended the Jacobins, and

passions and to rouse all the active powers of human nature. With the view of operating on the sentiments of religious people, Scripture was pressed into his service; and the powers and name of a king were rendered odious in the eyes of numerous colonists who had read and studied the history of the Jews,

towards the close of the year 1793 he was excluded from the convention, was arrested and committed to the prison of the Luxembourg. Just before his confinement he had finished the first part of his 'Age of Reason,' and confided it to the care of his friend Joel Barlow for publication. He was now taken ill, to which circumstance he ascribed his escape from the guillotine; and on the fall of Robespierre was released. In 1795 he published, at Paris, the second part of his 'Age of Reason.' He returned to America in 1802, bringing with him a woman named Madame Bonneville, whom he had seduced away from her husband, with her two sons, and whom he seems to have treated with the utmost meanness and tyranny. His friend and American biographer, Mr. Cheetham, in continuation, gives the following account of Paine's arrival at New York in 1802: 'The writer,' says Mr. Cheetham, 'supposing him (Paine) to be a gentleman, was employed to engage a room for him at Lovett's hotel, New York. On his arrival, in 1802, about ten at night, he wrote me a note, desiring to see me immediately. I waited on him at Lovett's, in company with Mr. George Clinton, jun. We rapped at the door. A small figure opened it within, meanly dressed, having an old top-coat, without an under one; a dirty silk handkerchief loosely thrown around his neck, a long beard of more than a week's growth, a face well carbuncled as the setting sun, and the whole figure staggering under a load of inebriation. I was on the point of inquiring for Mr. Paine, when I noticed something of the portraits I had seen of him. We were desired to be seated. He had before him a small round table, on which were a beefsteak, some beer, a pint of brandy, a pitcher of water and a glass. He sat eating, drinking, and talking with as much composure as if he had lived with us all his life. I soon perceived that he had a very retentive memory, and was full of anecdote. The Bishop of Llandaff (Dr. Watson) was almost the first word he uttered, and it was followed by his informing us that he had in his trunk a manuscript reply to the bishop's 'Apology for the Bible.' He then calmly mumbled his steak, and ever and anon drinking his brandy and beer, repeated the introduction to his reply, which occupied nearly half an hour. This was done with deliberation and the utmost clearness, and a perfect apprehension, intoxicated as he was, of all that he repeated. Scarcely a word would he allow us to speak. He always, I afterwards found, in all companies, drunk or sober, would be listened to; in his regard, there were no *rights of men* with him—no equality, no reciprocal immunities and obligations—for he would listen to no one.'

"On the 13th of October, 1802, he arrived at Baltimore, under the protection of Mr. Jefferson. But it appears that curiosity induced no one of distinction to suffer his approach. While at his hotel he was principally

as recorded in the Old Testament. Hereditary succession was turned into ridicule. The absurdity of subjecting a great continent to a small island on the other side of the globe was represented in such striking language as to interest the honour and pride of the colonists in renouncing the government of Great Britain. The necessity, the advantage and practicability of independence were forcibly demonstrated.

"Nothing could be better timed than this performance. It was addressed to freemen, who had just received convincing proof that Great Britain had thrown them out of her protection, and engaged foreign mercenaries to make war upon them, and seriously designed to compel their unconditional submission to her unlimited power. It found the colonists most thoroughly alarmed for their liberties, and disposed to do and suffer anything that promised their establishment. In union with the feelings and sentiments of the people, it produced surprising effects. Many thousands were convinced, and were led to approve and long for a separation from the mother country. Though that measure, a few months before, was not only foreign to their wishes, but the object of their abhorrence, the current suddenly became so strong in its favour that it bore down all opposition. The multitude was hurried down the stream; but some worthy men could not easily reconcile themselves to the idea of an eternal separation from a country to which they had long been bound by the most endearing ties. * * The change of the public mind of America respecting connection

visited by the lower class of emigrants from Scotland, England, and Ireland, who had read and admired his 'Rights of Man.' With them, it appears, 'he drank grog in the tap-room morning, noon, and night, admired and praised, strutting and staggering about, showing himself to all and shaking hands with all. The leaders of the party to which he had attached himself paid him no attention.'"

Paine's subsequent years, until his miserable death in 1809, were characterized by the lowest degradation, blasphemy, drunkenness, and filthiness, which rendered him unfit for any human society, as his biographies, written even by his friends, abundantly testify.

Those who knew Paine in his earlier years were, of course, not responsible for the depravity and degradation of his subsequent years; but from the beginning he was an infidel and an enemy of all settled government.

Such was the author of American republicanism and of American hatred to England, to all British institutions, to all monarchy, and the advocate of the abolition of kings.

with Great Britain is without a parallel. In the short space of two years, nearly three millions of people passed over from the love and duty of loyal subjects to the hatred and resentment of enemies."*

The American press and all the American historians of that day speak of the electric and marvellous influence of Tom Paine's appeal against kings, against monarchy, against England, and in favour of American independence.

The following remarks of the London *Athenæum* are quoted by the New York *Observer* of the 10th of April, 1879:

"A more despicable man than Tom Paine cannot be found among the ready writers of the eighteenth century. He sold himself to the highest bidder, and he could be bought at a very low price. He wrote well; sometimes as pointedly as Junius or Cobbett (who had his bones brought to England). Neither excelled him in coining telling and mischievous phrases; neither surpassed him in popularity-hunting. He had the art, which was almost equal to genius, of giving happy titles to his productions. When he denounced the British Government in the name of 'Common Sense,' he found willing readers in the rebellious American colonists, and a rich reward from their grateful representatives. When he wrote on behalf of the 'Rights of Man,' and in furtherance of the 'Age of Reason,' he convinced thousands by his title-pages who were incapable of perceiving the inconclusiveness of his arguments. His speculations have long since gone the way of all shams; and his charlatanism as a writer was not redeemed by his character as a man. Nothing could be worse than his private life; he was addicted to the most degrading vices. He was no hypocrite, however, and he cannot be charged with showing that respect for appearances which constitute the homage paid by vice to virtue. Such a man was well qualified for earning notoriety by insulting Washington. Only a thorough-paced rascal could have had the assurance to charge Washington with being unprincipled and unpatriotic."

* Dr. Ramsay's History of the United States, Vol. II., Chap. xii., pp. 161, 162, 163.

CHAPTER XXXIII.

HIRING OF FOREIGNERS AND EMPLOYMENT AND TREATMENT OF INDIANS IN THE AMERICAN WAR.

No two acts of the British Government in connection with the American war were more deprecated on both sides of the Atlantic than the employment of foreign troops and Indians against the colonists; they were among the alleged and most exciting causes of the Declaration of Independence; they weakened British influence throughout the colonies; they roused thousands to arms who would have otherwise remained peacefully at home. In England they were denounced by the highest personages both in and out of Parliament, and by the public at large.*

---

* The royal historian, Dr. Andrews, says:

"The colonies were particularly exasperated at the introduction of foreign troops into this quarrel. They looked upon this measure as an unanswerable proof that all regard for their character as Englishmen was fled, and that Great Britain viewed them as strangers, whom, if she could not conquer and enslave, she was determined to destroy. This persuasion excited their most violent indignation; they considered themselves as abandoned to plunder and massacre, and that Britain was unfeelingly bent on their ruin, by whatsoever means she could compass it.

"While the colonists represented this measure in so sanguinary a light, it was depicted at home in the same colour by their partisans. It was even reprobated by many individuals who were not averse to the other parts of the Ministerial plan, but who could not bring themselves to approve of the interference of foreign mercenaries in our domestic feuds.

"It was not only throughout the public at large this measure occasioned so much discontent; after having in Parliament undergone the keenest censure of the Opposition, it fell under the displeasure of a considerable number of those who sided with the Minister and were generally used to

These Hessian mercenaries, though much lauded at first, and dreaded by the colonists, proved to be inferior to the British soldiers, were not reliable, deserted in large numbers, and plundered everywhere, without regard to Loyalists or Disloyalists, and strengthened the American resistance far more than they strengthened the British army.*

support the measures of Government; but on this occasion they loudly dissented from them. Several quitted the House without voting; others, who voted in his favour, obliged him previously to give them an assurance that he would remove all their doubts and scruples, and satisfy them clearly on this subject." (Dr. Andrews' History of the Late War, Vol. II., Chap. xviii., pp. 76, 77.)

* "The employment of foreign troops to reduce America was an object animadverted upon by the Opposition with peculiar violence and indignation. This, indeed, of all the Ministerial measures, met with the most acrimonious notice both in and out of Parliament. * * Foreigners said the Opposition were now taught that Britain, with all its boasted greatness, could not find people at home to fight its battles. * * Who could behold so disgraceful a measure without feeling for that loss of national honour which it must occasion? * * But exclusive of the disgrace entailed upon our character, the danger of the system was no less apparent. What reason had we to trust an army of foreigners, who could possibly harbour no motives of enmity to the people against whom they were to be employed? The country where these foreigners were to wage war for us, was precisely that to which we had so often enticed numbers to emigrate from their native homes by promises of more *ease* and happiness than they could enjoy in their own country. * * Of all the measures that had been taken against the Americans, that of hiring foreigners to invade their country had given the highest offence. British soldiers, though acting in the capacity of foes, still retained the feelings of countrymen, and would not shed blood without some compunction. They were born and bred in a country noted for humanity, and the constitution of which inculcated mildness. But the Hessians were of a ferocious disposition; educated under a despotic Government, they knew no rights but those of force. They carried destruction wherever they were masters, plundering all before them without distinction, and committing the most barbarous ravages.

"They had, it was said, been told before their departure from Germany that they were to be put in possession of the lands of those whom they conquered, and they were full of this expectation at their arrival. But upon discovering their mistake, they resolved, however, to make themselves amends by appropriating whatever they could lay their hands upon. * * The conduct of the Hessians was extremely offensive to the British commanders, but they were too powerful a body to restrain by compulsion, as they composed almost one-half of the army. Notwithstanding the prudence and steadiness with which General Howe conducted himself upon this

But if the hiring of foreign troops at an enormous expense was disgraceful and impolitic, the employment *of Indians* against the colonists was still more impolitic and unnatural an outrage upon civilization and humanity; and what is still even more to be lamented is that this enlistment of savages in the warfare of one branch of the British family against another was sanctioned if not instigated by the King himself.*

emergency, it was not possible to restrain their excesses, nor even prevent them from spreading among the English troops in a degree to which they would not have certainly been carried had they not such examples for a plea.

"The depredations of the Hessians grew at last, it was said, so enormous, that the spoils they were loaded with became an absolute incumbrance to them, and a frequent impediment to the discharge of their military duties.

"The desolation of the Jerseys was one of the consequences of this spirit of rapine. The Americans who adhered to Britain attributed to it the subsequent decline of the British cause in these and other parts. As the devastation was extended indiscriminately to friend and foe, it equally exasperated both parties; it confirmed the enmity of the one, and raised up a new enemy in the other; and it injured the British interest in all the colonies." (Dr. Andrews' History of the Late War, Vol. II., Chaps. xvii. and xxii., pp. 53, 54—268, 269.)

Dr. Andrews adds, in another place, that—

"The resentment occasioned by the depredations that had been carried on in the Jerseys had left few, if any, friends to Britain in that province. The dread of seeing those plunderers return, who had spared neither friend nor foe, rendered all parties averse to the cause in which they were employed. To this it was owing that their motions were observed with such extreme vigilance, that they stood little or no chance of succeeding in any of their enterprises. So many had suffered through them, that there was no deficiency of spies to give instant information of whatever they were suspected to have in view; and as much mischief was done them by such as acted secretly from motives of private revenge, as by those who took an open part against them in the field." (Dr. Andrews' History of the American War, etc., Vol. II., Chap. xxiii., pp. 301, 302.)

* "At the north, the King called to mind that he might 'rely upon the attachment of his faithful allies, the Six Nations of Indians,' and he turned to them for immediate assistance. To insure the fulfilment of his wishes, the order to engage them was sent directly in his name to the unscrupulous Indian agent, Guy Johnson, whose functions were made independent of Carleton. 'Lose no time,' it was said; 'induce them to take up the hatchet against his Majesty's rebellious subjects in America. It is a service of very great importance; fail not to exert every effort that may tend to accomplish it; use the utmost diligence and activity.'" (Bancroft's History of the United States, Vol. VII., Chap. xxxiii., p. 349.)

During the war between France and England, which commenced in 1755, both parties sought the alliance and support of the Indians, and employed them in the savage work of border warfare. The French succeeded in securing the greater number of the Indians, and used them with dreadful effect, murdering and scalping thousands of the British colonists along the inland frontiers of the several colonies. At the termination of the war by the Treaty of Paris, in 1763, and the extinction of French power in America, the French authorities commended the Indians to cultivate the friendship of England, whose great superiority and success in the war tended to turn the Indian affections and interest in favour of the British. Dr. Ramsay observes: "The dispute between Great Britain and her colonies began to grow serious, and the friendship of the Indians became a matter of consequence to both parties. Stretching for fifteen hundred miles along the whole north-western frontier of the colonies, they were to them desirable friends and formidable enemies. As terror was one of the engines by which Great Britain intended to enforce the submission of the colonies, nothing could be more conducive to the excitement of this passion than the co-operation of the Indians. Policy, not cruelty, led to the adoption of this expedient, but it was of that over-refined species which counteracts itself. In the competition for the friendship of the Indians, the British had advantages far superior to any possessed by the colonists. The expulsion of the French from Canada—an event which had taken place only thirteen years before—was still fresh in the memory of many of the savages, and had inspired them with high ideas of the martial superiority of the British troops. The first steps taken by Congress to oppose Great Britain put it out of their power to gratify the Indians. Such was the effect of the non-importation agreement of 1774. While Great Britain had access to the principal Indian tribes through Canada on the north, and Florida on the south, and was abundantly able to supply their many wants, the colonists had debarred themselves from importing the articles which were necessary for the Indian trade."*

* Dr. Ramsay's History of the United States, Vol. II., Chap. xix., pp. 320, 321.

"It was unfortunate for the colonies that since the peace of Paris, 1763,

The employment of the Indians in this civil war was in every respect disadvantageous to England. It was disapproved and denounced throughout England and Europe, as unnatural and inhuman; it was disapproved by the English commanders and even Loyalists in America, and inflamed the colonists to the highest degree. Wherever the Indians were employed, they were a source of weakness to the English army, while their ravages and cruelties disgusted the Loyalists and brought disgrace upon the English arms and cause. Sir Guy Carleton forbade their crossing from Canada into the colonies, and was afterwards accused in England for disobedience in not employing them;* and General Burgoyne gave the strictest orders against their murdering and plundering. His defeat near Saratoga was largely owing to the conduct of the Indians in his army.

the transactions with the Indians had been mostly carried on by superintendents appointed and paid by the King of Great Britain. These being under obligations to the Crown, and expectants of further favours from it, generally used their influence with the Indians in behalf of the mother country and against the colonies. * * The Americans were not unmindful of the savages on their frontier. They appointed commissioners to explain to them the grounds of their dispute, and to cultivate their friendship by treaties and presents. They first sought to persuade the Indians to join them against Great Britain, but having failed in that, they endeavoured to persuade the Indians that the quarrel was by no means relative to them, and that therefore they should take part with neither side.

"For the greater convenience of managing the intercourse between the colonies and the Indians, the latter were divided into three departments—the northern, southern, and middle—and commissioners were appointed for each. Congress also resolved to import and distribute among them a suitable assortment of goods, to the amount of £40,000 sterling, on account of the United States; but this was not executed." (Dr. Ramsay's History of the United States, Vol. II., Chap. xix., p. 321.

* "Anxious (1775, October) to relieve St. John's, Carleton, after the capture of Allen, succeeded in assembling about nine hundred Canadians at Montreal; but a want of mutual confidence, and the certainty that the inhabitants generally favoured the Americans, dispirited them, and they disappeared by desertions thirty or forty of a night, till he was left almost as forlorn as before. The Indians, too, he found of little service; 'they were easily dejected, and chose to be of the strongest side, so that when they were most wanted they vanished. But history must preserve the fact that though often urged to let them loose on the rebel provinces, in his detestation of cruelty he would not suffer a savage to pass the frontier." (Bancroft's History of the United States, Vol. VIII., Chap. lii., p. 186.)

American historians dilate with much eloquence and justice upon the employment of Indians against the colonists, and narrate, with every possible circumstance of aggravation, every act of depredation and cruelty on the part of the Indians against the white inhabitants that espoused the cause of Congress; but they omit to state in like manner that Congress itself endeavoured to enlist the Indians in its quarrel with the mother country; that General Washington recommended their employment against the English,* and that the very idea of

* "Reading at the present day, we can see how the passionate and declamatory rhetoric of the Declaration of Independence has left its stain to this hour on most of the political writing and oratory of America, and may wish that the birth of a nation had not been screamed into the world after this fashion. Nothing could have been easier than, in the like rhetorical language, to draw up a list of lawlessness and utter outrage committed by the colonists. Some of the charges will not bear examination.

"For instance, the aid of the Indians had been willingly accepted by the colonists in the Canadian expedition since September, 1775; the general question of their employment had been considered by Washington in conference with a Committee of Congress and delegates of New England Governments in October of the same year; and the main objection which Washington and other officers urged against it, as shown by a letter of his to General Schuyler, January 27, 1776, and the answer from the latter, was that of expense. He had, nevertheless (April 19, 1776), advised Congress 'to engage them on our side,' as 'they must, and no doubt soon will, take an active part either for or against us;' and the Congress itself had, on June 3rd—not a month before the Declaration of Independence was actually accepted—passed a resolution to raise 2,000 Indians for the Canadian service, which, shortly afterwards, was extended by another (referred to in a letter of Washington's of June 20), authorizing General Washington to employ such Indians as he should take into the service in any place where he might think that they would be most useful, and to offer them bounties, not indeed for scalps, but for every officer and soldier of the King's troops whom they might capture in the Indian country or on the frontiers of the colonies. When all this had been done, it needed the forgetfulness and the blind hypocrisy of passion to denounce the King to the world for having 'endeavoured to bring on the inhabitants of our frontiers the merciless Indian savages;' yet the American people have never had the self-respect to erase this charge from a document generally printed in the fore-front of their Constitution and Laws, and with which every schoolboy is sedulously made familiar.

"Perhaps, indeed, it would have been otherwise had not the charge been one which circumstances appeared to confirm. For, in fact, owing to causes already indicated, the Americans never could make friends of the Indians in the contest, and consequently the 'merciless savages' continue in history to figure on the side of the British. Who could wonder at it? At the date

engaging the Indians in this civil war originated with the first promoters of the revolution in Massachusetts. Nor do American historians state frankly and fairly that for every aggression and outrage committed by the Indians, the American soldiers, even under the express order of Congress, retaliated with a tenfold vengeance—not in the manner of civilized warfare, but after the manner and destruction of the savages themselves. The American writers had also great advantages in representing everything in regard to the proceedings of the revolutionists in the brightest light, and everything connected with the Loyalists and the English in the darkest colours, as they had the reports, letters, and all other papers relating to these subjects in their own exclusive possession, and published only such and so much of them as answered their purpose; even the internal proceedings of Congress were secret,* and only became known

of the Declaration of Independence, the Indian child had only just reached man's estate, who in the year of his birth might have escaped being a victim to the bounty of £20, held out for the scalp of every Indian woman and child, by Massachusetts, in 1775, whilst one of £40 had been offered for that of his father, raised in 1776 to £300. It did not require the retentive memory of the redskin to make him look with suspicion on solicitations of friendship from men who might have been parties to such schemes of extermination to his race." (The. Ludlow's History of the War of Independence, 1777—1783, Chap. v., pp. 124—126.)

"But Jefferson's violent pamphlet should, in fact, be looked upon less as a Declaration of Independence than as a Declaration of War—less as an assertion of right than as a cry of defiance uttered in the hour of grave peril, and in the face of a formidable foe."—*Ib.*, p. 126.

* Some of the members of Congress were, at times, not so reticent as their oaths of secrecy required, and the squabbles of Conference became known abroad. It is a curious illustration of the dignity and character of a body, when the least publication of its proceedings becomes its disgrace.

"In those days (1779), far unlike our own, the Congress resembled a Committee or a Junta, much rather than a chamber of debate. The speeches, it is said, were all in the style of private conversation. There were never more than forty members present, often no more than twenty. These small numbers, however, by no means ensured harmony, nor precluded violent and unseemly quarrels, rumours of which were not slow in passing the Atlantic. 'For God's sake,' thus wrote La Fayette from France, 'for God's sake, prevent the Congress from disputing loudly together. Nothing so much hurts the interest and reputation of America.' Thus the object of concealment, unless, perhaps, for private purposes, was most imperfectly attained, although, in name at least, the deliberations of Congress at this time were secret. Historically, even the Journal which they kept

after the close of the war. And many of the most important historical facts relating to the war have been brought to light in the biographies and correspondence of the men who figured in the revolution; and many letters and papers of great historical value in throwing light upon the events and conduct of parties during that period have only been published during the present century, and some of them for the first time during the present generation. This is true in regard to much that relates to the employment and proceedings of the Indians, as well as in regard to those of the Loyalists and various events of the American revolution. According to American historians, the idea of employing the Indians in the civil war was the wicked conception of British malignity, and everywhere reprobated in America; while the idea was actually first conceived and embodied in a resolution by the Provincial Congress of Massachusetts. At Cambridge a new Provincial Congress had assembled, with the popular feeling in their favour, and with several thousands of militia or minute men under their command. But the most determined of all their measures was to enlist a company of Stockbridge Indians residing in their province. Further still, they directed a secret letter—and a secret it has been kept for more than fifty years—to a missionary much esteemed by the Indians in the western parts of New York, entreating "that you will use your influence with them to join us in the defence of our rights,"—in other words, to assail and scalp the British soldiers.* It is worthy of remark, that the Massachusetts delegates, the framers of this letter, were among those who expressed the highest astonishment and indignation when, at a later period, a similar policy was adopted on the British side.†

"Under date of the 27th of July, 1776, General Washington

gives little light as to their true proceedings. An American gentleman, who has studied that document with care, laments that it is 'painfully meagre, the object being apparently to record as little as possible.'" (Lord Mahon's History of England, Vol. VII., Chap. lviii., pp. 420, 421; quoting as his authority, "Letter of La Fayette to Washington, June 12, 1779," and "Life of President Reed," by Mr. Wm. Reed, Vol. II., p. 18.)

* Lord Mahon's History of England, etc., Vol. VII., Chap. lii., pp. 52, 53.

† This letter, dated Concord, April 4, 1775, may be seen at length in the Appendix to Sparks' edition of Washington's Writings, Vol. III., p. 495.

wrote to Congress," says Mr. Allen, "expressing respectful anxiety that the Stockbridge Indians shall be employed, and remarks that they were dissatisfied at not being included in the late order for enlisting their people, and had inquired the cause of General Putman.

"The reasons he assigns for recommending their employment are such as have influenced, and probably determined, the Americans from that time to the termination of the last war (1812—1815) with Great Britain—that is, the impossibility of keeping them neutral; the fear of their joining the enemy; while the customs of savage warfare are so repulsive to all the feelings of humanity and pride of the soldier, that it would seem no palliation could be received for the crime of having sanctioned them by example. Indians are active and serviceable when properly employed. They are the best defence against Indians. Acquainted from their birth with wiles and stratagems, they can trace the enemy, and tell its numbers, its footsteps, when the eye of the white man cannot discover a trace; and the moving of grass or rushes, which would be unregarded by a regular soldier, as the natural effect of winds, leads the Indian to be prepared for an ambush. The certainty that Indians can be restrained when it is wished, reconciles the opposite contradictions which are so often seen between the complaints made by the Americans that the enemy employed savages, at the very moment that they also employed them."*

The letter, it will be seen, was written a fortnight before the affair of Concord and Lexington, which took place the 19th of April, when the first blood was shed in the revolution.

* Allen's History of the American Revolution, Vol. I., Chap. xiv., pp. 423, 424.

"Lord Suffolk, in his speech (in reply to Lord Chatham), undertook to defend the employment of the savages. 'The Congress,' he said, 'endeavoured to bring the Indians over to their side, and if we had not employed them they would most certainly have acted against us.' This statement, which at the time was doubted or denied, has been, it must be owned, in no small degree borne out by documents that have subsequently come to light. Even several months later, we find Congress in treaty to engage several parties of Indians in their service." (Lord Mahon's History, etc., Vol. VII., Chap. lvi., p. 305.)

"See Washington's Writings, Vol. V., p. 273, and Appendix to Vol. III., p. 494. 'Divesting them,' says Washington, 'of the savage customs exercised

It is thus clear that both parties courted the co-operation of the Indians, and employed them to the utmost of their power; and therefore one party has no just ground of reproach against or advantage over the other party for the inhuman policy of enlisting the Indians in their cause, though the British had larger means and greater facilities in securing this savage co-operation.

It has been alleged, and no doubt truly, that the American commanders restrained the cruel and plundering propensities of the Indians, and the English commanders did the same; but neither the English nor the Americans were always able to control their Indian allies on or after the day of battle. American writers have, however, charged the outrages of the Indians in the English army, and scouting parties, to the sanction of the British generals,* and the prompting of the British Loyalists, and some English writers have retorted the charge. The employment of the Indians at all was against the judgment of both General Burgoyne and Sir Guy Carleton,† and only submitted to in obedience to the King's authority. As early as the 11th of July, 1776, Burgoyne (while pursuing his enterprise from Montreal to Albany) complains as follows of the conduct of the Indians to the Secretary of State: "Confidentially to your Lordship, I may acknowledge that in several instances I have found the Indians little more than a name. If, under the management of their conductors, they are indulged for interested reasons in all the caprices and humours of spoiled children like them, they grow more unreasonable and importunate upon every new favour. Were they left to themselves,

in their wars against each other, I think they may be made of excellent use as scouts and light troops, mixed with our own parties.' But what more did the English ever design or desire?" (Lord Mahon's History, etc., Vol. VII., Chap. lvi., p. 305.)

* Even so amiable and generous a man as Burgoyne did not escape these imputations. "It may well be imagined that while Burgoyne was advancing, declamations against his and the Indians' cruelty (for no distinction was admitted) were rife on the American side. By such means, and still more, perhaps, by the natural spirit of a free-born people when threatened with invasion, a resolute energy against Burgoyne was roused in the New England States."—*Ib.*, p. 261.

† "Carleton from the first abhorred the measure of employing the Indians, which he was yet constrained to promote." (Bancroft, Vol. VII., p. 119.)

enormities too horrid to think of would ensue ; guilty and innocent, women and infants, would be a common prey."*

While the Indians were an incumbrance to Burgoyne's army during his whole campaign, and forsook him in the eventful hour when he most needed them, their barbarities contributed

---

* Quoted in Lord Mahon's History, Vol. VII., Chap. lvi., p. 259. After quoting this letter, Lord Mahon adds :

"It is due to Burgoyne to state, that from the first he had made most strenuous exertions, both by word and deed, to prevent any such enormities. The testimony, for example, of his aide-de-camp, Lord Petersham, when examined before the House of Commons, is clear and precise upon that point. (See Burgoyne's Narrative and Collection of Documents, pp. 65, 66, second edition.) But in spite of all restraints, the cruel temper and lawless habits of these savages would sometimes burst forth—sometimes not more fatally to their enemies than to their friends. The tragical fate of Miss MacRea raised one loud cry of indignation on both sides of the Atlantic. This lady, in the bloom of youth and beauty, the daughter of an American Loyalist, was betrothed to an officer in the British provincial troops. Anxious for her security, the officer engaged some Indians to escort her from her home and convey her to the British camp, where the marriage would be solemnized. As a further precaution, he promised to reward the person who should bring her safe to him with a barrel of rum. But this very precaution, as it seemed to be, was the cause of the disaster which ensued. Two of the Indians who took charge of her began a quarrel on the way, as to which of them should first present her to the bridegroom. Each was eager for the rum ; each resolute that his companion should not receive it in his place. At last one of them in sudden fury raised his tomahawk, struck Miss MacRea upon the head, and laid her a corpse at his feet. General Burgoyne at this news displayed his utmost resentment and concern. He compelled the Indians to deliver up the murderer, and designed to put him to death. He was only induced to spare his life upon the Indians agreeing to terms which the General thought would be more effectual than any execution, in deterring them from similar barbarities. Deterred, indeed, they were. But when they found themselves precluded from their expected delights of plundering and scalping, they began to desert and go home. Of nearly five hundred who at the outset had joined Burgoyne, less than threescore at last remained beneath his banner."—*Ib.*, pp. 259—261.

At the first general encampment of Burgoyne's army on the western side of Lake Champlain, he met a deputation of the Indians in alliance with Great Britain, and made an animated speech to them. "He exhorted them to behave with courage and fidelity to their friends, and to avoid all barbarity towards their enemies. He entreated them to be particularly careful in distinguishing between the adherents and foes to the British nation. He earnestly requested that they would put none to death but such as actually opposed them with arms in their hands, and to spare old men, women,

greatly to swell the revolutionary army, and to alienate great numbers of Loyalists, weakening Burgoyne's army in the very country where he expected most support from the inhabitants, and giving the American general, Gates, a great preponderance of strength over him—the army of Burgoyne being reduced to 3,500 men fit for actual service, while that of Gates was increased to upwards of 16,000 fit for actual service.*

But if the British exceeded the Americans in gaining the greater part of the Indians to their cause, and the corresponding disgrace and disadvantage of their accompanying the army,

children, and prisoners ; to scalp only such as they had killed in action, and to treat compassionately the wounded and dying. He promised them a reward for every prisoner they brought in, but assured them he would look narrowly into every demand for scalps." (Dr. Andrews' History of the Late War, Vol. II., Chap. xxviii., p. 383.)

* " The apprehensions of those who had been averse to the employment of the Indians in the British army began to be justified. Notwithstanding the care and precautions taken by General Burgoyne to prevent the effects of their barbarous disposition, they were sometimes carried to an excess that shocked his humanity—the more, as it was totally out of his power to control them in the degree that he had hoped and proposed. The outrages they committed were such as proved highly detrimental to the royal cause. They spared neither friend nor foe, and exercised their usual cruelties with very little attention to the threats that were held out in order to restrain and deter them.

"Several instances of this nature happened about this time, which contributed powerfully to alienate the minds of many from the cause in which they served. One was recorded, in particular, that equally struck both parties with horror. A young lady, the daughter of Mr. MacRea, a zealous royalist, being on her way to the British army, where she was to be married to an officer, unhappily fell into the hands of the Indians, who, without regarding her youth and beauty, murdered her with many circumstances of barbarity.

"Scenes of this nature served to render the royal party extremely odious. However the Americans might be conscious that the Indians were as offensive, and as much abhorred by their enemies as by themselves, still they could not forgive them the acceptance of such auxiliaries as must necessarily disgrace the best cause.

"The resentment occasioned by the conduct of the Indians, and no less the dread of being exposed to their fury, helped considerably to bring recruits from every quarter to the American army. It was considered as the only place of refuge and security at present. The inhabitants of the tracts contiguous to the British army took np arms against it almost universally. The preservation of their families was now become an object of immediate concern. As the country was populous, they flocked in multitudes to the

the Americans far outdid the English and the Indians themselves in the work of desolation and destruction. Dr. Ramsay remarks:

"The undisturbed tranquillity which took place in South Carolina and the adjacent States after the British had failed in their designs against them in the spring and summer of 1776, gave an opportunity of carrying war into the Indian country. This was done, not so much to punish what was past, as to prevent all future co-operation between the Indians and British in that quarter. Virginia, North Carolina, South Carolina, and Georgia sent about the same time a considerable force, which traversed the Indian settlements, burned their towns, and destroyed their fields of corn. Above 500 of the Cherokees were obliged, from want of provisions, to take refuge in Florida, and were fed at the expense of the British Government."*

It is to be observed that this was not an invasion of the white settlements by the Indians, but an invasion of the Indian settlements by the whites; it was a "carrying war into the Indian country;" it was not provoked by the Indians, but "was done to prevent all future co-operation between the Indians and British in that quarter." Yet this war of *invasion*, this war of *precaution*, was also a war more destructive to the Indians than any which they, even under the French, had inflicted on the white colonists; for not an Indian cornfield was left undestroyed, nor an Indian habitation unconsumed.

American general's camp; and he soon found himself at the head of an army which, though composed of militia and undisciplined men, was animated with that spirit of indignation and revenge which so often supplies all military deficiencies." (Dr. Andrews' History of the Late War, Vol. II., Chap. xxviii., pp. 393, 394.)

* Dr. Ramsay's History of the United States, Vol. II., Chap. xix., p. 322.

CHAPTER XXXIV.

THE MASSACRE OF WYOMING—FOUR VERSIONS OF IT BY ACCREDITED AMERICAN HISTORIANS, ALL DIFFERING FROM EACH OTHER—THE FACTS INVESTIGATED, AND FALSE STATEMENTS CORRECTED.

It would be useless and tedious to attempt even a condensed account of the battles and warfare in which the Indians took part between the English and the Congress; but there is one of these revengeful and murderous occurrences which must be minutely stated, and the American accounts of it thoroughly investigated, as it has been the subject of more misrepresentation, more declamation, more descriptive and poetic exaggeration, and more denunciation against the English by American historians and orators than any other transaction of the American revolution—namely, what is known as the " Massacre of Wyoming." There are four versions of it, by accredited American histories.

The account of this massacre is thus given in the words of Dr. Ramsay's history:

"A storm of Indian and Tory vengeance burst in July, 1778, with particular violence on Wyoming, a new and flourishing settlement on the eastern branch of the Susquehanna. Unfortunately for the security of the inhabitants, the soil was claimed both by Connecticut and Pennsylvania. From the collision of contradictory claims, founded on Royal Charters, the laws of neither were steadily enforced. In this remote settlement, where government was feeble, the Tories were under less control, and could easily assemble undiscovered. Nevertheless, twenty-seven of them were taken and sent to Hartford, in Connecticut, but they were afterwards released. These and others of the same description, instigated by revenge against the Americans, from whom some of them had suffered banishment and loss of property, made common cause with the Indians, and attacked the Wyoming settlement with their combined forces, estimated at 1,100 men, 900 of whom were Indians. The whole was commanded by Colonel John Butler, a Connecticut Tory. One of the forts which had been constructed for the security of the inhabitants, being very weak, surrendered to this party; but some of the garrison had retired to the principal fort at Kingston, called Forty Fort. Colonel John Butler next demanded the surrender thereof. Colonel Zebulon Butler, a continental officer, who commanded, sent a message to him, proposing a conference at a bridge without the fort. This being agreed to, Colonel Zebulon Butler, Dennison, and some other officers repaired to the place appointed, and they were followed by the whole garrison, a few invalids excepted. None of the enemy appeared. The Wyoming people advanced, and supposed that the enemy were retiring. They continued to march on till they were about three miles from the fort. They then saw a few of the enemy, with whom they exchanged a few shots; but they presently found themselves ambuscaded and attacked by the whole bodies of Indians and Tories. They fought gallantly, till their retreat to the fort was cut off. Universal confusion ensued. Out of 417 who had marched out of the fort, about 360 were instantly slain. No quarter was given. Colonel John Butler again demanded the surrender of Forty Fort. This was agreed to, under articles of capitulation, by which the effects of the people therein were secured to them. The garrison, consisting of thirty men and two hundred women, were permitted to cross the Susquehanna, and retreat through the woods to Northampton county. The most of the other scattered settlers had previously retired, some through the woods to Northampton, others down the river to Northumberland. In this retreat, some women were delivered of children in the woods, and many suffered from want of provisions. Several of the settlers at Wyoming had erected good houses and barns, and made considerable improvements. These and the other houses in the vicinity were destroyed. Their horses, cattle, sheep, and hogs were, for the most part, killed or driven away by the enemy. A large proportion of the male inhabitants were in one day slaughtered. In a single engagement, near two hundred women became widows, and a much greater number of children were left fatherless." (Dr. Ramsay's History of the United States, Vol. II., Chap. xix., pp. 323, 324.)

REMARKS UPON DR. RAMSAY'S ACCOUNT.

Such is the account of this melancholy affair by Dr. Ramsay, a friend of General Washington, and a distinguished officer in the American army. Let us note Dr. Ramsay's admissions and his omissions. He admits that the Tories or Loyalists had been persecuted, imprisoned, plundered, and banished; that no less than twenty-seven of them had been taken, and sent to Hartford, in Connecticut, but were afterwards released; yet he might have added that they were kept prisoners nearly a year, and then discharged for want of any evidence against them. It is also admitted that "others of the same description (as those who had been sent prisoners to Connecticut) were instigated by *revenge* against the Americans, from whom some of them had suffered banishment and loss of property." It is likewise admitted that the whole invading party consisted of but 1,100 men, of whom only 200 were Tories, the remaining 900 being Indians. But it is not stated that those Indians were neighbours, and many of them the connections of the northern tribes of those Indians whose settlements had been invaded, their fields and towns destroyed, as a precaution lest they should co-operate with the British; nor is it said that many of these Indians were residents in the neighbourhood, and were treated like the Tories.

It furthermore appears from this narrative that the Americans in Wyoming were not even taken by surprise, but were prepared for their enemy; that none were killed except in the conflict of the battle; that the thirty men and two hundred women in the garrison were not murdered, but were "permitted (with their effects) to cross the Susquehanna and retreat to Northampton." The taking of the cattle and burning of the houses and barns was after the example of the Americans in invading and destroying the Indian settlements. It is therefore clear, according to Dr. Ramsay's own narrative, that the "Massacre of Wyoming" was not an *unprovoked aggression*, like that of the Americans against the more Southern

Indians, but a *retaliation* for injuries previously inflicted by the aggressors.*

But as the "Massacre of Wyoming" is the case selected by American historians and poets to exhaust their indignation against English cruelty in employing the Indians in the civil war, we will not dismiss it with the above cursory remarks, but will examine it with some degree of minuteness.

Wyoming was a pleasant and fertile valley, situated on the eastern branch of the Susquehanna, and consisted of eight townships, five square miles each. It had been claimed as part of Pennsylvania; but Connecticut, relying upon the authority of a more ancient Charter, had since the last war made a large settlement on the banks of that beautiful river. "The exquisitely beautiful valley of Wyoming, where, on the banks of the Susquehanna, the wide and rich meadows, shut in by walls of wooded mountains, attracted emigrants from Connecticut, through their claim of right under the Charter of their native colony, was in conflict with the territorial jurisdiction of the proprietaries of Pennsylvania."†

Such was the scene of a tragedy which thrilled all America and Europe; for the accounts published in Europe were the repetitions of the exaggerated American statements, omitting for the most part the causes of the tragedy and the retaliation which followed it.

I will now present and collate the three other accounts, with that of Dr. Ramsay, of those tragical events on both sides.

Mr. Bancroft states as follows:

"The Seneca tribe, fresh from the memory of their chiefs and braves who fell in conflict with the New York husbandmen at Oriskany. Their king, Sucingerachton, was, both in war and in

---

* "The aggressors on this occasion were a troop of wild Indians, in conjunction with some Tory exiles. They were headed by Colonel Butler, a partisan commander of note, and by Joseph Brant, a half Indian by birth, a whole Indian in cruelty. Unhappily, at Wyoming, the soil was claimed both by Connecticut and Pennsylvania. From this conflict of pretensions and consequent laxity of law, there had been the freer license for rigours against the Loyalists. Few of them in that district but had undergone imprisonment, or exile, or confiscation of property; and thus they were provoked to form a savage alliance and to perpetrate a fierce revenge." (Lord Mahon's History, etc., Vol. VII., Chap. lviii., pp. 382, 383.)

† Bancroft's History of the United States, Vol. V., Chap. ix., p. 165.

council, the foremost man of all the Six Nations. Compared with him, the Mohawk Brant, who had been but lately known upon the war-path, was lightly esteemed.* His attachment to the English increased to a passion on the alliance of the Americans with the French, for whom he cherished implacable hate. Through his interest, and by the blandishments of gifts and pay and chances of revenge, Colonel John Butler lured the *Seneca* warriors to cross the border of Pennsylvania under the British flag.

"The party of savages and rangers, numbering between five hundred and seven hundred men, fell down the Tioga river, and on the last day of June hid in the forests above Wyoming. The next day the two northernmost forts capitulated. The men of Wyoming, old and young, with one regular company, in all hardly more than three hundred, took counsel with one another, and found no hope of deliverance for their families but through a victorious encounter with a foe twice their number, and more skilful in the woods than themselves. On the 3rd day of July, the devoted band, led by Colonel Zebulon Butler, who had just returned from the continental service, began their march up the river.† The horde of invaders, pretending to retreat, crouched themselves on the ground in the open wood. The villagers of Wyoming began firing as they drew near, and at the third volley stood within a hundred yards of the ambush, when the Seneca braves began the attack, and were immediately seconded by the rangers. The Senecas gave no quarter, and in less than half an hour took two hundred and twenty-five scalps, among them those of two field officers and seven captains. The rangers saved but five of their captives. On the British side only two whites were killed and eight Indians wounded. The next day the remaining forts, filled chiefly with women and children, capitulated. The long and wailing procession of survivors flying from their fields of corn, their gardens, the flames of their cottages, the unburied bodies of their beloved defenders, escaped by a pass through

---

* Brant was not at Wyoming. This appears from Butler's report; and compare Broadhead documents, Vol. VIII., p. 572 (note by Mr. Bancroft).

† This is what Dr. Ramsay, in his account quoted above, on pages 85 and 86, erroneously states was a proposed conference as to terms of capitulation.

the hills to the eastern settlements. Every fort and dwelling was burned down.

"The Senecas spread over the surrounding country, adepts in murder and ruin. The British leader boasted in his report that his party had burned a thousand houses and every mill (a great exaggeration). Yet, marauders came to destroy and deal deaths, not to recover or hold; and the ancient affection for England was washed out in blood (more truly, the revenge for wrongs previously received). When the leader of the inroad turned to desolate other scenes, Pennsylvania was left in undisputed possession of her soil." (Bancroft's History of the United States, Vol. X., Chap. v., pp. 137, 138.)

Mr. Tucker briefly states the affair in the following words:

"The settlement of Wyoming, in Pennsylvania, was assailed in July by a large body of savages, who, having obtained easy possession of it, indiscriminately butchered both the garrison and the inhabitants; and soon afterwards Wilkesbarre shared the same fate. Near three thousand had succeeded in effecting their escape.*

"To prevent their return to the scenes of their former happiness, everything that could contribute to their comfort—houses, crops, animals—were, with an industry equal to their malignity, destroyed by the savages." (Tucker's History of the United States, Vol. I., Chap. iii., p. 239.)

The following account of the "Wyoming Massacre" appears more intelligible and consistent than any of the preceding. Says Mr. Hildreth:

"There had come in among the Connecticut settlers at Wyoming a number of Dutch and Scotch from New York, some thirty of whom, shortly after the commencement of the war, had been seized under the suspicion of being Tories, and sent to Connecticut for trial. They were discharged for want of evidence; but if not Tories before, they soon became so.

---

* *Note.* Mr. Hildreth says that "Wyoming did not number three thousand inhabitants." (History of the United States, Vol. III., Chap. xxxviii., p. 262.) The number of the slain could not have been greater than those mentioned above by Dr. Ramsay (p. 86), who states that, instead of those in the garrison being "indiscriminately butchered," they were allowed to cross the Susquehanna and make their way through the woods to neighbouring settlements.

Returning to the valley of the Mohawk, whence they had emigrated to Wyoming, they enlisted into the partisan corps of Johnson and Butler, and waited eagerly for chances of revenge.

"Though Wyoming did not number three thousand inhabitants, it had furnished two full companies (one writer says, a thousand men) to the continental army, and had thus in a manner deprived itself of the means of defence. Congress, upon rumours of intended Indian hostilities, had ordered a third company to be raised as a local garrison ; but this corps was as yet hardly organized, and very imperfectly armed. Such was the state of the settlement when there appeared at the head of the valley an overwhelming force of Tories and Indians, principally of the Seneca tribe of the Six Nations, led by Colonel Butler. Some of the inhabitants were waylaid and slain. The upper fort, held by disaffected persons, surrendered at once. The continentals, with such others as could be mustered, marched out to meet the enemy; but they were surrounded, defeated, and driven back with heavy loss, and several who were taken prisoners were put to death by the Indians with horrible tortures. Those who escaped fled to Fort Wyoming, which was speedily invested. The surviving continentals, to avoid being taken prisoners, embarked and escaped down the river ; after which the fort surrendered, upon promise of security of life and property. Desirous to fulfil these terms, Butler presently marched away with his Tories, but he could not induce the Indians to follow. They remained behind, burned the houses, ravaged the fields, killed such as resisted, and drove the miserable women and children through the woods and mountains to seek refuge where they might.

"These barbarities, greatly exaggerated by reports embodied since in poetry and history, excited everywhere a lively indignation. Wyoming was presently re-occupied by a body of continental troops. A continental regiment of the Pennsylvania line, stationed at Schoharie, penetrated to the neighbouring branches of the Upper Susquehanna, and *destroyed the settlement* of Unadilla, occupied by a mixed population of Indians and refugees. The Indians and Loyalists soon took their *revenge* by surprising Cherry Valley. The fort, which had a continental garrison, held out; Colonel Alden, who lodged in the town, was killed, the lieutenant-colonel was made prisoner, and the settlement suffered almost the fate of Wyoming." (Hildreth's History of the United States, Vol. III., Chap. xxxviii., pp. 262, 263.)

REMARKS ON THESE FOUR ACCOUNTS OF THE MASSACRE.

The attentive reader has doubtless observed that the four versions given above, by four accredited American historians, in regard to the "Massacre of Wyoming," differ from each other in several essential particulars.

1. Two of these versions imply that the "massacre" was a mere marauding, cruel, and murderous invasion of an inoffensive and peaceful settlement; while the other two versions of Dr. Ramsay and Mr. Hildreth clearly show the provocation and cruel wrongs which the Loyalists, and even Indians, had experienced from the continentals and inhabitants of Wyoming; that the settlement of Wyoming was the hot-bed of revolutionism, in which, out of three thousand inhabitants, several hundred had volunteered into the continental army, while they, as may be easily conceived, insulted, imprisoned, banished and confiscated the property of those who regarded their oath of allegiance as inviolate as their marriage vow, "for better for worse," until death released them from it. Instead of treating a solemn oath as secondary to caprice and passion, the Loyalists carried it to an excess of integrity and conscience; they were to be the more respected and honoured, rather than made on that account criminals and outlaws, subject to imprisonment and banishment of their persons and the confiscation of their property.

2. Two of these four versions import that the inhabitants, men, women, and children, were "indiscriminately butchered;" the other two versions import that none were "butchered" except in battle, and none were "scalped" except those who had fallen in battle.

3. In two of these versions it is stated that those who were in the forts after their surrender were "massacred," without respect to age or sex; in the other two versions it is stated that not one of them was massacred, but they were all permitted to cross the Susquehanna with their effects.

4. In one of these versions, Colonel John Butler is repre-

sented as not only the commander of the whole party of invasion, but the author of all the cruelties perpetrated in the "massacre" of Wyoming; yet Mr. Hildreth's statement shows the reverse—that Colonel Butler had accepted the surrender of Fort Wyoming "upon the promise of security to life and property;" that "desirous to fulfil these terms, he presently marched away with his Tories; but he could not induce the Indians to follow;" that "the depredations which followed were inflicted by the Indians alone, and whom Colonel Butler could not command, and against his remonstrance and example and that of his Tories."

It is therefore plain that the accounts at the time of the "Massacre of Wyoming," published by the Congress party, were of the most exaggerated and inflammatory character, containing the grossest misrepresentation, and doing the greatest injustice to the leaders and conduct of the expedition, of which accounts they had no knowledge, nor any means of correcting them. These partial and shamefully exaggerated accounts and misrepresentations were spread through Europe, and produced the most unfavourable impression in regard to the "Tories" and their mixture with the Indians—the only place of refuge for them, as they were driven from their homes to escape the sentences of death, imprisonment, or banishment, subject in all cases, of course, to the destruction and confiscation of their property. The English Annual Register for 1779, after reproducing these unjust and inflated accounts, candidly says:

"It is necessary to observe, with respect to the destruction of Wyoming, that as no narrative of the exploits of the leaders in that transaction, whether by authority or otherwise, has yet appeared in this country, we can only rely for the authenticity of the facts which we have stated upon the accounts published by the Americans.

"Happy should we deem it, for the honour of humanity that, the whole account was demonstrated to be a fable." (Vol. IV., p. 14.)

The testimony furnished by the four versions of the transaction by American historians shows how largely the original accounts of it were fabulous.

Since compiling and analysing the foregoing four historical versions of the "Massacre of Wyoming," I have read Colonel Stone's *Life of Joseph Brant, Thayendanegea, including the Border Wars of the American Revolution*, and have carefully examined his account of the "Massacre of Wyoming." Colonel Stone visited the place (1838), and obtained all the information which the oldest inhabitants and family letters could give, and examined all the papers in the State Paper Office, and obtained much information from correspondence and personal interviews with aged and distinguished inhabitants, well acquainted with all the particulars of the alleged "Massacre." The result of his researches was to justify the hopes of the British Annual Register, quoted on previous page, which, after having republished the American accounts of the "Massacre," says: "Happy should we deem it, for the honour of humanity, that the whole account were demonstrated to be a fable."

This has been done by Colonel Stone after the lapse of more than half a century. In the fifteenth chapter of the first volume of his eloquent and exhaustive work he gives a history of the settlement, and of the many years' wars between the rival claimants of Connecticut and Pennsylvania—the former styled "the Susquehanna Company," and the latter "the Delaware Company." The question was also complicated by Indian claims, as the land had been once acquired by the Six Nations, and alleged to have been sold to both companies. Many of the Mohawks and other Indians resided in and near the settlement. On the breaking out of the war, politics largely entered into the disputes, and armed conflicts ensued, and no less than ten forts were erected in the settlement.

According to Colonel Stone, the "Massacre" was not the result of surprise, nor did it involve the indiscriminate massacre of women and children, but was the result of a pitched battle between the Loyalists and Continentals, in which the latter were the assailants and were defeated, and whatever "massacre" there was followed the battle.*

Colonel Stone, after having given an account of the battle, as

---

* Colonel Stone states that the Provincials "intended to make a quick movement, and take the enemy by surprise;" but their purpose was dis-

stated in previous note, and having corrected several erroneous statements, makes the following correction of what had been often written and generally believed respecting the famous Chief Brant:

"There is another important correction to be made in reference to every written history of this battle extant, not even covered by an Indian scout. He then gives the following account of the battle and of the "massacre" which followed:

"The Provincials pushed rapidly forward; but the British and Indians were prepared to receive them, 'their line being formed a small distance in front of their camp, in a plain thinly covered with pine, shrub, oaks and undergrowth, and extending from the river to a marsh at the foot of the mountain' (Marshall). 'On coming in view of the enemy, the Americans, who had previously marched in a single column, instantly deployed into a line of equal extent, and attacked from right to left at the same time' (Col. Z. Butler's letter). 'The right of the Americans was commanded by Colonel Zebulon Butler, opposed to Colonel John Butler, commanding the enemy's left. Colonel Dennison commanded the left of the Americans, and was opposed by the Indians forming the enemy's right' (Chapman). The battle commenced at about forty rods distance, without much execution at the onset, as the brushwood interposed obstacles to the sight. The militia stood the fire well for a short time, and as they pressed forward there was some giving way on the enemy's right. Unluckily, just at this moment the appalling war-whoop of the Indians rang in the rear of the Americans' left; the Indian leader, having conducted a large party of his warriors through the marsh, succeeded in turning Dennison's flank. A heavy and destructive fire was simultaneously poured into the American ranks; and amidst the confusion, Colonel Dennison directed his men to 'fall back,' to avoid being surrounded, and to gain time to bring his men into order again. This direction was mistaken for an order to 'retreat,' whereupon the whole line broke, and every effort of their officers to restore order was unavailing. At this stage of the battle, and while thus engaged, the American officers mostly fell. The flight was general. The Indians, throwing away their rifles, rushed forward with their tomahawks, making dreadful havoc; answering the cries for mercy with the hatchet, and adding to the universal consternation those terrific yells which invest savage warfare with tenfold horror. So alert was the foe in his bloody pursuit, that less than sixty of the Americans escaped either the rifle or the tomahawk. Of the militia officers, there fell one lieutenant-colonel, one major, ten captains, six lieutenants, and two ensigns. Colonel Durkee and Captains Hewett and Ransom were likewise killed. Some of the fugitives escaped by swimming the river, and others by flying to the mountains. As the news of the defeat spread down the valley, the greater part of the women and children, and those who had remained to protect them, likewise ran to the woods and mountains, while those who could not escape thus

excepting the revised edition of the Life of Washington, by Chief Justice Marshall. This correction regards the name and just fame of Joseph Brant, whose character has been blackened with all the infamy, both real and imaginary, connected with this bloody expedition. Whether Captain Brant was at any time in company with this expedition, is doubtful; but it is certain, in the face of every historical authority, British and American,

sought refuge in Fort Wyoming. The Indians, apparently wearied with pursuit and slaughter, desisted and betook themselves to secure the spoils of the vanquished.

"On the morning of the 4th, the day after the battle, Colonel John Butler, with the combined British and Indian forces, appeared before Fort Wyoming and demanded its surrender. 'The inhabitants, both within and without the fort, did not on that emergency sustain a character for courage becoming men of spirit in adversity. They were so intimidated as to give up without fighting; great numbers ran off; and those who remained all but betrayed Colonel Zebulon Butler, their commander' (Col. Z. Butler's letter). 'The British Colonel Butler sent several flags, requiring an unconditional surrender of his opposing namesake and the few continental troops yet remaining, but offering to spare the inhabitants their property and effects. But with the American colonel the victor would not treat on any terms ; and the people thereupon compelled Colonel Dennison to comply with conditions which his commander had refused.' The consequence was that Colonel Zebulon Butler contrived to escape from the fort with the remains of Captain Hewett's company of regulars (*Idem*.), and Colonel Dennison entered into articles of capitulation. 'By these it was stipulated that the settlers should be disarmed, and their garrison demolished ; that all prisoners and public stores should be given up ; that the property of the people called Tories should be made good, and they be permitted to remain peaceably upon their farms. In behalf of the settlers it was stipulated that their lives and property should be preserved, and that they should be left in the unmolested occupancy of their farms' (Chapman's History).

"Unhappily, however, the British commander either could not or would not enforce the terms of capitulation (see page 91, where Mr. Hildreth says that 'Colonel Butler, desirous to fulfil these terms of capitulation, presently marched away with his Tories, but he could not induce the Indians to follow. They remained behind, burned the houses, ravaged the fields, killed such as resisted, and drove the miserable women and children through the woods and mountains to seek refuge where they might.'), which were to a great extent disregarded as well by the Tories as the Indians. Instead of finding protection, the valley was again laid waste, the houses and improvements were destroyed by fire, and the country plundered. Families were broken up and dispersed, men and their wives separated, mothers torn from their children and some of them carried into captivity, while far the greater number fled to the mountains, and wandered through the wilderness

that so far from being engaged in the battle, he was many miles distant at the time of its occurrence. Such has been the uniform testimony of the British officers engaged in the expedition, and such was always the word of Thayendanegea (Brant's Indian name) himself. It will, moreover, be seen toward the close of the present work that after the publication of Campbell's 'Gertrude of Wyoming,' in which poem the Mohawk chieftain is denounced as 'the Monster Brant,' his son repaired to England, and in correspondence with the poet, successfully vindicated his father's memory from the calumny."—*Ib.*, p. 338.

To all this Colonel Stone adds the following important note. He says: "Since the present chapter was written, and while the work was under revision, the author received a letter from Mr. Samuel C. Frey, of Upper Canada, a son of the late Philip Frey, Esquire, a Loyalist of Tryon County, who was ensign in H. B. M.'s Eighth Regiment, and who, with his regiment, was engaged in the campaign and battle of Wyoming Philip R. Frey, the ensign spoken of, died at Palatine, Montgomery (formerly Tryon) County, in 1823. It was his uniform testimony that Brant was not at Wyoming. Mr. Frey writes to the author that there were no chiefs of any notoriety with the Indians in that expedition, and that the Indians themselves were led from Detroit by Captain Bird, of the Eighth Regiment. Bird had been engaged in a love affair at Detroit, but being very ugly, besides having a hare-lip, was unsuccessful. The affair getting wind, his fellow-officers made themselves merry at his expense; and in order to steep his grief in forgetfulness, he obtained permission to lead an expedition somewhere against the American frontier. Joining the Indians placed under him and a detachment of his regiment to Butler's Rangers, they concerted the descent upon Wyoming. Ensign Frey stated that Bird was ill-natured during the whole march,

---

to the older settlements. Some died of their wounds, others from want and fatigue, while others were still lost in the wilderness or were heard of no more. Several perished in a great swamp in the neighbourhood, which, from the circumstance, acquired the name of 'the Shades of Death,' and retains it to this day. These were painful scenes. But it does not appear that anything like a massacre followed the capitulation." (Life of Joseph Brant, and Border Wars of the American Revolution, Vol. I., Chap. xv., pp. 334—336.)

and acted with foolhardiness at the battle. He further stated, according to the letter of his son, that the American colonel challenged them to a fair field-fight, which challenge was accepted. 'The next morning, about nine o'clock, the Americans poured out of the fort, about 340 in number; the Indians fell back over a hill; the troops on both sides drew up in battle array and soon commenced. After a few rounds fired, the American colonel ordered his drum-major to beat a charge; the drum-major mistook the order, and beat a retreat; the Americans became disordered immediately, and ran helter-skelter; the moment the Indians saw them running, they poured down upon them from their hiding-places, so that no more than about forty survived out of 340.'"

"Rarely, indeed," adds Colonel Stone, "does it happen that history is more at fault in regard to facts than in the case of Wyoming. The remark may be applied to nearly every writer who has attempted to narrate the events connected with the invasion of Colonel John Butler. Ramsay and Gordon and Marshall—nay, the British historians themselves have written gross exaggerations. Marshall, however, in his revised edition, has made corrections, and explained how and by whom he was led into error. My excellent friend, Charles Miner, Esq., long a resident of Wyoming, a gentleman of letters and great accuracy, furnished the biographer of Washington with a true narrative of the transactions which he made the basis of the summary account contained in his revised edition. Other writers, of greater or less note, have gravely recorded the same fictions, adding, it is to be feared, enormities not even conveyed to them by tradition. The grossest of these exaggerations are contained in Thatcher's Military Journal and in Drake's Book of the Indians. The account of the marching out of a large body of the Americans from one of the forts to hold a parley, by agreement, and then being drawn into an ambuscade and all put to death, is false; the account of seventy continental soldiers being butchered after having surrendered, is totally untrue. No regular troops surrendered, and all escaped who survived the battle of the 3rd. Equally untrue is the story of the burning of the houses, barracks, and forts, filled with women and children."—*Ib.*, p. 338, 339.

CHAPTER XXXV.

American Retaliation for the Alleged "Massacre of Wyoming," as narrated by American Historians.

We will now state from the same historical authorities the *revenge* which the continentals took for the "Massacre of Wyoming."

Dr. Ramsay says: "Soon after the destruction of the Wyoming settlement, an expedition was carried on against the Indians by Colonel Zebulon Butler, of the Pennsylvania troops. He and his party having gained the head of the Delaware, October 1st, marched down the river two days, and then struck across the country to the Susquehanna. They burnt or destroyed the Indian villages both in that quarter and the other settlements; but the inhabitants escaped. The destruction was extended for several miles on both sides of the Susquehanna. They completed the expedition in sixteen days."*

* Dr. Ramsay's History of the United States, Vol. II., Chap. xix., p. 325.
"About four weeks after Colonel Zebulon Butler's return, some hundreds of Indians, a large body of Tories, and about fifty regulars, entered Cherry Valley, within the State of New York. They made an unsuccessful attempt on Fort Alden; but they killed and scalped thirty-two of the inhabitants, mostly women and children; and also Colonel Alden and ten soldiers."—*Ib.*, p. 325. Then, on the side of the continentals, "Colonel G. Van Shaick, with fifty-five men, marched from Fort Schuyler to the Onondago settlements, and on the 19th of April, 1779, burnt the whole, consisting of about fifty houses, together with a large quantity of provisions. Horses and stock of every kind were killed. The arms and ammunition of the Indians were either destroyed or brought off, and their settlements were laid waste. Twelve Indians were killed and thirty-four made prisoners. This expedition was performed in less than six days, and without the loss of a man."—*Ib.*, pp. 326, 327.

This destruction of "Indian villages" and "other settlements" to the extent of "several miles on both sides of the Susquehanna" was more than an equivalent revenge for the destruction of Wyoming. But it was only the beginning of vengeance and destruction, not only against the immediate offenders in the case of Wyoming, but the pretext for a resolution and order of Congress itself for the entire destruction of the Six Indian Nations, though their chiefs had held no council and given no order as to the attack upon the settlement of Wyoming, and had nothing to do with it, except that one of their tribes, with possibly a few stragglers from some of the other tribes. With this exception, as is shown by the narratives above quoted, the Six Nations had no connection with the destruction of Wyoming; were living quietly and industriously on their well-cultivated farms, though friendly to the royal cause. Yet Congress, by an order which, we believe, has no parallel in the annals of any civilized nation, commands the complete destruction of those people as a nation. It is cruel, indeed, and revolting to humanity, to kill and scalp ever so small a number of individuals, including women and children; but is it less cruel and revolting to render them houseless by thousands, to destroy the fruits of their labours, to exile them from their homes (after having destroyed them), and leave them to nakedness and starvation? Yet such was the case in the execution of the order of Congress for the extermination of the Six Nations.

"The determination," says Dr. Andrews, "was now taken by Congress to destroy this Indian nation. * * The intelligence of the preparations that were making against them was received by the Indians with great courage and firmness. * * They took a strong position in the most woody and mountainous part of the country, which they fortified with great judgment. * * General Sullivan attacked them in this encampment on the 29th of August. They stood a hot cannonade for more than two hours; but the breastwork of logs being almost destroyed, and the Americans having reached the top of the hill on their left, they were apprehensive of being surrounded, and retreated immediately with the utmost speed. * * The behaviour of the Indians on this day was very courageous; they returned the fire of the Americans with great spirit and regularity; and would, it was thought, have maintained their ground had not the Americans been provided with a train of artillery, to which the defeat of the Indians was principally owing. * * This engagement proved decisive. After their trenches were forced, they fled without making any further endeavour to rally. They were pursued two or three miles; but their flight was so swift that they could not be overtaken. Their loss in slain and wounded was very considerable, though few prisoners were made.

"The consternation occasioned among the Indians by this defeat was such, that they lost all hope of retrieving their fortunes, and dropped all idea of further resistance. As the Americans advanced, they retreated before them with the utmost precipitation, and suffered them to proceed, without any obstruction, in the destructive operations they were commissioned to perform.

"In pursuance of the orders he had received, General Sullivan penetrated into the heart of the country inhabited by the Five Nations, spreading everywhere the most extensive desolation. His letter to the Congress, giving an account of the progress and proceedings of the army under his command, was as complete a journal of destruction as ever was penned. No less than forty towns and settlements were destroyed, besides detached habitations. All their fields of corn and all their orchards and plantations; whatever, in short, was in a state of cultivation, underwent the same fate. The devastation was such, that on the American army's leaving that country not a house was left standing to their knowledge, nor an Indian to be seen.

"Such was the issue of this celebrated expedition, undertaken by way of retaliation for the outrages which the Indians (Senecas) had committed on the frontiers, and particularly in destroying the unfortunate settlement of Wyoming during the preceding summer.

"What rendered this total ruin of the country possessed by the Five Nations the more remarkable was the degree of knowledge and expertness in agriculture and in various domestic arts to which it was now for the first time discovered that the Indians had attained. It appeared by General Sullivan's account that the lands about the towns were excellently cultivated, and their houses large and elegantly constructed. The extent of their industry may be conjectured by his asserting that the quantity of corn destroyed could not, by a moderate computation, amount to less than 160,000 bushels; that their orchards were so well stocked that no less than 1,500 trees were cut down in one orchard only, numbers of which had evidently been planted many years; and that their garden grounds contained immense quantities of vegetables of every kind."*

Mr. Bancroft represents what he in one place terms "the great expedition" as a mere raid for the chastisement of the Seneca Indians. He says: "Moved by the massacres of Wyoming and Cherry Valley, Congress, on the 25th of February, had directed Washington to protect the inland frontiers and chastise the Seneca Indians. * * The best part of the season was gone when Sullivan, on the last of July, moved from Wyoming. His arrival at Tioga sent terror to the Indians. * * Several of the chiefs said to Colonel Bolton, in council, ' Why does not the great king, our father, assist us? Our villages will be cut off, and we can no longer fight his battles.'

"On the 22nd of August, the day after he was joined by New York troops under General James Clinton, Sullivan began his march up the Tioga into the heart of the Indian country. On the same day, Little David, a Mohawk chief, delivered a message from himself and the Six Nations to General Haldimand, then Governor of Canada: 'Brother! for these three years past the Six Nations have been running a race against fresh enemies, and are almost out of breath. Now we shall see whether you are our loving strong brother, or whether you deceive us. Brother! we are still strong for the King of England, if you will show us that he is a man of his word, and that he will not abandon his brothers the Six Nations.' * * The march into the country of the Senecas, on the left, extended to Genesee; on the right, detachments reached Cayuga lake. After destroying eighteen villages and their fields of corn, Sullivan, whose army had suffered for want of supplies, returned to New Jersey."†

* Dr. Andrews' History of the Late War, Vol. III., Chap. xli., pp. 436—439.

† Bancroft's History of the United States, Vol. X., Chap. x., pp. 230, 231, 232.

Mr. Bancroft's tame account of "the great expedition" against the Five Nations, limiting it to a chastisement of the Senecas, can only be accounted for from his contempt of General Sullivan, his desire to pass over as slightly

Mr. Hildreth's account of this expedition, though brief, is more comprehensive and satisfactory than that of Mr. Bancroft. Mr. Hildreth says:

"The command of the enterprise against the Indians, declined by Gates, was given to Sullivan. Three brigades from the main army, under Poor, Hand, and Maxwell—New Hampshire, Pennsylvania, and New Jersey troops—were assembled at Wyoming. A New York brigade ('upwards of 1,000 men,' says Dr. Ramsay), under General James Clinton, hitherto employed in guarding the frontier of that State, crossed from the Mohawk to Lake Otsego (one of the sources of the Susquehanna), dammed the lake, and so raised its level, and then by breaking away the dam produced an artificial flood, by the aid of which the boats were rapidly carried down the north-east branch of the Susquehanna, to form a junction with Sullivan. * *

"Sullivan's army, amounting to 5,000 men, passed up the Chemung branch of the Susquehanna. At Newton, now Elmira, they encountered a strong body of the enemy,* partly Indians and partly Tories, under Brant, the Butlers and Johnson, entrenched on a rising ground and disposed in ambuscade. Sullivan detached Poor to gain the rear, while he attacked them in front with artillery. Having put them to rout, he crossed to

as possible an expedition of destruction so disproportionate to the alleged cause of it, and against a whole rural and agricultural people for the alleged depredations of some of them. There were, as might be expected, marauding parties along the borders on the part of both the Indians and Americans, but the former always seem to have suffered more, and the latter to have excelled the former in their own traditionary mode of savage warfare.

"Other expeditions," says Mr. Holmes, "besides this decisive one were conducted against the Indians in course of the year. In April, Colonel Van Shaick, with fifty-five men, marched from Fort Schuyler, and burnt the whole Onondago settlements, consisting of about fifty houses, with a large quantity of provisions, killed twelve Indians and made thirty-four prisoners, without the loss of a single man. In the month of August, Colonel Broadhead made a successful expedition against the Mingo, Munsey, and Seneca Indians." (American Annals, Vol. II., p. 302.)

* Mr. Bancroft says that "the British Rangers and men of the Six Nations (who constructed the defensive breastwork at Newton) *were in all about* 800." (History of the United States, Vol. X., Chap. x., p. 232.)

It was certainly no great feat of military courage and skill for 5,000 men, with the aid of artillery, to defeat and disperse 800 Indians and Tories, without artillery, and then ravage and devastate an undefended country.

the hitherto unexplored valley of the Genesee. That want of food might compel the Indians and their Tory allies to emigrate, everything was ravaged. The ancient Indian orchards were cut down; many bushels of corn were destroyed, and eighteen villages, composed largely of frame houses, were burned. Provisions failed. Such at least was the reason that Sullivan gave, and the attack upon Niagara, the great object of the enterprise, was abandoned.

"A simultaneous expedition from Pittsburg ascended the Alleghany, and visited with similar devastation all the villages along the river. Pending these operations, and to prevent any aid from Canada, divers artifices were employed by Washington to create the belief of an intended invasion of that province."*

The account of this expedition given by Dr. Ramsay corresponds, with some additional particulars, with that given by Dr. Andrews, as above quoted, and almost in the same words. He says:

"The Indians who form the confederacy of the Six Nations, commonly called Mohawks, were the objects of this expedition. They inhabit that immense and fertile tract of country which lies between New England, the Middle States, and the Province of Canada. * * The Indians, on hearing of the expedition projected against them, acted with firmness. They collected their strength, took possession of proper ground, and fortified it with judgment. General Sullivan, on the 29th of August, attacked them in their works. They stood a cannonade for more than two hours, but then gave way. This engagement proved decisive. After the trenches were forced, the Indians fled without making any attempt to rally. The consternation occasioned among them by this defeat was so great, that they gave up all ideas of further resistance. As the Americans advanced into their settlements, the Indians retreated before them, without throwing any obstruction in their way. General Sullivan penetrated into the heart of the country inhabited by the Mohawks, and spread desolation everywhere. Many settlements in the form of towns were destroyed. All their fields of corn, and whatever was in a state of cultivation, underwent the same

* Hildreth's History of the United States, Vol. III., Chap. xxxix., pp. 287—289.

fate. Scarcely anything in the form of a house was left standing, nor was an Indian to be seen.

"To the surprise of the Americans, they found the lands about the Indian towns well cultivated, and their houses both large and commodious. The quantity of corn destroyed was immense. Orchards, in which were several hundred fruit trees, were cut down; and of them many appeared to have been planted for a long series of years. Their gardens, replenished with a variety of useful vegetables, were laid waste."*

* Dr. Ramsay's History of the United States, Vol. II., Chap. xix., pp. 327—329.

We will select from the same historian, though the same facts may be found in other histories of the time, a few examples in addition to those already given of the terrible retribution which the Americans inflicted upon the Indians in retaliation for any incursions which they may have made into the white settlements.

"The Cherokee Indians made an incursion into Ninety-Six district, in South Carolina, massacred some families and burned several houses. General Pickens, in 1781, collected a party of the militia, and penetrated into their country. This he accomplished in fourteen days, at the head of 394 horsemen. In that short space he burned thirteen towns and villages, killed upwards of forty Indians, and took a number of prisoners. Not one of his party was killed, and only two were wounded. The Americans did not expend over two pounds of ammunition, and yet only three Indians escaped after having been once seen. * *

"Towards the end of the war, in 1782, there was a barbarous and unprovoked massacre of some civilized Indians who had settled near the Muskingum. These, under the influence of some pious missionaries of the Moravian persuasion, had been formed into some degree of religious order. They abhorred war, and would take no part therein, giving for a reason that 'the Great Spirit did not make men to destroy men, but to love and assist each other.' From love of peace they advised those of their own colour, who were bent on war, to desist from it. They were also led from humanity to inform the white people of their danger, when they knew their settlements were about to be invaded. This provoked the hostile (American) Indians to such a degree, that they carried these quite away from Muskingum to a bank of the Sandusky Creek. They, finding corn dear and scarce in their new habitations, obtained liberty to come back in the fall of the same year to Muskingum, that they might collect the crops they had planted before their removal.

"While the white (American) people at and near the Monongahela heard that a number of Indians were at the Moravian towns on the Muskingum, they gave out that their intentions were hostile. Without any further enquiry, 160 of them crossed the Ohio, and put to death these harmless,

From this review of the invasions and contests between the Americans and Indians, it is clear that the Indians were the greater sufferers in life and property. The mutual hatreds of former years, when the colonies were warring with the French (instead of being, as now, in alliance with them), and the Indians were in the interest and service of the French, seems to have been perpetuated on both sides, and to have become more intense on the part of the Americans after the failure of

inoffensive people, though they made no resistance. In conformity to their religious principles, these Moravians submitted to their hard fate, without attempting to destroy their murderers. Upwards of ninety of this pacific race were killed by men who, while they called themselves Christians, were more deserving of the name of savages than those whom they inhumanly murdered." (Dr. Ramsay's History of the United States, Vol. II., Chap. xix., pp. 330—332.)

Mr. Hildreth gives the following account of the proceedings of the eighty or ninety men who murdered the peaceful Indians : " Arrived at the middle Moravian village, they found a party of Christian Indians gathering corn. The Indians at another neighbouring village were sent for, and the whole were placed together in two houses. A council was then held to decide upon their fate. Williamson, their commander, heretofore accused of too great lenity to the Indians, referred the matter to his men. Only sixteen voted for mercy ; all the rest, professing a faith common on the frontier, that 'an Indian has no more soul than a buffalo,' were for murder. They rushed on their prey, scalping-knife in hand, and upwards of ninety Indians, men, women, and children, soon lay bleeding and gasping." (History of the United States, Vol. III., Chap. lxv., p. 423.)

" Soon after this unprovoked massacre, a party of Americans set out for Sandusky, to destroy the Indian towns in that part; but the Delawares, Wyandots, and other Indians opposed them. An engagement ensued, in which some of the white people were killed, and several were taken prisoners. Among the latter were Colonel Crawford and his son-in-law. The colonel was sacrificed to the manes of those Indians who were massacred in the Moravian towns. The other prisoners were put to death with the tomahawk.

" Throughout the American war, the desolation brought by the Indians on the frontier settlements of the United States, and on the Indians by the Americans, was sufficient to excite compassion in the most obdurate heart.

" Not only men and warriors, but women and children indiscriminately murdered, while whole settlements were involved in promiscuous desolation. Each was made a scourge to the other ; and the unavoidable calamities of war were rendered doubly distressing by the dispersion of families, the breaking up of settlements, and an addition of savage cruelties, to the most extensive devastation of those things which conduce to the comfort of human life."

their efforts to secure the Indians to their side. The old contests between the Southern colonists and the Indians were renewed and repeated with intense bitterness; and in the Northern colonies the policy of Congress and its agents was to crush and exterminate the Indians altogether. In acts of individual cruelty, their historical and characteristic mode of war, the Indians exceeded the Americans; but in acts of wholesale destruction of life and property, the Americans far outdid the Indians, adopting the Indian instead of a civilized mode of warfare, and including in their sweep of destruction women and children as well as men.

The employment of Indians at all on the part of Great Britain against the colonists, is, in our opinion, the blackest crime recorded in the annals of the British Government, prompted apparently by the cowardly and execrable General Gage, but condemned by Generals Carleton and Burgoyne, as well as by General Howe. The use, however, which the Americans sought to make of the Indians, and their cruel and exterminating mode of warfare against them, leave them no ground of boasting on the score of humanity against either the British Government or the Indians.

To this may be added the unfortunate condition and treatment of the Loyalists or "Tories" among the Indians. For adhering, or suspected of adhering to the faith of their fathers, and even of the present persecution down to within less than six years, they were, however peaceably they might be living, driven from their homes and their property seized and alienated, and they left no place for the soles of their feet except among the Indians, and then termed monsters and treated as traitors, for joining their protectors in the defence of their places of refuge, and, as far as possible, for the recovery of their homes. What else, as men, as human beings, could they do? They were denied and banished from the homes which they had, unless they would reverse their political faith and oath of allegiance, and forswear allegiance, to enrol themselves in arms against the country of their forefathers and of their affection. They could not but be chafed with the loss of their freedom of speech and of conviction of their citizenship and their property, and of being driven into exile; and they must have been more or less than men had they not acted loyally and to the best of their ability with their protectors, however abhorrent to their views and feelings were many acts of the Indians—acts imitated and even excelled, in so many respects, by the Americans themselves, in their depredations into the Indian territories.

COLONEL STONE'S ACCOUNT, IN DETAIL, OF GENERAL SULLIVAN'S EXPEDITION OF EXTERMINATION OF THE SIX NATIONS OF INDIANS.

In his *Life of Brant, including the Border Wars of the American Revolution*, Colonel Stone gives a much more elaborate account of this expedition of destruction against the Six Nations, or rather the Five Nations, for the Oneidas and some of the Tuscaroras joined the Americans. Colonel Stone narrates the progress and work of General Sullivan from place to place. We will add a few extracts from his narrative, after some preliminary explanations.

Colonel Stone corrects a very common error, which views the whole race of North American Indians as essentially alike—" all as the same roving, restless, houseless race of hunters and fishermen, without a local habitation and with scarce a name." He gives examples of the varieties of Indian character, not less marked than between the English and the French—some following the buffalo in his migrations, others finding a precarious subsistence in the forest chase, others again fishing and trapping: tribes who pass most of their time in canoes, while others, woodland tribes, cultivate the soil, and gradually become organized, and acquire a higher state of civilization, and present a marked difference of character and taste from the hunter and fishermen tribes. "This higher state of social organization among the Six Nations," says Colonel Stone "greatly increased the difference. They had many towns and villages giving evidence of perseverance. They were organized into communities whose social and political institutions, simple as they were, were still as distinct and well-defined as those of the American Confederacy. They had now acquired some arts, and were enjoying many of the comforts of civilized life. Not content with small patches of cleared lands for the raising of a few vegetables, they possessed cultivated fields and orchards of great productiveness at the West. Especially was this the fact with regard to the Cayugas and Senecas. The Mohawks having been driven from their own rich lands (in the valley of the Mohawk and Susquehanna rivers), the extensive domains of the westernmost tribes of the confederacy (in the Genesee country) formed the granary of the whole. And in consequence of the superior social and political organization just referred to, and the Spartan-like character incident to the forest life, the Six Nations, though not the most numerous, were beyond doubt the most formidable of the tribes then in alliance with the Crown. It was justly considered, therefore, that the only way *to strike them effectively would be to destroy their homes* and the growing produce of their farms, and thus, *by cutting off their means of supply, drive them from their own country deeper into the interior, and perhaps throw them altogether upon their British allies for subsistence.*"

These facts will go far to account for the desire of the Mohawks to recover the homes from which they had been driven, and for the relations between the Six Nations to the Crown of Great Britain and the revolting portion of the colonists.

It has been intimated that the Oneida Indians and part of the Onondagos adhered to the revolting colonists. Colonel Stone observes: " It was the intention of General Sullivan that General Clinton should employ in his division as large a number of the Oneida warriors as could be induced to engage in the service. The latter officer was opposed to this arrangement; but through the importunities of Sullivan, the Rev. Mr. Kirkland, their missionary, who was now a chaplain in the army, had been summoned to Albany for consultation. From thence Mr. Kirkland was despatched to Pennsylvania, directly to join Sullivan's division; while to Mr. Deane, the interpreter connected with the Indian Commissioner at Fort Schuyler (formerly Fort Stanwix), was confided the charge of negotiating with the Oneida chiefs on the subject. The Oneidas volunteered for the expedition almost to a man; while those of the Onondagos who adhered to the cause of the Americans were equally desirous of proving their fidelity by their deeds. Under these circumstances, Clinton wrote to Sullivan on the 26th, that on the following Saturday Mr. Deane, with the Indian warriors, would join him at the head of the lake. A sudden revolution, however, was wrought in their determination by an address to the Oneidas from General Haldimand (Governor of Canada), received at Fort Schuyler the 22nd. This document was transmitted to them in their own language; and its tenor was so alarming as to induce them suddenly to change their purpose, judging very correctly, from the threats of Haldimand, that their presence was necessary at home for the defence of their own castles. Still Mr. Deane wrote that an arrangement was on foot by which he hoped to obtain the co-operation of a considerable number of the Oneida warriors."

"General Haldimand's address was written in the Iroquois (Mohawk) language, of which a translation was made by Mr. Deane and enclosed to General Clinton."

In this address General Haldimand charged the Oneida Indians with having "taken a different course from the rest of the Five Nations, your confederates, and have likewise deserted the King's cause through the deceitful machinations and snares of the rebels, who intimidated you with their numerous armies, by which means you became bewildered and forgot all your engagements with and former care and favour from the Great King of England, your Father. You also soon forgot the frequent bad usage and continual encroachments of the Americans upon the Indian lands throughout the continent. I say, therefore, that at the breaking out of these troubles, you firmly declared to *observe a strict neutrality in the dispute,* and made your declaration known to Sir Guy Carleton, my predecessor, *who much approved of it, provided you were in earnest.** I have hitherto strictly observed and examined your conduct, and find that you did not adhere to your assertion, although I could trace no reason, on the side of Government as well as the Indians, why you should act so treacherous and double a part; by which means we, not mistrusting your fidelity, have had many losses among the King's subjects, and the Five Nations, your friends and connections."

---

* The biographer of Brant and historian of the Border Wars of the American Revolution thinks that Sir Guy Carleton was not opposed to the employment of the Indians in the war with the Congress (Vol. I., pp. 89, 90), and quotes Brant as his authority; but General Haldimand (who himself favoured the employment of the Indians in the war) appears to be the safest interpreter of the views of Sir Guy Carleton, who intended, by the friendly alliance of the Indians with the King, that they should be neutral.

After further reproaches, admonitions, and threatenings, General Haldimand concluded in the following severe words: "These are facts, Brothers, that, unless you are lost to every sense of feeling, cannot but recall in you even a most hearty repentance and deep remorse for your past vile actions."

The effect of General Haldimand's address was to cause a conference—Mr. Deane, at the head of thirty-five Oneida warriors—with General Clinton, to apologize for the absence of their brethren from the expedition, and to make those explanations in regard to their own situation already communicated by Mr. Deane by letter, together with the address of General Haldimand. In his reply, General Clinton, among other things, said: "It is not my desire that the whole of your warriors should leave their castles. I have given a general invitation to our brethren the Oneidas, the Tuscaroras, and such of the Onondagos as have entered into friendship with us. In order to give all our Indian friends an equal chance of evidencing their spirit and determination to partake of our fortune, I am entirely satisfied that such only should join me as think proper."

Colonel Stone, after stating that on the 22nd of August General Clinton arrived at Tioga, and formed a junction with General Sullivan, says: "The entire command amounted to 5,000, consisting of the brigades of Generals Clinton, Hand, Maxwell, and Poor, together with Proctor's artillery and a corps of riflemen." Then, after relating the battle of Newton (the present site of Elmira), as described in extracts from the historians in previous pages, Colonel Stone narrates the progress and work of the invading army of extermination and destruction. We give the following extracts from his narrative:

"It is apprehended that but few of the present generation are thoroughly aware of the advances which the Indians, in the wide and beautiful country of the Cayugas and Senecas, had made in the march of civilization. They had several towns and many large villages laid out with a considerable degree of regularity. They had framed houses, some of them well furnished, having chimneys, and painted. They had broad and productive fields; and in addition to an abundance of apples, were in the enjoyment of the pear, and the still more delicious peach. But after the battle of Newton, the Indians everywhere fled at Sullivan's advance, and the whole country was swept as with a besom of destruction. On the 4th (September), as the army advanced, they destroyed a small settlement of eight houses, and two days afterwards reached the more considerable town of Kendaia, containing about twenty houses, neatly built and well finished. These were reduced to ashes, and the army spent nearly a day in destroying the fields of corn and the fruit trees. Of these there were great abundance, and many of them appeared to be ancient."

"On the 7th, Sullivan crossed the outlet of Seneca Lake, and moved in three divisions upon the town of Kanadaseagea, the Seneca capital, containing about sixty houses, with gardens and numerous orchards of apple and peach trees. It was Sullivan's object to surround the town and take it by surprise. But although Butler had endeavoured to induce the Indians to make a stand at the place, his importunities were of no avail. They said it was no use to contend with such an army; and their capital was consequently abandoned as the other towns had been before the Americans could reach it. A detachment of 400 men was sent down on the west side of the lake to destroy Gotheseunquean, and the plantations in the neighbourhood; while at the same time a number of volunteers, under Colonel Harper, made a forced march in the direction of Cayuga Lake, and destroyed Schoyere. Meantime the residue of the army was employed, on the 8th, in the destruction of the town, together with the fruit trees and fields of corn and beans. Here, as elsewhere, *the work of destruction was thorough and complete.*"

"The main army then moved forward upon Kanandaigua, at which place it arrived in two days. Here they 'found twenty-three very elegant houses, mostly framed, and in general large, together with very extensive fields of corn—all of which were destroyed. From Kanandaigua they proceeded to the small town of Honeoye, consisting of ten houses, which were immediately burnt to the ground. A post was established by General Sullivan at Honeoye, to maintain which a strong garrison was left, with heavy stores and one field-piece. With this precautionary measure the army prepared to advance upon the yet more considerable town of Genesee—the great capital of the western tribes of the confederacy—containing their stores and their broadest cultivated fields."

"The valley of the Genesee, for its beauty and fertility, was beheld by the army of Sullivan with astonishment and delight. Though an Indian country, and peopled only by wild men of the woods, its rich intervales presented the appearance of long cultivation, and were then smiling with the harvests of ripening corn. Indeed, the Indians themselves professed not to know when or by whom the lands upon that stream were first brought into cultivation. Instead of a howling wilderness, Sullivan and his troops found the Genesee flats, and many other districts of the country, resembling much more the orchards and farms and gardens of civilized life. But all was now doomed to speedy devastation. The Genesee Castle was destroyed. The troops scoured the whole region round about, and burnt and destroyed everything that came in their way. The town of Genesee contained 128 houses, mostly large and very elegant. It was beautifully situated, almost encircled with a clear flatt, extending a number of miles, over which extensive fields of corn were waving, together with every kind of vegetable that could be conceived. But the entire army was immediately engaged in destroying it, and the axe and the torch soon transformed the whole of that beautiful region from the character of a garden to a scene of sickening desolation. Forty Indian towns, the largest containing 128 houses, were destroyed. Corn, gathered and ungathered, to the amount of 160,000 bushels, shared the same fate; the fruit trees were cut down; and the Indians were hunted like wild beasts, till neither house, nor fruit tree, nor field of corn, nor inhabitant remained in the whole country. The gardens were enriched with great quantities of useful vegetables of different kinds. The size of the corn-fields, as well as the high degree of cultivation, excited wonder, and the ears of corn were so remarkably large that many of them measured twenty-two inches in length. So numerous were the fruit trees, that in one orchard they cut down 1,500."

"Having completed the objects contemplated by the expedition to the point at which he had arrived, General Sullivan recrossed the Genesee with his army the 16th of September, and set out on his return. Why he did not follow up his success, and strike the enemy's citadel at Niagara, which at that time was in no situation for formidable resistance, is a question difficult of solution. Unquestionably, in the organization of the expedition, the conquest of Niagara, the headquarters of the foe of all descriptions, and the seat of British influence and power among the Indians, was one of the principal objects in view. Certain it is, that the most important feature of the enterprise was not undertaken; and it will be seen in the sequel that but small ultimate advantage resulted from the campaign. Stimulated by a keener thirst for revenge, clouds of savages were again and again seen to sweep through the valley of the Mohawk with the scalping knife and the torch."

"The return of the army was along the same tract by which it had advanced. On the 20th, having recrossed the outlet of Seneca Lake, Colonel Zebulon Butler was detached with the rifle corps of 500 men to pass round the foot of Cayuga Lake, and lay waste the Indian towns on its eastern shore; while Lieutenant-Colonel Dearborn, with 200 men, was detached to perform the same service on the south-western shore. The main army pursued the most direct route to the Chemung and Tioga. On the 26th Colonel Dearborn's detachment returned, and on the 28th they were rejoined by Colonel Zebulon Butler, who had burnt three towns of the Cayugas, including their capital. Dearborn had burnt six towns in his route, destroying at the same time large quantities of corn. On the same day, Colonels Van Courtlandt and Dayton were detached upon a similar service—for the destruction of large fields of corn growing upon the banks of the Tioga and its tributaries."

"The army then resumed its march, and passing through Wyoming, arrived at Easton on the 15th of October. The distance thence to Genesee Castle was 280 miles. With the exception of the action at Newton, the achievements of the army in battle were not great. But it had scoured a broad extent of country, and had laid more towns in ashes than had ever been destroyed on the continent before. The red men were driven from their beautiful country, their habitations left in ruins, their fields laid waste, their orchards uprooted, and their altars and the tombs of their fathers overthrown."*

All the devastations of settlements, burnings and slaughter committed by the "Tories and Indians" during the whole war shrink into insignificance in regard to extent of territory, the

---

* Stone's Life of Joseph Brant, including the Border Wars of the American Revolution, Vol. II., Chap. i.

number of inhabitants and towns, the extent of cultivated farms and gardens, when compared with General Sullivan's one vast sweep of ruin and misery, in the course of which, as the historian says, "*the Indians were hunted like wild beasts, till neither house nor fruit tree, nor field of corn nor inhabitant, remained in the whole country.*"

All this was done by an express order of Congress to the Commander-in-Chief; and for doing this General Sullivan and his army received the cordial approbation and thanks of the Congress.

It was very natural that the survivors of the Six Nations and the "Tories," who took refuge and resided among them, should seek revenge on every possible occasion, in months following, in the regions of their own sufferings, especially upon those individuals and communities who they knew had prompted and aided the executioners of Congress. There were partizan leaders, with adventurous followers, on both sides, in the Southern as well as in the Northern States, who inflicted many acts of barbarity and desolation; but these retaliatory cruelties and raids of destruction acquired a greater intensity of bitterness and cruelty after the terrible ravages and cruelties perpetrated by General Sullivan and his army.

Besides, the history of the Indians, as well as of the "Tories," throughout the whole war, was written by their adversaries, and it was considered a master-stroke of policy to exaggerate the alleged misdeeds and paint the character of both the Indians and Tories in the blackest colours. The story of the "Massacre of Wyoming" is a sample of the manner in which the American writers of the day made history against the Indians and the "Tories." When facts could not be sufficiently seasoned to stimulate recruits for the army and appropriations from the people for its support, fiction pure and simple was resorted to; and Dr. Franklin himself did not think it unworthy of his antecedents, age and position to employ this method to bring disrepute upon the "Tories," the Indians, and the British Government itself, and to excite the hatred of his countrymen against them. The accomplished author of the *Life of Brant and the Border Wars of the American Revolution* forcibly observes:

"The Indians of the Six Nations, in common with their chief, were loaded with execrations for atrocities of which all were alike innocent, because the deeds recorded were never committed, it having been the policy of the public writers and those in authority, not only to magnify actual occurrences, but sometimes, when those were wanting, to draw upon their imaginations for such deeds of ferocity and bloodshed as might best serve to keep alive the strongest feelings of indignation against the parent country, and likewise induce the people to take the field in revenge, if not driven thither by the nobler impulse of patriotism."*

Such deliberate fictions, for political purposes, as that by Dr. Franklin, just referred to, were probably rare; but the investigations into which the author has been, in the preparation of the present work, have satisfied him that, from other causes, much exaggeration and falsehood has obtained a permanent footing in American history. Most historians of that period, English and American, wrote too near the time when the events they were describing occurred, for a dispassionate investigation of the truth; and other writers who have succeeded, have too often been content to follow the beaten track, without incurring the labour of diligent and calm inquiry. Reference has been made above to Wyoming, concerning which, to this day, the world has been abused with monstrous fictions, with tales of horror never enacted. Nor were the exaggerations in regard to the invasion of Wyoming greater than were those connected with the irruption into and destruction of Cherry Valley, as the reader will discover in the course of the ensuing pages. Indeed, the writer, in preparation of materials for this work, has encountered so much that is false recorded in history as sober verity, that he has at times been disposed almost to universal scepticism in regard to uninspired narration.

The "deliberate fictions, for political purposes, by Dr. Franklin," as the biographer of Brant expresses it, "were written as facts;" or, as the author quoted expresses it, "the well-known scalp story of Dr. Franklin was long believed, and recently revived and included in several books of authentic history." The details of Dr. Franklin's publication were so minute and varied as to create a belief that they were perfectly true. "It was long supposed to be authentic," as the author quoted says

* Life of Brant, including the Border Wars of the American Revolution.

in introducing the document, in Appendix No. 1 to Volume I., "but has since been ascertained to be a publication from the pen of Dr. Franklin, for political purposes."

The names introduced are of course fictitious, as well as the statements, but introduced with such an air of plausibility as to preclude the suspicion that they were fictitious. The publication will be a curiosity to most of the readers of these pages, as it has been to the writer. It is as follows:

Extract of a letter from Captain Gerrish, of the New England Militia, dated Albany, March 7th, 1782:

"The peltry taken in the expedition will, as you see, amount to a good deal of money. The possession of this booty at first gave us pleasure; but we were struck with horror to find among the packages eight large ones, containing scalps of our unhappy folks taken in the last three years by the Seneca Indians, from the inhabitants of the frontiers of New York, New Jersey, Pennsylvannia, and Virginia, and sent by them as a present to Colonel Haldimand, Governor of Canada, in order to be transmitted by him to England. They were accompanied by the following curious letter to that gentleman:

"TIOGA, January 3rd, 1782.

"May it please Your Excellency,

"At the request of the Seneca chiefs, I send herewith to your Excellency, under the care of James Boyd, eight packs of scalps, cured, dried, hooped, and painted with all the Indian triumphal marks, of which the following is invoice and explanation:

"No. 1, containing forty-three scalps of Congress soldiers killed in different skirmishes; these are stretched on black hoops, four inch diameter; the inside of the skin painted red, with a small black spot to note their being killed with bullets. Also sixty-two farmers, killed in their houses, the hoops red; the skin painted brown, and marked with a hoe; a black circle all round, to denote their being surprised in the night; and a black hatchet in the middle, signifying their being killed with that weapon.

"No. 2, containing ninety-eight farmers killed in their houses; hoops red; figure of a hoe, to mark their profession; great white circle and sun, to show they were surprised in the daytime; *a little red foot*, to show they stood upon their defence, and died fighting for their lives and families.

"No. 3, containing ninety-seven farmers; hoops green, to show they were killed in the fields; a large white circle, with a little round mark on it for the sun, to show that it was in the daytime; black bullet mark on some, hatchet on others.

"No. 4, containing 102 farmers, mixed of the several marks above; only eighteen marked with a little yellow flame, to denote their being prisoners burnt alive, after being scalped, their nails pulled out by the roots, and other torments; one of these latter supposed to be of a rebel clergyman; his band being fixed to the hoop of his scalp. Most of the farmers appear by the hair to be young or middle-aged men; there being but sixty-seven grey heads among them all, which makes the service more essential.

"No. 5, containing eighty-eight scalps of women; hair long, braided in the Indian fashion, to show they were mothers; hoops blue; skin yellow ground, with red tadpoles, to represent, by way of triumph, the tears of grief occasioned to their relations; a black scalping-knife or hatchet at the bottom, to mark their being killed with these instruments; seventeen others, hair very grey; black hoops; plain brown colour, no mark but the short club or cassetete, to show that they were knocked down dead, or had their brains beat out.

"No. 6, containing 193 boys' scalps, of various ages; small green hoops; whitish ground on the skin, with red tears in the middle, and black bullet marks, knife, hatchet, or club, as their death happened.

"No. 7, 211 girls' scalps, big and little; small yellow hoops; white ground; tears, hatchet, club, scalping knife, etc.

"No. 8. This package is a mixture of all the varieties above mentioned, to the number of 122; with a box of birch bark, containing twenty-nine little infants' scalps of various sizes; small white hoops, white ground.

"With these packs, the chiefs send to your Excellency the following speech delivered by Conciogatchie in council, interpreted by the elder Moore, the trader, and taken down by me in writing:

"'*Father!*—We send you herewith many scalps, that you may see that we are not idle friends.—A blue belt.

"'*Father!*—We wish you to send these scalps over the water to the Great King, that he may regard them and be refreshed; and that he may see our faithfulness in destroying his enemies, and be convinced that his presents have not been made to ungrateful people.—A blue and white belt with red tassels.

"'*Father!*—Attend to what I am going to say; it is a matter of much weight. The Great King's enemies are many, and they grow fast in number. They were formerly like young panthers; they could neither bite nor scratch; we could play with them safely; we feared nothing they could do to us. But now their bodies are become big as the elk and strong as the buffalo; they have also got great and sharp claws. They have driven us out of our country by taking part in your quarrel. We expect the Great King will give us another country, that our children may live after us, and be his friends and children as we are. Say this for us to the Great King. To enforce it we give this belt.—A great white belt with blue tassels.

"'*Father!*—We have only to say further, that your traders exact more than ever for their goods; and our hunting is lessened by the war, so that we have fewer skins to give for them. This ruins us. Think of some remedy. We are poor, and you have plenty of everything. We know you will send us powder and guns, and knives and hatchets; but we also want shirts and blankets.—A little white belt.'

"I do not doubt but that your Excellency will think it proper to give some further encouragement to those honest people. The high prices they complain of are the necessary effect of the war. Whatever presents may be sent for them through my hands shall be distributed with prudence and fidelity. I have the honour of being

"Your Excellency's most obedient and most humble servant,
"JAMES CRAUFURD."

This chapter of Congress vengeance to exterminate the Six Nations of Indians, and of its writers to picture them as human monsters, cannot be better concluded than in the words of the historian of Brant,* and of the Border Wars of the American Revolution:

"No Indian pen traces the history of their tribes and nations,

---

* Brant himself was educated at Philadelphia, married and lived quietly

or records the deeds of their warriors and chiefs, their prowess and their wrongs. Their spoilers have been their historians; and although a reluctant assent has been awarded to some of the nobler traits of their nature, yet, without yielding a due allowance for the peculiarities of their situation, the Indian character has been presented with singular uniformity as being cold, cruel, morose, and revengeful; unrelieved by any of those varying traits and characteristics, those lights and shadows which are admitted in respect to other people no less wild and uncivilized than they.

"Without pausing to reflect that, even when most cruel, they have been practising the trade of war—always dreadful—as much in conformity to their own usages and laws as have their more civilized antagonists, the white historian has drawn them with the characteristics of demons. Forgetting that the second of Hebrew monarchs did not scruple to saw his prisoners with saws, and harrow them with harrows of iron; forgetful likewise of the scenes of Smithfield, under the direction of our own British ancestors; the historians of the poor untutored Indians, almost with one accord, have denounced them as monsters *sui generis*, of unparalleled and unapproachable barbarity; as though the summary tomahawk were worse than the iron tortures of the harrow, and the torch of the Mohawk hotter than the faggots of Queen Mary.

"Nor does it seem to have occurred to the 'pale-faced' writers that the identical cruelties, the records and descriptions of which enter so largely into the composition of the earlier volumes of American history, were not barbarities in the estimation of those who practised them. *The scalp lock was an emblem of chivalry.* Every warrior shaving his head for battle was careful to leave *the lock of defiance upon his crown*, as for the bravado, 'Take it if you can.' The stake and the

---

on his land in the Mohawk Valley, entertained the missionaries, and assisted in translating portions of the New Testament; but when the revolution commenced he was not allowed to live in peace unless he joined the revolutionary party. He determined to maintain, as he said, the covenant faith of his forefathers to the King of England, and entered upon the "war-path," in which he became so distinguished a hero; in the course of which he perpetrated many deeds of cruelty, but also, as his biographer records, performed many acts of humanity, kindness, and generosity.

torture were identified with their rude notions of the power of endurance. They were inflicted upon captives of their own race, as well as upon whites; and with their own braves these trials were courted, to enable the sufferer to exhibit the courage and fortitude with which they could be borne—the proud scorn with which all the pain that a foe might inflict could be endured.

"But (it is said) they fell upon slumbering hamlets in the night and massacred defenceless women and children. This, again, was their own mode of warfare, as honourable in their estimation as the more courteous methods of committing wholesale murder laid down in the books.

"But of one enormity they were ever innocent. Whatever degree of personal hardship and suffering their female captives were compelled to endure, their persons were never dishonoured by violence; a fact which can be predicated, we apprehend, of no other victorious soldiery that ever lived.

"In regard, moreover, to the countless acts of cruelty alleged to have been perpetrated by the savages, it must still be borne in mind that the Indians have had no writer to relate their own side of the story. The annals of man, probably, do not attest a more kindly reception of intruding foreigners than was given to the Pilgrims landing at Plymouth by the faithful Massassoit, and the tribes under his jurisdiction. Nor did the forest kings take up arms until they but too clearly saw that either their visitors or themselves must be driven from the soil which was their own—the fee of which was derived from the Great Spirit. And the nation is yet to be discovered that will not fight for their homes, the graves of their fathers, and their family altars. Cruel they were in the prosecution of their contests; but it would require the aggregate of a large number of predatory incursions and isolated burnings to balance the awful scene of conflagration and blood which at once extinguished the power of Sassacus, and the brave and indomitable Narragansets over whom he reigned. No! until it is forgotten that by some Christians in infant Massachusetts it was held to be right to kill Indians, as the agents and familiars of Azazel; until the early records of even tolerant Connecticut, which disclose the fact that the Indians were seized by the Puritans, transported to the British West Indies, and sold as slaves, are lost; until the Amazon and La Plata shall have washed away the bloody history of the Spanish American conquest; and until the fact that Cortez stretched the unhappy Guatimozin naked upon a bed of burning coals (or General Sullivan's devastation of the Six Indian Nations) is proved to be a fiction, let not the American Indians be pronounced the most cruel of men."*

* Stone's Brant and the Border Wars of the American Revolution, Vol. I., Introduction, pp. 13, 14, 15.

CHAPTER XXXVI.

SITUATION AND TREATMENT OF THE LOYALISTS DURING THE WAR.

THE condition of the United Empire Loyalists for several months before, as well as after, the Declaration of Independence, was humiliating to freemen and perilous in the extreme ; and that condition became still more pitiable after the alliance of the revolutionists with the French—the hereditary enemies of both England and the colonies. From the beginning the Loyalists were deprived of the freedom of the press, freedom of assemblage, and under an espionage universal, sleepless, malignant—subjecting the Loyalists to every species of insult, to arrest and imprisonment at any moment, and to the seizure and confiscation of their property.

Before the Declaration of Independence, both parties were confessedly British subjects, professing allegiance to the same sovereign and constitution of government, both professing and avowing their adherence to the rights of British subjects ; but differing from each other as to the extent of those rights in contradistinction to the constitutional rights of the Crown and those of the people—as in the case of party discussions of all constitutional questions, whether in the colonies or mother country for centuries past. Both parties had their advocates in the British Parliament ; and while the prerogative advocates supported the corrupt Ministry of the day—or the King's party, as it was called—the Opposition in Parliament supported the petitions and remonstrances of those colonists who claimed a more popular colonial government ; but all the advocates of the constitutional rights of the colonists, in both Houses of Parliament, disclaimed, on the part of those whom they represented, the least idea of independence or separation from England. The Declaration of Independence essentially changed the relations of parties, both in Great Britain and America. The party of independence—getting, after months of manipulation by its leaders, first a majority of one in the Congress, and afterwards increasing that majority by various means—repudiated their former professed principles of connection with England; broke faith with the great men and parties in England, both in and out of Parliament, who had vindicated their rights and professions for more than ten years; broke faith also with their numerous fellow-subjects in America who adhered to the old faith, to the old flag, and connection with England, and who were declared by resolutions of Conventions, from Congress, provinces, counties, to townships and towns, enemies of their country, rebels and traitors, and treated as such.* Even before the Declaration of Independence, some of these popular meetings, called Conventions, assumed the highest functions of legislation and government, and dealt at pleasure with the rights, liberties, property, and even lives of their Tory fellow-citizens. There had been violent words, terms of mutual reproach, as in all cases of hot political contests; but it was for the advocates of independent liberty to deny to the adherents of the old faith all liberty of speech or of opinion, except under penalties of imprisonment or banishment, with confiscation of property. For a large portion of the community† to be thus stript of their civil rights by resolutions of a Convention, and reduced to the position of proscribed aliens or slaves, must have been galling to Loyalists beyond expression,

---

* "Committees exercised legislative, executive, and judicial powers. It is not to be doubted that, in many instances, these were improperly used, and that private resentments were often covered under the specious veil of patriotism. The sufferers, in passing over to the Royalists, carried with them a keen remembrance of the vengeance of Committees, and when opportunity presented were tempted to retaliate." (Dr. Ramsay's History of the United States, Vol. II., Chap. xxvi., pp. 467, 468.)

† "Until the Declaration of Independence they were by far the largest party, who not only expected but prayed for a reconciliation. England was their home, and by that affectionate name was always spoken of; all the wrongs which were heaped upon the children could not make them forget their home, or entirely alienate them from their parent. The ligaments that connect nations are never less powerful, though less tender, than those

and well calculated to prompt them to outbreaks of passion, and retaliations of resentment and revenge, each such act followed by a corresponding act from the opposite party.*

It might be supposed that forbearance and respect would have been shown to those who remained "steadfast and immovable" in the traditional faith of British monarchy and British connection, notwithstanding a corrupt and arbitrary party was in power for the time being; but the very reverse of this was the case on the part of those who professed, as one cardinal article of their political creed, that "all men are born free and equal," and therefore that every man had an equal right to his opinions, and an equal right to the expression of them; but all this was reversed in the treatment of the Loyalists. Mr. Hildreth well describes the position and treatment of the Loyalists, both before and after the Declaration of Independence, in the following words:

"In the position of that considerable class of persons who had remained in doubt, the Declaration of Independence and the assumption of State government made a decided change. It was now necessary to choose one side or the other.

"Very serious, too, was the change in the legal position of the class known as Tories, in many of the States a large minority, and in all respectable for wealth and social position. Of those thus stigmatized, some were inclined to favour the utmost claims of the mother country; *but the greater part, though*

which unite individuals, families, and clans. Consanguinity, affinity, alliance, operate alike on each." (Allen's History of the American War.)

"The disaffected, or rather the Loyalists, were a formidable party in the Middle States. They might be forgiven—many of them acted from principle, from a conscientious regard to their duty, from affection to their 'Sovereign,' and however mistaken they may have been, they deserve no censure. It is the infirmity of men's nature to err, and the majority cannot complain if the minority insist on the same privilege for which the predominant party are contending—the liberty of judging for themselves."— *Ib.*, Vol. I., p. 483.

* Even in South Carolina. Mr. Hildreth remarks:

"Not, however, by armies alone were hostilities carried on. All the scattered settlements bristled in hostile array. Whigs and Tories pursued each other with little less than savage fury. Small parties, everywhere under arms, some on one side, some on the other, with very little reference to greater operations, were desperately bent on plunder and blood." (Hildreth's History of the United States, Vol. III., Chap. xli., p. 329.)

determined to adhere to the British connection, yet deprecated the policy which had brought on so fatal a quarrel. This loyal minority, especially its more conspicuous members, as the warmth of political feeling increased, had been exposed to the violence of mobs, and to all sorts of personal indignities, in which private malice or a wanton and insolent spirit of mischief had been too often gratified under the disguise of patriotism. The barbarous and disgraceful practice of tarring and feathering and carting Tories, placing them in a cart and carrying them about as a sort of spectacle, had become in some places a favourite amusement. To restrain these outrages, Congress had specially committed the oversight of Tories and suspected persons to the regularly appointed Committees of Inspection and Observation for the several counties and districts. But even these Committees were not always very judicious or discriminating in the exercise of despotic powers implied in that delicate trust.

"By the recent political changes, Tories and suspected persons became exposed to dangers from the law as well as from mobs. Having boldly seized the reins of government, the new State authorities claimed the allegiance of all residents within their limits, and under the lead and recommendation of Congress, those who refused to acknowledge their authority, or who adhered to their enemies, were exposed to severe penalties, confiscation of property, imprisonment, banishment, and finally death."*

It does not appear that these lawless outrages upon "Tories" were ever checked or discountenanced, or their authors ever even reproved by the so-called authorities, but were actively or tacitly encouraged; so that before and during the very first months of Independence, the Loyalists were subject to the penalties of the mobs on one side and to the more cruel penalties of new-made law by a newly self-created authority on the other side. Perhaps no one did as much to promote this cruel policy against the Loyalists as Mr. John Adams, who was the ruling spirit in all the proceedings of Boston for years, the advocate of the Declaration of Independence, and the chief

---

* Hildreth's History of the United States, Vol. III., Chap. xxxiii., pp. 137, 138.

member of the Secret Committee of Congress for years, and was at length appointed Ambassador from the American Congress to Holland, whence he wrote a letter to Thomas Cushing, then Lieutenant-Governor of Massachusetts, but which was intercepted on board of the prize brigantine *Cabot*, and carried to St. Christopher's, in the West Indies. This letter was published in the Annual Register for 1781, pp. 259—261. It is dated "Amsterdam, December 15th, 1780," more than four years after the Declaration of Independence, and fully indicates the source of all those cruel acts against the Loyalists at the commencement and during the early years of the American civil war. Mr. Adams says:

"It is true, I believe, what you suggest, that Lord North showed a disposition to give up the contest, but was diverted from it not unlikely by the representation of the Americans in London, who, in connection with their coadjutors in America, have been thorns to us indeed on both sides of the water; but I think their career might have been stopt on your side if the executive officers had not been too timid in a point which I so strenuously recommended at the first—namely, to fine, imprison, and hang all inimical to the cause, without favour or affection. I foresaw the evil that would arise from that quarter, and wished to have timely stopt it. I would have hanged my own brother had he taken a part with our enemy in the contest."

Such was the "strenuously recommended" wholesale hanging policy of Mr. John Adams for the extermination of the "Tories" —a curious illustration of his professed doctrine, that "all men are born free and equal," and which largely accounts for the treatment of Loyalists during the war, and for the exasperated feelings which existed between them and their persecutors and oppressors of the Independence party. One of the first manifestations of this relentless feeling against the Loyalists occurred in Mr. Adams' native city of Boston, on its evacuation by General Howe, who, as Lord Mahon says, "had taken with him, at their own urgent request, above a thousand of the inhabitants of Boston, who had espoused the cause of the parent State, and who dreaded on that account the vengeance of their countrymen. Before they had embarked, they had, as Washington informs his brother, publicly declared that 'if they thought the most abject submission would procure them peace, they never would have stirred.'"* (Letter to John Augustine Washington, March 13th, 1776, as printed in the American Archives.)

"Indeed, throughout this contest, and amidst all those qualities displayed by the Americans, many of those qualities being entitled to high respect and commendation, there was none certainly less amiable than their merciless rancour against those among them who adhered to the royal side. In reference to those, a ferocious saying came to be current in America, that though we are commanded to forgive our enemies, we are nowhere commanded to forgive our friends. In reference to them, true Jetburgh justice was more than once administered—first the punishment, then the accusation, and last of all the evidence."†

The Convention of the State of New York (1776) resolved that "any person being an adherent to the King of Great Britain should be guilty of treason and suffer death."‡

The Loyalists experienced similar treatment in other provinces.

"Previous to their evacuation of Philadelphia, the Congress

---

* Having thus recovered their capital (Boston), one of the first acts of government exercised by the Provincial Assembly was to order the effects and the estates of those who fled with the British troops to Halifax to be publicly disposed of, and their produce applied to the use of the State. Such adherents to Britain as had risked to remain behind, were treated with great severity. They were prosecuted as enemies and betrayers of their country, and their estates were confiscated accordingly. (Dr. Andrews' History of the Late War, Vol. II., Chap. xix., p. 159.)

† Lord Mahon's History, etc., Vol. VI., Chap. liii., pp. 127, 128.

"The American Loyalists, in arms on the side of England, had grievous cause throughout the war to complain of the merciless treatment of such among them as fell into their countrymen's hands."—*Ib.*, Vol. VII., Chap. lxvi., p. 250.

"The Legislature of North Carolina passed a law (1780) to put a stop to the robbery of poor people under the pretence that they were Tories—a practice carried on even to the plundering of their clothes and household furniture." (Hildreth's History of the United States, Vol. III., Chap. xli., p. 329.)

"In New York, in 1776, a rage for plundering, under pretence of taking Tory property, infected many of the common soldiery, and even some of the officers." (Dr. Ramsay's History of the United States, Vol. II., Chap. xi., p. 154.)

‡ Dr. Ramsay's History of the United States, Vol. II., Chap. xi.

had ordered some of the principal Quakers and other gentlemen of the first consideration in that place, above twenty in number, to be taken into custody, as strongly attached to the royal cause, and known enemies to the ruling powers. These gentlemen had repeatedly refused to give any written or verbal acknowledgment of allegiance or submission to the American Government, or promise of holding no correspondence with its enemies. Notwithstanding the evident danger their persons were in, they had even the resolution to refuse confining themselves to their respective dwellings. The spirit of these gentlemen was unconquerable to the last, as they still persisted, in defiance of threats, and in spite of all solicitations and entreaty, immovable in their principles and in their determination to reject the test that was proposed to them. They were sent prisoners to Stanton, in Virginia, as soon as it was apprehended that the British troops would take possession of Philadelphia."*

After the surrender of Lord Cornwallis, at Yorktown, the defenceless Loyalists were the objects of vengeance as they went further north. The army of Lord Cornwallis received civil treatment from Washington's army,† and great kindness from the French officers and soldiers. Lord Mahon observes:

"The followers of the English army, left defenceless at Yorktown, were exposed to much ill-treatment on the part of the native soldiers, thirsting, it was said, for vengeance. Abbé

---

* Dr. Andrews' History of the Late War, Vol. II., Chap. xxvi., pp. 370, 371.

† In connection with these transactions, we have an illustration of the uniform and generous treatment of Loyalists by General Washington, although he once gave expression to ill-feeling towards them at Boston in the spring of 1775; for says Lord Mahon:

"Cornwallis, on his part, was honourably anxious to protect from harm the native Loyalists within his lines; and he proposed, as the tenth Article, that no such men were to be punished on account of having joined the British army. Washington wrote in reply: 'This cannot be assented to, being altogether of civil resort.' Means were found, however, with Washington's connivance, to obtain the same object in another form. It was stipulated that, immediately after the capitulation, the *Bonetta* sloop-of-war was to sail for New York, unsearched, with despatches from Lord Cornwallis to Sir Henry Clinton, and with as many soldiers on board as he should think fit to send; provided only that the vessel was returned, and that the soldiers were accounted for as prisoners in a future exchange. By this expedient was the British chief enabled to secure a safe conduct for his American adherents." (Lord Mahon's History, etc., Vol. VII., Chap. lxiv., p. 179.)

Robin* saw an English lady, a colonel's wife, come in tears to implore for herself and for her children the protection of French generosity against American outrage. On the other hand, we find the English officers and soldiers, the actual prisoners of war, bear willing testimony to the kindness they received. Thus speaks Lord Cornwallis in his letter to Sir Henry Clinton: 'The treatment in general that we have received from the enemy since our surrender has been perfectly good and proper. But the kindness and attention that has been shown us by the French officers in particular, their delicate sensibility of our situation, their generous and pressing offer of money, both public and private, to any amount, has really gone beyond what I can possibly describe, and will, I hope, make an impression on the breast of every English officer, whenever the fortune of war should put any of them into our power.'" (Lord Mahon's History of England, etc., Vol. VII., Chap. lxiv., pp. 181, 182.)

APPENDIX TO CHAPTER XXXVI.

The Acts of Legislative Bodies for the Punishment of the Adherents to the Crown were numerous.

"In *Rhode Island*, death and *confiscation* of estate were the penalties by law for any person who communicated with *the Ministry* or their agents, *or* who afforded supplies to the forces, *or* piloted the armed ships of the King. Besides these general statutes, several Acts were passed in that State to confiscate and sequester the property of certain persons who were designated by name.

"In *Connecticut*, the offences of supplying the royal army

---

* "The abbé was struck at seeing, from several indications, how much keener was at that time the animosity between the English and Americans than between the English and French. Thus the English officers, when they laid down their arms and were passing along the enemy's lines, courteously saluted every French officer, even of the 'lowest rank,' a compliment which they withheld from every American man of the highest." (Voyage en Amerique, par l'Abbé Robin, p. 141, ed. 1782; quoted in Lord Mahon's History, Vol. VI., Chap. lxiv., p. 181.)

or navy, of giving them information, of enlisting or procuring others to enlist in them, and of piloting or assisting naval vessels, were punished more mildly, and involved only the loss of estate and personal liberty for a term not exceeding three years. To *speak* or *write* or act against the doings of Congress or of the Assembly of Connecticut, was punishable by *disqualification for office, imprisonment*, and the disarming of the offender. Here, too, was a law for seizing and confiscating the estates of those who sought royal protection, and absented themselves from their homes or the country.

"In *Massachusetts*, a person *suspected* of enmity to the Whig cause could be *arrested* under a magistrate's warrant and banished, unless he would swear fealty to the friends of liberty; and the select men of towns could prefer charges of political treachery in town meetings, and the individual accused, if convicted by a jury, could be sent into the enemy's jurisdiction (banished). Massachusetts also designated by name, and generally by occupation and residence, 380 of her people, of whom seventeen had been inhabitants of Maine, who had fled from their homes, and denounced against any one of them who should return, apprehension, imprisonment, and transportation to a place possessed by the British; and for a second voluntary return, without leave, *death* without the benefit of clergy. By another law, the property of twenty-nine persons who were denominated 'notorious conspirators,' was confiscated —two had been governors, one lieutenant-governor, one treasurer, one attorney-general, one chief justice, and four commissioners of customs.

"*New Hampshire* passed Acts similar to these, under which seventy-six of her former citizens were prohibited from coming within her borders, and the estates of twenty-eight were declared to be forfeited.

"*Virginia* passed a resolution to the effect that persons of a given description should be deemed and treated as aliens, and that their property should be sold, and the proceeds go into the public treasury for future disposal; and also a law prohibiting the migration of certain persons to that commonwealth, and providing penalties for the violation of its provisions.

"In *New York*, the County Committees were authorized to apprehend and decide upon the guilt of such inhabitants as were *supposed* to hold correspondence with the enemy, or had committed some other specified act; and they might punish those whom they adjudged to be guilty with imprisonment for three months, or banishment. There, too, persons opposed to liberty and independence were prohibited from practising law in the Courts; and the effects of fifty-nine persons, of whom three were women, and their rights of remainder and reversion, were to pass by confiscation from them to the people. So, also, a parent whose sons went off and adhered to the enemy was subjected to a tax of ninepence on the pound of the parents' estate for each and every such son; and until a revision of the law, Whigs were as liable to this tax as others.

" In *New Jersey*, one Act was passed to punish traitors and disaffected persons; another, for taking charge of and leasing the real estates, and for forfeiting the personal estates of certain fugitives and offenders; and a third for forfeiting to, and vesting in the State, the real property of the persons designated in the second statute; and a fourth, supplemental to the Act first mentioned.

" In *Pennsylvania*, sixty-two persons, who were designated by name, were required by the Executive Council to surrender themselves to some Judge of a Court, or Justice of the Peace, within a specified time, and abide trial for *treason*, or in default of appearance to stand attainted; and by an Act of a subsequent time, the estates of thirty-six other persons, who were also designated by name, and who had been previously attainted of treason, were declared to be confiscated.

" The Act of *Delaware* provided that the property, both real and personal, of certain persons who were named, and who were forty-six in number, should be forfeited to the State, 'subject, nevertheless, to the payment of the said offenders' just debts,' unless, as in Pennsylvania, they gave themselves up to trial for *the crime of treason in adhering to the royal cause.*

" *Maryland* seized, confiscated, and appropriated all property of persons in allegiance to the British Crown, and appointed Commissioners to carry out the terms of three statutes which were passed to effect these purposes.

" In *North Carolina*, the Confiscation Act embraced sixty-five specified individuals, and four mercantile firms, and by its terms not only included the 'lands' of these persons and commercial houses, but their 'negroes and other personal property.'

"The law of *Georgia*, which was enacted very near the close of the struggle, declared certain persons to have been gulity of treason against that State, and their estates to be forfeited for their offences."*

* *Note* by the Author.—The above statement of the confiscating law of Georgia gives a very inadequate idea of that law. Savannah was taken, and General Lincoln and his army were driven out of Georgia by Lieutenant-Colonel Campbell, in 1778, who treated all classes with such kindness and generosity that the Legislature and Government, as previously existed, was restored and remained until 1782, when Savannah was evacuated by the British. Just at the juncture of Colonel Campbell's conquest of Georgia, the Legislature of that State was passing a Confiscation Act against "Tories" and preparing to carry it into effect. During the latter part of the nearly four years of British occupation, the Congress party elected a Governor and organized their Legislature, meeting at Augusta. Two months before the evacuation of Savannah by the British, the Legislature of the Congress party passed the Confiscation Act referred to in the text. We find a copy of this act in a pamphlet published in London in 1783, entitled *The Particular Case of the Georgia Loyalists*. This Act may serve as a specimen of Confiscation Acts passed in other States. We give it entire, remarking that it curiously assumes in the preamble that there had been no break in the Government of the State from 1778 to 1782, though the English had ruled the State during the whole of that period. The Act is as follows:

"Whereas on the 1st day of March, which was in the year of our Lord 1778, an Act was passed for attainting certain persons therein mentioned of treason, and confiscating their estates for the use and benefit of this State, which said Act has not yet been carried into full execution: And whereas it is necessary that the names of the said persons so attainted by the same law should be inserted in a law, with the names of various other persons who have since the aforesaid time been guilty of treason against this State, and the authority of the same, by traitorously adhering to the King of Great Britain, and by aiding, assisting, abetting, and comforting the generals and other officers, civil and military, of the said King, to enforce his authority in and over this State, and the good people of the same: And whereas the *aforesaid treason*, and other atrocious crimes, justly merit forfeiture of protection and property:

"Be it enacted, by the representatives and freemen of the State of Georgia in General Assembly met, and by the authority of the same, that all and each of the following persons, viz. (here follow the names of 286 persons, late inhabitants of Georgia), be and they are hereby declared to be banished from this State for ever; and if any of the aforesaid shall remain in this State sixty days after the passing of this Act, or shall return to this State, the Governor or Commander-in-Chief for the time being is hereby authorised

"*South Carolina* surpassed all the other members of the confederacy, Massachusetts excepted. The Loyalists of the State, whose rights, persons, and property were affected by legislation, were divided into four classes. The persons who had offended the least, who were forty-five in number, were and required to cause such persons so remaining in or *returning* to this State to be apprehended and committed to jail, there to remain without bail or mainprize, until a convenient opportunity shall offer for transporting the said persons beyond the seas to some part of the British King's dominions, which the Governor or Commander-in-Chief for the time being is hereby required to do ; and if any of the said persons shall return to this State after such transportation, then and in such case he or they shall be adjudged and hereby declared to *be guilty of felony*, and shall, on conviction of their having so returned as aforesaid, *suffer death* without the benefit of clergy.

"And be it further enacted, by the authority aforesaid, that all and singular the estates, real and personal, of each and every one of the aforesaid persons, which they held, possessed or were entitled to, in law or equity, on the 19th of April, 1775, or which they have held since, or do hold in possession, or others hold in trust for them, or to which they are or may be entitled in law or equity, or which they may have, hold, or be possessed of, in right of others, together with all debts, dues, and demands that are or may be owing to the aforesaid persons, or either of them, *be confiscated to and for the use and benefit of this State;* and the monies arising from the sales which take place by virtue of and in pursuance of this Act, to be applied to such uses and purposes as the Legislature shall hereafter direct.

"And whereas divers others persons, citizens of this State, and owing allegiance thereto (whose names are not herein recited), did, in violation of said allegiance, traitorously assist, abet, and participate in the aforesaid treasonable practices : Be it therefore enacted, by the authority of the aforesaid, that all and every of the person or persons under this description shall, on full proof and conviction of the same in a court of law, be liable and subjected to all the like pains, penalties, and forfeitures inflicted by this Act on those offenders whose names are particularly mentioned therein.

"And be it further enacted, that all debts, dues, or demands due or owing to merchants and others residing in Great Britain, be and they are hereby sequestered, and the Commissioners appointed by this Act, or a majority of them, are hereby empowered to recover, receive, and deposit the same in the Treasury of this State, in the same manner and under the same regulations as debts confiscated, there to remain for the use of this State until otherwise appropriated by this or any other House of Assembly.

"And whereas there are various persons, subjects of the King of Great Britain, possessed of or entitled to estates, real and personal, which justice and sound policy require should be applied to the benefit of this State : Be it therefore enacted, by the authority aforesaid, that all and singular the

allowed to retain their estates, but were amerced twelve per cent. of their value. Soon after the fall of Charleston, and when disaffection to the Whig cause was so general, 210 persons, who styled themselves to be 'principal inhabitants' of the city, signed an address to Sir Henry Clinton, in which they state that they have every inducement to return to their allegiance, and ardently hope to be re-admitted to the character and condition of British subjects. These 'addressers' formed another class. Of these 210, sixty-three were banished and lost their property by forfeiture, either for this offence or the graver one of affixing their names to a petition to the royal general, to be armed on the royal side. Another class, composed of the still larger number of eighty persons, were *also banished and divested of their estates*, for the crime of holding civil or military commissions under the Crown, after the conquest of South Carolina. And the same penalties were inflicted upon thirteen others, who, on the success of Lord Cornwallis at Camden, presented his lordship with congratulations. Still fourteen others were *banished and deprived of their estates* because they were *obnoxious*. Thus, then, the 'addressers,' 'petitioners,' 'congratulators,' and 'obnoxious Loyalists,' who were proscribed, and who suffered the loss of their property (in South Carolina), were 170 in number; and if to these we add the forty-five who were fined twelve pounds in the hundred of the value of their estates, the aggregate will be 215.

"Much of the legislation of the several States appears to

estates, real and personal, belonging to persons being British subjects, of whatever kind or nature, of which they may be possessed, or others in trust for them, or to which they are or may be entitled in law or equity, and also all debts, dues, or demands owing or accruing to them, be confiscated to and for the use and benefit of this State; and the monies arising from the sale which shall take place by virtue of and in pursuance of this Act, to be applied to such uses and purposes as the Legislature shall hereafter direct.

"And be it further enacted, by the authority aforesaid, that the State will and do guarantee and defend the Commissioners appointed by this Act, or a majority of them, in all their proceedings for carrying the powers and authorities given them by the same into full effect; and will also warrant and for ever defend all and every sale or sales which the said Commissioners, or a majority of them, shall make to any purchaser or purchasers of any part or parts of the real and personal estates confiscated by this Act.

"Augusta, State of Georgia, 4th May, 1782."

have proceeded from the recommendations made from time to time *by Congress*, and that body passed several acts and resolutions of its own. Thus they subjected to *martial law* and to *death* all who should furnish provisions and certain other articles to the King's troops in New Jersey, Pennsylvania, and Delaware; and they resolved that all Loyalists taken in arms should be sent to the States to which they belonged, there to be *dealt with as traitors*" (not as prisoners of war, as were Americans taken in arms against the British).*

REMARKS ON THE CONFISCATION ACTS ABOVE CITED.

The Draconian Code or the Spanish Inquisition can hardly be said to exceed in severity and intolerance, the acts of the several State Legislatures and Committees above quoted, in which mere opinions are declared to be treason, as also the refusal to renounce a solemn oath of allegiance. The very place of residence, the non-presenting one's self to be tried as a traitor, the mere *suspicion* of holding Loyalist opinions, involved the loss of liberty and property. Scores of persons were made criminals, not after trial by a verdict of a regularly empannelled jury, but by name, in acts or resolutions of Legislatures, and sometimes of Committees. No modern civilized country has presented such a spectacle of the wholesale disposal, by name, of the rights, liberties and properties, and even lives of citizens, by inquisition and various bodies, as was here presented against the Loyalists, guilty of no crime against their neighbours except holding to the opinions of their forefathers, and the former opinions of their present persecutors, who had usurped the power to rob, banish, and destroy them—who embodied in themselves, at one and the same time, the functions of law makers, law judges, and law executioners, and the receivers and disposers, or, as was the case, the possessors of the property which they confiscated against the Loyalists.

Is it surprising, then, that under such a system of oppression and robbery, Loyalists should be prompted to deeds of heroism, and sometimes of desperation and cruelty, to avenge themselves for the wrongs inflicted upon them, and to recover the liberties and properties of which they had thus been deprived, rendering

* Historical Introduction to Col. Sabine's Biographical Sketches of the American Loyalists, pp. 77—81.

themselves and their families homeless, and reducing them to
poverty and distress? No one can justify many deeds of the
Loyalists; but who could be surprised had they been more
desperate than they were? And this the more so as they were,
probably, superior in wealth and nearly equal in numbers to
their oppressors, who had suddenly seized upon all military
sources of power, disarmed the Loyalists, and erected tribunals
for their ruin.* American writers often speak of the havoc
committed by the "Tories," but the acts of Legislatures and
Committees above quoted furnish ample causes and provocation
for retaliation, and the most desperate enterprises and efforts to
recover lawful rights and hard-earned property. Where these
Confiscating Acts had been most sweeping and severe, as in the
case of South Carolina, and the two parties nearly equal, this
internecine war against life and property was the most relentless.†

It is as easy as it is unfair for American writers to narrate and

---

* In the historical essay above quoted, the author says: "The examination
now completed of the political condition of the colonies, of the state of
parties, and of the divisions in particular classes in society, and avocations
in life, leads to the conclusion that the number of our countrymen who
wished to continue their connection with the mother country was very large.
In nearly every Loyalist letter or other paper which I have examined, and
in which the subject is mentioned, it is either assumed or stated in terms
that the LOYAL were *the majority;* and this opinion, I am satisfied, was very
generally entertained by those who professed to have a knowledge of public
sentiment. That the adherents of the Crown were mistaken, is certain.
But yet in the Carolinas, and Georgia, and possibly in Pennsylvania, the
two parties differed but little in point of strength, while in New York the
Whigs were far weaker than their opponents." (Historical Introduction to
Col. Sabine's Biographical Sketches of the American Loyalists, p. 65.)

† In the historical essay above quoted we have the following words:
"What was the nature of the conflict between the two parties in South
Carolina? Did the Whigs and their opponents meet in open and fair fight,
and give and take the courtesies and observe the rules of civilized warfare?
Alas, no! They murdered one another. I wish it were possible to use a
milder word; but murder is the only one that can be employed to express
the truth. Of this, however, the reader shall judge. I shall refrain from
a statement of my own, and rely on the testimony of others.

"Gen. Greene thus spoke of the hand-to-hand strifes, which I stigmatize
as murderous. 'The animosity,' said he, 'between the Whigs and Tories
renders their situation truly deplorable. The Whigs seem determined to
extirpate the Tories, and the Tories the Whigs. Some thousands have fallen

magnify the murderous acts of the "Tories," and omit those perpetrated by the "Whigs," as well as the cruel laws against the liberties, property, and lives of the "Tories," which gave rise to these barbarous acts.

in this way in this quarter, and the evil rages with more violence than ever. If a stop cannot be soon put to these massacres, the country will be depopulated in a few months more, as neither 'Whig' nor 'Tory' can live." (Historical Introduction to Colonel Sabine's Biographical Sketches of the American Loyalists, p. 33.)

CHAPTER XXXVII.

TREATMENT OF THE LOYALISTS BY THE AMERICANS, AT AND AFTER THE AMERICAN REVOLUTION.

IT remains now to ascertain the reception with which the applications of Loyalists were met in the several State Legislatures. During the last three years of the war, the principal operations of the British army were directed to the Southern States; and there the exasperations of party feeling may be supposed to have been the strongest.*

No where had arbitrary authority been exercised more unmercifully towards the revolutionists than by Earl Cornwallis and Lord Rawdon in South and North Carolina. Dr. Ramsay says: "The troops under the command of Cornwallis had spread waste and ruin over the face of all the country, for

---

* Writing under date of January, 1782, Mr. Hildreth says: "The surrender of Cornwallis was soon felt in the Southern department. Wilmington was evacuated, thus dashing all the hopes of the North Carolina Tories. Greene approached Charleston, and distributed his troops so as to confine the enemy to the neck and adjacent islands.

"In re-establishing the State Government of *South Carolina, none were allowed to vote who had taken British protection.* John Matthews was elected Governor. Among the earliest proceedings of the Assembly was the passage of a law *banishing the most active British partizans and confiscating their property.* The services of Greene were also gratefully remembered in a vote of 10,000 guineas, or $50,000, to purchase him an estate.

"The Georgia Assembly, in meeting at Augusta, chose John Martin as Governor, *and passed a law of confiscation and banishment very similar to that of South Carolina.* Greene presently received from this Province, also, the present of a confiscated plantation. *North Carolina* acknowledged his services by a grant of wild lands." (History of the United States, Vol. III., Chap. xliii., p, 373.)

400 miles on the sea coast, and for 200 miles westward. Their marches from Charleston to Camden, from Camden to the River Dan, from the Dan through North Carolina to Wilmington, from Wilmington to Petersburg, and from Petersburg through many parts of Virginia, till they finally settled in Yorktown, made a route of more than 1,100 miles. Every place through which they passed in these various marches experienced the effects of their rapacity. Their numbers enabled them to go where they pleased ; their rage for plunder disposed them to take whatever they had the means of removing ; and their animosity to the Americans led them often to the wanton destruction of what they could neither use nor carry off. By their means, thousands had been involved in distress."[*]

It was therefore in South Carolina, more than any other State, that animosity might be expected to be intense and prolonged against the Loyalists ; but among these men of the South, with their love of freedom, and dash and energy in war, there was a potent element of chivalry and British generosity which favourably contrasts with the Massachusetts school of persecuting bigotry and of hatred, from generation to generation, to

---

[*] Dr. Ramsay's History of the United States, Vol. II., Chap. xxv., p. 456.

"Under the immediate eye of Cornwallis," says Mr. Bancroft, "the prisoners who had capitulated in Charleston were the subjects of perpetual persecution, unless they would exchange their paroles for oaths of allegiance. Mechanics and shopkeepers could not collect their dues except after promises of loyalty.

"Lord Rawdon, who had the very important command on the Santee, raged equally against deserters from his Irish regiment and against the inhabitants. The chain of forts for holding South Carolina consisted of Georgetown, Charleston, Beaufort, and Savannah on the sea ; Augusta, Ninety-Six, and Camden in the interior. Of these, Camden was the most important, for it was the key between the north and south. On the rumour of an advancing American army, Rawdon called on all the inhabitants round Camden to join in arms. One hundred and sixty who refused he shut up during the heat of midsummer in one prison, and loaded more than twenty of them with chains, some of whom were protected by the capitulation of Charleston." (Bancroft's History of the United States, Vol. X., Chap. xv., pp. 311, 312, 313.)

"Peace was restored to Georgia (July, 1782), after having been four years in possession of the British. That State is supposed to have lost 1,000 of its citizens and 4,000 slaves." (Moultrie's Memoirs, Vol. II., p. 340 ; quoted in Holmes' American Annals, Vol. II., p. 340.)

England and English institutions. Accordingly we learn from Moultrie's Memoirs, Vol. II., p. 326, that "after the peace, a Joint Committee from the Senate and House of Representatives in South Carolina, chosen to hear the petitions of Loyalists who had incurred the penalties of the confiscation, banishment, and amercement laws, made a report to the separate Houses in favour of the great majority of the petitioners; and a great part of those names which were upon the confiscation, banishment and amercement lists were struck off."

"The petitions of others were afterwards presented from year to year, and ultimately almost the whole of them had their estates restored to them, and they were received as citizens."*

As to the proceedings of the other States, after the close of the war, in regard to the United Empire Loyalists, the following summary, from the *Historical Introduction* to Colonel Sabine's *Biography of the American Loyalists*, will be sufficient:

"At the peace, justice and good policy both required a general amnesty, and the revocation of the acts of disability and banishment, so that only those who had been guilty of flagrant crimes should be excluded from becoming citizens. Instead of this, however, the State Legislatures generally continued in a course of hostile action, and treated the conscientious and pure, and the unprincipled and corrupt, with the same indiscrimination as they had done during the struggle. In some parts of the country there really appears to have been a determination to place these misguided but then humbled men beyond the pale of human sympathy. In one legislative body, a petition from the banished, praying to be allowed to return to their homes, was rejected without a division; and a law was passed which denied to such as had remained within the State, and to all others who had opposed the revolution, the privilege of voting at the elections or of holding office. In another State, all who had sought royal protection were declared to be aliens, and to be incapable of claiming and holding property within it, and their return was forbidden. Other Legislatures refused to repeal such of their laws as conflicted with the conditions of the treaty of peace, and carried out the doctrines of the States

* Quoted in Holmes' Annals, Vol. II., p. 351.

alluded to above without material modification. But the temper of South Carolina was far more moderate. Acting on the wise principle that 'when the offenders are numerous, it is sometimes prudent to overlook their crimes,' she listened to the supplications made to her by the fallen, and restored to their civil and political rights a large portion of those who had suffered under her banishment and confiscation laws. The course pursued by New York, Massachusetts, and Virginia was different. These States were neither merciful nor just; and it is even true that Whigs, whose gallantry in the field, whose prudence in the Cabinet, and whose exertions in diplomatic stations abroad, had contributed essentially to the success of the conflict, were regarded with enmity on account of their attempts to produce a better state of feeling and more humane legislation. Had these States adopted a different line of conduct, their good example would not have been lost, probably, upon others, smaller and of less influence; and had Virginia especially been honest enough to have permitted the payment of debts which her people owed to British subjects before the war, the first years of our freedom would not have been stained with a breach of our public faith, and the long and angry controversy with Great Britain, which well-nigh involved us in a second war with her, might not have occurred.

"Eventually, popular indignation diminished; the statute book was divested of its most objectionable enactments, and numbers were permitted to occupy their old homes, and to recover the whole or part of their property; but by far the greater part of the Loyalists who quitted the country at the commencement of, or during the war, never returned; and of the many thousands who abandoned the United States after the peace, and while these enactments were in force, few, comparatively, had the desire or even the means to revisit the land from which they were expelled. Such persons and their descendants form a very considerable proportion of the population of Nova Scotia, New Brunswick, and Upper Canada.

"It is equally to be regretted on grounds of policy that the *majorities** in the State Legislatures did not remember, with

* "I say *majorities*, because I am satisfied that in almost every State there were minorities, more or less numerous, who desired the adoption of a more moderate course. In New York it is certain that the first political

Mr. Jefferson, that separation from England was contemplated with affliction by all,' and that, like Mr. Adams, many sound Whigs 'would have given everything they possessed for a restoration to the state of things before the contest began, provided they could have had sufficient security for its continuance.' Then they might have done at an early moment after the cessation of hostilities, what they actually did do in a few years afterwards—namely, have allowed the banished Loyalists to return from exile, and, excluding those against whom enormities could have been proved, have conferred upon them, and upon those who had remained to be driven away at the peace, the rights of citizens. Most of them would have easily fallen into respect for the new state of things, old friendships and intimacies would have been revived, and long before this time all would have mingled in one mass. * *

"As a matter of *expediency*, how unwise was it to perpetuate the feelings of the opponents of the revolution, and to keep them a distinct class for a time, and for harm yet unknown! How ill-judged the measures that caused them to settle the hitherto neglected possessions of the British Crown! Nova Scotia had been won and lost, and lost and won, in the struggle between France and England, and the blood of New England had been poured out upon its soil like water. But when the Loyalists sought refuge there, what was it? Before the war, the fisheries of its coast, for the prosecution of which Halifax itself was founded, comprised, in public estimation, its chief value; and though Great Britain had quietly possessed it for about seventy years, the emigration to it of the adherents of the Crown from the United States, in a single year, more than doubled its population. Until hostile events brought Halifax into notice, no civilized people were poorer than the inhabitants of that colony; since, in 1775, the Assembly estimated that £1,200 currency—a sum less than $5,000—was the whole amount of money which they possessed. By causing the expatriation, then, of many thousands of our countrymen, among whom were the well-educated, the ambitious, and the well-versed in politics, we became the founders of two agricultural and commercial parties, after the peace, were formed in consequence of divisions which existed among the Whigs as to the lenity or severity which should be extended to their vanquished opponents."

colonies; for it is to be remembered that New Brunswick formed a part of Nova Scotia until 1784, and that the necessity of the division then made was of our own creation. In like manner we became the founders of Upper Canada. The Loyalists were the first settlers of the territory thus denominated by Act of 1791; and the principal object of the line of division of Canada, as established by Mr. Pitt's Act, was to place them, as a body, by themselves, and to allow them to be governed by laws more congenial than those which were deemed requisite for the government of the French on the St. Lawrence. Our expatriated countrymen were generally poor, and some of them were actually without the means of providing for their common wants from day to day. The Government for which they had become exiles was as liberal as they could have asked. It gave them lands, tools, materials for building, and the means of subsistence for two years; and to each of their children, as they became of age, two hundred acres of land. And besides this, of the offices created by the organization of a new Colonial Government, they were the chief recipients. The ties of kindred and suffering in a common cause created a strong bond of sympathy between them, and for years they bore the appellation of 'United Empire Loyalists.'"*

APPENDIX A. TO CHAPTER XXXVII.

REVIEW OF THE PRINCIPAL CHARACTERISTICS OF THE AMERICAN REVOLUTION, AND REMARKS ON THE FEELINGS WHICH SHOULD NOW BE CULTIVATED BY BOTH OF THE FORMER CONTENDING PARTIES.

The entire failure of the Americans to conquer Canada in the war of 1812—1815 is an illustration of the folly of coercing the allegiance of a people against their will. Upper Canada at that time consisted of less than 100,000 inhabitants; yet, with the extra aid of only a few hundred English

---

* Historical Essay, introductory to Colonel Sabine's Sketches of the American Loyalists, pp. 86—90.

soldiers, she repelled for three years the forces of the United States—more than ten times their number, and separated only by a river.

Mr. J. M. Ludlow, in his brief but comprehensive "History of the War of American Independence, 1775—1783," Chapter vii., well states *the folly of England in endeavouring to conquer by arms the opinions* of three millions of people, and the impossibility of the American colonists achieving their independence without the aid of men and money, and ships from France, to which, in connection with Spain and Holland, the Americans are actually indebted for their independence, and not merely to their own sole strength and prowess, as American writers so universally boast. Mr. Ludlow observes:

"At a time when steam had not yet baffled the winds, to dream of conquering by force of arms, on the other side of the Atlantic, a people of the English race, numbering between 3,000,000 and 4,000,000, with something like 1,200 miles of seaboard, was surely an act of enormous folly. We have seen in our own days the difficulties experienced by the far more powerful and populous Northern States in quelling the secession of the Southern, when between the two there was no other frontier than at most a river, very often a mere ideal line, and when armies could be raised by 100,000 men at a time. England attempted a far more difficult task, with forces which, till 1781, never exceeded 35,000 men, and never afterwards exceeded 42,075, including 'Provincials,' *i.e.*, American Loyalists." (But England, repeatedly on the verge of success, failed from the incapacity and inactivity of the English generals.)

"Yet it is impossible to doubt that not once only, but repeatedly during the course of the struggle, England was on the verge of triumph. The American armies were perpetually melting away before the enemy—directly, through the practice of short enlistments; indirectly, through desertions. These desertions, if they might be often palliated by the straits to which the men were reduced through arrears of pay and want of supplies, arose in other cases, as after the retreat from New York, from sheer loss of heart in the cause. The main army, under Washington, was seldom even equal in numbers to that opposed to him. In the winter of 1776-77, when his troops were only 4,000 strong, it is difficult to understand how it was that Sir William Howe, with more than double the number, should have failed to annihilate the American army."

"WEAKNESS OF THE AMERICAN ARMY.

"In the winter of 1777-78 the 'dreadful situation of the army for want of provisions,' made Washington 'advise' that they should not have been excited to a general mutiny and desertion. In May, 1779, he hardly knew any resource for the American cause *except in reinforcements from France*, and did not know what might be the consequence if the enemy had it in their power to press the troops hard in the ensuing campaign. In December of that year his forces were 'mouldering away daily,' and he considered that Sir Henry Clinton, with more than twice his numbers, could 'not justify remaining inactive with a force so superior.' A year later he was compelled, for want of clothing, to discharge the levies which he had always so much trouble in obtaining; and 'want of flour would have disbanded the whole army' if he had not adopted this expedient.

"In March, 1781, again the crisis was 'perilous,' and though he did not doubt the happy issue of the contest, he considered that the period for accomplishment might be too far distant for a person of his years. In April he wrote: 'We cannot transport provisions from the States in which they are assessed to the army, because we cannot pay the teamsters, who will no longer work for certificates. It is equally certain that our troops are approaching fast to nakedness, and that we have nothing to clothe them with; that our hospitals are without medicines, and our sick without nutriment, except such as well men eat; and that all our public works are at a stand, and the artificers disbanding. * * It may be declared in a word that we are at the end of our tether, and that now or never our deliverance must come.' Six months later, when Yorktown capitulated, the British forces remaining in North America, after the surrender of that garrison by Cornwallis, were more considerable than they had been as late as February, 1779, and Sir Henry Clinton even then declared that with a reinforcement of 10,000 he would be responsible for the conquest of America.

"*The main hope of success on the English* side lay in the idea that the spirit and acts of resistance to the authority of the mother country were in reality only on the part of a turbulent minority—that the bulk of the people desired to be loyal. It is certain indeed that the struggle was, in America itself, much more of a civil war than the Americans are now generally disposed to admit. In December, 1780, there were 8,954 'Provincials' among the British forces in America, and on March 7th, 1781, a letter from Lord George Germaine to Sir H. Clinton, intercepted by the Americans, says: 'The American levies in the King's service are more in number than the whole of the enlisted troops in the service of the Congress.' As late as September 1st, 1781, there were 7,241. We hear of loyal 'associations' in Massachusetts, Maryland, and Pennsylvania; of 'associated Loyalists' in New York; and everywhere of 'Tories,' whose arrest Washington is found suggesting to Governor Trumbull, of Connecticut, as early as November 12th, 1775. But New York, New Jersey, and Pennsylvania remained long full of Tories. By June 28th, 1776, the disaffected on Long Island had taken up arms, and after the evacuation of New York by Washington a brigade of Loyalists was raised on the island, and companies were formed in two neighbouring counties to join the King's troops. During Washington's retreat through New Jersey, 'the inhabitants, either from fear or disaffection, almost to a man refused to turn out.' In Pennsylvania, the militia, instead of giving any assistance in repelling the British, exulted at their approach and over the misfortunes of their countrymen. On the 20th of that month the British were 'daily gathering strength from the disaffected.' In 1777, the Tories who joined Burgoyne in his expedition from the North are said to have doubled his force. In 1778, Tories joined the Indians in the devastation of Wyoming and Cherry Valley; and although the indiscriminate ravages of the British, or of the Germans in their pay, seem to have aroused the three States above mentioned to self-defence, yet, as late as May, 1780, Washington still speaks of sending a small party of cavalry to escort La Fayette safely through the 'Tory settlements' of New York. Virginia, as late as the spring of 1776, was 'alarmed at the idea of independence.' Washington admitted that his countrymen (of that State), 'from their form of government, and steady attachment heretofore to royalty,' would 'come reluctantly' to that idea, but trusted to 'time and persecution.' In 1781, the ground for transferring the seat of war to the Chesapeake was the number of Loyalists in that quarter. In the Southern States the division of feeling was still greater. In the Carolinas, a royalist regiment was raised in a few days in 1776, and again in 1779. In Georgia and in South Carolina the bitterest partisan warfare was carried on between Whig and Tory bands; and a body of New York Tories contributed powerfully to the fall of Savannah in 1778, by taking the American forces in the rear.

"On the other hand, the British generals did not receive that support from the Loyalists which they had expected. They seem to have looked upon the Loyalists as an inferior class of aids to the regular soldiery; their advice seems to have been unsought, and the mode of war pursued was European, and not adapted to the peculiar circumstances of America. The Loyalist volunteers were looked upon as the rivals to rather than fellow-soldiers of the regular army; and no provincial Loyalist was promoted to lead any expedition or command any position of importance. This depreciation of the Loyalists by the English (utterly incompetent) generals exactly answered the purposes of American writers. *But the real cause of its protraction*, though it may be hard to an American to admit the fact, lay in the incapacity of the American politicians, and, it must be added, in the supineness and want of patriotism of the American people. If indeed importing into the views of later date, we look upon it as one between two nations, the mismanagement of the war by the Americans on all points save one—the retention of Washington in the chief command—is seen to have been so pitiable, from first to last, as to be in fact almost unintelligible."

"DESCRIPTION OF THE AMERICAN ARMY, AND THE MANNER OF RAISING IT.

"We can only understand the case when we see there was no such thing as an American nation in existence, but only a number of revolted colonies, jealous of one another, and with no tie but that of common danger. Even in the army divisions broke out. Washington, in a General Order of August, 1776, says: 'It is with great concern that the general understands that jealousies have arisen among the troops from the different provinces, and reflections are frequently thrown out which can only tend to irritate each other and injure the noble cause in which we are engaged.'"

"WANT OF PUBLIC SPIRIT AND PATRIOTISM IN THE STATES.

"It was seldom that much help could be obtained in troops from any State, unless the State were immediatly threatened by the enemy; and even then these troops would be raised by that State for its own defence, irrespectively of the general or 'continental army.' 'Those at a distance from the seat of war,' wrote Washington, in April, 1778, 'live in such perfect tranquillity, that they conceive the dispute to be in a manner at an end, and those near it are so disaffected that they serve only as embarrassments.' In January, 1779, we find him remonstrating with the Governor of Rhode Island, because that State had 'ordered several battalions to be raised for the State only; and this before the proper measures are taken to fill the continental regiments.' The different bounties and rates of pay allowed by the various States were a constant source of annoyance to him."

"DECLINE OF CONGRESS.

"After the first year, the best men were not returned to Congress, and did not return to it. Whole States remained frequently unrepresented. In the winter of 1777-78, Congress was reduced to twenty-one members. But even with a full representation it could do little. 'One State will comply with a requisition,' writes Washington in 1780, 'another neglects to do it, a third executes by halves, and all differ either in the manner, the matter, or so much in point of time, that we are always working up-hill.'

"At first, Congress was really nothing more than a voluntary Committee. When the Confederation was completed, which was only, be it remembered, on March 1, 1781, it was still, as Washington wrote in 1785, 'little more than a shadow without a substance, and the Congress a nugatory body;' or, as it was described by a late writer, 'powerless for government, and a rope of sand for union.'"

"DECLINE OF ENERGY AND SPIRIT AMONG THE COLONISTS AND ARMY.

"Like politicians, like people. There was, no doubt, a brilliant display of patriotic ardour at the first flying to arms of the colonists. Lexington and Bunker's Hill were actions decidedly creditable to their raw troops. The expedition to Canada, foolhardy though it proved, was pursued up to a certain point with real heroism. But with it the heroic period of the war (individual instances excepted) may be said to have closed. There seems little reason to doubt that the revolution would never have been commenced if it had been expected to cost so tough a struggle. 'A false estimate of the power and perseverance of our enemies,' wrote James Duane to Washington, 'was friendly to the present revolution, and inspired that confidence of success in all ranks of the people which was necessary to unite them in so arduous a cause.' As early as November, 1775, Washington wrote, speaking of military arrangements: 'Such a dearth of public spirit, and such want of virtue—such stock-jobbing and fertility in all the low arts to obtain advantage of one kind or another, I never saw before, and pray God's mercy that I may never be witness to it again.' Such a 'mercenary spirit' pervaded the whole of the troops that he should not have been 'at all surprised at any disaster.' At the same date, besides desertion of thirty or forty soldiers at a time, he speaks of the practice of plundering as so rife that 'no man is secure in his effects, and scarcely in his person.' People were 'frightened out of their houses under pretence of those houses being ordered to be burnt, with a view of seizing the goods;' and to conceal the villainy more effectually, some houses were actually burned down. On February 28th, 1777, 'the scandalous loss, waste, and private appropriation of public arms during the last campaign' had been 'beyond all conception.' Officers drew 'large sums under pretence of paying their men, and appropriated them.'

"'Can we carry on the war much longer?' Washington asks in 1778, after the treaty with France and the appearance of the French fleet off the coast. 'Certainly not, unless some measures can be devised and speedily executed to restore the credit of our currency and restrain extortion and punish forestallers.' A few days later: 'To make and extort money in every shape that can be devised, and at the same time to decry its value, seems to have become a mere business and an epidemical disease.' On December 30th, 1778, 'speculation, peculation, and an insatiable thirst for riches seems to have got the better of every consideration, and almost of every order of men; * * party disputes and personal quarrels are the great business of the day (in Congress), whilst the momentous concerns of an empire, a great and accumulating debt, ruined finances, depreciated money, and want of credit, which in its consequences is the want of everything, are but secondary considerations."

"DECLINE OF PATRIOTIC FEELING ON THE PART OF THE AMERICANS.

" After the first loan had been obtained from France and spent, and a further one was granted in 1782, so utterly unpatriotic and selfish was known to be the temper of the people that the loan had to be kept secret, in order not to diminish such efforts as might be made by the Americans themselves. On July 10th of that year, with New York and Charleston still in British hands, Washington writes: 'That spirit of freedom which at the commencement of the contest would have gladly sacrificed everything to the attainment of its object, has long since subsided, and every selfish passion has taken its place.' But, indeed, the mere fact that from the date of the battle of Monmouth (July 28th, 1778), Washington was never supplied with sufficient means, even with the assistance of the French fleets and troops, to strike one blow at the English in New York—though these were but very sparingly reinforced during the period—shows an absence of public spirit, one might almost say of national shame, scarcely conceivable, and in singular contrast with the terrible earnestness exhibited on both sides, some eighty years later, in the Secession War."

"INCAPACITY OF ENGLISH GENERALS IN AMERICA.

" Why, then, must we ask on the other side, did the English fail at last?

" The English were prone to attribute their ill success to the incompetency of their generals. Lord North, with his quaint humour, would say, ' I do not know whether our generals will frighten the enemy, but I know they frighten me whenever I think of them.' When, in 1778, Lord Carlisle came out as Commissioner, in a letter speaking of the great scale of all things in America, he says, ' We have nothing on a great scale with us but our blunders, our losses, our disgraces and misfortunes.' No doubt, it is difficult to account for Gage's early blunders; for Howe's repeated failure to follow up his own success, or profit by his enemy's weakness: and Cornwallis's movement, justly censured by Sir Henry Clinton, in transferring the bulk of his army from the far south to Virginia, within marching distance of Washington, opened the way to that crowning disaster at Yorktown, without which it is by no means impossible that Georgia and the Carolinas might have remained British."

"INEFFECTIVE MILITARY ARRANGEMENTS IN AMERICA.

"Political incapacity was, of course, charged upon Ministers as another cause of disaster; and no doubt their miscalculation of the severity of the struggle was almost childish. But no mistakes in the management of the war by British statesmen can account for their ultimate failure. However great British mismanagement may have been, it was far surpassed by the Americans. There was nothing on the British side equal to that caricature of a recruiting system in which different bounties were offered by Congress, by the States, by the separate towns, so as to make it the interest of the intended soldier to delay enlistment as long as possible, in order to sell himself to the highest bidder; to that caricature of a war establishment, the main bulk of which broke up every twelvemonth in front of the enemy, which was only paid, if at all, in worthless paper, and left continually without supplies. On the whole, no better idea can be had of the nature of the struggle on the American side, after the first heat of it had cooled down, than from the words of Count de Rochambeau, writing to Count de Vergennes, July 10th, 1780: 'They have neither money nor credit; their means of resistance are only momentary, and called forth when they are attacked in their own homes. They then assemble for the moment of immediate danger and defend themselves.'"

"FRENCH MONEY, TROOPS, AND SHIPS TURN THE SCALE IN FAVOUR OF AMERICAN INDEPENDENCE.

"A far more important cause in determining the ultimate failure of the British was the aid afforded by France to America, followed by that of Spain and Holland. It was impossible for England to re-conquer a continent and carry on a war at the same time with the three most powerful naval States of Europe. The instincts of race have tended on both the English and American side to depreciate the value of. the aid given by France to the colonists. It may be true that Rochambeau's troops, which disembarked on Rhode Island in July, 1780, did not march till July, 1781; that they were blockaded soon after their arrival, threatened with attack from New York, and only disengaged by a feint of Washington's on that city. But more than two years before their arrival, Washington wrote to a member of Congress: 'France, by her supplies, has saved us from the yoke thus far.' The treaty with France alone was considered to afford a 'certain prospect of success' to 'secure' American independence. The arrival of D'Estaing's fleet, although no troops joined the American army, and nothing eventually was done, determined the evacuation of Philadelphia. The discipline of the French troops, when they landed in 1780, set an example to the Americans; chickens and pigs walked between the lines without being disturbed. The recruits of 1780 could not have been armed without fifty tons of ammunition supplied by the French. In September of that year, Washington, writing to the French envoy, speaks of the 'inability' of the Americans to expel the British from the South unassisted, or perhaps even to stop their career;' and he writes in similar terms to Congress a few days later. To depend ' upon the resources of the country, unassisted by foreign loans,' he writes to a member of Congress two months later, 'will, I am confident, be to lean upon a broken reed.' In January, 1781, writing to Colonel Laurens,[*] the American envoy in Paris, he presses for 'an immediate, ample, efficacious succour in money from France,' also for the maintenance on the American coasts of 'a constant naval superiority,' and likewise for 'an additional succour in troops.' And since the assistance so requested was in fact granted in every shape, and the surrender of Yorktown was obtained by the co-operation both of the French army and fleet, we must hold that Washington's words were justified by the event."[†]

[*] War of American Independence, 1777—1783, by John Malcolm Ludlow, Chap. vii., pp. 215—227.

[†] Dr. Ramsay says: " Pathetic representations were made to the Ministers of his Most Christian Majesty by Washington, Dr. Franklin, and particu-

APPENDIX B. TO CHAPTER XXXVII.

REFLECTIONS OF LORD MAHON ON THE AMERICAN CONTEST AND ITS RESULTS — APOLOGY FOR GEORGE THE THIRD — UNHAPPINESS OF AMERICANS SINCE THE REVOLUTION — UNITY OF THE ANGLO-SAXON RACE.

At this period (Declaration of Independence), the culminating point in the whole American war, I may be forgiven for desiring to interrupt its narrative in order to review its course and its results. That injurious and oppressive acts of power had been inflicted by England upon America, I have in many places shown, and do most fully acknowledge. That from the other side, and above all from Massachusetts, there had been strong provocation, I must continue to maintain. I should not deem it consistent with candour to deny that the Americans had sufficient ground for resisting, as they did resist, the Ministerial and Parliamentary measures. But whether these had yet attained a pitch to justify them in discarding and renouncing their allegiance to the Throne is a far more doubtful question—a question on which perhaps neither an Englishman nor yet an American could quite impartially decide.

"The time has come, however, as I believe and trust, when it is possible to do equal justice to the many good and upright men who in this great struggle embraced the opposite sides. The great mass of the people meant honestly on both shores of the Atlantic. The two chief men in both countries were alike pure-minded. On the one side there were deeds that savoured of tyranny; on the other side there were deeds that savoured of rebellion; yet at heart George the Third was never a tyrant, nor Washington ever a rebel. Of Washington I most firmly believe, that no single act appears in his whole public life proceeding from any other than public, and those the highest

larly by Lieutenant-Colonel John Laurens, who was sent to the Court of Versailles as a special Minister on this occasion. The King of France *gave* the United States a subsidy [as a present] of six millions of livres, and became their security for ten millions more, borrowed for their use in the United Netherlands." (History of the United States, Vol. II., Chap. xxiii., p. 407.)

motives. But my persuasion is no less firm that there would be little flattery in applying the same terms of respect and commendation to the 'good old king.' I do not deny, indeed, that some degree of prejudice and pride may, though unconsciously, have mingled with his motives. I do not deny that at the outset of these troubles he lent too ready an ear to the glozing reports of his governors and deputies, the Hutchinsons or Olivers, Gateses, Dunmores, etc., assuring him that the discontents were confined to a factious few, and that measures of rigour and repression alone were needed. For such measures of rigour he may deserve, and has incurred, his share of censure. But after the insurgent colonies had proclaimed their independence, is it just to blame King George, as he often has been blamed, for his steadfast and resolute resistance to that claim? Was it for him, unless after straining every nerve against it, to forfeit a portion of his birthright and a jewel of his crown? Was it for him, though the clearest case of necessity, to allow the rending asunder his empire—to array for all time to come of several millions of his people against the rest? After calling on his loyal subjects in the colonies to rise, after requiring and employing their aid, was it for him, on any light grounds, to relinquish his cause and theirs, and yield them over, unforgiven, to the vengeance of their countrymen? Was it for him to overlook the consequences, not even yet, perhaps in their full extent unfolded, of such a precedent of victory to popular and colonial insurrection? May not the King, on the contrary, have deemed that on such a question, touching as it did both his honour and his rights, he was bound to be firm—firmer than even the firmest of his Ministers? Not, of course, that he could be justified for persevering; but, in truth, he did not so persevere after every reasonable hope had failed. Not, of course, that he could be excused from continuing to demand, or to expect, unconditional submission; but, as his own letters to Lord North assure us, such an idea was never harboured in his mind. To do his duty conscientiously, as he should answer it to God hereafter, and according to the lights he had received, such was his unceasing aim and endeavour from the day when, young but superior to the frailties of youth, he first assumed the reins of government, until that dismal period, half a century later, when, bowed down by years and sorrows, and blind, doubly blind, he concluded his reign, though not, as yet, his life.

"Before the American war had commenced, and during its first period, nearly all the statesmen and writers of England argued, or rather took for granted as too plain to stand in need of argument, that separation from our colonies would most grievously impair, if not wholly ruin, the parent State. * * It is worthy of note how much our experience has run counter to the general prognostication—how little the loss was felt, or how quickly the void was supplied. An historian of high and just authority—Mr. Macaulay—has observed that England was never so rich, so great, so formidable to foreign princes, so absolutely mistress of the sea, as since the alienation of the American colonies. (Essays, Vol. II.) The true effect of that alienation upon ourselves, as time has shown, has been not positive, but by comparison it has lain not in the withdrawal of wealth and population and resources, but in raising up a rival State from the same race, and with powers and energies not inferior to our own.

"But how far, and in what degree, has the new form of government promoted the happiness of the United States themselves? * * It would be folly, or worse than folly, to deny that since their independence the prosperity of the United States has advanced with gigantic strides; that they have grown to be a first-rate power; that immense works of public utility have been achieved with marvellous speed; that the clearing of new lands and the building of new cities have been such as to outstrip the most sanguine calculations; that among them the working classes have been, in no common degree, well paid and prosperous; that a feeling for the national honour is in no country stronger; that the first elements of education have been most widely diffused; that many good and brave men have been trained and are training to the service of the Commonwealth. But have their independent institutions made them, on the whole, a happy and contented people? That, among themselves, is often proclaimed as undeniable; and certainly among themselves it may not always be safely denied. That, however, is not always the impression conveyed to him who only sojourns in their land, by the careworn faces, by the hurried steps, by the unsocial meals which he sees, or by the incessant party cries which he hears around him; by the fretful aspirations and the feverish hopes resulting from the unbounded space of competition open to them without check or barrier; and by the innumerable disappointments and heartburnings which in consequence arise. On the true condition of North America, let us mark the correspondence between two of the greatest and most highly gifted of her sons. There is now open before me a letter which, in August, 1837, and on the annexation of Texas, Dr. Channing wrote to Mr. Clay. In that letter, as published in Boston, I find the following words (and what Dr Channing said in 1837 has been illustrated in scores of instances since that time, and greatly enhanced by the events of the civil war):

"'I cannot do justice to this topic without speaking freely of our country, as freely as I should of any other; and unhappily we are so accustomed, as a people, to receive incense, to be soothed by flattery, and to account reputation a more important interest than morality, that my freedom may be construed into a kind of disloyalty. But it would be wrong to make concessions to this dangerous weakness. * * Among us a spirit of lawlessness pervades the community which, if not repressed, threatens the dissolution of our present forms of society. Even in the old States, mobs are taking the government into their hands, and a profligate newspaper finds little difficulty in stirring up multitudes to violence. * * Add to all this the invasions of the rights of speech and of the press by lawless force, the extent and toleration of which oblige us to believe that a considerable portion of our citizens have no comprehension of the first principles of liberty. It is an undeniable fact that, in consequence of these and other symptoms, the confidence of many reflecting men in our free institutions is very much impaired. Some despair. That main pillar of public liberty—mutual trust among citizens—is shaken. That we must seek security for property and life in a stronger government is a spreading conviction. Men who in public talk of the ability of our institutions, whisper their doubts, perhaps their scorn, in private.

"'Whether the people of the United States might have been as thriving and more happy had they remained British subjects, I will not presume to say. Certainly not if violent men like Lord Hillsborough, or corrupt men like Mr. Rigby, had continued to take part in the administration. With other hands at the helm the case might have been otherwise. Jefferson, at least, in his first draft of the Declaration of Independence, said of his countrymen and of the English: "We might have been a free and great people together." One thing, at all events, is plain, that had these colonies shared the fate of the other dominions of the British Crown, the main curse and shame—the plague spot of the system of slavery—would have been long since removed from them (before it was); but, as in the case of Jamaica, not without a large compensation in money to the slave owners. It is also plain that in the case supposed they would have equally shared in our pride and glory at the wondrous growth of the Anglo-Saxon race—that race undivided and entire, extending its branches as now to the furthest regions of the earth, yet all retaining their connection with the parent stem—all its members bound by the same laws, all animated by the same loyalty, and all tending to the same public-spirited aim. How great a nation should we and they be together!—how great in the arts both of peace and war! scarcely unequal now to all other nations of the world combined!" * *

"Since 1782 at the latest, views like these are merely day-dreams of the past. In place of them, let us now indulge the hope and expectation that the American people may concur with ours in desiring that no further resentment may be nourished, no further strife be stirred, between the kindred nations; so that both, mindful of their common origin, and conscious of their growing greatness, may both alike discard, as unworthy of them, all mean and petty jealousies, and be ever henceforth what nature has designed them—friends."*

* Lord Mahon's History of England, etc., Vol. VI., Chap. liii., pp. 150—160.

CHAPTER XXXVIII.

TREATMENT OF THE LOYALISTS BY THE BRITISH GOVERNMENT AND PARLIAMENT AFTER THE REVOLUTION.

PART I.

PROCEEDINGS IN PARLIAMENT—REFUSAL OF THE STATES TO COMPENSATE THE LOYALISTS.

It has been seen, by the fact stated in the last preceding chapter, that the promised recommendations of Congress to the several States, as agreed upon by the English and American Commissioners of the peace negotiations at Paris, were, as had been expected and predicted by Dr. Franklin at the time, without any result, the State Legislatures passing Acts to proscribe rather than compensate the Loyalists. In justification of these Acts, the American writers of that period, and largely down to the present time, assailed the character of the Loyalists in the grossest language of calumny and abuse; but the most respectable American writers of the present age bear testimony to the intelligence, wealth, and respectability of the Loyalists; and the fact, no longer questionable, that they sacrificed wealth, liberty, country, and chose poverty and exile, in support of their principles, has fully vindicated their character and presented their conduct in advantageous contrast with that of those who deprived them of their liberty, and largely profited by the confiscation of their immense property, while they and their families were pining in exile and want.

The only resource of the exiled and impoverished Loyalists, under such circumstances, was the Government and Parliament of the mother country to which they had so faithfully adhered, and nothing could be more honourable than the testimony borne in the British Parliament to their character and merits, and the consideration given to their wants and claims. The fifth Article of the Treaty of Paris, leaving the Loyalists to the recommendation of the Congress to the Legislatures of the several States, was severely reprobated in both Houses of Parliament. In the House of Commons, Mr. Wilberforce said that " when he considered the case of the Loyalists, he confessed he felt himself conquered: there he saw his country humiliated; he saw her at the feet of America; still he was induced to believe that Congress would religiously comply with the Article, and that the Loyalists would obtain redress from America. Should they not, this country was bound to afford it them. They *must be compensated;* Ministers, he was persuaded, meant to keep *the faith of the nation with them.*"

Lord North (who had been Prime Minister during twelve years, including the war) said:

"And now let me, Sir, pause on a part of the treaty which awakens human sensibility in a very irresistible and lamentable degree. I cannot but lament the fate of those unhappy men, who, I conceive, were in general objects of our *gratitude* and *protection.* The Loyalists, from their attachments, surely had some claim to our affection. But what were not the claims of those who, in conformity to their *allegiance,* their *cheerful obedience* to the *voice of Parliament,* their confidence in the proclamation of our generals, invited under every assurance of *military, parliamentary, political, and affectionate protection,* espoused with the hazard of their lives, and the forfeiture of their properties, the cause of Great Britain ? *I cannot but feel for men thus sacrificed for their bravery and principles*—men who have sacrificed all the dearest possessions of the human heart. They have exposed their lives, endured an age of hardships, deserted their interests, forfeited their possessions, lost their connections, and ruined their families *in our cause.* Could not all this waste of human enjoyment excite one desire of protecting them from a state of misery, with which the implacable resentment of the States has desired to punish their loyalty to their Sovereign and their attachment to their mother country? Had we not espoused their cause from a *principle of affection and gratitude,* we should, at least, have *protected* them *to have preserved our own honour.* If not tender of *their feelings*, we should have been tender *of our own character.* Never was the *honour*, the *principles*, the policy of a nation so grossly abused as in the desertion of those men, who are now exposed to *every punishment* that *desertion* and *poverty* can inflict, *because they were not rebels.*"

Lord Mulgrave said: "The Article respecting the Loyalists he never could regard but as a lasting monument of *national disgrace.* Nor was this Article, in his opinion, more reproachful and derogatory to the *honour and gratitude* of Great Britain than it appeared to be wanton and unnecessary. The honourable gentleman who had made the motion had asked if those gentlemen who thought the present peace not sufficiently advantageous to Great Britain, considering her circumstances, could consent to pay the amount which another campaign (twenty millions) would have put us to, for the degree of advantage they might think we had a right to expect? In answer to this, he declared, for one, he had rather, large as the estimated sum in question was, have had it stipulated in the treaty, *that Great Britain should apply it to making good the losses of the Loyalists*, than that they should have been so *shamefully deserted and the national honour so pointedly disgraced* as it was by the fifth Article of the treaty with the United States."

Mr. Secretary Townsend (afterwards Lord Sydney) said "he was ready to admit that many of the Loyalists had the strongest claims upon the country; and he trusted, should the recommendation of Congress to the American States prove unsuccessful, which he flattered himself would not be the case, *this country* would feel itself bound *in honour to make them full compensation for their losses.*"

Mr. Burke said: "At any rate, it must be agreed on all hands that a vast number of Loyalists had been deluded by this country, and had risked everything in our cause; to such men the *nation owed protection, and its honour was pledged for their security at all hazards.*"

The Lord Advocate said: "With regard to the Loyalists, they merited *every possible effort on the part of this country.*"

Mr. Sheridan "execrated the treatment of those unfortunate men, who, without the least notice taken of their civil and religious rights, were handed over as subjects to a power that would not fail to take vengeance on them for their zeal and attachment to the religion and government of this country. This was an instance of *British degradation not inferior* to the unmanly petitions to Congress for the wretched Loyalists. Great Britain at the feet of Congress, suing in vain, was not a humiliation or a stigma greater than the infamy of consigning over the loyal inhabitants of Florida, as we had done, without any conditions whatsoever."

"*The Honourable Mr. Norton* said that 'Under the circumstances, he was willing to approve of the two former (European treaties with France and Spain); but on account of the Article relating to the Loyalists, he felt it impossible to give his assent to the latter."

Sir Peter Burrell said: "The fate of the Loyalists claimed the compassion of every human breast. These helpless, forlorn men, abandoned by the Ministers of a people on whose *justice, gratitude,* and *humanity* they had the best-founded claims, were left at the mercy of a Congress highly irritated against them. He spoke not from party zeal, but as an independent country gentleman, who, unconnected with party, expressed the emotions of his heart and gave vent to his honest indignation."

Sir William Bootle said: "There was one part of the treaty at which his heart bled—the Article relative to the Loyalists. Being a man himself, he could not but feel for men so cruelly abandoned to the malice of their enemies. It was scandalous; it was disgraceful. Such an Article as that ought scarcely on any condition to have been admitted on our part. They had fought for us and run every hazard to assist our cause; and when it most behoved us to afford them protection, we deserted them."

Several other members spoke to the same effect. The treaty recognizing the Independence of America could not be reversed, as an Act passed the previous session had expressly authorized the King and his Cabinet to make it; but it was denied that a treaty sacrificing the Loyalists and making the concessions involved had been authorized; in consequence of which an express vote of censure was passed by the Commons by a majority of seventeen. The Earl of Shelburne, the Prime Minister, forthwith resigned in consequence of this vote of censure, and it was nearly three months before a new Administration could be formed; and during this administrative interregnum affairs were in great confusion.

In the *House of Lords, Lord Walsingham* said that " he could neither think nor speak of the dishonour of leaving these deserving people to their fate with patience." *Lord Viscount Townsend* considered that " to desert men who had constantly adhered to loyalty and attachment, was a circumstance of such cruelty as had never before been heard of." *Lord Stormont* said that " Britain was bound in justice and honour, gratitude and affection, and by every tie, to provide for and protect them." *Lord Sackville* regarded " the abandonment of the Loyalists as a thing of so atrocious a kind, that if it had not been painted in all its horrid colours he should have attempted the ungracious task but never should have been able to describe the cruelty in language as strong and expressive as were his feelings ;" and again, that " peace on the sacrifice of these unhappy subjects must be answered in the sight of God and man." *Lord Loughborough* said that " the fifth Article of the treaty had excited a general and just indignation, and that neither in ancient nor modern history had there been so shameful a desertion of men who had sacrificed all to their duty and to their reliance on British faith."

In reply, *Lord Shelburne*, the Prime Minister, frankly admitted that the Loyalists were left without better provision being made for them " from the unhappy *necessity* of public affairs, which induced the extremity of submitting the fate of their property to the discretion of their enemies;" and he continued: " I have but one answer to give the House—it is the answer I gave my own bleeding heart—a *part* must be wounded, that the whole of the empire may not perish. If better terms could be had, think you, my lords, that I would not have embraced them ? *I had but the alternative either to accept the terms proposed or continue the war.*" The *Lord Chancellor* held that the stipulations of the treaty were " specific," and said : " My own conscious honour will not allow me to doubt the good faith of others, and my good wishes to the Loyalists will not let me indiscreetly doubt the disposition of Congress, since the understanding is that all these unhappy men shall be provided for ; yet, if it were not so, Parliament could take cognizance of their case, and impart to each suffering individual that relief which reason, perhaps policy, certainly virtue and religion, required."

Such were the sentiments of members in both Houses of Parliament, and of both parties, as to the character and merits of the Loyalists. But there were no prospects of the States compensating them for their losses. Indeed, this idea was entertained by Lord Shelburne himself, and that compensation would have to be made to the Loyalists by Parliament when, in the speech above quoted, he said that "without one drop of blood spilt, and without one-fifth of the expense of one year's campaign, happiness and ease can be given to them in as ample a manner as these blessings were ever in their enjoyment." This was certainly a very low and mercenary view of the subject. It was one thing for the Loyalists to have their rights as British subjects maintained while they were obeying the commands of the King and maintaining their allegiance to the empire, and another thing for them to become pensioners upon the bounty of the British Parliament, to be paid in pounds, shillings, and pence for the rights and privileges which should have been secured to them by national treaty as British subjects. The House of Commons had adopted a resolution against continuing the American war for the *purpose of enforcing the submission of the colonies;* but it had not resolved against continuing the war to protect the rights and property of British subjects in the colonies. A campaign for this purpose, on the refusal of the American Commissioners to recognise what was sanctioned by the laws and usages of nations, would have been honourable to the British Government, would have been popular in England, and would have divided America; for there were many thousand "Whigs" in America, who believed in the equity of treating the Loyalists after the war as all others were treated who conformed to the laws, as has been the case in Holland, Ireland, and Spain. England was then mistress of the seas, held New York, Charleston, Rhode Island, Penobscot, and other military posts, and could soon have induced the Americans to do what their Peace Commissioners at Paris had refused to do —place British subjects in America upon the same footing as to property that they possessed before the war, and that they possess in the United States at this day. England could have easily and successfully refused granting to the United States a foot of land beyond the limits of the thirteen colonies, and thus have secured those vast western territories now constituting the larger part of the United States, and retained the garrisons of New York, Rhode Island, and Charleston as guarantees until the stipulated conditions in regard to the Loyalists should be fulfilled. A joint Commission in America could have settled upon equitable grounds all disputed claims in much less time than the six years occupied by a Parliamentary Commission in examining into and deciding upon the individual claims of Loyalist claimants. If the war to reduce the colonies to absolute submission had been unpopular in England, the peace upon the terms submitted to by the English Commissioners and the Ministry was equally unpopular. If England had been wrong in its war of coercion against the revolting colonists, was she not equally wrong, and more than wrong, in abandoning to their enemies those who had abided faithful to her laws and commands? The language of the speeches of members of both Houses of Parliament, above quoted, is as just as it is severe; although much could be and was said in justification of the policy of the Government in promoting peace upon almost any terms, seeing that England was at war with the three most powerful naval nations of Europe, besides that in America.

The fallacy of the argument employed by the advocates of the treaty, that the Americans would honourably fulfil the recommendations of Congress, was illustrated by the following facts:

"The province of Virginia, a short time before the peace, had come to an unanimous conclusion 'that all demands or requests of the British Court for the restoration of property confiscated by the State were wholly impossible; and that their delegates should be instructed to move Congress that they should direct the deputies for adjusting peace not to agree to any such restitution.'"

The State of New York resolved, "That it appears to this Legislature that divers of the inhabitants of this State have continued to adhere to the King of Great Britain, after these States were declared free and independent, and persevered in aiding the said king, his fleets and armies, to subjugate the United States to bondage: Resolved, That as on the one hand the scales of justice do not require, so on the other the public tranquillity will not permit, that such adherents who have been attainted should be restored to the rights of citizens, and that there can be no reason for restoring property which has been confiscated or forfeited."

PART II.

AGENTS OF LOYALISTS—PROCEEDINGS OF PARLIAMENTARY COMMISSION—RESULTS.

Of course all hope of obtaining relief under the stipulations of the treaty was abandoned by the Loyalists, who "now applied to the Government which they had ruined themselves to serve, and many of them, who had hitherto been 'refugees' in different parts of America, went to England to state and recover payment for their losses. They organized an agency, and appointed a Committee composed of one delegate or agent from each of the thirteen States,* to enlighten the British public, and adopt measures of proceeding in securing the attention and action of the British Ministry in their behalf. In a tract printed by order of these agents (which now lies before us, entitled *The Case and Claim of American Loyalists impartially Stated and Considered*, published in 1783), it is maintained that 'it is an established rule, that all sacrifices made by individuals for the benefit and accommodation of others shall be equally sustained by all those who partake of it,' and numerous cases are cited from Puffendorf, Burlamaqui and Vattel, to show that the 'sacrifices' of the Loyalists were embraced in this principle. As a further ground of claim, it is stated that in case of territory alienated or ceded away by one sovereign power to another, the rule is still applicable; for that in the treaties of international law it is held, 'The State ought to

---

* The names of the agents, or delegates, are as follows:

W. Pepperell, for the Massachusetts Loyalists; J. Wentworth, jun., for the New Hampshire Loyalists; George Rowe, for the Rhode Island Loyalists; Ja. Delancey, for the New York Loyalists; David Ogden, for the New Jersey Loyalists; Joseph Galloway, for the Pennsylvania and Delaware Loyalists; Robert Alexander, for the Maryland Loyalists; John R. Grymes, for the Virginia Loyalists; Henry Eustace McCulloch, for the North Carolina Loyalists; James Simpson, for the South Carolina Loyalists; William Knox, for the Georgia Loyalists.

indemnify the subject for the loss he has sustained beyond his proportion.' And in the course pursued at the close of the civil war in Spain, when the States of Holland obtained their independence, under the Treaty of Utrecht, and at various other periods, proved that the *rights* of persons similarly situated had been respected and held inviolate. The conclusion arrived at from the precedents in history, and diplomacy, and in the statute-books of the realm, is, that as the Loyalists were as 'perfectly subjects of the British State as any man in London or Middlesex, they were entitled to the same protection and relief.' The claimants had been 'called by their sovereign, when surrounded by tumult and rebellion, to defend the supreme rights of the nation, and to assist in suppressing a rebellion which aimed at their destruction. They have received from the highest authority the most solemn assurances of protection, and even reward, for their meritorious services;' and that 'His Majesty and the two Houses of Parliament having thought it necessary, as the *price of peace*, or to the interest and safety of the empire, or from some other motive of public convenience, to ratify the Independence of America, *without securing any restitution whatever to the Loyalists*, they conceive that the nation is bound, as well by the fundamental laws of society as by the invariable and external principles of natural justice, to make them compensation.' "*

Though the treaty of peace left the Loyalists to the mercy— rather to the resentment (as the result proved)—of the American States, and as such received the censure of the House of Commons, British justice and honour recognized the claims of the Loyalists to compensation for their losses, as well as to gratitude for their fidelity to the unity of the empire. The King, at the opening of the session of Parliament, said: " I have ordered inquiry to be made into the application of the sum to be voted in support of the American sufferers; and I trust you will agree with me, that a due and generous attention ought to be shown to those who have relinquished their properties or professions from motives of loyalty to me, or attachment to the

---

* Another very able pamphlet was issued some time afterwards, entitled "Claims of the American Loyalists Reviewed and Maintained upon the Incontrovertible Principles of Law and Justice;" printed in London, 1788.

mother country." Accordingly, a Bill was introduced and passed without opposition in June, 1783, entitled "An Act Appointing Commissioners to Inquire into the Losses and Services of all such Persons who have Suffered in their Rights, Properties, and Professions, during the late Unhappy Dissensions in America, in consequence of their Loyalty to his Majesty and Attachment to the British Government."

The Commissioners named were John Wilmot, M.P., Daniel Parker Coke, M.P., Esquires, Col. Robert Kingston, Col. Thomas Dundas, and John Marsh, Esquire, who, after preliminary preparations, began their inquiry in the first week of October, and proceeded, with short intermissions, through the following winter and spring. The time for presenting claims was first limited by the Act to the 25th of March, 1784; but the time was extended by the renewal of the Act, from time to time, until 1789, when the Commissioners presented their *twelfth* and last report, and Parliament finally disposed of the whole matter in 1790, seven years after its commencement.

The Commissioners, according to their first report, divided the Loyalists into *six* classes, as follows: 1. Those who had rendered service to Great Britain. 2. Those who had borne arms for Great Britain. 3. Uniform Loyalists. 4. Loyal English subjects resident in Great Britain. 5. Loyalists who had taken oaths to the American States, but afterwards joined the British. 6. Loyalists who had borne arms for the American States, but afterwards joined the British navy or army. The reason for this classification is not very apparent; for all showed alike who were able to establish their losses, without reference to differences of merit, or the time or circumstances of their adhering to the Crown.

Every applicant was required to furnish proof of his loyalty, and of every species of loss for which he claimed compensation; in addition to which each claimant was put upon his oath as to his alleged losses; and if in any case *perjury* or *fraud* were believed to have been practised, the claimant was at once cut off from his whole claim. The rigid rules which the Commissioners laid down and enforced in regard to claimants, examining each claimant and the witnesses in his behalf separately and apart, caused much dissatisfaction, and gave the proceeding more the character of an Inquisition than of Inquiry.

It seemed to place the claimants almost in the position of criminals on whom rested the burden of proof to establish their own innocence and character, rather than in that of Loyalists who had faithfully served their King and country, and lost their homes and possessions in doing so. Very many, probably the large majority of claimants, could not possibly prove the exact value of each species of loss which they had sustained years before, in houses, goods, stocks of cattle, fields with their crops and produce, woods with their timber, etc., etc. In such a proceeding the most unscrupulous would be likely to fare the best, and the most scrupulous and conscientious the worst; and it is alleged that many false losses were allowed to persons who had suffered no loss, while many other sufferers received no compensation, because they had not the means of bringing witnesses from America to *prove* their losses, in addition to their own testimony.

The chairman of the Commission admits the delay and difficulty caused by the mode of proceeding adopted by the Commissioners. He says: "The investigation of the property of each claimant, and of the value of each article of that property, real and personal, could not but be attended with a good deal of time as well as much caution and difficulty, each claim in fact branching out into so many articles, or rather distinct causes, in which the Commissioners were obliged to execute the office of both judge and jury, or rather of arbitrators between the nation on one side, and the individual on the other, whose whole patrimony as well as character depended on their verdict."*

The Act passed in 1783, authorizing the inquiry, being limited to two years, expired in July, 1785, but was renewed with some additions, one of which was a clause to empower the Commissioners to appoint proper persons to repair to America "to inquire into such circumstances as they might think

* "Historical View of the Commission for Inquiry into the Losses, Services, and Claims of the American Loyalists, at the Close of the War between Great Britain and her Colonies in 1783; with an Account of the Compensation granted to them by Parliament in 1785 and 1788." By John Eardley Wilmot, Esq. London, 1815. Dedicated "To His Most Gracious Majesty George the Third, equally distinguished for justice and beneficence to his subjects and for humanity to his enemies."

material for better ascertaining the several claims which had been or should be presented to them under this or the former Act of Parliament." The Commissioners appointed John Anstey, Esq., a barrister-at-law, as agent to the United States, "to obtain information as to the confiscation, sale, and value of landed estates, and the total loss of the property of the claimants," respecting which he procured much valuable and authentic information and testimony. They sent Colonel Thomas Dundas and Mr. Jeremy Pemberton, two members of the Board, to visit Nova Scotia and Canada, "to inquire into the claims of such persons as could not without great inconvenience go over to Great Britain."

Before the 25th of March, 1784, the latest period allowed by the first Act for presenting claims, the number of claimants was 2,063, and the property alleged by them to have been lost, according to their schedules, amounted to £7,046,278, besides debts to the amount of £2,354,135. The sum was very large, but the losses were undoubtedly very great. The Commissioners made their first report in July, 1784; and after having detailed their assiduous proceeding in the fulfilment of their trust, and care in examining and deciding on individual cases, reported on the part of the cases submitted, and awarded £201,750 for £534,705 claimed, reducing the amount by more than half the amount claimed.

The *second* report of the Commissioners was made in December of the same year, and states that 128 additional cases had been examined and disposed of, the amount claimed being £693,257, and the amount allowed was £150,935—less than one-fourth the amount claimed.

One hundred and twenty-two (122) cases were examined into and disposed of in May and July, 1785, according to the third and fourth reports—the amount claimed being £898,196, and the amount allowed being £253,613—less than one-third of the amount claimed.

In April, 1786, the fifth report of the Commissioners was presented, announcing that 142 other claims had been considered and decided, the claims amounting to £733,311, on which the Commissioners allowed £250,506—a little more than one-third of the amount claimed.

The Commissioners proceeded in the same manner with their

investigations, and with about the same results, in 1786 and 1787.*

On the 5th of April, 1788, the Commissioners reported that they had examined into and declared upon 1,680 claims, and had allowed the sum of £1,887,548 for their payment.

Under all the circumstances, it appears scarcely possible that the Commissioners could have proceeded with more despatch than they did. But the delay caused much dissatisfaction among the Loyalists, whose agents petitioned both King and Parliament on the delay, or on the course pursued by the Commissioners, or on some subject connected with the claims of the Loyalists. Essays and tracts were published; letters and communications appeared in the newspapers on the subject; in 1786, the agents of the Loyalists presented a petition to Parlia-

* It has already been mentioned that the Legislature of South Carolina (the only State of the American Republic) had taken steps to restore the estates of several of her Loyalists. This "caused the withdrawal of the claims of their owners (before the English Commissioners), except that in instances of alleged strip and waste, amercements, and similar losses, inquiries were instituted to ascertain the value of what was taken compared with that which was returned."

The English Commissioners, in their twelfth and last report, remark on this subject as follows:

"We thought it our duty to state, in our second report of the 24th December, 1784, that the State of South Carolina had, by an Act of the 24th March, 1784, restored the confiscated property of certain Loyalists, subject to the restrictions therein mentioned; and that in consequence thereof many had withdrawn the claims they had before presented to us. We find, however, that in many instances the parties have not been able to reap that advantage they had expected, and which the Act above-mentioned held out to them. In some instances the property restored has been so wasted and injured as to be of little value; in others, the amercements and charges have been nearly equal to the value of the fee simple of the estates; and in many, where the indents (a), being the species of money received by the State, have been restored to the former proprietors, an inevitable and considerable loss has been sustained by the depreciation. In all these cases we have made minute inquiry into the real benefit that has been derived from such restitution, whether of the property itself, or of the *indents* in lieu of it; and having endeavoured to ascertain, as nearly as the circumstances would admit, the value of what was lost and the value of what was restored, we have considered the difference as the real loss of the party."

(a) *Indent*—A certificate, or indented certificate, issued by the Government of the United States at the close of the revolution, for the principal or interest of the public debt.—Webster.

ment, which contained among other things the following touching words: "It is impossible to describe the poignant distress under which many of these persons now labour, and which must daily increase should the justice of Parliament be delayed until all the claims are liquidated and reported; * * ten years have elapsed since many of them have been deprived of their fortunes, and with their helpless families reduced from independent affluence to poverty and want; some of them now languishing in British jails; others indebted to their creditors, who have lent them money barely to support their existence, and who, unless speedily relieved, must sink more than the value of their claims when received, and be in a worse condition than if they had never made them; others have already sunk under the pressure and severity of their misfortunes; and others must, in all probability, soon meet the same melancholy fate, should the justice due them be longer postponed. But, on the contrary, should provision be now made for payment of those whose claims have been settled and reported, it will not only relieve them from their distress, but give credit to others whose claims remain to be considered, and enable all of them to provide for their wretched families, and become again useful members of society."

Two years later, in 1788, a tract was published by a Loyalist, entitled "The Claim of the American Loyalists Reviewed and Maintained upon Incontrovertible Principles of Law and Justice." The writer of that tract thus forcibly states the situation of the Loyalists: "It is well known that this delay of justice has produced the most melancholy and shocking events. A number of sufferers have been driven into insanity and become their own destroyers, leaving behind them their helpless widows and orphans to subsist upon the cold charity of strangers. Others have been sent to cultivate the wilderness for their subsistence, without having the means, and compelled through want to throw themselves on the mercy of the American States, and the charity of former friends, to support the life which might have been made comfortable by the money long since due by the British Government; and many others with their families are barely subsisting upon a temporary allowance from Government, a mere pittance when compared with the sum due them."

Shortly after the publication of the pamphlet containing these statements, the Commissioners submitted their eleventh report, April, 1788, and Mr. Pitt, Chancellor of the Exchequer, yielded the following month to the pressing entreaties of the claimants to allow their grievances to be discussed in Parliament. "Twelve years had elapsed since the property of most of them had been alienated under the Confiscation Acts, and five since their title to recompense had been recognized by the law under which their claims had been presented and disposed of."

We will give an abridged account of the proceedings in Parliament and by the Commissioners in their own words:

"The business came on in the House of Commons on the 6th of June, 1788, which Mr. Pitt opened in a very handsome and eloquent speech respecting the merits of the American Loyalists, and which, he did not doubt, would meet with the unanimous acknowledgment of the House; and he trusted, therefore, there would be no difference of opinion as to the principle, though there might be as to the mode of compensation and the distribution which he thought it his duty to propose.

"The first principle he laid down was, that however strong their claims might be on the generosity of the nation, the compensation could not be considered *as a matter of right and strict justice;** in the mode, therefore, he had pursued, he had marked

---

* The principle thus laid down was neither just, nor true, nor generous. The claimants had not asked for *charity*, but for *compensation*, and that not as a favour, but upon the principles of "right and of strict justice." The British Ministry and Parliament alone originated and were responsible for the policy and measures which had led to the calamities so ruinous to the Loyalists, who now claimed compensation. The claimants had had nothing to do with passing the Stamp Act; with imposing duties on tea and other articles imported into the colonies; with making naval officers collectors of customs; with erecting courts of admiralty, and depriving the trading colonists of trial by jury, and of rendering the officers of the admiralty courts, and the complainants before them, the recipients of the first confiscations imposed by such events; with the acts to close the Port of Boston, and supersede the chartered constitution of Massachusetts, all of which, separately and collectively, with other like measures, roused and united the colonists to resistance, from Maine to Georgia, and in consequence of which a majority of the General Congress of the colonists seized the opportunity to renounce their allegiance to the British Throne, and to declare their separation from the mother country. And even after the character of the contest became thus changed from one for British constitutional rights to one for Republican independence, the Loyalists had nothing to do

the principle in the various quotas of compensation he should propose to be made to the various classes of the American Loyalists.

"He considered the three first classes of them, stated by the Commissioners in their reports as the most meritorious, and who were likewise the most numerous, viz.:

"1st. Loyalists who had rendered services to Great Britain. Number, 204.

"2nd. Loyalists who had borne arms in the service of Great Britain—481.

"3rd. Zealous and uniform Loyalists—626.

"Total number of these three classes—1,311.

"The number of the remaining classes were much fewer, viz. :

"4th. Loyal British subjects resident in Great Britain—20.

"5th. Who took the oath to the Americans, but afterwards joined the British—27.

"6th. Who bore arms for the Americans, but afterwards joined the British—23.

"7th. Ditto, losses under the Prohibitory Act—3.

"8th. Loyal British proprietors—2.

"9th. Subject or settled inhabitants of the United States—25.

"10th. Claims disallowed and withdrawn—313.

"11th. Loyal British subjects who appear to have relief by the Treaty of Peace, but state the impossibility of procuring it—4.

"Mr. Pitt proposed to pay classes 1, 2, 3, 4, 5, 6, 7, whose liquidated losses did not amount to more than £10,000 each, the full amount of their losses ; and if they should exceed the

with the selection of British generals, or with their incapacity, their want of tact and energy, their mistakes and rapacity, together with that of their officers and soldiers, from all which the Loyalists grievously suffered. In the camp, on the march, and in the field of battle, the Loyalists were always on the alert, and performed the severest and most perilous services. No class of men had stronger claims on the nation, upon the principles of right and strict justice, than the Loyalist claimants before Parliament. This was acknowledged by all the speakers on both sides, and in both Houses of Parliament, and even by Mr. Pitt himself, and the objectionable and offensive principle which he laid down at the outset was contravened by the whole tenor and spirit of his speech.

sum of £10,000, to deduct the sum of ten per cent. from excess only of £10,000, provided such losses did not exceed £35,000; and if they exceeded £35,000, then fifteen per cent. from the excess of £10,000, and not above £50,000; and if they exceeded £50,000, then to deduct twenty per cent. from the excess of £10,000; and which principle, he informed the Committee, he meant to follow in every other class.

"With regard to the 4th and 8th classes, viz., of loyal British subjects and loyal British proprietors resident in Great Britain during the war, he did not mean to propose any deduction from the losses under £10,000; but from the losses which amounted from £10,000 to £50,000 he proposed a deduction of twenty per cent. should be made; and a further deduction from those losses amounting to above £50,000, and a still further deduction of seventy per cent. from those from £50,000 to £200,000; and so on in proportion.

"He next considered the case of those Loyalists whose losses principally, if not solely, arose from their loss of office or profession, by which they had been deprived of their livelihood, or means of support, both for themselves or families. These persons were distinct from those who had been in trade or other branches of business, or gained their livelihood by their manual labour. Though these losses were not of so substantial a nature as those who lost property real or personal, yet they could not be easily reinstated in the same lucrative professions which they had enjoyed—civil employment, in the law, in the Church, or in physic—and therefore he thought them entitled to a liberal compensation. But as they were not precluded from exercising their industry and talents in this country, he proposed that all those persons who were reported by Commissioners to have lost incomes not exceeding £400 *per annum*, should receive pensions at the rate of £50 *per cent.* of such income, and £40 *per cent.* for every £100 above £400 per annum; where the value did not exceed £1,500 *per annum*, £30 *per cent.* for every £100 per annum exceeding £400; thus the *percentage* would be governed by and diminish in proportion to the increase of the income lost.

"Having expatiated on these various classes of claimants, Mr. Pitt said he meant to propose that the amount of these various sums should be issued in debentures bearing interest at three and a half per cent., which would be nearly equal to a money payment, and that the whole should be paid off by instalments.

"He began, therefore, by moving 'that provision should be made accordingly.'

"This plan met with general approbation and applause from all sides of the House; not only from the friends of the Minister, but from leaders of the Opposition, particularly from Mr. Fox and Mr. Burke; and Mr. Pitt congratulated the House on their concurrence with him in the plan he laid before the Committee.

"Soon after a motion was made for continuing the Act another year, for the purpose principally of enabling the Commissioners to inquire into claims of certain other persons therein specified, who, it was stated, appeared to have been prevented by particular circumstances from preferring their claims before; provided the Commissioners were satisfied, by proof made on oath, with the reasons assigned by those persons for not having before preferred their respective claims; and the Act passed, including these and other purposes.

"As the Commissioners who had gone to Nova Scotia and Canada had by this time returned to England, and Mr. Anstey was daily expected from the United States, there was more than sufficient to employ the Commissioners, independent of the Act for carrying into effect the plan of relief and compensation into execution.

"The Commissioners immediately, viz., in August, 1788, proceeded with the various matters referred to them.

"Colonel Dundas and Mr. Pemberton, having returned from Nova Scotia and Canada, made a separate report of the proceedings to the Board of Treasury and the Secretaries of State;* but the Commissioners, before they finished their deliberations, united the proceedings of both Boards in order to give a comprehensive view of the whole.

"Mr. Anstey also having returned from the United States in September, the Commissioners took a general review of the whole of their proceedings from the commencement of the inquiry, and were thus enabled to supply any defects, to

---

* The number of claims examined by the Commissioners in Nova Scotia and Canada was 1,272; the amount of claims was £975,310; the losses allowed were £336,753.

correct any mistakes, and to reconsider any points in which, perhaps, too great humanity to the individuals on the one hand, or too great anxiety to reduce claims which appeared exaggerated on the other, might have led them into error.

"Having thus wound up the business in the spring of 1789, they presented their twelfth and last Report on the 15th of May; and likewise, pursuant to the order of the House of Commons of the 10th of June, 1789, presented a statement of them to that House, comprising the whole of their proceedings in one view, specifying what had been granted by Parliament and what still remained for consideration; but as the inquiring into these claims was not completed, and the Minister thought proper to give way once more to strong applications from various persons, who had been still prevented from preferring or prosecuting their claims under the former Acts of Parliament, the Commission was renewed once more, and it was not till the spring of 1790 that the business was finally settled and adjusted by Parliament. In the beginning of April, in consequence of an order of the House of Commons, on the 31st of March, 1790, the Commissioners laid before the House a statement of the claims and losses of the American Loyalists up to the 25th of March, 1790, with the terms already granted, and of what remained for the consideration of Parliament.

"The general result of this was, that the number of claims preferred in England and Nova Scotia was 3,225—

"Of which were examined.. 3,225
"Disallowed............. 343
"Withdrawn .... 38 } 934
"Not prosecuted 553

"The amount of the claims preferred was £10,358,413.
"The amount of the claims examined was £8,216,126.
"The amount allowed in liquidation thereof amounted to £3,033,091.
"Of which had been provided £2,096,326.
"There remained for consideration of Parliament £936,764.*
"The amount of pensions paid to 204 Loyalists, on account

* What remained for consideration, and which was afterwards granted by Parliament, consisted of seven Articles, and was as follows:

"1. Additional claims liquidated since 1788, to the
    amount of £224,406

of losses of office or profession, was £25,785 *per annum*, besides annual allowances to 588 persons, chiefly widows, orphans, and merchants, who had no means of livelihood, but had lost no real or personal estate except debts due them,* and which had not been gone into for reasons before given.

"As many of the Loyalists who had received pensions or allowances are since deceased, the Lords of the Treasury, by his Majesty's direction, have continued some part of those annual payments to their widows.

" 2. The proprietary claims of Messrs. Pennes..........	£500,000
" 3. Do. do. Trustees under the will of Lord Granville, North Carolina..............	60,000
" 4. The proprietary claims of Robert Lord Fairfax, proprietor of Virginia.........................	60,000
" 5. Claims of subjects, settled inhabitants of the United States, many of which were cases of great merit and peculiar hardship	32,462
" 6. Claims of persons who appeared to have relief under the Treaty of Peace	14,000
" 7. Claims of creditors on ceded lands in Georgia......	45,885

* The case of such merchants was peculiarly distressing. In the "Historical Review of the Commission," the Commissioners state:

"The claims for debts due from subjects of the United States, as well from the magnitude of their amount as the peculiar hardship and injustice under which the claimants labour respecting them, form a subject which appears strongly to press for the attention and interposition of Government. The Treaty of Peace having provided that 'Creditors on either side should meet with no lawful impediment to the recovery of the full value of their debts in sterling money,' losses of this nature have not been considered as within the inquiry directed by the Act, because we cannot consider any right or property as lost to the party where the Government of the country has expressly provided and stipulated for a remedy by a public treaty. We think it, however, incumbent upon us to represent that the claimants uniformly state to us the insuperable difficulties they find themselves under, as individuals, in seeking the recovery of their debts according to the provision of the treaty, whilst themselves are the objects of prosecution in courts of justice here for debts due to the subjects of the United States. Under such circumstances, the situation of this class of sufferers appears to be singularly distressing—disabled on the one hand by the laws or practice of the several States from recovering the debts due them, yet compellable on the other to pay all demands against them; and though the stipulation in the treaty in their favour has proved of no avail to procure them the redress it holds out in one country, yet they find themselves excluded by it from all claims to relief in the other."

"Thus had the nation extended an inquiry for seven successive years into the losses of those who, from motives of loyalty to his Majesty and attachment to the British Government, had risked their lives and sacrificed their fortunes in support of the constitutional dependence of the colonies on Great Britain.

"Whatever may be said of this unfortunate war, either to account for, to justify, or to apologize for the conduct of either country, all the world has been unanimous in applauding the virtue and humanity of Great Britain in rewarding the services, and in compensating, with a liberal hand, the losses of those who suffered so much for their firm and faithful adherence to the British Government."

We will conclude these extracts by giving the Commissioners' account of their mode of proceeding and the reasons for it, together with the acknowledgment of the agents of the claimants in a formal address to the King:

"The principle which has directed our mode of conducting the inquiry," say the Commissioners, "has been that of requiring the very best evidence which the nature and circumstances of the case would admit. We have in no instance hitherto thought fit to dispense with the personal appearance and examination of the claimant, conceiving the inquiry would be extremely imperfect and insecure against fraud and misrepresentation if we had not the advantage of cross-examining the party himself, as well as his witnesses; nor have we, for the same reason, allowed much weight to any testimony that has not been delivered on oath before ourselves. We have investigated with great strictness the titles to real property, wherever the necessary documents could be exhibited to us; and where they have not been produced we have required satisfactory evidence of their loss, or of the inability of the claimant to procure them."*

---

* It is certain that but a small proportion of the American Loyalists presented claims before the Parliamentary Commissioners in England for compensation for services or loss of property; and many of those who presented claims did not prosecute them. The Commissioners give the following explanation on this point:

"It may, perhaps, appear singular that so many claims presented, viz., 448, have been withdrawn; but it may be owing, in the first place, to the circumstance of many of these claimants having recovered possession of

The Commissioners conclude their twelfth and last Report in the following words:

"Great as is the length of time which hath been consumed in the prosecution of this inquiry, it may without difficulty be accounted for by a survey of the multiplicity and complicated nature of the objects to which the Acts of Parliament extended our scrutiny; and when to these are added the investigation (delegated to us by your lordships) of the numerous claims for present relief and temporary support (which alone formed a heavy branch of business, demanding daily attention), the several reviews and modifications of pension lists, and the various other extraneous matters which have incidentally devolved upon us, we trust we shall, on due consideration of this extensive scene of employment, at least stand exculpated by your lordships of inactivity and unnecessary delay. We have felt with anxious solicitude the urgency as well as the importance and delicate nature of the trust reposed in us, and to this impression our exertions towards the speedy, faithful, and honourable execution of it have been proportioned. We cannot flatter ourselves that no errors have been committed; but we have this consolation, that the most assiduous endeavours have not been wanting on our part to do justice to the individuals and to the public. Supported by this reflection in our retirement from this arduous and insidious employment, we shall feel no inconsiderable satisfaction in having been instrumental towards the completion of a work which will ever reflect honour on the character of the British nation.

    (Signed)   "JOHN WILMOT.
            "ROBERT KINGSTON.
            "JOHN MARSH.

"Office of American Claims,
  "Lincoln's Inn Fields,
    "May 15th, 1789."

A proper sequel to this whole proceeding will be the following Address of the Agents for the American Loyalists, presented to the King by Sir William Pepperell, Bart., and the other

their estates, and, in the next place, to the uncertainty, at the commencement of the inquiry, as to the nature of the Commission, and the species of loss which was the object of it, and perhaps to the consciousness of others that they were not able to establish the claims they had presented."

agents, being introduced by the Lord of his Majesty's Bedchamber in waiting; which address his Majesty was pleased to receive very graciously, and they all had the honour to kiss his Majesty's hand:

"*To the King's Most Excellent Majesty.*
"The Humble Address of the Agents for the American Loyalists.
"Most Gracious Sovereign,—

"Your Majesty's ever dutiful and loyal subjects, the agents of the American Loyalists, who have heretofore been the suppliants of your Majesty in behalf of their distressed constituents, now humbly beg leave to approach your Throne, to pour forth the ardent effusions of their grateful hearts for your most gracious and effectual recommendation of their claims to the just and generous consideration of Parliament.

"To have devoted their fortunes and hazarded their lives in defence of the just rights of the Crown and the fundamental principles of the British Constitution, were no more than their duty demanded of them, in common with your Majesty's other subjects; but it was their peculiar fortune to be called to the trial, and it is their boast and their glory to have been found equal to the task.

"They have now the distinguished happiness of seeing their fidelity approved by their Sovereign, and recompensed by Parliament, and their fellow-subjects cheerfully contributing to compensate them for the forfeiture their attachment to Great Britain incited them to incur; thereby adding dignity to their own exalted character among the nations of the world, and holding out to mankind the glorious principles of justice, equity, and benevolence as the firmest basis of empire.

"We should be wanting in justice and gratitude if we did not upon this occasion acknowledge the wisdom and liberality of the provisions proposed by your Majesty's servants, conformable to your Majesty's gracious intentions for the relief and accommodation of the several classes of sufferers to whose cases they apply; and we are convinced it will give comfort to your royal heart to be assured they have been received with the most general satisfaction.

"Professions of the unalterable attachment of the Loyalists to your Majesty's person and government we conceive to be unnecessary; they have preserved it under persecution, and gratitude cannot render it less permanent. They do not presume to arrogate to themselves a more fervent loyalty than their fellow-subjects possess; but distinguished as they have been by their sufferings, they deem themselves entitled to the foremost rank among the most zealous supporters of the British Constitution. And while they cease not to offer up their most earnest prayers to the Divine Being to preserve your Majesty and your illustrious family in the peaceful enjoyment of your just rights, and in the exercise of your royal virtues in promoting the happiness of your people, they humbly beseech your Majesty to continue to believe them at all times, and upon all occasions, equally ready, as they have been, to devote their lives and properties to your Majesty's service and the preservation of the British Constitution.

"W. Pepperell, for the Massachusetts Loyalists.
"J. Wentworth, for the New Hampshire Loyalists.
"George Rowe, for the Rhode Island Loyalists.
"Ja. Delancey, for the New York Loyalists.
"David Ogden, for the New Jersey Loyalists.
"Joseph Galloway, for the Pennsylvannia and Delaware Loyalists.
"Robert Alexander, for the Maryland Loyalists.
"John R. Grymer, for the Virginia Loyalists.
"Henry Eustace McCulloch, for the North Carolina Loyalists.
"James Simpson, for the South Carolina Loyalists.
"William Knox, for the Georgia Loyalists.
"John Graham, late Lieutenant-Governor of Georgia, and joint agent, for the Georgia Loyalists."

CHAPTER XXXIX.

THE LOYALISTS DRIVEN FROM THE UNITED STATES TO THE BRITISH PROVINCES.

THE Loyalists, after having been stripped of their rights and property during the war, and driven from their homes, and hunted and killed at pleasure, were exiled from all right of residence and citizenship at the close of the war ; and though the Treaty of Peace engaged that Congress should recommend the several States to compensate them for the losses of their property, the Legislatures of the several States (with one exception) refused any compliance with this stipulation of the national treaty ; and the Legislature of New York actually ordered the punishment of those Loyalists who applied for compensation. At the close of the war, therefore, instead of witnessing, as in the case of all other civilized nations at the termination of a civil war, however rancorous and cruel, a general amnesty and the restoration of all parties to the rights and property which they enjoyed at the commencement of the strife, the Loyalists found themselves exiled and impoverished, and their enemies in possession of their homes and domains. It is true about 3,000 of the Loyalists were able to employ agents, or appear personally, to apply to the English Government and Parliament for compensation for their losses ; and the preceding chapter records the noble appreciation of their character and services by British statesmen, and the liberality of Parliament in making them compensation for their losses and sufferings in maintaining their fidelity to the mother country. But these 3,000 constituted not one-tenth of the Loyalists who had suffered losses and hardships during the civil war ; upwards of 30,000 of them were driven from the homes of their birth, and of their forefathers, to wildernesses of everlasting snow. It was a policy as inhuman and impolitic as that of Spain in expelling upwards of 600,000 Moors, the most skilful and profitable of their manufacturers and artizans; or of France, in compelling the escape of above 500,000 of the best workers in the finest manufactures to other countries where they laid the foundation of industries which have proved a source of boundless wealth to England at the expense of the commerce and manufactures of France. The Democrats were then the ruling party in most of the States; the more moderate voice and liberal policy of the Conservative Republicans were hushed and fanned down by the Democratic leaders, who seemed unable to look beyond the gratification of their resentment and avarice; they seemed to fear the residence and presence of men of intelligence, ability, and energy, who might in the future rival if not eclipse them. The maxim of the Loyalists was, obedience to law; heretofore they looked upon the enactments of the States and of Congress as usurpation; those enactments were now recognized as law by England herself, in the acknowledgment of American Independence; and the Loyalists would have been among the most obedient and law-abiding citizens had they been allowed to remain in the land of their nativity and forefathers, and would have largely added to its social advancement, literature, and wealth, and would undoubtedly, before now, have led to the unity of the Anglo-Saxon race under one free and progressive government. Historians and statesmen have long since condemned this resentful and narrow-minded policy of the States against the Loyalists after the close of the revolutionary war, as do now even American historians.*

---

* " Had we pursued a wise course, people of our own stock would not have become our rivals in ship-building, in the carriage of our great staples, in the prosecution of the fisheries, and in the production of wheat and other breadstuffs. Nor is this all: we should not have had the hatred, the influence and the talents of persons of Loyalist origin to contend against in the questions which have and may yet come up between us and England.

" Thus, as it seems to me, humanity to the adherents of the Crown, and prudent regard for our own interests, required a general amnesty; as it was, we not only dealt harshly with many, and unjustly with some, but doomed

The Americans inaugurated their Declaration of Independence by enacting that all adherents to connection with the mother country were rebels and traitors; they followed the recognition of Independence by England by exiling such adherents from their territories. But while this wretched policy depleted the United States of some of their best blood, it laid the foundation of the settlement and institutions of the then almost unknown and wilderness provinces which have since become the wide-spread, free and prosperous Dominion of Canada.

Until very recently, the early history of the Loyalists of America has never been written, except to blacken their character and misrepresent their actions; they were represented as a set of idle office-seekers—an imputation which has been amply refuted by their braving the forests of northern countries, and converting them into fruitful fields, developing trade and commerce, and establishing civil, religious, and educational institutions that are an honour to America itself. Yet, when exiled from their native land, they were bereft of the materials of their true history. A living American writer truly observes:

"Of the reasons which influenced, of the hopes and fears which agitated, and of the miseries and rewards which awaited the Loyalists—or, as they were called in the politics of the time, the Tories—of the American Revolution, but little is known. The most intelligent, the best informed among us, confess the deficiency of their knowledge. The reason is obvious. Men who, like the Loyalists, separate themselves from their friends and kindred, who are driven from their homes, who surrender the hopes and expectations of life, and who become outlaws, wanderers, and exiles—such men leave few memorials behind them. Their papers are scattered and lost, and their very

to misery others, whose hearts and hopes had been as true as those of Washington himself. Thus in the divisions of families which everywhere occurred, and which formed one of the most distressing circumstances of the conflict, there were wives and daughters, who, although bound to Loyalists by the holiest ties, had given their sympathies to the right from the beginning, and who now, in the triumph of the cause which had their prayers, went meekly—as woman ever meets a sorrowful lot—into hopeless, interminable exile." (Introductory Historical Essay to Sabine's Sketches of the Loyalists of the American Revolution, pp. 90, 91.)

names pass from human recollection. * * Of several of the Loyalists who were high in office, of others who were men of talents and acquirements, and of still others who were of less consideration, I have been able, after long and extensive researches, to learn scarcely more than their names, or the single fact that for their political opinions or offences they were proscribed and banished."*

The circumstances under which the Loyalists were banished from the States and deprived of their property will largely account for the alienation of feeling which long existed between the Americans and Canadians, which gave intensity to the war of 1812-15, which exists to some extent at this day, but which is gradually subsiding, and is being gradually superseded by feelings of mutual respect and friendship, strengthened by large commercial and social relations, including many intermarriages.

To understand the sacrifices which the Loyalists made, and the courage and energy they evinced, in leaving their old homes and associations in the sunny parts of America, and in seeking a refuge and a home in the wilds of the remaining British Provinces, it will be necessary to notice what was then known, and the impression then existing, as to the climate, productions, and conditions of these provinces.†

At that time New Brunswick formed a part of Nova Scotia, and was not organized into a separate province until 1784. The impressions then entertained as to the climate of Nova Scotia (including New Brunswick) may be inferred from the following extracts from a pamphlet published in England in 1784:

"It has a winter of almost insufferable length and coldness; * * there are but a few inconsiderable spots fit to cultivate, and the land is covered with a cold spongy moss in place of grass. * * Winter continues at least seven months in the year; the country is wrapt in the gloom of a perpetual fog;

---

* Preface to Colonel Sabine's Biographical Sketches of the American Loyalists, or Adherents to the British Crown, in the War of the Revolution.

† The Loyalists who were attached to military corps raised in the extreme South were principally of the Southern States, and a large portion of them settled in the Bahamas, Florida, and the British West Indies. "Some of the officers who belonged to the 'Maryland Loyalists,' and some of the privates of that corps, embarked for Nova Scotia, but were wrecked in the Bay of Fundy, and a part perished." (Sabine.)

the mountains run down to the sea coast, and leave but here and there a spot to inhabit." Some of the officers, embarking at New York for Nova Scotia, are said to have remarked that they were "bound for a country where there were nine months of winter and three months of cold weather every year." Lower Canada was known as a region of deep snow, intense cold, and little fertility; a colony of the French; its capital, Quebec, the scene of decisive battles between the English and French under Wolfe and Montcalm, and afterwards between Murray and Montgomery, the latter the leader of the American revolters and invaders. Montreal was regarded as the place of transit of the fur trade from the Hudson's Bay Company to England.

Upper Canada was then unknown, or known only as a region of dense wilderness and swamps, of venomous reptiles and beasts of prey, the hunting grounds and encampments of numerous Indian tribes, intense cold of winter, and with no other redeeming feature except abundance of game and fish.*

The entire ignorance of the climate of Upper Canada which prevailed at the close of the revolutionary war, may be inferred from the facts stated in a succeeding chapter, when the British commander of New York, being unable to transport any more Loyalists to Nova Scotia and New Brunswick, sent for a Mr. Grass, who had been a prisoner during the French war for two

---

* "The western part of Canada, abandoned after the conquest *as an Indian hunting ground*, or occupied at its western extremity on Lake Erie by a few of the ancient French colonists, began now to assume importance, and its capability of supporting a numerous population along the Great River and the lakes became evident. Those excellent men, who, preferring to sacrifice life and fortune rather than forego the enviable distinction of being British subjects, saw that this vast field afforded a sure and certain mode of safety and of honourable retreat, and accordingly, in 1783, ten thousand (10,000) were enumerated in that portion of Canada, who, under the proud title of United Empire Loyalists, had turned their backs for ever upon the new-fangled republicanism and treason of the country of their birth.

"The obstacles, privations, and miseries these people had to encounter may readily be imagined in a country where the primeval forest covered the earth, and where the only path was the river or the lake. They ultimately were, however, blessed with success; and to this day the original letters U. E., after the name of an applicant for land, ensure its grant." (Sir Richard Bonnycastle's Canada Before 1837, Vol. I., pp. 24, 25.)

or three years at Kingston, then Frontenac, to inquire of him what sort of a country Upper Canada was, and whether people could live there. Grass replied that he thought Upper Canada was a good country, and that people could live there. The British commander expressed much joy at the reply, and asked Mr. Grass if he would undertake to conduct a colony of Loyalists to Canada; the vessels, provisions, etc., would be furnished for that purpose. Mr. Grass asked three days to consider the proposal, and at length consented to undertake the task. It appears that five vessels were procured and furnished to convey this first colony of banished refugee Loyalists to Upper Canada; they sailed around the coast of New Brunswick and Nova Scotia, and up the St. Lawrence to Sorel, where they arrived in October, 1783, and where they built themselves huts or shanties and wintered; and in May, 1784, they prosecuted their voyage in boats, and reached their destination, Cataraqui, afterwards Kingston, in July. The manner of their settlement and providing for their subsistence is described in a succeeding chapter.

Other bands of Loyalists made their way to Canada by land; some by the military highway to Lower Canada, Whitehall, Lake Champlain, Ticonderoga, Plattsburg, and then turning northward proceeded to Cornwall; then ascending the St. Lawrence, along the north side of which many of them settled. This Champlain route was the common one to Lower Canada, descending the River Richelieu from St. John's to Sorel.

But the most common land route from New York to Upper Canada, chosen by the Loyalists at the close of the war, was to Albany 180 miles up the Hudson river, which divides into two branches about ten miles north of Albany. The western branch is called the Mohawk, leading to Rome, formerly Fort Stanwix. A branch of the Mohawk, called Wood Creek, leads towards the Oneida lake, which was reached by a portage. From Oneida Lake, Lake Ontario was reached by the Oswego river. Flat-bottom boats, specially built or purchased for the purpose by the Loyalists, were used in this journey. The portages over which the boats had to be hauled, and all their contents carried, are stated to be thirty miles. On reaching Oswego, some of the Loyalists coasted along the eastern shore of Lake Ontario to

Kingston, and thence up the Bay of Quinté ; others went westward, along the south shore of the lake to Niagara and Queenston ; some pursued their course to the head of the lake at Burlington ; others made their way up the Niagara river to Queenston, conveyed their boats over the portage of ten or twelve miles to Chippewa, thence up the river and into Lake Erie, settling chiefly in what was called the "Long Point Country," now the county of Norfolk. This journey of hardship, privation, and exposure occupied from two to three months. The parents and family of the writer of this history were from the middle of May to the middle of July, 1799, in making this journey in an open boat. Generally two or more families would unite in one company, and thus assist each other in carrying their boats and goods over the portages.

A considerable number came to Canada from New Jersey and the neighbourhood of Philadelphia on foot through the then wilderness of New York, carrying their little effects and small children on pack horses, and driving their cattle, which subsisted on herbage of the woods and valleys. Some of the families of this class testified to the relief and kindness they received in their extreme exigencies from the Indians.

The hardships, exposures, privations and sufferings which the first Loyalists endured in making their way from their confiscated homes to Canada, were longer and more severe than anything narrated of the Pilgrim and Puritan Fathers of New England in their voyages from England to Massachusetts Bay ; and the persecutions to which the emigration of the Puritans from England is attributed were trifling indeed in comparison of the persecutions, imprisonments, confiscations, and often death, inflicted on the loyal adherents to the Crown of England in the United States, and which drove the survivors among them to the wilderness of Canada. The privations and hardships experienced by many of these Loyalist patriots for years after the first settlement in Canada, as testified by the papers in the subsequent chapter, were much more severe than anything experienced by the Pilgrim Fathers during the first years of their settlement in Massachusetts. These latter could keep a "Harvest Home" festival of a week, at the end of the first year after their landing in the Bay of Massachusetts ; but it was years after their arrival in Canada before the Loyalists could command means to keep any such festival. The stern adherence of the Puritans to their principles was quite equalled by the stern adherence of the Loyalists to their principles, and far excelled by their sacrifices and sufferings.

Canada has a noble parentage, the remembrance of which its inhabitants may well cherish with respect, affection, and pride.

CHAPTER XL.

BRIEF SKETCHES OF SOME INDIVIDUAL LOYALISTS—FIRST SETTLERS IN CANADA AND OTHER BRITISH PROVINCES.

It is not possible to give biographical sketches of all the old Loyalists, officers and soldiers. To do justice to their character and merits would require a massive volume. Besides, the data for such a volume are for the most part wanting. It is not the object of this history to give a biography of the Loyalists; that must be done by others, if attempted at all. The Loyalists were not writers, but workers. Almost the only history of them has been written by their enemies, whose object was to conceal the treatment they received, to depreciate their merits and defame their character, for the vindication of which it is only of late years that materials have been procured. It is the object of this history to vindicate their character as a body, to exhibit their principles and patriotism, and to illustrate their treatment and sufferings.

The best, and indeed only biography of the Loyalists extant is Sabine's "*American Loyalists, or Biographical Sketches of Adherents to the British Crown in the War of the Revolution*,"— especially the first, not the second edition. The author has more than once quoted the excellent historical essay introductory to the sketches of this work, and from which Dr. Canniff has enriched the pages of his valuable "*History of the Settlement of Upper Canada, with special reference to the Bay of Quinté.*" From these sources we will condense brief notices of some of the early Loyalists, preliminary to the information in regard to others furnished us in the interesting letters and papers which follow. These notices will further illustrate the character and sacrifices of the Loyalist combatants—the treatment they received and the courage they displayed.

1. *Samuel Anderson*, of New York, entered the service of the Crown, and was a captain in the regiment of Sir John Johnson. In 1783 he settled near Cornwall, Upper Canada, and received half-pay; held several civil offices, such as those of Magistrate, Judge of the District Court, Associate Justice of King's Bench, etc. He continued to reside on his property near Cornwall until his decease in 1836, at the age of one hundred and one. His property in New York was abandoned and lost.

2. *Rev. John Bethune* (father of the late Bishop of Toronto), of North Carolina, was chaplain to the Loyal Militia; was taken prisoner at the battle of Cross Creek; was confined in jail, first at Halifax and finally in Philadelphia. After his release, his continued loyalty reduced him to great distress. He was appointed to the 84th Regiment and restored to comfort. At the peace, he settled in Upper Canada, at Williamston, near Cornwall, and died in 1815, at the age of sixty-five.

3. *Doane*, of Bucks County, Pennsylvania. Of this family there were five brothers—Moses, Joseph, Israel, Abraham, and Mahlon. They were men of fine figure and address, elegant horsemen, great runners and leapers, and excellent at stratagems and escapes. Their father was respectable, and possessed a good estate. The sons themselves, prior to the war, were men of reputation and proposed to remain neutral; but harassed personally, their property sold by the Whigs, because they would not submit to the exactions of the time, they determined to avenge themselves by a predatory warfare upon their persecutors, and to live in the open air as best they could. They became the terror of the surrounding country; they spared the weak, the poor, and the peaceful; they aimed at public property and at public men. Generally their expeditions were on horseback. Sometimes the five went together; at other times separately, with accomplices. Whoever of them was apprehended, broke jail; whoever of them was assailed, escaped. In a word, such was their course, that a reward of £300 was offered for the head of each. Ultimately, three were slain; Moses, after a desperate fight, was shot by his captor; and Abraham and Mahlon were living at Philadelphia. Joseph, before the revolution, taught school. During the war, while

on a marauding expedition, he was shot through the cheeks, and was taken prisoner. He was committed to await his trial, but escaped to New Jersey. A reward of $800 was offered for his apprehension, but without success. He resumed his former employment in New Jersey and lived there under an assumed name for nearly a year, but finally fled to Canada. The only mention of Israel is that "in February, 1783, he appealed to the Council of Pennsylvania to be released on account of his own sufferings and the destitute condition of his family, and that his petition was dismissed."

4. *Stephen Jarvis*, in 1782 was a lieutenant of cavalry in the South Carolina Royalists; was in several battles; was in New Brunswick; after the revolution came to Upper Canada, and died at Toronto in 1840, aged eighty-four.

5. *William Jarvis* was an officer of cavalry in the Queen's Rangers; was wounded at the siege of Yorktown. At the Peace he settled in Upper Canada, became Secretary of the Province, and died at York (Toronto) in 1817.

6. *David Jones* was captain in the royal service, and the reputed spouse or husband of the "beautiful and good Jane McCrea," whose cruel death in 1777, by the Indians, on her way to join him, is so universally known and lamented. He lived in Canada to an old age, but never married. Jane McCrea was the daughter of the Rev. James McCrea, a Loyalist.

7. *Jonathan Jones*, of New York, was brother of Captain David Jones, and assisted in the latter part of 1776 in raising a company in Lower Canada, and joined the British garrison at Crown Point. Later in the war he was captain under General Frazer.

8. *Captain Richard Lippincott* was born in Shrewsbury, New Jersey, on the 2nd of January, 1745. He was descended from an old colonial family, and served during the revolution as a captain in the New Jersey volunteers. He was married on the 4th of March, 1770, to Esther Borden, daughter of Jeremiah and Esther Borden, of Bordentown, New Jersey. On the outbreak of the revolution he warmly espoused the side of the Crown, and was early in the war captured and confined in Burlington jail, from which he escaped in the year 1776, and made his way to the British army at Staten Island. During the remainder of the war he served with his regiment. His

connection with the execution of Captain Joshua Huddy, of the rebel service, attracted a great deal of attention both in Europe and America. Captain Huddy was a partisan officer of some repute in New Jersey, and had been concerned in the murder of a Loyalist named Philip White, who was a relative of Lippincott, and a resident of Shrewsbury. One Edwards of the same neighbourhood had also been put to death about the same time. Shortly after, Captain Huddy was captured and taken as prisoner to New York. The "Board of Associated Loyalists of New York" sent Captain Lippincott to Middleton Point, or Sandy Hook, with Captain Huddy and two other prisoners, to exchange them for prisoners held by the rebels. He was authorized to execute Huddy in retaliation for White, who had already been put to death. Therefore, on the 12th of April, 1782, having exchanged the two other prisoners, Captain Lippincott hung Huddy on a tree by the beach, under the Middleton Heights. In 1867 the tree was still to be seen, and tradition keeps alive in the neighbourhood the story connected with it. Captain Lippincott, who was evidently only obeying orders, pinned a paper on Huddy's breast with the following inscription:

"We, the Refugees, having long with grief beheld the cruel murders of our brethren, and finding nothing but such measures carrying into execution,—we therefore determine not to suffer without taking vengeance for the numerous cruelties, and thus begin, having made use of Captain Huddy as the first object to present to your view, and further determine to hang man for man while there is a refugee existing.

"UP GOES HUDDY FOR PHILIP WHITE."

Washington, upon hearing of Huddy's death, demanded the surrender of Captain Lippincott from the Royalist authorities, in order that he might be put to death. This demand was refused, and Washington then ordered the execution of one officer of equal rank to be chosen by lot from among the prisoners in his hands. The lot fell upon Captain Asgill, of the Guards, who was only nineteen years of age. The British authorities secured a respite under promise of trying Captain Lippincott by court-martial. After a full inquiry, Lippincott was honourably acquitted. In the meantime, Lady Asgill, Captain Asgill's mother, appealed to the Count de Vergennes, the French Minister, and, in response to her most pathetic appeal, the Count was instructed by the King and Queen of France, in their joint names, to ask of Washington the release of Captain Asgill "as a tribute to humanity." Washington, after a long delay, granted this request, but Asgill and Lippincott were not set at liberty till the close of the war. Asgill lived to become a general, and to succeed to his father's baronetcy.

After the war Captain Lippincott moved to New Brunswick, to a place called Pennfield, where he lived till the fall of 1787, when he went to England, where he remained till the end of 1788. He was granted half pay as a captain of the British army, and in 1793 he moved from New Brunswick to Canada, when he was granted for his U. E. Loyalist services 3,000 acres of land in the township of Vaughan, near Toronto.

He lived near Richmond Hill for many years. His only surviving child, Esther Borden Lippincott, was married in 1806 to the late Colonel George Taylor Denison, of Bellevue, Toronto, at whose house Captain Lippincott died in 1826, aged eighty-one years. The family of Denisons of Toronto are all descendants of Captain Lippincott through this marriage.

9. *McDonald.*—There were many of this name who took part with the loyal combatants, and of whom several settled in Canada.

Alexander McDonald was a major in a North Carolina regiment, and was the husband of the celebrated Flora McDonald, who was so true and devoted to Prince Charles Edward, the last of the Stuarts who sought the throne of England. They had emigrated to North Carolina; and when the revolution broke out, he, with two sons, took up arms for the Crown. Those who settled in Canada were Donald McDonald, of New York, who served under Sir John Johnson for seven years, and died at Wolfe Island, Upper Canada, aged 97; and Allan McDonald, of Tryon (afterwards Montgomery), New York, who was associated with Sir John Johnson in 1776, and died at a great age, at Three Rivers, in Lower Canada, 1822.

10. *John McGill* was, in 1782, an officer of infantry in the Queen's Rangers, and at the close of the war went to New Brunswick; removed thence to Upper Canada, became a man

of note and member of the Legislative Council, and died at Toronto, in 1834, at the age of eighty-three.

11. *Donald McGillis* resided at the beginning of the revolution on the Mohawk river, New York. Embracing the royal side in the contest, he formed one of a "determined band of young men," who attacked a Whig post, and, in the face of a superior force, cut down the flag-staff and tore in strips the stars and stripes attached to it. Subsequently he joined a grenadier company called the Royal Yorkers, and performed efficient service throughout the war. At the peace he settled in Canada; and entering the British service again in 1812, was appointed captain in the colonial corps by Sir Isaac Brock. He died at River Raisin, Canada, in 1844, aged eighty years.

12. *Thomas Merrit*, of New York (father of the late Hon. W. Hamilton Merrit), was in 1782 cornet of cavalry in the Queen's Rangers. He settled in Upper Canada, and held the office of high sheriff of the Niagara district. He died at St. Catharines, May, 1842, at the age of eighty years.

The Robinson family was one of the distinguished families in America before, during, and after the revolution, and its members have filled some of the most important offices in the provinces of Nova Scotia, New Brunswick, Lower and Upper Canada.

13. *Beverley Robinson*, of New York, was the son of the Honourable John Robinson, of Virginia, who was President of that colony on the retirement of Governor Gooch. He removed to New York, and married Susanna, daughter of Frederick Phillipse, Esquire, who owned an immense landed estate on the Hudson river. By this connection Mr. Robinson added greatly to his wealth and became very rich. When the revolutionary controversy commenced, he was living on that portion of the Phillipse estate which had been given to his wife, and there he desired to remain in the quiet enjoyment of country life, and in the enjoyment of his large domains. That such was his inclination is asserted by the late President Dwight, and is fully confirmed by circumstances and by his descendants. He *was opposed to the measures of the British Ministry, gave up the use of imported merchandize, and clothed himself and family in fabrics of domestic manufacture.*

But *he was opposed to the separation of the colonies from the mother country.* Still he wished to take no part in the conflict of arms. The importunity of friends overruled his own judgment, and he entered the military service of the Crown. Of the Loyal American Regiment, raised principally in New York by himself, he was commissioned the colonel. He also commanded the corps called Guides and Pioneers. Of the former, or the Loyal Americans, his son Beverley was lieutenant-colonel, and Thomas Barclay, major. He and Washington had been personal friends until political events produced separation between them.

At the peace, Colonel Robinson, with a part of his family, went to England. His name appears as a member of the first Council of New Brunswick; but he never took his seat at the Board. His wife, with himself, was attainted for high treason; in order to secure her property to the Americans, she was included in the Confiscation Act of New York, and the whole of the estate derived from her father passed from the family. The value of her interest may be estimated from the fact that the British Government granted her and her husband the sum of £17,000 sterling, which, though equal to $80,000, *was considered only a partial compensation.*

Colonel Robinson has highly respectable descendants in New Brunswick as well as in Canada. William Henry, who was afterwards King William the Fourth, enjoyed Colonel Robinson's hospitality in New York at a later date. The Robinsons were unquestionably immediate sufferers from the events which drove them into exile. But though Colonel Robinson was not amply compensated in money by the Government for which he sacrificed fortune, home, and his native land, yet the distinction obtained by his children and grand-children in the colonies, though deprived of their inheritance, has not been without other and substantial recompense, as no persons of the Loyalist descent have been more favoured in official stations and powerful family alliances than the heirs of the daughters of Frederick Phillipse, Susanna Robinson, and Mary Morris (see under the names of Colonel Ragier Morris and Colonel Thomas Barclay).

14. *Beverley Robinson (jun.)* was son of Colonel Beverley Robinson, and lieutenant-colonel in the Loyal American Regiment, commanded by his father; was a graduate of Columbia

College, New York, and at the commencement of the revolutionary troubles was a student of law in the office of James Duane. His wife, Nancy, whom he married during the war, was daughter of the Reverend Henry Barclay, D.D., rector of Trinity Church, New York, and sister of Colonel Thomas Barclay. At the evacuation of New York, Lieutenant-Colonel Robinson was placed at the head of a large number of Loyalists who embarked for Shelburne, Nova Scotia, and who laid out that place in a very handsome manner, in the hope of its becoming a town of business and importance. The harbour of Shelburne is represented to be one of the best in North America; the population rapidly increased to about 12,000 persons, but soon as rapidly declined, being outrivalled by Halifax—and many abandoned Shelburne for other parts of the British provinces. Lieutenant-Colonel Robinson went to New Brunswick, and resided near the city of St. John. His deprivations and sufferings for a considerable time after leaving New York were great, but were finally relieved by the receipt of half-pay as an officer in the service of the Crown. In New Brunswick he was a member of his Majesty's Council; and at the period of the French revolution, and on the occurrence of the Napoleonic war between England and France, he was entrusted with the command of the regiment raised in that colony, possessed great energy, and contributed much by his exertions and influence to settle and advance the commercial emporium of New Brunswick. In the Confiscation Act of New York, by which his estate was taken from him, he was styled "Beverley Robinson the younger." He died in 1816, at New York, while on a visit to two of his sons who were residing in that city.

15. *Christopher Robinson*, of Virginia, was kinsman of Colonel Beverley Robinson; entered William and Mary College with his cousin Robert, escaped with him to New York, and received a commission in the Loyal Canadian Regiment: served at the South, and was wounded. At the peace he went first to New Brunswick, and then to Nova Scotia, receiving a grant of land in each province. He soon removed to Upper Canada, where Governor Simcoe gave him the appointment of Deputy-Surveyor-General of Crown Lands. His salary, half pay, and an estate of 2,000 acres, placed him in comfortable circumstances.

16. *Sir John Beverley Robinson* was a son of Christopher Robinson, of Virginia; received his early legal education in England, and was admitted to the English bar. He returned to Upper Canada while yet young; served with distinction in the war of 1812, and was in several battles. He was early appointed Attorney-General, and held a seat in the House of Assembly for ten years; after which he was appointed Member and Speaker of the Legislative Council. During the insurrection of 1837, in Upper Canada, he took his musket and went into the ranks, accompanied by his two sons. He was born in 1791; was appointed Attorney-General of Upper Canada in 1818; was raised to the Bench as Chief Justice in 1829; was created Baronet in 1854; and died in 1863, aged seventy-two.

17. *Sir Charles Frederick Phillipse Robinson*, G.C.B., of New York, was the son of Colonel Beverley Robinson; entered the King's service early in the Revolution, and at the peace returned with his father to England, where he was continued in the British army; became Lieutenant-General, and received the honour of knighthood. He was with the Duke of Wellington, and saw much hard service. At the storming of St. Sebastian he was dangerously wounded. He was in the battle of Vittoria, Nive, Orthes, and Toulouse. During the war of 1812 he came to America, and was employed in Canada. He commanded the British force in the attack on Plattsburg, under Prevost, and protested against the order of his superior, when directed to retire, because from the position of his troops he was of opinion that his loss of men would be greater in retreat than in advance upon the American works. After the conclusion of hostilities he embarked at New York for England.

18. *Morris Robinson*, of New York, was also son of Colonel Beverley Robinson, and was captain of the Queen's Rangers. When that corps was disbanded at the close of the war, most of the officers were dismissed on half pay, and settled in New Brunswick; but Captain Robinson, by good fortune, was continued in commission, and at the time of his decease he was lieutenant-colonel, and assistant-barrackmaster-general in the British army. He had three sons officers in the British army, and two daughters, Susan and Joane; the former became the wife of Robert Parker, judge of the Supreme Court of New Brunswick; and the latter the wife of Robert T. Hagien, Esq.,.

barrister-at-law, master in chancery, and formerly mayor of the city of St. John.

19. *John Robinson*, of New York, likewise a son of Colonel Beverley Robinson, was during the revolution a lieutenant of the Loyal American Regiment, commanded by his father; and when the corps was disbanded at the close of the war, he settled in New Brunswick, and received half pay. He embarked, and successfully, in mercantile pursuits, and held distinguished public stations, being deputy-paymaster-general of his Majesty's forces in the Province, a member of the Council, treasurer of New Brunswick, mayor of St. John, and president of the first bank chartered in the colony. He died at St. John in 1828, aged sixty-seven.

Several other Robinsons were engaged on the royal side in the American Revolution, but none of them so prominently connected with the British provinces as those above mentioned.

20. *Roger Morris*, of New York, was a captain in the British army, in the French war, and one of the aides of the ill-fated Braddock. He married Mary, daughter of Frederick Phillipse, Esq., and settled in New York. At the commencement of the revolution he was a member of the Council of the colony, and continued in office until the peace, although the Whigs organized a government, under a written Constitution, as early as 1777. A part of the Phillipse estate was in possession of Colonel Morris in right of his wife, and was confiscated. In order that the whole property should pass from the family into the hands of the Americans, Mrs. Morris was included with her husband in the New York Confiscation Act of attainder. It is believed that this lady, her sister Mrs. Robinson, and Mrs. Ingles, were the only ladies who were attainted of treason during the revolution, and that merely to get possession of their property. "Imagination," says Sabine, "dwells upon the attainting of a lady whose beauty and attractions had won the admiration of Washington.* Humanity is shocked that a woman was

---

* An interesting incident occurred in the early life of Mrs. Morris—no other than that Washington desired to become her suitor—a fact which rests on the highest authority. In Sparks' Life of Washington there is the following passage: "While in New York, in 1756, Washington was lodged and kindly entertained at the house of Mr. Beverley Robinson, between whom and himself an intimacy of friendship subsisted, which indeed, con-

attainted of treason for no crime but that of clinging to the fortunes of the husband whom she had vowed on the altar of religion never to desert."

But it appeared in due time that the Confiscation Act did not affect the rights of Mrs. Morris's children, who were not named in, and therefore not disqualified by the Act of Confiscation. In 1787, the Attorney-General of England examined the case and gave the opinion that the reversionary interest (or property of the children at the decease of the parents) was not included in their attainder, and was recoverable under the principles of law and of right. In the year 1809, their son, Captain Henry Gage Morris, of the Royal Navy, in behalf of himself and his two sisters, sold his reversionary interest to John Jacob Astor, Esquire, of New York, for the sum of £20,000 sterling. In 1828, Mr. Astor made a compromise with the State of New York, by which he received for the rights thus purchased by him (with or without associates) the large amount of $500,000. The terms of the arrangement required that he should execute a deed of conveyance in fee simple, with warranty against the claims of the Morrises, husband and wife, their heirs, and all persons claiming under them; and that he should obtain the judgment of the Supreme Court of the United States, affirming the validity and perfectibility of his title. These conditions were complied with, and the purchasers of the confiscated lands were thus quieted in their titles derived from the sales of the Commissioners of Confiscated Property.

tinued without change till severed by their opposite fortunes twenty years afterwards in the revolution. It happened that Miss Mary Phillipse, a sister of Mrs. Robinson, and a young lady of rare accomplishments, was an inmate of the family. The charms of the lady made a deep impression upon the heart of the Virginia colonel. He went to Boston, returned, and was again welcomed to the hospitality of Mr. Robinson. He lingered there till duty called him away; but he was careful to entrust his secret to a confidential friend, whose letters kept him informed of every important event. In a few months intelligence came that there was a rival in the field, and that consequences could not be answered for if he delayed to renew his visits to New York. Whether time, the bustle of the camp, or the scenes of war, had moderated his admiration, or whether he despaired of success, is not known. He never saw the lady again, till she was married to that same rival, Captain Morris, his former associate in arms, and one of Braddock's aide-de-camps."

21. *Allan McNab* was a lieutenant of cavalry in the Queen's Rangers, under Colonel Simcoe. During the war he received thirteen wounds. He accompanied his commander to Upper Canada, then a dense unpeopled wilderness. He was appointed Sergeant-at-Arms of the House of Assembly of Upper Canada, and held the office for many years. He was father of the late Sir Allan McNab, who was born at Niagara, in 1798, of Scotch extraction, whose grandfather, Major Robert McNab, of the 42nd Regiment, or Black Watch, was Royal Forester in Scotland, and resided on a small property called Dundurn, at the head of Loch Earn. Sir Allan McNab, though very young, distinguished himself in the war of 1812. In the insurrection of 1837 he was appointed to the command of the militia, dispersed the rebels, and cut out and burnt the rebel steamer *Caroline*, at Black Rock, for which he was knighted. He was Speaker of the House of Assembly of Upper Canada before the union of the two Canadas, and was afterwards Speaker of the Legislative Council of United Canada.

22. *Luke Curscallan* (resident of Bay of Quinté) was an Irishman by birth, and had served in the British army; he had retired and emigrated to the American colonies prior to the revolution. He desired to remain neutral and take no part in the contest. The rebels, however, said to him, that inasmuch as he was acquainted with military tactics, he must join them or be regarded as a King's man. His reply was that he had fought for the King, and he would do it again, consequently an order was issued to arrest him; but when they came to take him, he had secreted himself. The escape was a hurried one, and all his possessions were at the mercy of the rebels—land to the amount of 12,000 acres. They, disappointed at not catching him, took his young and tender son, and threatened to hang him if he would not reveal his father's place of concealment. The brave little fellow replied, "Hang away!' and the cruel men, under the name of liberty, carried out their threat, and three times was he suspended until he was almost dead, yet he would not tell; and then, when taken down, one of the monsters actually kicked him." (Canniff.)

23. *John Diamond* was born in Albany, with several brothers. An elder brother was drafted, but he tried to escape a service so repugnant to his fellings; was concealed for some

time, and upon a sick bed. The visits of the doctor led to suspicion, and the house was visited by rebels. Although he had been placed in a bed so arranged that it was thought his presence would not be detected, his breathing betrayed him. They at once required his father to give a bond for $1,200 that his son should not be removed while sick. He got well, and some time after again sought to escape, but was caught, and handcuffed to another. Being removed from one place to another, the two prisoners managed to knock their guards on the head, and ran for life through the woods, chained together. One would sometimes run on one side of a sapling, and the other on the opposite side. At night they managed to rub their handcuffs off, and finally escaped to Canada. Of the other brothers, two were carried off by the rebels and were never more heard of; John was taken to the rebel army when old enough to do service, but he also escaped to Canada, and enlisted in Rogers' Battalion, in which he served until the end of the war, when he settled with the company at Fredericksburg. He married Miss Loyst, a native of Philadelphia, whose ancestors were German. She acted no inferior part, for a woman, during the exciting times of the revolution. They were married in Lower Canada. They spent their first summer in Upper Canada in clearing a little spot of land, and in the fall got a little grain in the ground. They slept during the summer under a tree, but erected a small hut before winter set in.

24. *Ephraim Tisdale*, of Freetown, Massachusetts. In 1775, he fled from home, and went to New York. During the war, while on a voyage to St. Augustine, Florida, he abandoned his vessel at sea to avoid capture, and gained the shore in safety. Though nearly destitute of money, he accomplished an overland journey to New York, a distance, by the route which he travelled, of fifteen hundred miles. In 1783 he embarked at New York for New Brunswick, in the ship *Brothers*, Captain Walker; and on the passage his wife gave birth to a son, who was named for the master of the ship. Mr. Tisdale held civil and military offices in New Brunswick. He removed to Upper Canada in 1808, settled in the Township of Charlotteville, near Vittoria, and died in 1816. He left eight sons and four daughters. Walker Tisdale, Esq., of St. John (the son above referred to), was in Canada in 1845, when the descendants of his father

there were 169, of whom he saw 163. The Tisdales were active on the side of the Crown in the insurrection of 1837. The whole family have always been distinguished for loyalty.

25. *Lemuel Wilmot*, of Long Island, New York, entered the King's service as an officer, and at the peace was captain in the Loyal American Regiment. In 1783 he settled on the River St. John, New Brunswick, near Fredericton, where he continued to reside until his death, which took place in 1814. Five sons survived him. The Honourable Lemuel A. Wilmot, the son of his younger son William, was a member of the Legislative Assembly, and leader of the Liberal party; became Attorney-General, and afterwards Chief Justice, and ultimately Lieutenant-Governor of the province. He had for many years been superintendent of the Sunday-school, and leader of the choir in the (Methodist) Church to which he belonged, and continued to discharge the duties of both offices during the five years that he was Lieutenant-Governor, and until his death, which occurred suddenly in May, 1878.

I have not space to extend these notices of individual combatants in the American Revolution, though I might add scores to the number of those I have already noticed, equally loyal and courageous, and equal in their energy, sacrifices and sufferings in fleeing to Canada from American Republican persecution, far beyond anything endured by the Pilgrim and Puritan Fathers of New England, to whose enterprise, energy, and privations I have done ample justice in the first volume of this history.

The Loyalists fled to Canada, and settled chiefly in Lower Canada, on the northern banks of the St. Lawrence, between Montreal and Kingston, on the Bay of Quinté, Prince Edward, the frontiers of the Niagara district, and the northern shores of Lake Erie. In the following chapter I will present an epitome of the immigration of the first Loyalists to the Bay of Quinté, to the Niagara frontier, and to the northern shores of Lake Erie, especially of what was called the "Long Point" country, their modes of struggling their way thither, the privations and labours of their early settlement. I will here add a few passages from Dr. Canniff's *Settlement of Upper Canada, with Special Reference to Bay Quinté*, in regard to the Loyalists fleeing into Lower Canada, and making their way up the St. Lawrence to Kingston and Bay Quinté.

"The batteaux," says the late Sheriff Sherman, of Brockville, "by which the refugees emigrated were principally built at Lachine, nine miles from Montreal. They were calculated to carry four or five families, with almost two tons weight. Twelve boats constituted a brigade, and each brigade had a conductor, with five men in each, one of whom steered. The duty of the conductor was to give directions for the safe management of the boats, to keep them together, and when they came to a rapid they left a portion of the boats in charge of one man. The boats ascending were doubly manned, and drawn by a rope fastened at the bow of the boat, having four men in the boat with setting poles; thus the men walked along the side of the river, sometimes in the water or on the edge of the bank, as circumstances occurred. Having reached the head of the rapids the boats were left with a man, and the other men went back for the other boats;" and so they continued until the rapids were mounted. Lachine was the starting place—a place of some twenty dwellings.

It was by these batteaux that the Loyalist refugee officers and their families, as well as the soldiers and their families, passed from the shores of Lake Champlain, from Sorel and St. Lawrence, where they had temporarily lived, to Upper Canada. It was also by these or the Schenectady or Durham boat that the pioneer Loyalists made their way from Oswego.

"Thus it is seen that to gain the northern shore of the St. Lawrence and Lake Ontario was a task of no easy nature, and the steps by which the Loyalists came were taken literally inch by inch, and were attended by hard and venturesome labour. Records are not wanting of the severe hardships endured by families on their way to their wooded lands. Supplied with limited comforts, perhaps only the actual necessaries of life, they advanced slowly by day along dangerous rapids, and at night rested under the blue sky. But our Loyalist forefathers and mothers were made of stern stuff, and all was borne with noble heroism.

"This toilsome mode of travelling continued for many a year. John Ferguson, writing in 1788 from Fredericksburg, Bay Quinté, to a friend in Lachine, Lower Canada, says of his journey: 'After a most tedious and fatiguing journey I arrived here, nineteen days on the way, sometimes for whole days up to the waist in water or mire.' But the average time required to ascend the rapids was from ten to twelve days, and three or four to descend.

"With the later coming loyal refugees was introduced another kind of flat-bottomed boat. It was generally small, rigged with an ungainly sail; and usually built in the town of Schenectady; hence its name. Schenectady is a German word, and means *pine barren*. Families about to come to Canada would build one or more of these boats to meet their requirements.

"The Loyalists not only came in summer, by batteaux or the Schenectady boat, but likewise in winter. They generally followed, as near as possible, some one of the routes taken in summer. To undertake to traverse a wilderness with no road, and guided only by rivers and creeks, or blazed trees, was no common thing. Several families would sometimes join together to form a train of sleighs. They would carry with them their bedding, clothes, and the necessary provisions. We have received interesting accounts of winter journeyings from Albany along the Hudson, across to the Black River country, and to the St. Lawrence. Sometimes the train would follow the military road, along by Champlain, St. George, as far as Plattsburg, and then turn north to the St. Lawrence, by what was then called the Willsbury wilderness, and 'Chataquee' woods. At the beginning of the present century there was but one tavern through all that vast forest, and that of the poorest character. Indeed, it is said that while provision might be procured for the horses, none could be had for man. Those who thus entered Canada in winter found it necessary to stay at Cornwall until spring. Two or more of the men would foot it along the St. Lawrence to the Bay Quinté, and at the opening of navigation, having borrowed a batteau, descend to Cornwall for the women, children, and articles brought with them. While the families and sleighs were transported in the batteaux, the horses were taken along the shore by the larger boys, if such there were among them. The French train was occasionally employed in these winter journeys. It consisted of a long rude sleigh, with several horses driven tandem style; this allowed the passage among the trees to be made more easily.

"Travellers from Montreal to the west would come by a batteau, or Durham boat, to Kingston. Those who had business further west, says Finkle, 'were conveyed to Henry Finkle's, in Ernest Town, where they commonly stopped a few days. Thence they made their journey on horseback. A white man conducted them to the River Trent, where resided Colonel Bleecker, who was at the head and had control of all Mississauga Indians, and commanded the entire country to Toronto. At this place the traveller was furnished with a fresh horse, and an Indian guide to conduct him through an unsettled country, the road being little better than a common Indian path, with all its windings. The road continued in this state until about the year 1798. Sometimes the traveller continued his journey around the head of Lake Ontario, on horseback, to Queenston, where resided Judge Hamilton."

CHAPTER XLI.

FIRST SETTLEMENT OF LOYALISTS IN THE BRITISH PROVINCES, ESPECIALLY UPPER CANADA—THEIR ADVENTURES AND HARDSHIPS, AS WRITTEN BY THEMSELVES OR THEIR DESCENDANTS.

IN 1861 I addressed a printed circular to the United Empire Loyalists and their descendants in the British Provinces of North America, stating the design and scope of the history I proposed to write respecting them, in compliance with a call which had been made upon me by the press and members of all parties, and requesting the surviving Loyalists and their descendants to communicate to me, at my expense, any letters or papers they might possess which would throw light upon the early history of the fathers and founders of our country.

This chapter contains the letters and papers which I received in answer to my circular. These letters and papers, with repetitions of some incidents, contain, in a variety of style, statements and narratives of a remarkable character, and of intense interest, and introduce the reader to the inner life and privations of the bold, self-denying, and energetic pioneers of Canada and of other British provinces.

First Settlement of the First Company of Loyalists, after the close of the Revolutionary War.

Letter from the Rev. Dr. Richardson, late Bishop of the Methodist Episcopal Church in Canada:

" *To the Rev. Dr. Ryerson.*

" DEAR SIR,—

" The following is the narrative of which I spoke to you, relative to the early settlement of Upper Canada, as related to me by the late Mr. John Grass, of the Township of Kingston, some years since, and which you requested might be furnished for insertion in your forthcoming history of our country. I give it to you as near as may be in Mr. Grass's own words. The old gentleman, his father, I knew well when I was a boy; his residence was next to my father's for several years in Kingston. He was a genuine sample of an honest, plain, loyal German. The narrator was about eleven years old at the time he migrated with his father and the company of Loyalists from New York to 'Frontenac,' and therefore had a distinct recollection of all the incidents he relates. Being seated in his parlour one evening, while partaking of his hospitality, the conversation naturally turned on events connected with the first settlement of the township of Kingston and its early inhabitants, most of whom had descended to their graves; Mr. Grass was led to state as follows:

"My father had been a prisoner among the French at Frontenac (now Kingston), in the old French war, and at the commencement of the American revolution he resided in a farm on the borders of the North River, about thirty miles above New York. Being solicited by General Herkimer to take a captain's commission in the American service, he replied, sternly and promptly, that he had sworn allegiance to one King, meaning George the Third, and could not violate his oath, or serve against him.

"For this he was obliged to fly from his home and take refuge within New York, under British protection. His family had soon to follow him, being driven from their home, which by the enemy was dilapidated and broken up. They continued in that city till the close of the war, living on their own resources as best they could. On the return of peace, the Americans having gained their independence, there was no longer any home there for the fugitive Loyalists, of which the city was full; and the British Governor was much at a loss for a place to settle them. Many had retreated to Nova Scotia or New Brunswick; but this was a desperate resort, and their immense numbers made it difficult to find a home for them all, even there. In the meantime, the Governor, in his perplexity, having heard that my father had been a prisoner among the French at Frontenac, sent for him and said: 'Mr. Grass, I understand you have been at Frontenac, in Canada. Pray tell me what sort of a country is it? Can people live there? What think you?' My father replied: 'Yes, your Excellency, I was there a prisoner of war, and from what I saw I think it a fine country, and that people might live there very well.' 'Oh! Mr. Grass,' exclaims the Governor, 'how glad I am to hear that, for the sake of these poor Loyalists. As they cannot all go to Nova Scotia, and I am at a loss how to provide for them, will you, Mr. Grass, undertake to lead thither as many as may choose to accompany you? If so, I will furnish a conveyance by Quebec, and rations for you all till such time as you may be able to provide for yourselves.' My father requested his Excellency to allow him three days to make up his mind. This was granted, and accordingly, at the expiration of the three days, my father went to the Governor and said he would undertake it. Notices were then posted up through the city, calling for all that would go to Frontenac to enrol their names with Mr. Grass; so in a short time the company of men, women, and children was completed, a ship provided and furnished, and off they started for the unknown and far distant region, leaving the homes and friends of their youth, with all their endearing recollections, behind them—the fruits of all their former toil and suffering—a sacrifice to their loyalty. The first season they got no further than Sorel, in Lower Canada, where they were obliged to erect log huts for the winter. Next spring they took boats, and proceeding up the St. Lawrence, at length reached *Frontenac*, and pitched their tents on *Indian Point*, where the marine docks of Kingston now stand. Here they awaited the surveying of the lands, which was not accomplished so as to be ready for location before July. In the meantime several other companies had arrived by different routes under their respective leaders, who were all awaiting the completing of the surveys. The Governor, also, who by this time had himself come to Quebec, paid them a visit, and riding a few miles along the lake shore on a fine day, exclaimed to my father: 'Why, Mr. Grass, you have indeed got a fine country! I am really glad to find it so.' While the several companies were together waiting for the survey, some would say to my father: 'The Governor will not give you the first choice of the townships, but will prefer Sir John Johnson and his company, because he is a great man.' But my father replied that he did not believe that, for if the Governor should do so he should feel himself injured and would leave the country, as he was the first man to mention it to the Governor in New York, and to proceed hither with his company for settlement.

"At length the time came, in July, for the townships to be given out. The Governor came, and having assembled the companies before him, called for Mr. Grass, and said: 'Now, you were the first person to mention this fine country, and have been here formerly as a prisoner of war. You must have the first choice. The townships are numbered first, second, third, fourth, and fifth. Which do you choose?' My father says: 'The *first* township (Kingston).' Then the Governor says to Sir John Johnson, 'Which do you choose for your company?' He replies, 'The *second* township (Ernest Town).' To Colonel Rogers, 'Which do you choose?' He says, 'The *third* township (Fredericksburgh).' To Major Vanalstine, 'Which do you choose?' He replies, 'The *fourth* township (Adolphustown).' Then Colonel McDonell, with his company, got the fifth township (Marysburgh). So after this manner the first settlement of Loyalists in Canada was made.

"But before leaving, the Governor very considerately remarked to my father, 'Now, Mr. Grass, it is too late in the season to put in any crops.' What can you do for food? My father replied, 'If they were furnished with turnip seed, they might raise some turnips.' 'Very well,' said the Governor, 'that you shall have. Accordingly from Montreal he sent some seed, and each man taking a handful thereof, they cleared a spot of ground in the centre of where the town of Kingston now stands, and raised a fine crop of turnips, which served for food the ensuing winter, with the Government rations.

"The above is at your service.

"With much respect,
"JAS. RICHARDSON.
"Clover Hill, Toronto, 1st December, 1859."

Transmitted to the Author by a gentleman in Nova Scotia, taken from the "Political Magazine," published in London 1783:

"When the loyal refugees from the Northern provinces were informed of the resolution of the House of Commons against offensive war with the rebels, they instantly saw there were no hopes left them of regaining their ancient settlements, or of settling down again in their native country.

"Those of them, therefore, who had been forward in taking up arms, and in fighting the battles of the mother country, finding themselves deserted, began to look out for a place of refuge, and Nova Scotia being the nearest place to their old plantations, they determined on settling in that province. Accordingly, to the number of 500 embarked for Annapolis Royal; they had arms and ammunition, and one year's provisions, and were put under the care and convoy of his Majesty's ship the *Amphitrite*, of 24 guns, Captain Robert Briggs. This officer behaved to them with great attention, humanity, and generosity, and saw them safely landed and settled in the barracks at Annapolis, which the Loyalists soon repaired. There was plenty of wild fowl in the country, and at that time, which was last fall, a goose sold for two shillings, and a turkey for two shillings and sixpence. The captain was at £200 expense out of his own pocket in order to render the passage and arrival of the unfortunate Loyalists in some degree comfortable to them. Before Captain Briggs sailed from Annapolis, the grateful Loyalists waited on him with the following address:

"*To Robert Briggs, Esquire, Commander of His Majesty's Ship* '*Amphitrite.*'

"The loyal refugees who have emigrated from New York, to settle in Nova Scotia, beg your acceptance of their warmest thanks for the kind and unremitted attention you have paid to their preservation and safe conduct at all times during their passage.

"Driven from their respective dwellings for their loyalty to our King, after enduring innumerable hardships, and seeking a settlement in a land unknown to us, our distresses were sensibly relieved during an uncomfortable passage by your humanity, ever attentive to our preservation.

"Be pleased to accept of our most grateful acknowledgments, so justly due to you and the officers under your command, and be assured we shall remember your kindness with the most grateful sensibility.

" We are, with the warmest wishes for your health, happiness, and a prosperous voyage,
" With the greatest respect,
" Your most obedient humble servants,
" In behalf of the refugees,
" AMOS BOTSFORD,
" TH. WARD,
" FRED. HANSIR,
" SAM. CUMMINS,
" ELIJAH WILLIAMS.*
" Annapolis Royal, the 20th of October, 1782."

Letter with Enclosure from the Hon. R. Hodgson, Chief Justice of Prince Edward Island.

" CHARLOTTETOWN, Prince Edward Island, 12th June, 1861.
" SIR,—
" I recently perused, in a newspaper published in Halifax, Nova Scotia, called the 'British Colonist,' a statement to the purport that you contemplate publishing a history of 'The British United Empire Loyalists of America,' and have issued a circular to the descendants of the Loyalists, asking for information relating to the lives and adventures of their forefathers.

" I have not seen your circular, and possibly the whole thing may be a mere newspaper fabrication; but it is stated so circumstantially as to carry with it an air of truth, and I have been induced to copy a brief memoir of my maternal grandfather, Lieut.-Colonel Joseph Robinson, in his own handwriting, now in my possession, and to enclose it to you herewith, to be made use of as you think fit in your intended publication. The memoir would appear, from a statement contained in it, to be written in obedience to some order from the then Secretary at War, possibly calling upon the Loyalists in receipt of half-pay from the British Government for a record of their services, to meet parliamentary enquiry; it is marked on the back of the draft, in Colonel Robinson's handwriting, as 'transmitted.' He died in this Island (formerly St. John's Island, now Prince Edward Island) in 1808 or 1809. Colonel Robinson was a native of Virginia, and emigrated from somewhere about James River,

---

* This must be the grandfather of General W. Fenwick Williams, of Kars.

in that province, to South Carolina, where he resided at the commencement of the revolution. After a reward had been offered for his life, as stated in his memorial, and he had been compelled to abscond, a party of rebels visited his plantation and burned to the ground his dwelling-house and every building upon it, scarcely giving time to my grandmother (as she has often told me) to drag out of the house her two female children in time to save their lives. My grandmother was a woman of heroic spirit, and she, accompanied by a single faithful negro slave, made her way on horseback, in an overland journey of several hundred miles, to East Florida, where she joined her husband. In this journey she carried one of her children before her on the same horse, and the negro man carried the other in the same way on the horse he rode.

"At the termination of the contest, my grandfather's property, a large and valuable one, was confiscated by the victors, and he embarked with his family for the island of Jamaica, was unfortunately shipwrecked by the way, and lost every particle of property he had left, he, his wife and children, with difficulty escaping drowning. After a short residence in that island he emigrated to St. John's, in the Province of New Brunswick, and ultimately came to this island.

"He was a member of the House of Assembly of this colony, and its Speaker afterward; an Assistant-Justice of the Supreme Court, and member of the Executive Council, such Council at that time also exercising legislative functions. These last-named offices of Judge and member of Council he held up to his decease.

"I was much too young at his death to be enabled to say anything of my personal knowledge of him; but from his papers which I have perused, I am warranted in saying that he was a man of a refined mind, an excellent classical scholar, with a great taste for astronomy, and possessing no ordinary talent in that science, which seems to have amused and occupied his mind in his latter years. The only reward he received was the half-pay of a lieutenant-colonel (his Judgeship was an honorary one, having no salary or emolument); this he enjoyed up to the period of his decease.

"I have somewhat hurriedly put together these observations. You may rely upon the truth of the facts stated, and they are at your service if coming within the scope and meaning of your intended history. At the same time, if the thing be a newspaper hoax, I must beg you to excuse the liberty I have taken in addressing you, and please burn this and the copy of the memoir.

"I have the honour to be, Sir,
"Your obedient servant,
"R. HODGSON,
"Chief Justice of Prince Edward Island."

Report of Joseph Robinson, Lieutenant-Colonel of the late Regiment of South Carolina Royalists, now residing in the Island of St. John, in the Gulf of St. Lawrence.

"To the Right Honourable William Wyndham, Secretary at War.

"At the commencement of the American rebellion, I was an inhabitant of the Province of South Carolina, and major of a regiment of the King's Militia in Cambden District.

"The insurgents formed a camp in Ninety-six district, and were recruiting men, declaring that as soon as they had forces sufficient for their purpose they would burn and destroy the houses and property of all persons who refused to join them in opposing the King and the authority of Great Britain.

"I then waited upon Lord William Campbell, the Governor of the Province, and received written orders from his lordship to levy forces and march against the rebels, in consequence of which I advanced with about 2,000 men, and found them fortified at Ninety-six Court-house. We defeated them and destroyed their fortifications.

"But in the meantime the violence of the insurgents obliged Lord William Campbell to depart from his Province, and our small army of Royal Volunteers was left without further orders, money, or military stores; wherefore, with much reluctance, I was under the necessity of desiring the men to return to their respective habitations, and by all means not to suffer any false pretences of the rebel party to deceive them, or to efface their principles of loyalty, until we should enjoy a more favourable opportunity.

"A reward being then offered for my life, personal safety induced me to retire to the Cherokee Indian nation, afterwards to the Creek Indians, and, passing through many dangers and suffering various hardships, at length arrived at Saint Augustine, in the Province of East Florida, in the year 1777. Soon afterwards, a party of about 300 men, being some of those I formerly commanded in South Carolina, joined me there.

"I formed the regiment, which was styled the South Carolina Royalists, of which General Prevost appointed me lieutenant-colonel, and soon after I received my commission from Sir Henry Clinton, the Commander-in-Chief.

"The said regiment acted in East Florida, Georgia, and South Carolina, in the course of which service I was in several engagements against the enemy—viz., at the Alligator Bridge, in East Florida; at Doctor Brimstone's Plantation, in Georgia; at New Port Meeting-house, in Georgia; at New Port Bridge, in Georgia; at Stone Ferry, in South Carolina; and afterwards at the reduction of Sunbury Fort, in the Province of Georgia, and the fortifications of Charlestown, in South Carolina. The order from the office of the Secretary at War was not seen or known by me until the 24th of April, 1797; and that I am now fifty-five years of age.

(Signed) "JOSEPH ROBINSON,
"*Lieut.-Colonel of the late South Carolina Royalist Regiment.*
"Charlottetown, Island of St. John,
    "April 26th, 1797.
"Half-pay commenced 7th November, 1783."

Letter from Colonel John C. Clark, respecting his Father's Sufferings in the Revolutionary War, and Settlement in the Midland District.

"ERNEST TOWN, July 9th, 1861.
"Rev. Egerton Ryerson, D.D.
    "REVEREND SIR,—
"Having seen your circular, I write to inform you of my late father's connection with the war of the revolution in the then British colonies. My father, Robert Clark, Esq., late of the township of Ernest Town, in the county of Addington, deceased, was born March 16th, 1744, on Quaker Hill, in Dutchess county, and Province of New York. He learned the trade of carpenter and millwright, and was the owner of two farms. When the war commenced, his loyal proclivities made it danger-

ous for him to remain at home, and he joined the British standard as a volunteer in 1776. He had a few opportunities of visiting his family privately, who consisted then of a wife and two children (boys); another son was born during his absence, who was called Robert (after his father), on which occasion the nurse—being a violent *Tory*—whispered the secret to some of the rebels' wives in the vicinity, that Robert Clark was at home, well knowing the secret would be divulged; and for several days and nights after 'there were liers-in-wait' about the house to capture the Tory when he made his exit. At length the said nurse told them they had been hoaxed.

"I have a powder-horn now in my possession, which my father owned in the time of the war, with his name cut on it, with the date 'Fort Edward, November 4th, 1776.' His family were driven from their home and his lands confiscated. Being with General Burgoyne's army on the 16th of October, 1777, the day previous to the general's surrender of his army to Generals Gates and Arnold, Burgoyne mustered the provincial volunteers, and told them that he was obliged to surrender his army; that they must leave the camp that night, and, if possible, avoid the army, and try to find their way to Canada.

"They left accordingly, and after some weeks of great suffering and privation, my father reached Canada. He subsequently served two years in his Majesty's provincial regiment called 'Loyal Rangers,' commanded by Major Edward Jessup, and was in Captain Jonathan Jones' company, and was discharged the 24th of December, 1783.

"In 1782-83 he was employed by Government to erect the Kingston Mills (then Cataraqui), preparatory to the settlement of the Loyalists in this section of the Province of Quebec. While there employed, his wife and three children arrived in Canada, in the autumn of 1783; they wintered at Sorel, where they all were afflicted with the small-pox, and being entirely among strangers, most of whom spoke a language not understood by them, they were compelled to endure more than the usual amount of suffering incident to that disease; the husband being at a distance, and in the employ of Government, could not leave to administer to their necessity.

"In 1784 his family joined him at the Mills, after immense

suffering, having been separated by the vicissitudes of war for the term of *seven years.*

"In 1785 he removed with his family to lot No. 34, in the 1st concession of Ernest Town (where he had three children born, and of the six I am the only survivor), in which year he was again employed by Government to build the Napanee Mills.

"He was appointed a Justice of the Peace for the (then) district of Mecklenburg in July, 1788, and subsequently an officer in the militia; he joined the first Methodist class formed in Ernest Town by the Rev. William Losee, in 1791, and remained a consistent member during his life. He died the 17th December, 1823.

"If you can glean anything from the above sketch to assist you in your new work, I shall be much gratified.

"I have the honour to be, Rev. Sir,

"Your obedient servant,

"JOHN C. CLARK."

Adventures and Sufferings of Captain William Hutchison, and his Settlement in Walsingham, County of Norfolk; communicated by his grandson, J. B. Hutchison, Esquire.

"In the beginning of the wars of 1776, William Hutchison (my grandfather) was urged to join the rebel army (he living at that time in New Jersey); but he boldly declared, *death before dishonour.* After being harassed about for some time, and leaving a wife and eight children to the mercy of their enemies, he with a number of others tried to make their way to the British army, and were followed by a large force of the enemy; but when they found themselves so greatly outnumbered (being about ten to one), they tried to make their escape to an old barn; but every one of the unfortunate men was caught and hanged but himself. They did not succeed in finding him, he hiding among the bushes. While he lay hidden among some elder bushes, one of the enemy pulled up the bush where he lay, saying 'this would be a d—d good place for a —— to hide,' but the shadow falling on him completely hid him from sight. His captain, James J. Lett, was among the unhappy victims, grandfather being lieutenant under him at the time. His comrades being all killed, he tried to escape from his covert, but they had stationed sentries all around; he could hear them swearing vengeance on him if they could find him. It being bright moonlight, he could see quite a long distance. He crawled along on his hands and knees across a field, and got into the middle of the road; when the sentries, one on either side of him, got into a quarrel and came close to him before they settled their dispute; having done so, they turned to go away; he then made his escape and got to the British army. After suffering all the horrors of a war lasting seven years, losing his property—everything but his loyalty—and that, having extended faithfully through the *whole family*, is not likely to be lost. His wife and six of his children died from the sufferings consequent upon such a war. Previous to this he had received a captain's commission. After the war closed, he went to New Brunswick, and remained there fourteen years, coming to Canada in 1801, and settled in the township of Walsingham. My father, Alexander Hutchison, was the only surviving son by his first wife. In the war of 1812, my grandfather went out against the enemy with his sons, Alexander, David, and James, in which war my father lost his life.

" Hoping you may be able to find something in these fragments which will be interesting to you,

" I remain, with the greatest respect,
" Yours most faithfully,
"J. B. HUTCHISON."

Patriotic feelings—Early Settlement of Prince Edward County and Neighbouring Townships.

Extracts of an address entitled "Scraps of Local History," delivered by Canniff Haight, Esq., before the Mechanics' Institute of Picton, March 16th, 1859:

"If I feel a pride in one thing more than another, it is that I am a Canadian. I rejoice more in being the descendant of these early pioneers of Canada, than if noble blood coursed my veins. I point you back with more unmitigated pleasure to that solitary log cabin in the wilderness which once bordered your fine bay, as the home of my fathers, than I would to some baronial castle in other lands.

"' Is there for honest poverty,
  That hangs his head, and a' that?

> The coward slave we pass him by—
> We dare be poor for a' that.
> For a' that, and a' that,
> Our toils obscure and a' that;
> The rank is but the guinea's stamp,
> The man's the gowd for a' that!"

"We love our country. Thousands of sweet recollections cluster round our childhood's homes, and as we think of them the words of Scott occur to us:

> "'Breathes there a man with soul so dead,
> Who never to himself hath said,
> This is my own, my native land;
> Whose heart hath ne'er within him burned,
> As home his footsteps he hath turned'——

"What part of the world can you point me to to show such rapid changes as have occurred here? Where among the countries of the earth shall we find a quicker and more vigorous growth? Seventy years ago this beautiful and wealthy county of Prince Edward was one dense and untrod forest. We can hardly realize the fact, that even one century has not passed away since those strong-hearted men pushed their way into the wilderness of Upper Canada. Were they not heroes?

"In the summer of the year 1795, or thereabouts, a company of six persons, composed of two married men and their wives, with two small children, pushed a rough-looking and somewhat unwieldy little boat away from the shore in the neighbourhood of Poughkeepsie, and turned its prow up the Hudson. A rude sail was hoisted, but it flapped lazily against the slender mast. The two men betake themselves to the oars. The sun was just showing his face above the eastern woods as they pulled out into the river. The boat was crowded with sundry household matters—all carefully packed up and stowed away; a very small place was left at the stern, and was occupied by the two women and the children. The mother was a small and delicate-looking creature, well and neatly dressed. Had you been there, you would have observed tear after tear dropping from the pale cheek, as she bent in silence over her youngest babe; and see, the eyes of that young father, too, are suffused with tears. Why do they weep? Whither are they bound? Not a word is spoken. They are too sad to talk. Still the oar keeps its measured stroke, and they glide slowly on, and thus may we follow them day after day. Now and then a gentle breeze fills the sail, and wafts the small boat on. When the shades of evening begin to fall around them, they push to shore, and rear a temporary tent. Then the frugal supper is spread upon the green grass, and they gather round it, and forget their toils in speculations upon the future. But the morrow draws on, with its demands upon their strength; so they lay them down to rest. In due course they reach Albany, then a small Dutch town filled with Dutch people, Dutch comforts and frugality, and Dutch cabbage. This in those days was one of the outposts of civilization. Beyond was a wilderness-land but little known. Some necessaries are purchased, and again our little company launch away. They reach the place where the city of Troy now stands, and turn away to the left into the Mohawk river, and proceed slowly, and often with great difficulty, up the rapids and windings of the stream. The rich and fertile valley of the Mohawk of to-day was then the home of the Indian. There the celebrated Chief Brant had lived but a short time before, but had now withdrawn into the wilds of Western Canada. The voyagers, after several days of hard labour and difficulty, emerge into the little lake Oneida, lying in the northwestern part of the State of New York, through which they pass with ease and pleasure. The most difficult part of their journey had been passed. They reach the Onondago river, and soon pass down it to Oswego, then an old fort which the French had reared when they possessed the country as a barrier against the encroachments of the wily Indian. Several bloody frays have occurred here, but our friends did not pause to learn their history. Their small craft now danced upon the wide bosom of Ontario, but they did not push out into the lake, and away across it. No; they are careful sailors, and they believed no doubt 'that small boats should not venture far from shore,' and so they wind along it until they reach Gravely Point, now known by the more dignified name of Cape Vincent. Here they strike across the channel, and thence around the lower end of Wolf Island, and into Kingston Bay, when they come to shore and transact some business. There were not many streets or fine store-houses in Kingston at this time. A few log-houses composed the town. An addition was made to their diminished stock of eatables, and away they push again. They steer now up the Bay of Quinté; and what a wild and beautiful scene that must have been! Could those toil-worn voyagers have failed to mark it? Why do they slacken their pace? Why do they so often rest upon their oars and look around? Why do they push into this little cove and that? Why do they laugh and talk more than usual? Perhaps their journey is drawing to an end! We shall see. They go up the bay until they reach township number five. This township, now known as Adolphustown, is composed of five points or arms of land, which run out into the bay. They run round three of these points, and turn down an arm of the bay called Hay-bay, and after proceeding some two miles pull to shore. Their journey it would seem had come to an end, for they begin at once to unload their boat and build a tent. The sun sinks down behind the western woods, and they, weary and worn, lay down to rest. Six weeks had passed since we saw them launch away in quest of this wilderness home. Look at them, and tell me what you think of the prospect. Is it far enough away from the busy haunts of men to suit you? or would you not rather sing,

"'Oh, Solitude, where are the charms
Which sages have seen in thy face?
Better dwell in the midst of alarms,
Than reign in this horrible place.'

"With the first glimmer of the morning's light, all hands are up and at work. A small spot is cleared away; trees are felled and a house is built. I fancy that it was not large nor commodious; that the rooms were not numerous nor spacious. The furniture, I suppose, did not amount to much either in quality or quantity; an inventory thereof would probably run somewhat after this fashion—a pot or two, perhaps a few quite common plates, cups and saucers, knives and forks, a box or two of linen, a small lot of bed-clothes, etc., with a

"'Chest contriv'd a double debt to pay—
A bed by night, a chest of drawers by day.'

"This, ladies and gentlemen, is no fancy sketch, but one drawn from the shadows of the past. You may find hundreds of similar adventures in the past history of our country. Such was the first home of the young wife whom I have mentioned.

She had once lived in comfort, but by the fate of war the home of a father and husband had been confiscated, and hence they had sought for a dwelling-place in Canada, when England offered other homes to those who had fought her battles. A grandchild of that couple now stands before you.

"We can form no correct idea of the difficulties which beset these early inhabitants, nor of the hardships and privations they endured. They were not unfrequently reduced to the very verge of starvation, yet they struggled on. Tree after tree fell before the axe, and the small clearing was turned to immediate account. A few necessaries of life were produced, and even these, such as they were, were the beginnings of comfort—comfort indeed, but far removed from the idea we associate with the term.

"But time rolled on. The openings in the forest grew larger and wider. The log cabins began to multiply, and the curling smoke told a silent but cheerful tale. There dwelt a neighbour, miles perhaps away, but a neighbour nevertheless. The term bears a wide difference now-a-days. If you would like an idea of the proximity of humanity and the luxury of society in those days, just place a few miles, say six or eight, of dense woods between you and your neighbour, and you may get a faint conception of the delights of a home in the woods.

"There are some here, I presume, who have heard their parents or their grandparents tell of the dreadful sufferings they endured the second year after the settlement of the Bay of Quinté country. The Government was to provide food, etc., for two years. It could hardly be expected that men could go into the woods with their families, and clear up and raise enough for their support, the first or even the second year. The second year's Government supply, through some bad management, was frozen up in the lower part of the St. Lawrence, and in consequence the people were reduced to a state of famine. Men willingly offered pretty much all they possessed for food. I could show you one of the finest farms in Hay-bay that was offered to my grandfather for a half hundred of flour, and refused. A very respectable old lady, whom numbers of you knew, but who some time since went away to her rest—whose offspring, some at least, are luxuriating in comfort above the middle walks of life—was wont in those days to wander away early in the spring to the woods and gather and eat the buds of the basswood, and then bring an apron or basketfull home to the children. Glad were they to pluck the rye and barley heads, as soon as the kernel had formed, for food; and not many miles from Picton a beef's bone passed from house to house, and was boiled again and again in order to extract some nutriment. It seems incredulous, but it is no fiction, and surely no homœopathist would desire to be placed on a lower regimen.

"I feel it unnecessary almost for me to tell you that the largest proportion of the first settlers of this province were Americans who had adhered to the cause of England. After the capture of General Burgoyne, many of the Royalists with their families moved into Canada; and upon the evacuation of New York, at the close of the war, a still greater number followed. A large proportion of these were soldiers, disbanded and left without employ. Some there were who had lost their estates by confiscation; so that nearly all were destitute and dependent upon the liberality of the country whose battles they had fought, and for whose cause they had suffered. In order, therefore, to reward their loyalty and relieve their present necessities, as well as to supply some means of future subsistence, the British Government determined upon making liberal grants of the land in Upper Canada and other provinces to the American Loyalists. The measure was not only an act of justice and humanity, but it was sound in policy and has been crowned with universal success.

"The grants were made free of expense and upon the following scale: A field-officer received 5,000 acres; a captain, 3,000; a subaltern, 2,000; and a private soldier, 200 acres. A survey was accordingly made, commencing near Lake St. Francis, then the highest French settlement, and extended along the shores of the St. Lawrence up to Lake Ontario, and thence along the lake, and round the Bay of Quinté. Townships were laid out, and then subdivided into concessions and lots of 200 acres. These townships were numbered, but remained without names for many years afterwards. Of these numbers there were two divisions—one including the townships below Kingston on the river, east to the St. Francis settlement; the others from Kingston, west to the head of the Bay of Quinté. This will at once explain to you the reason why the old people used to talk of first, second, third, fourth town, etc., as far back as we can remember and up to the present. No names were given to the townships by legal proclamation, as we said before, until long after they were settled, and hence the habit was formed of designating them by numbers.

"The settlement of the surveyed portion of the Midland district, so named because of its then central position, commenced in the summer of 1784. The new settlers were supplied with farming utensils, building materials, provisions, and some clothing, for the two first years, at the expense of the nation; and in order that the love of country may take deeper root in the hearts of these true men, the Government determined to put a mark of honour, as the Orders of Council expressed it, upon the families who had adhered to the unity of the empire, and joined the Royal standard in America before the treaty of separation in the year 1783. A list of such persons was directed in 1789 to be made out and returned, to the end that their posterity might be discriminated from the future settlers. From these two emphatic words, the Unity of the Empire, it was styled the U. E. List, and they whose names were entered upon it were distinguished as U. E. Loyalists. You are aware of the fact that this was not a mere empty distinction, but was, in reality, a title of some consequence; for it not only provided for the U. E.'s themselves, but guaranteed unto all their children, upon arriving at the age of twenty-one years, 200 acres of land free from all expense. I always look back on these early acts of the English nation with the fathers of this growing Canada with pleasure, and I venerate the memory of those true and noble-hearted men, who loved their fatherland so well that they even preferred to live under the protection of her flag in the wild woods of Canada, and endure hunger and want, than enjoy the comforts of home under the banner of a rebellious but now independent people. And I hope, ladies and gentlemen, that we, the sons and daughters of those whom our mother country was wont to honour, may never love our country and its institutions less than they.

"Kingston is the oldest Upper Canadian town by many years. Here the white man found his way over a century before any settlement was made or thought of. The crafty and industrious

French Governor, De Courcelles, in order to check the encroachments of the Five Nations, despatched a messenger from Quebec to their chiefs, stating that he had some business of great importance to communicate, and desired them to proceed to Cataraqui, where he would meet them. (I observe here that Cataraqui is an Indian name, and means 'Rocks above water.') As soon as the deputies of the Indians arrived, a Council was held. The Governor informed them that he was going to build a fort there, simply to facilitate the trade between them and to serve as a depot for merchandise. The chiefs, ignorant of the real intent of the design, readily agreed to a proposition which seemed to be intended for their advantage; but this, so far from being the case, or what the Indians expected, was really to be a barrier against them in future wars. While measures were being completed to build the fort, Courcelles was recalled and Count de Frontenac sent out in his place. Frontenac carried out the designs of his predecessor and completed the fort in 1672, which received and retained his name for many years. Kingston was subsequently substituted, and the county received the name of Frontenac."

Letters from the late Rev. George J. Ryerse, dated June 12th and June 23rd, 1861, give some particulars of his father's coming to Canada, and of the earliest settlement of the London District.

His father, Colonel Samuel Ryerse, was appointed Lieutenant of the county, and authorized to organise the militia and appoint the officers, as also the local civil court, of which he was the first Judge. The following letters indicate what he sacrificed and endured for his allegiance to the unity of the empire, and for which allegiance he and thousands of others were banished from the United States and their property confiscated; but the writer has never heard a word from any one of these veteran Loyalists regretting the part he had taken:

"PORT RYERSE, 12th June, 1861.

"MY DEAR COUSIN,—

"I received your circular some time since, but, through forgetfulness, I did not at once give an answer. I am highly gratified with your noble undertaking, and humbly trust that you may live to succeed and be amply rewarded. I am sorry that I have no documents that would be of use to you. You are aware of the staunch loyalty that was inherent in our parents, that made them sacrifice everything out of regard for the British Throne, and endure every privation in their early settlement in this country. It was in 1794 my father came here, and gave orders to his family that if he should decease while on his way through the United States, to take his body to British soil for burying. At that time there were but eight families residing within thirty miles of this place, except Indians; no roads; the nearest mill 100 miles distant by water (at Niagara Falls). My father purchased corn of the Indians at the Grand River, thirty miles from home, and carried it home on his shoulders. Afterwards he bought a yoke of oxen of the Indians, and on a toboggin sled put his son, and with his axe and compass made his way through the woods and streams to his beloved home. Two years afterwards he built a saw mill, and afterwards a grist mill. These nearly proved his ruin, not understanding the business, and very little to sustain them; they were badly built, and proved a bother to him, but still a great help to the settlement for a long time. Merchandise was so very expensive and produce so very cheap that the early settlers could barely exist; but they loved their country, and they have gone to their rest, and I feel proud that so many of their children inherit their spirit.

"I am, yours truly,
"GEORGE J. RYERSE.
"Rev. E. Ryerson."

"PORT RYERSE, 23rd June, 1861.
"DEAR COUSIN,—
"Your kind letter I received, and in answer to your suggestions I have to state that my father was a captain in the New Jersey Volunteers during the American Revolution; and at its close in 1783, having his property confiscated in the United States, he went to New Brunswick and drew lands according to his rank as captain; but being disappointed both in soil and climate, finding it to be sterile and uncongenial, he determined to remove to Canada. In the spring of 1794 he started and went to Long Island, the place where the city of Brooklyn now

stands, and there left his family. While on foot, he went to Canada (U.C.) to better his condition by looking out a more congenial place. Having accomplished his purpose, he started, at the opening of navigation, with his family, in company with Captain Bonta's family, first on board a sloop (as all was then done by sloops) to Albany, thence by land to Schenectady, where they procured a flat-bottomed boat, in which families and baggage were put; thence, with poles and oars, against a strong current, they made their way up the Mohawk river a long distance, until they came to a place called Wood Creek, which they again navigated for a long distance toward Lake Ontario, until they approached a stream called the Oswego, which to enter they had to draw their boat by hand across a portage (I think some two miles); thence down this stream to the lake to Oswego; thence up the lake in this boat westward to the Niagara river; thence up the Niagara as far as Queenston, where again they had to pass over a portage of nine miles around the Falls to Chippawa; thence up the river eighteen miles to Lake Erie; thence up the lake westward eighty miles to the place my father had selected (and which is now my home), arriving here 1st July, 1795. It was in this boat that they went to mill, as before stated to you. A kind Providence furnished plenty of fish and game at this early day, or the people could not have survived. The total absence of roads, schools, and religious teachers for many years were among the heavy privations that the early settlers had to endure.

"I remain, yours truly,
"GEORGE J. RYERSE.

"Rev. E. Ryerson."

Historical Memoranda by Mrs. Amelia Harris, of Eldon House, London, Ontario, only daughter of the late Colonel Samuel Ryerse, and sister of the late Rev. Geo. J. Ryerse, writer of the foregoing short letters.

The husband of Mrs. Harris was an active and scientific officer in the Royal Navy, having been employed with the late Admirals Bayfield and Owen in the survey of the Canadian lakes and rivers, by the Admiralty, during the years 1815 to 1817. It was during the progress of this survey that Miss

Ryerse married. After a few years' residence at Kingston, Mr. and Mrs. Harris returned to a beautiful homestead on Long Point Bay, intending to reside there permanently. In the days of the early settlement, a more refined and cultivated society was to be found in the country than usually in the towns and villages. Mr. Harris was at once selected by the various Governments of the day to be the recipient of various Government offices. During the years 1837-38 he took an active part in quelling the rebellion, and is believed by many to have been the head and front and organizer of the expedition which sent the steamer *Caroline* over the Falls. He was the first man on her deck, and the last to leave, having set her on fire.

The late Edward Ermatinger, in his Life of Colonel Talbot, refers to the Harris family as follows:

A.D. 1834. "By degrees the officers of the Court removed to London, and Mr. Harris was the first to build a house of considerable dimensions on a handsome piece of ground highly elevated above the banks of the River Thames. This house was long the resort of the first men in Canada, and in this house the venerable founder of the Talbot settlement lay during his first serious illness, while on his way to England. Every man of rank or distinction who visited this part of Canada became the guest of Mr. Harris—the late Lord Sydenham, the various lieutenant-governors and governor-generals, and the present Lord Derby, were among the number."

In the following memoranda, which Mrs. Harris wrote more than twenty years since, at the wish of her children, but not for publication, she gives a graphic and highly interesting account of her father's early settlement in Canada, and the circumstances of the first settlers, and the state of society of that time:

"Captain Samuel Ryerse, one of the early settlers in Canada, was the descendant of an old Dutch family in New Jersey, and both his father and grandfather held judicial appointments under Kings George II. and III. When the rebellion commenced in 1776, and the British Government was anxious to raise provincial troops, they offered commissions to any young gentlemen who could enlist a certain number of young men; sixty, I think, entitled them to a captaincy. My father, Captain Ryerse, being popular in his neighbourhood, found no difficulty in enlisting double the number required, and on presenting himself and men at headquarters, New York, was gazetted captain in the 4th Battalion New Jersey Volunteers, in which regiment he served with distinction during the seven years' war.

"After the acknowledgment of American Independence by England, and the British troops were about to be disbanded, the British Government offered them a free transport to New Brunswick, and a grant of land. When there, little choice was left to those who had sacrificed all for connection with the mother country. On my father's arrival in New Brunswick he obtained a lot of land in or near Fredericton, the present seat of government; and there he met my mother, who was a refugee also, and they were married.

"After remaining there several years, his friends entreated him to return to New York, holding out great inducements if he would consent to do so. He accepted the offer of his friends and returned, but he soon discovered that the rancorous, bitter feelings which had arisen during the war were not extinct, and that it was too soon for a British subject to seek a home in the United States. My mother loved her native city, and might not have been induced again to leave it had it not been for domestic affliction. She brought from the healthy climate of New Brunswick four fine children, all of whom she buried in New York in eight weeks. She gave birth to four more; three of those had died also, and she felt sure if she stayed there she would lose the only remaining one. Therefore she readily consented to my father's proposal to come to Canada, where his old friend, General Simcoe, was at that time governor. In the summer of 1794 my father and a friend started for Canada The journey was then a most formidable one, and before commencing it wills were made and farewells given, as if a return was more than doubtful.

"On his arrival at Niagara he was warmly greeted by his old friend, General Simcoe, who advised him by all means to settle in Canada, holding out many inducements for him to do so. He promised my father a grant of 3,000 acres of land as a captain in the army, 1,200 as a settler, and that my mother and each of her sons should have a grant of 1,200, and each of her daughters a grant of 600 acres.

"My father was pleased with what he saw of the country,

and heard a favourable account of the climate, and decided at once to return as early the ensuing year as possible. On his return to New York he commenced making arrangements for his move the ensuing spring.

"It would be much easier for a family to go from Canada to China now, than it was to come from New York to Canada then. He had to purchase a boat large enough to hold his family and goods, with supplies of groceries for two or three years, with farming utensils, tools, pots, boilers, etc., and yet the boat must not be too large to get over the portage from the Hudson to the Mohawk. As there were no waggon roads from Albany to the Niagara frontier, families coming to Canada had to come down the Mohawk to Lake Ontario, and enter Canada in that way. My father found it a weary journey, and was months in accomplishing it.

"On my father's arrival at Niagara, at that time the seat of government, he called on his Excellency General Simcoe, who had just returned from a tour through the Province of Canada West, then one vast wilderness. He asked General Simcoe's advice as to where he should choose his resting-place. He recommended the county of Norfolk (better known for many years as Long Point), which had been recently surveyed.

"As it was now drawing towards the close of summer, it would require all their time to get up a shanty and prepare for the winter. Consequently, arrangements were made immediately for continuing their journey. The heavy batteau was transported from Queenston to Chippawa, around the Falls, a distance of twelve miles. Supplies were added to those brought from New York, and they once more started on their journey, bidding goodbye to the last vestige of civilization. They were twelve days making 100 miles—not bad travelling in those days, taking the current of the river and lake, adverse winds, and an unknown coast into consideration.

"When my father came within the bay formed by Long Point, he watched the coast for a favourable impression, and, after a scrutiny of many miles, the boat was run into a small creek, the high banks sloping gradually on each side.

"Directions were given to the men to erect the tent for my mother. My father had not been long on shore before he decided that that should be his home. In wandering about, he came to an eminence which would, when the trees were felled, command a view of the harbour. He gazed around him for a few moments and said, 'Here I will be buried,' and there, after fourteen years' toil, he sleeps in peace.

"The men my father hired in New York all wished to settle in Canada, and were glad to avail themselves of an opportunity of coming free of expense, and promised to remain with him until he had a log-house built, and had made himself comfortable. He had paid them a great portion of their wages in advance, to enable them to get necessaries in New York. Immediately on his arrival at Niagara they left him, with one exception, and went in search of localities for themselves, very little regard at that time being paid to engagements, and there being no means to enforce them; consequently, he had to hire fresh hands at Niagara, who were men, like the former, on the look-out for land. After one day's rest at Ryerse Creek, they re-embarked, and went fourteen miles further up the bay, to the house of a German settler who had been there two years, and had a garden well stocked with vegetables.

"The appearance of the boat was hailed with delight by those solitary beings, and my mother and child were soon made welcome, and the best that a miserable log-house, or rather hut, could afford was at her service. This kind, good family consisted of father, mother, one son and one daughter. Mr. Proyer, the father, was a fine-looking old man with a flowing beard, and was known for many years throughout the Long Point settlement as 'Doctor Proyer.' He possessed a thorough knowledge of witches, their ways and doings, and the art of expelling them, and also the use of the divining rod, with which he could not only find water, but could also tell how far below the surface of the earth precious metals were concealed, but was never fortunate enough to discover any in the neighbourhood of Long Point. Here my father got his goods under shelter and left my mother, and returned to Ryerse Creek, intending to build a log-house as soon as possible. Half a dozen active men will build a very comfortable primitve log-house in ten or twelve days; that is, cut and lay up the logs and chink them, put on a bark roof, cut holes for the windows and door, and build a chimney of mud and sticks. Sawing boards by hand for floor and doors, making sash and shingles, is an after and longer process.

"But soon after my father returned he fell ill with Lake fever; his men erected a shanty, open in front like an Indian camp, placed my father in it, and left him with his son, a lad of fifteen years of age, the son of a former wife, as his only attendant. When my father began to recover, my half brother was taken ill, and there they remained almost helpless, alone for three weeks.

"My mother hearing nothing of or from them, became almost frantic, as some of the party were to have returned in a few days. She prevailed upon Mike Proyer, the son, to launch his bark canoe, and to take her and my brother, then a year and a half old, in search of my father. On approaching Ryerse Creek, after a many days' paddle along the coast, they saw a blue smoke curling above the trees, and very soon my mother stood in front of the shanty, where my father sat with a stick, turning an immense turkey, which hung, suspended by a string, before a bright fire. The day previous, a large flock of wild turkeys had come very near his camp, and commenced fighting. Without moving from his shanty, he killed six at one shot. He afterwards, at single shots, killed eight more, and the united strength of him and my brother was scarcely sufficient to bring them into camp. My mother used to look back upon that evening as one of the happiest of her life. She had found her loved ones, after torturing her mind with all sorts of horrors —Indians, wild beasts, snakes, illness, and death had all been imagined. The next day, Mike Proyer's canoe was laden with wild turkeys, and he returned alone, as my mother refused to separate herself again from my father. A few days after, a party of pedestrians arrived, on the look-out for land, and they at once set to work and put up the wished-for log-house or houses, for there were two attached, which gave them a parlour, two bedrooms, and a kitchen and garret. On removing from the shanty to this house, my mother felt as if in a palace. They bought a cow from Mr. Proyer and collected their goods, and when cold weather set in they were comfortable.

"My father found it necessary to return to Niagara to secure the patent for the lands he had selected, and also to provide for wants not previously known or understood. The journey was long and tedious, travelling on foot on the lake shore, and by Indian paths through the woods, fording the creeks as he best could. At the Grand River, or River Ouse, there was an Indian reservation of six miles on each side of the river from its mouth to its source, owned by two tribes of Indians, Mohawks and Cayugas, whose wants were well supplied with very little exertion of their own, as the river and lake abounded with fish, the woods with deer and smaller game, and the rich flats along the river yielded abundance of maize with very little cultivation. They were kind and inoffensive in their manner, and would take the traveller across the river, or part with their products for a very small reward.

"On my father's application for the lots he had chosen, he was told by the Council that the two at Ryerse Creek could only be granted conditionally, as they possessed very valuable water privileges, and that whoever took them must build both a flour and a saw-mill. My father accepted the conditions, secured the grant for his own lands, but left my mother's for a future day, and at once made arrangements for purchasing the necessary material for his mills—bolting cloths, mill-stones, iron, and screws, etc.—and then with a back load of twine, provisions for his journey, and his light fusee, he commenced his return home, where he arrived in good health, after an absence of twelve days. It is only the settlers in a new country that know what pleasure a safe return can give.

"Long Point now boasted four inhabitants in twenty miles, all settled on the lake shore. Their nearest neighbour, Peter Walker, at the mouth of Patterson's Creek [now Port Dover], was three miles distant by water and six by land. But from this time, 1795, for several years to come, there was a constant influx of settlers.

"Few days passed without some foot traveller asking a night's rest. The most of the travellers would set to work cheerfully for a few days, and assist in cutting roads, making sheds, sawing boards, or felling timber. The winter was now fast approaching, and much was to be done in preparation for the coming spring. My father succeeded in hiring five or six men for as many months. The great object was to get some land cleared, so that they could plant maize, potatoes, and garden vegetables for the next year's consumption. They had also to make preparations for sugar-making, by hollowing out troughs, one to each tree that was tapped, sufficiently large to hold the sap that would run in one day.

"Their evenings were devoted to netting the twine, which my father had purchased at Niagara for that purpose. My mother hired Barbara Proyer as a help, and time passed less heavily than she had imagined. My father had brought with him a sufficient quantity of flour and salt pork to last them a year; for fresh meat and fish he depended upon his gun and spear, and for many years they had always a good supply of both. My father had a couple of deer-hounds, and he used to go to the woods for his deer as a farmer would go to his fold for a sheep. Wild turkey and partridge were bagged with very little skill or exertion, and when the creek and lake were not frozen he need scarcely leave his own door to shoot ducks; but the great sporting ground—and it is still famous, and the resort of sporting gentlemen from Toronto, Woodstock, and indeed all parts of Canada West—is at the head of Long Point Bay. I have known him, several years later, return from there with twenty wild geese and one hundred ducks, the result of a few days' shooting. Pigeons were so plentiful, so late as 1810 and 1812, that they could be knocked down with poles. Great would have been the sufferings of the early settlers had not a kind and heavenly Father made this provision for them. But deer were not the only animals that abounded in the woods; bears and wolves were plentiful, and the latter used to keep up a most melancholy howl about the house at night, so near that my mother could scarcely be persuaded that they were not under the window. The cow, for security, was tied to the kitchen door every night; during the day she accompanied the men to the field they were chopping, and fed upon browse, which kept her fat and in good heart,—the men making a point of felling a maple tree each morning for her special benefit. Their first sugar-making was not very beautiful, but they made sufficient of a very bad quality for the year's consumption. The potatoes gave a great yield; the maize was eaten and destroyed by the racoons; the apple and pear pips grew nicely, as did the peach, cherry, and plum stones, and my mother's balsams and few flowers from the new rich soil were beautiful.

"The summer of 1796 passed away with few incidents at Ryerse Creek, except the arrival of settlers.

"This year there was a total failure of the grain crops, not only in the new settlements, but throughout the United States. The Indians alone had preserved the maize from destruction by the racoons, squirrels and bears, which had invaded the settlements by thousands in search of food, as there were no nuts in the woods. The settlers had now to depend upon the Indians at the Grand River for their bread, and they continued to sell their maize at the same price as formerly, and during the year of scarcity never raised it. My father procured his year's supply, but there were no mills; the nearest ones were south of the Short Hills, seventy miles distant. Lucky was the family that owned a coffee mill in the winter of 1797. My father had a number of hands getting out timber for his mills and clearing land, and when they returned from their work in the evenings they used to grind in the coffee-mill maize for the next day's consumption. They soon learned the exact quantity required, and each man ground his own allowance, dividing that of the rest of the household amongst them. The meal was made into johnny-cakes, eaten hot for breakfast, cold for dinner, and the remainder in mush with milk for supper; and upon this fare they enjoyed perfect good health, were always cheerful, and apparently happy.

"The greatest good-feeling existed amongst the settlers, although they were of all nations and creeds and no creeds. Many of those families who had remained neutral during the revolution to save their property, and still retained their preference for the British Government, now sought homes in Canada, or assisted their sons to do so. The Quakers and Yunkers were amongst the best settlers, as they always brought some property with them, and were generally peaceable and industrious.

"Lands were so easily obtained, and so much encouragement was given by Government to settlers, that many of the half-pay officers and soldiers who had gone to New Brunswick found their way here, as well as many of the idle, discontented, dissipated, vicious and worthless of the United States. But at the Settler's Home all were made welcome; the meals, victuals and night's lodging were freely given to all, and for years after, to my recollection, during the summer season our house was never free from travellers; not that there was any particular merit due to our hospitality, for the man that would have closed his door against a traveller would have been looked upon as worse than a savage. My mother, this summer, had a dreadful alarm, which she used to describe to me with great feeling many years after. My little brother (George), for whose sake she had encountered all the privations and hardships of an early settler, gave rise to numerous fears and anxieties if he was out of her sight a few minutes. Endless misfortunes might befall him; he might be eaten up by wild beasts; or, he might be stolen by the Indians (their stealing children not being a very uncommon occurrence in those days, and during the summer season there used to be hundreds encamped on the beach); or, he might be drowned; or, he might wander away and be lost in the woods; and he would steal away and follow the men to the field when not closely watched. One day George was missing, and great was the commotion. Search was made everywhere, and George's name sounded through the forest in every direction. At last his hat was found in the creek. My mother sat perfectly quiet on the bank, with feelings not easily described, while my father probed the deep holes, and thrust his spear under the driftwood, expecting every time he drew it out to see George's red frock rise to the surface, when she heard with delight a little voice say 'Mamma,' from the opposite side of the creek. And there was George, with his little bare head peeping through the bushes, with his pet cat by his side. The reaction was too much for my mother; she fell fainting to the ground. George had lost his hat walking over a log which the men used as a bridge.

"The settlement was now considered in a most prosperous state; in a half-circle of twenty miles, probably there was a population of a hundred. People had ceased to count the families on their fingers, but no census was taken. The mills were fast advancing towards completion. Some few of the settlers grew wheat sufficient for their own consumption, and a little to sell; but the squirrels, racoons, and pigeons were very destructive to the grain of the early settlers. A dog that was trained for hunting the racoons, or a 'coon dog,' as they were called, was of great value, and the young lads, for many years after, used to make coon parties on fine moonlight nights, and go from farm to farm, killing those animals; and, although the necessity has long passed away, these parties still continue; and, though a virtue and kindness in the commencement, have ended in vice, and the coon parties now meet together to rob orchards and gardens of their best fruit and melons. One bitter cold night in February, 1798, the household was alarmed by the announcement of my mother's illness. No assistance was to be had nearer than three miles; no horses and no roads—only a track through the woods. Mr. Powel, who had just secured a lot near us, volunteered to go in search of Granny McCall, with the ox-team. After some weary hours' watching, the 'gee haw!' was heard on the return in the woods, and Mrs. McCall soon stood beside my mother, and very soon after the birth of a daughter was announced. That daughter is now making this record of the past. The settlement was now increasing so fast that the general voice was for a town, and my father was petitioned to lay one out at the mouth of Ryerse Creek, and was at last prevailed upon to do so, and called it Clarence. The first applicant for a lot was a Mr. Corklin, a very good blacksmith, a mechanic that was very much wanted in the settlement. He was a very intelligent young man for his class, and a great favourite with everyone, although he had one fault, that of indulging in strong drinks occasionally. He bargained for a lot, and put up a frame for a house. My father bought him a set of blacksmith's tools to commence with, and built him a shop. The next thing was a wife. My mother soon saw that a tender feeling was growing up between the young blacksmith and her nurse, a pretty girl, to whom she was much attached. My mother's advice was against the marriage, on account of his one bad habit; but of course she was not listened to, and they were married.

"A few months after the marriage, Mr. Corklin went in a log canoe to the head of the bay, on business, and was to return the next day; but day after day passed, and no Mr. Corklin appeared. At last the poor wife's anxiety became so great that a messenger was sent in search of him. He had been at Dr. Proyer's, but left the day he was expected home. The alarm was given, and search commenced along the lake shore. They found his canoe drifted on shore, laden with game, vegetables and a few apples, his hat, and an empty bottle that smelt of rum; but he was gone. They supposed that he had fallen overboard without upsetting the canoe. His body they could not find for days after, and his wife used to wander along the lake shore, from early dawn until dark, with the hope that she might find his body. One day she saw a number of birds on a drift log that was half out of the water. By the side of this log lay the remains of her husband. The eagles had picked his eyes out, but had only commenced their feast. This was the first death in the settlement. My father took back the lot, paid for the frame house, kept his smith's tools, and so ended his town.

"Upon more mature reflection, he decided that the neighbourhood of a small town would be the reverse of agreeable, as the first inhabitants would be those that were too idle to improve a farm for themselves, and bad habits are generally the attendants of idleness, and that he, in place of being the owner of all, would only be proprietor in common with all the idle and dissipated of a new country.

"On my father's arrival in the country he had been sworn in a justice of the peace for the London and Western districts—a very extensive jurisdiction over wild lands with few inhabitants; for those districts embraced all the lands between Lake Erie and Lake Huron, the Grand River, and Rivers Detroit and St. Clair. Courts were held at Sandwich, a distance of nearly two hundred miles, without roads, so that magistrates had to settle all disputes as they best could, perform all marriages, bury the dead, and prescribe for the sick. In addition to the medicine chest, my father purchased a pair of tooth-drawers, and learned to draw teeth, to the great relief of the suffering. So popular did he become in that way, that in after years they used to entreat him to draw their teeth in preference to a medical man—the one did it gratuitously, the other, of course, charged. My father put up two or three small log-houses which were tenanted by very poor people whose labour he required. From one of these houses my mother hired a nurse, Poll Spragge, who was a merry, laughing, 'who-cares' sort of girl. Upon my mother remarking the scantiness of her wardrobe, which was limited to one garment, a woollen slip that reached from the throat to the feet, Poll related a misfortune which had befallen her a short time before. She then, as now, had but the one article of dress, and it was made of buckskin, a leather something like chamois; and when it became greasy and dirty, her mother said she must wash it that afternoon, as she was going visiting, and that Poll must have her slip dry to put on before her father and mother returned from the field. During the interval, she must, of necessity, represent Eve before her fall. Poll had seen her mother, in the absence of soap, make a pot of strong ley from wood ashes, and boil her father's and brother's coarse linen shirts in it. She subjected her leather slip to the same process. We all know the effect of great heat upon leather. When Poll took her slip from the pot it was a shrivelled-up mass, partly decomposed by the strong ley. Poor Poll was in despair. She watched for the return of her family with no enviable feelings, and when she heard them coming she lifted a board and concealed herself in the potato hole, under the floor. Her mother soon discovered what had befallen Poll, and search was made for her. After a time, a feeble voice was heard from under the floor, and Poll was induced to come forth, by the promise of her mother's second petticoat, which was converted into the slip she then wore. She ended her recital with a merry laugh, and said now she had got service she would soon get herself clothes. But clothing was one of the things most difficult to obtain then. There were very few sheep in the settlement, and if a settler owned two or three, they had to be protected with the greatest care, watched by the children during the day that they might not stray into the woods, and at night penned near the house in a fold, built very high, to secure them from the bears and wolves, which could not always be done.

"There were instances of wolves climbing into pens that they could not get out of. On these occasions they did not hurt the sheep, but were found lying down in a corner like a dog, It is said that the first thought of a wolf on entering a fold is how he is to get out again; and if he finds that difficult, his heart fails him and he makes little effort.

"Wolves were the pests of the country for many years, and, even after they were partially expelled by the settlers, they used to make occasional descents upon the settlements, and many a farmer that counted his sheep by twenties at night, would be thankful if he could muster half a score in the morning. It was flax, the pedlar's pack, and buckskins that the early settlers had to depend upon for clothing when their first supply was run out. Deerskins were carefully preserved and dressed, and the men had trowsers and coats made of them. Though not very becoming, they were said to be very comfortable and strong, and suitable to the work they had to do. Chopping, logging, and clearing wild lands required strong clothing.

"One part of the early clearing was always appropriated to flax, and after the seed was in the ground the culture was given up to the women. They had to weed, pull and thrash out the seeds, and then spread it out to rot. When it was in a proper state for the brake, it was handed over to the men, who crackled and dressed it. It was again returned to the women, who spun and wove it, making a strong linen for shirts and plaid for their own dresses. Almost every thrifty farmhouse had a loom, and both wife and daughters learnt to weave. The pedlar's pack supplied their little finery, the pack generally containing a few pieces of very indifferently printed calicoes at eight and ten shillings, New York currency, a yard; a piece of book-muslin at sixteen and eighteen shillings a yard, and a piece of check for aprons at a corresponding price; some very common shawls and handkerchiefs, white cotton stockings to match, with two or three pieces of ribbon, tape, needles, pins and horn combs; these, with very little variety, used to be the contents of the pedlar's pack. Opening the pack caused much more excitement in a family then than the opening of a fashionable shopkeeper's show-room does at the present day.

"About this time, 1799, a great number of old soldiers, who had served under and with my father, found their way to the Long Point Settlement. One of these soldiers had been taken prisoner with my father at Charleston, and when they were plundered of everything he managed to conceal a doubloon in his hair. With this he supplied my father's wants, who was wounded and suffering. My father now exchanged with him one of his choice lots, that he might be in the settlement and near a mill; and took his location, which was far back in the woods. My uncle [Joseph Ryerson], and several other half-pay officers, came from New Brunswick to visit my father. The pleasure of seeing those loved and familar faces, and again meeting those who had fought the same battles, shared the same dangers, and endured the same hardships, fatigues, and privations for seven long years, and had the same hopes and fears, and the bitter mortification of losing their cause, was indeed great. How many slumbering feelings such a reunion awakened! how many long tales of the past they used to tell, of both love and war! Those officers that came from New Brunswick to visit the country all returned, after a few years, as settlers. The climate of Canada was much preferable, and as an agricultural country was very superior. The population was now becoming so great that the Government thought it necessary to have all the male population, between the ages of sixteen and sixty, enrolled in the Militia. My father was requested to organize a regiment, and to recommend those whom he thought, from their intelligence, good conduct, and former service, most entitled to commissions. He was appointed Lieutenant-Colonel of Militia and Lieutenant of the County, a situation that was afterwards done away with. This duty of selecting officers gave rise to the first awkward feelings that had been exhibited towards him in the settlement. Every man thought he ought to be a captain at the least, and was indignant that my father did not appreciate his merits. Some threatened to stone him; others, to shoot him. The more moderate declared they would not come to his mill, although there was no other within seventy miles. John McCall did not care for my father; he would be a captain without his assistance. He built a large open boat and navigated her for several years, and gloried in the designation of Captain McCall. But, notwithstanding all opposition, the regiment of militia was formed. They used to meet one day in the year for company exercise, and there was a general muster on the 4th of June, the King's birthday, for a general training. These early trainings presented a strange mixture. There were a few old officers, with their fine military bearing, with their guns and remains of old uniforms; and the old soldier, from his upright walk and the way he handled his gun, could easily be distinguished, though clothed in home-spun and buckskin, with the coarse straw hat. The early settlers all had guns of some description, except the very juvenile members, who used to carry canes to represent guns. Those trainings used to be looked forward to with intense interest by all the boys of the neighbourhood, and afforded subjects of conversation for the ensuing year. It was no easy thing in that day to find a level piece of ground that was tolerably clear from stumps sufficiently large to serve for their general trainings.

"Amongst the early settlers there were very few who could afford to hire assistance of any kind. Those that could pay found it easy to get men as labourers; but women servants, unless by mere chance, were not to be had. The native American women would not and will not, even at the present day, go out to service, although almost any of the other neighbours' daughters would be glad to go as helps, doing the same work and eating at the table with their mistress. My father, for many years, used occasionally to take the head of the table with his labourers, to show them he was not too proud to eat with them. My mother was exempt from this, but the help ate at her table, which was considered a sufficient proof of her humility. Many of those helps of early days have since become the wives of squires, captains, majors and colonels of Militia, and are owners of large properties, and they and their descendants drive in their own carriages.

"In the summer of 1800 my mother had a very nice help as nurse. Jenny Decow had been apprenticed to a relative, and, at the age of eighteen, she received her bed, her cow, and two or three suits of clothing (those articles it was customary to give to a bound girl), and was considered legally of age, with the right to earn her own living as she best could.

"My mother soon discovered that Jenny had a wooer. On Sunday afternoon, young Daniel McCall made his appearance, with that peculiar, happy, awkward look that young lads have when they are 'keeping company,' as it is called. At that time, when a young man wanted a wife, he looked out for some young girl whom he thought would be a good help-mate, and, watching his opportunity, with an awkward bow and blush he would ask her to give him her company the ensuing Sunday evening. Her refusal was called 'giving the mitten,' and great was the laugh against any young man if it was known that he had 'got the mitten,' as all hopes in that quarter would be at an end. But young McCall had not got 'the mitten;' and it was customary on those occasions, when the family retired to bed, for the young man to get up and quietly put out the candles, and cover the fire, if any; then take a seat by the side of his lady-love, and talk as other lovers do, I suppose, until twelve o'clock, when he would either take his leave and a walk of miles to his home, that he might be early at work, or he would lie down for an hour or two with some of the boys, and then be away before daylight. Those weekly visits would sometimes continue for months, until all was ready for marriage. But they did not always end in matrimony. Sometimes those children of the woods were gay Lotharios in their way, as well as in more refined society, and it would be discovered that a favourite Adonis was keeping company with two or three young girls at the same time, and *vice versa* with some young coquettes. But such unprincipled conduct would furnish gossip for a whole neighbourhood, and be discountenanced by all. Nor must you for a moment imagine that there was anything wrong in this system of wooing. It was the custom of the country in an early day, and I think it is still continued in settlements remote from towns. But the lives of hundreds of estimable wives and mothers have borne testimony to the purity of their conduct. When Jenny had been with my mother about six months, young McCall made his appearance in the middle of the week, and my father and some visitors commenced bantering him why he did not marry at once. Why did he spend his time and wear out his shoes in the way he was doing? He said he would go and talk to Jenny, and hear what she said. He returned in a few minutes and said they would be married. In an hour afterwards they were man and wife. They married in their working dresses—he in his buckskin trowsers, and she in her homespun. She tied up her bundle of clothes, received her wages, and away they walked to their log-house in the woods. Thirty years afterwards they used to show me some little articles that had been purchased with Jenny's wages; and they appeared to look back upon that time with pleasure. They became rich; he was colonel of militia, and some of their descendants are worth thousands. During their early struggles, Mrs. McCall was in the field with her husband, pulling flax, when she felt what she thought was a severe blow on her foot. A rattlesnake had bitten her. Her husband killed the snake; vulgar prejudice thought that, by killing the snake, the poison would be less severe. He then put his lips to the wound, sucked it, and, taking her in his arms, carried her to the house. Before he reached it, her foot had swollen and burst. They applied an Indian remedy, a peculiar kind of plantain, which relieved her, but she was years before she perfectly recovered from the effects of the poison. Two children that were born during that time turned spotted, became sore and died; but her third child was strong and healthy, and is still living. These reptiles, that are now almost unknown in the country, were then plentiful. They had a den at the mouth of the Grand River, and there was another at the Falls. For many years the boatmen going up and down Lake Erie used to stop at the mouth of the Grand River for an hour or two's sport, killing rattlesnakes. My father and boat's crew, on one of these occasions, killed seventy. The oil of the rattlesnake was thought to possess great medicinal virtues.

"There was a sad want of religious instruction amongst the early settlers. For many years there was no clergyman nearer than Niagara, a distance of 100 miles, without roads. My father used to read the Church Service every Sunday to his household, and any of the laborers who would attend. As the country became more settled, the neighbours used to meet at Mr. Barton's, and Mr. Bostwick, who was the son of a clergyman, used to read the service, and sometimes a sermon. But there were so few copies of sermons to be obtained, that after reading them over some half-a-dozen times they appeared to lose their interest. But it was for the children that were growing up that this want was most severely felt. When the weekday afforded no amusements, they would seek them on Sunday; fishing, shooting, bathing, gathering nuts and berries, and playing ball, occupied, with few exceptions, the summer Sundays. In winter they spent them in skating, gliding down the hills on hand sleighs. And yet crime was unknown in those days, as were locks and bolts. Theft was never heard of, and a kindly, brotherly feeling existed amongst all. If a deer was killed, a piece was sent to each neighbour, and they, in turn, used to draw the stream, giving my father a share of the fish. If anyone was ill, they were cared for by the neighbours and their wants attended to. But the emigrant coming to the country in the present day can only form a very poor idea of the hardships endured by the early pioneers of the forest, or the feelings which their isolated situation drew forth. Education and station seemed to be lost sight of in the one general wish to be useful to each other, to make roads and improve the country.

"I think it was in 1802 that I first saw Colonel Talbot, a distinguished settler, who had a grant of lands seventy miles further up the lake, at a place afterwards called Port Talbot, where he had commenced building mills. People were full of conjecture as to the cause that could induce a young gentleman of his family (the Talbots of Malahide) and rank in the army to bury himself in Canada.

"He and Sir Arthur Wellesley had been at the same time on the staff of the Duke of Buckingham, when Lord Lieutenant of Ireland, and it was said the field of glory was equally open to both. Colonel Talbot afterwards came to this country, and was on the staff of General Simcoe when he made a tour through the Upper Province. At that time he selected his future home. Some said that he left the army in disgust at not getting an appointment that he felt himself entitled to; others, again, said that neither Mars nor Venus presided at his birth. But one thing was certain: he had chosen a life of privation and toil, and right manfully he bore the lot he had chosen. When in the army, he was looked upon as a dandy; but my first impressions would place him in a very different light. He had come to Port Ryerse with a boat-load of grain to be ground at my father's mill. The men slept in the boat, with an awning over it, and had a fire on shore. In front of this fire, Colonel Talbot was mixing bread in a pail, to be baked in the ashes for the men. I had never seen a man so employed, and it made a lasting impression upon my childish memory. My next recollection of him was his picking a wild goose, which my father had shot, for my mother to dress for dinner. Thus commenced an acquaintance which lasted until his death in 1853.

"My father, on his arrival at Long Point, promised my mother that if she would remain contented for six years at Port Ryerse, and give the country a fair trial, if she then disliked it, and wished to return to New York, he would go back with her—that party feeling would by that time have greatly subsided. My mother now claimed my father's promise. He at once acquiesced, and left it to her to decide when they should go, my father well knowing that however much my mother might wish to return, when left to her to decide, her better judgment would say 'Not yet,' as his improvements must all be a sacrifice. To sell his property was impossible. My mother postponed the return for a few years, but could not relinquish the hope of emerging from the woods, and being once more within the sound of the church-going bell. My father's property was fast improving. He had planted an orchard of apple, peach, and cherry trees, which he procured from Dr. Proyer, whose young trees were a year or two in advance of his own, and he had procured a few sheep which were pastured in a field immediately in front of the house. But all their watching could not preserve them from the wolves. If they escaped by the greatest care for a year or two, and the flock increased to twenty or thirty, some unlucky day they would find them reduced to ten or a dozen.

"A tree sometimes unobserved would fall across the fence, and the sheep would stray into the woods, which was fatal to them; or, the fastening to their pen would be left just one unlucky night not secured, and the morning would show a melancholy remainder of the fine flock that had been folded the night before. All of these mishaps were serious vexations to the early settlers. The mill was a constant draw upon my father's purse. A part of his lands had been sold at a very low price (but not low at that time)—one dollar the acre—to assist in building it, and now it had to be kept in repair. The dam breaking, machinery getting out of order, improvements to be made, bolting cloths wanted, and a miller to be paid—to meet all this was the toll, every twelfth bushel that was ground. During the summer season the mill would be for days without a bushel to grind, as farmers got their milling done when they could take their grists to the mill on ox-sleds upon the snow. Few grew more than sufficient for their own consumption and that of the new-coming settler; but had they grown more, there was no market, and the price of wheat, until the war of 1812, was never more than half a dollar a bushel; maize, buckwheat, and rye, two shillings (York) a bushel. The flour mill, pecuniarily speaking, was a great loss to my father. The saw-mill was remunerative; the expense attending it was trifling, its machinery was simple, and any commonly intelligent man with a day or two's instruction could attend to it. People brought logs of pine, oak, and walnut from their own farms, and my father had half the lumber for sawing; and this, when seasoned, found a ready sale, not for cash (cash dealings were almost unknown), but for labour, produce, maple sugar or anything they had to part with which my father might want, or with which he could pay some of his needy labourers. There were some wants which were almost unattainable with poor people, such as nails, glass, tea, and salt. They could only be procured in Niagara, and cash must be paid for them. There was not yet a store at Long Point. Great were the advantages of the half-pay officers and those who had a little money at their command, and yet their descendants appear not to have profited by it. It is a common remark in the country that very many of the sons of half-pay officers were both idle and dissolute; but I am happy to say there are many honourable exceptions. At the head of the list of these stand our present Chief Justice (Sir John Robinson), and Dr. Ryerson, the Superintendent of Education, and many others who deem it an honour to be descended from an United Empire Loyalist. From a multiplicity of care, my father had postponed, from time to time, going to Toronto, or Little York, as it was then called (where the seat of government had been removed), to secure the grant of land which had been promised to his family, until after the departure of his friend General Simcoe, who was succeeded as Governor by General Hunter.

"When my father made application to General Hunter, he was told that an order from the Home Government had limited the grants to the wives and children of the U. E. Loyalists to 200 acres each; but said that if the Order in Council had passed for the larger grants, of course my father should have the lands he had selected; but he, not foreseeing the change, had not secured the order, and General Simcoe's verbal promise could not be acted upon.

"The autumn of 1804 found us still in the original log-house. It had been added to and improved, but the stick chimney had not been replaced by brick, as my father looked forward from year to year to building a better house in a better situation;

but he found so many improvements actually necessary, and so much to be done each spring and summer, that although a great deal of material had been prepared, the house was not yet commenced. One fine bright morning, as some visitors were taking their departure, there was an alarm of fire, and, sure enough, the stick chimney had caught and communicated to the garret, and in a few minutes the whole of the upper part of the house was in flames. Our visitors, who had not gone beyond the threshold, joined with the family and labourers in getting out the furniture as fast as possible. Nearly everything was saved from the lower part of the house, but all that was in the garret was lost. The garret had been used as a store-room, and contained cases which had not been unpacked since they came from New York, but were left until a better house could be built. These things—linen, bedding, and some nice little articles of furniture, and various little nicknacks which were prized beyond their value—were a great loss; but the greatest loss was a box or two of books. These were not to be replaced this side of New York, and to a young family the loss was irreparable. A part of Pope's works, a copy of Milton's Paradise Lost, Buchan's Family Medicine, and a Testament with commentaries, were all that were saved. A small quantity of plate also, which had not been unpacked, was found in a very unsatisfactory state. The family took shelter in a house built for and occupied by the miller and his family, sending them to a smaller tenement. The situation was airy and beautiful, and, with a few alterations and improvements, was more comfortable than the first log-house. This my mother rather regretted, as discomfort would have hastened the new house. Although allusions were made to New York, no time had yet been named for their return. My father used to assure my mother and friends that he would go as soon as she said the word; yet these remarks were always accompanied by a particularly humorous expression of countenance.

"About this time the London district was separated from the Western, and composed what now forms the counties or districts of Middlesex, Elgin, Huron, Bruce, Oxford, and Norfolk. The necessary appointments were made, and the London district held its own courts and sessions at Turkey Point, six miles above us on the lake shore. The people, in a most patriotic manner, had put up a log-house, which served the double purpose of court-house and jail. The courts were held in the upper story, which was entered by a very rough stairway, going up on the outside of the building. The jail consisted of one large room on the ground floor, from which any prisoner could release himself in half an hour unless guarded by a sentinel. The juries for some years held their consultations under the shade of a tree. Doubtless it was pleasanter than the close lock-up jury-room of the present day. My father, in addition to his other commissions, was appointed Judge of the District Court and Judge of the Surrogate Court. Turkey Point is a very pretty place; the grounds are high, and from them there is a very fine view of the bay and lake. General Simcoe had selected it for the county town, and the site of a future city. Now it boasted of one house, an inn kept by Silas Montross. There was also a reservation of land for military purposes. But the town never prospered; it was not in a thoroughfare, and did not possess water privileges. Twenty years afterwards it contained but the one solitary house. The county town was changed to a more favourable situation, Vittoria. My father's young family now gave him great anxiety. How they were to be educated was a question not easily solved. Schools there were none, nor was it possible to get a tutor. A man of education would not go so far into the woods for the small inducement which a private family could offer.

"Magistrates were not allowed to marry by license, nor could the parties be called in church, for there were no churches in the country. The law required that the parties should be advertised—that is, that the banns should be written out and placed in some conspicuous place for three Sundays. The mill door was the popular place, but the young lads would endeavour to avoid publicity by putting the banns on the inside of the door; others would take two or three witnesses and hold it on the door for a few minutes for three successive Sundays, allowing no one but their friends to see it. In many places marriages used to be solemnized by persons not authorized, and in a manner that made their legality very doubtful; but the Legislature have very wisely passed Acts legalizing all marriages up to a certain date. The marriages that took place at my father's used to afford a good deal of amusement. Some very odd couples came to be united. The only fee my father asked was a kiss from the bride, which he always insisted on being paid; and if the bride was at all pretty, he used, with a mischievous look at my mother, to enlarge upon the pleasure that this fee gave him, and would go into raptures about the bride's youth, beauty, and freshness, and declare that it was the only public duty he performed that he was properly remunerated for.

"Application had several times been made to the Rev. Mr. Addison, the only clergyman in the country, who was living at Niagara, entreating him to come to Long Point and baptize the children. All who had been born there remained unbaptized. This summer his promised visit was to take place, and was looked forward to with intense anxiety by both parents and children. I used to discuss it with my elder brother, and wonder what this wonderful ceremony of christening could mean. My mother had explained it as well as she could, but the mystical washing away of sin with water, to me was incomprehensible, as was also my being made member of a Church which was to me unknown. I wondered what God's minister could be like, and whether he was like my father, whom I looked up to as the greatest and best of anyone in my little world. At last Parson Addison arrived, and my curiosity was satisfied on one point, and in my estimation my father stood higher than the clergyman.

"The neighbourhood was notified, and all the children, from one month to eight or nine years old, were assembled to receive baptism. The house was crowded with people anxious to hear the first sermon preached in the Long Point Settlement by an ordained minister. Upon my own mind I must confess that the surplice and gown made a much more lasting impression than the sermon, and I thought Mr. Addison a vastly more important person in them than out of them; but upon the elder part of the community, how many sad and painful feelings did this first sermon awaken, and recall times long past, friends departed, ties broken, homes deserted, hardships endured! The cord touched produced many vibrations, as Mr. Addison shook hands with every individual, and made some kind inquiry about their present or future welfare. The same God-hopeful smile passed over every face, and the same 'Thank you, sir, we find ourselves every year a little better off, and the country is improving.' 'If we only had a church and a clergyman we should have but little to complain of.' But it was a hope deferred for many long years. A Baptist minister, the Rev. Mr. Finch, was the first clergyman who came to the little settlement to reside. His meetings were held in different parts of the settlement each Sunday, so that all might have the opportunity of hearing him if they chose to attend. He preached in houses and barns without any reward, labouring on his farm for his support. He, like all the early Dissenting ministers who came to the province, was uneducated, but possessed and sincerely believed a saving knowledge of the Gospel, and in his humble sphere laboured to do all the good in his power. Many of the young people joined his Church. He was soon followed by the Methodists. Too much cannot be said in praise of the early ministers of these denominations; they bore every privation and fatigue, praying and preaching in every house where the doors were not closed against them— receiving the smallest pittance for their labour. A married man received $200 a year and a log-house for his family; an unmarried man had half that sum, the greater portion of which was paid in home-made cloth and produce. Their sermons and prayers were very loud, forcible and energetic, and if they had been printed *verbatim*, would have looked a sad jumble of words. They encouraged an open demonstration of feeling amongst their hearers—the louder the more satisfactory. But notwithstanding the criticisms cast upon these early preachers, were they not the class of men who suited their hearers? They shared their poverty and entered into all their feelings; and although unlearned, they taught the one true doctrine—to serve God in spirit and in truth—and their lives bore testimony to their sincerity. In this world they looked forward to neither preferment nor reward; all they expected or could hope for was a miserable subsistence. Nor was it surprising that in twenty years afterwards, when the path was made smooth, the church built, and the first clergyman, the Rev. Mr. Evans, came, that he found a small congregation. Every township had one or two Methodist and Baptist chapels. I do not recollect one Roman Catholic family in the neighbourhood. Although the Long Point Settlement was in existence thirty years before we had a resident clergyman of the Church of England, yet I cannot recollect one member who had seceded from the Church. Many had died, and many communed with the Methodists, who did not belong to them."

POSTSCRIPT.—At the author's request, Mrs. Harris, in June, 1879, brought down her recollections to the close of the war of 1812—1815. The following pages are the result—written by Mrs. Harris, twenty years after writing the previous memoranda, in the eighty-first year of her age, containing some interesting particulars of the war, and stating the cause of the loss of the British fleet on Lake Erie, and the disasters which followed.

The author has not seen cause to alter a sentence or a word of Mrs. Harris's manuscript, written by herself in a clear, bold hand, notwithstanding her advanced age:

"In 1810 my father showed signs of failing health. A life of hardship and great exertion was telling upon a naturally strong constitution. He decided upon resigning all his offices, and his resignation was accepted upon this assurance, that from ill-health he could no longer fulfil the duties they involved. The Hon. Thomas Talbot was appointed his successor as colonel commandant of the militia, and the late Judge Mitchell succeeded him as Judge of the District and Surrogate Courts. At this time there were strong rumours of war between America and England, and the militia anticipated being called into active service. At the close of 1811, a large body of the militia which my father had organized waited upon him, and urged him to resume the command, as in him they had confidence. Colonel Talbot was a stranger amongst them, and lived at a distance. My father at that time was in the last stage of consumption, and died in the June following, in 1812, aged sixty years. In six days after his death war was declared, and then came troubles to my widowed mother in various shapes. My father in seventeen years had seen a lonely wilderness changed into a fruitful country. Most of the original log-houses had given place to good frame buildings, and the inhabitants generally seemed prosperous and content. Immediately after the declaration of war, the militia had to do military duty and neglect their farms. British troops passed through Port Ryerse, on their way to Amherstburg and Sandwich, and every available building was used as barracks. All merchant vessels were converted into ships of war, and they, with one or two small ships belonging to the Provincial Navy, were placed under the command of Captain Barclay, of the Royal Navy; Captain Finnes, R. N., was second in command. His ships were all of light tonnage; there were several transports, which were in constant use conveying troops and army supplies to Sandwich and Amherstburg. The lake was clear of enemies, as the Americans were blockaded within Erie Harbour, where they had two or three large ships on the stocks. They could not cross the bar at Erie without lightening their ships and taking out part of their guns. This they could not do in the presence of Barclay's fleet. When the weather was too rough for the blockading squadron to remain outside the harbour, it was too rough for the American fleet to get over the bar; consequently we felt very safe. This was during the summer of 1813. During this summer General Brock called out the militia of Norfolk, and asked for volunteers to go with him to Detroit; every man volunteered. He made his selection of the strong and active young men. Right gallantly the militia throughout the province behaved during the three years' war, casting no discredit upon their parentage—the brave old U. E. Loyalists. During the summer, Captain Barclay used to have private information—not very reliable, as the result proved—of what progress the ships were making on the stocks. He used occasionally to leave the blockade and go to Amherstburg and come to Ryerse. The Americans took note of this, and made their plans and preparations for his doing so. There was a pretty widow of an officer of some rank in Amherstburg, who was very anxious to go to Toronto. Captain Barclay offered her a passage in his ship and brought her to Ryerse, and then escorted her to Dr. Rolph's, where he and some of his officers remained to dinner the following day. When they came in sight of Erie, they saw all the American fleet riding safely at anchor outside the bar. The Americans had everything in readiness; and as soon as the watched-for opportunity came, and the British fleet left the station, they got their own ships over the bar, their guns in, and all things ready for defence or attack. They far outnumbered the British fleet, and were of heavier tonnage. Captain Barclay consulted his senior officers whether it would be best to come into Long

Point Bay to winter, where they could get supplies across the country from Burlington Bay of all the munitions of war, and leave the ship on the stocks at Amherstburg (the *Detroit*) to her fate, as neither the guns to arm nor the men to man her had yet been forwarded, and now could not unless by land, which for heavy guns and the munitions of war was the next thing to an impossibility. It was with great difficulty that food and clothing could be forwarded, where there was little more than an Indian path and no bridges. The wisdom of the fleet decided upon going to Amherstburg and trusting to arming the ships with the guns from the fort, and manning them with sailors from the fleet, and with soldiers and volunteers. They landed Captain O'Keefe, of the 41st Regiment, who was doing marine duty at or near Otter Creek, to find his way to Ryerse, and to tell the militia commandant that the whole frontier on Lake Erie was now open to American invasion, the new ship was launched, imperfectly armed and manned; and without a sufficient supply of ammunition for the fleet, and with little more than a day's rations for his men, Commodore Barclay was necessitated to risk an action. The result is too well known. Nearly all the officers were killed or severely wounded. Captain Barclay, who had already lost one arm, was disabled in the other arm; but they did not strike their colours to Commodore Perry's superior force until their ammunition in some ships was all exhausted, and in others nearly so. No one could have fought more bravely than Captain Barclay. At the same time, those who knew of his leaving the blockade could not help feeling that all the disasters of the upper part of the province lay at his door. In May of 1814 we had several days of heavy fog. On the morning of the 13th, as the fog lifted, we saw seven or eight ships under the American flag anchored off Ryerse, with a number of small boats floating by the side of each ship. As the fog cleared away they hoisted sail and dropped down three miles below us, opposite Port Dover. Of course an invasion was anticipated. Colonel Talbot was then in Norfolk, and he ordered all the militia to assemble the next day at Brantford, a distance of thirty miles, which they did with great reluctance, as many of both officers and men thought that an effort should have been made to prevent the Americans landing; but no resistance was offered. On the 14th, the

Americans burnt the village and mills of Dover; on the 15th, as my mother and myself were sitting at breakfast, the dogs kept up a very unusual barking. I went to the door to discover the cause; when I looked up, I saw the hill-side and fields, as far as the eye could reach, covered with American soldiers. They had marched from Port Dover to Ryerse. Two men stepped from the ranks, selected some large chips, and came into the room where we were standing, and took coals from the hearth without speaking a word. My mother knew instinctively what they were going to do. She went out and asked to see the commanding officer. A gentleman rode up to her and said he was the person she asked for. She entreated him to spare her property, and said she was a widow with a young family. He answered her civilly and respectfully, and expressed his regret that his orders were to burn, but that he would spare the house, which he did; and he said, as a sort of justification of his burning, that the buildings were used as a barrack, and the mill furnished flour for British troops. Very soon we saw columns of dark smoke arise from every building, and of what at early morn had been a prosperous homestead, at noon there remained only smouldering ruins. The following day Colonel Talbot and the militia under his command marched to Port Norfolk (commonly known as Turkey Point), six miles above Ryerse. The Americans were then on their way to their own shores. My father had been dead less than two years. Little remained of all his labours excepting the orchard and cultivated fields. It would not be easy to describe my mother's feelings as she looked at the desolation around her, and thought upon the past and the present; but there was no longer a wish to return to New York. My father's grave was there, and she looked to it as her resting-place. Not many years since a small church was built on a plot of ground which my father had reserved for that purpose; in the graveyard attached are buried two of the early settlers—my father and my mother.   "A. H."

The writer of the following paper seems to have been perfectly acquainted with the subject on which he writes, but is entirely unknown to the author of this history. The paper appears to have been written shortly after the decease of Colonel Ryerse, and was enclosed to the author on a printed slip. It throws much light on the history and character of the times of which it speaks:

"*Last of the Old U. E. Loyalists.*

"Died, at his residence, near Vittoria, county of Norfolk, on Wednesday, the 9th of August, 1854, after a short illness of three days, Colonel Joseph Ryerson (father of the Rev. Messrs. George, William, John, Egerton, and Edwy Ryerson), in the ninety-fourth year of his age.

"Colonel Ryerson was born near Paterson, New Jersey, about fourteen miles from the city of New York, the 28th of February, 1761. His ancestors were from Holland; he was the seventh son; he lost his father in childhood. At the breaking out of the American revolution, two of the brothers entered the British army. Samuel (father of Mrs. Harris, Eldon House, London) was nine years older than Joseph, and was the first in that part of the country to join the Royal standard. On arriving at New York, he was informed by the British commander that if he would raise sixty men he would receive a captain's commission. He returned to his native place, and raised the complement of men in a few days. Joseph, who was then only fifteen years of age, entered the army the 6th of May, 1776, as a cadet. He was too small and weak to handle a musket, and received a light fowling-piece, with which he learned the military exercise in a few days. In the course of a few months an order was received to embody a portion of these New Jersey volunteers into a corps of Light Infantry, to go to the South to besiege Charleston. Joseph Ryerson was one of the 550 volunteers for this campaign. When Colonel Ennis (the Inspector-General of the troops at New York) came to Joseph Ryerson, he said, 'You are too young and too small to go.' The lad replied, 'Oh! sir, I am growing older and stouter every day.' The colonel laughed heartily, and said, 'Well, you shall go then.' These Light Infantry volunteers were attached at different times to different regiments; and Mr. Ryerson was successively attached to the 37th, 71st, and 84th Regiments. Such was the hard service performed by these Light Infantry volunteers, that out of 550 men, rank and file, exclusive of officers, only eighty-six of them returned, three years afterwards, after the evacuation of Charleston.

"The Light Infantry corps having been broken up, the few remains of the men composing it returned to the regiments out of which they had volunteered. About eighteen months after leaving New York, before he was seventeen years of age, Mr. Ryerson received an ensign's commission, and he was, in the course of a year, promoted to a lieutenancy in the Prince of Wales' Regiment. His first commission was given him as the immediate reward of the courage and skill he displayed as the bearer of special despatches from Charleston, 196 miles into the interior, in the course of which he experienced several hair-breadth escapes. He was promoted to his lieutenancy for the manner in which he acquitted himself as the bearer of special despatches by sea to the north, having eluded the enemy in successive attacks and pursuits. He was in six battles, besides several skirmishes, and was once wounded. At the close of the war in 1783, he, with his brother Samuel, and many other Loyalists and discharged half-pay officers and soldiers, went to New Brunswick, where he married in 1784, and settled and resided in Majorville, on the River St. John, near Fredericton, in 1799, when he removed to Upper Canada and settled in Charlotteville, near his brother—they both having drawn land from the Government for their services.

"While in New Brunswick he was appointed captain of militia; on his arrival in Canada he was appointed major, and a few years afterwards colonel. On the organization of London district in 1800 (including the recent districts of Talbot, London, Brock, and Huron), he was appointed high sheriff—an office which he resigned, after a few years, in favour of his son-in-law, the late Colonel Bostwick, of Port Stanley.

"During the late war with the United States, in 1812, Colonel Ryerson and his three eldest sons took an active part in the defence of the country. He was for many years a magistrate and Chairman of the Quarter Sessions; but he would never accept of any fees as a magistrate.

"Some ten years since he resigned whatever offices he held. In 1850 he lost his wife, aged eighty-four years—a woman of sound understanding and rare excellence. He continued healthy and vigorous to the last—having the Friday before his decease rode several miles, and walked from Vittoria to his own house

—a distance of nearly two miles—after which he conversed with much animation and cheerfulness.

"Shortly after his attack on Sunday night, he expressed his belief that he should not recover, and stated his entire trust in God, through the merits of Jesus Christ, in whom he felt that he had good hope of eternal life.

"His funeral was attended by a large concourse of people—especially of the old inhabitants. Six of his old neighbours acted as pall-bearers—namely, Colonel Potts, F. Walsh, Aquilla Walsh, Abner Owen, Joseph Culver, and S. Ellis, Esquires—whose joint ages amounted to almost 400 years. The Scripture lesson was read, and prayers offered up at the house by the Rev. Mr. Clement, Wesleyan minister; and the service was read at the grave by the Rev. George Salmon (an old friend of the family), in the absence of the Rev. Mr. Evans, rector of Woodhouse, to the erection of the church of which rectory Colonel Ryerson had been the largest contributor.

"Colonel Ryerson is probably the last of the old United Empire Loyalists in Canada who joined the British army in 1776—a race of men remarkable for longevity and energy, and a noble enthusiasm for British institutions."[*]

Interesting piece of Local History by the Rev. Dr. Scadding.

"NIAGARA, Aug. 3rd, 1861.

"DEAR SIR,—

"I have deferred acknowledging the circular announcing your intended work on the U. E. forefathers of the Canadian people, until now, from not having had before a moment of leisure to prepare the contribution which I intended to offer for your acceptance and use. I only hope that my delay may not have rendered the communication too late.

---

[*] Dr. Canniff, in his excellent "History of the Settlement of Upper Canada," with special reference to Bay Quinté, has the following respecting Colonel Ryerson, who commanded a company and was called captain, though not yet gazetted :

"One of Captain Joseph Ryerson's old comrades, Peter Redner, of the Bay Quinté, says: 'He was a man of daring intrepidity, and a great favourite in his company.' He represented Captain Ryerson as one of the most determined men he ever knew. With the service of his country uppermost in his mind, he often exposed himself to great danger to accomplish his desires." (p. 119.)

"Such a work as that which you propose to bring out is a desideratum, and cannot fail to be interesting, and increasingly so as years roll on. I am glad that you have been moved to this undertaking, as I feel sure that it will be executed with vigour and thoroughness, in a patriotic spirit, and with a real affection. Our neighbours in the United States have long since seen the propriety of collecting and permanently recording the otherwise rapidly evanescent memorials of their past. The volumes put forth by their Historical Societies and State Government and by individuals amongst them, on this subject, possess extraordinary interest not only for United States' citizens, but also for the general reader, and particularly for the inhabitants of the existing British North American Colonies. I have often wished that we could have for Canada some such publication as Lossing's Field Book of the Revolution, to preserve for the eye, by woodcuts worked into the text, sketches and plans of historic places and buildings as they were in their primitive state—objects which, in a country like this, from the perishing nature of materials in many instances, from the levelling of streets, straightening of roads, railway excavations, esplanades, building and other processes and causes, are being so rapidly obliterated.

"As you invite information in regard to early settlers generally, I have thought it simply a duty to send some memoranda—which I hope may be deemed not unworthy of use—respecting my father, whom I have supposed you might, perhaps, find an occasion of noticing in connection with a mention of Whitby, in a note or otherwise.

"I am, dear Sir,
"Very truly yours,
"H. SCADDING."

"The Rev. Dr. Ryerson."

"This town was, at its commencement, about the year 1819, named Windsor, by its projector, Mr. John Scadding, the original grantee of a thousand acres in this locality. On a natural harbour of Lake Ontario, popularly known as 'Big Bay,' Mr. S. laid out the town, built the first house, and named the streets, three of them, after his three sons—John, Charles, and Henry. The appellation 'Windsor' had no reference to the world-renowned royal residence, but to a very humble property so designated, once possessed by Mr. S. in the parish of Luppitt, in Devonshire, from which neighbourhood, viz., Dunkeswell, he first emigrated to Upper Canada in 1793. Before this transplantation, his family, with numerous kith and kin, had had their home in these old Wessex regions for many a generation. Local registries, tombstones, and other records constantly exhibit the name, which will also be found in the minute Ordnance maps of England, attached to a small hamlet in the vicinity of Wellington, in the closely adjoining county of Somerset. Through the instrumentality of Governor Simcoe, to whom he was personally and in the most friendly manner known in Devonshire before his emigration, Mr. S. was also the owner and first cultivator of a section of land watered through its whole length by the River Don, from the second concession to the lake's edge, in the township of York. It was while putting off trespassers on a portion of this last-mentioned property, which is now to a great extent included within the limits of the city of Toronto, but which was at the time, for the most part, in its primitive natural state, that he was, at the age of seventy, unfortunately killed by the falling of a tree in 1824. His widow, Mrs. Melicent Scadding, survived until 1860, attaining the age of ninety-three years. In 1854, the town of Windsor was incorporated by the Act of Parliament 18 Vic., c. 28, on which occasion its name was changed to 'Whitby,' ambiguities and inconveniences having arisen from the existence of another Windsor on the Detroit river."

Loyalty and Sufferings of the Hon. John Munroe, of Fowlis.

"Born in Scotland, in 1731; came to America in 1756; married in Albany Miss Brower, of Schenectady, in 1760; lived at Matilda, U.C., and died at Dickenson's Landing in October, 1800, aged sixty-nine.

"During the revolutionary war he resided near Fort Bennington, where he possessed considerable property, which was confiscated by the United States' Government. He was captain in Sir John Johnston's regiment, and his son Hugh was a lieutenant. The appended certificates state his services, sufferings and merits."

The above summary statement, and the following certificates, were enclosed to the writer of this history several years since by a son of Captain Munroe, who held several situations in Upper Canada, such as judge, sheriff, etc.

Brigadier-General Allen Maclean's Certificate.

"I do hereby certify that the bearer hereof, Captain Munroe, was the first man that joined me at New York, on the 3rd of June, 1775, to take up arms in defence of his King and country, and that he was of infinite service to me at that time. That during the time I was engaged at Boston he remained in and about New York, till my return, when he gave me every information in respect to the danger of my being taken prisoner; in consequence of which I divested myself of every military appearance, and secured my papers, etc., on board the *Asia* man-of-war, and at the risk of his life he conducted me upwards of 200 miles through the province of New York to a gentleman's house near Schenectady, whose son conducted me up the Mohawk river, on my journey to Canada by way of Oswego, the communication on all other places being shut up. I do also certify that Captain Munroe did engage a great number of men to serve his Majesty against the rebels, and that an information was lodged against him on that account, and was taken up and tried; that though many of the men were never able to join the King's troops in Canada, yet numbers joined Sir John Johnston's regiment, and others joined the 84th, under my command; and that in defiance of all the hardships, difficulties, and dangers he was exposed to, he has ever adhered to the same loyal principles, notwithstanding he was eighteen months a close prisoner, mostly in irons; that he made his escape from prison in Albany; was unfortunately retaken and confined at Esopsus, on the Hudson river, and would infallibly have been hanged (his sentence having been pronounced) had he not made his escape; that I am acquainted with Mrs. Munroe and her family of eight children, which has hitherto been brought up in a genteel sphere of life; and that I always understood Captain Munroe to be a gentleman of considerable property in the province of New York, and as an officer always behaved with becoming spirit and resolution.

"ALLEN MACLEAN,
"Late Brigadier-General in Canada."

Captain Duncan Campbell's Certificate, Late of the 84th Regiment.

"I do hereby certify, that I have been well acquainted with Captain John Munroe, late of the King's Regiment, of New York, for many years, while he followed the mercantile way of business in America's last war, and ever since; that he always bore the character of an honest and respectable gentleman amongst his numerous acquaintances. I also knew him to be a zealous friend to the interest of his King and country, and that he and his family have suffered the greatest cruelties by the rebels, and the loss of all his property. I also know that he laid a permanent foundation for his family in the province of New York by his indefatigable industry; that I have been different times at his last place of abode, where I have seen most part of the improvements he had made, though at that time in a manner beginning, where he had an excellent dwelling-house, a saw and grist mills, with other improvements.

"That I know him to have a very large family, and a thriving and growing property in the county of Albany, and province of New York.

"DUNCAN CAMPBELL,
"Late Captain of the 84th Regiment.
"No. 8 Fley Market, St. James."

General Tryon's Certificate.

"I do certify that I know Captain Munroe, during the time that I was Governor of the Province of New York, to be an active magistrate; that in the year 1776, at the period I was on board the *Duchess of Gordon*, he came from his place of abode, two hundred miles through the rebel posts, on the Hudson river, and with difficulty got on board, when he informed me of several particulars relative to the situation of the rebel armies, and the preparations they were making for defence in the highlands.

"He also communicated to me his distress for want of money to pay the recruits he had engaged for General Maclean's regiment, on which I advanced him such a sum as he thought he could carry with safety. About that time a packet arrived from England, which brought dispatches for the Bishop of Quebec. These I requested he would take charge of, and forward them with diligence and secrecy. To facilitate this business, I offered him fifty pounds to defray the expense thereof. He took charge of the dispatches, which I heard were safely delivered, though he declined accepting the fifty pounds. Such conduct, and his indefatigable diligence to forward his Majesty's service, merits the attention of Government, particularly as he has lost his property and suffered imprisonment in the royal cause.

"Wm. Tryon,
"Upper Grosvenor St., 14th February, 1785."

SUFFERINGS OF THE U. E. LOYALISTS DURING THE REVOLUTIONARY WAR—VINDICATION OF THEIR CHARACTER—THEIR PRIVATIONS AND SETTLEMENT IN CANADA.

A Letter from the late Mrs. Elizabeth Bowman Spohn, of Ancaster, County of Wentworth, dated July 3rd, 1861, together with an Introductory Letter by the Writer of this History, dated February 15, 1875.

"*To the Editor of the Christian Guardian.*

"My Dear Sir,—

"At the request of the family, I have prepared, and I send you herewith, a brief obituary notice of Mrs. Elizabeth Bowman Spohn, only child of the honoured and widely-known late Peter and Elizabeth Bowman, near the village of Ancaster, in the county of Wentworth.

"I here subjoin for publication a remarkable letter which I received from Mrs. Spohn in 1861, in answer to a circular which I sent out to the United Empire Loyalists of Canada and their descendants, to procure information and testimonies from themselves as to their early history and settlement in this country.

"I had long been impressed with the injustice done to the character and acts of our Canadian forefathers by the partial and often unfounded statements of American historians and utter neglect of English historians. I had, in accordance with my own strong convictions and in compliance with many solicitations, determined to attempt an act of justice and gratitude to that noble generation of men and women. I have been favoured with a large number of letters similar to that which follows, and which will form an interesting Appendix of information and testimony to any history which may be written of them. I have not been able to complete my task; but if my life and strength be spared, and if I can be released from official labours which weigh so heavily upon my time and strength, I shall be able to complete what I have undertaken and long prosecuted, namely, contribute something to settle many unsettled and disputed facts of American and Canadian history, and to do, at least, a modicum of justice to a Canadian ancestry whose heroic deeds and unswerving Christian patriotism form a patent of nobility more to be valued by their descendants than the coronets of many modern noblemen.

"The following letter is founded on the testimony of those who were incapable of knowingly perverting the truth in any particular, and tends to prove and illustrate, by its artless statements, the true disinterested loyalty and Christian patriotism of those who adhered to British connection in the American revolution; their cruel treatment from the professed friends of liberty; their privations, sufferings, courage, and industry in settling this country; or who, as it is beautifully expressed in the following letter, 'with their hoes planted the germ of its future greatness.'

"Yours very faithfully,
"E. RYERSON.
"Toronto, February 15, 1875."

"ANCASTER, July 23rd, 1861.
"REV. AND DEAR SIR,—
"I have long wished some person would give the world a true history of that much-traduced and suffering people, the U. E. Loyalists; and I assure you that when your circular came I was greatly rejoiced to learn that they would at least get justice from such an able source as yourself; and if the plain narrative of the sufferings of my forefathers will assist you in the least in your arduous and praiseworthy undertaking, I will be exceedingly gratified.

"My great-grandfather emigrated from Germany in the reign of Queen Anne. He settled near the Mohawk river, at a creek that still bears his name (Bowman's Creek). My grandfather, Jacob Bowman, joined the British army in the French war; at the conclusion of peace he was awarded 1,500 acres of land on the Susquehanna river, where he made improvements until the revolutionary war broke out. The delicate state of my grandmother obliged him to remain at home, while nearly all that remained firm to their allegiance left for the British army.

"He was surprised at night, while his wife was sick, by a party of rebels, and with his eldest son, a lad of sixteen years of age, was taken prisoner; his house pillaged of every article except the bed on which his sick wife lay, and that they stripped of all but one blanket. Half an hour after my grandfather was marched off, his youngest child was born. This was in November. There my grandmother was, with an infant babe and six children, at the commencement of winter, without any provisions, and only one blanket in the house. Their cattle and grain were all taken away.

"My father, Peter Bowman, the eldest son at home, was only eleven years old. As the pillage was at night, he had neither coat nor shoes; he had to cut and draw his firewood half a mile on a hand-sleigh to keep his sick mother from freezing; this he did barefooted. The whole family would have perished had it not been for some friendly Indians that brought them provisions. One gave my father a blanket, coat and a pair of mocassins. A kind squaw doctored my grandmother, but she suffered so much through want and anxiety that it was not until spring that she was able to do anything. She then took her children and went to the Mohawk river, where they planted corn and potatoes; and in the fall the commander of the British forces at Niagara, hearing of their destitute situation, sent a party with some Indians to bring them in. They brought in five families: the Nellises, Secords, Youngs, Bucks, and our own family (Bowman), five women and thirty-one children, and only one pair of shoes among them all. They arrived at Fort George on the 3rd of November, 1776; from there they were sent first to Montreal, and then to Quebec, where the Government took care of them—that is, gave them *something to eat* and barracks to sleep in. My grandmother was exposed to cold and damp so much that she took the rheumatism, and never recovered.

"In the spring of 1777 my father joined Butler's Rangers,

and was with Colonel Butler in all his campaigns. His brother, only nine years old, went as a fifer.

"But to return to my grandfather, Jacob Bowman: his captors took him and his son to Philadelphia, where he was confined in jail eighteen months. An exchange of prisoners then took place, and they were sent to New York; from there he, with his son and Philip Buck, started for their homes, not knowing that these homes they never would see again, and that their families were far away in the wilds of Canada. The third evening after they started for their homes, they came to a pond, and shot some ducks for their supper. The report of their guns was heard by some American scouts, who concealed themselves until our poor fellows were asleep, when they came stealthily up and fired. Six shots took effect on my uncle, as he lay with his hat over his ear. Five balls went through it, and one through his thigh. My grandfather and Buck lay on the opposite side of the fire. They sprang into the bushes, but when they heard the groans of my uncle, grandfather returned and gave himself up. Buck made his escape. They then marched off, carrying the wounded boy with them.

"They were taken to the nearest American station, where grandfather was allowed the privilege of taking care of his wounded son. As he began to recover, grandfather was again ordered to abjure the British Government, which he steadfastly refused to do. He was then taken to Lancaster jail, with Mr. Hoover. They were there fastened together by a band of iron around their arms, and a chain with three links around their ankles, the weight of which was ninety-six pounds; and then fastened by a ring and staple to the floor. In that condition they remained either three years and a half or four years and a half, until the flesh was worn away and the bones laid bare four inches.

"Men, women, and children all went to work, clearing land. There were none to make improvements in Canada then but the U. E. Loyalists, and they, *with their hoes, planted the germ of its future greatness.* About this time, my father with his brother returned from the army; they helped their father two years, and then took up land for themselves near Fort Erie.

"My father married the daughter of a Loyalist from Hudson, North River (Mr. Frederick Lampman); he was too old to serve in the war, but his four sons and two sons in-law did. They were greatly harassed, but they hid in the cellars and bushes for three months, the rebels hunting them night and day. At length an opportunity offered, and they made their escape to Long Island, where they joined the British army. One of his sons, Wilhelmus Lampman, returning home to see his family, was caught by the rebels within a short distance of his father's house, and *hanged*, because, as they said, he was a Tory.

"At the restoration of peace, the whole family came to Canada. They brought their horses and cattle with them, which helped to supply the new country. They settled in the township of Stamford, where their descendants are yet.

"My father settled on his land near the fort; he drew an axe and a hoe from Government. He bought a yoke of yearling steers; this was the amount of his farming utensils. Mother had a cow, bed, six plates, three knives, and a few other articles. It was the scarce year, on account of the rush of Loyalists from the States, who had heard that Canada was a good country, where they could live under their own loved institutions, and enjoy the protection of England.

"The amount of grain that the U. E. Loyalists had raised was hardly sufficient for themselves; still they divided with the new comers, as all were alike destitute. After planting corn and potatoes, they had nothing left. My father cleared two acres, on which he planted corn, potatoes, oats, and flax; his calves were not able to work, and he had to carry all the rails on his shoulders until the skin was worn off them both. This was the way he made his first fence. In the beginning of May [1789], their provisions failed; none to be had; Government promised assistance, still none came. All eyes turned toward their harvest, which was more than three months away; their only resource was the leaves of trees. Some hunted ground nuts; many lived on herbs; those that were near the river, on fish. My father used to work until near sun-down, then walk three miles to the river, get light wood, fish all night, in the morning divide the fish, carry his share home on his back, which they ate without bread or salt. This he did twice a week, until the middle of June, when the moss became so thick in the river that they could not see a fish; still they worked on, and hoped on every day. My father chopped the logs and they had milk for their breakfast, then went to work until noon; took their dinner on milk; to work again till night, and supped on milk. I have frequently heard my mother say she never was discouraged or discontented; thankful they were that they could eat their morsel in peace.

"Their only crime was loyalty to the Government which they had sworn fealty to. The God of Heaven saw all this, and the sword of vengeance is now, in 1861, drawn over the American people (now they know how to appreciate loyalty), and will perhaps never be sheathed again until they make some restitution for the unheard-of cruelties they inflicted upon those most brave and loyal people.

"At the close of the war they were liberated. Grandfather was sent to the hospital for nearly a year, but his leg never got entirely well. As soon as he was able to walk, he sent for his family (it had been eight years since he saw them): they had suffered everything but death. Coming in the boats from Quebec, they got out of provisions and were near starving. He never had his family all together again. He drew land near the Falls of Niagara, where he went to work in the woods, broken down with suffering, worn out with age; his property destroyed, his land confiscated, and his family scattered; without money or means, and worse than all, without provisions. Still, to work they went with willing hands and cheerful hearts, and often did he say he never felt inclined to murmur. He had done his duty to God and his country; his own and his family's sufferings he could not help. Theirs was not a solitary case; all the Loyalists suffered. The Government found seed to plant and sow the first year; they gave them axes and hoes, and promised them provisions. How far that promise was fulfilled, you well know; they got very little; they soon found that they had to provide for themselves.

"As soon as the wheat was large enough to rub out, they boiled it, which to them was a great treat. Providence favoured them with an early harvest; their sufferings were over, and not one had starved to death. They now had enough, and they were thankful. Heaven smiled, and in a few years they had an abundance for themselves and others.

"I have no memorandum to refer to. I have just related the tale I have often heard my parents tell, without any exaggeration, but with many omissions. I have not told you about my father's sufferings in the army, when, upon an expedition near Little Miamac, he and some others were left to carry the wounded. They got out of provisions: went three days without anything to eat, except one pigeon between nine. I will give you his own words. He says: 'The first day we came to where an Indian's old pack-horse had mired in the mud; it had lain there ten days in the heat of summer; the smell was dreadful; still some of our men cut out slices, roasted and ate it; I was not hungry enough. The next day I shot a pigeon, which made a dinner for nine; after that we found the skin of a deer, from the knee to the hoof. This we divided and ate. I would willingly, had I possessed it, have given my hat full of gold for a piece of bread as large as my hand. Often did I think of the milk and swill I had seen left in my father's hog-trough, and thought if I only had that I would be satisfied.'

"Such were some of the sufferings of my forefathers for supremacy. They have gone to their reward. Peace to their ashes!

"Yours, respectfully,
"Dr. E. Ryerson." "ELIZABETH BOWMAN SPOHN.

"P. S.—One thing more I must add: My father always said there never was any cruelty inflicted upon either man, woman or child by Butler's Rangers, that he ever heard of, during the war. They did everything in their power to get the Indians to bring their prisoners in for redemption, and urged them to treat them kindly; the officers always telling them that it was more brave to take a prisoner than to kill him, and that none but a coward would kill a prisoner; that brave soldiers were always kind to women and children. He said it was false that they gave a bounty for scalps. True, the Indians did commit cruelties, but they were not countenanced in the least by the whites. "E. S."

"N. B.—To this last statement of Mrs. Spohn's it may be added that it is also true that the Indians were first employed by the Revolutionists against the Loyalists, before they were employed by the latter against the former. The attempt to enlist the Indians in the contest was first made by the Revolutionists. Of this the most conclusive evidence can be adduced.
"E. R."

CHAPTER XLII.

Governments of the British Provinces—Nova Scotia.

To the painful narrative given of the banishment of the Loyalists, and confiscation of their property, at the close of the revolutionary war, and their settlement in the British provinces of Nova Scotia, New Brunswick, Lower and Upper Canada, so fully detailed in the preceding pages, it is proper to add some account of the Provincial Governments.

Nova Scotia is the oldest of the present British American Provinces. This territory had the general appellation of New France, or Acadia, and comprehended, until 1784, New Brunswick and Cape Breton. It was originally regarded as a part of Cabot's discovery of Terra Nova, and as such claimed by the English Government, and was afterwards comprehended within the boundary of a large portion of America, called North Virginia. In the wars between France and England this country changed masters several times; but in 1710 Nova Scotia was again re-conquered by the forces of her Britannic Majesty Queen Anne, sent from New England, under the command of General Nicholson; and by the Treaty of Utrecht, in 1712, it was finally ceded and secured to Great Britain, and has ever since continued in her possession.*

" There were originally three sorts of government established by the English on the continent of America : Charter Governments, such as those of Massachusetts, Rhode Island, and Connecticut; Proprietary Governments, as Pennsylvania and

---

* General Description of Nova Scotia. Printed at the Royal Canadian School, 1825, p. 13.

Maryland; and Royal Government, as Nova Scotia. A Royal Government is immediately dependent upon the Crown, and the King appoints the Governor and officers of State, and the people only elect the representatives, as in England."*

"Peace was declared between France and England the 8th of November, 1762; and by the treaty which followed, all the French possessions in Canada, with Nova Scotia, Cape Breton, and the islands in the Gulf of the St. Lawrence, were ceded to Great Britain. In the year 1764, the Island of St. John, named Prince Edward Island in 1799, in honour of the Duke of Kent, was annexed to Nova Scotia.

"Of Acadia, and accordingly of Nova Scotia, during its early government by the English, the province now known as New Brunswick formed a part, and to the colony was added, in 1758. the Island of Cape Breton, then finally taken from the French, In the same year the military rule which had prevailed was exchanged for a regular Constitution, in which a Governor, representing the British Crown, presided over a Legislative Council and a House of Assembly modelled to some extent from the two estates of the English Parliament."†

---

* General Description of Nova Scotia, p. 17.
† Bourne's Our Colonies and Emigration, pp. 100, 101.

"The proclamation inviting emigrants to Nova Scotia *guaranteed them the same form of government and rights as the other colonies;* but owing to alleged difficulties in the way of electing an Assembly, no Assembly was chosen, and laws were made and the affairs of the colony were administered by the Governor and Council, until Chief Justice Belcher raised the question in 1755, in a letter to the Lords of Trade, as to the constitutionality of several laws passed by the Governor and Council without the endorsement of a representative Assembly. The question was referred to the Attorney and Solicitor-General of England, who decided that the Governor and Council alone had not the right to make laws, and that any laws so made were unconstitutional. The Lords of Trade *advised* the Governor (Lawrence) to convene an Assembly without delay, but he objected to it as needless and impracticable; when the Lord of Trade replied sharply, that "he knew their desires on the subject; and as he did not seem disposed to gratify them, they were obliged to *order him to do so;* adding, that they knew that many had left the province and gone to other colonies on account of the discontent at the delay of calling an Assembly."

In obedience to these instructions, Governor Lawrence brought the subject before his Council the 20th of May, 1758, and a resolution (prepared by Chief Justice Belcher the year before) was passed, to the effect "That a

The first Assembly of Nova Scotia met on the 7th of October, 1758, at Halifax, and elected Robert Sanderson as Speaker. A number of laws passed by the Governor and Council were passed with slight alterations; and the Assembly, on the question being put whether any money should be paid them for their services, unanimously resolved that the members should serve without any remuneration that session. (This was repealed by the members of the next elected Assembly.) The usual Speech from the Throne was made, and a complimentary address was moved in reply; and the Governor and his new Assembly got on better together than he had expected.*

"On October 19th, 1760, Governor Lawrence died from inflammation of the lungs, brought on by a cold taken at a ball

House of Representatives of the inhabitants of this province be a civil Legislature thereof, in conjunction with the Governor for the time being, and the Council; that the first House shall be known as the General Assembly, and shall consist of sixteen members, to be elected by the province at large—four by the township of Halifax, and two by the township of Lunenburg; and that as soon as any other township which might be erected had fifty electors (freeholders), it should be entitled to elect two representatives to the Assembly, as well as having the right of voting for representatives for the Province at large. Eleven members besides the Speaker were to form a quorum." (Tuttle's History of the Dominion of Canada, Chap. li., pp. 238, 239.)

* *Ib.*, p. 239.

"Lawrence was an active and able officer, and paid great attention to developing the resources of the province and promoting the welfare of the people. He opposed the Government scheme of making the colony a military settlement, and was permitted to invite a more desirable class of emigrants, farmers, mechanics, etc. A proclamation was issued, and inquiry soon followed as to the inducements offered to settlers. The terms were liberal. The townships were laid out at twelve miles square, or one hundred thousand acres each; and each settler was entitled to one hundred acres for himself, and fifty acres for every member of his family, on condition that he cultivated the land within thirty years; and each township was to have the right to send two members to the Legislature as soon as it contained fifty families. Agents from parties in Connecticut and Rhode Island visited Halifax in 1759, with a view to emigration, and selected Minas, Chignecto, and Cobequid, which had formerly been settled by the Acadians, as sites for townships. Emigration soon set in steadily towards the province; six vessels, with two hundred settlers, arrived from Boston; four schooners, with one hundred, came from Rhode Island; New London and Plymouth furnished two hundred and eighty; and three hundred came from Ireland, under the management of Alexander McNutt."—*Ib.*

at the Government House. He was deeply mourned by the colony, and his loss was severely felt. He was accorded a public funeral, and the Legislature caused a monument to be erected to his memory in St. Paul's Church, Halifax, as a mark of their sense of the many important services he had rendered the province. He was a wise and impartial administrator, and zealous and indefatigable in his endeavours for the public good; even his opposition to calling a General Assembly made him few enemies, and his strongest opponent in the matter, Chief Justice Belcher, who succeeded him in the administration, remained on good terms with him."*

In the same month that Governor Lawrence died, occurred the death of George the Second, in consequence of which the first House of Assembly of Nova Scotia was dissolved, and a new election, with some changes in the electoral districts, took place. The first meeting of the new Assembly was held the 1st of July, 1761, and the members of the House again agreed to give their services gratuitously. From the death of Governor Lawrence to the close of the American Revolution in 1783, there were ten governors and lieutenant-governors of Nova Scotia, under whose administration the colony was quiet and prosperous, though there was little increase in the population (until the influx of the U. E. Loyalists), and domestic manufactures were discouraged in the interests of English manufacturers.†

Down to the year 1783, at the close of the American revolutionary war, the population of Nova Scotia amounted to only a few thousand; but in the following year, by the forced exodus

---

* Tuttle's History of the Dominion of Canada, Chap. li., p. 239.

† Governor Francklin wrote to the Earl of Shelburne, in 1766, that "The country, in general, work up for their own use, into stockings and a stuff called homespun, what little wool their few sheep produce; and they also make part of their coarse linen from the flax they produce."—" I cannot omit representing to your lordship on this occasion, *that this Government has at no time given encouragement to manufactures which could interfere with those of Great Britain*, nor has there been the least appearance of any association of private persons for that purpose."—" It may be also proper to observe to your lordship, that all the inhabitants in this colony are employed either in husbandry, fishing, or providing lumber; and that all the manufactures for their clothing, and the utensils for farming and fishing, are made in Great Britain." (Tuttle, Chap. lxvi., p. 325.)

of the Loyalists from the United States, the population more than doubled. " Even before hostilities began, a number of loyal families emigrated from Boston, and settled on the River St. John, founding the town of Parrtown, now St John, N. B. They found the climate and soil both much better than they had expected; and the colony soon began to thrive apace. Settlements were made at Oromocto, where a fort was built, and one bold explorer penetrated as far as the present site of Fredericton, and cleared a farm there for himself. These emigrants numbered about 500, and the district they settled in was made the county of Sunbury. This, however, was only the advance guard of the immense army of emigrants which was to be attracted to the colony at the close of the war, and which was destined to play so important a part in the history of the Maritime Province. The exodus of the Loyalists from New England commenced immediately after the opening of negotiations for peace in November, 1782; for so bitter was the action of the different State Legislatures against them that Sir Guy Carleton (afterwards Lord Dorchester) could not await the action of Parliament, but took upon himself to commence their removal to Nova Scotia. On the 18th of May, 1783, the ships bearing the first instalment of Loyalist emigrants arrived at Navy Island, and during the summer they continued to arrive, until about 5,000 had settled between Parrtown (St. John) and St. Anne's. The peninsula now occupied by the city of St. John was then almost a wilderness, covered with shrubs, scrubby spruce, and marsh. Large numbers of emigrants also arrived at Annapolis, Port Roseway, and other points; and Governor Parr, in a letter to Lord North in September, 1783, estimates the whole number that had arrived in Nova Scotia and the island of St. John (Prince Edward's Island) at 13,000.

"These emigrants included all classes—disbanded soldiers, lawyers, clergymen, merchants, farmers, and mechanics; all in indigent circumstances, but willing to build up their own fortunes, and those of the land of their adoption, by honest labour and industry."*

* Tuttle's History of the Dominion of Canada, Chap. lxvi., p. 327.

" The Loyalists who settled at the St. John River did not agree very well with the original settlers. They grew angry with the Governor because their grants of land had not been surveyed. He in turn charged them with refusing to assist in the surveys, by acting as chairmen, unless they were well paid for it. Then they demanded additional representation in the Assembly. Nova Scotia was then divided into eight counties, and there were thirty-six representatives in the Assembly, the districts where a number of Loyalists had settled being included in the county of Halifax. Governor Parr opposed an increase of representation, as his instructions forbade his increasing or diminishing the number of representatives in the Assembly.

"The Loyalists then began to agitate for a division of the province—a policy which was strongly opposed by the Governor, and which gave rise to much excitement and ill-feeling. Parr went so far as to remove some of the Loyalists to the other side of the Bay of Fundy, in the hope that that would settle the agitation; but it only increased it, and the Loyalists, who had many warm and influential friends at court, urged a division so earnestly that the Ministry yielded to their wishes, and the Province of New Brunswick was created (in 1784), so called out of compliment to the reigning family of England. The River Missiquash was constituted the boundary line between the two provinces, and the separation took place in the fall of 1784, and the first Governor of New Brunswick, Colonel Thomas Carleton (brother of Lord Dorchester), arrived at St. John on the 21st of November. In the same year Cape Breton was made a separate colony (*a*); and as the Island of St. John (Prince Edward Island) had been separated from Nova Scotia in 1770, there were now four separate governments in what at present constitute the Maritime Provinces." (Tuttle's History of the Dominion of Canada, Chap. lxvi., pp. 328, 329.)

(*a*) In 1829, Cape Breton was restored to Nova Scotia, of which it now forms a part.

CHAPTER XLIII.

New Brunswick.

THE population of New Brunswick at the time of its separation from Nova Scotia, in 1784, was about 12,000. The governments of both provinces were similarly constituted—a Governor, an Executive and Legislative Council, members of the latter appointed by the Crown for life, and an Assembly or House of Commons, elected periodically by the freeholders; and both provinces were prosperous and contented for many years under successive governors, who seemed to have ruled impartially, and for the best interests of the people, though with narrower views of free government than those which obtained at a later period. The Loyalists not only obtained the establishment of New Brunswick as a province, but constituted the principal members of its Legislature, the officers of its government, and founders of its institutions; and the chief public men of the province have been from that day to this either U. E. Loyalists or their descendants.

Mr. Andrew Archer, in his excellent *History of Canada for the Use of Schools*, prescribed by the Board of Education for New Brunswick, gives the following account of the formation of the government of that province, and its founders:

"On Sunday, the 21st of November, 1784, Colonel *Thomas Carleton* (brother to Sir *Guy Carleton*), the first Governor of New Brunswick, arrived in St. John harbour and landed at Reed's Point. He had commanded a regiment during the revolutionary war, and was much esteemed by his Majesty's exiled Loyalists. The province was formally proclaimed the next day.

"The government of New Brunswick consisted of a Governor

and a Council that united both executive and legislative functions, and a House of Assembly of twenty-six representatives. The Council was composed of twelve members. They were men of great talent, and had occupied before the war positions of influence in their native States. Chief Justice *Ludlow* had been a judge of the Supreme Court of New York; *James Putman* was considered one of the ablest lawyers in all America; the Rev. and Hon. *Jonathan Odell*, first Provincial Secretary, had acted as chaplain in the Royal army, practised physic and written political poetry; Judge *Joshua Upham*, a graduate of Harvard, abandoned the Bar during the war, and became a colonel of dragoons; Judge *Israel Allen* had been colonel of a New Jersey Volunteer corps, and lost an estate in Pennsylvania through his devotion to the Loyalist cause; Judge *Edward Winslow*, nephew of Colonel *John Winslow*, who executed the decree that expelled the Acadians from Nova Scotia, had attained the rank of colonel in the Royal army; *Beverley Robinson* had raised and commanded the Loyal American Regiment, and had lost great estates on Hudson river; *Gabriel G. Ludlow* had commanded a battalion of Maryland Volunteers; *Daniel Bliss* had been a commissary of the Royal army; *Elijah Willard* had taken no active part in the war; *William Hagen* and *Guildford Studholme* were settled in the province before the landing of the Loyalists; Judge *John Saunders*, of a cavalier family in Virginia, had been captain in the Queen's Rangers, under Colonel Simcoe, and had afterwards entered the Temple and studied law in London. He was appointed to the Council after the death of Judge Putman. The government of the young province was governed with very few changes for several years.

"The town and district of Parr was incorporated in 1785, and became the city of *St. John*. It was the first, and long continued to be the only incorporated town in British America. It was governed by a mayor and a board of six aldermen and six assistants. The first two sessions of the General Assembly (1786-87) met in St. John. On meeting the Legislature at its first session, Governor Carleton expressed his satisfaction at seeing the endeavours of his Majesty to procure for the inhabitants the protection of a free government in so fair a way of being finally successful. He spoke of the peculiar munificence which had been extended to New Brunswick—the asylum of loyalty—and all the neighbouring States; and expressed his conviction that the people could not show their gratitude in a more becoming manner than by promoting sobriety, industry, and religion; by discouraging all factious and party distinctions, and by inculcating the utmost harmony between the newly-arrived Loyalists and the subjects formerly settled in the province.

" Two years afterwards (1788), the seat of government was removed to St. Anne's Point, Fredericton, which was considered the most central position in the province. It is said that Fredericton was chosen to be the seat of government because Albany, the seat of the Legislature of New York (from which State the great body of the Loyalists came), is situated many miles up the River Hudson, and is thus removed from the distracting bustle, the factious and corrupting influences of the great commercial metropolis at its mouth."*

* Chap. xxvi., pp. 260—262.

CHAPTER XLIV.

Prince Edward Island.

Prince Edward Island was first called by the French St. John's Island, on account of the day on which the French landed on it; but in 1799 its name was changed, and it was called Prince Edward's Island in honour of the Duke of Kent, (William Edward) afterward William IV. After the close of the American Revolution in 1783, a considerable number of the exiled Loyalists went to Prince Edward's Island and became merchants and cultivators of the soil.

"In 1763 the island was incorporated with Nova Scotia; but in 1770 it was made a separate province, in fulfilment of a curious plan of civilization. It was parcelled out in sixty-seven townships, and these were distributed by lottery among the creditors of the English Government, each of whom was bound to lodge a settler on every lot of two hundred acres that fell to him. The experiment was not at first very successful, but gradually the shares passed from the original speculators to men who knew how to use the rich soil and usually healthy climate of the island."*

* Bourne's "Our Colonies and Emigration," Chap. viii., p. 105.

CHAPTER XLV.

LOWER CANADA.

Lower Canada was first possessed by the French, and under the rule of France the government was purely despotic, though not cruel or harsh. On the conquest of Lower Canada in 1759, and its final ceding to England by the Treaty of Paris, 1763, a military government was instituted, which continued until 1774, when the famous "Quebec Act" was passed by the Imperial Parliament, known as the 14th George the Third, Chapter 83; or as "the Quebec Act"—it was introduced into the House of Lords on the 2nd of May, 1774—" for Making more Efficient Provision for the Province of Quebec." By the provisions of this famous Act, the boundaries of the province of Quebec were extended from Labrador to the Mississippi, embracing in one province the territory of Canada, together with all the country north-west of the Ohio to the head of Lake Superior and the Mississippi, and consolidating all authority over this boundless region in the hands of a Governor and Council of not less than seventeen or more than twenty-three members, with power to pass ordinances for the peace, welfare, and good government of the province. At the close of the war between England and France by the Peace of Paris, 1763, English emigration was invited to Lower Canada, with the promise, by Royal Proclamation, of *representative government*, as in the other colonies. That promise, however, was not fulfilled by the Act of 1774; but the Catholics were not displeased that the promise of a Representative Assembly was not kept, as a Representative Assembly, to which none but Protestants could at that time be chosen, was less acceptable to them than the despotic rule of a Governor and Council nominated by the Crown. The Quebec Act authorized the Crown to confer places of honour and business upon Catholics. The owners of estates were further gratified by the restoration of the French system of law. The English emigrants might complain of the want of jury trials in civil processes, but the French Canadians were grateful for relief from statutes which they did not comprehend. The nobility of New France, who were accustomed to arms, were still further conciliated by the proposal to enrol Canadian battalions, in which they could hold commissions on equal terms with English officers. The great dependence of the Crown, however, was on the clergy. The capitulation of New France had guaranteed to them freedom of public worship, but the laws for their support were held to be no longer valid. By the Quebec Act they were confirmed in the possession of their ancient churches and their revenues; so that the Roman Catholic worship was as effectually established in Canada as the Presbyterian Church in Scotland.*

This Act encountered very strong opposition both in England and America. The Mayor, Aldermen, and Council of the city of London presented a petition to the King against the Bill, praying his Majesty not to sign it. In that long and ably drawn up petition, occur the following words:

"We beg leave to observe that the English law, and that wonderful effort of human wisdom, the trial by jury, are not admitted by this Bill in any civil cases, and the French law of Canada is imposed on all the inhabitants of that extensive province, by which both the persons and properties of very many of your Majesty's subjects are rendered insecure and precarious. We humbly conceive that this Bill, if passed into a law, will be contrary not only with the compact entered into with the various settlers of the Reformed religion, who were invited into the said province under the sacred promise of enjoying the benefit of the laws of your realm of England, but likewise repugnant to your Royal Proclamation of the 7th of October, 1763, for the speedy settlement of the said new government. * * That the whole legislative power of the

---

* Bancroft, Vol. VII., Chap. xiv., pp. 157, 158.

province is vested in persons to be wholly appointed by your Majesty, and removable at your pleasure, which we apprehend to be repugnant to the leading principles of this free Constitution, by which alone your Majesty now holds, or legally can hold, the Imperial Crown of these realms."

In the House of Commons the Bill was strongly opposed by Messrs. Fox, Burke, Townsend and others, chiefly on the ground of its unconstitutionality, and every effort was made to amend it, but without success. The Bill was finally passed by a vote of 56 to 20.

In the House of Lords, the Bill was vehemently opposed by the Earl of Chatham, who protested against it "as a most cruel, oppressive, and odious measure, tearing up justice and every good principle by the roots," and "destructive of that liberty which ought to be the groundwork of every constitution." The Bill, however, passed the Lords by a vote of 26 to 7, and received the royal assent on the prorogation of Parliament, the 22nd of June, the King stating in regard to it that "it was founded on the clearest principles of justice and humanity, and would, he doubted not, have the best effect in quieting the minds and promoting the happiness of his Canadian subjects."

The feeling against the Act was intense both in England and the colonies, regarding it as a type of Imperial legislation for the colonies. "The strongest excitement prevailed in England for some months after the passing of the Act; and the papers were filled with little else than letters and remarks upon it." The British Loyalist settlers in Canada were indignant, and meetings were held in Quebec and Montreal, at which strong resolutions were passed, and petitions unanimously signed to the King, Lords and Commons, praying for the repeal of the Act, and forwarded to England.

"On the 17th of May, 1775, Lord Camden moved in the House of Lords for the repeal of the Act, but the motion was defeated by a vote of 88 to 28." A similar motion by Sir George Saville, in the Commons, was likewise defeated by a vote of 174 to 86.* The feeling of the Loyalists throughout

---

* "The excitement in England and Canada on the passage of the Act was, however, only a breeze compared to the storm of indignation which it raised in the thirteen other provinces when the news reached them; and

Canada was very strong against this Act; and its operations gave no satisfaction to any party.*

From the prevalent dissatisfaction among all parties in Canada with the Quebec Act of 1774, the Imperial Government having, in 1788, sanctioned ordinances to restore the *Habeas Corpus* Act, and the *trial by jury* in civil cases, and obtained

there is no doubt but that the passage of this Act was 'the last drop' which overflowed the cup of colonial patience, and led directly to the Declaration of Independence." (Tuttle's History of the Dominion of Canada, Chap. lix., pp. 295, 296.)

* "The provisions of the Quebec Act dissatisfied all parties when they came to be executed. The French majority, being represented by less than one-fourth of the number of members in the Council, thought themselves but little better off than when a purely military government. The English party considered themselves injured because the trial by jury, in civil cases, had been taken away. The absence of a representative form of government, and of the privileges of the *Habeas Corpus* Act, made them feel that they were denied the rights of British subjects.

"Nobody being satisfied, and the Governor (Sir Frederick Haldimand, whose governorship lasted from 1778 to 1785) being very arbitrary, discontent reigned in the provinces. There were loud complaints, not only of the Governor's tyranny, but also that justice was not fairly administered by the judges in the course of law.

"Many persons, on slight grounds, were thrown into prisons, were sent to England, and at length, 1785, the unpopular Governor demanded his own recall.

"The English Government saw that steps must be taken to put an end to the general discontent. But this could not be done without making such changes as might satisfy the increasing English and Protestant population as well as the French and Roman Catholics. Nor could such changes be made on the instant, or without due preparation. Accordingly, in the first instance, *trial by jury* in civil cases, and the law of *habeas corpus*, was introduced into the province (in 1788). Next it was determined to procure further and more perfectly reliable information about all its internal affairs, and find out, if possible, the best modes of removing the causes of complaint.

"Lastly, as a proof of the desire to deal impartially with the King's Canadian subjects, it was decided to send out, as governor, one who had rendered himself acceptable to all classes. This was no other than the popular Sir Guy Carleton, who had been made a peer with the title of *Lord Dorchester*, who reached Quebec in October, 1786. During the succeeding five years, until 1791, when he again departed (for a short time) to England, the Governor did all in his power to mitigate the bad feelings growing out of the differences of race, creed and language. In order to procure for the English Ministers the information they needed about the internal affairs of the province, he appointed Committees of Inquiry to inquire into all

full and minute information as to the internal state of Canada, a Bill was prepared and introduced into the House of Commons by Mr. Pitt, pursuant to a message from the King, on the 4th of March, 1791, establishing a representative government for Canada, after the model as far as possible of the British Constitution. This Act is sometimes called the "Grenville Act," having been chiefly prepared by Grenville, and conducted by him through the House of Lords; it is sometimes called the "Pitt Act," having been introduced and carried through the House of Commons by Pitt; but it is generally known in Canada as the Constitutional Act, 31 George III., Chapter 31—the Act which gave to Canada its first constitutional government, and under the provisions of which Canada was governed for fifty years, until the union of the two Canadas in 1841.

Mr. Pitt in introducing his Bill stated "that the division of the province into Upper and Lower Canada, he hoped would put an end to the competition between the old French inhabitants and the new settlers from Britain and the British colonies. This division he trusted would be made in such a manner as to give each a majority in their own particular part; although it could not be expected to draw a complete line of separation. Any inconvenience, however, to be apprehended from ancient Canadians being included in the one or British settlers in the other, would be averted by a local Legislature to be established in each.

"In imitation of the Constitution of the mother country, he would propose a Legislative Council and House of Assembly for each; the Assembly to be constituted in the usual manner, and the members of the Council to be for life; reserving to his Majesty to annex to certain honours an hereditary right of sitting in Council (a power never exercised). All laws and ordinances of the province to remain in force till altered by the new Legislature. The *Habeas Corpus* Act was already law by an ordinance of the province, and was to be continued as a fundamental principle of the Constitution.

particulars relating to *commerce, education, justice,* the *militia,* and the *tenure of lands;* to make full reports upon these; to suggest changes and improvements by which existing evils might be remedied." (Dr. Miles' School History of Canada, Chap. v., pp. 181, 182.)

See also Tuttle's History of the Dominion of Canada, Chap. v., p. 322.

"It was further meant to make a provision for a Protestant clergy in both divisions, by an allotment of lands in proportion to those already granted.

"The tenures were to be settled in Lower Canada by the local Legislature. In Upper Canada, the settlers being chiefly British, the tenures were to be soccage tenures.

"To prevent any such dispute as that which separated the thirteen colonies from the mother country, it was provided that the British Parliament should impose no taxes but such as might be necessary for the regulation of trade and commerce; and to guard against the abuse of this power, such taxes were to be levied and disposed of by the Legislature of each division."

The Bill was opposed in the House of Commons by Mr. Fox and others, upon the grounds that it created two provinces and two Legislatures, and made the members of the Legislative Councils nominees of the Crown for life, instead of leaving their election to the people; but the Bill was supported by Edmund Burke, who, with Fox, had voted side by side against the Quebec Act of 1774, but who opposed each other on the Canada Bill of 1791.*

Mr. Pitt, in reply to the objection of Mr. Fox and others, stated among other things, "That the population of *Upper*

---

* It was the discussion on this Bill which produced the first separation between Fox and Burke. The mind of Burke was excited to the highest degree by the principles and horrors of the French revolution, and he had frequently denounced it with the full force of his lofty eloquence; while Fox had repeatedly expressed his admiration of the French revolution. When the Canada Bill was discussed in the House of Commons, Burke commenced his speech by a philippic against the republican principles of the revolutionary Government of France; and concluded by declaring that if by adhering to the British Constitution would cause his friends to desert him, he would risk all, and, as his public duty taught him, exclaim in his last words, "Fly from the French Constitution!" Fox said in a low voice, "There is no loss of friendship, I hope." "Yes," retorted Burke, "there is a loss of friendship. I know the price of my conduct. Our friendship is at an end." Such a scene followed as had seldom, if ever, been witnessed in the House of Commons. Members were veritably affected by such an open rupture between those two celebrated statesmen and orators. Fox shed tears; and it was some time before he could sufficiently command his emotions to reply.

Canada amounted to only 10,000 inhabitants, and that of *Lower Canada* to not more than 100,000.*

With such preparation and explanations the Bill passed both Houses of Parliament and received the royal assent, conferring on Canada a new Constitution.

This Act separated the province of Quebec into two provinces, *Upper* and *Lower Canada*, the division line between which was the River Ottawa.

For each province a Legislature was established consisting of a *Governor*, a *Legislative Council* and *House of Assembly*—in imitation of the Constitution of England; for the Governor was to represent the Sovereign, the Legislative Council the House of Lords, and the Assembly the House of Commons.

The members of the Legislative Council were to be discreet persons, appointed by Royal authority for life; the members of the Assemblies were to be chosen by the people, once in four years, unless oftener called upon, by dissolution, to elect new members.

The Act was to come in force not later than the 31st of December, 1791; and the date of meeting of the new Legislature was not to be later than the 31st December, 1792.

Thus in fulfilment of a promise made in a Royal Proclamation in 1763, Canada obtained a *representative* form of government in 1791.

It has been seen that *the representative* form of government was obtained both for *Nova Scotia* and *New Brunswick* by the

---

* This was an under-estimate of the population of both provinces. Later and reliable authorities estimate the population of Lower Canada in 1791 at 150,000, of whom about 15,000 were British; in 1763 the population of Lower Canada was estimated at 65,000; the population had therefore more than doubled during the twenty-seven years of English rule. Before 1782, the English-speaking Protestant inhabitants were very insignificant in number; but after 1782 they increased rapidly, and are estimated at upwards of 15,000, and by some writers as high as 30,000 in the year 1791. The great majority of them, besides, were of classes of people accustomed to think for themselves, also officers and disbanded soldiers belonging to the army, and emigrants from the British Isles, who came to make homes for their families in Canada. (Miles' School History of Canada, Part II., Chap. v., pp. 183, 184.)

It is stated on the best authorities that 10,000 Loyalist emigrants arrived in what was afterwards designated Upper Canada, during the year 1783; in 1791 the population of Upper Canada is stated to have been 12,000.

representation and influence of the *United Empire Loyalists*; it was so in Canada. Thus are we indebted to the *United Empire Loyalists* not only for our unity with the British empire, but for the original constitution of representative government which, with enlarged application, is the basis of that free government which now prevails throughout all the provinces of the Dominion of Canada.

GOVERNMENT OF LOWER CANADA.

In 1786, Lord Dorchester had been appointed Governor of Canada and Commander-in-Chief of the British forces in North America.* But he left for England in August, 1791, on a year's leave, and in his absence the administration of the Government was entrusted to the Lieutenant-Governor, General Alured Clarke, a retired British officer. The elections took place in June, 1792, and were in some instances warmly contested. Lower Canada had been divided into twenty-one counties, eighteen of which elected two members each, and three—the counties of Gaspé, Bedford, and Orleans—returned one member each; the cities of Quebec and Montreal were each represented by four members, and Three Rivers by two. Of the fifty members elected to the first House of Assembly, fifteen were of British origin, and thirty-five were of French origin.†

The Legislative Council consisted of fifteen members.

* "In June, 1786, Sir Guy Carleton, now raised to the peerage as Lord Dorchester, was appointed Governor-General of all the provinces, and Commander-in-Chief of all the forces in British America. He arrived at Quebec on the 23rd of October, and was joyfully received by all classes, but especially by the Canadians, with whom he was a great favourite on account of the mildness and justice with which he had treated them during his former administrations. At the same time there also arrived a new Chief Justice for Quebec, Mr. Smith, who had been Attorney-General for New York, but had been forced to leave on account of his loyalty to the British Crown." (Tuttle's History of the Dominion of Canada, Chap. lxv., p. 321.

† "The elections came off during June, and the people exercised their new privilege with prudence and judgment, returning good men; and although the elections were warmly contested in some places, everything passed off quietly. There were fifteen English-speaking members elected, amongst whom were some of the leading merchants, such as James McGill, Joseph Frobisher, John Richardson and others, whose descendants are still amongst our leading citizens. Amongst the French elected were many of

On the 30th of October, the Provincial Parliament was commanded to meet at Quebec the 17th of December, 1792, for the actual despatch of business. On the meeting of the Legislative Council that day, the Hon. Chief Justice William Smith was appointed Speaker. The House of Assembly did not agree upon the election of Speaker on the first day—the French and English-speaking members advocating respectively the election of a Speaker of their own language; but at length Mr. J. A. Panet was elected by a large majority—he speaking both languages with equal fluency.*

the most prominent seignors, such as Louis De Salaberry, M. H. De Rouville, Philip Rocheblave, M. E. G. C. De Lotbiniere, M. La Vatrice and others. Altogether, it is generally claimed that the first Assembly of Lower Canada was the best the province ever had." (Tuttle's History of the Dominion of Canada, Chap. lxviii., p. 330.)

* The French-speaking members nominated Mr. J. A. Parret (Panet), a leading advocate of Quebec ; and the English party nominated successively Mr. James McGill, one of the most prominent merchants of Montreal, and William Grant, of Quebec. The feeling was strong on each side to have in the Speaker a gentleman of their own language ; but Mr. Parret (Panet) was ultimately chosen by a large majority, to some extent because *he understood and spoke both languages fluently.* This gentleman occupied the position of Speaker for upwards of twenty years, and fully justified the wisdom of the first Assembly in electing him."—*Ib.*, p. 330.

It is singular that in some histories of Canada it should have been stated that the Speaker elected by the first House of Assembly could speak no other tongue than the French language. Mr. Archer, in his History of Canada for the Use of Schools, says : " By a vote of twenty-eight to eighteen, M. Panet, *who could speak no language but his native French,* was chosen" (p. 269). Mr. Withrow, in his excellent History of Canada, says : " Mr. Panet, a distinguished advocate, *who spoke no language but his native French,* was elected Speaker of the Assembly" (p. 291). The very discussion which took place on the election of Speaker turned chiefly on the point whether a Speaker should be elected who could speak one or both languages. Mr. P. L. Panet, brother to Mr. J. A. Panet, who was elected Speaker, in reply to some of his own countrymen who advocated the exclusive use of the French language, while he advocated the ultimate use of the English language alone in the Legislature and in the courts of law, commenced and concluded his speech in the following words : " I will explain my mind on the necessity that the Speaker we are about to choose *should possess and speak equally well the two languages.*"—" I think it is but decent that the Speaker on whom we may fix our choice be one who can express himself in English when he addresses himself to the representative of our Sovereign." (Christie's History of Canada, Vol. I., Chap. iv., pp. 127, 128, in a note.) Mr. Christie, after stating in the text about " J. A. Panet, Esq., an old and eminent advo-

The Lieutenant-Governor made a speech expressing the solicitude and consideration of the King for his Canadian subjects, in recommending to his Parliament such a change in their colonial government as circumstances might require and admit. "On a day like this," said his Excellency, "signalized by the commencement in this country of that form of government which has raised the kingdom to which it is subordinate to the highest elevation, it is impossible not to feel emotions difficult to be expressed.

"To give an opportunity for your loyal and grateful acknowledgments to his Majesty is one of my motives for calling you together, and that debt discharged, your Council will doubtless be next employed for enacting the laws necessary to confirm and augment the property of your country."

The Lieutenant-Governor concluded in the following words:

"Great Britain being happily at peace with all the world, and I hope without apprehension of its interruption, the present moment must be most fit and urgent for all those arrangements best made at a season of tranquillity, and falling within the sphere of our trust. The conviction I feel of your disposition to cultivate that harmony amongst yourselves and each branch of the Legislature, which is always essential to the public good and private satisfaction, makes it unnecessary for me to enlarge upon this subject.

"Such objects as it may become my duty to recommend to your consideration, shall be occasionally communicated to you by message."

The address of the Assembly in answer to his Excellency's speech breathed a spirit of grateful affection and loyalty. After expressing their warmest gratitude to the King and Parliament of Great Britain, "in granting to his Majesty's subjects in this province a new and liberal Constitution for their colonial government," the Assembly proceeds:

cate of the Quebec bar, returned a member for the Upper Town of Quebec, was chosen by the Assembly for its Speaker," remarks, in a note, before giving the speech of Mr. P. L. Panet quoted above, that "this excellent man and good citizen (J. A. Panet) served, as we shall see in proceeding, many years as Speaker, and without other remuneration or reward than the approbation of his fellow-citizens and subjects." (Tuttle's History of the Dominion of Canada, Chap. lxvii., p. 127.)

"We cannot express the emotions which arose in our breasts, on that ever-memorable day when we entered on the enjoyment of a Constitution assimilated to that form of government which has carried the glory of our mother country to the highest elevation. * *

"It is an unparalleled happiness for us to have an opportunity of presenting to his Majesty our loyal thanks, and of expressing to him our gratitude; such homage is the language of our hearts, and it is due from us, for all the favours with which we have been loaded. That duty fulfilled, we will turn our attention with most ardent zeal to framing such laws as may tend to the prosperity and advantage of our country.

"We hear with pleasure that Great Britain is at peace with all the world, and we consider this as the most favourable time for the consideration of the objects that fall within the sphere of our charge, to cultivate harmony among ourselves and each branch of the Legislature; that it is a condition essentially necessary to the public good and our own private satisfaction.

"We will at all times give the most speedy and deliberate consideration to such messages as we may receive from your Excellency."

Throughout this address of the Assembly there is the true ring of manly sincerity, and heartfelt loyalty to the Throne and to the unity of the empire. The Governor soon sent several messages to the Assembly, submitting, by command of the King, various subjects for their consideration, for which he received their cordial thanks, and assurances that the subjects submitted would receive their best consideration.

There was one subject of discussion which created much feeling and protracted debate—namely, the language in which the proceedings of the Assembly should be conducted, recorded, and published; but the rising storm was allayed and unity restored by the decision to leave each member at liberty to address the House in French or English at his pleasure—to have all motions, before being put to the House, read in both languages, and the record of the proceedings kept and published in both languages—a happy arrangement, which has been continued to this day.

The House of Assembly, in their reply to the opening speech of the Lieutenant-Governor, expressed their intention of presenting their heartfelt thanks to his Majesty for the new and liberal Constitution conferred upon them. That truly loyal address was as follows, and does lasting honour to its authors and the Imperial Government:

"We, your Majesty's most dutiful and loyal subjects, the representatives of Lower Canada, met in Assembly for the first time under our new Constitution, humbly approach the Throne, to express to your most gracious Majesty our sentiments of gratitude and joy on the happy change which has taken place in the forms of our government.

"The Constitution which it hath pleased your Majesty and Parliament to give us, modelled upon that of Great Britain—a Constitution which has carried the empire to the highest pitch of glory and prosperity—assures to this colony the most solid advantages, and will for ever attach it to the parent State.

"Now, partaking without distinction the benefits of a government which protects all equally, we offer our thanks to Divine Providence for the happiness prepared for us. Our prayers are for the general prosperity of the nation of which we make a part, and for the preservation and felicity of our august and virtuous Sovereign.

"May it please your Majesty to receive favourably our respectful homage, and permit us anew to express our loyalty and attachment.

"May it please your Majesty and Parliament to receive our most humble thanks for the favour conferred upon this colony.

"Such are the heartfelt wishes of the representatives of the people of Lower Canada."

Such were the auspicious circumstances and cordiality of feeling attendant upon the inauguration of constitutional government in Lower Canada. The session continued upwards of four months —from December until May—during which time a great many subjects were introduced respecting expenses and revenues, salaries of officers, affairs appertaining to legislation, to the militia, to the administration of justice, and the welfare of the country; but only eight *Bills* were passed, and which were assented to in the King's name by the Lieutenant-Governor, who prorogued the Legislature on the 9th of May, 1793, with a short and complimentary speech.

It is not my object to narrate in detail the legislation or

proceedings of any of the colonies, except in so far as may be necessary to illustrate the history of *the Loyalists of America*. A most impressive illustration of true loyalty was given by the Assembly of Lower Canada before the close of its first session. In the Lieutenant-Governor's speech at the opening of the session, he informed the Legislature that Great Britain was at peace with all the world, and that there was no apprehension of its interruption. But before the close of the session intelligence was received at Quebec that the revolutionary authorities of France had declared war against Great Britain.

On the 25th of April, 1793, the Lieutenant-Governor sent a message to the Assembly, informing them that he had received a letter from the Secretary of State, of the 9th of February previous, stating that "the persons exercising the supreme authority in France had declared war against his Majesty."*

The answer to the message breathes the *Loyalists*' spirit. They thanked his Excellency for his message, and assured him that "it was with horror they had heard that the most atrocious act which ever disgraced society had been perpetrated in France (alluding to the recent decapitation of the unfortunate Louis XV.), and that it was with concern and indignation they now learned that the persons exercising the supreme authority there had declared war against his Majesty.

"His Majesty's faithful subjects earnestly pray that his arms may be crowned with such signal success over his enemies as shall speedily bring about a peace honourable, safe, and advantageous to his Majesty and the empire."

In conclusion, the Assembly assured his Excellency that "the House would immediately proceed to a revision of the Militia

---

* The transmission of this letter occupied *ten weeks*, it being dated the 9th of February, and reaching Quebec the 25th of April. In the *Quebec Gazette* of the 10th of November, 1792, it is stated that the latest news from Philadelphia and New York was to the 8th of October, giving accounts of a battle on the Wabash and Arguille rivers, between an expedition of American forces under General Wilkinson and a body of Indians, in which the latter were routed. In a notice from the "General Post Office, Quebec, 17th of November, 1791," information is given that "a mail for England will be closed at this office on Monday, the 5th of December next, at four o'clock p.m., to be forwarded by way of New York, in H.M. packet-boat which will sail from thence in January." (Christie's History of Canada, Vol. I., Chap. iv., p. 142.)

laws, and if alterations and amendments were necessary they would make such amendments as should be deemed the most fit and proper to secure and protect the province from every insult and injury of his Majesty's enemies."

At the close of the session, after assenting, on behalf of the King, to the eight Bills which had been passed, the Lieutenant-Governor delivered the proroguing speech, in which he thanked the Assembly for the diligent and practical consideration which they had given to the various subjects which had been submitted to them, and the "further regulations necessary for the better organizing and more effectually calling forth the militia for the defence of this extensive and valuable country, when our enemies of any description shall make it necessary." His Excellency alluded to the war of the rulers of France against England in the following words :

"Gentlemen, at the first meeting of the Legislature, I congratulated you upon the flattering prospects which opened to your view and upon the flourishing and tranquil state of the British empire, then at peace with all the world. Since that period, I am sorry to find its tranquillity has been disturbed by the unjustifiable and unprecedented conduct of the persons exercising the supreme power in France, who, after deluging their own country with the blood of their fellow-citizens, and imbruing their hands in that of their Sovereign, have forced his Majesty and the surrounding nations of Europe into a contest which involves the first interests of society. In this situation of public affairs, I reflect with peculiar pleasure upon the loyal and faithful attachment of his Majesty's subjects of this province to his royal person, and to that form of government we have the happiness to enjoy."*

* "Thus ended the first session of the first Parliament of Lower Canada, and as a whole we may say that the session was a satisfactory one. The demons of party spirit and of national prejudice had indeed shown themselves; but only enough to show that they were in existence, and would become potent agents of discord as the heat of political contest warmed them into life. The war of races, which had been going on between the French and English on this continent for over a century and a half, was not ended by the capitulation and cession of Canada ; only the scene of action was changed from the battle field to the council chamber, and words and ballots took the place of swords and bullets. The French Canadians showed at the very commencement of constitutional government that they considered the

The second session of the Parliament was summoned by Lord Dorchester himself, the 11th of November, 1793.* This session lasted seven months and a half, though only six Bills were passed. In his speech at the opening of the session, Lord Dorchester recommended the due administration of justice, together with the arrangements necessary for the defence and

French language, the French people, the French laws, and the French religion, the language, people, laws, and religion of Canada, and that the English were only interlopers who had no business there, and with whom they were to affiliate as little as possible." (Tuttle's History of the Dominion of Canada, Chap. lxviii., p. 332.)

With the exception of the first sentence, we have no sympathy with the spirit or sentiment of the above quoted passage. The addresses to the Governor and the King show that the French did not regard the British as intruders, but as the legitimate rulers of the country, to whom they expressed all possible respect and loyalty. All that they asked on the question of language was, that in legislative and judicial proceedings the French language might be equally used with the English language; and was this unreasonable on the part of those who then comprised nine-tenths of the population, and whose laws and exercise of worship had been guaranteed by the articles of capitulation and the Quebec Act of 1774 ?

* "The Provincial Parliament met again at Quebec on the 11th of November, 1793, and was opened by Lord Dorchester, who had arrived at Quebec from England on the 24th of September, and re-assumed the government; his Excellency Major-General Clarke returning to England, bearing with him the best wishes of those whose Constitution he had fairly started, and put in operation to their satisfaction. His government had been popular, and he received several flattering addresses at departing.

"Lord Dorchester's return was cordially welcomed, a general illumination taking place at Quebec the evening of his arrival." (Christie's History of Canada, Chap. v., p. 145.)

"The great French revolution, causing France such awful scenes of distress and bloodshed as the world had never seen before, was in progress. It made the Canadians feel that their transfer to the Crown of England now saved them from innumerable evils which would have been their lot had Canada been again restored to France.

"Lord Dorchester's popularity and personal influence were made useful in preventing the people of the provinces from being misled by seditious persons who came from France on purpose to tamper with them." (Miles' School History of Canada, Part Third, Chap. i., p. 190.)

"All Europe was engaged in war, and the emissaries of the French republic were busily at work trying to gain sympathy in the United States, and stir up that country to war with England—an effort which would probably have succeeded had it not been for the firmness of Washington. The consul for France in the United States was also endeavouring to spread republican

safety of the province, as matters of the first importance. His Excellency also informed the Assembly that he would order to be laid before them an account of all the receipts of the provincial revenues of the Crown since the division of Upper and Lower Canada.

The purport of his Excellency's speech, and the spirit of the Assembly, and the relations between the colony and the parent state, may be inferred from the following cordial and complimentary address of the Assembly in answer to the Governor's opening speech:

"Fully convinced of the happy effects to be derived from a solid and invariable administration of justice, and of the indispensable necessity for an establishment for assuring the defence and safety of the province, we will lose no time in resuming the consideration of these important subjects, and in making such amendments in the existing laws as may best protect the persons and property of its inhabitants.

"By receiving from your Excellency an account of the receipts of the provincial revenues of the Crown, we shall be enabled to deliberate on the means by which they may be rendered more productive; and penetrated with gratitude to the parent state for having hitherto defrayed the surplus expenditure of the province, we flatter ourselves that, in consideration of our situation, we shall continue to receive her generous assistance—a hope further strengthened by your Excellency's intention of not requiring from us any subsidy at present, which confirms the benevolence of the mother country.

"In the infancy of our Constitution, we perceive the necessity of greater circumspection in the formation of laws that may tend to support and establish it; and also to cultivate amongst the different branches of the Legislature that cordial harmony and concord so necessary to promote the measures essential to the happiness and well-being of our country."

ideas in Canada, to incite the people to revolt against British authority, and to declare themselves in favour of the republic. It was no wonder then that the great bulk of the law-abiding and peace-loving citizens of Canada welcomed Lord Dorchester with delight—one who had for so many years been associated in their recollections with peace and prosperity, and who had successfully resisted the attack of the only foe who had assailed Quebec during his many administrations." (Tuttle, Chap. lxviii., p. 333.)

The Assembly bestowed much attention upon the Judicature Bill of the previous session, and on the Militia Bill, and brought them to maturity ; also an Alien Bill was introduced and passed, establishing "regulations respecting aliens and certain subjects of his Majesty, who have resided in France, coming into this province and residing therein, and for empowering his Majesty to receive and detain persons charged with or suspected of high treason, and for the arrest and commitment of all persons who may individually, by seditious practices, attempt to disturb the government of this province.*

It happened at the commencement of this session that Edward, Duke of Kent, the father of our beloved Queen Victoria, was in Canada, and held military command of the troops. The day after the assembling of the Legislature, the Assembly presented him with a most cordial and affectionate address, as did subsequently the Legislative Council, clergy, and citizens of Quebec, Montreal, and Three Rivers, styling the prince "the son of the best of sovereigns." The prince delighted all by his answers, his amiable manners and exemplary conduct. All were especially delighted with his declared disapprobation of the terms *the King's old and new subjects ;*"

* It appears by a proclamation of Lord Dorchester, dated the 26th of November, a fortnight after the commencement of the session of the Legislature, that there were emissaries of France and others in the province, who were busy in propagating among the inhabitants the revolutionary principles of the infidel and bloody rulers of France. He says : " Whereas divers evil-disposed persons had lately manifested seditious and wicked attempts to alienate the affections of his Majesty's loyal subjects by false representations of the cause and conduct of the persons at present exercising supreme authority in France, and particularly certain foreigners, being alien enemies, who are lurking and lie concealed in various parts of this province, *acting in concert with persons in foreign dominions* (evidently alluding to parties in the United States), with a view to forward the criminal purposes of such persons, enemies of the peace and happiness of the inhabitants of this province, and of all religion, government, and order." His Excellency therefore called upon all magistrates, captains of militia, peace-officers, and others of his Majesty's good subjects throughout the province, to be vigilant, and to do their utmost to discover and secure all and every person who might hold seditious discourses, or utter treasonable words, spread false news, publish or distribute libellous papers, written or printed, tending to excite discontent or lessen the affections of his Majesty's subjects, or in any manner to disturb the peace and happiness under his Majesty's government in this colony," etc.

"*French and English inhabitants.*" He said all were "the King's Canadian subjects."*

Lord Dorchester transmitted to the Assembly, on the 29th of April, 1794, a message peculiarly interesting from its being the first financial statement laid before the Legislature of Lower Canada. The message commences: " The Governor has given directions for laying before the House of Assembly an account of the provincial revenue of the Crown from the commencement of a new Constitution to the 10th of January, 1794."†

The House, by an address, thanked his Excellency for the message and papers accompanying it; they observed that they

---

* " The prince, shortly after this, receiving notice of his promotion to the rank of major-general, and appointment to a command in the West Indies, was presented, previous to his departure from Quebec, with several congratulatory letters of a most gratifying character. The Legislative Council, the Roman Catholic clergy, the citizens of Quebec, and the burgesses of William Henry paid his Royal Highness spontaneous respects in this manner, to whom he responded feelingly and affectionately, for the spontaneous proofs of esteem which in parting they gave him; and which in truth were not the effusions of adulation, but an homage of a grateful people to the intrinsic virtues and the social and manly character of a son of, as he was truly called, ' the best of sovereigns.'" (Christie's History of Canada, Vol I., Chap. v., p. 140.)

† The account transmitted was under six heads:

1. " The casual and territorial revenue established prior to the conquest, which his Majesty has been most graciously pleased to order to be applied towards defraying the civil expenses of the province."

2. " The duties payable to his Majesty under the Act of the 14th of his reign, chap. 88 (the ' Quebec Act '), on articles imported into the province of Quebec, and on licenses to persons for retailing spirituous liquors."

3. " The duties imposed by the Provincial Legislature, with the appropriation and balance."

4. " Amount of cash received from fines and forfeitures imposed by the courts of justice."

5. " The naval officers' returns inwards since the division of the province, which were originally intended as a check on the customs, but seem not to answer the end imposed."

6. " A statement of the monies taken out of the pocket of the subject on this account; its progress and diminution before it lodges in the public coffers, with the after diminution on account of the collection, that every circumstance of this important business may be constantly before their eyes; that in the outset of the Constitution, and its progress, they may guard this important branch from those corruptions and abuses which have brought so many miseries on other nations."

saw in it an additional proof of the paternal solicitude of his Majesty to ease the burdens of his subjects, and of his Excellency's anxiety to promote the interests of this province; and that the magnitude and utility of the objects recommended to their consideration could not fail engaging their serious attention as soon as the important matters now before them, and in a state of progression, were accomplished.*

In closing the session, the 31st of May, 1794, Lord Dorchester assented, in the King's name, to five Bills, reserving the Judicature Bill for the royal pleasure (which was approved and became law the following December), and one for appointing Commissioners to treat with Commissioners on behalf of Upper Canada, relating to duties and drawbacks to be allowed to that province on importations through the lower province. The closing speech of his Excellency, among other things, contained the following words:

"I have no doubt that, on returning to your respective homes, you will zealously diffuse among all ranks of people those principles of justice, patriotism, and loyalty which have distinguished your public labours during this session, and that you will use your best exertions to find out and bring to justice those evil-disposed persons who, by inflammatory discourses, or the spreading of seditious writings, endeavour to deceive the unwary and disturb the peace and good order of society; and that you will avail yourselves of every opportunity to convince your fellow-subjects that the blessings they enjoy under a truly free and happy Constitution can be preserved only by a due obedience to the laws, all breaches of which are the more inexcusable as the Constitution itself has provided for the safe and easy repeal or modification of such as may not answer the good intentions of the Legislature."

The interval between the close of the second and the opening of the third session of the Legislature, from the 31st of May, 1794, to 5th of January, 1795, quiet and contentment prevailed in the province; and the short speech of Lord Dorchester (for his speeches were always short and to the point) at the opening of this third Session was chiefly one of congratulation, commendation and suggestion. Among other things he said:

* Christie's History of Canada, Vol. I., Chap. v., where the accounts referred to are given in detail.

"Gentlemen, I shall order to be laid before you a statement of the provincial revenues of the Crown for the last year, together with such part of the expenditure as may enable you to estimate the ways and means for the most necessary supplies, in bringing forward which you will keep in view the advantages of providing for the public exigencies by a prudent restraint on luxuries, and by regulations which may, at the same time, encourage and extend commerce.

"Gentlemen, the judges and law officers of the Crown have been directed to draw up and report their opinion on the subject of your address to me on the 28th of May last" (this related to the establishment of forms of proceeding in the courts of justice, and a table of fees to which the different civil officers, advocates, notaries, and land surveyors should be entitled in their respective offices); "and I have much satisfaction in perceiving this early disposition on your part to prevent and guard against abuses which might impede the course of justice, or give rise to customs that would establish oppressive demands, and gradually efface from our minds a due sense of their unwarrantable origin.

"Your own disinterested conduct in your legislative capacity; your zealous endeavours to promote a general obedience to the laws, connected with a benevolent attention to the interests of the subject, form a solid foundation for government, and afford me great hopes that our new Constitution will be firmly established, and ensure, for ages to come, the happiness of the people."

Referring to this speech of Lord Dorchester, Mr. Christie well remarks: "The foresight, the rectitude, the wisdom of this most upright man and virtuous governor, cannot fail to strike the reader, and command his respect and admiration."

As might be expected, the address of the House of Assembly in answer to the Governor's speech was equally cordial and assuring, concluding with the following words:

"It is highly flattering to us that our conduct in our legislative capacity has met with your Excellency's approbation. Being thoroughly sensible of the happiness we enjoy under the free and liberal Constitution which has been granted to us by the parent state, under your Excellency's prudent and wise administration, we will continue to exert our most zealous endeavours to promote a general obedience to the laws, and to establish that Constitution in such a manner as may ensure for ages to come the happiness of the people."

On the 16th of February, 1795, the Governor sent a message to the Assembly, transmitting "the accounts of the provincial scheme of the Crown from the 6th of January, 1794, to the 5th of January, 1795, also of the civil expenditure for the same period."*

The Commissioners appointed under the Act of the previous session, to treat with Commissioners on behalf of Upper Canada concerning duties and drawbacks to be allowed in favour of that province, reported that they had met and finally adjusted with them the sum to be reimbursed to Upper Canada for 1793 and 1794.†

Several important Acts were passed this session relating to revenue, defraying the charges for the administration, the

---

* This return contained all the accounts transmitted the year before, under the six heads mentioned in a previous note, page 298, and other accounts under fourteen additional heads, the eighth of which is as follows:

"No. 8. Estimate of such part of the civil expenditure for the ensuing year as may enable the House of Assembly to calculate the ways and means for the most necessary supplies; all the pensions, amounting to £1,782 6s. 6d. sterling, though chiefly granted for services rendered in Canada, are deducted, these services being considered as rendered to the empire at large; it is from thence, therefore, their rewards, with other acts of benevolence, may be expected to flow. The salaries of sundry officers, to the amount of £782 10s., appearing to belong to the military rather than the civil expenditure, are also deducted."

† The following extract from their report illustrates the amicable spirit in which the Commissioners of the two provinces entered upon their work and arranged the matters committed to their trust:

"The Commissioners, as well as those for Upper Canada, being authorized to enter into an agreement for a further period, and being equally desirous to treat on the subject, which if unprovided for might give rise to difficulties hereafter; being at the same time most solicitous on both sides to preserve the harmony and cordiality which prevail between the two provinces, the article of the provisional agreement for two years was cheerfully assented to. By that article the province of Upper Canada is entitled to one-eighth part of the revenue already payable on goods, wares, or merchandise coming into Lower Canada, under an Act of the Legislature thereof; and to assure the most perfect freedom of trade with the sister province, it is provided that no imposts or duties shall be imposed or shall be laid by Upper Canada, which renders unnecessary the establishing of Custom-houses on the line

support of the civil government, and for other purposes. On the 7th of May, his Excellency prorogued the Legislature with a speech which contained the following paragraphs:

"Gentlemen, I cannot put an end to this session of our Provincial Parliament without expressing my approbation and thanks for that zeal for the public welfare which has distinguished all your proceedings.

"Gentlemen of the House of Assembly, the cheerfulness with which you have granted a supply towards defraying the civil expenditure of the province gives me great satisfaction; the judicious choice you have made of the means for this purpose, evinces a tender regard for the interests and condition of this country; and the unanimity in this tribute of gratitude and attachment to the King's government cannot but be highly pleasing to his Majesty."

The fourth and last session of this Parliament was summoned for the 20th of November, 1795, and continued until the 7th of May, 1796, during which twelve Bills were passed that received the royal assent. In his opening speech, his Excellency expressed his "great satisfaction to observe, during the present session, a continuance of the same zealous attention to their legislative duties, and to the general interests of the province, which he had occasion to notice in their former proceedings." His concluding words were:

"Gentlemen of the Legislative Council, and Gentlemen of the House of Assembly, in expressing my approbation of your proceedings, I must further observe that the unanimity, loyalty, and disinterestedness manifested by this first Provincial Parliament of Lower Canada, have never been surpassed in any of his Majesty's provincial dominions; and I feel convinced that the prosperity and happiness of this country will continue to increase in proportion as succeeding Parliaments shall follow your laudable example."

Thus ended the first Parliament of Lower Canada; thus was inaugurated and consolidated its government, which, without

which divides the two provinces, but saves to both an expense which, in all probability, would far exceed any trifle of revenue that this agreement may take from one or the other of the provinces more than their legitimate proportion."

the strife of partizanship or the machinery of party, was pure, just, mild, economical, patriotic, and progressive.

Thus also ended, in the course of a few weeks, Lord Dorchester's connection with Canada; for having obtained his Majesty's leave of absence, he embarked with his family for England the 9th of July, 1796. He was far advanced in life; he had been, with few interruptions, connected with Canada, as officer, military commander, and governor, more than thirty-six years. He was with General Wolfe at the siege and taking of Quebec in 1759, where he was wounded; he was colonel of the Grenadiers, and quartermaster-general of Wolfe's army. In the various capacities in which he served, whether as governor or commander-in-chief or diplomatist, he was equally distinguished for his courage and prudence, his justice and humanity, as well as for his many social and private virtues.*

His departure from Canada was a matter of universal regret. Farewell addresses were presented to him by the citizens of Quebec, Montreal, and other places—all expressing to him the highest respect and warmest gratitude for his long and valuable services to Canada. The general spirit of these addresses may be inferred from the following expressions:

"Having experienced for many years your lordship's mild and auspicious administration of his Majesty's Government, and being aware that during that period the resources,

---

* The conduct and character of Lord Dorchester as governor and commander-in-chief of the army may be inferred from the following among many other notices in the Index to Bancroft's History of the United States, Vol. X., p. 616:

"Carleton, Guy, afterwards Lord Dorchester, colonel of Grenadiers in Wolfe's army; is wounded; is at Havana (one of the commanders in taking it); Governor of Canada; has full authority to arm and employ the Canadians and Indians against the Americans; abhors the scheme; takes measures for the defence of the province; the command of Canada assigned to him, he will not turn the savages loose on the frontier; returns no answer to Montgomery's summons; repels the assault made by that general; is lenient to his prisoners; his humanity to sick Americans left behind; blamed for restraining the Indians; restrains the ravages of the Indians; the King and Ministers are displeased at this; Carleton prepares to invade the United States; is displeased at being superseded by Burgoyne; refuses to assist Burgoyne; is complained of by that officer; supersedes Clinton in America; his humanity; restrains Indian hostility."

prosperity, and happiness of this province have increased in a degree almost unequalled, we, the inhabitants of the city of Quebec, respectfully request your lordship to accept our sincere and most grateful thanks and acknowledgments.

"The length of your residence in the province; the advantages derived to our society from the example of private virtues shown by yourself and your family; your lordship's uniform prudent and paternal attention, under every change of time and circumstance, to the true interests of his Majesty's subjects entrusted to your immediate care, and that gratitude which we feel (and must be permitted to repeat), excite in our minds the warmest sentiments of personal attachment, of which allow us to tender you the strongest assurance.

"Under these impressions, we view your lordship's intended departure with the deepest regret; and submitting to your determination to leave us with unfeigned reluctance, we entreat you to accept our most sincere wishes for the future prosperity of yourself and all your family."

In the Montreal address we have the following expressions of sentiment and feelings:

"The inhabitants of Montreal, penetrated with gratitude for the happiness enjoyed by them under your lordship's administration of the government of this province during a great number of years, embrace the present opportunity of your intended departure for Great Britain to entreat you to receive their humble acknowledgments and accept their most sincere wishes for your health and prosperity, and for that of all your family.

"The prudence and moderation which distinguished your conduct in the province assured internal peace and tranquillity, and in reflecting infinite honour on your lordship, have fully justified the confidence reposed in you by our august Sovereign, and assured to you the affections of the inhabitants."

The grateful and affectionate answers of Lord Dorchester to both addresses may be easily conceived. The comparatively happy state of things indicated by these addresses continued, with interruptions, for about ten years after Lord Dorchester's departure.

Lord Dorchester was succeeded by General Prescott, who became lieutenant-governor, until he was relieved the 31st of July, 1799, by the appointment of Sir Robert S. Milnes, who acted as lieutenant-governor of the province during the ensuing six years, when the senior Executive Councillor, Thomas Dunn, succeeded to the administration of the government for two years, until the appointment, in 1807, of Sir James Craig as lieutenant-governor and commander-in-chief, under whose administration the reign of discord and strife of race became predominant, with the natural results which in long years afterwards ensued. These matters, however, do not come within the province of my history of the Loyalists of America.

But it is to be observed that though the French had much to complain of, having scarcely any representation in the Legislative Council, none in the Executive, and none in the Provincial Board of Education, called the "Royal Institution," which had the care of education in the province,* and therefore had to depend alone upon their own elected representatives in the House of Assembly for the protection of their rights and feelings; yet they evinced a loyalty through all these years, and through the war of 1812—1815, not excelled by the British inhabitants of Lower Canada, or of any other colony, notwithstanding the efforts of French and American emissaries to create disaffection in the province. A remarkable illustration of the loyalty of the French in Lower Canada occurred in 1805: "The horrors of the French revolution had passed by, but Great Britain and France were still engaged in a desperate war. By land, on the continent of Europe, the French, under Napoleon I., were everywhere victorious against the countries in alliance with Great Britain. But England by sea was more than a match for France; and on October 21st, 1805, won the battle of *Trafalgar*, by which the French naval power was destroyed. The news of this victory reached Canada early in January, 1806. The Canadians of French origin immediately showed that they felt less sympathy for their own

---

* "It was also one of the grievances in Lower Canada that Protestants alone were appointed Executive Councillors, and that while the chief Protestant ecclesiastic was admitted, the Roman Catholic Church was not allowed to be represented. Great offence was also caused by this to the great majority of the inhabitants, which was made to be felt the more keenly by the determination of the Council not to acknowledge the title, or even existence, of a Roman Catholic bishop in the province." (Miles' School History of Canada, Part III., Chap. ii., pp. 195, 196.)

race, and less pride in its military prowess, than gratification at the naval success of the empire of which they formed a part. They indulged in patriotic songs, and testified their interest by illuminations and other modes of rejoicing."*

* Miles' School History of Canada, Part III., Chap. i., pp. 192, 193.

CHAPTER XLVI.

GOVERNMENT OF UPPER CANADA.

THE Constitution of Upper Canada was the same as that of Lower, established by the same *Constitutional Act of 1791*, the Act 31 George III., Chapter 31.

Before the Constitution of Upper Canada was established, when it formed part of the province of Quebec, Lord Dorchester, by proclamation, divided the now western part of the province, afterwards Upper Canada, into four districts with German names—namely, *Lunenburg*, extending from the River Ottawa to Gananoque; *Mecklenburg*, extending from Gananoque to the Trent; *Nassau*, extending from the Trent to Long Point, on Lake Erie; and *Hesse*, including the rest of the western part of Upper Canada to the Lake St. Clair. To each of these four districts a judge and a sheriff were appointed, who administered justice by means of Courts of Common Pleas.

Under the new Constitution, Upper Canada, like Lower Canada, had a Legislature consisting of a Governor, appointed by the Crown, and responsible only to it; a Legislative Council, appointed by the Crown, and the members appointed for life; and a Legislative Assembly, elected by the freeholders of the country. The Assembly was to be elected once in four years, but might be elected oftener if dissolved by the Governor, and was empowered to raise a revenue for public services, roads, bridges, schools, etc.; the Legislative Council consisted of seven members, appointed for life by the Crown; the House of Assembly consisted of sixteen members, elected by the people.

By usage and by approbation of the Imperial Government, though not by the provisions of the Constitutional Act, the

Lieutenant-Governor was assisted, mostly ruled, by an Executive Council, consisting for the most part of salaried officers, judges, and members of the Legislative Council, who were not responsible either to the Governor or to the Legislative Council, or to the House of Assembly—an independent, irresponsible body—an oligarchy which exercised great power, was very intolerant, and became very odious.

The first Lieutenant-Governor of Upper Canada was General John Graves Simcoe, who had commanded the Queen's Rangers in the revolutionary war; he was a landed gentleman, elected to the British House of Commons, in which he supported the Constitutional Act of 1791, and afterwards accepted the office of Lieutenant-Governor of Upper Canada created by that Act, and did all in his power to give beneficial effect to it. He arrived in Upper Canada the 8th of July, 1792, when the members of the Executive and Legislative Councils were sworn in at Kingston, and writs were issued for the election of members of the Legislative Assembly.

After much hesitation and perplexity, the seat of government was first established at a village then called Newark, now Niagara, at the mouth of the Niagara River, where the Governor built a small frame house which had to serve as a Parliament House, as well as residence for the Lieutenant-Governor. The Governor, with the usual state and ceremony, opened the first session of the first Parliament of Upper Canada the 17th of September, 1792. There were present three members of the Legislative Council and five members of the House of Assembly. The members of the Assembly have been represented as "plain, home-spun clad farmers and merchants, from the plough and the store." The members of the Legislature have always, for the most part, been such from that day to this, but many of the members of the first Parliament of Upper Canada had possessed respectable, and some of them luxurious homes, from which they had been exiled by narrow-minded and bitter enemies; they had fought on battle fields for the country whose forests they now burned and felled; their home-spun garments were some of the fruits of their own industry, and that of their wives and daughters. Eight years had elapsed since 10,000 of these United Empire Loyalists, driven from their homes in the States, came into the dense wilderness of Upper Canada, to hew out homes for themselves and their families in the vast solitude, the silence of which was only broken by the barking of the fox, the howl of the wolf and the growl of the bear, and the occasional whoop of the Indian.*

The population of Upper Canada was, in 1792, about 12,000 souls. The Loyalist pioneers of Upper Canada fought as bravely against privations, hardships, and dangers in founding their forest homes, as they had done in the Royal ranks in the defence of the unity of the empire. During the first ten years of their hard enterprise and labours, the forest began to yield to the axe of industry, and the little cabins, and clearings, and growing crops gave evidence of human life and activity; but there were no towns or large settlements; the inhabitants were scattered in little groups, or isolated log-houses, along the north shores of the River St. Lawrence, Lakes Ontario and Erie, and of the Detroit river, the only gathering of houses or villages being Kingston, Newark, and Amherstburg.

The first session of the first Parliament of Upper Canada lasted only four weeks, commencing the 17th of September, and closing the 15th of October, 1792; the first session of the Parliament of Lower Canada lasted nearly five months— from the 17th of December, 1792, to the 9th of May, 1793. During these nearly five months, the Legislature of Lower Canada passed eight Bills, all well prepared and useful, but with much ceremony and delay from the polite French seignors; the Legislature of Upper Canada, in their session of four weeks,

---

* But the Indians were friendly to white settlers, as they have always been. Almost the entire Mohawk tribe, with other loyalist Indians, under their chief, Joseph Brant, followed the fortunes of their white loyalist brethren, and settled on their reservation on the Grand River. Brant had been educated in a Christian school in Philadelphia; had a comfortable home, and lived respectably on the Mohawk river before the American revolution; had entertained missionaries, and had assisted one of them in translating a part of the New Testament and Prayer Book into the Mohawk language. Colonel Stone, in his "Life of Brant" and the "History of the Border Wars of the American Revolution," has nobly vindicated the character of Brant, and of his brethren of the Six Nations, from the misrepresentations and calumnies of American historians. Brant was a member of the Church of England, and built a church in his settlement in 1786, in which was placed the first church bell ever heard in Upper Canada.

also passed eight Bills, indicating no haste, well prepared, and of importance and useful. The Bills passed provided for the introduction of English law; the trial by jury; for the charge of millers, limiting their allowance for grinding and bolting grain to the rate of one bushel for every twelve bushels ground; for the easy recovery of small debts; for the change of the German names of the four districts into which Lord Dorchester had divided what now constituted Upper Canada, and granted to the United Empire Loyalists. *Lunenburg*, extending from the River Ottawa to the River Gananoque, was now called the *Eastern District*; *Mecklenburg*, extending from Gananoque to the River Trent, was called the *Middle* or *Midland District*; *Nassau*, extending from the Trent to Long Point, on Lake Erie, was called the *Home* or *Niagara District*; and *Hesse*, embracing the rest of Canada, west to the Lake St. Clair, was called the *Western* or *Detroit District*. These districts were again divided into twelve counties. An Act was also passed to erect a jail and court-house in each district.

Governor Simcoe closed this session of the Parliament the 15th of October, 1792, and after complimenting both Houses on the business-like manner in which they had performed their legislative duties, concluded his proroguing speech with the following significant words:

"I cannot dismiss you without earnestly desiring you to promote, by precept and example, regular habits of piety and morality, the surest foundations of all private and public felicity; and at this juncture I particularly recommend you to explain *that this province is signally blessed, not with a mutilated Constitution, but with a Constitution which has stood the test of experience, and is the very image and transcript of that of Great Britain*, by which she has long established and secured to her subjects as much freedom and happiness as is possible to be enjoyed under the subordination necessary to civilized society."

When Governor Simcoe selected Newark as the seat of government, he thought that Fort Niagara, on the opposite side of the river, would be ceded to England, as it was then occupied by a British garrison; but when he found that the Niagara river was to be the boundary line between Great Britain and the United States, and that the British garrison was to be withdrawn from Fort Niagara, he judged it not wise that the capital of Upper Canada should be within reach of the guns of an American fort. He made a tour through the wilderness of the western peninsula, and proposed to found a new London for the Canadian capital, on the banks of what he then called the River Thames, the site of the present city of London, in the heart of the western district, and secure from invasion; but Lord Dorchester preferred Kingston, which he had made the principal naval and military station of the province. To this Governor Simcoe objected. It was at length agreed to select York, as it was then called, the site of an old French fort. Though the surrounding land was low and swampy, the harbour was excellent.

Governor Simcoe removed to the new capital before a house was built in it, and lodged some time in a large canvas tent, pitched on the site of the old fort, at the west end of the bay. He employed the Queen's Rangers, who had accompanied him, to open a main road—Yonge Street—from York to Lake Simcoe, called after the Governor himself. He proposed to open a direct communication between Lakes Ontario and Huron, and then with the Ottawa; and projected an enlightened and vigorous policy for promoting the development of the country, its agriculture, fisheries, population, trade, etc.; but before he had time to mature and give effect to his plans, he was suddenly removed, in 1796, from the government of Upper Canada to that of St. Domingo, in the West Indies. He was succeeded in the government by the senior member of the Executive Council, the Hon. Peter Russel, who improved his two years' administration, not by carrying out the patriotic plans of his predecessor, but by granting lands to himself and his friends for speculation, to the impediment of settlements and often to the disappointment and wrong of real settlers, whose applications for lands were rejected, which were afterwards granted to the land-speculating friends of the Governor, or to himself— whose grants to himself are said to have run something on this wise: "I, Peter Russel, Lieutenant-Governor, etc., do grant to you, Peter Russel, etc."*

---

* "During Colonel Simcoe's administration he had been exceedingly careful with regard to the distribution of lands; but immediately on his

General Simcoe zealously encouraged emigration to and settlement in the country, and during the four years of his administration the population increased to 30,000. There was a very considerable emigration from the United States of persons who did not like the new system of government there, and to whom the first Loyalist settlers had written, or visited, giving a favourable account of the climate and productiveness of the country.

Though the seat of government was removed to Toronto in 1795, the Parliament continued to meet at Niagara until 1797. During its successive sessions at Niagara (then Newark), the Parliament passed Acts for the civil and municipal administration of the country, the construction of roads, fixing duties on goods imported from England and the United States, etc., etc. The Legislature gave a reward of twenty and ten shillings respectively for the heads or scalps of wolves and bears, an Act

---

departure, irregularities began to creep into the Crown Land Department, just as it had in Lower Canada, and great injustice was done to the actual settlers. Large tracts of the most eligible sites were seized upon by Government officials and speculators, and the actual settlers found themselves in many instances thrust into out-of-the-way corners, and cut off from intercourse with any near neighbours for want of roads." (Tuttle's History of the Dominion of Canada, Chap. lxxxiii., p. 387.)

"On the removal of Governor Simcoe, (a) most of his wise schemes fell through. Land designed for settlements was seized by speculators, especially in the vicinity of Toronto, and the general development of the country was greatly retarded." (Withrow's History of Canada, Chap. xvi., p. 293.)

Scarcely any—if any—of these early land speculators had served as *United Empire Loyalists* during the revolutionary war; and their descendants, if existing, are as little known as if their fathers had never lived.

(a) Lord Dorchester did not endorse Governor Simcoe's policy, as the latter had not concurred with the former in giving German names to the four first districts of Upper Canada, and in the selection of the seat of government. The American Government represented Governor Simcoe as exciting the Iroquois or Mohawks, both in Canada and Western New York, against it—representations in which there was not a shadow of truth, though Americans were endeavouring to excite disaffection to the British Government and sympathy with republican France against England in both Upper and Lower Canada, especially in the latter province. But by these representations, and those of disappointed local speculators, the Home Government removed Governor Simcoe, the father of constitutional, pure, and progressive government in Upper Canada.

suggestive of the exposures of the early settlers; and allowed the members of the Assembly ten shillings per day each. In the second session, the first Parliament passed an Act forbidding the introduction of slavery into the province—ten years in advance of Lower Canada on this subject.

Major-General Hunter succeeded the Hon. Peter Russel, in 1799, as Lieutenant-Governor of Upper Canada. He possessed little energy or enterprise, and did little or nothing except as advised by his Executive Council of five; so that the Government of Upper Canada was practically an oligarchy, irresponsible alike to Governor and people, each member receiving £100 per annum as Councillor, besides the lands he was able to obtain. Yet the Government, upon the whole, was satisfactory to the country, and commanded for many years the support of its elected representatives.

When General Hunter first met the Parliament in Toronto, the 2nd of June, 1800, the growth of Upper Canada having been rapid, its population now numbered upwards of 50,000. This year, 1800, the Legislature passed an Act prohibiting the sale of spirituous liquors to the Indians. In 1802, the Legislature of Upper Canada, as had that of Lower Canada, passed an Act appropriating £750 to encourage the growth of hemp, in order to render England independent of Russia in the supply of hemp for cordage for the navy, as was being rapidly the case in the supply of timber to build ships. As obstructions on the St. Lawrence rendered communication more difficult between Upper and Lower Canada than with Albany and New York, articles of commerce from Europe could be more readily brought in by that route than by the St. Lawrence; a considerable trade sprang up with the United States, which rendered necessary the establishment of custom-houses on the frontiers. Accordingly, ports of entry were established at Cornwall, Brockville, Kingston, Toronto, Niagara, Queenston, Fort Erie, Turkey Point, Amherstburg, and Sandwich, the duties being the same on American as on English goods. The Governor was authorized to appoint collectors, at salaries not exceeding £100 currency per annum, except when the amount of duties collected at a port was less than £100, in which case the collector was allowed one-half of the amount collected in lieu of salary.

In 1807 Parliament made provision for eight masters of grammar schools, one for each district, and at a salary of £100 currency ($400) for each master.

In the meantime emigration continued large. Many of the emigrants were from the United States. The troubles of '98 in Ireland were followed by a large Irish emigration to Canada; there were also a considerable number of Scotch and a few English emigrants; but the larger number of emigrants were from Ireland and the United States.*

The Legislature continued from session to session to pass Bills for the various improvements of the country; after doing which its members did not give much attention to politics, but devoted themselves to the culture and enlargement of their farms, of which their descendants are at this day reaping large advantages.†

Mr. McMullen, in his History of Canada, speaking of the year 1809, says:

"No civilized country in the world was less burdened with taxes than Canada West at this period. A small direct tax on property, levied by the District Courts of Session, and not amounting to £3,500 for the whole country, sufficed for all local expenses. There was no poor rate, no capitation tax, no tithes, or ecclesiastical rates of any kind. Instead of a road tax, a few days' statute labour annually sufficed. Nowhere did the working man find the produce of his labour so little diminished by exactions of any kind. Canada West literally teemed with abundance; while its people, unlike the early

---

* "In Upper as well as Lower Canada the first sixteen years' experience of the new Constitution had been very encouraging. All concerned in working it out during that period kept as clear as possible from causes of discord. The consequence was that harmony and good progress marked the early career of the province." (Miles' School History of Canada, Part III., Chap. i., pp. 193, 194.)

† "Meanwhile the country had steadily prospered, undisturbed in its forest isolation by the great European war, which was deluging with blood a hundred battle fields and desolating thousands of homes. By the year 1809, the population had increased to about 70,000. Taxes were exceedingly light. The Customs revenue, derived principally from the imports of groceries —for clothing was chiefly home-spun—amounted to £7,000." (Withrow's History of Canada, Chap. xxi., p. 296.)

French and Americans, had nothing to fear from the red man, and enjoyed the increase of the earth in peace."

I have thus given a brief narrative of the formation of the government of Upper Canada, and of the first seventeen years of its operations, down to the period when the anticipated hostilities between Great Britain and the United States—the latter being the tools of Napoleon to rescue Canada from Great Britain—rendered preparation necessary on the part of the Loyalists of Canada to defend their country and homes against foreign invasion.

I have also given some account of the first settlement of the country, and the privations and hardships of the first settlers. But believing that a narrative from a single pen could not do justice to this subject, or could present to the reader, in so vivid and interesting a light, the character, sufferings, courage, and enterprise of our country's forefathers and founders, as narratives from themselves, with the diversity of style characteristic of communications from various sources, I have therefore inserted in Chapter XLI. those interesting papers transmitted to me from time to time, at my request, during the last twenty years.

CHAPTER XLVII.

WAR BY THE UNITED STATES AGAINST GREAT BRITAIN, FROM 1812 TO 1815—INTRODUCTORY AND GENERAL REMARKS.

THE war between Great Britain and the United States, from 1812 to 1815, furnishes the strongest example of the present century, or of any age or country, of the attachment of a people to their mother country, and of their determination, at whatever sacrifice and against whatever disparity, to maintain the national life of their connection with it. The true spirit of *the Loyalists of America* was never exhibited with greater force and brilliancy than during the war of 1812—1815.

England was engaged in a death struggle for the independence of the continental nations of Europe and the rights of mankind. At the darkest hour of that eventful contest, when the continent was drenched with the blood of nations, and the Tyrant had his feet upon their neck, and England alone stood erect, taxing her resources to the utmost and shedding her best blood for human freedom, the Democratic party in the United States—the ever anti-British party—the pro-slavery party—the party in the United States least subordinate to law and most inimical to liberty—at such a crisis such a party declared war against Britain, and forthwith invaded Canada, before the declaration of war was known in England.

At that time the population of Lower Canada was 225,000 souls—200,000 of whom were French; the population of Upper Canada was 75,000; the population of the United States was upwards of 8,000,000: so that the population of the *two Canadas* was to that of the United States as one to twenty-seven; and the population of *Upper Canada* was to that of the United States as one to one hundred and six.

Yet the Canadas, with a frontier of more than 1,000 miles, and aided by a few regiments of regular soldiers, sent as a mere guard for the principal cities, from Halifax to Amherstburg, resisted the whole military power of the United States for two years, at the end of which not an inch of Canadian ground was in possession of the invaders; and within six months after England had given freedom and peace to Europe—chaining its Tyrant to the island rock of Elba, sweeping with its fleet the coasts of the United States, and sending 16,000 veteran soldiers to aid the struggling Canadas—the boasting Madison and his Government sued for peace, without even mentioning the original pretexts of war, which Great Britain generously granted.

It does not come within our purpose to write a history of this war; we present only such phases and events of it as will illustrate the Loyalist spirit and courage of the Canadians, French as well as English, and even true Americans; for the American settlers in Canada were, with few exceptions, as loyal subjects and as bold defenders of their adopted country as the U. E. Loyalists themselves; and even the most virtuous and intelligent part of the citizens of the United States protested against the alliance of the Democratic rulers at Washington with the tyrant and scourge of Europe.

We shall notice, in the first place, the alleged and real causes of the war; secondly, the preparations for it made by the Governments and Legislatures of the two Canadas; thirdly, the invasions of each province, each year, separately, and the battles fought. There were no less than eleven invasions of the Canadas by the American armies during the three years of the war, besides naval engagements, and various incursions of marauding and plundering parties.

CHAPTER XLVIII.

ALLEGED AND REAL CAUSES OF THE WAR.

FROM the first—from the treaty of peace between Great Britain and the United States in 1783—there was a large party in the United States bitterly and actively hostile to England and its colonies; that party had persecuted and driven the Loyalists from the United States, and compelled them to seek homes in the Canadian wilderness, and had even followed them with its enmities in their new abodes; that party had sympathized with the revolutionists of France, who crimsoned the streets of Paris with the blood of their Sovereign and fellow-citizens, and who sent emissaries to Canada to subvert legal authority, and excite the strife of anarchy and bloodshed. The base of the operations of all the emissaries of French revolutionists in Canada was for twenty years the United States, aided directly and indirectly by American sympathizers; that same party sympathized and even leagued with Napoleon against England while she was defending the liberties of Europe and of mankind; it was the same party that in subsequent years aided the rebel Mackenzie and the rabble Fenians to invade Canada, allowing the United States to be the base of their organizations, and opening to them the American arsenals of arms and ammunition; it was the same party that, in conspiracy with the Tyrant of France and the enemy of human freedom, declared war against Great Britain in 1812, in order to wrest Canada from her possession, and make it an appendage of France and the United States.*

---

* "The war party in the United States was not very strong, numerically speaking, and it was not composed of the most respectable portions of the

The American Government alleged two reasons as the ground of its declaration of war against Britain: the one was, that the British Government had issued Orders in Council which injured the American commerce with other countries; the other was, that the British Government had infringed the rights of the United States by authorizing the boarding of American vessels in search of deserters from the English army and navy, and seizing them.

As to the first of these reasons, namely, the English Orders in Council, the facts are as follow: "After the annihilation of the naval power of France at *Trafalgar* in 1805, by Lord Nelson, the principal transactions of France at sea were the fitting out and arming of privateers to prey upon the English merchant vessels and commerce. To accomplish his purpose more effectually, Napoleon promulgated the following year after the destruction of his fleet what is called the Berlin Decree."*

"No nation was allowed to trade with any other country in any articles the growth, produce, or manufactures of any of the

---

community; but what it lacked in these two requisites it made up in loud and demonstrative clamour, and the more serious-minded and important portions of the people were being forced, against their better judgment, into a position hostile to Great Britain, by the continued cry of a few demagogues, who were more anxious to give vent to their old feeling of spite against Great Britain than to consult the best interests of their country." (Tuttle's History of the Dominion of Canada, Chap. lxxii., p. 349.)

* This Decree is dated "Imperial Camp, Berlin, November 21st, 1806." Its principal Articles are as follow :

"Art. 1. The British islands are in a state of blockade.

"Art. 2. *All commerce and correspondence with them is prohibited;* consequently, all letters or packets written *in* England, or *to* an Englishman, *written in the English language,* shall not be dispatched from the post-offices, and shall be seized.

"Art. 3. Every individual, a subject of Great Britain, of whatever rank or condition, who is found in countries occupied by our troops or those of our allies, shall be made prisoner of war.

"Art. 4. Every warehouse, all merchandise or property whatsoever, belonging to an Englishman, are declared god-prize.

"Art. 6. No vessel coming directly from England or her colonies, or having been there since the publication of this Decree, shall be admitted into any port.

"Art. 7. Every vessel that by a false declaration contravenes the foregoing

British dominions, all of which, as well as the island of Great Britain itself, were declared to be in a state of blockade. He appointed residents in every trading country, and no ship was to be admitted into any of his ports without a *certification of origin;* that is, of the nature of the goods they carried, and that no part of these was English. In consequence of these Decrees, the English commerce, during the months of August, September, and October, 1807—that part of the year in which the Berlin Decree of November, 1806, was carried into full effect—was not only greatly cramped, but lay prostrated on the ground, and motionless, before a protecting and self-defensive system was adopted by our Orders in Council."*

The British Orders in Council were dated January 7th, 1807, and were a measure of retaliation for the protection of British commerce in response to Napoleon's Berlin Decree of the 21st of November, 1806. By these Orders in Council, "all trade to France or her dependencies was strictly prohibited; all vessels, of whatever nation, which ventured to engage in this trade were declared liable to seizure, and France and her dependencies were thus reduced to that state of blockade with which she had vainly threatened the British islands. The Orders in Council admitted but of one exception to this general blockade of the French empire. The French had declared all vessels liable to seizure which had touched at a British port; the Orders in Council, to counteract this provision, declared, on the other hand, that only such ships as were in that situation should be permitted to sail for France. Thus did the utter extinction of the foreign trade of France result as a natural consequence of the very measures of her own Government; measures which no despotism, how ignorant soever, would have ventured to adopt, had it not trusted to a power which effectually silenced all popular opinion."†

As France was the aggressor upon the rights of neutrals by

---

disposition, shall be seized, and the ship and cargo confiscated as English property.

"Art. 10. Our Ministers of Foreign Relations, etc., are charged with the execution of the present Decree."

* British Annual Register, 1807, Vol. XLII., Chap. xii., p. 227.

† Thompson's History of the War of 1812, between Great Britain and the United States, Chap. III., pp. 23, 24.

the Berlin Decree, and as the Orders in Council were a defensive retaliation upon France for her attempt to destroy English commerce, the American Government should have first remonstrated with France and demanded reparation; but this was not the case; the outcry of the Madison partizans was against England alone. It is true some grumbling words were uttered by some parties against the policy and acts of the French Government; but mere words to save appearances, not followed up by any acts; for by a collusion between Napoleon and Madison, it was understood that the Articles of the Berlin Decree were not intended to apply to ships of the United States—would not be executed against them—and were intended to destroy the commerce of Great Britain. An American writer (Lossing) remarks, " *With a partiality towards the Americans that was practical friendship,* the French cruisers did not, for a whole year, interfere with American vessels trading with Great Britain;" and Mr. Alex. Baring, M. P. (afterwards Lord Ashburton), in his *Inquiry into the Causes and Consequences of the Orders in Council,* said that "*no condemnation of an American vessel had ever taken place under it.*'

By this collusion between the Tyrant of Europe and the President of the United States, the necessities of France were supplied, and the shipping interests of the United States largely promoted, at the expense of the commerce and shipping interests of England.

But the collusion, or conspiracy, between Napoleon and Madison were carried on to weaken the English navy by the desertion of its sailors, as well as to injure English commerce by connivance in behalf of American trading vessels. The seduction of deserters from the British navy, and even army, was carried on successfully on a large scale. The safety of England consisted chiefly in her navy, which she was increasing and strengthening by every possible means. Therefore every skilled sailor was of importance to England, while every practicable scheme was resorted to by her enemies to induce and facilitate the desertion of her seamen and soldiers—especially of her seamen, several thousands of whom were detected and seized on board of American vessels—constituting as they did the best sailors on board American merchant vessels, and the vital strength of the French privateers. To stop this depleting of her naval resources, England put in exercise her right of boarding vessels of neutral powers in search of deserters from her navy. The only neutral power in Europe was Sardinia; so that the United States was the only neutral power that had vessels upon the ocean; and the President of the United States was conniving against England with the usurper and oppressor of Europe.

The right of a belligerent power to search the vessels of neutral powers in search of deserters had never been denied, though the modification of its exercise had frequently been sought; but under the teachings of Napoleon, his American pupils now began to exclaim against it as an infringement of national dignity and rights. The English Government had directed the exercise of this right with the greatest caution and courtesy, and only in regard to vessels on board of which, from specific information, there was reason to believe there were English deserters. These deserters, on getting smuggled on board of American vessels, would forthwith take the oath of allegiance to the United States, and be recognized and claimed as American citizens.*

An event now occurred which enabled President Madison to excite his partizans throughout the United States to a flame of

* The justice of the proceedings and demands of the British Government, the fairness of its proposals, and the injustice and unreasonableness of the conduct of the Madison U. S. Government, are forcibly presented in the following preamble to resolutions adopted by the Legislature of the State of Massachusetts, as late as the 5th of February, 1813:

"Whereas the President, in his message to Congress, has made known to the people of the United States that the British Orders in Council have been repealed 'in such manner as to be capable of explanations meeting the views of the Government' of the United States; and therefore none of the alleged causes of war with Great Britain now remain except the claim of the right to take British subjects from the merchant ships of the United States:

"And whereas, during the administration of General Washington and President Adams, this claim of Great Britain was not considered a reasonable cause of war; and under the administration of President Jefferson, the Government of Great Britain did offer to make an arrangement with the United States, which in the opinion of Messrs. Montrose and Pinkey, their Ministers, placed this subject on a ground that was both honourable and advantageous to the United States, and highly favourable to their interests, and was, at the same time, a concession which had never before been made;

indignation against England. Information had been received that there were English deserters on board the American ship *Chesapeake*; the British warship *Leopard* sought their restoration, and on being refused fired into the *Chesapeake*, and recovered the four deserters claimed. The attendant circumstances being omitted, the simple fact announced by the President to Congress, that the English warship *Leopard* had fired into the American ship *Chesapeake*, and in American waters, killing several persons, and had seized and carried off four American citizens, produced the excitement he was anxious to create against England, preparatory to the war on which he was then determined—in the zenith of Napoleon's success and power, and in the extremity of England's struggle for her own existence and the liberties of mankind. The statement of the American President as to the affair of the ships *Leopard* and *Chesapeake* has been repeated to this day by American historians, and is used in American school books to illustrate England's arrogance and cruelty; whereas all the facts of the case prove directly the reverse. We give the account of the affair from one American writer, who, though partial, was too honest to omit essential facts, much less to pervert them; we refer to Dr. Holmes, author of *American Annals*, and quote at length his account of the affair. He says:

"The frigate *Chesapeake*, being ordered to cruise in the Mediterranean Sea, under the command of Commodore Barron, sailing from Hampton Roads, was come up with by the British ship-

and it is highly probable that the Government of Great Britain would still be willing to make an arrangement on this subject which should be alike honourable and advantageous to the United States:

"And whereas, under the administration of President Madison, when the arrangement of matters in controversy between the United States and Great Britain was made with his Britannic Majesty's Minister, David Montague Erskine, Esq., the impressment of seamen was not considered of sufficient importance to make it a condition of that arrangement:

"And whereas *the European powers, as well as the United States, recognize the principle that their subjects have no right to expatriate themselves, and that the nation has a right to the services of all its citizens, especially in time of war; and none of those powers respect the neutralization laws of others so far as to admit their operation in contravention of that principle—and it is manifestly unjust for a neutral power to make war upon one nation in order to compel it to relinquish a principle which is maintained by the others, etc.*"

of-war *Leopard*, one of a squadron then at anchor within the limits of the United States. An officer was sent from the *Leopard* to the *Chesapeake* with a note from the captain respecting some deserters from his Britannic Majesty's ships, supposed to be serving as part of the crew of the *Chesapeake* and enclosing a copy of an order from Vice-Admiral Berkeley requiring and directing the commanders of ships and vessels under his command, in case of meeting with the American frigate at sea, and without the limits of the United States, to show the order to her captain, and to require to search his ship for the deserters from certain ships therein named, and to proceed and search for them; and if a similar demand should be made by the American, he was permitted to search for deserters from their service, according to the custom and usage of civilized nations on terms of amity with each other. Commodore Barron gave an answer that he knew of no such men as were described; that the recruiting officers for the *Chesapeake* had been particularly instructed by the Government, through him, not to enter any deserters from his Britannic Majesty's ships; that he knew of none such being in her; that he was instructed never to permit the crew of any ship under his command to be mustered by any officers but her own; that he was disposed to preserve harmony, and hoped his answer would prove satisfactory. The *Leopard*, shortly after this answer was received by her commander, ranged alongside of the *Chesapeake*, and commenced a heavy fire upon her. The *Chesapeake*, unprepared for action, made no resistance, but remained under the fire of the *Leopard* from twenty to thirty minutes; when, having suffered much damage, and lost three men killed and eighteen wounded, Commodore Barron ordered his colours to be struck, and sent a lieutenant on board the *Leopard* to inform her commander that he considered the *Chesapeake* her prize. The commander of the *Leopard* sent an officer on board, who took possession of the *Chesapeake*, mustered her crew, and, carrying off four of her men, abandoned the ship. Commodore Barron, after a communication, by writing, with the commander of the *Leopard*, finding that the *Chesapeake* was very much injured, returned, with the advice of his officers, to Hampton Roads." (American State Papers, 1806–08.)

"On receiving information of this outrage, the President, by proclamation, interdicted the harbours and waters of the United States to all armed British vessels, forbade all intercourse with them, and ordered a sufficient force for the protection of Norfolk, and such other preparations as the occasion appeared to require. An armed vessel of the United States was dispatched with instructions to the American Minister at London to call on the British Government for the satisfaction and security which the outrage required." (American State Papers, 1806-08, pp. 183, 184, 248—252.)*

Such is the American State Paper account of this affair, published some years afterwards; and from this it will be seen that what was asked by the captain of the *Leopard* was what had been granted by all neutral nations to belligerents— to seek for and take their own deserters on board of neutral vessels, in order to prevent neutrals from being, or suspected of being, in collusion with either belligerent party. The American Government being in sympathy with the French Government during the whole of its twenty years' war with England, sought to change and evade this hitherto undisputed usage of mutually friendly nations in regard to belligerents. The *Chesapeake* seems to have been selected to make up a cause of war with Great Britain, by the warlike proceedings of the President before communicating with the British Government on the subject. The American people had nothing but a complete perversion of the facts of the case until years afterwards.

It is plain from the true version of the affair that the captain of the *Leopard* acted courteously and fairly, though in excess of the authority granted by the British Government; that he

* Holmes' American Annals, Vol. II., pp. 434, 435.
The manner in which this affair was presented to the public by the President and American writers may be inferred from the following:

" This vessel (the *Chesapeake*) was suddenly attacked within our waters in the time of profound peace, compelled to surrender, and several seamen, alleged to be British, were then forcibly taken from her. The burst of indignation which followed was even more violent than that which was produced by the Orders in Council in 1793 [1807]. Party animosity was suspended; meetings were assembled in every village; the newspapers were filled with formal addresses; volunteer companies were everywhere set on foot; and, in the first frenzy of the moment, the universal cry was for immediate war. Although hostilities were not declared, the feelings of America were from

offered the same facilities to the captain of the *Chesapeake*, in regard to examination for deserters, that he asked himself; that the commander of the *Chesapeake* stated what he knew to be untrue when he asserted that there were no deserters on board the *Chesapeake*, which he knew would be detected on examination of his crew.

In all the American accounts and discussions on the question, they ignore the usage or customary law of civilized nations as to neutral or mutually friendly nations in respect to belligerent powers, and are silent as to France and England being at war with each other, and that in encouraging desertions from the English ships, and then claiming them as American citizens, they were playing into the hands of Bonaparte against England.

It appears that President Madison, without awaiting or asking satisfaction or explanation on this affair of the *Leopard* and *Chesapeake*, forthwith prohibited the anchoring of British war ships in American waters, and then sent a special messenger and communication to the American Minister in London to demand satisfaction of the British Government for the alleged "outrage" upon the *Chesapeake*. But did the British Government show the passion and violence of the President of the United States? Let the American author above quoted be our witness again on this point. Dr. Holmes says:

"Reparation was made by the British for the attack on the *Chesapeake*. Augustus J. Foster, the British envoy, informed the Secretary of the United States that he was instructed to repeat to the American Government the prompt disavowal made by his Majesty, on being apprised of the unauthorized act of the officer in command of his naval forces on the coast of America, whose recall from a highly important and honourable command immediately ensued, as a mark of his Majesty's disapprobation; that he was authorized to offer, in addition to that disavowal on the part of his Majesty, to order the immediate restoration, as far as circumstances would admit, of the men who [though deserters], in consequence of Admiral Berke-

that day at war with England." (Breckenridge's History of the War of 1812.)

This state of feeling was precisely what President Madison wished to create, preparatory to his meditated war with England, in connection with the French usurper.

ley's orders, were forcibly taken out of the *Chesapeake*, to the vessel from which they were taken ; or, if that ship were no longer in commission, to such seaport of the United States as the American Government may name for the purpose ; and that he was authorized to offer to the American Government a suitable pecuniary provision for the sufferers in consequence of the attack on the *Chesapeake*, including the families of those seamen who fell in the action, and of the wounded survivors. The President acceded to these propositions; and the officer commanding the *Chesapeake*, then lying in the harbour of Boston, was instructed to receive the men, who were to be restored to that ship."—*Ib.*, p. 443.

It might be supposed that such a spontaneous, courteous, and just proceeding on the part of England would have satisfied even the bellicose President Madison ; but he was bent on joining the Tyrant of Europe in war against England ; the American public were kept in ignorance of the instigating circumstances, and the just and generous conduct of the British Government in regard to the affair of the *Leopard* and the *Chesapeake*, and availed himself of every occurrence or incident to excite and increase the war feeling in the United States against England.

An incident soon occurred answerable to President Madison's purpose. A renegade by the name of *Henry*, who had in youth emigrated from Ireland, and who had, by the interest of friends, got appointed captain of militia; but not succeeding in the United States to the extent of his ambition, emigrated to Montreal, where, by some talents and address, and professed love of British institutions, he ingratiated himself in the good graces of the principal persons at Montreal, and commenced his studies at law there, with a view of qualifying himself for a seat on the judicial bench of *Upper Canada*, to which he was vain and ambitious enough to aspire. He at length got access to the Governor-General, Sir James Craig, into whose confidence he so wormed himself as to obtain a letter of recognition and recommendation to visit Massachusetts and other eastern States to ascertain and report upon the state of feeling there in regard to the sympathy of those States with England in case of war with England ; but neither the British Government nor even Sir James Craig's Canadian Executive Council had the slightest knowledge of this confidential epistolary intrigue between his Excellency and the renegade American militia captain, who professed to be familiar with the politics and parties of the New England States, where there was vehement opposition to the democratic and war government of President Madison, and supposed to cherish a strong leaning to England. While this unprincipled "Captain Henry" was sauntering in the public-houses and brothels of Boston, he wrote from time to time letters to Sir James Craig and other principal persons in Quebec; but the Governor and others who received his ostentatious and pretentious letters—though amused by them—derived no more information from his epistles than from the public newspapers of the day. Henry, however, estimated his own worthless services of the greatest importance; and failing to get from Sir James Craig the amount of his demands, he appealed for compensation to the Government in England. He addressed a memorial to the Earl of Liverpool, Principal Secretary of State for the Colonies, stating his services, and suggesting that the appointment of Judge Advocate General of Lower Canada, with the salary of £500 per annum, or a consulate in the United States, *sine cura*, would be considered by him as a fair discharge of the obligation of the Government to him for his services. Lord Liverpool was not disposed to prostitute such favours upon a mercenary and intriguing vagrant, and referred him to the Government of Lower Canada, then in charge of Sir George Prevost, who had succeeded Sir James Craig. Henry knew the little estimate that was placed upon his services in Canada; he therefore betook himself back to the United States, and offered his traitorous letters to the American Government for $50,000, which he obtained, paid out of the United States Secret Service Fund.* President Madison,

* "Indignant at this neglectful treatment, Henry returned to Boston, and obtained a letter of introduction from Governor Gerry to Madison, to whom he offered to divulge the whole conspiracy, *of which he had been the head and soul*, for a certain sum of money. Madison gave him $50,000, and the swindler embarked for France. There is but little doubt that Henry made a fool of the Governor of Canada, and completely overreached the President. The publication of the correspondence, however, increased the hatred both against the Federalists and the English nation." [The object President Madison had in view.] (Headley's History of the War of 1812—1815 with England, p. 49.)

instead of laying the correspondence before the British Government for explanation and satisfaction, communicated it to Congress, as a discovery and illustration of a conspiracy by the British Government to subvert the Constitution and Government of the United States, and by his message inflamed the Congress to the highest pitch of excitement, in the climax of which he got a vote in favour of a declaration of war against Great Britain. The President, in his message to Congress, referring to the Henry documents said: "They prove that at a recent period, while the United States, notwithstanding the wrongs sustained by them, ceased not to observe the laws of neutrality towards Great Britain, and in the midst of amicable professions and negotiations on the part of the British Government through its public Minister here [Mr. Erskine], a *secret agent of that Government* was employed in certain States—more especially at the seat of government in Massachusetts—in fomenting disaffection to the constituted authorities of the nation, and in intrigues with the disaffected, for the purpose of bringing about resistance to the laws, and eventually, in concert with a British force, of destroying the Union, and forming the eastern part thereof into a political connection with England."

Two days before the transmission of President Madison's message of accusation against England, the British Minister at Washington declared in the public prints his entire ignorance of any transaction of the kind, and asked the United States Government to consider the character of the individual who had made these disclosures,* and to "suspend any further

---

* "The *Henry Plot* (as it was denominated) was clamoured through America as a crime of the deepest dye on the part of Great Britain, tending to disorganize the Government, to dismember the Union, and to destroy the independence of the States. The fictitious and exaggerated importance which the American Government affected to attach to this trivial matter had, however, some influence in confirming the spirit of hostility towards Great Britain which at that time pervaded America, and shortly after broke out in open war. This self-sufficient miscreant having, as he fancied, taken ample vengeance upon the Government of his native country, could not, with any degree of decency, remain in the States, from whence he sailed for France in an American sloop-of-war, carrying with him the reward of his treason and the universal contempt of mankind." (Christie's History of the War of 1812, p. 55.)

Yet, at this very time, there were American and French emissaries in both

judgment on its merits until the circumstances shall have been made known to his Majesty's Government." But such fairness to England did not answer President Madison's purpose to get himself re-elected President, by exciting hostility and declaring war against England.

the Canadas (as the proclamations of the Governors show), with a view of exciting disaffection to the British Canadian Government, in order to wrest the Canadas from England and subject them to France and the United States.

"The Americans had been declaring, for several years, that they would take the provinces. They had even boasted of the ease with which the intended conquest could be made by them whenever they pleased. They believed, or pretended to believe, that the majority of the people, owing to dissensions and a desire to be free from the mother country, would not take part against them in this contest with Great Britain." (Dr. Miles' History of Canada, Part III., Chap. iii., p. 201.)

CHAPTER XLIX.

DECLARATION OF WAR BY THE UNITED STATES AGAINST GREAT BRITAIN, AND PREPARATIONS FOR THE INVASION OF CANADA.

THE Bill for declaring war against Britain passed the Congress June 18th, 1812, after protracted discussions: by the House of Congress, by a majority of forty—seventy-nine to thirty-nine—by the Senate, by a majority of six.* The vote

* In the report of the Committee recommending the Bill for the declaration, it was, of course, attempted to make England the aggressive and the United States the injured party. "On presentation of this report," says Lossing, "the doors were closed, and a motion to open them was denied by a vote of seventy-seven against forty-nine. Mr. Calhoun [the democratic leader of the war party of the South] then presented a Bill, as part of the report, declaring war between Great Britain and her dependencies and the United States and its territories. Amendments were offered. Ten votes were given for a proposition by Mr. McKee, of Kentucky, to include France. Mr. Quincy (of Boston) endeavoured, by an addition to the Bill, to provide for the repeal of all restrictive laws bearing upon commerce; and John Randolph, of Virginia, moved to postpone the whole matter until the following October. All were rejected, and the Bill, as Mr. Calhoun presented it, was passed on the 4th day of June by a vote of seventy-nine for it and thirty-nine against it.

"When the Bill reached the Senate it was referred to a Committee already appointed to consider the President's message. It remained under discussion twelve days. Meanwhile the people throughout the country were fearfully excited by conflicting emotions. A memorial against the war went from the Legislature of Massachusetts; and another from the merchants of New York, led by John Jacob Astor. War-meetings were held in various places, and the whole country was in a tumult of excitement. Finally, on the 17th of June, the Bill, with some amendments, was passed in the Senate by a vote of nineteen against thirteen. It was sent back to the House on the morning of the 18th, when the amendments were concurred in.

for the declaration of war was a purely party vote; the war itself was a purely partizan war—the carrying out of intrigue between the American Democratic President and the French despoiler of Europe—a war against the intelligence and patriotism of the American people, as well as against the independence and liberties of nations; a war in which the very selection of generals and officers were, as a general rule, partizan appointments.*

The Bill was engrossed on parchment, and at three o'clock in the afternoon of that day became law by the signature of the President [who next day declared war against Great Britain]. In the House, the members from Pennsylvania, and the States of the South and West, gave sixty-two votes for it to seventeen against it. In the Senate, the same States gave fourteen for it, to five against it. 'Thus,' says a late writer [Edwin Williams], "the war may be said to have been a measure of the South and West to take care of the interests of the North, much against the will of the latter.'" (Lossing's Field Book of the War of 1812, Chap. xi., pp. 227, 228.)

The minority of the members of the House of Representatives who voted against the war, addressed a protest, signed by them all, to their constituents, exposing the impolicy and objects of the war, and indicating their own conduct. We quote two sentences of this able paper:

"As to the invasion and seizure of Canada, which was a part of the programme of the war party, they considered an attempt to carry out that measure as unjust and impolitic in itself, very uncertain in the issue, and unpromising as to any good results."—" It cannot be concealed that to engage in the present war against England is to place ourselves on the side of France, and expose us to the vassalage of States serving under the banner of the French Emperor."

* The distinguished Joseph Quincy, of Boston, leader of the Federalist party, said, in his place in Congress, "I have evidence satisfactory in my own mind, that the Secretary of War has made it a principle not to appoint any man to a command in that army who is not an open partizan of the existing Administration. If it be denied, appoint a Committee of Inquiry. If the intention had been to unite the nation as one man against a foreign enemy, is not this the last policy that any Administration ought ever to have adopted? Is not a partizan army the most dreadful and detestable of all engines, and most likely to awaken suspicions and to inspire discontent?" (Hildreth, Second Series, Vol. III., Chap. xxi., p. 123.)

"The place of the first major-general, with the command of the Northern Department, had been given to the petted favourite, Henry Dearborn, late Secretary of War, and, since Madison's accession, collector of the port of Boston —a lucrative post, kept in his family by his son's appointment to it."— "Wilkinson, the senior brigadier, just acquitted by court-martial of long-pending charges against him, had been sent to New Orleans [afterwards to Canada] to relieve Hampton [who was afterwards sent to Canada], whose

The war party consisted largely of the mob or refuse of the nation—of those who had nothing to lose and everything to gain by such a war—facts which will go far to account, with three or four exceptions, for the inferior character of the American generals and officers in the war; men appointed to offices for which they had no qualifications, and to situations in which they could, without stint, rob their country of its money, if not of its reputation.

In New York, a Convention of delegates from several counties of the State was held at Albany, on the 17th and 18th days of September, 1812, in which the war was denounced as unjustifiable, unprincipled, and unpatriotic, and as subservient, simply subservient to the cause of the French Emperor against England.*

command there had been a constant scene of collision and turmoil with his officers. Commissions as brigadiers, under the late Acts, had been given to Bloomfield, Governor of New Jersey; to James Winchester, of Tennessee; and to Hull, Governor of Michigan Territory. * * Hampton and Smythe had been civilians for more than thirty years, and were indebted for their present appointments rather to political than to military considerations. Of the inferiors of the old army, presently distinguished, Alexander MacNab, of the Engineers, was now a colonel, and Winfield Scott and Edmund Gaines lieutenant-colonels. A lieutenant-colonelcy in one of the new regiments had been given to Eleazar W. Ripley, a young Democrat from Maine, who had succeeded Storey, of the late Democratic Massachusetts House of Representatives. Ripley's subsequent conduct justified his appointment; but the colonel of that same regiment was afterwards cashiered for peculation; and as few of the new regimental officers had any military knowledge, so numbers of them were quite destitute of those qualities without which even that knowledge would have been of little avail." (Hildreth's History of the United States, Second Series, Vol. III., Chap. xxiv., pp. 308—310.)

* "The following are extracts from the resolutions of this famous Convention:

"Taking solely into consideration the time and circumstances of the declaration of the present war, the condition of the country, and state of the public mind, we are constrained to consider, and feel it our duty to pronounce it a most rash, unwise, and inexpedient measure, the adoption of which ought forever to deprive its authors of the esteem and confidence of an enlightened people; because, as the injuries we have received from France are at least equal in amount to those we have sustained from England, and have been attended with circumstances of still greater insult and aggravation, if war were necessary to vindicate the honour of the country, consistency and impartiality required that both nations should have been included in the declaration; because, if it were deemed expedient to exercise

The address of the House of Representatives of the State of Massachusetts presented in a still stronger light and with unanswerable argument the causes of this unjust and cruel war, as wanton and unprovoked, and the climax of the various outrages committed against Great Britain.

Yet even the English Orders in Council—made the pretext for the war by President Madison and his partizans—impolitic as those Orders were on the part of England, being founded not on sound national policy, but dictated by revenge on Napoleon on account of his Berlin and Milan decrees for the destruction of British commerce—even these British Orders in Council were actually a source of profit to American merchants

our right of selecting our adversary, prudence and common sense dictated the choice of an enemy from whose hostility we had nothing to dread. A war with France would equally have satisfied our insulted honour, and at the same time, instead of annihilating, would have revived and extended our commerce; and even the evils of such a contest would have been mitigated by the sublime consolation, that, by our efforts, we were contributing to arrest the progress of despotism in Europe, and essentially serving the great interests of freedom and humanity throughout the world ;" * * "because, before the war was declared, it was perfectly well ascertained that a vast majority of the people in the Middle and Northern States, by whom the burden and expenses of the war must be borne almost exclusively, were strongly opposed to the measure." * *

"Whereas the late revocation of British Orders in Council (a) has removed the great and ostensible cause of the present war, and prepared the way for an immediate accommodation of existing differences, inasmuch as, by the concession of the present Secretary of State, satisfactory and honourable arrangements might easily be made, by which abuses resulting from the impressment of our seamen might in future be effectually prevented. Therefore,

"Resolved,—That we shall be constrained to consider the determination on the part of our rulers to continue the present war, after official notice of revocation of the British Orders in Council, as affording conclusive evidence that the war has been undertaken from motives entirely distinct from those which have been hitherto avowed, and for the promotion of objects wholly unconnected with the interest and honour of America.

"Resolved,—That we contemplate with abhorrence even the possibility of an alliance with the present Emperor of France, every action of whose life has demonstrated, that the attainment, by any means, of universal empire,

(a) These Orders in Council were cancelled five days after President Madison's declaration of war—weeks before that declaration could have been known in England.

from the indulgent way in which they were administered by the British authorities. The American historian, Hildreth, says:

"The comparative indulgence of the British, their willingness to allow to Americans a certain margin of profitable employment, contrasted very favourably in the minds of shipowners with the totally anti-commercial system of France. Forgetting their late pretensions to a neutral trade, perfectly unshackled, and the loud outcry they had raised against British invasions of it, they were now ready, with characteristic commercial prudence, to accept as much of the views of British Ministers and merchants still left within their reach. A trade still profitable, however shackled and curtailed, they regarded as decidedly preferable to no trade at all. In fact, by the calculations of eminent merchants, fully confirmed by subsequent experience, the trade still allowed under the British Orders, while far more profitable, was also quite as extensive as there could be any reasonable expectation of enjoying after the restoration of general peace.

"The merchants and ship-owners had, however, but a limited influence over public opinion. Their vast profits of late years had made them objects of envy. Though their accumulations were but an index of the general enrichment of the nation, there were multitudes who more or less openly rejoiced over their present distress [arising from the American embargo.] Unfortunately, too, they were divided among themselves. Some even of the wealthiest of their number were among those who applauded the embargo, of which conduct this not very charitable explanation was given: that it would enable those who

---

and the consequent extinction of every vestige of freedom, are the sole objects of his incessant, unbounded, and remorseless ambition. His arms, with the spirit of freemen, we might openly and fearlessly encounter; but of his secret arts, his corrupting influences, we entertain a dread we can neither conquer nor conceal. It is therefore with the utmost distrust and alarm that we regard his late professions of attachment and love to the American people, fully recollecting that his invariable course has been, by perfidious offers of protection, by deceitful professions of friendship, to lull his intended victims into the fatal sleep of confidence and security, during which the chains of despotism are silently wound round and riveted on them.

(Signed) "JACOB MORRIS, *President.*
"WILLIAM HENDERSON, *Secretary.*"

were able to wait for the revival of trade to buy up at a great discount the ships and produce of their poorer neighbours."*

President Madison having declared a professedly defensive war against Great Britain for the purpose of defending maritime rights on the Atlantic Ocean, commenced by invading Canada in three "Grand Armies." The one was the Grand Army of the West, consisting of 5,000 men, under General Hull, and the base of whose operations was Detroit; the second was the Grand Army of the Centre, under the command of General Van Rensellaer, consisting of 5,000, which was to operate against Canada from Lewiston; and the third, but first in command, was the Grand Army of the North, under General Dearborn, consisting of 10,000 men, to operate from Lake Champlain against Montreal and the rest of Lower Canada.

Such, then, was the declaration of war against England by President Madison and his democratic faction; such were the false pretensions for the war; such was the confederacy between the democratic President of the United States and the Tyrant of Europe against the liberties of mankind, under pretence of war with England; such was the noble opposition of the States of New York and New England to that unholy coalition between the American President and the oppressor of Europe against human liberty—States which had been the head and the sinews and the backbone of American resistance to Great Britain during the struggle for American independence, and which, having achieved that independence, abhorred being buccaneers against the independence of Canada, and the acquisition of the Indian territories of the West and North of the United States.

* Hildreth's History of the United States, Second Series, Vol. III., Chap. xxi., pp. 86, 87.

CHAPTER L.

PREPARATIONS BY CANADA AGAINST THE AMERICAN INVASIONS.

1. LOWER CANADA.

IT now becomes our duty to state the preparations made by the Canadians for their own defence against the American invasions. Though so few in number and modest in pretensions to their multitudinous and boasting invaders, they had the hearts of freemen and patriots, and trusted to the Divine blessing in the justness of their cause.* We shall notice first the preparations of Lower Canada, and then those of Upper Canada.

Sir George Prevost, in the autumn of 1811, succeeded Sir James H. Craig in the government of Lower Canada, and in the chief command of the North American provinces. He had been Lieutenant-Governor of Nova Scotia. The known mildness of his character, and the popularity of his administration

* "A war with Great Britain had been long contemplated by the rulers in America, and a seasonable moment only was sought for, to grasp the provinces which they had fallaciously been induced to believe were ripe for revolt, and would therefore fall a willing conquest to America. The Peninsular war had engrossed the attention and resources of the mother country, and the Canadas were necessarily the less provided with means to encounter the struggle in which they were likely soon to be engaged. The coffers were exhausted, nor were hopes entertained of their being speedily replenished from home; the regular forces were too thin to preserve an extensive frontier of some hundred miles against the pressure of an enemy which, if united, must become irresistible; and the Canadians, though naturally brave and hardy, and attached to their Constitution, might from recent occurrences be fairly presumed to have been so far disgusted as to leave doubt of their hearty co-operation and zeal in the cause." (Christie's History of the War of 1812, Chap. iii., p. 48.)

in Nova Scotia, caused his arrival at Quebec to be heartily welcomed by the friends of just and liberal government. The narrow-mindedness and harshness of Sir James Craig's administration had caused serious agitation and differences in Lower Canada, which Sir George Prevost, by his impartiality and kindness, soon succeeded in allaying and reconciling. He called the first meeting of the Legislature on the 21st of February, 1812, and, in his opening speech, stated that he had hastened, in obedience to his orders, to assume the administration of Lower Canada; congratulated the Legislature on the brilliant achievements of the British arms in rescuing Portugal and Spain " from the tyranny of the Ruler of France;" and recommended an increased and unremitted care and vigilance in securing the country from either open invasion or insidious aggression, and hoped the Parliament would testify its loyalty by an early attention to those Acts which experience had proved essential for the preservation of his Majesty's government, as also by its readiness in supplying the Government with such aid as should be suitable to the exigence of the times, by enabling the loyal Canadian subjects to assist in repelling any sudden attack made by a tumultuary invasion, and effectually to participate in the defence of their country against a regular invasion at any future period.

The Assembly, in answer, among other things assured the Governor that they would give attention to those acts recommended by him. The Assembly passed a Militia Bill, by which the Governor was authorized to embody 2,000 unmarried men, between the ages of eighteen and twenty-five years, for three months in the year; and in case of invasion or imminent danger, to retain them for one year, relieving one-half the number embodied, by fresh drafts at the expiration of that period. In the event of war, invasion, insurrection, or imminent danger thereof, he was empowered to embody the whole militia of the province, should it become necessary. No substitutes were allowed, nor commissioned officers permitted to take any militiamen for their servants, under a penalty of £10 for every offence of that nature. These provisions, from their harshness and inconsistency, were, however, winked at in practice. It was penal to enlist any militiamen into the regular forces, and such enlistments were declared null.

Twelve thousand pounds were granted by the Legislature, one moiety thereof for drilling and training the local militia, the other moiety for other purposes of the Militia Act. *Twenty thousand pounds* were granted to be employed for such services as the safety of the province and the exigence of the times might require. And a further sum of *thirty thousand pounds* currency, to be at the Governor's disposal in case of war between Great Britain and America.

These liberal supplies enabled the Government to meet the approaching crisis with confidence in the patriotism and support of the Provincial Legislature, and the whole mass of the Canadian population. In closing the session, the Governor thanked the House for the labour they had bestowed upon the improvement of the militia system, and for the increased means thereby afforded him for the defence of the province. He also expressed his best thanks for the proofs he had received of their confidence in his administration, by the liberal provision they had made for the exigencies of the public service.*

After the declaration of war by President Madison, June 19th, 1812, which was made known at Quebec the 28th of

* Christie's History of the War of 1812, Chap. iii., pp. 49—53.

"The Governor, by a General Order of the 28th of May, 1812, organized four battalions of embodied militia, in virtue of the late Act. The first battalion rendezvoused at Point-aux-Trembles, near Quebec, under the command of Colonel De Salaberry; the second at Laprairie, near Montreal, commanded by Colonel De Rouville; the third at Berthier, in the district of Montreal, commanded by Lieutenant-Colonel Cuthbert; and the fourth at St. Thomas, near Quebec, commanded by Lieutenant-Colonel Tascherean. The alacrity with which they were filled, and the cheerfulness with which the young men submitted to the restraints of discipline, reflected credit upon the military character of the Canadians. This proof of the zeal and the loyalty of the people inspired Government with hopes of successful resistance against the approaching war, and a reciprocal confidence between the Governor and the people seems to have resulted, as much from the danger of the moment as from any studied policy on the part of the present Administration. They who had incurred the displeasure of the late Government were treated with confidence, and gradually appointed to situations of trust.

"A regiment of Canadian Voltigeurs was recruited, and placed under the command of Major De Salaberry, of the 60th Regiment of Foot, which in the course of the war became eminent for discipline and its steadiness in action, as well as for the fatiguing duties on which it was unremittingly employed."—*Ib.*, pp. 55, 56.

June, a notification was immediately made by the police that all Americans must leave Quebec by the 1st of July, and be out of the district by the 3rd of the same month. On the last day of June the period was extended by the Governor's proclamation; fourteen days were allowed to such Americans as were in the province, they being principally persons who had entered the same in good faith, and in prosecution of commercial pursuits.

"On the same day a proclamation issued imposing an embargo upon the shipping in port, and convoking the House of Assembly on the 16th of July."*

"At the opening of the session, the Governor, after informing the Legislature of the recent declaration of war by the United States against Great Britain, expressed his reliance upon the spirit of his Majesty's subjects in the province, their loyalty to their Sovereign, and their ardent love for the true interests of their country; and that he should depend implicitly, under Divine Providence, upon their best exertions, aided by the courage and loyalty of the militia, and by the valour, skill, and discipline of his Majesty's regular forces, for repelling every hostile attempt that might be made upon the colony. He observed with concern that the necessary establishment of the militia forces, together with the various services and operations of the approaching campaign, would be attended with considerable expense, but that he relied upon their wisdom and public spirit for such supplies as the exigencies of affairs might be found to require: he at the same time expressed his approbation of the embodied militia, and his confidence in their increased discipline, which encouraged an expectation that they would materially contribute to the defence of their country." * *

"A Bill to Facilitate the Circulation of Army Bills was introduced, and the liberality of the House of Assembly surpassed the hopes of the Executive. Fifteen thousand pounds were granted to pay the interest that might become due upon army bills, of which £250,000 were authorized to be put in circulation (large bills of twenty-five dollars and upwards bearing interest at the rate of fourpence per day for every hundred pounds). They were made current in the revenue, were to

---

* Christie's History of the War of 1812, Chap. iii., pp. 36, 37.

have the effect of a legal tender, and were redeemable at the Army Bill Office, either in cash or Government bills of exchange on London, at the option of the commander of the forces. Small bills of four dollars were at all times payable in cash at the Army Bill Office. On the 1st day of August, 1812, this Bill received the royal sanction, and the Governor prorogued the Parliament, with acknowledgments for the liberal aid they had granted him to meet the exigencies of the public service."*

Such were the provisions made spontaneously, and with wonderful unanimity, in Lower Canada for the defence of the province against the impending American invasion. These provisions were prior to corresponding provisions made in Upper Canada, and the statement of which has been made in so much detail that the English reading public might be reminded, or informed, of what has been too little known—the loyalty, liberality, and courage of the French as well as of the English inhabitants of Lower Canada, from the very beginning of the contest, and followed by deeds of heroism and fortitude (to be noticed hereafter), which successfully repelled successive American invasions, and prevented the American armies, ten times as numerous as the Voltigeurs and all other Canadian volunteers, from gaining a single foothold in Lower Canada.

2. UPPER CANADA.

Upper Canada was not second to Lower Canada. Sir Francis Gore left for England in 1811, and was succeeded by General Brock as President of Upper Canada, and commander of the forces, who called the Legislature together as early as possible after the declaration of war. Colonel John Clarke, Adjutant-General of Militia, in his manuscripts (with the use of which I have been favoured by the learned and excellent librarian of the Dominion at Ottawa, entitled " U. E. Papers "), says:

" Whilst the Americans were busily preparing for the campaign, we were not idle in Canada. On the 27th of July, 1812, General Brock proceeded to York and called a meeting of the Legislature, to which he delivered an animated and spirited address, concluding with the following remarkable words:

"' We are engaged in an awful and eventful contest.

---

* Christie's History of the War of 1812, Chap. iii., pp. 57—60.

"'By unanimity and dispatch in our councils, and by vigour in our operations, we may teach the enemy this lesson, that a country defended by FREE MEN, enthusiastically devoted to the cause of their King and Constitution, cannot be conquered.'"

The Legislature heartily responded to the noble appeal of General Brock at the opening of the session ; passed the necessary Acts for the security of the country, for the organization and training of the militia, and for the expenses and support of the war, and concluding their work by an earnest and patriotic address to the people of Upper Canada. We will extract some passages of this "Address of the House of Assembly to the People of Upper Canada, on the Declaration of War." This powerful address, which occupies twelve pages, is signed " Allan MacLean, Speaker," and dated "Commons House of Assembly, August 5th, 1812"—just ten days before General Brock took Detroit :

"The House of Assembly having nearly completed the necessary business for which they were called together, beg leave, before they return home, to lift up their warning voice at this eventful crisis. The declaration of war issued against Great Britain by the United States, when first announced, appeared to be an act of such astonishing folly and desperation as to be altogether incredible, and not only excited the greatest surprise among the inhabitants of this province, but among the great majority of our enemies themselves. That that Government, professing to be the friend of man and the great supporter of his liberty and independence, should light up the torch of war against the only nation that stands between itself and destruction, exhibited a degree of infatuation or madness, altogether incomprehensible. But the men at present ruling the States, infatuated, or, as their more enlightened countrymen say, 'bribed by the Tyrant of France,' regardless of the best interests of their country, and the feelings and affections of a great majority of their own people, have commenced hostilities against our mother country whilst treating their vessels with hospitality, and instead of threatening their liberties, offering most equitable terms of accommodation.

"This war, on the part of the United States, includes

an alliance with the French usurper, whose dreadful policy has destroyed all that is great and good, memorable and holy, on the continent of Europe. The government of this bloody tyrant penetrates into everything; it crushes individuals as well as nations; fetters thoughts as well as motives; and delights in destroying forever all that is fair and just in opinion and sentiment. It is evidently this tyrant who now directs the rulers of America, and they show themselves worthy disciples of such a master." * *

"We turn with joy to you, many of whom have already risked your lives for the unity of the empire. We are confident that the same spirit still animates your breasts and those of your children—that you still retain the same love of your excellent King, the same veneration for a free and happy Constitution, that you exhibited during the American war. * * When we picture to ourselves the sublime prospect the world would have exhibited this day, had the population of the neighbouring States preserved, like you, their filial love, we should not now behold the continent of Europe groaning under the yoke of a sanguinary tyrant, nor his satellites in America studiously imitating his example.

"It is therefore from former experience that we look to you for the same patriotic principles—principles which enabled you to face death in its most dreadful attire—principles which exalt human nature, and which have been warmly cherished by the most virtuous and renowned of every age; and surely when we are attacked by the same enemies who once, aided by the mistaken lenity of the mother country and the misconduct of her commanders, were able to drive us from our native homes and possessions to this province—a people whose lands are manured with the blood of our friends and kinsmen, who drove our wives and children from their homes in the woods, or threw them into dungeons, and who now envy us the habitations which, through the blessing of Providence, the beneficence of our parent state, and our own industry, we have gained from the wilderness, we are confident that you will display the same energy, and certainly with better hopes of success. Great Britain will not now consider such Americans as perverse children who may be reclaimed, but as her most malignant foes. Her commanders will not, as formerly, temporize and raise hosts of enemies by their misconduct and delays, but they will hasten to punish them with all the rigour of war.

"Already have we the joy to remark, that the spirit of loyalty has burst forth in all its ancient splendour. The militia in all parts of the province have volunteered their services with acclamation, and displayed a degree of energy worthy of the British name. * * When men are called upon to defend everything they call precious—their wives and children, their friends and possessions—they ought to be inspired with the noblest resolutions, and they will not be easily frightened by menaces, or conquered by force. And beholding, as we do, the flame of patriotism burning from one end of the Canadas to the other, we cannot but entertain the most pleasing anticipations.

"Our enemies have indeed said that they could subdue this country by Proclamation; but it is our part to prove to them that they are sadly mistaken—that the population is determinedly hostile to them, and that the few who might be otherwise inclined will find it their safety to be faithful. * *

"Innumerable attempts will be made by falsehood to detach you from your allegiance; for our enemies, in imitation of their European master, trust more to treachery than to force; and they will, no doubt, make use of many of those lies, which, unfortunately for the virtuous part of these States, and the peace and happiness of the world, had too much success during the American rebellion: they will tell you that they are come to give you freedom—yes, the base slaves of the most contemptible faction that ever distracted the affairs of any nation —the minions of the very sycophants who lick the dust from the feet of Bonaparte will tell you that they are come to communicate the blessing of liberty to this province; but you have only to look at your own situation to put such hypocrites to confusion. * *

"Trusting more to treachery than to open hostility, our enemies have already spread their emissaries through the country, to seduce our fellow-subjects from their allegiance, by promises as false as the principles on which they are founded. A law has been enacted for the speedy detection of such emissaries, and for their condign punishment on conviction."*

"Remember, when you go forth to the combat, that you fight not for yourselves alone, but for the whole world. You are defeating the most formidable conspiracy against the civilization of man that was ever contrived; a conspiracy threatening greater barbarism and misery than followed the downfall of the Roman Empire—that now you have an opportunity of proving your attachment to the parent state, which contends for the relief of oppressed nations—the last pillar of true liberty, and the last refuge of oppressed humanity.

(Signed) "ALLAN MACLEAN,
"*Speaker, Commons House of Assembly, August 5th*, 1812."

The effect of this manly and animated address to the people of Upper Canada was most beneficial, and contributed greatly to unite and encourage the people to face the struggle impending over them. There was no inflated boasting—no undervaluing of danger and sacrifice, but a plain statement of facts, and a heartfelt appeal to loyalty, patriotism, and manly courage.

* Colonel Clarke remarks that "the moderation of the different Acts which were then passed, for the preservation and defence of the province, is an additional proof that *internal treachery* was not one of the causes which were found."

CHAPTER LI.

FIRST AMERICAN INVASION OF UPPER CANADA BY GENERAL HULL, FROM DETROIT, WHOSE PROCLAMATION "TO THE INHABITANTS OF CANADA" IS GIVEN ENTIRE, AND GENERAL BROCK'S NOBLE ANSWER TO IT, IN AN ADDRESS TO THE PEOPLE OF UPPER CANADA.

IN the meantime Canada, in its western extremity, had been invaded. The American Government had been for several months collecting an army of some 3,000 or 4,000 regular troops and militia, around and west of Detroit, in order to strike a blow upon Canada the moment war should be declared. General Hull was the Governor of the territory of Michigan, and Commander-in-Chief of the "Grand Army of the West." On the 12th of July he crossed the River Detroit with a force of 2,500 of the above troops, and a strong park of artillery, and planted the American standard on the shores of Canada, at Sandwich. He forthwith issued a pretentious, inflated, cajoling, patronising, threatening proclamation to the inhabitants of Canada, and pronouncing instant death to any one who should be fighting in company with the Indians, while at the same time the Americans were employing in their army all the Indians they could induce to join them. The American democratic party which ruled at Washington had persecuted and driven the fathers of Canada from their homes in the United States, and had always been the enemies of their peace and prosperity in Canada; yet they were under the strange delusion that the people of Canada must be still as much in love with them as they were with themselves, and that the magnetism of their star-spangled banner planted in Canada would draw all

Canadians to it; that an address from their commanding general would supply the place of armies, and that taking Canada would be but a holiday march, in which, as their language of the time was, they would "breakfast at Sandwich, take dinner at York (Toronto), and sup at Montreal." It was in this spirit of vanity and delusion that General Hull issued his famous proclamation, on his landing at Sandwich, and which I give entire in a note.*

* The following is General Hull's Proclamation:

"PROCLAMATION.

"Head-quarters, Sandwich, 12th July, 1812.
"*Inhabitants of Canada*,—

"After thirty years of peace and prosperity, the United States have been driven to arms. The injuries and aggressions, the insults and indignities of Great Britain have once more left them no alternative but manly resistance or unconditional submission. The army under my command has invaded your country. The standard of the Union now waves over the territory of Canada. To the peaceable, unoffending inhabitants it brings neither danger nor difficulty. I come to find enemies, not to make them; I come to protect, not to injure you.

"Separated by an immense ocean and an extensive wilderness from Great Britain, you have no participation in her councils, nor interest in her conduct. You have felt her tyranny; you have seen her injustice; but I do not ask you to avenge the one, or to redress the other. The United States are sufficiently powerful to afford every security consistent with their and your expectations. I tender you the invaluable blessings of civil, religious, and political liberty, and their necessary result—individual and general prosperity; that liberty which gave decision to our councils and energy to our conduct, in a struggle for independence—which conducted us safely and triumphantly through the stormy period of the revolution—the liberty which has raised us to our elevated rank among the nations of the world, and which afforded us a greater measure of peace and security, of wealth and improvement, than ever fell to the lot of any people.

"In the name of my country and the authority of Government, I promise you protection to your persons, property, and rights. Remain at your homes; pursue your peaceful and customary avocations; raise not your hands against your brethren. Many of your fathers fought for the freedom and independence we now enjoy. Being children, therefore, of the same family with us, and heirs of the same heritage, the arrival of an army of friends must be hailed by you with a cordial welcome. You will be emancipated from tyranny and oppression, and restored to the dignified status of freemen.

"Had I any doubt of eventual success, I might ask your assistance; but I

In a noble address to the people of Upper Canada, General Brock answered the proclamation of General Hull, repelling and exposing with overwhelming power his misstatements, and answering with withering sarcasm General Hull's attack upon the Indians, and the " barbarous and savage policy of Great Britain" in recognizing the Indians as allies and fellow-subjects, and their right to defend their homes and liberties against American invasion and rapine. We present the reader with the following extracts of this masterly address, transcribed from the manuscripts of the Dominion Library at Ottawa.

do not. I come prepared for every contingency—I have a force which will break down all opposition, and that force is but the vanguard of a much greater. If, contrary to your own interest, and the just expectations of my country, you should take part in the approaching contest, you will be considered and treated as enemies, and the horrors and calamities of war will stalk before you.

"If the barbarous and savage policy of Great Britain be pursued, and the savages are let loose to murder our citizens, and butcher our women and children, this war will be a war of extermination. The first stroke of the tomahawk, the first attempt with the scalping knife, will be the signal of one indiscriminate scene of desolation. No white man found fighting by the side of an Indian will be taken prisoner—instant death will be his lot. If the dictates of reason, duty, justice, and humanity, cannot prevent the employment of a force which respects no rights, and knows no wrongs, it will be prevented by a severe and relentless system of retaliation.

"I doubt not your courage and firmness. I will not doubt your attachment to liberty. If you tender your services voluntarily, they will be accepted readily. The United States offer you peace, liberty, and security. Your chance lies between these and war, slavery, and destruction. Choose, then, but choose wisely; and may He who knows the justice of our cause, and who holds in His hands the fate of nations, guide you to a result the most compatible with your rights and interests, your peace and happiness.

" By the General,
" A. P. Hull."

Note.—It is a curious commentary on the above proclamation, that within six weeks of its being so pompously put forth, General Hull himself, with all his army, was a prisoner in the hands of the Lieutenant-Governor of Upper Canada, to whom was surrendered nearly 3,000 prisoners, Fort Detroit, an immense quantity of arms and munitions of war, together with the whole territory of Michigan, and the secured alliance of the numerous Indian tribes to the west and north.

In the course of his Address to the People of Canada, General Brock says:

"The unprovoked declaration of war by the United States of America against Great Britain and Ireland and its dependencies, has been followed by the actual invasion of this Province, in a remote frontier of the Western District, by a detachment of the armed force of the United States.

"The officer commanding that detachment [General Hull] has thought proper to invite his Majesty's subjects not merely to a quiet and unresisting submission, but insults them by offering with a call to seek the protection of his Government.

"Without condescending to notice the epithets bestowed, in this appeal of the American commander to the people of Upper Canada, on the administration of his Majesty, every inhabitant of the Province is desired to seek the confutation of such indecent slander in the review of his own particular circumstances.

"Where is the Canadian subject who can truly affirm to himself that he has been injured by the Government in his person, his property, or his liberty?

"Where is to be found in any part of the world a growth so rapid in prosperity and wealth as this colony exhibits? Settled not thirty years, by a band of veterans exiled from their former possessions on account of their loyalty, not a descendant of these brave people is to be found who has not, under the fostering care of their Sovereign, acquired a property and means of enjoyment superior to what were possessed by their ancestors.

"This unequalled prosperity would not have been attained by the utmost liberality of the Government or the persevering industry of the people, had not the maritime power of the mother country secured to the colonists a safe access to every market where the produce of their labour was in request. * *

"The restitution of Canada to the empire of France was the *stipulated* reward for the aid afforded to the revolted colonies, now the United States. The debt is still due; and there can be no doubt but that the pledge has been renewed as a consideration for commercial advantages, or rather for an expected relaxation in the tyranny of France over the commercial world.

"Are you prepared, inhabitants of Canada, to become willing subjects, or slaves, to the Despot who rules the nations of continental Europe with a rod of iron?

"If not, arise in a body; exert your energies; co-operate cordially with the King's regular forces to repel the invader, and do not give cause to your children, when groaning under the oppression of a Foreign Master, to reproach you with having so easily parted with the richest inheritance of this earth—a participation in the name, character, and freedom of Britons.
* * *

"Be not dismayed at the unjustifiable threat of the commander of the enemy's forces, to refuse quarter should an Indian appear in the ranks.

"The brave bands of aborigines which inhabit this colony were, like his Majesty's other subjects, punished for their zeal and fidelity by the loss of their possessions in the late colonies, and rewarded by his Majesty with lands of superior value in this Province.

"The faith of the British Government has never been violated. The Indians feel that the soil they inherit is to them and their posterity protected from the base arts so frequently devised to overreach their simplicity.

"By what principle are they to be prohibited from defending their property? If their warfare, from being different to that of other people, be more terrific to the enemy, let him retrace his steps; they seek him not—and cannot expect to find women and children in an invading army.

"But they are men, and have equal rights with all other men to defend themselves and their property when invaded, more especially when they find in the enemy's camp a ferocious and mortal enemy, using the same warfare which the American commander affects to reprobate.

"This inconsistent and unjustifiable threat of refusing quarter, for such a cause as being found in arms with a brother sufferer, in defence of invaded rights, must be exercised with the certain assurance of retaliation, not only in the limited operations of war in this part of the King's dominions, but in every quarter of the globe; for the national character of Britain is not less distinguished for humanity than strict retributive justice, which will consider the execution of this inhuman threat as deliberate murder, for which every subject of the offending power must make expiation.

      (Signed) "ISAAC BROCK,
        "*Major-General and President.*
"HEAD-QUARTERS,
 "Fort George, July 22nd, 1812."
   "By order of his Honour the President,
      (Signed) "J. B. GLEGG, A.D.C.,
           "*General.*"

CHAPTER LII.

GENERAL BROCK PREPARES FOR AN ATTACK ON DETROIT, AND WITH A SMALL FORCE TAKES GENERAL HULL AND HIS ARMY PRISONERS, AND ACQUIRES POSSESSION OF DETROIT AND THE TERRITORY OF MICHIGAN—INCIDENTS PRECEDING AND ATTENDING THE TAKING OF DETROIT—GENERAL BROCK'S PROCLAMATION TO THE INHABITANTS OF THE MICHIGAN TERRITORY—HIS COUNCIL WITH THE INDIANS, AND CONVERSATION WITH THE GREAT CHIEF TECUMSEH, AND ESTIMATE OF HIM—GENERAL BROCK RETURNS TO YORK (TORONTO)—WHAT HE DID IN NINETEEN DAYS.

GENERAL BROCK did not content himself in replying to General Hull on paper, in defence of the British Government and the people of Canada; he answered him in a more substantial way on the battle-field. General Brock lost no time in collecting the few soldiers in Upper Canada, and the militia volunteers, and proceeding by boats, vessels, and by land, from Niagara to Detroit, to meet face to face the boasting commander of the Grand Army of the West, and, in less than four weeks of his manly reply to Hull's inflated proclamation, he made Hull and all his army prisoners of war, with the surrender of the whole Michigan territory. It was an achievement worthy of perpetual remembrance, that General Brock, with forces hastily collected, "consisting of thirty of the Royal Artillery with three six-pounders, under the command of Lieutenant Troughton, two hundred and fifty of the 41st Regiment, fifty of the Newfoundland Fencibles, and four hundred Canadian militia—in all amounting to seven hundred and thirty, to whom six hundred Indians attached themselves—making an aggregate of one thousand three hundred and thirty; we say, it is an achievement worthy of all remembrance and honour, that General Brock should, with such motley and slender forces, cross the Detroit river, and, by the skilful arrangement of his handful of soldiers, take, without shedding a drop of blood, a fort strongly protected by—*iron* ordnance, nine twenty-four-pounders, eight twelve-pounders, five nine-pounders, three six-pounders; *brass* ordnance, three six-pounders, two four-pounders, one three-pounder, one eight-inch howitzer, one five and a-half inch howitzer—in all thirty-three pieces of ordnance; and defended by upwards of 2,500 regular soldiers and militia.

But there was this essential difference between the two armies: the little Canadian army had homes, families, and liberties to defend, connection with the mother country to maintain, and the consciousness of right; the great American army, with its fortifications, had the consciousness of long-continued and wide-spread wrongs in depredations against their western Indian neighbours, bloated avarice for conquest, and inveterate hatred of Great Britain.

There are several incidents connected with this remarkable military achievement. Mr. Thompson, in his History of the War of 1812, says: " General Brock having made such arrangements, in the government of the province, as were necessary during his absence from York, proceeded thence to Fort George, and thence to *Long Point, on Lake Erie, where he was joined by two hundred and sixty of the militia, who had, in a few days, and in the very height of their harvest, gallantly volunteered their services to share the dangers of the field in defence of their country*, together with the detachment of the 41st Regiment, who had been previously sent to that quarter." (Thompson's History of the War of 1812, p. 106.)

Among the 260 volunteers from the county of Norfolk—Long Point, Lake Erie—were the elder brother and brother-in-law of the writer of these pages (he being then ten years of age); the one of them was lieutenant and the other captain, who, with a great number of their neighbours, proceeded in a vessel from Port Ryerse to Amherstburg—making the passage in forty-eight hours—General Brock marching by land. The vessel with the militia volunteers reached Amherstburg some five days before General Brock, and, under the command of Colonel Proctor and the direction of a skilful engineer, commenced erecting a battery at Windsor, opposite to Detroit, behind a tuft of trees which skirted the river shore. Sentries were stationed at convenient distances along the north shore of the river, to prevent any intercourse with the American side; while the militia, officers and men, worked each night with the utmost quietness, in the erection of the battery, retiring at the approach of day. In four nights the battery was erected and mounted with cannon, when General Brock arrived, approved of what had been done, called a Council of the Indian allies, as well as of his officers, and determined forthwith to cross the river and attack Fort Detroit. The Indians were to cross in the night, which they did some three or four miles below Detroit, and spread themselves in the woods that surrounded the town, which then contained from 6,000 to 8,000 inhabitants. The night-erected battery was unmasked by felling the trees and underwood in front of it, when, to the astonishment and terror of the Americans, they saw a battery fully equipped, and already firing effectually upon their town and fort. Early in the morning of the 15th of August, General Brock, with his little army of 730 men (the militia being accoutred as regular soldiers), crossed the river unopposed about three miles below the fort (which was in the centre of the town), and marched in order of battle, under cover of corn fields, to within half a mile of the fort, from which, not cannon balls, but a flag of truce was sent out, proposing the surrender to the British commander of the fort, army, town, and territory.*

* The brother-in-law and elder brother of the writer were ordered by General Brock to select the fleetest horses of those captured from the Americans, in order to convey the intelligence of the capture of Detroit, and of General Hull and army, to Colonel Talbot, at Port Talbot, and to General Vincent, commander of the forces at Burlington Heights. They had wrought all night before they received their orders, and travelled, one of them two days and two nights, and the other two nights and three days without sleep. But these deeds were not peculiar; similar deeds were performed on the Niagara and Lower Canada frontiers during that and the following years. The Loyalist defenders of Canada of those days were patriots and soldiers to the heart's core; and they had wills, and nerves, and muscles " to endure hardness as good soldiers," in the hardest and darkest hours of our country's trials and struggles.

It may be added, that the horse on which the elder brother of the writer of these pages rode, in execution of the orders of General Brock, was afterwards stolen by the traitor Wilcox, who escaped to the United States, but was afterwards killed while invading Fort Erie.

The terrific war-whoop of the dreaded Indians, who seemed to swarm in the woods around the town, filled the people and General Hull with irresistible terror; and at the very moment that General Hull was holding a council of war with his officers in a room within the fort, a shell, thrown from the British battery at Windsor, fell into the council room, killed some officers, and wounded several more. This catastrophe, with the terrible yells of the surrounding Indians, seemed to have decided General Hull and his advisers that *surrender* " was the better part of valour."

A *second* incident connected with the surrender of Detroit and the Michigan territory is the council which General Brock held with the Indians the day before the attack upon and surrender of Detroit, and his interview with them the day after, for the account of which I am indebted to Colonel John Clarke's manuscripts in the Dominion Library at Ottawa :

" On General Brock's arrival at Sandwich, a council of war was assembled on the following morning. Along with others were 1,000 Indians, whose equipment generally might be considered very imposing.

" The council was opened by General Brock, who informed the Indians that he was ordered by their great Father, the King, to come to their assistance, and with them to drive the enemy from Fort Detroit. His speech was highly applauded, and Tecumseh was unanimously called upon to speak in reply. He commenced with expressing his joy that their great Father beyond the Salt Lake (meaning the King of England) had at length awoke from his long sleep, and sent his warriors to the assistance of his red children, who had roused themselves in their honour, and were now ready to shed the last drop of their blood in their great Father's service.

"Previously to passing over to Detroit, General Brock inquired of Tecumseh what kind of country he should have to pass through, in the event of his proceeding further. Tecumseh, taking a roll of elm bark, and extending it on the ground, drew forth his scalping knife, and presently etched upon the bark a plan of the country ; which, if not so neat, was as fully intelligible as if a surveyor had prepared it. Pleased with this talent in Tecumseh, and with his characteristic boldness, General Brock induced the Indians to cross the river for the attack on Detroit, prior to the embarkation of the white troops.

"Soon after Detroit was surrendered, General Brock took off his sash, and publicly placed it around the body of the chief Tecumseh, who received the honour conferred on him with evident gratification; but was seen the next day without his sash. The British general, fearing that something had displeased the Indian chief, sent his interpreter for an explanation. Tecumseh told him that he did not wish to wear the sash as a mark of distinction, when an older warrior than himself was present; he had transferred the sash to the Wyandot chief, Roundhead.

"In his correspondence, General Brock states that 'of many Indians whom he met at Amherstburg, he who most attracted his notice was the Shawnee chief, Tecumseh, brother of the Prophet—a more gallant or sagacious warrior does not, I believe, exist; he was the admiration of every one, and was as humane as he was brave.'

"General Brock, in General Orders of the 16th of August, 1812, after the capture of Detroit, states that two fortifications had been already captured, Michilimackinac and Detroit, without a drop of blood being shed by the hands of the Indians; the moment the enemy surrendered, his life became sacred."

"On congratulating General Brock, after the capture of Detroit, Tecumseh said to the General, 'We observed you from a distance standing the whole time in an erect position, and when the boats reached the shore, you were the first man on the land; your bold and sudden movements frightened the enemy, and so compelled them to surrender to half their number.'

"General Brock engaged the Indians to throw away the scalping knife—implanting in their hearts the virtue of clemency, and teaching them to feel pleasure and pride in compassion extended to a vanquished enemy. In return, they revered him as their common Father, and whilst under his control, were guilty of no excesses; and thereby the noble Tecumseh was humane as well as brave."*

---

* I think the reader will be interested in the following particulars, which I have collected of this remarkable Indian Chief:

"In the year 1809, Tecumseh, attended by several hundred warriors, encamped near Vincennes, then capital of Indiana, and demanded an inter-

Such was the character and results of the first American invasion of Canada.

It may be worth while to notice some events which preceded the taking of Detroit, and which doubtless disappointed and disheartened General Hull. In the island of St. Joseph, in Lake Huron, there was a fort or blockhouse, under the command of Captain Roberts, with thirty regulars. General Brock, in communicating to Captain Roberts the American declaration of war against Great Britain, instructed him to take every precaution for the protection of St. Joseph, and, if possible, to get

view with the Governor of the State ; for which interview was assembled a Council, when it was observed there was no vacant seat for the noble chief, Tecumseh. One of the Council officers hastily offered his seat, and having respectfully said to him, 'Warrior, your Father, General Harrison, offers you a seat.' 'My Father,' exclaimed Tecumseh, extending his arms towards the heavens, 'There, son, is my Father, and the earth is my mother ; she giving me nourishment, and I dwell upon her bosom.' He then sat himself upon the ground."

"The Indian warrior Tecumseh, a Shawnee chief, himself and warriors, attached themselves to the cause of Great Britain, on the declaration of the American war of 1812. * *

"Tecumseh's first engagement, under the British Colonel Proctor, then in command of the Western District, was attacking and defeating a detachment of Americans under Major Howe, from Detroit to the Beaver river. In this affair, General Hull's despatches, and correspondence of his troops, fell into the hands of Tecumseh ; and it was partly from the discouraging nature of their contents that General Brock attempted the capture of the American army under General Hull."

"On the 16th of July, Tecumseh and a few of his warriors pursued near Sandwich [on the Canadian side of the river] a detachment of the American army, under Colonel McArthur, and fired on the rear guard. 'The colonel suddenly faced about and gave orders for a volley, when all the Indians fell flat on the ground, with the exception of Tecumseh, who stood firm on his feet, with apparent unconcern."

"As Colonel Proctor retired to Nassau (Moravian town), on the Thames, and when the regulars and militia had surrendered on the right, the Indians carried on the contest on the left, and did not retreat until the day was lost, and thirty-three of their number had been slain, including the noble warrior, Tecumseh. After his fall, his lifeless corpse was recovered with great interest by the American officers, who declared that the contour of his features was majestic even in death. He left a son who fought by his side when he fell, and was seventeen years of age.

"The Prince Regent, in 1815, as a mark of respect to the memory of his father, sent a handsome sword as a present to his son."

possession of Michilimackinac, now called Mackinac, and pronounced Mackinaw, an island about nine miles in circumference, commanding the entrance from Lake Huron into Lake Michigan, on which the Americans had a fort with a captain in command, and a garrison of seventy-five men. Captain Roberts was aided by Mr. Pothier, a gentlemen of the South-west Fur Company, who volunteered his own services, attended by about 160 Canadian voyageurs, and placed the contents of the stores at the disposal of Captain Roberts, who, with his little armament, consisting of thirty regulars, two artillerymen and a sergeant, 160 Canadians, and two iron field-pieces, set out on the 16th of July with his flotilla of boats and canoes, convoyed by the *Caledonia* brig, belonging to the North-West Company, loaded with stores and provisions. On the ensuing morning he reached Mackinac, a distance of about forty miles, landed without opposition, and immediately summoned the garrison to surrender, which was complied with in a few minutes Thus was this key of the West taken without the effusion of a drop of blood.

The Americans had carried on a brisk trade in schooners and sailing vessels from Detroit, through Lake Huron, to the head of Lake Michigan, now Chicago. The capture of Mackinac—which was a surprise to the commander, who had not heard of the declaration of war—interrupted this trade, and gave confidence to the Canadian voyageurs and Indians in the British interests employed in the fur trade in these distant countries.

"This achievement, effected by the promptitude and judicious arrangements of Captain Roberts, not only inspired the people with confidence, and gave a turn to the present campaign fatal to the views of the United States, by enabling us to maintain our influence among the Indians of the West, which otherwise must have been lost, but it essentially contributed to the successful struggle afterwards maintained against the American arms in Upper Canada. General Hull, after the capture of his army and the fall of Detroit, in his official despatch relative to these events, attributes his disasters to the fall of Mackinac; after the surrender of which, almost every tribe and nation of Indians, except a part of the Miamis and Delawares, north from beyond Lake Superior, west from beyond the Mississippi, south from Ohio and the Wabash, and east from every part of

Upper Canada, and from all the intermediate country, joined in open hostility against the army he commanded."*

"General Hull remained some time inactive, under pretext of making preparation to prosecute the campaign with vigour; but it was the fallacious hope of an early insurrection in his favour that lulled him into a supineness fatal to the safety of his army. Amherstburg lay about eighteen miles below him, and the mud and picketed fortifications of that post was not in a condition to make resistance against a regular siege. The Americans, confident of an easy conquest, had not as yet a single cannon or mortar mounted, and to endeavour to take it at the point of the bayonet he thought inexpedient. During this delay his situation became more and more precarious; three detachments from his army were, on three successive days, beaten back by a handful of the 41st Regiment and a few Indians, from a bridge over the River Canard, three miles from Amherstburg, which they endeavoured to seize, in order to open the route to that port. Another detachment, in attempting to ford the river (Canard) higher up, was put to flight by a small party of eighteen or twenty Indians who lay concealed in the grass. The enemy, panic-struck at their sudden and hideous yell, fled with precipitancy, leaving their arms, accoutrements, and haversacks. The British sloop of war *Queen Charlotte*, carrying eighteen twenty-four pounders, lay in the Detroit river, opposite the mouth of the River Canard, so that it was impossible for the Americans to convey by water to Amherstburg any artillery, of which, after much labour, they had at last mounted two twenty-four-pounders. Lieutenant Rolette, commanding the armed brig *Hunter*, had on the 3rd of July, at about ten o'clock in the forenoon, by a bold attempt in his barge, with only six men, succeeded in capturing the *Cuyahaya* packet, bound from Miami river to Detroit with troops, and loaded with baggage, and the hospital stores of the American army, the loss of which was now severely felt. Mackinac, in his rear, had been taken since the commencement of the invasion, while the Indians from that quarter were flocking to the British standard. Our naval force being superior on the lake, Colonel Proctor pushed over to Brownstown, a village nearly

* Christie's War of 1812, pp. 65, 66.

opposite to Amherstburg, twenty miles below Detroit, with a small detachment of the 41st Regiment, under the command of Captain Tallon, with a few Indians, who on the 5th of August surprised and routed a party of 200 Americans under Major Vanhorne, on their way from Detroit to River Raisin, to meet a detachment of volunteers from Ohio, under Captain Brush, with a convoy of provisions for the army. In this affair a quantity of booty, and General Hull's despatches to the Secretary at War, fell into the hands of the victors, whereby the deplorable state of the American army was disclosed." * *

"In the interim, the American general received a despatch from General Hull, on the Niagara frontier, intimating that he could not expect co-operation in that quarter, which would have created a diversion in his favour. Such was the hopeless state of things when the American general began to be sensible of his danger. His army hemmed in on every side, cut off from its resources, and hourly wasting away with defeat, death, sickness, and fatigue, unsupported by an expected insurrection of Canadians in his favour, and unaided by any co-operating army, and, above all, dismayed at the report of General Brock's resolution to advance against him; his schemes of conquest vanquished, and in the sinking state of his affairs, he saw no other alternative than to retreat back to Detroit, under pretence of concentrating his main army, and after re-opening his communications with the Rivers Raisin and Miami, through which he received his whole supplies, to resume offensive operations against Upper Canada. Accordingly, on the evening of the 7th and the morning of the 8th of August, the whole of his army, except a garrison of 250 men and a few artillery left in charge of a small fortress they had thrown up on the British side, a little below Detroit, *recrossed the river.*

"General Hull now detached a body of 600 men, under Lieutenant-Colonel Miller, to dislodge the British from Brownstown, and open the communication with the Rivers Raisin and Miami, upon which the existence of the army depended. On the 9th, this detachment was met by the British and Indians under Major Muir at Magnogo, between Brownstown and Detroit, which, after a desperate battle, in which the Americans lost seventy-five men, was obliged to retreat with inconsiderable loss compared with that of the Americans.

On the 7th, Lieutenant Rolette, with the boats of the *Queen Charlotte* and *Hunter*, under cover of the guns of the latter, attacked and captured a convoy of eleven batteaux and boats, having on board fifty-six of their wounded, and two English prisoners, on their way from Magnogo to Detroit, escorted by 250 American troops on shore.

"Amidst these reverses of fortune, the American general was startled at the summons to surrender the fort of Detroit, by General Brock, who, after having closed the public business at York, and prorogued Parliament, and collecting a few regulars and militia with incredible exertion, had reached Amherstburg by the 13th of August. So resolute a demand struck the American commander with dismay, who, at the most, had never contemplated a pursuit into his own territory by the British. He still, however, maintained sufficient presence of mind to return a prompt and positive refusal, upon receipt of which, the British, who now occupied the ground so lately in possession of the enemy, in front of Detroit, where they had thrown up a battery (erected by night) under the direction of Captain Dixon, of the Royal Engineers, commenced, on the afternoon of the 15th, a brisk cannonade on Detroit, from two five-and-a-half-inch mortars, and two twelve-pounders, under the management of Captain Hall, of the Provincial Navy, with a party of sailors, which was continued for upwards of an hour with great effect. Early in the morning of the 16th the cannonade recommenced, while General Brock, with about 700 regulars and militia, and 600 Indians, crossed the river without opposition at the Spring Wells, three miles below Detroit, under cover of the *Queen Charlotte* and *Hunter*. This small but resolute force, after forming upon the beach, advanced in column, flanked on the left by the Indians, with the river of Detroit on their right, and took (at the distance of a mile) position in line, in front of the American fort, into which the enemy had retired. Here every preparation was making for an immediate assault, when, to the surprise of both armies, a white flag was seen flying upon the walls of the fort, and a messenger advancing with proposals from the American general to *capitulate*. Lieutenant-Colonel McDowell, of the Militia, and Major Glegg, of the 49th Regiment, aide-de-camp to General Brock, immediately proceeded by his orders to the tent of the American general, where, in a few minutes, they dictated the terms of capitulation. By this the whole American army, including a detachment of 350 men, under Colonels M'Arthur and Cass, dispatched on the 14th for River Raisin to escort the provisions in charge of Captain Brush from thence to Detroit, became prisoners of war; and Detroit, with the Michigan territory, were surrendered to the British arms, without the effusion of a single drop of British blood.

"The American statements of their own strength nearly coincide with British reports, which make it 2,500 men, regulars and militia. The militia were paroled, and permitted to return home, on condition of not serving during the present war. The regulars were sent down to Quebec.

"The British force, including Indians, is acknowledged by the enemy to have consisted of only 1,030 men or thereabout. Our own, and perhaps more correct reports, state it to have consisted of 350 regular troops, 400 militia, and 600 Indians, who, upon the present occasion, are said not to have sullied the glory of the day by any wanton acts of savage barbarity incident to the Indian mode of warfare. Twenty-five pieces of iron and eight pieces of brass ordnance, with an immense quantity of stores of every description, and one armed brig, called the *John Adams* (afterwards named *Detroit*), fell into the hands of the British" [besides nearly 3,000 stand of small arms, much ammunition, and three weeks' provisions for the whole army]. (Thompson's History of the War of 1812, pp. 67—72.)

"Thus ended this (first) rash and imbecile attempt at the conquest of Canada. The loss of Mackinac and Detroit, with the flower of their army, at the outset of the war, was a disgrace that filled the American Government with consternation and alarm, as their plans of aggrandisement were not only totally defeated, but their whole western frontier was laid open to the inroads of the hostile Indians, and at the mercy of a people still warm with indignation at the late invasion."—*Ib.*, pp. 72, 73.

General Brock, the day after taking Detroit, addressed to the inhabitants of the Michigan territory the following Proclamation:

"Whereas the territory of Michigan was this day, by capitulation, ceded to the arms of his Britannic Majesty, without any other condition than the protection of private property; and wishing to give an early proof of the moderation and justice of his Majesty's government, I do hereby announce to all the inhabitants of the said territory, that the laws heretofore in existence shall continue in force until his Majesty's pleasure be known, and so long as the peace and safety of the said territory will admit thereof; and I do hereby also declare and make known to the said inhabitants, that they shall be protected in the full exercise and enjoyment of their religion—of which all persons, both civil and military, will take notice, and govern themselves accordingly.

"All persons having in their possession, or having knowledge of any public property, shall forthwith deliver in the same, or give notice thereof to the officer commanding, or to Lieutenant-Colonel Nicholl, who are duly authorized to receive and give the proper receipts for the same.

"Officers of militia will be held responsible that all arms in possession of the militiamen be immediately delivered up; and all individuals whatever who have in possession arms of any kind, will deliver them up without delay.

"Given under my hand, at Detroit, this 16th day of August, 1812, and in the 52nd year of his Majesty's reign. God save the King.

(Signed) "ISAAC BROCK,
"*Major-General.*"

The purport and spirit of this proclamation was very different from those issued by successful American commanders in former years, when they required the conquered to take a new oath of allegiance, to enrol themselves in a new army under pain of confiscation of property, imprisonment, and even death. The true genius of English government is justice, law, and liberty; the genius of democratic government is the domination of party, and the spoils to the victors. In the conquest of a vast territory by General Brock, there was no plunder or sacrifice of life, by Indian or soldier, much less plunder for the benefit of the general. It was not so with the promising, threatening, ostentatious, grasping General Hull, who, according to the Patriotic Society of Upper Canada (of which hereafter), is thus reported:

"In 1812, General Hull invaded the British province of Upper Canada, and took possession of the town of Sandwich. He threatened (by proclamation) *to exterminate the inhabitants if they made any resistance. He plundered* those with whom he had been on habits of intimacy years before the war. Their plate and linen were found in his possession after his surrender to General Brock. He marked out the loyal subjects of the King as objects of his peculiar resentment, and consigned their property to pillage and conflagration."

General Brock left Colonel Proctor in command of Detroit, and returned to York (Toronto), where he arrived the 27th of August, amidst the heartfelt acclamations of a grateful people.

"In the short space of nineteen days he had, with the assistance of the Provincial Parliament, settled the public business of the province, under the most trying circumstances that a commander could encounter, and having united and prepared his little army, had effected a long and fatiguing march of several hundred miles; and with means incredibly limited, had repelled an invading enemy of double his force, pursued him into his own territory, and finally compelled him to surrender his whole army and jurisdiction; thus extending the British dominions, without bloodshed, over an extent of territory almost equal to Upper Canada."—"Our little navy on Lake Erie, and on Lake Ontario, though the enemy were making the most active exertions, still maintained a decided ascendency, and upon it depended the safety of Upper Canada and the future fate of the British provinces. General Brock intended to have followed up his first success by an attempt on Niagara, a fort nearly opposite to Fort George; which, in all probability, as well as Oswego and Sackett's Harbour, the nursery of the enemy's fleet and forces, would have yielded to the terror of his name and the tide of success that attended his arms; but, *controlled by his instructions*, he was prevented from adopting measures which probably might have for ever blasted the hopes of the United States in Upper Canada." (Christie.)

CHAPTER LIII.

SECOND AMERICAN INVASION OF UPPER CANADA AT QUEENSTON—DISPRO-
PORTION OF AMERICAN AND CANADIAN FORCES—DEATH OF GENERAL
BROCK—DEFEAT AND LOSS OF THE AMERICANS—ARMISTICE—INCI-
DENTS WHICH OCCURRED ON THE NIAGARA FRONTIER, AT FORT ERIE,
AS RELATED BY LIEUTENANT DRISCOLL, OF THE 100TH REGIMENT.

THE *second invasion* of Upper Canada took place on the Niagara frontier, at Queenston. We will give the account of it (condensed) from the History of the War by Mr. Thompson, of the Royal Scots:

"Dispirited at such a total failure in General Hull's expedition, it became late in the season before the American Government could collect a force on the frontiers with which, with any safety, another descent upon Canada could be made. At length, Major-General Van Rensellaer, of the New York Militia, with a force of *four thousand men* under his command (1,500 of whom were regular troops), established his camp at Lewiston, on the Niagara river, nearly half-way between Lake Ontario and the Falls.

"Before daylight on the morning of the 13th of October, a large division of General Van Rensellaer's army, under Brigadier-General Wadsworth, effected a landing at the lower end of the village of Queenston (opposite to Lewiston), and made an attack upon the position, which was defended with the most determined bravery by the two flank companies of the 49th Regiment, commanded by Captains Dennis and Williams, aided by such of the militia forces and Indians as could be collected in the vicinity.

"Major-General Brock, on receiving intelligence, immediately proceeded to that post, from Fort George, and arrived at the juncture when the handful of British regulars was compelled to retire for a time before an overwhelming force of the enemy. However, on the appearance of their gallant chief, the troops were seized with a fresh animation, and were led on by that brave general to a renewed exertion to maintain the post; but at the moment of charging the enemy's position, within pistol-shot of the line, General Brock was killed by a musket ball, and with him the position was for a short time lost. Colonel Macdonell, his provincial aide-de-camp, was mortally wounded about the same time, and died shortly afterwards of his wounds.

"A reinforcement of the 41st Regiment, commanded by Captain Derenzy, with a few of the Lincoln Militia and a party of Indians, were immediately marched from Fort George to the succour of the troops at Queenston, under the direction of Major-General Sheaffe, who now assumed the command; and persons who were, by their situations in life and advanced age, exempt from serving in the militia, made common cause, seized their arms, and flew to the field of action as volunteers.

"The conflict was again renewed, and from the advantageous position of Norton, the Indian chief, with his warriors, on the woody brow of the high grounds, a communication was opened with Chippewa, from whence Captain Bullock, of the 41st Regiment, with a detachment of that corps, was enabled to march for Queenston, and was joined on the way by parties of militia who were repairing from all quarters, with all the enthusiasm imaginable, to the field of battle. The fight was maintained on both sides with a courage truly heroic. The British regulars and militia charged in rapid succession against a force in number far exceeding their own, until they succeeded in turning the left flank of their column, which rested on the summit of the hill. The event of the day no longer appeared doubtful."

"Major-General Van Rensellaer, commanding the American army, perceiving his reinforcements embarking very slowly, re-crossed the Niagara river to accelerate their movements; but, to his utter astonishment, he found that at the very moment when their services were most required, the ardour of the engaged troops had entirely subsided. He rode in all directions through his camp, urging the men by every consideration to pass over.

Lieutenant-Colonel Bloome, who had been wounded in the action and re-crossed the river, together with Judge Peck, who happened to be in Lewiston at the time, mounted their horses and rode through the camp, exhorting the companies to proceed—*but all in vain.* Crowds of the United States Militia remained on the American bank of the river, to which they had not been marched in any order, but run as a mob; *not one of them would cross.* They had seen the wounded re-crossing; they had seen the Indians, *and were panic-struck."* (American Report of the Battle of Queenston.)

"No sooner had the British forces succeeded in turning the left flank of the enemy, than he visibly began to give way; one grand effort was therefore made upon the crest of his position, in which the heights were carried at the point of the bayonet.

"General Van Rensellaer, having found that it was impossible to induce a man to cross the river to reinforce the army on the heights, and that the army had nearly expended its ammunition, immediately sent boats to cover their retreat; but the fire, which was maintained upon the ferry from a battery on the bank of the lower end of Queenston, completely dispersed the boats, and many of the boatmen re-landed and fled in dismay.

"Brigadier-General Wadsworth was therefore compelled, after a vigorous conflict had been maintained for some time on both sides, to surrender himself and all his officers, with 900 men, between three and four o'clock in the afternoon, to a force far inferior to his in numbers—a circumstance which speaks loudly in favour of the plan of defence and attack adopted by Major-General Sheaffe.

"The loss of the British in this battle did not exceed 100 men, including killed, wounded, and missing; while that on the side of the Americans, including deserters, was not less than 2,000; but amongst the killed, the British Government and the country had to deplore the loss of Sir Isaac Brock, one whose memory will long live in the warmest affections of every British subject in Canada."*

* Such was the high esteem in which the character of General Brock was held even by the enemy, that during the movement of the funeral procession of that brave man from Queenston to Fort George, a distance of seven miles, minute guns were fired at every American post on that part of the lines; and even the appearance of hostilities was suspended.

"On the morning subsequent to the battle of Queenston, General Sheaffe entered into an armistice with the American general commanding at Lewiston, to be confined to that part of the frontier comprised between Lakes Ontario and Erie, subject to a condition that forty-eight hours' notice should be given by either party for a recommencement of hostilities [a condition violated by the American commander]. This arrangement [considered disadvantageous to the British cause] was at first censured by individuals unaware of the motives by which General Sheaffe was actuated. It was not, in the flush of victory, taken into consideration that the number of American prisoners then in his charge far exceeded the numerical strength of his army, when the Indian force was withdrawn; and that, with his very limited means of defence, he had a frontier of forty miles to protect."*

Before noticing the *third* American invasion of Canada, in 1812, or the second on the Niagara frontier, we will conclude this Chapter by adding a few incidents on the Niagara river frontier, at Fort Erie, after the death of General Brock, October 13, 1812, by Lieutenant Driscoll, of the 100th Regiment :

"I was stationed at Fort Erie on the memorable 13th of October, 1812. At daybreak, having returned with my escort as visiting rounds, after a march of about six miles in muddy roads through the forests, and about to refresh the inward man, after my fatiguing trudge, I heard a booming of distant artillery, very faintly articulated.

"Having satisfied myself of the certainty of my belief, hunger, wet, and fatigue were no longer remembered; excitement banishes these trifling matters from the mind; and I posted off to my commanding officer to report the firing, now more audible and rapid.

"I found my chief, booted, spurred, and snoring—lying, as was his wont, on a small hair mattrass on the floor in his barrack-room, which boasted of furniture, one oak table covered with green baize, a writing-desk, a tin basin containing water, and a brass candlestick, which had planted in it a regulation mutton-dip, dimly flickering its last ray of light, paling before

---

* Thompson's History of the War of 1812, Chap. xv.

the dawn, now making its first appearance through the curtainless window.

"The noise I made on entering the major's sleeping and other apartment awoke him. As he sat up on his low mattrass, he said, 'What is the matter?' 'Heavy firing down the river, sir.' 'Turn the men out.' 'All under arms, sir.' 'That 'll do.'

"By this time he was on his legs—his hat and gloves on. His hutman was at the door with his charger, and his spurs in his horse's flanks in an instant—leaving the orderly, hutman, and myself to double after him up to the fort, some hundred yards off.

"As we reached it, the men were emerging through the gate in measured cadence, and we were on our way to the batteries, opposite the enemy's station at Black Rock.

"Before we reached our post of alarm the sun was up and bright. We had not assumed our position long before an orderly officer of the Provincial Dragoons rode up, and gave us the information that the enemy were attempting to cross at Kingston, and that we must annoy them along the whole line, as was being done from Niagara to Queenston, by any and every means in our power short of crossing the river. Everything was ready on our parts. The enemy all appeared asleep, judging from the apparent quiet that prevailed on their side of the river.

"The command to annoy the enemy was no sooner given than, bang! bang! went off every gun we had in position.

"Now there was a stir. The enemy's guns were in a short time manned, and returned our fire; and the day's work was begun, which was carried on briskly the greater part of the day on both sides of the Niagara.

"About two o'clock, another Provincial dragoon, bespattered, horse and man, with foam and mud, made his appearance—not wearing his sword or helmet.

"Said an old Green Tiger to me, 'Horse and man jaded, sir; depend upon it, he brings bad news.' 'Step down and ascertain what intelligence he brings.' Away my veteran doubles, and soon returns at a funeral pace. 'Light heart, light step,' were my inward thoughts. I knew by poor old Clibborn's style of return something dreadful had occurred.

"'What news, Clibborn? What news, man? Speak out,'

said I, as he advanced towards the battery, that was still keeping up a brisk fire. Clibborn walked on, perfectly unconscious of the balls that were ploughing up the ground, uttered not a word, but shook his head.

"When in the battery, the old man sat down on the platform; still no word, but the pallor and expression of his countenance indicated the sorrow of his soul.

"I could stand it no longer. I placed my hand on his shoulder, 'For Heaven's sake, tell us what you know.' In choking accents he revealed his melancholy information: 'The general is killed; the enemy has possession of Queenston Heights.'

"Every man in the battery was paralyzed; the battery ceased firing.

"A cheer by the enemy from the opposite side of the river recalled us to our duty. They had heard of their success down the river. Our men, who had in various ways evinced their feelings—some in weeping, some in swearing, some in mournful silence—now exhibit demoniac energy. The heavy guns are loaded, traversed and fired, as if they were field-pieces—too much hurry for precision. 'Take your time, men; don't throw away your fire, my lads.' 'No, sir, but we will give it to them hot and heavy.'

"All the guns were worked by the 49 men of my own company, and they wished to avenge their beloved chief Brock, whom they knew and valued with that correct appreciation peculiar to the British soldier. They had all served under him in Holland and at Copenhagen.

"I had a very excellent reconnoitring-glass; and as I kept a sharp look-out for the effect of our fire, and the movements of the enemy, I observed that powder was being removed from a large wooden barrack into ammunition waggons. The only man of the Royal Artillery I had with me was a bombardier, Walker. I called his attention to the fact I had observed, and directed him to lay a gun for that part of the building wherein the powder was being taken. At my request he took a look through my glass, and, having satisfied himself, he lay the gun as ordered. I, with my glass, watched the spot aimed at. I saw one plank of the building fall out, and at the same instant the whole fabric went up in a pillar of black smoke, with but little noise, as it was no more. Horses, waggons, men, and building all disappeared; not a vestige of any was seen.

"Now was our turn to cheer; and we plied the enemy in a style so quick and accurate, that we silenced all their guns just as a third dragoon come galloping up to us, shouting 'Victory! Victory!' Then again we cheered lustily; but no response from the other side. Night now hid the enemy from our sight.

"The commissariat made its appearance with biscuit, pork, rum, and potatoes; and we broke our fast for that day about nine p.m.

"How strange and unaccountable are the feelings induced by war! Here were men of two nations, but of a common origin, speaking the same language, of the same creed, intent on mutual destruction, rejoicing with fiendish pleasure at their address in perpetrating murder by wholesale, shouting for joy as disasters propagated by the chances of war hurled death and agonizing wounds into the ranks of their opponents! And yet the very same men, when chance gave them the opportunity, would readily exchange, in their own peculiar way, all the amenities of social life, extending to one another a draw of the pipe, and quid, or glass; obtaining and exchanging information from one and the other of their respective services, as to pay, rations, and so on—the victors, with delicacy, abstaining from any allusion to the victorious day. Though the vanquished would allude to their disaster, the victors never named their triumphs.

"Such is the character of acts and words between British and American soldiers which I have witnessed, as officer commanding a guard over American prisoners.

"J. DRISCOLL,
"Of the 100th Regiment."

CHAPTER LIV.

THIRD AMERICAN INVASION OF UPPER CANADA, AT AND NEAR FORT ERIE, ON THE NIAGARA RIVER, UNDER GENERAL SMYTH—HIS ADDRESS TO HIS SOLDIERS—THE LUDICROUS AND DISGRACEFUL FAILURE OF HIS EXPEDITION—THREE AMERICAN EXPEDITIONS REPELLED IN 1812 BY THE SPARTAN BANDS OF CANADIAN VOLUNTEERS, ASSISTED BY A FEW REGIMENTS OF ENGLISH SOLDIERS.

SUCH was the result of the *second invasion of Canada*—the first invasion on the Niagara frontier by the American " Grand Army of the Centre."

The Americans, after recovering in some measure from their disastrous defeat at Queenston, commenced gigantic preparations for assembling another army near Buffalo, for a second descent on the Niagara frontier, under the command of General Smyth, with an army which, according to the latest accounts of the American reports themselves, was 8,000 strong, with fifteen pieces of field ordnance—sustained in the rear by a populous and fertile country, and the facility afforded by good roads to draw the supplies for his army and to bring into the field a formidable artillery. So confident was General Smyth himself of a successful result of his expedition, that he boasted on the 10th of November "that in a few days the troops under his command would plant the American standard in Canada," and issued an order to the commandant of Fort Niagara to save the buildings at Fort George and the adjacent town of Newark (Niagara), as they would be required for winter quarters for the " Army of the Centre."

It was a difficult if not doubtful task for General Sheaffe and the regular and militia officers under his command to provide for the defence of the country against such formidable odds;

for up to the time at which the American general had violated the terms of the armistice not a single British soldier had arrived to reinforce the little Canadian army; and "after the conflict at Queenston, the militia, which constituted the majority of the British force, had been permitted to return home to secure the remainder of their harvest." (Thompson.)

"However, on the first alarm being given of the hostile movements of the American army, those already harassed but loyal Canadian militiamen promptly returned to their posts, fully determined to dispute every inch of ground while a man was left to defend it."—(*Ib*). Nor were these volunteer Loyalists intimidated by General Smyth's extended columns of cavalry and infantry with which he lined the American shore, his marching and countermarching of countless battalions, and all the pomp of war and parade of martial bombast with which the fertile mind of General Smyth hoped to terrify the apparently defenceless Canadians; to which he added a flaming proclamation, not excelled in pomposity and brag by that of General Hull issued to Canadians three months before. We give this proclamation, as we have done that of General Hull, in a note.*

This proclamation, ridiculous as it is, and appealing to the lowest mercenary as well as better motives of democratic

---

* The following is General Smyth's proclamation, issued to his soldiers, on his intended invasion of Canada:

"*General Smyth to the Soldiers of the Army of the Centre.*

"Companions in arms!—The time is come when you will cross the stream of Niagara to conquer Canada, and to secure the peace of the Canadian frontier.

"You will enter a country that is to be one of the United States. You are to arrive among a people who are to become your fellow-citizens. It is not against *them* that we come to make war. It is against that Government which holds them as vassals.

"You will make this war as little as possible distressful to the Canadian population. If they are peaceable, they are to be secure in their persons; and in their property as far as our imperious necessities will allow.

"Provided that, plundering is absolutely forbidden. Any soldier who quits his rank to plunder on the field of battle, will be punished in the most exemplary manner.

"But your just rights as soldiers will be maintained; whatever is booty by the usages of war, you shall have. All horses belonging to the artillery and cavalry; all waggons and teams in the public service, will be sold for

Americans, produced a considerable effect in Pennsylvania, and caused an accession of some 2,000 volunteers to General Smyth's already large forces; but when the crisis of action arrived, this grandiloquent General Smyth was not to be found on the

the benefit of the captors. Public stores will be secured for the service of the United States. The Government will, with justice, pay you the value.

"The horses drawing the light artillery of the enemy are wanted for the service of the United States. I will order $200 for each to be paid to the party who may take them. I will also order $40 to be paid for the arms and spoils of each savage warrior who shall be killed.

"*Soldiers!*—You are amply provided for war. You are superior in number to the enemy. Your personal strength and activity are greater. Your weapons are longer. The regular soldiers of the enemy are really old, whose best years have been spent in the sickly climate of the West Indies. They will not be able to stand before you—you who charge with the bayonet. You have seen Indians, such as those hired by the English to murder women and children, and kill and scalp the wounded. You have seen their dances and grimaces, and heard their yells. Can you fear *them?* No; you hold them in the utmost contempt.

"*Volunteers!*—Disloyal and traitorous men have endeavoured to dissuade you from your duty. Sometimes they say, if you enter Canada you will be held to service for five years. At others they say that you will not be furnished with supplies. At other times they say that if you are wounded, the Government will not provide for you by pensions. The just and generous course pursued by Government towards the volunteers who fought at Tippecanoe, furnishes an answer to that objection. The others are too absurd to deserve any.

"*Volunteers!*—I esteem your generous and patriotic motives. You have made sacrifices on the altar of your country. You will not suffer the enemies of your fame to mislead you from the path of duty and honour, and deprive you of the esteem of a grateful country. You will show the *eternal* infamy that awaits the man who, having come in sight of the enemy, basely shrinks in the moment of trial.

"*Soldiers of every corps!*—It is in your power to retrieve the honour of your country, and to cover yourselves with glory. Every man who performs a gallant action shall have his name made known to the nation. Rewards and honours await the brave. Infamy and contempt are reserved for cowards.

"*Companions in arms!*—You come to vanquish a valiant foe; I know the choice you will make. Come on, my heroes! And when you attack the enemy's batteries, let your rallying word be 'The cannon lost at Detroit, or death.'

    (Signed)   "ALEXANDER SMYTH,
              "*Brigadier-General Commanding.*

"Camp near Buffalo, 17th Nov., 1812."

field of action; and of the twenty boats which were provided to convey across the river the first instalment of invaders of Canada, fourteen boats were sunk or driven back, and only six boats reached the Canadian shore and gained a temporary hold, but some of them were driven back with loss before the next morning, and the remainder were taken prisoners. The next day General Smyth promised to do very great things; but we will narrate these doings and the results in the words of the American writer Lossing, in his *Field Book of the War of 1812*. Lossing says:

"November 27th [1812].—It was sunrise when the troops began to embark, and so tardy were the movements that it was late in the afternoon when all was ready. General Smyth did not make his appearance, and all the movements were under the direction of his subordinates. A number of boats had been left to strand upon the shore, and became filled with water, snow, and ice; and as hour after hour passed by, dreariness and disappointment fell upon the spirits of the shivering troops. Meanwhile the enemy had collected on the opposite [British] shore, and were watching every movement. At length, when all seemed ready and impatience had yielded to hope, an order came from the commanding general '*to disembark and dine.*' The wearied and worried troops were deeply exasperated by this order, and nothing but the most positive assurances that the undertaking would be immediately resumed kept them from open mutiny. The different regiments retired sullenly to their respective quarters, and General Porter, with his dispirited New York volunteers, marched in disgust to Buffalo.

"November 28th [1812].—Smyth now called a council of officers. They could not agree. The best of them urged the necessity of crossing in force at once, before the (Canadian) enemy could make formidable preparations for their reception. The General decided otherwise; and doubt and despondency brooded over the camp that night. The ensuing Sabbath brought no relief. Preparations for another embarkation were indeed in progress, while the (Canadian) enemy, too, was busy in opposing labour. It was evident to every spectator of judgment that the invasion must be attempted at another point of the river, when, towards evening, to the astonishment of all, the General issued an order perfectly characteristic of the man—

for the troops to be ready at eight (November 30) o'clock the next morning for embarkation. 'The General will be on board,' he pompously proclaimed. 'Neither rain, snow, or frost will prevent the embarkation,' he said. 'The cavalry will soon scour the fields from Black Rock to the bridge, and suffer no idle spectators. While embarking, the bands will play martial airs; *Yankee Doodle* will be the signal to get under way. * * The landing will be effected in despite of cannon. The whole army has seen that cannon is to be but little dreaded. * * Hearts of war! to-morrow will be memorable in the annals of the United States.'

"'To-morrow' came, but not the promised achievement. All the officers disapproved of the time and manner of the proposed embarkation, and expressed their opinions freely. At General Porter's quarters a change was agreed upon. Porter deferred the embarkation until Tuesday morning, the 1st of December, an hour or two before daylight, and to make the landing-place a little below the upper end of Grand Island. Winder suggested the propriety of making a descent directly upon Chippewa, 'the key of the country.' This Smyth consented to attempt, intending as he said, if successful, to march down to Queenston, and lay siege to Fort George. Orders were accordingly given for a general rendezvous at the Navy Yard, at three o'clock on Tuesday morning, and that the troops should be collected in the woods near by on Monday, where they should build fires, and await the signal for gathering on the shore of the river. The hour arrived, but when day dawned only fifteen hundred were embarked. Tannehill's Pennsylvania Brigade were not present. Before their arrival rumours had reached the camp that they, too, like Van Rensellaer's militia at Lewiston, had raised a constitutional question about being led out of their State. Yet their scruples seem to have been overcome at this time, and they would have invaded Canada cheerfully under other auspices. But distrust of their leader, created by the events of the last forty-eight hours, had demoralized nearly the whole army. They had made so much noise in embarkation that the startled Canadian had sounded his alarm bugle and discharged signal guns from Fort Erie to Chippewa. Tannehill's Pennsylvanians had not appeared, and many other troops lingered upon the shore, loth to embark. In this dilemma Smyth hastily called a Council of the regular officers, utterly excluding those of the volunteers from the conference; and the first intimation of the result of that Council was an order from the commanding general, sent to General Porter, who was on a boat with the pilot, a fourth of a mile from shore, in the van of the impatient flotilla, *directing the whole army to debark, and repair to their quarters*. This was accompanied by a declaration that the *invasion of Canada was abandoned at present*, pleading in bar of just censure, that his orders from his superiors were, not to attempt it with less than 3,000 men. The regulars were ordered into winter quarters, and the volunteers were dismissed to their homes.

"The troops, without order or restraint, discharged their muskets in all directions, and a scene of insubordination and utter confusion followed. At least a thousand of the volunteers had come from their homes in response to his invitation, and the promise that they should be led into Canada by a victor [without personal danger, and with the promise of plunder and glory]. They had implicit confidence in his ability and in the sincerity of his great words, and in proportion to their faith and zeal were now their disappointment and resentment. Unwilling to have their errand to the frontier fruitless of all but disgrace, the volunteers earnestly requested permission to be led into Canada under General Porter, promising the commanding general the speedy capture of Fort Erie if he would furnish them with four pieces of artillery.* But Smyth evaded their request, and the volunteers were sent home uttering imprecations against the man whom they considered a mere blusterer without courage, and a conceited deceiver without honour. They felt themselves betrayed, and the inhabitants in the vicinity sympathized with them. Their indignation was greatly increased by the ill-timed and ungenerous charges made by Smyth in his report to General Dearborn against General Porter, in whom the volunteers had

* We are inclined to think that those volunteers and others who professed such patriotic indignation against Smyth, and promised such great things, were, in general, no less poltroons than Smyth himself. It was as easy for them to denounce Smyth, and to boast of what they could and would do, as for Smyth, in his proclamation, to denounce those who opposed the invasion of Canada.

the greatest confidence. General Smyth's person was for some time in danger. He was compelled to double the guards around his tent, and to move it from place to place to avoid continual insults. He was several times fired at when he ventured out of his marquee. Porter openly attributed the abandonment of the invasion of Canada to the cowardice of Smyth." * *

"Thus ended the melodrama of Smyth's invasion of Canada. The whole affair was disgraceful and humiliating. 'What wretched work Smyth and Porter have made of it!' wrote General Wadsworth to General Van Rensellaer from his home at Genesee at the close of the year. 'I wish those who are disposed to find so much fault could know the state of the militia since the day you gave up the command. It has been "confusion worse confounded."' The day that saw Smyth's failure was indeed 'memorable in the annals of the United States,' as well as in his own private history. Confidence in his military ability was destroyed; and three months afterwards he was 'disbanded,' as the *Army Register* says; in other words, he was deposed without a trial, and excluded from the army."*

Such was the third and last American invasion of Upper Canada in 1812. Three large American armies defeated—two of them taken prisoners by less than one-third their number of Canadian volunteers, aided by a few hundred regular soldiers and as many Indians, who, notwithstanding the abuse

---

* Lossing's Field Book of the War of 1812, Chap. xx., p. 430—432.

Mr. Lossing adds, in a note, that "General Smyth petitioned the House of Representatives to reinstate him in the army. That body referred the petition to the Secretary of War—the General's executioner. Of course, its prayer was not answered. In that petition Smyth asked the privilege of 'dying for his country.' This phrase was the subject of much ridicule. At a public celebration of Washington's birth-day, in 1814, at Georgetown, in the District of Columbia, the following sentiment was offered during the presentation of toasts : 'General Smyth's petition to Congress to die for his country ; may it be ordered that the prayer of said petition be granted.'

"A wag wrote on a panel of one of the doors of the House of Representatives :

> "'All hail, great chief, who quailed before
> A Bishop on Niag'ra's shore ;
> But looks on Death with dauntless eye,
> And begs for leave to bleed and die,
>
> "'Oh my !'"

of them by the American generals, never murdered a woman or child during the year, or killed a prisoner, and who were no more "savages" than the men who maligned them.

The Spartan bands of Canadian Loyalist volunteers, aided by a few hundred English soldiers and civilized Indians, repelled the Persian thousands of democratic American invaders, and maintained the virgin soil of Canada unpolluted by the foot of the plundering invader.

CHAPTER LV.

FOURTH AMERICAN INVASION—FIRST INVASION OF LOWER CANADA, COMPLETELY DEFEATED BY THE COURAGE AND SKILL OF THE CANADIANS; AND GENERAL DEARBORN RETIRES INTO WINTER QUARTERS AT PLATTSBURG.

BUT in addition to these three abortive invasions of Upper Canada in 1812, was one of *Lower Canada*, which will be narrated in the words of Mr. Christie, illustrating as it does the ardent loyalty and noble heroism of the French Canadians:

"The American forces, under General Dearborn, gradually approached the frontier of Lower Canada; and early on the morning of the 17th of November, 1812, Major (now Lieutenant-Colonel) De Salaberry, Superintendent of the Canadian Voltigeurs, commanding the cordon of advanced posts on the lines, received information at St. Philip's that the enemy, to the number of ten thousand (10,000), were advancing to Odletown. He immediately despatched two companies of the Voltigeurs, under the command of Captain Perrault, of the same regiment, with 300 Indians under Captain Duchesne, of the Indian Department, to reinforce Major Laforce, of the 1st Battalion embodied militia, who was posted with the two flank companies of that battalion at the River La Cole. This detachment, after a fatiguing march of thirty-six miles, chiefly through *morasses* and *abatis*, arrived early in the afternoon of the same day at Burtonville, and took a position within the River La Cole, a mile distant from it, in conjunction with a party of thirty Algonquin and Abenaki Indians, and a few Voyageurs under Captain McKay, a gentleman of the North-West Company in the Voyageurs' corps. Major De Salaberry arrived the day following, with the remainder of the Voltigeurs and the Voyageurs, commanded by Lieutenant-Colonel McGillivray, and four companies of the volunteer Chasseurs from the parishes of Chateauguay, St. Constant, St. Philip, and l'Acadie.

"In the meantime the enemy occupied Champlain Town, two or three miles from the lines, and an earnest invasion was momentarily expected. Nothing occurred of any consequence until the 20th, in the morning, when Captain McKay, visiting the picquet between three and four o'clock, perceived the enemy fording the River La Cole, and at the same instant heard them cock their firelocks in the surrounding bushes. He had scarcely time to apprise the picquet under Captain Bernard Panet, of their danger, when the enemy, who had surrounded the guard-hut on all sides, discharged a volley of musketry so close that their wads set fire to the roof and consumed the hut. The militia and Indians discharged their pieces, and dashing through the ranks of the enemy, escaped unhurt, while the Americans, who had forded the river in two places, mistaking each other for the enemy in the darkness and confusion of the night, kept up a brisk fire for near half an hour, in which they killed and wounded several of their own people. After discovering their error they retired back to Champlain Town, leaving five of their men wounded, and three or four killed, who were found by the Indians on the same day. The American party is said to have consisted of fourteen hundred (1,400) men and a troop of dragoons, and was commanded by Colonels Pike and Clarke.

"This movement of the enemy gave room to expect another more vigorous attempt to invade Lower Canada; and on the 22nd, the Governor, by a General Order, directed the whole of the militia of the province to consider themselves commanded for active service, and to be prepared to move forward to meet the enemy as soon as required.

"Lieut.-Colonel Deschambault was ordered to cross the St. Lawrence at Lachine to Cahuaugo, with the Point Claire, Riviere du Chene, Vaudreuil, and Longue Point Battalions, and to march upon l'Acadie. The volunteers of the 1st Battalion of Montreal Militia, the flank companies of the 2nd and 3rd Battalions, and a troop of Militia Dragoons, crossed the river to Longueuil and Laprairie; and the whole mass of population in the district of Montreal made a spontaneous movement towards the point of invasion with an enthusiasm unsurpassed in any age or country.

"General Dearborn, who, no doubt, was well informed of the state of the public mind in Lower Canada at this crisis, foresaw, from the multitude assembled to oppose his progress, and the hostile spirit of the Canadians, the fruitlessness of an attempt to invade Lower Canada, and began to withdraw his sickly and already enfeebled host into winter quarters at Plattsburg and Burlington.

"All apprehensions of an invasion of Lower Canada for the present season having disappeared, the troops and embodied militia were, on the 27th of November, ordered into winter quarters."*

---

* Christie's History of the War of 1812, Chap. iv., pp. 90—92.

"The armistice between General Smyth and Sheaffe after the battle of Queenston was terminated on the 20th of November, pursuant to notification to that effect from the former. This and the former armistice, without affording any present advantage, proved in the event materially prejudicial to the British on Lake Erie. The Americans availed themselves of so favourable an occasion to forward their naval stores unmolested from Black Rock to Presqu' Isle [Erie] by water, which they could not otherwise have effected, but with immense trouble and expense by land, and equipped at leisure a fleet which afterwards wrested from us the command of that lake."—*Ib.*, pp. 92, 93.

CHAPTER LVI.

PART I.

WAR CAMPAIGNS OF 1813—THREE DIVISIONS OF THE AMERICAN ARMY—
BATTLE OF FRENCHTOWN, AMERICANS DEFEATED—MISREPRESENTATIONS
CORRECTED.

THE campaign of 1813 opened auspiciously for the Canadians, in both Upper and Lower Canada, notwithstanding the fewness of their defenders in regulars, militia, and Indians, and though they suffered severely in several instances towards the close of the year.

It was manifest from the movement of the American army to the frontiers of Upper and Lower Canada, before the close of the year 1812, that on the opening of the campaign of 1813 they intended to retrieve the disasters and disgraces of the first year of the war, and make descents upon the colonies in good earnest. Sir George Prevost, Governor-General, was placed at great disadvantage for their general defence, as the small British force then occupying the Canadas, and the wide extent of frontier the British commander-in-chief had to defend, rendered it impossible for him to cope with the American enemy in point of numbers.

The American army, to whom was committed this year *the honour of conquering Canada*, was divided, as the year before, into three divisions: first, the Army of the North, consisting of 18,000 men, commanded by General Hampton, and stationed along the southern shore of Lake Champlain, on the south precincts of Lower Canada; the second, the Army of the Centre, consisting of 7,000 effective men, which was again subdivided into two divisions, commanded by Generals Dearborn and Wilkinson, and were posted from Buffalo, at the lower extremity of Lake Erie, to Sackett's Harbour, at the lower end of Lake Ontario; and the third, the Army of the West, consisting of "8,000 effective men," according to the American account, commanded by Generals Harrison and Wilkinson, whose limits extended from Buffalo westward, as far as the British frontier extended.

After the capture of Detroit by General Brock and his little army, Colonel Proctor was appointed to command that fort, with a force of about 600 regulars and a number of Indians—an entirely insufficient force, but all that could be spared and provided from the slender forces of Upper Canada. The American General, Harrison, who succeeded Hull in the command of the West, organized a large force by the end of 1812, of over 5,000 men, consisting principally of men from Ohio and Kentucky. Among the small outposts which Proctor had established in the neighbourhood of Detroit, was one at *Frenchtown*, on the River Raisin, twenty-six miles from Detroit, which consisted of thirty of the Essex Militia, under Major Reynolds, and about 200 Indians. On the 17th of January, 1813, Brigadier-General Winchester, commanding a division of the American army, sent Colonel Lewis with a strong force to dislodge the British—which he succeeded in doing, after a sharp encounter in which the Americans lost twelve killed and fifty wounded. Reynolds retreated to Brownstown, sixteen miles in his rear, and gave information to Colonel Proctor of the advance of Winchester's brigade, which now occupied *Frenchtown*, and *was over one thousand strong.*

Colonel Proctor knew that his only hope of success was by prompt action to fight the enemy in detail, before General Harrison could unite his whole force to bear on Detroit. He therefore forthwith assembled all his available force at Brownstown, and on the 21st pushed on to attack the American camp at Frenchtown, with about 500 regular soldiers and militia and 600 Indians. The attack upon the American camp was made on the morning of the 22nd; and the Indians, under the Wyandot chief Roundhead, speedily turned the enemy's flank and caused him to retreat—Chief Roundhead with his Indians taking General Winchester himself prisoner, and delivering him unharmed to Colonel Proctor. About 500 of General Winchester's men had thrown themselves into the houses, where they were making deadly resistance from fear of falling into the hands of the Indians, who were greatly exasperated by this mode of warfare, and assailed and pursued their retreating but resisting enemies with a ferocity unequalled during the whole three years' war. Colonel Proctor informed General Winchester that the houses would be set on fire, and he would be utterly unable to restrain the Indians, if this kind of warfare were persisted in, and they refused to surrender. They at length surrendered, on being assured that they would be protected from the Indians. Thirty-two officers and upwards of 500 men were taken prisoners, not one of whom sustained any injury from their captors, whether regular soldiers, militia, or Indians.

But many Americans were slaughtered in refusing to surrender for fear of the Indians, and determined to fight and retreat in hopes of making their escape. They suffered severely; and on that account several American writers have represented the Indians at the battle of Frenchtown as committing unheard-of cruelties upon helpless men, women, and children. Even President Madison joined in the misrepresentation, as he was always ready to seize upon any pretext to assail the British Government for admitting the alliance of the Indians in the war—forgetful that his Government had repeatedly sought to do the same thing, but had only succeeded in a few instances. But in vindication of the Indians and their commander, Colonel Proctor, the following facts may be stated, which are conclusive on the subject. In the first place, General Winchester, the commander of the American detachment, was taken prisoner by the Indians, and instead of being butchered and scalped, was delivered unharmed by the Wyandot chief Roundhead into the hands of Colonel Proctor.

However, many of the Americans refused to surrender from fear of falling into the hands of the Indians, and attempted to retreat and fight, in hopes of escape, but were mostly killed in the attempt by the Indians, so greatly exasperated by the mode of warfare adopted against them from the houses. Under this pretext most American writers have represented the Indians, with the sanction of the English, as having committed unheard-of cruelties against helpless men, women, and children at the battle of Frenchtown—statements which were pure fiction, as has been proved to demonstration in Chapter XXXV. of this history, in the fictions of the alleged "Massacre of Wyoming."

For example, General Harrison, who was one of the few old American generals employed by the democratic President Madison in the war, and who was one or two days' march from Frenchtown, was informed and wrote in a despatch two days after the battle (24th of January), that "General Winchester had been taken by the Indians, *killed and scalped; his body was cut up and mangled in a shocking manner, and one of his hands cut off*; when not a hair of General Winchester's head was injured, and he was afterwards exchanged, and appeared on the Niagara frontier, and was again taken prisoner, safe and sound, by the British at the battle of Stony Creek.

General Harrison, in his despatches written five days afterwards, after having ascertained all the facts of the battle, makes no mention of any cruelties practised by the Indians, which he doubtless would have done had there been any truth in the imputations against the Indians or the English soldiers with whom they acted. He speaks of General Winchester as among the prisoners, notwithstanding his statement five days before that he had been killed, scalped, and cut to pieces. The following facts, given by Mr. Thompson in his "History of the War of 1812," are conclusive on this affair of the battle of Frenchtown, the 22nd of January, 1813:

"Much has been said by American writers regarding the conduct of the combined forces of the affair of Frenchtown. They have not even stopped to charge British officers and soldiers with the most enormous cruelties, committed in conjunction with the Indians, when it was in their power to have prevented them. Such have been the contemptible misrepresentations to which many publications, otherwise deserving of merit, have descended, as well of this as of many other affairs during the war; and even amongst a few British subjects they have gained credence.

"General Harrison, however, in writing his despatches to Governor Meigs, as well as several officers of his army who avail themselves of the general express to write to their friends in Chillicothe, in most of their letters give the details of the battle, *but seem to be ignorant as regards the greatest part of that 'Massacre,'* as it has been gravely termed. It is gathered from these despatches and letters by a Chillicothe journal of the 2nd of February, 1813, that '*those who surrendered themselves on the field of battle were taken prisoners by the British, while those who attempted to escape were pursued, tomahawked, and scalped.*' Now, even this account, in part, is incorrect; for the Indians, by whom they were assailed, were posted there for the express purpose of cutting off their retreat; and *those who surrendered to the Indians were safely conducted to the British camp;* but such was the panic with which these unfortunate fugitives were seized, that no persuasions on the part of the Indian chiefs, *who were fully disposed to comply with the orders of Colonel Proctor*, could prevail on them to surrender until they were either wounded and taken, or overtaken in the chase by their pursuers, when no efforts of the chiefs could save them from their fury.

"In a letter containing copies of despatches from General Harrison, dated 24th January, 1813, it is stated that 'when the attack commenced, General Winchester ordered a retreat, but from the utter confusion which prevailed, this could not be effected; and he then told them that every man must take care of himself, and attempted to make his own escape on horseback, but was overtaken by the Indians before he had gone a mile, and killed and scalped. His body was cut up and mangled in a most shocking manner, and one of his hands cut off.'

"Now, here is an awful Indian tale, manufactured, as many others have been of like description, which turns out to be a mere fabrication; for when General Winchester found himself pursued in his attempt to escape, he with a few others surrendered themselves to a chief of the Wyandot nation, and not a hair of their heads was hurt, *except the injury received from the fight.*

"It is also stated in the same letter that Colonels Allen and Lewis were among the slain; in contradiction of which, in General Harrison's letter to Governor Meigs, dated 29th January, it is stated that General Winchester and Colonel and Brigade-Major Gerrard are among the prisoners.

"The conclusion is plain, that had those deluded people not

been overcome by fear, and surrendered themselves at once, they might have enjoyed the same safety as did General Winchester and his companions."*

"This spirited and vigorous measure (on the part of Colonel Proctor) completely disconcerted the arrangements made by General Harrison for the recovery of Michigan territory, and secured Detroit from any immediate danger. The House of Assembly of Lower Canada [as also of Upper Canada] passed a vote of thanks to Colonel Proctor for the skill and intrepidity with which he planned and carried into effect this enterprise. A vote of thanks was also passed to the officers, non-commissioned officers, and privates who assisted in its accomplishment; and Colonel Proctor was immediately promoted to the rank of brigadier-general by Sir George Prevost, the commander of the forces, until the pleasure of the Prince Regent should be known, who was pleased to approve and confirm the appointment."†

PART II.

AMERICANS ATTACK AND PLUNDER IN AND ABOUT BROCKVILLE—SUCCESSFUL RETALIATORY ATTACK ON OGDENSBURG.

The next military affairs in the order of time, illustrative of the loyalty and courage of the Canadians, occurred on the River St. Lawrence, in the neighbourhoods of Prescott and Brockville. Most of the American invasions were mere raids for destruction and plunder of property. In the winter of 1813 several of these raids were made from Ogdensburg on the British settlements. "After winter (1813) had fairly set in, and the St. Lawrence was frozen over, the Americans on several occasions sent marauding parties across the ice to pillage and destroy the Canadian settlements. [The American

* Thompson's History of the War of 1812, Chap. xxii., pp. 179—181.

"Terms of capitulation were agreed upon, by which the whole of General Winchester's command that had survived the fury of the battle were surrendered prisoners of war, amounting to upwards of 600. In this sanguinary engagement, the loss of the Americans, in killed and wounded, was nearly 500; while that of the British was only twenty-four killed and 161 wounded."—*Ib.*, pp. 176, 177.

† Christie's History of the War of 1812, Chap. v., pp. 100, 101.

mode of giving liberty to Canada.] On the night of the 6th of February, two companies of riflemen from Ogdensburg, under command of Captain Forsyth, made a descent on the town of Brockville, wounded a sentry, fired several houses, and carried off a quantity of plunder, together with fifty of the inhabitants. Several inroads from Ogdensburg were made; and the British were anxious to retaliate." (Tuttle.) On the closing of the session of the Legislature of Lower Canada, the 17th of February, 1813, the Governor-General, Sir George Prevost, made a tour of inspection of the forts of Upper Canada. On his arrival at Prescott he was importuned to authorize an attack upon Ogdensburg, in retaliation for an attack upon Brockville by the enemy some days previous. He consented to a demonstration on the river to ascertain the enemy's force; and on the ensuing morning (22nd February), as the Governor-General departed, accompanied to Kingston by Lieut.-Colonel Pearson (commander of Prescott), Lieut.-Colonel M'Donnell, second in command, moved with his party across the river on the ice, towards Ogdensburg. The enemy, perceiving the movement, were prepared to receive him; and Lieut.-Colonel M'Donnell, impelled by that spirit characteristic of British soldiers, turned the demonstration into a real attack.

"The enemy was driven from the town after a short contest, leaving about twenty killed and a considerable number wounded. Four brass field-pieces, seven pieces of iron ordnance, complete, with several stand of arms and a considerable quantity of stores, fell into the hands of the victors, who lost seven killed, and seven officers (including Lieutenant-Colonel M'Donnell) and forty-one men wounded. After having destroyed two small schooners and two gun-boats left there to winter, they removed the stores and arms to their own side of the river at Prescott. This brilliant achievement prevented any further American forays on the Canadians from Cornwall to Gananoque for the rest of the winter

PART III.

WINTER PREPARATIONS IN LOWER CANADA FOR THE CAMPAIGN—UNPRECEDENTED MARCH ON SNOW-SHOES OF LOYALIST VOLUNTEERS FROM NEW BRUNSWICK TO LOWER CANADA—AMERICAN PLAN OF OPERATIONS.

The greatest exertions were made in Canada during the winter to prepare for the ensuing campaign. The Canadian regiment of Fencibles, the Voltigeurs, the Glengarries, were recruited with diligence and success, though still without reinforcements from England—too much engrossed with her European wars to afford much assistance to the colonies. A volunteer regiment from New Brunswick came, by permission and authority, to the assistance of the beleaguered but hitherto successful Canadians. "The King's Regiment of New Brunswick was mustered into the regular army as the 104th Regiment, and sent to Canada for active service. The regiment was first formed amongst the Loyalists who had settled in York county, about Fredericton, in 1784, and on its voluntary enrolment in the regular army, the Legislature passed complimentary resolutions to officers and men, and presented the regiment with a handsome silver trumpet. A portion of this regiment was conveyed to Quebec by sea; but several companies made a very trying march on snow-shoes, through an unbroken country, during very cold weather, to arrive in Canada in time for the spring campaign." *

"The plan of the American campaign for 1813 was that a large army under General Dearborn was to threaten Lower Canada, whilst a determined effort was to be made to retake Michigan territory, capture the forts of Niagara frontier, and thus reduce the whole of Upper Canada. This accomplished, all the armies were to make a joint descent upon Montreal and Quebec, which would be followed by the occupation of the

---

* Tuttle, Chap. xxxviii., p. 396.

"The 104th (or New Brunswick Regiment) marched through from Fredericton to Upper Canada, several hundreds of miles, with extraordinary celerity, in the month of March, though their route from Fredericton to the River St. Lawrence lay through an uninhabited wilderness buried in snow, and never before traversed by troops." (Christie's History of the War of 1812, p. 103.)

Maritime Provinces, and thus the British would be driven from the American continent."*

PART IV.

AMERICAN FLEET ON LAKE ONTARIO SUPERIOR TO THE BRITISH FLEET, AND, WITH THE ARMY, ATTACKS AND TAKES YORK (TORONTO), AND AFTER OCCUPYING IT LESS THAN TWO WEEKS, RETIRE WITH MUCH HASTE.

The American fleet on Lake Ontario was superior to that of the British, and was being daily augmented at Sackett's Harbour —their principal navy yard on Lake Ontario. The first descent was expected to be upon Kingston ; but the American Government deemed it too hazardous a game to risk their Lake armament upon an enterprise against this principal military depot of the British in Upper Canada, and resolved to direct their forces against more distant and defenceless places on the lake.

Commodore Chauncey having equipped his fleet for an expedition, and received on board upwards of 1,700 troops under the command of Generals Dearborn and Pike, sailed from Sackett's Harbour as early as the 25th of April, and on the following evening arrived off York (Toronto) with fourteen sail of armed vessels ; and on the following day commenced landing their troops about three miles west of the town—the British being compelled to retire after making a strong resistance. The grenadiers of the 8th Regiment, who lost their captain, M'Neal, were, after a desperate contest, almost annihilated by the overwhelming numbers of the enemy.

The best account we have read of this expedition against, or rather raid upon, the town of York, is given by Thompson, and which I quote at length, relating as it does to what was then and now is the capital—the defenceless capital—of Upper Canada:

"In the month of April, the ice having completely broken up in the port of Sackett's Harbour, where the American squadron under Commodore Chauncey had wintered, General Dearborn, commanding the right division of the Army of the

* Tuttle, Chap. xxxviii., pp. 396, 397.

Centre, consisting of 4,000 men stationed in that vicinity, selected 2,000 of the most efficient of his division [American History of the War, published in New York], and on the 22nd of the month embarked them on board the fleet, with which he ascended the lake, and with this force appeared off the harbour of York, the capital of Upper Canada, on the morning of the 27th.

"The enemy appearing to threaten an attack upon the town, General Sheaffe collected his forces, which consisted of nearly 700 men, including regulars and militia, with about 100 Indians; and with these he made a most determined resistance to the landing of the enemy; but at length, overcome by numbers, he was compelled to retire; by which means the enemy was enabled to effect his landing a short distance above the fort, which was situated about two miles to the west of the town, at the entrance of the harbour.

"So soon as the American troops, who were led on by General Pike, had made good their landing, they formed into two lines (the first of which was commanded personally by General Pike, and the rear or reserve line by General Pearce), and in this order advanced upon the first battery and carried it by assault; they then advanced towards the citadel in the same order, and by the same means captured an intervening battery.

"Here the columns halted, in order to dress the lines for an attack upon the main works. At this moment a large magazine accidentally exploded, by which a quantity of stones and timbers were thrown into the air, and in their fall killed and wounded a number on both sides, amongst whom was the American general, Pike.

"The British regulars and militia performed prodigies of valour, but were overpowered by a force three times their number, and in a high state of discipline;* they were compelled to retreat towards the town.

"General Sheaffe then held a Council with his principal officers and civil authorities of the town, by whom it was advised that he should retreat towards Kingston with the remainder of his troops; and that the commandant of the militia,

---

* "The American troops had been preparing for this expedition the whole winter; and no pains had been spared in their discipline."

Lieutenant-Colonel Chewett, should treat with the American commander for terms for the surrender of York. .

"At the capture of York the British lost not less than 400 men, 300 of whom were made prisoners of war, and about forty killed and wounded by the explosion. The Americans lost 378, thirty-eight of whom were killed and two hundred and twenty-two wounded by the explosion of the magazine. General Pike died of his contusions a few minutes after being carried on board of one of the vessels.*

"On the 8th of May, the American army under General Dearborn once more evacuated York, after having occupied it twelve days, and secured much booty.

PART V.

AMERICAN FLEET AND ARMY RETURN TO SACKETT'S HARBOUR—MAKE PREPARATIONS FOR ATTACKING FORT GEORGE AND THE TOWN OF NEWARK, WHICH, AFTER A SEVERE BATTLE, THEY TAKE AND OCCUPY.

After evacuating York, the American fleet and army proceeded again to Sackett's Harbour, where preparations were immediately made for invading the Niagara frontier. On the 20th of May the American fleet again ascended Lake Ontario, and on the morning of the 23rd they appeared off the mouth of the Niagara river, soon after which, the weather being favourable to their purpose, they attacked Fort George and the town of Newark (now Niagara), by land and water. Early in the morning of the 27th of May the enemy commenced a combined attack upon the fort, having previously, on the 24th and 25th,

* "The people, hitherto unaccustomed to hear of reverses, were irritated at this success of the enemy, and, as usual upon such occasions, clamoured against the General [Sheaffe], who a few weeks afterwards was succeeded in the administration of the civil government by Major-General De Rottenburg, and on his return to the Lower Province assumed the command of the forces in the district of Montreal. It is not ascertained whether his removal was the result of the displeasure of the commander of the forces [Sir George Prevost]; but upon a cool survey of the battle of York, it must be owned that the honour of the British arms was strenuously and ably maintained by the small party of men under his command, who, including regulars, militia, and Indians, did not exceed 600." (Christie's History of the War of 1812, Chap. v., p. 105.)

materially injured the works by a warm cannonade from their ships and batteries. A body of about 800 riflemen, under Colonel Winfield Scott, landed near the Two Mile Creek, while the fleet ranged up in the form of a crescent, extending from the north of the Lighthouse to the Two Mile Creek, so as to enfilade the British batteries by a cross fire. The riflemen, after forming and ascending the bank, were met by the British, and compelled to give way in disorder, and return to the beach, from whence they kept up a smart fire under cover of the bank. In the meantime, another body of upwards of 2,000 men, under the command of General Lewis, made a landing, and formed on the beach under cover of a tremendous cannonade of round shot, and showers of grape and canister from the fleet, that swept the adjacent plain, and compelled the British to retire. General Vincent, finding the works torn to pieces by the enemy's artillery, and no longer tenable against so overwhelming a force, caused the fort to be dismantled, and the magazines to be blown up, and retreated to Queenston, leaving the Americans to take possession of the ruins of the fort. The British loss consisted of fifty-two killed and upwards of three hundred wounded and missing [more than half the entire force]. The Americans state their loss at thirty-nine killed and a hundred and eleven wounded.*

PART VI.

THE BRITISH RETREAT TO BURLINGTON HEIGHTS—BATTLE OF STONY CREEK—DEFEAT OF THE AMERICANS, AND THEIR DISORDERLY RETREAT TO FORT GEORGE.

"General Vincent, on the ensuing day, having collected all the forces from Chippewa and Fort Erie, and destroyed or rendered useless the posts and stores along the frontier, commenced his retreat towards Burlington Heights, at the head of Lake Ontario." (Christie.)

* Among the killed of the British party was Mr. Allan MacLean, Clerk of the House of Assembly of Upper Canada, who volunteered his services with a musket.

"The Americans moved forward in three strong brigades, under Generals Chandler, Winder, and Boyd, with an advance of light troops and riflemen, under Colonels Scott and Forsyth, the whole commanded by

"General Vincent continued his retreat as far as Burlington Heights; and on the 1st day of June was followed by an American army of 3,500 infantry, and about 300 cavalry, commanded by Generals Chandler and Winder, for the purpose, as was vainly boasted, of making prisoners of the whole British army, and thus terminate the contest of the north-western frontier."

This expected conquest of the whole British army was commenced by the affair of Stony Creek, when both of the American generals themselves were taken prisoners.

On the evening of the 5th of June, the American forces encamped at the village of Stony Creek, about nine miles from the British camp at Burlington Heights, with the purpose of attacking and taking the British position next day. But General Vincent was on the alert to obtain information as to the enemy's strength and movements, and dispatched Colonel (afterwards Major-General) Harvey, with two companies, to reconnoitre their camp at Stony Creek, and, from the report received, determined to attack them that very night.

"All the troops, both regulars and militia, that could possibly be spared from the garrison at Burlington Heights, together with those who had retreated from Fort George, amounting in all to 700, were ordered to be in readiness for a movement. Immediately after dark they commenced an advance towards Stony Creek, where, after several halts in order to reconnoitre the country through which they were marching, they arrived between one and two o'clock on the morning of the 6th of June. Immediately the quarter guard of the enemy was surprised and taken, and the assailants rushed into the camp, where all was in apparent security. But such a scene of carnage commenced —the huzzas of the besiegers; the yells of the Indians, led on by Captain Brant; the clashing of bayonets, and, above all, the thunder of the cannon and musketry, rendered it truly appalling. A column of the enemy was at length formed into some kind of order, but to no purpose; they were by this time completely unnerved and dispirited, which, together with the

---

General Lewis, the next in command to General Dearborn, whose low state of health compelled him to keep his bed, from whence he issued his orders." (Thompson's History of the War of 1812, Chap. xxiii., p. 185.)

darkness of the night and the clouds of smoke, threw them into the greatest confusion and disorder. Not so, however, with the British troops; their plans had been so well concerted, that every man knew his rallying signal; they were, therefore, at all times beyond surprise. The American army, being completely discomfited, retreated from their bivouac in the greatest confusion.

"As soon as General Vincent had completed the defeat of the enemy, he again fell back upon Burlington Heights, taking as trophies of his victory three field-pieces and a brass field howitzer, captured from the enemy, besides both their generals, and about 150 officers, sergeants, and rank and file.

"After the defeat at Stony Creek, the American army, in the most indescribable manner [helter-skelter, every man for himself] retreated towards Fort George [whence they came] without the least military order or subordination; in fact, such officers as could avail themselves of horses on the road, regardless of the means employed for that purpose, took them and made their way to the lines with all possible speed, and left the rest of the army to shift for themselves; they, therefore, retreated [or scampered] in small detached parties, some of whom had exonerated themselves of their arms and equipments. Thus did they travel [at double-quick] towards their head-quarters from two or three to a dozen; and were, in compassion for their sufferings, succoured by those very people whose houses, a day or two previous, they had ransacked and plundered."*

* Thompson's War of 1812, Chap. xxiii.

In General Vincent's official despatch relating to this brillant and intrepid action, he gives the credit of it to Lieutenant-Colonel Harvey. He says: "To Lieutenant-Colonel Harvey, the Deputy-Adjutant-General, my obligations are particularly due. From the first moment the enemy's approach was known, he watched his movements, and afforded me the earliest information. To him, indeed, I am indebted for the suggestion and plan of operations; nothing could have been more clear than his arrangements, nor more completely successful in the result." (Christie, Chap. v.)

PART VII.

GENERAL VINCENT, REINFORCED, PURSUES THE RETREATING ENEMY—BRILLIANT AFFAIR OF THE BEAVER DAMS, IN WHICH SEVERAL HUNDRED AMERICANS SURRENDER TO ONE-FIFTH OF THEIR NUMBER—THE AMERICANS COOPED UP IN FORT GEORGE—FORT SCHLOSSER AND BLACK ROCK ATTACKED BY THE BRITISH, AND THE PUBLIC FORTS AND MAGAZINES DESTROYED OR TAKEN—THE AMERICAN ARMY CANNOT BE INDUCED TO COME OUT OF FORT GEORGE INTO OPEN FIELD FIGHT.

In a short time General Vincent received some reinforcements, and assumed the offensive, advanced towards Fort George with a view to investing it—forming his line on the Four Mile Creek, with his left resting on the lake; but he ultimately extended his line from the Twelve Mile Creek (St. Catharines) to Queenston.

General Lewis, who now had full command (General Dearborn having resigned), finding his advance posts and foraging parties continually harassed and frequently made prisoners by small detachments of British and Canadian troops stationed at different posts through the country, in order to prevent the American camp at Fort George from obtaining supplies, dispatched Colonel Boerstler with about 600 or 700 men, by way of Queenston, with a view of dislodging a detachment or picquet posted at a place called the Beaver Dams, a few miles from Queenston. Colonel Boerstler was surprised by a small party of Indians under Captain Ker; and believing themselves hemmed in by superior numbers, surrendered to Lieutenant (afterwards Colonel) Fitzgibbon, of the 49th Regiment, who arrived in time to complete the victory with a detachment of forty-six rank and file. The prisoners were five to one to the captors, being 512 in number, including twenty-five officers, two field pieces, and a stand of colours.

By these successes, the Americans were compelled to confine themselves to Fort George and its neighbourhood; and before the 1st of July the British had formed a line extending from Twelve Mile Creek, on Lake Ontario (Port Dalhousie), across to Queenston, on the Niagara river; and the Canadians began now to retaliate the game of marauding which the Americans had been practising on the Niagara frontier. From Chippewa an attack was made on Fort Schlosser, on the American side of the river, during the night of the 4th of July, by a small party of militia and soldiers under Lieutenant-Colonel Clarke, who surprised the guard at that post, and brought away a brass six-pounder, upwards of fifty stand of arms, a small quantity of stores, with a gun-boat and two batteaux. At daybreak in the morning of the 11th of July, Lieutenant-Colonel Bishop, lately commanding Fort Erie, crossed over the river with 240 men, consisting of a small party of militia and detachments of the 41st and 49th Regiments, and effectually surprised the enemy's post at Black Rock, burning his block-houses, stores, barracks, dockyard, and a vessel, but were compelled to hasten their departure by a reinforcement of American militia and some Indians in their interest, who opened a smart fire under cover of the surrounding woods, killing thirteen of the British attacking party, and wounding a considerable number—among others, Lieutenant-Colonel Bishop, mortally; but the British party brought away seven pieces of ordnance, two hundred stand of small arms, and a great quantity of stores.

The two armies were almost in sight of each other at Fort George; the commander of the British wished to ascertain the extent of the enemy's works and his means of defence, and to draw him into an open field of battle, and therefore, on the 24th of August, made a demonstration as if to assault the fort, drove in the picquets; took several of them, advanced to within a few hundred yards of the enemy, who, though supported by the fire upon the British from their batteries on the American side of the river, could not be induced to leave their entrenchments and venture in the open field, although the force of the British did not exceed 2,000, while the American force exceeded 4,000, but wholly depending upon resources from the *American side for their subsistence, and compelled to act solely on the defensive, from the hostile front assumed by the British in the neighbourhood. The American army of 4,000 men, being cooped up within the limits of the fort, depending for their supplies from the United States, and not daring to go out of their fortifications, could do little harm and be of little use to the American cause, the British commander did not think it advisable to incur the loss and risk of an assault upon the fort.

PART VIII.

WAR IN THE WEST—GENERAL PROCTOR'S UNSUCCESSFUL SIEGE OF LOWER SANDUSKY.

In the meantime General Harrison was on the Sandusky river, making preparations to prosecute the war with vigour, in order to recover the Michigan territory, as soon as the fleet fitting out at Erie (Presqu' Isle), under Captain Perry, who had been dispatched thither by Commodore Chauncey towards the end of May, should be sufficiently strong to co-operate with the land forces. General Proctor resolved to make another effort to defeat General Harrison's purpose to recover Michigan, and immediately besieged the American fort at Lower Sandusky; but in consequence of the withdrawment of the Indians out of the reach of the enemy's guns, and disinclined to the delay of a siege, and General Harrison with a respectable force at no great distance, General Proctor thought proper to raise the siege and retire to Amherstburg.

PART IX.

FAILURE OF THE EXPEDITION OF SIR GEORGE PREVOST AND COMMODORE SIR JAMES YEO AGAINST SACKETT'S HARBOUR.

During the absence of Commodore Chauncey and his fleet from Sackett's Harbour, engaged in operations on the Niagara frontier, an expedition was planned and fitted out at Kingston against that chief depot of American naval supplies on Ontario. Sir George Prevost, Commander-in-Chief, and the British Commodore, Sir James L. Yeo (just arrived from England), were both at Kingston, and much was expected from their joint counsels, and the arrival of some naval officers and sailors from England. On the 27th of May a body of 800 or 1,000 men were embarked on board the British flotilla at Kingston, consisting of *Wolfe*, 24 guns; *Royal George*, 24; *Earl of Moira*, 18; and four schooners, carrying from ten to twelve guns each, with a sufficient number of batteaux; and at noon the following day they were off Sackett's Harbour. The weather was propitious, and the troops were transferred to the batteaux to make their landing under an escort of two gun-boats, commanded by Captain Mulcaster—the whole under the immediate direction of the land and naval commanders-in-chief. They had not proceeded far when a convoy of American boats, loaded with troops, was descried doubling Stanley Point, on their way from Oswego to Sackett's Harbour. The Indians, who had previously landed on an island, fired upon them as they passed, and threw them into confusion, while the British boats and batteaux bore down and captured twelve of them, with about 150 men; the remainder escaped to Sackett's Harbour.

The landing was deferred until next day, thus giving the Americans time to spread the alarm throughout the country —to collect reinforcements from all quarters—to collect and station their soldiers, with a field-piece, in the surrounding woods, and make every possible preparation for their defence. The fine day was followed by a dark, rainy, and stormy night, which scattered the boats, so that the British could not succeed in landing in the morning before the Americans had lined the woods with their men. Nevertheless the British succeeded in landing; the enemy retreated, but posting themselves securely behind large trees, kept up a smart fire on the British.

The fleet in the meantime, as well as small vessels intended to have been landed in time to support the advance of the troops, were, through the light and adverse wind, a long way in the rear. Under these circumstances, Colonel Baynes, the Adjutant-General of the Forces in British North America, who was charged with this service, found it impossible to bring up or wait for the arrival of the artillery, and ordered his detachment to divide and scour the woods. The enemy, dislodged from the woods at the point of the bayonet, fled to their fort and block-houses, whither they were pursued by the British, who set fire to their barracks.

At this juncture it was thought by the commanding officer, Colonel Baynes, that the enemy's block-houses and stockaded battery could not be carried by assault, even with the assistance of the field-pieces, had they been landed. The fleet were still too far out of reach to aid in battering them, while the men were exposed to the fire of the enemy, secure within the works. The *signal of retreat* was therefore given to the indignant assailants, and the enterprise was abandoned at a moment when the enemy had so far calculated upon a victory on the part of the British as to set fire to their naval stores, hospital, and marine barracks, by which all the booty previously taken at York, and the stores for their new ship, were consumed. They had also set fire to a frigate on the stocks; but on discovering the retreat of the British, they succeeded in suppressing the fire, and saved her. The troops were immediately re-embarked, and returned to Kingston, after having sustained a loss of 259 in killed, wounded, and missing, while the loss of the enemy must have been double that number.

Thus terminated this expedition, to the disappointment of the public, who, from the presence and co-operation of the two commanders-in-chief, fondly flattered themselves with a far more brilliant result. This miscarriage, with other reverses at the commencement of the present campaign, destroyed in the opinion of the enemy the invincibility our arms had acquired the preceding autumn.*

PART X.

OCCURRENCES ON LAKE ONTARIO—NAVAL MANŒUVRES AND BATTLES.

On Lake Ontario the two naval commanders strove with indefatigable emulation for the dominion of the lake. Chauncey, after the capture of Fort George, returned to Sackett's Harbour to await the equipment of his new ship, the *Pike*; while his adversary, Sir James Yeo, scoured the lake, and supplied the British army in the neighbourhood of Fort George with abundance of stores. In the early part of July, Sir James fitted out an expedition of boats for Sackett's Harbour, with a view of cutting out their new ship, then almost rigged and ready to appear on the lake. He arrived unobserved in the vicinity of that port, and would probably have effected his purpose had not the escape of two deserters from his party, which had landed for refreshments, and in order to remain concealed until night should favour the enterprise, given the alarm to the enemy. This unlucky incident induced him to relinquish the undertaking and return to Kingston.

Towards the end of July the American fleet again appeared

* Christie's History of the War of 1812, Chap. v.
VOL. II.—26

with augmented force upon the lake, and Commodore Chauncey having received a company of artillery, with a considerable number of troops under Colonel Scott, proceeded for the head of the lake, with a view of seizing and destroying the stores at Burlington Heights, the principal depot of the army on the Niagara frontier, then occupied by a small detachment under Major Maule. The design of the enemy against this depot being suspected, Lieutenant-Colonel Battersby, commanding the Glengarry Regiment, upon being notified to that effect by Lieutenant-Colonel Harvey, Deputy-Adjutant-General, moved forward from York, and, by a march of extraordinary celerity, arrived with a reinforcement in time to save the depot, which the enemy, on finding the British ready to receive them, did not deem it prudent to attack.

Commodore Chauncey, on learning that York, by the advance of Lieutenant-Colonel Battersby to Burlington Heights, was left destitute of troops, seized the opportunity and bore away for that port, which he entered on the 31st of July. Here the Americans landed without opposition, and having taken possession of a small quantity of stores found at that place, they set fire to the barracks and public store-houses, and having re-embarked their troops, bore away to Niagara.

It is a coincidence worthy of notice, that on the same day in which the American commander was employed in burning the barracks and stores at York, Lieutenant-Colonel Murray was no less actively employed on the same business at Plattsburg.

The British fleet sailed from Kingston on the last day of July, with supplies for the army at the head of the lake, and on the 8th of August looked into Niagara, where the enemy's fleet lay moored. The latter hove up and bore down upon the British fleet, with which they manœuvred until the 10th, when a partial engagement ensued, in which two small vessels (the *Julia* and *Growler*) were cut off and captured by the British.*

* The following graphic account of the manœuvres and conflicts of the two fleets is given by the American historian, Brackenridge, in his War of 1812:

"On Lake Ontario, a naval armament, which might be termed formidable for this inland sea, was arrayed on either side; and an interesting contest ensued between two skilful officers for the superiority. The *General*

Commodore Chauncey, somewhat disheartened with the loss of these, and two other small vessels—the *Scourge* of eight, and the *Hamilton* of nine guns—upset by press of sail to escape, with the loss of all hands, except sixteen men picked up by the English, bore up for Niagara, from whence he sailed almost immediately for Sackett's Harbour, where he arrived on the 13th of August. Here he provisioned his fleet, and instantly

Pike, of twenty-two guns, having been launched, and proving to be an excellent sailer, Commodore Chauncey was now fully equal, in point of strength, to his antagonist. Sir James Yeo, though somewhat inferior in force, had the advantage in an important particular: his ships sailed better in squadron, and he could therefore avoid or come to an engagement as he thought proper. It being a matter all-important to the British, to prevent the Americans from becoming masters of the lake, Sir James prudently avoided a general action; while, on the other hand, to bring him to action was the great object of Commodore Chauncey. On the 7th of August the two fleets came in sight of each other. Commodore Chauncey manœuvred to gain the wind. Having passed to the leeward of the enemy's line, and being abreast of his war-ship, the *Wolfe*, he fired a few guns to ascertain whether he could reach the hostile fleet. The shot falling short, he wore, and hauled upon a wind to the starboard tack; the rear of his schooners being six miles astern. Sir James wore also, and hauled upon a wind on the same tack; but observing that the American fleet would be able to weather him in the next tack, he tacked again and made sail to the northward. Commodore Chauncey pursued him. He continued the chase until night; but the schooners not being able to keep up, a signal was made to relinquish the pursuit, and to form in close order. The wind now blew heavily; and at midnight two of the schooners, the *Scourge* and the *Hamilton*, were found to have upset in the squall. Lieutenants Winter and Osgood, two valuable officers, were lost, and only sixteen men of the crews saved [picked up by the British]. The next morning, the enemy discovering this misfortune, and having now the superiority, manifested a disposition to engage the Americans, and bore up for the purpose. Two schooners were ordered to engage him; but when they were within a mile and-a-half of him, he attempted to cut them off. Failing in this, he hauled his wind, and hove to. A squall coming on, Commodore Chauncey was fearful of being separated from his dull sailing schooners, and ran in towards Niagara and anchored. Here he received on board, from Fort George, 150 men to act as marines, and distributed them through his fleet. On the morning of the 9th he again sailed. At eleven o'clock, after much manœuvring on both sides, the rear of the enemy's line opened its fire; and in fifteen minutes the action became general on both sides. At half-past eleven, the American weather line bore up and passed to the leeward, the *Growler* and *Julia* excepted, which soon after tacking to the southward, brought the British between them and the remainder of the American fleet. Sir James, after exchanging a few shots made sail for Niagara, where he remained at anchor until the British fleet appeared off the harbour, early in the morning of the 7th of September, when the American fleet again weighed and bore down upon the British fleet, with which they manœuvred until the 12th, when the latter returned into Amherst Bay, near Kingston. During these five days but few shots were exchanged between the larger ships, without any injury to either side. The Americans, however, had much the advantage in weight of metal and long guns.

The fleets again met on the 28th of September, off York, when an engagement ensued for nearly two hours, in which the *Wolfe*, commanded by Sir James Yeo, lost her main and mizen-top-masts, and would probably have been captured had not the *Royal George*, commanded by Captain Mulcaster, run in between the *Wolfe* and the *Pike*, taking the latter in a raking position, so as to afford the *Wolfe* an opportunity of hauling off and clearing away the wreck. This affair terminated in the retreat of the British fleet under Burlington Heights, whither the enemy did not think proper to pursue it.

On the 1st of October, the American fleet set sail from Fort George with a convoy of troops for Sackett's Harbour, where an expedition was preparing whose destination was as yet unknown. The British fleet left their anchorage under Burlington Heights on the next day, and came in sight of the enemy; but no attempt was made to bring on a general engagement. The American fleet, on their way to Sackett's Harbour; fell in with and captured five small vessels out of seven, with upwards of 250 men of De Watteville's Regiment, from York, bound for Kingston, where an attack was apprehended. This loss, though apparently trifling in itself, was severely felt, by reason of the few forces in the Upper Provinces.

with the American commodore's ship, pursued the *Growler* and *Julia*. A fire commenced between them, which continued until one o'clock in the morning of the 10th, when, after a desperate resistance, the two schooners were compelled to yield. The fleets had lost sight of each other in the night; but as Sir James, on the next day, when they were again visible, showed no disposition to renew the action, Commodore Chauncey returned to Sackett's Harbour. A victory for this affair was claimed for the British commander." (Brackenridge's History of the War of 1812, etc., Chap. viii., pp. 121, 122.)

For the remainder of the season nothing of moment occurred on this lake; and indeed the naval commanders appeared to have considered the question of too great importance to their respective Governments to stake the fate of war in Upper Canada upon a decisive naval engagement.*

PART XI.

OCCURRENCES ON LAKE ERIE AND IN THE WEST—LOSS OF THE BRITISH FLEET—EVACUATION OF DETROIT AND THE TERRITORY OF MICHIGAN BY GENERAL PROCTOR, WHO IS PURSUED IN HIS RETREAT UP THE THAMES, AND DEFEATED BY GENERAL HARRISON, AND IS AFTERWARDS TRIED AND CONDEMNED TO BE SUSPENDED AND DEPRIVED OF HIS PAY FOR SIX MONTHS.

The operations on Lake Erie and in the West were disastrous to the British cause during the latter part of the summer and early autumn of 1813. General Harrison, with an army of 8,000 men on the Miami river, only awaited for the equipment of the American fleet fitting out under Commodore Perry, at Presqu' Isle (Erie), to move his forces against Detroit, and to carry on offensive operations against the British in the neighbourhood of Lake Erie. Captain Barclay, who had early in the summer assumed the command of the British squadron on Lake Erie, blockaded the American fleet, so as to prevent their crossing the bar at Presqu' Isle (which they could not effect without unshipping their guns) until the end of August; when, having occasion to bear away for Long Point,† the enemy seized the moment of his absence and crossed the bar. Finding on his return the enemy ready for the lake, and too power-

---

* Christie, Chap. v., pp. 126—130.

† It was this episode in Captain Barclay's proceedings which resulted in the loss of British supremacy on Lake Erie, the loss of his fleet, his own wounding, the death of most of his officers and sailors, General Proctor's compulsory evacuation of Detroit and the Michigan territory, his retreat into Canada, his defeat on the Thames at the Moravian village, involving the loss of many of his men, with upwards of 100 Indians, including famous Chief Tecumseh. We do not desire to dwell upon this dark spot in the life of Captain Barclay; but the whole mystery is explained in the Mrs. Amelia Harris's Memoirs of her father and the early settlement of Long Point (and her authority cannot be questioned.) See Chapter XLI. of this History, pp. 425.

ful for his small squadron, he bore away for Amherstburg, to await the equipment of the *Detroit*, recently launched.

Commodore Perry sailed shortly after him for the head of the lake, and appeared at the commencement of September, for several days successively, off Amherstburg, in defiance of the British squadron, retiring every evening to his anchorage at *Put-in-Bay*. The British forces in Michigan territory and its neighbourhood, under General Proctor, falling short of supplies for which they depended solely upon the fleet, the captain had no other alternative than that of risking a general naval engagement. With this resolution he made sail from Amherstburg on the 9th of September, manned with only fifty or sixty seamen (including a small reinforcement of thirty-six men from Lake Ontario), and detachments from the 41st and Royal Newfoundland Regiment as marines. On the 10th, in the morning, the enemy's fleet was descried at anchor in *Put-in-Bay*, which immediately weighed and bore down upon the British squadron, while the wind blowing a gentle breeze from the south-west, turning round to the south-east, gave the enemy the weather gage. At a quarter before twelve the British commenced firing, which was in ten minutes afterwards returned by the enemy, who bore up for close action. The engagement continued with unabated fury until half-past two, when the enemy's principal ship being rendered unmanageable, Commodore Perry left her in charge of his first lieutenant, Yarnal, and hoisted the pendant on board the *Niagara*. Soon after Commodore Perry had left the *Lawrence*, her colours were struck, but the British, from weakness of their crews and destruction of their boats, were unable to take possession of her.

It was at this anxious and interesting juncture that the fate of the day seemed to poise in favour of the British; and Commodore Perry even despaired of the victory, when a sudden breeze revived his hopes, and turned the scale in his favour. This fortunate commander, finding the *Niagara* had suffered lightly in the engagement, made a desperate effort to retrieve the fortune of the day, and taking advantage of the breeze, shot ahead of the *Lady Prevost*, *Queen Charlotte*, and *Hunter*, raking them with her starboard guns, and engaged the *Detroit*, which, being raked in all directions, soon became unmanageable. The *Niagara* then bore around ahead of the *Queen*

Charlotte, and hauling up on starboard tack, engaged that ship, giving at the same time a raking fire with her larboard guns to the *Chippewa* and the *Little Belt*, while the smaller vessels, closing to grape and canister distance, maintained a most destructive fire. This masterly and but too successful manœuvre decided the contest. Captain Barclay being severely and dangerously wounded, Captain Finnis, of the *Queen Charlotte*, killed, and every commander and officer second in command either killed or disabled, the *Detroit* and *Queen Charlotte*, perfect wrecks, after a desperate engagement of upwards of three hours, were compelled to surrender.

By this decisive action, the whole of the British squadron on Lake Erie was captured by the enemy, who now became masters of the lake. The enemy lost in this action twenty-seven men in killed and ninety-six men wounded. The British lost three officers and thirty-eight men killed, and nine officers and eighty-five men wounded.

The prisoners were landed at Sandusky, and treated with the greatest humanity by the American commodore, who paroled Captain Barclay, and treated that gallant officer with all the kindness and attention which his unsuccessful bravery deserved.

The British army in possession of the Michigan territory and the neighbourhood of Detroit, by this disastrous defeat, were deprived of every prospect of obtaining future supplies from Kingston by way of Lake Ontario, and a speedy evacuation of Detroit, and a retreat towards the head of that lake became inevitable.

General Harrison having received reinforcements amounting to 7,000 or 8,000 men, including 4,000 volunteers from Kentucky under Samuel Shelby, the ex-governor of that State, and an old revolutionary officer, was conveyed by Commodore Perry, in his flotilla, with all the troops and stores, from the mouth of the Miami to the Canadian shore, except the thousand dragoons who were to advance by land, and so order their march that they might arrive in the neighbourhood of Malden at the same time with the infantry. General Harrison occupied Amherstburg the evening of the 23rd of September, General Proctor having previously abandoned it and fallen back upon Sandwich, after having set fire to the navy yard, barracks, and public stores at the former place.

General Harrison, on his arrival, having found the different points evacuated, invested General McArthur with the chief command of these garrisons, and prepared to pursue the retreating army up the River Thames, with a force of 3,000 men, including Colonel Johnson's corps of dragoons, consisting of 1,000. General Harrison occupied Sandwich the 27th of September, and on the 2nd of October he marched in pursuit of the shattered remains of the British forces under General Proctor. In this, his reverse of fortune, the Indians, under Colonel Elliot, of the Indian Department, with Tecumseh, still adhered to his standard with unshaken fidelity, and covered his retreat.

On the 4th of October, General Harrison came up with the rear-guard of the British, and succeeded in capturing the whole of their ammunition and stores. General Proctor, under this second reverse of fortune, by which he was left destitute of the means of subsistence or defence, found himself compelled to stake the fate of the remnant of his small army on a general engagement. Accordingly he assumed a position on the right bank of the River Thames, near the Indian village of Moravian Town—the left resting on the river supported by a field-piece, his right on a swamp, at a distance of 300 yards from the river, and flanked by the whole Indian force attached to the division. The intermediate ground, covered with lofty trees, was dry and somewhat elevated. Here General Proctor formed his troops into line, to the number of 500 or 600. The Indians under Tecumseh amounted to 1,200. In this position he awaited the approach of the enemy, who, on the morning of the 5th of October, passed the river at a rapid twelve miles below the Moravian village, and came up with the British in the afternoon. General Harrison drew up his men in two lines, and secured his left flank, which was opposed to the Indians, by a division thrown back *en potence;* and without any previous engagement by infantry, ordered his mounted Kentuckians (accustomed from their boyhood to ride with extraordinary dexterity through the most embarrassed woods) to charge at full speed upon (the *open* line of) the British, which had effected before the latter had time to discharge their third fire. This cavalry charge of the enemy on the British line decided the issue of the day. The line gave way at the charge; the troops, worn down with fatigue and hunger, dispirited by the unpromising appearance of the campaign, became totally routed, and for the most part surrendered themselves prisoners, while General Proctor and his personal staff sought safety in flight.

To the left of the enemy's position, which was opposed to the Indians, the battle raged with more obstinacy. This part of the enemy's line had even given way until a column under ex-Governor Shelby was brought up to its support. These faithful allies continued to carry on the contest with the left of the American line with furious determination, encouraged by the presence of Tecumseh, until finding all hopes of retrieving the day to be in vain—General Proctor and his soldiers having fled or surrendered—they yielded to the overwhelming numbers of the enemy, and left the field—upwards of 100 of them having fallen in battle, and the bodies of 33 of them being found around the dead body of their famous chief and warrior, Tecumseh; celebrated no less for his humanity than for his bravery, his eloquence, and his influence among the Indian allies of the British in the West.

Upwards of 600 of the British, including twenty-five officers, were made prisoners of war. Those who escaped made the best of their way to Ancaster, a few miles from Burlington Heights, exposed at an inclement season to all the horrors of the wilderness, of hunger, and famine. The number thus escaped to that place amounted to only 246, including the general and seventeen officers.

This disaster of the British arms in that quarter seems not to have been palliated by those precautions and that presence of mind which, even in defeat, reflects lustre on a commander. In rapid retreats from a pursuing enemy cumbrous and useless baggage is abandoned, and bridges and roads are destroyed and rendered as impassable as possible, in order to impede the progress of the pursuers; but General Proctor encumbered himself with a cumbrous load of baggage, and left the bridges and roads in his rear entire, to the advantage of his pursuers. Whether this error and neglect arose from contempt of the enemy, or from disobedience of the commanding officer's orders, is not well understood; but the defeat led to the harshest recrimination, and involved in unmerited disgrace the division of the brave troops that had served with honour in the Michigan territory; and General Proctor was subjected to a trial by court-martial for his conduct in the whole affair—censured and deprived of his pay for six months.

PART XII.

AMERICANS BURN MORAVIAN TOWN, BEFORE RETURNING TO DETROIT—FORM ALLIANCE WITH INDIANS, WHICH THEY HAD EXCLAIMED SO MUCH AGAINST ON THE PART OF THE BRITISH—ARE INTOXICATED WITH THEIR SUCCESSES IN THE WEST—MAGNIFICENT CLOSE OF THE YEAR 1813, AS OF 1812, IN BEHALF OF CANADIANS, BOTH IN UPPER AND LOWER CANADA —CANADIAN VICTORY OF ISLE-AUX-NOIS—SPLENDID CANADIAN VICTORIES OF CHATEAUGUAY AND CHRYSTLER'S FARM—AMERICAN ARMIES RETREAT INTO WINTER QUARTERS.

The American army returned to Detroit after the battle of Moravian Town; but before doing so, they consigned the town to the flames, assigning as a justification of the savage act against the unoffending Christian Moravian Indians, a retaliation for what they called the massacre of River Raisin.

During General Harrison's absence from Detroit, a few of the Indian tribes tendered their services to General McArthur, to raise the hatchet against the British, and their proffered services were readily accepted—showing that, according to the American rule of judging, the alliance of the Indians with the United States was quite right, while with England it was all wrong and barbarous.

The success of the American arms on Lake Erie and its surrounding shores so intoxicated and bewildered them, that, in their subsequent movements, they calculated upon nothing but victory and conquest, made no allowance for failure in any point. "Canada must now be ours" was their exulting and arrogant language. But they had overlooked the fact that, however gloomy the prospects of the Western Canadians were in October of the year 1813, there were remaining elements of strength with them—their courage and zeal were unabated, and even increased, by the transactions of the months of disaster; their loyalty to their principles, and their love of their independence, were intensified rather than enfeebled; they would not be a *conquered people;* and before the end of the year

1813, the American armies had to relinquish every inch of Canadian soil both in Upper and Lower Canada.

But to present a connected and intelligent view of the magnificent close of the year 1813, as was that of 1812, we must first turn to the American campaigns against Lower Canada in 1813; and the defeats and want of success for several months in Upper Canada were more than compensated by the heroic deeds and splendid success of both the English and French defenders of Lower Canada, as well as by victories gained in Upper Canada in the months of November and December.

The Isle-aux-Nois was termed the key of Lower Canada, and its old fortifications had been repaired, and three gun-boats sent thither from Quebec. The little garrison was under the command of Lieutenant-Colonel George Taylor, Inspecting General Field Officer (then major of the 100th Regiment), who, apprehending, from previous private information, a combined attack from the American naval force on Lake Champlain and the troops in the neighbourhood of his post, commanded by the Brigadier-Generals Smyth and Clarke, lost no time in equipping the three gun-boats lying unemployed for want of seamen; and Lieutenant-Colonel Taylor having no sailors, he manned the gun-boats from his regiment, with three artillerymen for each boat, and took the precaution to man two batteaux with a detachment of soldiers, for the double purpose of rendering assistance to the gun-boats in the event of their being either sunk or disabled in the engagement, or to assist in boarding if it should be found necessary. The enemy, discovered in approaching, consisted of the sloops of war *Growler* and *Eagle*, fitted out in the most complete manner, each carrying eleven guns (eighteens, twelves, and sixes), long eighteens on pivots, with complements each of fifty-five men, comprehending a company of marines, which they had received at Champlain the evening previous to the engagement; the whole under the command of the United States navy. The admirable execution with their small arms of the two small detachments of soldiers landed on the east side of the river, and the well-directed fire from the gun-boats, of round and grape shot, completely decided the fate of the action, which the enemy gallantly contested from half-past four to half-past eight in the morning, and did not surrender until further resistance became utterly unavailing—one of the vessels being run aground to prevent her from sinking.

The whole force of the British in this affair was only 108. The men killed on board the American vessels were thrown overboard by their surviving comrades; the prisoners amounted to 100 men, of whom many were wounded. Of the captors, not a man was killed, and only three severely wounded. The naval force of the enemy on Lake Champlain was, by the capture of these vessels, almost annihilated, while it afforded the British immediate and effectual means for offensive operations on that lake, and checked the invasion meditated on Lower Canada.

The American Government, with a view of conquering Lower Canada, had been at considerable pains and expense in erecting barracks, hospitals, and magazines at different points along Lake Champlain, particularly at Burlington, Plattsburg, Champlain, and Swanton, in the neighbourhood of the Canadian frontiers—all under the direction of the two American generals, Moore and Hampton. To counteract these movements, the captured vessels, *Growler* and *Eagle*—re-named the *Shannon* and *Brock*—were speedily put in commission, and the three gun-boats being put in repair, the small squadron was placed under the command of Captain Pring. Still there were no sailors; but, fortunately, at this juncture the *Wasp* sloop-of-war arrived from England at Quebec, and Captain Everard, her commander, was ordered to transfer his crew to the *Shannon* and other vessels, and take command of the little fleet on Lake Champlain.

On the 29th of July the fleet took 900 regulars from the 13th, 100th, and 103rd Regiments, with some artillery, and a number of Canadian militia, who acted as batteaux men, and proceeded up the lake, landing near Plattsburg on the 31st, without meeting any opposition—the American general, Moore, with 1,500 men, having retreated at the approach of the British. Colonel John Murray, who was in command of the British, took possession of the arsenals, etc., and after having embarked all the warlike stores, of which a considerable quantity was found in the arsenal, and having destroyed such as he could not conveniently take away, set fire to the enemy's arsenal, public buildings, commissariat stores, and barracks, recently erected, and capable of accommodating from 4,000 to 5,000 men. While the troops were thus employed during the whole of the night, Captains Everard and Pring, in the *Growler* and *Eagle*, with a gun-boat proceeded to Burlington, where General Hampton lay encamped with 4,000 men, and threw that place into the utmost consternation. Having captured and destroyed, within sight of the American forces, four vessels, Captain Everard returned to Plattsburg, where the troops were re-embarked, and proceeded to Swanton. Colonel Murray, while on the way thither, sent a detachment to Champlain for the purpose of destroying the barracks and block-house at that port. The main body having visited Swanton, and effected the purpose of the expedition to the fullest extent of his Excellency the Governor-General's orders, returned to the Isle-aux-Nois, where they arrived the 4th of August, without the loss of a man, and having been completely successful.

But these successes were only preliminary to two victories remarkable in the annals of military warfare, considering the disparity in the number and means of the parties concerned— known as the battles of *Chateauguay* and *Chrystler's Farm*.

General Hampton, after having transported his force across Lake Champlain, lay encamped some days at Cumberland Head, near Plattsburg. On the 20th of September he entered Lower Canada at Odletown, at the lower extremity of Lake Champlain, with upwards of 5,000 men. The road leading from thence to l'Acadie, and the open country in the neighbourhood of Montreal, lies through a swamp of about fifteen miles, which had been cut up and rendered almost impracticable by abatis since the preceding campaign, by the Voltigeurs under Lieutenant-Colonel De Salaberry, and guarded by some Voltigeurs and Indians. Deterred by these obstructions, General Hampton evacuated Odletown on the 22nd of September, and moved with his whole force westward, toward the head of Chateauguay river, under pretext of the impracticability of advancing through the Odletown road for want of water for his cavalry and cattle, owing to the extraordinary drought of the season. Colonel De Salaberry, with the Canadian Voltigeurs, on ascertaining the route the enemy had taken, moved in like manner to Chateauguay, and by his skilful precautions and arrangements of defence and attack, he gained advantage in several skirmishes with scouting and advance parties of the enemy—thus leading his Voltigeurs for the first time into action, and acquiring a just confidence in the valour of his countrymen, which a few days afterwards they nobly exemplified under their gallant leader at Chateauguay. Finally he assumed a judicious position in a thick wood on the left bank of the Chateauguay river, at a distance of two leagues above the Turk, or confluence of the English and Chateauguay rivers, where he threw up temporary breastworks of logs, covering his front and right flank with extended abatis, while his left was covered by the river. Here he resolved to await the enemy and maintain his ground with a Spartan handful of Canadians against the whole strength of the invading army. In his rear there was a small rapid where the river was fordable; this he covered with a strong breastwork and guard; keeping at the same time a strong picquet of the Beauharnois Militia in advance of the right bank of the river, lest the enemy, approaching under cover of the forest, might cross the ford and dislodge him from his ground.

The occupancy of this position General Hampton justly considered of the first importance to the ulterior object of the campaign against Montreal, as the country from thence to the mouth of the Chateauguay, being principally open and cultivated, afforded no strong points to check his progress to the St. Lawrence, and prevent his junction with General Wilkinson's division; but which in fact was not yet in readiness to move.

General Hampton, in the meantime, to distract and divide the attention of the British, directed Colonel Clarke to carry on a petty warfare on the eastern side of Lake Champlain; and that ruthless depredator invested the settlements in Missisquoi Bay, where he plundered the inhabitants in the most wanton manner.

On the 21st of October, General Hampton again entered Lower Canada, having early in the morning of that day dispatched his light troops and a regiment of the line, under Brigadier-General Izard, to dislodge a small picquet of sedentary militia, at the junction of the Outarde and Chateauguay rivers, where the main body arrived on the 22nd. On the 24th, having opened and completed a large and practicable road from his position at Four Corners (a distance of twenty-four miles), through woods and morasses, which Lieutenant-Colonel De Salaberry, on returning from the Four Corners, had broken up and embarrassed with abatis, General Hampton brought forward the whole of his artillery (ten field-pieces) and stores to his new position—about seven miles from Lieut.-Colonel De Salaberry's post.

From this point General Hampton dispatched Colonel Purdy with a light brigade, and a strong body of infantry of the line, at an early hour of the night of the 25th, with orders to gain the Ford, and fall on the rear of Lieutenant-Colonel De Salaberry's position; while the main body were to commence the attack in front. Purdy's brigade proceeded, but were misled and bewildered in the woods, and did not gain the point of attack as directed by the commanding officer. General Hampton, however, advanced next morning (26th October) under the expectation of having the intended attack at the Ford, and at ten o'clock made his appearance with about *three thousand five hundred men*, under General Izard, on the high road leading to the abatis, and drove in a picket of twenty-five men, who falling back on a second picket made a resolute stand, and maintained a smart fire upon the enemy. Lieutenant-Colonel De Salaberry, upon hearing the musketry, promptly advanced with the light company of the Canadian Fencibles, commanded by Captain Ferguson, and two companies of his Voltigeurs, commanded by Captains Chevalier and Jucheseau Duchesnay. The first of these companies he posted on the right, in front of the abatis, in extended order, its right skirting on the adjoining woods and abatis, among which were distributed a few Abena qui Indians. Captains Chevalier and Duchesnay's companies of Voltigeurs, in extended order, occupied the ground from the left of this company to the River Chateauguay, and the third company, under Captain L. Jucheseau Duchesnay, with the sedentary militia, under Captain Lougtain, were thrown back *en potence* along the margin of the river for the purpose of flanking, or preventing a flank fire from the enemy in the event of his appearing on the opposite side of the river. The enemy in the meantime advanced with steadiness in open column of sections to within musket shot, when Lieutenant-Colonel De Salaberry discharged his rifle as signal to commence firing, at which a mounted officer was seen to fall. The bugles sounded, and a quick fire was immediately opened upon the enemy who wheeled up into line, and commenced a fire in battalion vollies, which, from the position of their line, was almost totally thrown to the right of the Canadians, and of no effect whatever. They, however, soon changed their front parallel to their adversaries, by facing to the right, and filing up with speed, when the engagement became general.

The retirement of the few skirmishers, rather advanced in the centre of the line, being mistaken by the enemy for a flight, an universal shout ensued, which was re-echoed by the Canadians, and the reinforcements in reserve under Lieutenant-Colonel McDonnell, while Lieutenant-Colonel De Salaberry as a *ruse de guerre* (like Gideon with his trumpets and 300 men, Judges, vii.), ordered the bugles placed at intervals, in the abatis, to sound an advance; this had the desired effect, and checked the ardour of the enemy, who suspected that the Canadians were advancing in great numbers to circumvent them. The noise of the engagement brought Colonel Purdy's division on the opposite side of the river, which, having driven in the picket of the sedentary militia under Captain Bruguier, were pressing on for the ford at which Lieutenant-Colonel De Salaberry ordered the light company of the 3rd Battalion embodied militia, under Captain Daly, to cross and take up the ground abandoned by the picquet, Captain Daly with his company crossed the ford, and having advanced fell in with and drove back the advanced guard of the Americans on the main body, which still pressed forward and compelled him in his turn to fall back. Having repulsed Captain Daly's company, they were moving on in overwhelming numbers with eagerness and speed close to the bank of the river, until opposite to Captain L. Juchereau Duchesnay's company, which hitherto lay concealed, and now at the word of command from Lieutenant-Colonel De Salaberry, opened so unexpected and effectual a fire upon the enemy, as to throw him into the utmost disorder, and to occasion a tumultuous and precipitate retreat.

General Hampton finding his arrangements disconcerted by the total route of the division on the right bank, withdrew his forces in good order at half-past two in the afternoon, without having made a single effort to carry the abatis and entrenchments at the point of the bayonet, leaving Lieutenant-Colonel

De Salaberry, with scarcely 300 Canadians, masters of the field of action.

Towards the close of the engagement, Sir George Prevost, with Major-General De Watteville, arrived on the ground, and witnessed in person the judicious arrangements and successful exertions of Lieutenant-Colonel De Salaberry and his gallant comrades and countrymen, whose prowess on the occasion called forth the warmest encomiums of the commander of the forces, and gave them a just claim to the disinterested and impartial applause of history.

The fatigues and privations experienced by General Hampton's troops, exposed for several weeks to the inclemency of the season, demoralized them to the native rawness of new recruits, and rendered them no more capable of co-operating with General Wilkinson's division in the combined movement against Montreal. They shortly after fell back on Plattsburg and retired to winter quarters.

The Canadian Victory of "Chrystler's Farm."—The next expedition against Montreal was to proceed down the St. Lawrence, under the command of General Wilkinson.* The American forces to about 10,000 men rendezvoused towards the end of October on Grenadier Island, near Kingston, where General De Rottenburgh confidently expected an attack, and was prepared for it; but General Wilkinson was not so disposed, and, after experiencing much foul weather, commenced his movement under cover of the American fleet, and on the 3rd of November slipt into the St. Lawrence with a flotilla of upwards of *three hundred* boats of various sizes, escorted by a division of gun-boats. He proceeded to within three miles of Prescott and landed his troops on the American shore, who proceeded downwards by land to a bay or cove, two miles below Ogdensburgh, in order to avoid the British batteries at Prescott, while the flotilla passed them in the night of the 6th, with little injury from the cannonade of the British batteries.

The movements of the flotilla down the St. Lawrence having been ascertained at Kingston, General De Rottenburgh detached a small force from that port, consisting of the 49th

* "General Wilkinson was called from the South to assume the command of the American forces in the North, in the room of General Dearborn. which now with General Hampton's division, amounted to about 18,000, to

Regiment, commanded by Lieutenant-Colonel Plenderleath, of the 89th Regiment, and some Voltigeurs, which, when reinforced by Lieutenant-Colonel Pearson with a party of the Canadian Fencibles from Prescott, amounted to about 800 rank and file, the whole commanded by Lieutenant-Colonel Morrison, of the 89th Regiment, and accompanied by the Deputy-Adjutant-General.

This corps of observation proceeded under the escort of a small division of gun-boats, commanded by Captain Mulcaster, R.N., in pursuit of the enemy; and on the 8th came up with them at Point Iroquois. General Wilkinson had on the preceding day directed Colonel Macomb to land on the British shore with 1,200 men, in order to clear the coast to the head of the Long Sault, of the militia along the shore, from various parts of the country. On the 18th this division was reinforced by Brigadier-General Brown's Brigade, with a body of dragoons from the American shore. On arriving at the head of the Long Sault, the whole of the effective men, except such as were required to navigate the boats down the Rapids, were landed under the orders of Brigadier-General Boyd, who was to proceed down the land in the rear of General Brown's division to the foot of the Long Sault.

On the 10th Lieutenant-Colonel Morrison, with his gun-boats, visited the American post at Hamilton, where he landed and took possession of a considerable quantity of provisions and stores belonging to the American army, with two pieces of ordnance. Lieutenant-Colonel Harvey, in the meantime, followed up the enemy, who in the evening were observed advancing from the woods in considerable numbers, with a body of cavalry; but upon receiving a few rounds from three field-pieces fell back for the night. (Some smart cannonading took place in the meantime between the British and American gun-boats.)

Battle of Chrystler's Farm.—On the ensuing day, Lieutenant-Colonel Morrison pressed so closely upon the rear of General

which General Harrison's division was ordered to be added. Such were the gigantic and formidable preparations for the capture of Montreal, where the American soldiers were promised, as an additional inducement, good winter quarters." (Thompson's History of the War of 1812, Chap. xxvi., p. 209.)

Boyd's division as to compel him to concentrate his forces and give battle. The enemy's force, consisting of two brigades of infantry and a regiment of cavalry, amounting to *between three and four thousand men*, moved forward about two o'clock in the afternoon from Chrystler's Point, and attacked the British advance, which gradually fell back to the position which had been selected for the detachment to occupy—the right resting on the river, and the left on a pine wood, between which there were about 700 yards of open ground, the troops on which were thus disposed:

The flank companies of the 49th Regiment, the detachment from the Canadian regiment, with one field-piece, under Lieutenant-Colonel Pearson, on the right, a little advanced on the road. Three companies of the 89th Regiment, under Captain Barnes, with a gun, formed in echelon, with the advance on its left supporting it. The 49th and the 89th, thrown more to the rear, with a gun, formed the main body and reserve, extending to the woods on the left, which were occupied by the Voltigeurs under Major Herriot, and the Indians under Lieutenant Anderson.

At about half past two the action became general, and the enemy endeavoured, by moving forward a brigade from his right, to turn the British left, but was repulsed by the 89th Regiment forming *en potence* with the 49th Regiment, and moving forward in that direction, in echelon, followed by the 89th. When within half musket shot, the line was formed under a heavy but irregular fire from the enemy. The 49th was directed to charge the American guns, posted opposite the Canadian guns, but it became necessary, when within a short distance of them, to check this forward movement in consequence of a charge from the American cavalry on the right, lest they should wheel about and fall upon the rear; but they were received in so gallant a manner by the companies of the 89th under Captain Barnes, and the well-directed fire of the artillery, that they quickly retreated; and by a charge from those companies one gun was gained. The enemy immediately concentrated their force to check the British advance, but such was the steady continuance and well-directed fire of the troops and artillery that about half-past four they gave way at all points from an exceeding strong position, endeavouring by their light infantry to cover their retreat, who were soon driven away by a judicious movement made by Lieutenant-Colonel Pearson.

The British detachment for the night occupied the ground from which the enemy had been driven.

This (called the Battle of Chrystler's Farm, from the ground on which it occurred) is, in the estimation of military men, considered the handsomest affair during the war, from the professional skill displayed in the course of the action by the adverse commanders; and when we consider the prodigious preparations of the American Government for that expedition, with the failure of which their hopes of conquest banished, the battle of Chrystler's Farm may be classed as an event of the first importance in the defence of the Canadas.

The American division, after leaving the field, re-embarked in haste, while the dragoons, with five field-pieces of light artillery, proceeded down towards Cornwall, in the rear of General Brown's division, who, unaware of the battle of Chrystler's Farm, had continued his march for that place.

The loss of the enemy, by their own statements, amounted to three officers and ninety-nine men killed, and sixteen officers and one hundred and twenty-one men wounded. The loss of the British amounted to three officers (Captain Nairne of the 49th Regiment, and Lieutenants Lorimier and Armstrong), and twenty-one men killed, and one hundred and thirty-seven wounded, and twelve missing.

General Wilkinson, who, during the action, lay confined to his barge from a protracted illness, in his official despatch to his Government, bears strong testimony to the loyalty of the inhabitants on the Canada side of the St. Lawrence, and to the bravery and discipline of the troops he had to contend with at Chrystler's Farm.

The day after the engagement, the American flotilla proceeded down the Long Sault, and joined near Cornwall the division which had moved towards that place, where General Wilkinson confidently expected to hear of the arrival of General Hampton on the opposite shore, to whom he had written on the 6th, to that effect, not being then acquainted with his late defeat. Here, to his unspeakable mortification and surprise, he received a letter from General Hampton, informing him that the division under his command was falling back upon Lake Champlain.*

This information, with the countless difficulties momentarily crowding upon the American army, effectually blasted every prospect of further success. So circumstanced, the American commander immediately held a Council of War, in which it was unanimously resolved, "That the attack upon Montreal should be abandoned for the present season, and that the army near Cornwall should immediately cross to the American shore, in order to take up winter quarters," a resolution which was carried into effect the following day, by their proceeding for Salmon river, where their boats and batteaux were scuttled, and extensive barracks for the whole army were erected with extraordinary celerity, surrounded on all sides by abatis, so as to render a surprise unpracticable.

Every appearance of danger having subsided, the commander of the Canadian forces dismissed the sedentary militia, by a General Order of the 17th of November, with acknowledgments of the cheerful alacrity with which they had repaired to their posts, and the loyalty and zeal they had manifested at the prospect of encountering the enemy.

With these operations terminated the campaigns of 1813 in Lower Canada; but new triumphs still awaited the British

---

* "General Wilkinson had, at an early stage of the expedition, transmitted an order to General Hampton to join him at St. Regis; but that officer having learned the low state of General Wilkinson's supplies of provisions, and considering the state of the roads, conceived it the most prudent method to disobey the order, and not to place himself at too great a distance from his own magazines; he therefore availed himself of the nearest route to Montreal, the unsuccessful result of which manœuvre has just been detailed.

"The American army was again ordered to cross the line and take up their winter quarters in their own territory, after repeatedly suffering themselves to be defeated under the most mortifying and humiliating circumstances; with the blame of which the commander-in-chief (General Wilkinson) charged General Hampton, in consequence of his disobedience of orders, but with which the American Secretary of War more properly charged both. However, it had the effect of checking the military zeal which appeared to manifest itself in the American ranks at a distance from the theatre of hostile operations, and completely to extinguish the ardour of the American troops on the lines." (Thompson, Chap. xxvii. p. 215.)

arms in the Province of Upper Canada before the end of the year.*

PART XIII.

GENERAL DRUMMOND ARRIVES IN UPPER CANADA—COLONEL MURRAY SENT TO ARREST THE PREDATORY INCURSIONS OF THE BRUTAL GENERAL McCLURE UPON THE INHABITANTS IN THE NEIGHBOURHOOD OF FORT GEORGE—McCLURE'S BARBAROUS BURNING OF THE TOWN OF NEWARK (NIAGARA), EXPOSING 400 WOMEN AND CHILDREN TO THE INTENSE COLD OF THE 10TH OF DECEMBER—McCLURE'S FLIGHT TO FORT NIAGARA ON THE AMERICAN SIDE OF THE RIVER—COLONEL MURRAY, BY SURPRISING FORT NIAGARA, TAKES THE WHOLE GARRISON PRISONERS, AND SEIZES LARGE QUANTITIES OF MILITARY STORES—GENERAL RIALL RETALIATES IN THE SAME WAY, IN REGARD TO LEWISTON, BLACK ROCK, AND BUFFALO—GENERAL DRUMMOND ISSUES A PROCLAMATION DEPRECATING SUCH SAVAGE POLICY AS INITIALED BY THE AMERICAN GOVERNMENT.

Early in December, Major General De Rottenburgh was relieved in the command of Upper Canada by Lieutenant-General Drummond, who proceeded from Kingston to York, and from thence to the head of the lake, where the army again resumed an offensive position. The country along the St. Lawrence, being freed from the incursions of the enemy, Colonel Murray, of the 100th Regiment, was ordered to advance from Burlington Heights towards Fort George, with a view at that time to prevent predatory incursions of the enemy under General McClure (then in possession of that fort) on the defenceless inhabitants of the surrounding country. But General McClure, having heard of the disasters which had befallen the army destined for Montreal, and conscious that a like fate might probably await him and his army, with that dastardly cowardice peculiar to himself and a few of his compatriots and traitors who joined themselves to his train, and against the very spirit of the law of nations and of civilized warfare, immersed the flourishing town of Newark (Niagara) in one continued sheet of flame, and ignobly fled with his followers into his territory. The historian laments that it is

* The foregoing account of the transactions in Lower Canada is chiefly extracted from Mr. Christie's History of the War of 1812, and mostly in his words. What follows is mostly taken from Thompson's War of 1812.

not in his power to record one magnanimous act of that recreant General, to rescue his name from that gulf of infamy to which his nefarious conduct has forever doomed it.*

But retaliation was only delayed a week. On the evening of the 18th of December, preparations were made for taking Fort Niagara from the enemy, for which service Colonel Murray, of the 100th Regiment, was selected to take the command; and long before daylight next morning this gallant officer, at the head of the grenadier company of the Royal Scots, the grenadier and light companies of the 41st Regiment, and a detachment of his own corps, crossed the river about two miles above the fort, upon which they immediately advanced. On approaching the fortress, sentries, planted on the outer works, were surprised and taken, the countersign obtained, and in a few minutes the fort was carried at the point of the bayonet.

The loss on the part of the British in this affair was only

---

* The barbarous act of General McClure in burning Niagara is ascribed to directions from the American Secretary at War; but the many nefarious acts committed by McClure could hardly be owing to directions from Washington. Mr. Christie says that McClure "having, pursuant to the directions of the American Secretary at War, most inhumanly, on the 10th of December, set fire to the flourishing village of Newark, containing about 150 houses, which were reduced to ashes, leaving the wretched and forlorn inhabitants, with upwards of 400 women and children, exposed to the accumulated horrors of famine and the inclemency of a Canadian winter.

The British, under the command of Colonel Murray, scarcely amounting to 500 men, including Indians and militia, immediately occupied Fort George. The barbarous policy of the American Government in destroying Newark, exasperated the army as well as the inhabitants on the frontier, of whose impatience for retaliation General Drummond promptly availed himself after the occupation of Fort George, by adopting the resolution of carrying the American Fort Niagara by surprise." (Chap. vii., p. 156.)

Mr. Thompson remarks on the conduct of McClure and his soldiers, even before the burning of the town of Newark: "The American army had no sooner taken up a position in front of Fort George, than the foraging parties, or rather marauders, commenced a systematic course of plunder upon the defenceless inhabitants within the vicinity of their camp, most of whom, at the time, consisted of women and children; even amongst the general officers acts of pillage were perpetrated, that, had such occurred with private soldiers in the British army, would have stamped a stigma on the character of the British, in the eyes of America, for which no course of conduct which they could ever after have pursued would have sufficiently atoned." (War of 1812, Chap. xxix. pp. 227, 228.)

six killed and five wounded: that of the enemy amounted to sixty-five killed and fourteen wounded (all with the bayonet), and the whole garrison was made prisoners, consisting of nearly 350. There were in the fort, at the time of its capture, twenty-seven pieces of ordnance of weighty calibre, 3,000 muskets with apparatus, besides large magazines of camp equipage and military clothing, which of course fell into the hands of the victors.

On the same day on which Fort Niagara was captured, the town of Lewiston, about eight miles above Fort Niagara, was taken possession of by a British force under Major-General Riall, without opposition; in which place the public magazines were well filled with provisions and other military stores.

Towards the latter end of the same month, General Riall crossed the Niagara river at Black Rock, at the head of a force consisting of about 600 men, detachments from the 8th or the King's Regiment, 41st, 89th, and 100th Regiments, with a few Militia volunteers, exclusive of six or seven companies of the Royal Scots, under the command of Lieutenant-Colonel Gordon, who were directed to land between the villages of Buffalo and Black Rock, about two miles distant from each other, with a view to divert the garrison of Black Rock, while the other troops were landing in front of that port; but in consequence of the severity of the weather, a number of the boats were stranded; by which means the troops were unable to land in time to effect the object for which they had been intended; however, the enemy was driven from both positions in a short time.

The American loss in this affair was upwards of five hundred, 130 of whom were prisoners of war; the loss of the British was inconsiderable compared with that of the enemy.

The state of exasperation to which the mind of every British subject had been wrought by the conduct of McClure in burning the town of Newark, and exposing all to the inclemency of a Canadian winter, both the helpless infant and infirm old age, was such that nothing but a similar retaliation could assuage; the whole line of frontier, from Buffalo to Fort Niagara, was therefore burnt to ashes.

Ample vengeance having thus been taken for the wanton conflagration and cruel outrages committed upon the defenceless inhabitants of Newark and neighbourhood, Lieutenant-General Drummond, on the 12th of January, 1814, issued a proclamation, in which he strongly deprecated the savage mode of warfare to which the enemy, by a departure from the established usages of war, had compelled him to resort. He traced with faithful precision and correctness the conduct that had marked the progress of the war on the part of the enemy, and concluded by lamenting the necessity imposed upon him of retaliating upon the subjects of America the miseries inflicted upon the inhabitants of Newark, but at the same time declared it not to be his intention further to pursue a system so revolting to his own feelings, and so little congenial to the British character, unless he should be compelled by the future measures of the enemy.

CHAPTER LVII.

MOVEMENTS AND CAMPAIGNS OF 1814—THE THIRD AND LAST YEAR OF THE WAR.

PART I.

PREPARATIONS FOR THE CAMPAIGN—REINFORCEMENTS FROM NEW BRUNSWICK—ROYAL APPROBATION OF CANADIAN LOYALTY AND COURAGE—AMERICAN INVASION OF THE DISTRICT OF MONTREAL UNDER GENERAL WILKINSON—THE LARGE FORCE OF AMERICANS DEFEATED AT LA COLLE BY A SMALL FORCE OF CANADIANS—RETURN TO PLATTSBURG, WHERE GENERAL WILKINSON, DISAPPOINTED AND MORTIFIED, RETIRES FROM THE ARMY.

THE total failure for two years of the expeditions which had been fitted out at so much expense by the United States Government for the invasion of Canada, had considerably subdued that ardour for military renown which, at the commencement of the war—from the defenceless state of Canada, and the absorption of British strength in the European war—had promised so rich a harvest of laurels and territory to the United States. Nevertheless the most active exertions were made on both sides during the winter for the ensuing campaign. Stores of all descriptions were forwarded to Kingston from Quebec and Montreal on sleighs, at prodigious expense. The inhabitants of New Brunswick again evinced their loyalty and patriotism. Lieutenant-Colonel Robinson, with a regiment, marched through the woods from Fredericton to the St. Lawrence, in the month of February. A reinforcement of 220 seamen for the lakes came by the same route. To expedite the progress of these reinforcements, the Legislature of New

Brunswick voted £300, and the city of St. John gave a similar sum to defray the expense of conveying the troops and sailors on sleighs as far as the nature of the roads would permit.

On the 26th of March, His Excellency Sir George Prevost issued a General Order expressing the approbation of the Prince Regent of the affair of Chateauguay, and his "peculiar pleasure at finding that His Majesty's Canadian subjects had at length the opportunity of refuting, by their own brilliant exertions in defence of their country, the calumnious charges of disaffection and disloyalty with which the enemy had prefaced his first invasion of the province, to Lieutenant-Colonel De Salaberry in particular, and to all the officers and men under his command, the sense entertained by his Royal Highness of their meritorious and distinguished services, was made known.

The first movement of the Americans in the neighbourhood of Lake Champlain which gave room to expect an American invasion of the district of Montreal, was towards the conclusion of March, 1814, when Brigadier-General Macomb, with a division of American forces from Plattsburg, crossed Lake Champlain upon the ice, and entered St. Armand, where he remained some days, while General Wilkinson prepared for an attack upon the outposts of Odletown and the Le Colle Mill, which had been converted into a block-house. On the morning of the 13th of March (General Macomb having suddenly withdrawn his division from St. Armand's, and rejoined the main body), the American forces, consisting of 5,000 men, commanded by General Wilkinson in person, entered Odletown. The Americans repeated their attacks upon the coveted Le Colle Mill frontier; and the Canadian Fencibles, Frontier Light Infantry, and the Voltigeurs, repeated their deeds of bravery and heroism, and repelled the multitudinous invaders. "The Americans," says Mr. Christie, "exhausted with cold and fatigue, and finding it impossible to carry the place without heavy artillery, which, from the state of the roads, could not be brought forward, withdrew their forces in good order from the contest, at five o'clock in the afternoon, without being pursued in the retreat.

The British loss amounted to only ten men killed and four

men missing, and two officers and forty-four men wounded. The American loss, though considerable, could not be precisely ascertained.

Having failed in the attempt to carry the block-house (Le Colle Mill), scarcely deserving the appellation of a military post, the enemy fell back upon Champlain Town, from whence they returned to Plattsburg.

General Wilkinson, after this abortive attempt to retrieve his military fame, seems to have been removed from his command, or to have sought voluntary retirement from a service in which he had experienced nothing but disappointment and reverses.

PART II.

TAKING OF PRAIRIE DU CHIEN—DEFENCE OF MACKINAC—SUCCESS IN THE MARITIME PROVINCES.

Before noticing the military campaign of Upper Canada, we will complete the summary view of those which relate to the Maritime Provinces and Lower Canada.

During the occurrences of the taking of the post of *Prairie du Chién*, on the Mississippi, and the triumphant defence of *Michilimackinac*, Lieutenant-General Sir John C. Sherbrook, the Lieutenant-Governor of Nova Scotia, was successful in reducing a very populous and extensive portion of the enemy's territories adjacent to the Provinces of New Brunswick. He detached a small force from Halifax under Colonel Pilkington, while the Ramilies, commanded by Sir Thomas Hardie, took possession, on the 10th of July, of Mosé Island, in Passassamaquoddy Bay; the garrison at Fort Sullivan, consisting of six officers and eighty men, under the command of Major Putman, surrendering themselves prisoners of war.

On the 26th of August, Sir John C. Sherbrook, having embarked at Halifax the whole of his disposable forces on board of ten transports, set sail, accompanied by a small squadron under Rear-Admiral Griffith, for Castine, on the Penobscot river, where he arrived on the 1st of September, and took possession of the batteries at that place; the enemy finding it impossible to retain the post—having previously blown up the magazine, and retreated with the field-pieces.

The United States frigate *Adams* had, some days previous to the arrival of the British at Castine, run into the Penobscot river, and for security had gone up as far as Hampden, where her guns had been landed and a position taken, with a view of protecting her. Captain Barrie, of the *Dragon*, with a suitable naval force, and 600 picked men under the command of Colonel John, of the 6th Regiment, were detached up the river for the purpose of possessing or destroying the *Adams*. The enemy, who at first offered a spirited resistance, after setting fire to the frigate, fled in all directions, upon finding the British resolutely advancing against their positions. Several pieces of ordnance and three stands of colours fell into the hands of the British, whose loss amounted to no more than one man killed, and one officer and seven men wounded.

After the capture of Castine, Lieutenant-Colonel Pilkington was despatched with a brigade of troops for Madrias, which was taken possession of on the 11th of September by that officer—the detachment in Fort O'Brien having, on the approach of the British, precipitately retreated from the fort, leaving twenty-six pieces of ordnance, with a quantity of small arms and ammunition.

Lieutenant-Colonel Pilkington was on the point of marching into the interior of the country when he received a communication from Lieutenant-General Brewer, commander of the district, engaging that the militia forces within the County of Washington should not bear arms, or serve against his Britannic Majesty during the war. This, with a similar offer made by the civil officers and principal inhabitants of the county, brought on a cessation of arms.

By these judicious measures a populous extent of territory, stretching one hundred miles along the sea coast, including a valuable tract of country partly separating New Brunswick from Lower Canada, passed under the dominion of the British arms, without effusion of blood or the least waste of treasure.

PART III.

ENGLAND, FREE FROM THE EUROPEAN WAR, DETERMINES TO PUNISH THE UNITED STATES FOR THEIR JUNCTION WITH NAPOLEON AND INVASION OF CANADA—SWEEPS THE AMERICAN COASTS WITH HER FLEET, AND SENDS REINFORCEMENTS OF 16,000 MEN TO CANADA—FAILURE OF SIR GEORGE PREVOST'S ATTACK ON PLATTSBURG—HIS RECALL, AND SUMMONED TO BE TRIED BY COURT-MARTIAL—DIES BEFORE THE APPOINTED DAY OF TRIAL—ESTIMATE OF HIS CHARACTER.

Hitherto, for more than two years, the colonies had been thrown almost entirely upon their own prowess and resources, with the assistance of a few British soldiers, for their own defence against an invading enemy fifty times more populous than themselves. Up to this time England had been struggling against Napoleon for the liberties of Europe; but now the Corsican tiger was chained up in Elba; peace once more reigned in Europe, and England was now free to throw the whole weight of her victorious armies and unconquerable navy against the United States, whose treasury was bankrupt, whose people were disheartened at the reverses inflicted on their armies by handfuls of British and Canadians opposed to them, and whose loudest cry now was for peace; but the United States had refused peace when she could have had it, and Great Britain was now determined to punish her for her attacks on a peaceful colony, when the mother country was so thoroughly engaged elsewhere as to be almost forced to leave it to its own resources. Of the vigorous blockade of the American seaports, of the capture of Washington and burning of the capitol, etc., it is not necessary to speak in this place; we have only to do at present with the operations which took place in Canada during the summer of 1814.

During the summer about 16,000 British troops arrived at Quebec; but only 4,000 were sent to Upper Canada, under the command of General Kempt; and the Governor-General, Prevost, concentrated nearly the whole of the remainder of the reinforcements in the Richelieu district, with a view to a descent on the State of New York by way of Lake Champlain, at Plattsburg. In order to do this, the co-operation of the flotilla on the lake was considered necessary, and orders were given to put it in an efficient condition; but the flotilla was defeated and its vessels taken by the enemy; and the land forces, though they could have easily taken Plattsburg, did nothing, and were ordered to retreat within the British lines. The conduct of Sir George Prevost in this affair—undertaken for his own ambition, and without any public necessity—lost him all his military prestige; both officers and men felt the disgrace of retreating before an inferior force of militia; the valiant Colonel Murray and other officers protested against the retreat, and some of them indignantly broke their swords, declaring that they would never serve under him again. He was recalled to England, and under charges by Commodore Sir James Yeo, was arraigned before a court-martial, but died a week before the day appointed for his trial. Though Sir George Prevost was unsuccessful as a military commander—having disgracefully failed in the only two expeditions which he planned and personally superintended—the one against Sackett's Harbour and the other against Plattsburg—he was an excellent civil governor for Lower Canada, and an amiable and upright man.

It is alleged, however, that the Duke of Wellington and other high authorities approved of his conduct, and the Prince Regent showed marks of kindness to his family after his death. His health, which was never strong, suffered much, not only from mortification and mental anxiety in regard to his approaching trial (which he demanded at the earliest possible period), but by a winter's journey across the open country between the St. Lawrence and St. John, on his way home, that he died on the 5th of January, 1816, just one week before the court-martial appointed to examine into his conduct was to have been convened.

Mr. Christie, who was an English member of the Legislative Assembly of Lower Canada, and the author of an elaborate History of Canada, in six volumes, beside his excellent "History of the War of 1812," gives the following estimate of the character and Administration of Sir George Prevost:

"A warm and unswerving friend of the Canadian population, of French origin, he confided in and liberally patronized them from the commencement to the close of his administration; and they, it must be acknowledged, as generously responded to his confidence in them. No country or people ever exhibited greater unanimity or patriotism than did the people of Lower Canada of both origins, in the war of 1812 by the United States against Great Britain—a stand the more to be remembered by her Government, as these colonies, almost destitute of troops, wholly so of money, and scarcely possessing even a sufficiency of arms and other munitions of defence, owing to the more imperious calls from other quarters upon the Home Government, were, at the outset of the war, in a manner left to their own action and resources, and which they nobly exemplified, single-handed, as it were, throughout the first two campaigns. The principles of loyalty and duty, no doubt, were deeply implanted in the bosom of the people; but he it was who exalted them into enthusiasm and inspired the mass with a confidence in their own exertions and a reliance upon his wisdom, fitting them for the emergency, and that bore them successfully through the contest. Whatever may be the opinion now established of his talents, by the military world, the impression which the inhabitants of French origin in Lower Canada universally retain of him, is that of a conciliatory, wise, and able civil governor, and in all the relations of private life, an amiable and estimable man."*

PART IV.

UPPER CANADA—PREPARATIONS FOR THE CAMPAIGN—THE BRITISH FLEET INFERIOR ON LAKE ONTARIO—SUCCESSFUL EXPEDITION AGAINST OSWEGO—DESTRUCTION OF FORTIFICATIONS AND SEIZURE OF MUNITIONS OF WAR—BLOCKADES SACKETT'S HARBOUR—UNSUCCESSFUL ASCENT OF SANDY CREEK.

In Upper Canada the occurrences during the winter of 1814 were principally confined to incursions reciprocally practised by troops in advance along the frontiers with various successes, but with no important results on either side. After the winter's preparations, the campaign was opened in Upper Canada by Sir Gordon Drummond and Sir James L. Yeo, under most cheering circumstances. The American forces along the Lake Champlain, after leaving small garrisons at Plattsburg, Burlington, and Vergennes, moved early in the spring towards Lake

* History of the War of 1812.

Ontario and the Niagara frontier, with a view of assuming offensive operations against Upper Canada, as soon as the fleet in Sackett's Harbour (considerably augmented during the winter) should be in a state to co-operate with the land forces. The principal naval stores for the equipment of the fleet were forwarded to Sackett's Harbour by the way of Oswego; and as the British naval force at Kingston, strengthened by two additional ships, the *Prince Regent* and the *Princess Charlotte*, were ready to appear on the lake early in the season, it became an object of importance to intercept the enemy's supplies, and by that means retard his preparations for invasion. An *expedition against Oswego* was therefore determined upon, and General Drummond having embarked a considerable force, consisting of six companies of De Watteville's Regiment, the Light Company of Glengarries, the 2nd Battalion of Royal Marines, with a detachment of Royal Artillery, and two field-pieces, a detachment of the Rocket Company, with a few Sappers and Miners, set sail from Kingston the 4th of May, and at noon on the following day made the port of Oswego, when a heavy gale from the north-west sprung up and obliged the squadron to gain the offing. On the morning of the 6th, a landing was effected by about 140 of the troops, under Lieutenant-Colonel Fisher, and 200 seamen, armed with pikes, under the command of Captain Mulcaster, R.N., in front of a heavy discharge of round and grape from the battery, and of musketry from a detachment of about 300 men of the American army, posted on the brow of the hill, and in the skirts of the neighbouring wood. The British, on landing, pressed up the hill towards the enemy's battery, which the Americans (upon finding the British determined to carry it by storm) relinquished, leaving about sixty men, principally wounded.

The land and naval commanders having taken possession of the stores found in the fort and its neighbourhood, and having dismantled the fortifications and destroyed the barracks, re-embarked on the 7th of May, and returned to Kingston.

The loss of the British troops amounted to one captain (Holtaway, of the Marines) and eighteen men killed, and two officers and sixty men wounded. That of the navy amounted to three men killed, and four officers and seven men wounded. Captain Mulcaster, while entering the fort at the head of his men, received a very severe and dangerous wound. Captain Popham was also severely wounded.

Although the service derived much benefit from this expedition, the main object contemplated was not accomplished, the principal part of the naval stores being saved by the enemy, who had taken the precaution of depositing them at the Falls, some miles from Oswego, up the river.

The British squadron having, for the present, a decided ascendency on Lake Ontario, blockaded Sackett's Harbour, in order to intercept the supplies which might, from time to time, be forwarded from Oswego for the equipment of the American fleet. On the 29th of May, they captured a boat laden with two twenty-four-pounders, and a large cable for one of the American ships of war, and, with two gun-boats and five barges, pursued fifteen other boats, loaded with naval and military stores, and which took shelter in Sandy Creek; but they were met in the Creek by an American force, consisting of 150 riflemen, nearly 200 Indians, and a strong body of militia and cavalry, which overpowered the British party, of whom eighteen were killed and fifty wounded—the rest being taken prisoners. Captain Popham, in his official dispatch to Sir James L. Yeo, on this affair, acknowledged with warmest gratitude the humane exertions of the American officers of the Rifle Corps, commanded by Major Appling, in saving the lives of many of the officers and men, whom the American soldiers and Indians were devoting to slaughter.

CHAPTER LVIII.

LAST INVASIONS AND LAST BATTLES OF THE WAR.

PART I.

GENERAL BROWN TAKES FORT ERIE—DEFEATS GENERAL RIALL ON THE PLAINS OF CHIPPEWA—ADVANCES TO FORT GEORGE—HIS OFFICERS AND ARMY PLUNDER THE INHABITANTS—RETREATS BACK TO CHIPPEWA— BURNS THE VILLAGE OF ST. DAVID'S ON THE WAY.

ON the Niagara frontier, the American army commanded by General Brown, and consisting of about 7,000 men, began early in the summer to concentrate at Buffalo, Black Rock, and other points, and on the 3rd of July invaded Canada in two brigades, under the command of Brigadier-Generals Scott and Ripley. They embarked in boats and batteaux, and effected a landing on the Canada side of the river without opposition—one brigade landing about a mile above, and the other brigade a mile below Fort Erie. The fort was under the command of Major Buck, of the 8th Regiment, with about seventy men of his regiment; it had been put in a state of defence by that officer, with a view of causing a temporary check to an invading force, rather than for the purpose of defending it against a regular siege. But Major Buck was so careful of himself and his men as to abandon the fort without firing a shot—an error fatal to the British—for although Fort Erie could not have been held for any length of time against the overwhelming strength of the enemy, still a few hours' defence would have enabled General Riall to concentrate his forces and attack the Americans before they were firmly established on Canadian soil. The able dispositions which General Riall had made of the forces under his command along the Niagara line by the direction of General Drummond, who had anticipated an invasion at that point where it commenced, were such, that the least impediment to the progress of the invaders would have enabled General Riall to have concentrated his troops, and to have fallen upon and dispersed the enemy before they could have time to be prepared for an effectual resistance. As it was, the Americans were permitted to occupy this important post without resistance, and transfer, unmolested, to the Canadian side all the troops they pleased.

On the following day, General Brown advanced with his whole force, of over 4,000 men, down the river to the plains of Chippewa, with the intention of taking possession of the British post at the mouth of the Chippewa or Welland river. General Riall, having collected what forces he could, consisting of five companies of the Royal Scots, a part of the 8th or King's Regiment, a part of the 100th Regiment, and the 2nd Lincoln Militia, amounting in all to about 1,500 men, determined to check him, until further assistance should arrive. A series of manœuvres ensued on both sides, and the most furious battle hitherto occurring during the war, followed, when General Riall, finding himself no longer able to sustain the fight against a force so unequal in universal strength, gave orders to abandon the field—his troops retiring in the rear of the works at Chippewa and destroying the bridge across the river, which they had previously repaired.

The loss on both sides is said to have been nearly equal—amounting to between 400 and 500 on each side.

"The 2nd Lincoln Militia, under Major David Secord, distinguished themselves in this action by feats of genuine bravery and heroism, animated by the example of their gallant leader, which are seldom surpassed even by the most experienced veterans. Their loss was proportionate with that of the regular army.

"Three or four days subsequent to this sanguinary battle on the plains of Chippewa were mostly employed in burying their own dead, and in burning those of the British, after which several ineffectual efforts were made by General Brown to cross the Chippewa river, contemplating an advance on Fort George; but at each of his attempts he was promptly met by picket guards of the British, posted along the margin of the river for that purpose.

General Riall, however, in a few days gave orders that the remnant of his army should retire under the shelter of Fort George and Mississagua until reinforcements could be collected to place him on more equal ground with the enemy; after which General Brown moved his army towards those posts within a mile and a half of the British—his army forming a crescent; his right resting on Niagara river, his left on Lake Ontario.

The American army had no sooner taken up a position in front of Fort George than their foraging parties, or rather marauders, commenced a systematic course of plunder upon the defenceless inhabitants within the vicinity of their camp, most of whom, at the time, consisted of women and children. Even amongst general officers were acts of pillage perpetrated, that, had such occurred with private soldiers in the British army, would have stamped on the character of the British, in the eyes of America, for which no course of conduct which they could ever after have pursued, would have sufficiently atoned.

During the interval in which General Riall was receiving reinforcements from York and other military posts on that side of Lake Ontario, General Brown also received a strong reinforcement under General Izard, after which he made a few ineffectual assaults on Fort George; but, finding all his efforts to carry that fort fruitless, and the British army receiving fresh acquisitions of strength, all seemed to conspire to render the case of General Brown hopeless; who, now perceiving the situation in which he was placed—the forts in his front to him completely impregnable, and an army in his rear in full flow of spirits, and every day gathering new strength (though by no means equal to his as regarded numbers), a Canadian Militia, and unexpectedly to him, fervent beyond a parallel in the cause of their King and country—began now to think of a safe retreat, in pursuance of which, on the morning of the 25th of July, he commenced his retrograde movement; he retreated towards Chippewa, after burning the village of St. David's. Riall pushed on in pusuit, when the Americans halted at Lundy's Lane (called Bridgewater by the Americans), where took place the most stubborn fight of the war—known as *the Battle of Lundy's Lane*—which may be regarded as terminating the American invasions of Canada, and the last field battle of the war.

We will here give a brief account of this celebrated battle, from Thompson's History of the War of 1812, and the events which followed at Fort Erie, and afterwards we will review the transactions of this battle, together with the true principles of loyalty, the causes and character of the war, and the reciprocal relations between Great Britain, Canada and the United States.

PART II.

BATTLE OF LUNDY'S LANE—PRELIMINARIES.

"The British army, at the time General Brown commenced his retreat from Fort George and Queenston to Chippewa, was scattered in small cantonments over twenty or thirty miles of country; but like a well-ordered and systematic machine, every part was in a moment simultaneously in motion, to concentrate their united strength at a point where they would be likely to intercept the enemy.

"Detachments of the Royal Scots and 41st Regiments, and a small body of Indians, amounting in all to about 500 men, under the command of Colonel Tucker (supported on the river by a party of seamen and marines under the direction of Captain Dobbs, of the Royal Navy), passed over to the American side of the River Niagara, with a view to disperse or capture a body of the enemy stationed at Lewiston. The object of this movement being accomplished, the troops were again withdrawn at Queenston. The 41st and 100th Regiments, under Colonel Tucker, were sent back to garrison Fort George, Mississagua, and Niagara; General Drummond moving on towards the falls, with a force of about 800 strong, consisting of detachments of the Royal Scots, 89th, and King's, with the light company of the 41st Regiment, to join General Riall's division of the army as soon as it could arrive from the several bivouacs at which it had been stationed.

"As soon as the column of the British army under the command of Lieutenant-Colonel Morrison had arrived at the rising ground near the end of Lundy's Lane, on the main road leading from Queenston to Chippewa, the enemy was just taking possession of that position. Without a moment's delay, the troops which had arrived on the ground were formed in line on the north-east side of the height, their left resting on the Queenston road.

"The troops from the Twelve and Twenty Mile Creeks, together with a detachment of the King's Regiment, as they arrived, were formed on each side of Lundy's Lane. This line was supported in front by two twenty-four-pounders [fieldguns], which were covered by a small squadron of the 19th Light Dragoons and a detachment of the infantry.

"*The battle itself.*—The troops of the line being thus disposed, notwithstanding the superior strength of the enemy, in about ten minutes dislodged him from the position he had first taken, at the point of the bayonet.

"The sun was now fast descending towards the western horizon; and detachments of the 1st and 2nd Lincoln Militia continued to arrive from the different outposts they had been occupying, who joined in maintaining the summit of the hill until the whole of General Riall's division should come up.

"General Drummond, after dislodging the enemy from the partial possession he had gained on the hill, again formed his line with as much despatch as existing circumstances would admit, placing his artillery, which consisted of two twenty-pounders, two six-pounders [brass field-pieces], and a rocket party, in front of the centre of his position, near the right side of Lundy's Lane, leading down the hill to the Queenston road, supported by the 2nd battalion of the 89th Regiment, under Colonel Morrison. Scarcely had this arrangement been completed before the position was furiously assailed by General Winfield Scott's brigade at the point of the bayonet; but the enemy was repulsed with great slaughter. A tremendous fire was then commenced on the crest of the British position, by the first brigade of the enemy, stationed near the copse between Lundy's Lane and the Falls of Niagara, and the 9th and 22nd Regiments and Captain Lawson's brigade of artillery, stationed on the Queenston road.

"During this stage of the engagement, the Light Company of Royal Scots arrived on the ground from the Twenty Mile

Creek; and a courier was despatched to countermand the route of the 103rd Regiment, and the detachment of the King's and 104th Regiments, who had, in a mistake, taken the road to Queenston from the Beach Woods, and to hasten their movement to the field of action.

"On the brow of the hill, at the east end of Lundy's Lane, for the possession of which the armies hitherto had principally contended, General Drummond had now planted his artillery, as it appeared to form the key to the position. On this quarter, therefore, the enemy for a length of time directed his whole efforts; and notwithstanding the carnage was truly appalling, no visible impression had yet been made. Still on this part of the field did the whirlwind of the conflict rage with awful and destructive fury; columns of the enemy, not unlike the undulating surge of the adjacent cataract, rushed to the charge in close and impetuous succession.

"In this fearful and tremendous stage of the contest, the British forces, both regulars and militia, finding themselves pressed by an overwhelming force, simultaneously closed round the guns, apparently determined to contest their possession with the last drop of British blood on the ground, fully assured of their importance to a favourable termination of the engagement —in short both armies appeared to be roused to a state of desperation for victory.

"The enemy at length succeeded to make a slight turn on the left of the British position; at which period, General Riall, who commanded that division of the army, was severely wounded in the arm, and having passed to the rear for the purpose of having his wound dressed, on his return to resume the command, was intercepted by a column of the enemy and made prisoner of war.

"It was long before this crisis of the engagement that the curtain of night had enveloped the scene; but instead of this circumstance abating the fury of war, which had now completely drenched the field with the blood of the combatants, the rage of battle appeared only to increase as the night advanced. Still did the enemy continue to direct his strongest force against the crest of the British position; but his repeated charges were as often received and repelled by the regular, fencible, and militia forces engaged, with that intrepid gallantry for which the British army was ever characterized. Charges were made in such rapid succession and with such determined vigour that often were the British artillerymen assailed in the very act of springing and charging their guns; and often were the muzzles of the guns of the contending armies hauled up and levelled within a few yards of each other. The havoc of lives on both sides, under such circumstances, may be better conceived than described.

"The battle having raged with almost unprecedented fury for upwards of three hours, both sides appeared for a time mutually to suspend hostilities; during which the British troops were supplied with fresh ammunition, and the enemy employed himself actively in bringing up his reserve columns; after which, the fire was recommenced from the Queenston road, on the left of the British column; however, it was discovered that this was only a diversion to mask the intention of a large body of the enemy's fresh troops, which was actually moving on the right of the British position, to outflank it. General Drummond commenced immediately to draw his strength towards this flank of the army, forming a line in a field of grain, upon which the enemy were seen to advance in slow and silent pace The British line formed to repel this new attack was directed to kneel sufficiently low to prevent being perceived by the enemy; but scarcely had General Drummond completed this order of arrangement, before the enemy's column made its appearance and advanced within a few yards of the British line, when the signal was made to fire a volley and charge. The effect of that single fire upon the enemy's ranks was awful in the extreme—those of the enemy who were able made a precipitate retreat.

"'The enemy's efforts to carry the hill,' says General Drummond, in his official report, 'were continued until midnight, when he had suffered so severely from the superior steadiness and discipline of his Majesty's troops, that he gave up the contest and retreated with great precipitation to his camp beyond the Chippewa, burning, as he passed the (Street) flour mills at Bridgewater. On the following day he abandoned his camp, threw the greatest part of his baggage, camp equipage, and provisions into the rapids above the falls; and destroying the bridge at Chippewa, he continued his retreat in great disorder towards Fort Erie.

"'The loss sustained by the enemy,' adds General Drummond, 'in this severe action, cannot be estimated at less than 1,500 men, including several prisoners left in our hands. Generals Brown and Scott were among the wounded. His whole force, which was never rated at less than 5,000 men, were all engaged.'

"In General Drummond's report of this action, the total number of killed, wounded, and missing of the British army was 878.

"By the regimental returns of the British army, including those of the militia, both before and after this engagement, the whole British force consisted of 2,800; but before the arrival of the troops under Colonel Scott, of the 103rd Regiment, it did not exceed 1,600.

"Of all the battles (says a writer on this subject) fought in America, the action of Lundy's Lane was unquestionably the best sustained and by far the most sanguinary. The rapid charges and real contest with the bayonet were themselves sufficient to render this engagement conspicuous. Traits of real bravery and heroic devotion were that night displayed by those engaged, which would not suffer in comparison with those exhibited at the storming of St. Sebastian, or the conflict of Quatre Bras.

"Both the belligerent armies have offered their claims for victory in this engagement. Upon what grounds the American general could propose such a claim are best known to himself— General Brown not only abandoned the plans of operations which he had formed previous to the action at Lundy's Lane [of advancing to Queenston, Fort George, and Burlington Heights], but 'retreated in great disorder towards Fort Erie,' where his egress from the territory might be more easy; and in his way destroyed the bridge at Chippewa, in order to retard the advance of the British light troops in his rear."*

* Thompson's History of the War of 1812, Chap. xxx.

PART III.

AMERICAN ARMY RETREATS TO FORT ERIE, PURSUED BY GENERAL DRUMMOND, WHO INVESTS THE FORT—UNSUCCESSFUL ATTEMPTS TO STORM IT—SORTIE OF THE WHOLE AMERICAN FORCE, TWICE THAT OF GENERAL DRUMMOND, BUT DEFEATED—RAIN COMPELS THE RAISING OF THE SIEGE—GENERAL BROWN EVACUATES THE FORT AND CROSSES THE RIVER TO THE AMERICAN SIDE, AND THUS ENDS THE THREE YEARS' INVASIONS OF CANADA, WITHOUT ACQUIRING AN INCH OF ITS TERRITORY.

On the American army reaching Fort Erie, they entrenched and strengthened the fortifications of the fort. Thither General Drummond pursued, and immediately invested the fort, although his army was not half the strength of the American army. General Drummond having reconnoitred the enemy's position, determined to storm his entrenchments. On the 13th of August, General Drummond, having completed his batteries, commenced a brisk cannonade on the position of the enemy, which, with few interruptions, was continued for two days with great effect; after which he was determined to carry the fort and outworks by nocturnal assault. In pursuance of this purpose, he formed his troops into three divisions: the first, under Lieutenant-Colonel Fischer, of De Watteville's, consisting of the King's Regiment, the regiment of De Watteville, and flank companies of the 89th and 100th Regiments, directed against the enemy's entrenchments at and near Snake Hill; the second, under Lieutenant-Colonel Drummond, of the 104th Regiment, consisting of the 41st and 104th Regiments, and a body of seamen and marines under the direction of Captain Dobbs, of the Royal Navy, against the fort; and the third, under Colonel Scott, consisting of his own regiment, supported by two companies of the Royals, against the entrenchments adjoining the fort.

About two o'clock on the morning of the 15th, the several divisions of the British army moved towards the enemy's entrenchments; but as soon as the column against Snake Hill had emerged from the woods, it came in contact with an abatis within twelve or fifteen yards of the enemy's entrenchments, defended by a heavy column of infantry, under the command of Major Wood, and the artillery under Captain Towson. This for a time completely checked his advance.

However, it was soon announced by a tremendous fire from the guns in the fort, and from the columns of infantry defending the entrenchments near the shore of the lake, that the other two columns, under Lieutenant-Colonels Scott and Drummond, had commenced an assault upon the enemy's works.

At the first outset of the two last columns, the enemy succeeded in turning the column on the left, under Colonel Scott; but that under Colonel Drummond penetrated the enemy's works and charged through his ranks with such irresistible impetuosity that nothing seemed sufficiently impregnable to arrest its progress. Lieutenant-Colonel Scott in the meantime rallied his column, which had been partially turned on one flank, and the fort was assailed in almost every quarter by the besiegers; an escalade was effected, the enemy driven from the ramparts at the point of the bayonet, and the guns of the fort turned upon the garrison; all of which preludes to victory had actually been gained a few minutes after the first alarm.

The battle raged with a fury seldom equalled. The British troops, in pursuance of an order to that effect, having previously divested their muskets of the flints, every foot of ground was contested at the point of the bayonet, which rendered the carnage more dreadful and appalling.

Lieutenant-Colonel Drummond (brother of General Drummond), during the conflict within the fort, performed extraordinary acts of valour. In the hottest of the battle he presented himself, encouraging his men, both by example and precept. But at the very moment when victory was declaring in favour of the British arms, some ammunition which had been placed under the platform ignited, and a dreadful explosion was the result, by which the greater part of the British forces, which had entered the fort, were literally blown into the air.* All exertions of the few British troops who sur-

---

* As in the storming of the fort at York, the explosion which took place was and is a matter of dispute, and as to whether the explosion was accidental, or caused by the British; so it is a matter of unsettled dispute as to whether the explosion of Fort Erie was caused by the Americans, or was accidental. General Pike was killed in the explosion which took place in the fort at York, and Colonels Drummond and Scott were killed at the explosion of Fort Erie: many of the British and Canadians were killed in the explosion in the fort at York, but none of the Americans were killed at the explosion in Fort Erie.

vived the explosion were found ineffectual to maintain their ground, in the panic of the moment, against such an unequal force as the enemy was enabled to bring up against them, and the British forces were compelled to retire.

In this assault the loss of the British was severe. Colonels Scott and Drummond fell, while storming the works, at the head of their respective columns. General Drummond reported the killed, wounded, and missing, officers and men, as 904. The missing were reported at nine officers and 530 men—afterwards ascertained to have been principally killed. The American statement of their own loss made it 84 in killed, wounded, and missing.

A day or two after this assault, General Drummond was reinforced by the arrival of the 6th and 82nd Regiments from Lower Canada; but this reinforcement was barely sufficient to supply recent losses. He deemed it unadvisable to attempt a second storming of the fort against a force twice as numerous as his own; but by continuing the investment, he cut off all communication of the enemy with the surrounding country, cooped him up in the fort, compelled him to draw his provisions and other resources from his own country, and thus rendered his occupation of that fort for the remainder of the campaign of no service to the invaders.

At about the expiration of a month, General Brown, having recovered of his wounds, again resumed command of the army on the Niagara frontier, and brought with him a strong reinforcement, resolving to attempt the destruction of the British batteries in front of Fort Erie. Pursuant to this determination, General Brown, on the 17th of September, at about noon, ordered a sortie of the whole American force, including both regulars and militia, in three divisions, under Generals Porter, Miller, and Ripley; and before the ready and reserved columns of the British could be brought from the camp (about a mile in the rear), the enemy had succeeded in penetrating the batteries, destroying the works with one magazine of ammunition, and spiking the guns. But ere he could effect his retreat, the ready and reserve columns arrived, and immediately commenced a determined attack upon his columns, and after about half an hour's desperate fighting, notwithstanding his great superiority of numbers, he retired before the bayonets of the British line, in great precipitation, under the cover of his works, after losing nearly 600 of his force.

The incessant rains which had fallen that season rendered it impossible for General Drummond to repair his batteries, or, indeed, to keep the field, on account of the exposure and increased sickness of the troops; he therefore, on the 21st of September, raised the siege and retired into winter quarters, in rear of his works at the mouth of the Chippewa.

General Brown affected some inclination to follow on the rear of the British army; yet, notwithstanding all the efforts which could possibly be exercised by a general were called into contribution by General Drummond to bring General Brown into action, it all proved unavailing. The American general, "as soon as the coast was clear," having blown up the works, evacuated Fort Erie, and retreated across the river into his own country.

Thus terminated the campaign of 1814 on the Niagara frontier; and whatever might have been the object of the American Government when they sent that last army to invade Canada, it is certain that nothing was acquired, if we except a fresh proof (if such had been now necessary) of the loyalty of the Canadian people to their Sovereign, and their unshaken zeal to defend their country from the grip of its enemy, at whatever time he might think proper to invade it.*

PART IV.

REVIEW.

The author cannot better present a summary review of the true principles of loyalty, the origin, causes, characteristics, and results of the war of 1812-15, together with the conduct of the inhabitants of Canada in respect to it, than in the words of an address which he delivered to the York Pioneers at Queenston, in July, 1875, on the occasion of the anniversary celebration of the battle of Lundy's Lane. The address (which

---

* The greater part of the foregoing accounts of the campaign of 1814 are extracted and condensed from Thompson's and Christie's Histories of the War of 1812, compared with other histories of the same events.

was entirely extemporaneous in the delivery) is here reproduced, as reported in the newspapers at the time:

"CAUSES OF THE WAR DECLARED BY THE UNITED STATES AGAINST GREAT BRITAIN, JUNE 18, 1812—CANADIAN DEFENCE—BATTLE OF LUNDY'S LANE, FOUGHT JULY 25, 1814.

"Address delivered by the Rev. Dr. Ryerson before the York Pioneers and other Associations assembled on Queenston Heights, near Brock's Monument, met at a pic-nic on Monday, July 26th, 1875, to celebrate the battle of Lundy's Lane.

"The Chairman, Colonel R. Denison, called upon Dr. Ryerson, who was warmly received.

"After a few preliminary observations, he said that he felt it a great privilege to be called on to address a number of those Canadians who had laid the foundation of our country, who had given Canada a name that was honoured throughout the world, and whose hearts beat responsive to those noble principles that made England the glory of all nations, and British institutions the honour of mankind. (Loud applause.) He thought the York Pioneers might well be called the Canadian Pioneers —the pioneers of Canadian industry, enterprise, freedom, and civilization. The object of the Society in giving an intelligent intensity to those principles that constituted the loyalty of the people of Canada, in preserving the traditions of the country, and in uniting in one centre the various elements of scattered light which were connected with the earliest rays of its opening history, were works well worthy of the defenders of the liberties of this country. The very foundation of the York Pioneers was a spirit of loyalty. What was that loyalty itself? It was no other than an attachment to the institutions and laws of the land in which we live, and to the history of the nation to which we belong. It was not merely a sentiment of respect of the country to an individual, or even to the Sovereign. If it gathered round the person of the Sovereign, it was because that Sovereign represented the institutions of the people, the overshadowing laws of the people, the real and essential freedom, and the noblest development of the spirit of the people. Loyalty in its true essence and meaning was the principle of respect to our Sovereign, the freedom of our institutions, and the excellencies of our civilization, and it was therefore a feeling worthy to be perpetuated by the people. Shakespeare—that great apostle of human nature—has said :

> " ' Though *loyalty*, well held, to fools does make
> Our faith mere folly ; yet he that can endure
> To follow with allegiance a fallen lord,
> Does conquer him that did his master conquer.'

Loyalty is, therefore, faithful to its own principles, whether the personal object of it is in prosperity or adversity.

> " ' Loyalty is still the same,
> Whether it win or lose the game ;
> True as the dial to the sun,
> Though it be not shone upon.'

Hence, says Lord Clarendon, of a statesman of his time, ' He had no veneration for the Court, but only such loyalty to the King as the law required.' True loyalty is, therefore, fidelity to the Constitution, laws, and institutions of the land, and, of course, to the sovereign power representing them.

" Thus was it with our Loyalist forefathers. There was no class of inhabitants of the old British-American Colonies more decided and earnest than they in claiming the rights of British subjects when invaded ; yet when, instead of maintaining the rights of British subjects, it was proposed to renounce the allegiance of British subjects and destroy the unity of the empire, or ' the life of the nation ' (as our American neighbours expressed it, in their recent civil war to maintain the unity of their republic), then were our forefathers true to their loyalty, and adhered to the unity of the empire at the sacrifice of property and home, and often of life itself. Of them might be said, what Milton says of Abdiel, amid the revolting hosts:

> " ' Abdiel, faithful found ;
> Unshaken, unseduced, unterrified,
> His loyalty he kept.'

Our United Empire Loyalist forefathers 'kept their loyalty unshaken, unseduced, unterrified,' during seven long years of conflicts and sufferings ; and that loyalty, with a courage and enterprise, and under privations and toils unsurpassed in human history, sought a refuge and a home in the wilderness of Canada, felled the forests of our country, and laid the foundation of its institutions, freedom, and prosperity. (Loud applause.)

"Canadian loyalty is the perpetuation of that British national life which has constituted the strength and glory of Great Britain since the morning of the Protestant Reformation, and placed her at the head of the freedom and civilization of mankind. This loyalty maintains the characteristic traditions of the nation—the mysterious links of connection between grandfather and grandson—traditions of strength and glory for a people, and the violations of which are a source of weakness and disorganization. Canadian loyalty, therefore, is not a mere sentiment, or mere affection for the representative or person of the Sovereign; it is a reverence for, and attachment to, the laws, order, institutions and freedom of the country. As Christianity is not a mere attachment to a bishop, or ecclesiastic, or form of church polity, but a deep love of divine truth; so Canadian loyalty is a firm attachment to that British Constitution and those British laws, adopted or enacted by ourselves, which best secure life, liberty, and prosperity, and which prompt us to Christian and patriotic deeds by linking us with all that is grand and noble in the traditions of our national history.

"In the war of 1812 to 1815—one of the last and hardest-fought battles was that of Lundy's Lane, which we meet this day, on this historic ground, to celebrate—both the loyalty and courage of the Canadian people were put to the severest test, and both came out of the fiery ordeal as refined gold. Nothing could be more disgraceful and unprincipled than the Madison (I will not say American) declaration of war against Great Britain, which was at that moment employing her utmost strength and resources in defence of European nations and the liberties of mankind. That scourge of modern Europe—the heartless tyrant, but great soldier, Napoleon—had laid prostrate at his feet all the Governments of Western and Central Europe, England alone excepted. To destroy British power, he issued decrees first at Berlin, in 1806, and afterwards at Milan, excluding all British merchandize from French ports, and prohibiting the use of British commodities throughout France and her dependencies, under severe penalties; searching neutral vessels for British goods, and confiscating them when found, with the vessels carrying them; interdicting all neutral vessels from trading with any British port; declaring all the ports of Great Britain and of her dependencies to be in a state of blockade, though at the very moment the English fleet commanded the seas. These Napoleon decrees violated the laws of nations, and affected the national rights and independence of the United States, as well as of the European nations; and had not President Madison and his war faction been in league with Napoleon, they would have resented it, instead of silently submitting, and thus becoming a party to it. In self-defence and retaliation upon the tyrant Napoleon, Great Britain, in January, 1807, issued Decrees of Council, declaring all French ports in a state of blockade, and declaring all vessels of neutrals liable to seizure which should engage in trade with France; and as the Napoleon decrees had declared all vessels of any nation liable to seizure which had touched at any British port, the English Orders of Council, to counteract this decree, declared, on the other hand, that only such ships as had touched at a British port should be permitted to sail for a port of France. The American President, Madison, being in league with the French usurper against Great Britain, made no remonstrance against the Napoleon decrees of Berlin and Milan, but raised a great outcry against the counter English Orders in Council, and made them a pretext for declaring war against Great Britain. But President Madison not only thus leagued with Napoleon to destroy British commerce, but also to weaken the British army and navy by seducing some 10,000 British sailors and soldiers to desert on board of American vessels, where they were claimed as American citizen sailors.

"England had always claimed the right to search and claim her deserting sailors on board foreign vessels, and that right had never been disputed by the United States, until now, under the teachings of Napoleon. But though there was no occasion for the exercise of such a right in a time of general peace, the exercise of it then was a matter vital to the existence and strength of the British navy; but, under the promptings of Napoleon, President Madison made it not only a subject of loud complaint, but also an additional pretext for war. Yet, to keep up some appearance of fairness, but in secret intrigue with Napoleon, the Madison Administration issued a declaration to open commercial relations with either of the belligerent powers that should first rescind the prohibitory decrees or orders. In May, 1812, Napoleon rescinded the Berlin and Milan decrees so far as concerned the United States, but had the unparalleled meanness to antedate them *thirteen* months, and even apply them to 1810, dating them April, 1811, in order to play into the hands of his American confederates. Within a month after Napoleon had rescinded the Berlin and Milan decrees—June 23rd, 1812—the British Government cancelled the Orders in Council so far as related to the United States; but five days before that, the 18th of June, President Madison declared war against Britain, and then when, six weeks afterwards, he was duly informed of the cancelling of these Orders in Council, on which he had professed to declare war, he refused to ratify an armistice agreed upon between Sir George Prevost and General Dearborn, until the British and American Governments could confer with a view to prevent any further prosecution of the war. Madison and his faction of British haters and war adventurers naturally supposed, that as Upper Canada consisted of 70,000 inhabitants, and as the British troops were all engaged in the deadly war with France, except guards of regular soldiers in the Canadian garrisons, our country would fall an easy prey to his ambition; Great Britain would be humbled at the feet of Napoleon, and France and the United States would then divide the power and commerce of Europe and America. But British and Canadian loyalty, patriotism, and courage defeated their dark designs against the liberties of mankind. Even the patriotic and intellectual part of the American people denounced this unholy intrigue between their own President and the bloody ursurper of Europe, and this causeless war against Great Britain. The Legislative Assemblies of Massachusetts, Connecticut, Rhode Island, New Jersey, and Maryland condemned the war policy of President Madison, and some of them declared it to be but a party proceeding of the President and his minions to keep themselves in power and subsidize their hungry partizans. Only a small majority of Congress approved the declaration of war. A convention of the great State of New York, held at Albany, September, 1812, consisting of delegates from the several counties of the State, embodied, in elaborate resolutions, the intelligent American sentiment on the subject of the war. That convention declared: 'That, without insisting on the injustice of the present war, taking solely into consideration the time and circumstances of its declaration, the condition of the country, and the state of the public mind, we are constrained to consider and feel it our duty to pronounce it a most rash, unwise and inexpedient measure, the adoption of which ought forever to deprive its authors of the esteem and confidence of an enlightened people; because, as the injuries we have received from France are at least equal in amount to those we have sustained from England, and have been attended with circumstances of still greater insult and aggravation; if war were necessary to vindicate the honour of the country, consistency and impartiality required that both nations should have been included in the declaration; because, if it were deemed expedient to exercise our right of selecting our adversary, prudence and common sense dictated the choice of an enemy from whose hostility we had nothing to dread. A war with France would equally have satisfied our insulted honour, and, at the same time, instead of annihilating, would have revived and extended our commerce; and even the evils of such a contest would have been mitigated by the sublime consolation, that by our efforts we were contributing to arrest the progress of despotism in Europe, and effectually serving the great interests of freedom and humanity throughout the world.' 'That we contemplate with abhorrence, even the probability of an alliance with the present Emperor of France, every action of whose life has demonstrated, that the attainment, by any means, of universal empire, and the consequent extinction of every vestige of freedom, are the sole objects of his incessant, unbounded and remorseless ambition.' 'Whereas the late revocation of the British Orders in Council has removed the great and ostensible cause of the present war, and prepared the way for an immediate accommodation of all existing differences, inasmuch as, by the confession of the present Secretary of State, satisfactory and honourable arrangements might easily be made, by which the abuse resulting from the impressment of our seamen might, in future, be effectually prevented.'

"Such were the sentiments of the most intelligent and

patriotic American citizens in regard to the war of 1812-15; they had no more sympathy with the Madison-Napoleon war than with the recent Fenian invasion of our shores. And when the war was declared, our fathers knew their duty, and knew the worthlessness of the pompous proclamations and promises of President Madison's generals and agents. The blood of our United Empire Loyalist forefathers warmed again in their own bosoms, and pulsated in the hearts of their sons and grandsons, and in the hearts of hundreds of others who had adopted Canada, under the flag of British law and liberty, as their home. Our Legislative Assembly—specially called together by General Brock, on the declaration of war—struck the key-note for Canadian loyalty, sacrifice and action, in a calm, expository and earnest address to the people of Upper Canada, and truly represented the already roused spirit of the country. Some of the words of that noble address are as follows:

"'This war, on the part of the United States, includes an alliance with the French usurper, whose dreadful policy has destroyed all that is great and grand, venerable and holy, on the continent of Europe. The government of this bloody tyrant penetrates into everything—it crushes individuals as well as nations, fetters thoughts as well as motives, and delights in destroying forever all that is fair and just in opinion and sentiment. It is evidently this tyrant who now directs the rulers of America, and they show themselves worthy disciples of such a master.'

"After noting the juncture selected for declaring war, the address proceeds: 'It is certainly not the least wonderful among the occurrences of this astonishing age, that we should find a nation descended from Englishmen, connected still by the same language and laws, by consanguinity and many similar habits, not merely eulogizing the implacable enemy of their parent state, but joining him in the war; while pretending to nourish the purest principles of liberty, bowing the knee before the foe of all just and rational freedom, and supplicating his acceptance of tribute and adulation.' After sketching the origin and sustained loyalty of the first inhabitants of the country, the Assembly said: 'Already have we the joy to remark, that the spirit of loyalty has burst forth in all its ancient splendour. The militia in all parts of the Province have volunteered their services with acclamation, and displayed a degree of energy worthy of the British name. When men are called upon to defend everything they hold precious, their wives and children, their friends and possessions, they ought to be inspired with the noblest resolutions, and they will not be easily frightened by menaces, or conquered by force. And beholding, as we do, the flame of patriotism burning from end to end of the Canadas, we cannot but entertain the most pleasing anticipations. Our enemies have indeed said, that they can subdue this country by a proclamation; but it is our part to prove that they are sadly mistaken.' 'If the real foundations of true liberty, and consequently of solid happiness, consist in being amenable only to such laws as we or our representatives ordain, then are we in possession of that liberty and that happiness, for this principle was fully recognized in our excellent constitution.' 'It is not necessary for us to examine the causes alleged by our enemies for this unjust and unnatural war, because an address from the House of Representatives of Massachusetts, the most respectable in the Union, proves in the most satisfactory manner, that it is wanton and unprovoked, and is the climax of the various outrages previously committed against Great Britain. In this statement they have been joined by the minority in Congress, whose expositions of the secret reasons of the war, and the falsehood of those alleged by the President and his friends, is unanswerable, and must hand down the promoters of this diabolical measure to the execration of posterity.' 'Your representatives finished their labours with placing in the hands of His Honour the President (Sir Isaac Brock), all the public money they could collect, in order to contribute as much as possible to the extraordinary expenses which the war renders necessary, and they have the fullest confidence that it will be most faithfully applied. Having thus endeavoured, to the best of their abilities, to provide for the welfare and safety of the Province, your representatives take the liberty of reminding you that the best laws are useless without the zealous co-operation of the people. Unless you are prepared to endure the greatest privations and to make the severest sacrifices, all that your representatives have done will be of no avail. Be ready, then, at all times to rally round the Royal Standard, and let those who are not called into the service assist the families of those who are called into the field.' 'Remember, when you go forth to the combat, that you fight not for yourselves alone, but for the whole world. You are defeating the most formidable conspiracy against the civilization of man that ever was contrived; a conspiracy threatening a greater barbarism and misery than followed the downfall of the Roman Empire—that now you have an opportunity of proving your attachment to the parent State which contends for the relief of the oppressed nations—the last pillar of true liberty, and the last refuge of oppressed humanity.'

"Such were the views and spirit with which the 70,000 people of Upper Canada, and their score of parliamentary representatives, engaged in the unequal struggle against myriads of invaders—relying simply upon their principles, their duty, and their God; and, in three months after the declaration of war, they had, with the aid of a few hundred regular soldiers and noble officers, driven back three invading armies, capturing Hull and the territory of Michigan, driving the invaders commanded by General Van Rensellaer down Queenston Heights, taking hundreds of prisoners, driving 'proclamation' General Smyth, with his 8,000, from the Canadian side of the Niagara river, near Fort Erie, so that he had to run away and retire from the army to escape popular indignation and disgrace. It is not for me to dwell upon the incidents and progress of the war; raids were made into our country, many battles were fought, and much property destroyed and much suffering inflicted; but those raids were severely retaliated, and at the end of three years not a foot of Canadian territory was in possession of the invader, while the key of the North-west, Fort Mackinaw, was in the hands of the British.

"Of all the battles fought during the war, the most sanguinary and obstinate was that of Lundy's Lane—the battle, the anniversary of which we are this day assembled to commemorate—the battle fought the last few months of the war, the 25th of July, 1814. It was the most formidable and final effort of the American General Brown to get permanent footing in Canada. The smallest number of American soldiers engaged in the battle, according to General Brown's report, was upwards of 5,000; and the largest number of British soldiers and Canadian militia engaged, according to the British General

Drummond's report, was 2,800, although the greater part of the battle was fought with a force not exceeding 1,600. I shall not attempt to describe the order, or narrate the incidents of the battle; I will only say, that the high ground, near the east end of Lundy's Lane, was the centre of interest, and the position contended for by both parties in deadly strife for several hours. In no battle during the war did the Americans fight with such heroism and obstinacy; and in no battle was the courage, steadiness and perseverance of the British soldiers and Canadian volunteers put to so severe a test. The enemy was drawn up in order of battle within 600 yards of the coveted eminence, when General Drummond arrived on the ground, and he had barely time to plant his artillery on the brow of the hill, when the enemy concentrated all his power and efforts to obtain the key of the battle-field. An eye-witness says: 'Columns of the enemy, not unlike the surge of the adjacent cataract, rushed to the charge in close and impetuous succession.' The curtain of night soon enveloped the scene, now drenched with blood; but the darkness seemed to intensify the fury of the combatants, and the rage of the battle increased as the night advanced. An eye-witness truly observes, that 'nothing could have been more awful than this midnight contest. The desperate charges of the enemy were succeeded by a dead silence, interrupted only by the groans of the dying, and the dull sounds of the stupendous Falls of Niagara, while the adverse lines were now and then dimly discerned through the moonlight, by the dismal gleam of their arms. These anxious pauses were succeeded by a blaze of musketry along the lines, and by a repetition of the most desperate charges from the enemy, which the British received with the most unshaken firmness.' General Drummond, in his official report of the battle, says:—'In so determined a manner were these attacks directed against our guns, that our artillerymen were bayoneted by the enemy in the act of loading, and the muzzles of the enemy's guns were advanced within a few yards of ours. The darkness of the night, during this extraordinary conflict, occasioned several uncommon incidents; our troops having, for a moment, been pushed back, some of our guns remained for a few minutes in the enemy's hands; they were, however, not only quickly recovered, but the two pieces, a six-pounder and a five-and-a-half-inch howitzer, which the enemy had brought up, were captured by us, together with several tumbrils. About nine o'clock (the action having commenced at six) there was a short intermission of firing, during which it appears the enemy was employed in bringing up the whole of his remaining force; and he shortly afterwards renewed the attack with fresh troops, but was everywhere repelled with equal gallantry and success. The enemy's efforts to carry the hill were continued until about midnight, when he had suffered so severely from the superior steadiness and discipline of his Majesty's troops, that he gave up the contest, and retreated with great precipitation to his camp beyond the Chippewa. On the following day he abandoned his camp, threw the greatest part of his baggage, camp equipage and provisions into the Rapids; and having set fire to Street's Mills, and destroyed the bridge at Chippewa, he continued his retreat in great disorder towards Fort Erie.'

"In this bloody battle, the Canadian militia fought side by side with the regular soldiers; and General Drummond said, 'the bravery of the militia on this occasion could not have been excelled by the most resolute veterans.'

"Such was the loyalty of our grandfathers and fathers, and such their self-devotion and courage in the darkest hour of our country's dangers and sufferings, and though few in number in comparison of their invaders, they had

> "'Hearts resolved and hands prepared
> The blessings they enjoyed to guard.'

"There was doubtless as much true courage among the descendants of Great Britain and Ireland in the United States as in Canada; but the former fought for the oppressor of Europe, the latter fought for the freedom of Europe; the former fought to prostrate Great Britain in her death struggle for the liberties of mankind, and to build up the United States upon her ruin, the latter fought in the glorious cause of the mother country, and to maintain our own unity with her; the former fought for the conquest of Canada, the latter fought in her defence; the fire that kindled the military ardour of the former was the blown-up embers of old enmities against Great Britain, the gross misrepresentations of President Madison, the ambition of adventure, and the lust of booty—the fire that burned in the hearts of the latter, and animated them to deeds of death or freedom, was the sacred love of hearth and home, the patriotic love of liberty, and that hallowed principle of loyalty to truth, and law, and liberty combined, which have constituted the life, and development, and traditions, and strength, and unity, and glory of British institutions, and of the British nation, from the resurrection morn of the Protestant Reformation to the present day. A great writer has truly observed: 'The most inviolable attachment to the laws of our country is everywhere acknowledged a capital virtue;' and that virtue has been nobly illustrated in the history of our United Empire Loyalist forefathers, and of their descendants in Canada, and it grows with the growth and increases with the strength of our country.

"I have said that loyalty, like Christianity itself, is an attachment to principles and duties emanating from them, irrespective of rulers or teachers; but if the qualities of our chief rulers were necessary to give intensity to Canadian loyalty, those qualities we have in the highest degree in our Sovereign and in her representive in Canada; for never was a British Sovereign more worthy of our highest respect and warmest affection than our glorious Queen Victoria—(loud cheers)—and never was a British Sovereign more nobly represented in Canada than by the patriotic, the learned, and the eloquent Lord Dufferin. (Loud cheers.) And at no period were we more free or prosperous than now. The feelings of his (the speaker's) heart went far beyond anything that his tongue could express, and the language of his heart that day was, might loyalty ever be the characteristic trait of the people of Canada, might freedom ever be our possession, and might we ever have cause and heart to say 'God save the Queen!'" (Loud cheering.)

Note by the Author.—The Administration of President Madison, and his Declaration of War against Great Britain, are dark spots in the brilliant history of the United States of America, and the American narratives of the war are rather fiction than history—compiled largely from letters of officers and soldiers, who, in writing to their friends, sought to magnify their own heroism, even when suffering disgraceful defeats, and sometimes claiming victory when they were driven from the field. The usual tales on these occasions were that the Canadian forces were vastly superior in numbers and equipments, when it was known that the American armies were ten to one in numbers to those of Canada, and their invading forces were declared, by themselves, to be irresistible in strength and equipments.

The American account of the battle of Lundy's Lane is an example, and is repeated with exaggerations in the latest and most popular history of the war, namely, Lossing's Pictorial Field Book of the War of 1812, page 1084. Lossing says :

"The number of troops engaged in the battle of Niagara Falls was little over 7,000, the British having about 4,500, and the Americans a little less than 2,600." (p. 824.)

The very reverse of this was the fact, as quoted in the foregoing extract from the official report of General Drummond. When the American invading army consisted of 10,000 men, it is absurd to suppose that all but 2,600 would remain on the American side of the river, and the American historian states that every available soldier on the British side of the river was engaged in the battle.

Lossing likewise claims the battle for the Americans "because they drove the enemy from the field and captured his cannon" (p. 824). It is not true that the British were driven from the field at all ; they were once pushed back for a few minutes, and their cannon were for a few moments in the hands of the Americans, who, however, were forthwith driven back, the cannon retaken, with two pieces left by the Americans. And how could there possibly be any American victory, when Lossing himself admits that the American army retired from the field during the night to Chippewa (p. 823), with the intention of returning next morning to bring off the cannon and other booty. Is it the characteristic of a victorious army to leave the conquered field and retire two miles from it ? Lossing also admits that the Americans did not return to the battle-field next morning, but burnt the bridge which separated the British army from them, and retreated up the Niagara river. Is this the conduct of a conquering army, to flee from the enemy whom he pretends to have conquered ? Mr. Lossing's admissions of details contradict the pretence of American victory at Lundy's Lane, and prove American defeat.

It is by such fictions of victories where there were defeats, interspersed with fictitious incidents of individual heroism, that American vanity is fed, and American children taught in the schools what is purely apocryphal for history in regard to Great Britain and Canada.

But it is gratifying to observe a greatly improved feeling in the educated American mind towards Great Britain, and even the causes of the American Revolution, which were magnified in the American Declaration of Independence, and which have been exaggerated in every possible way in American histories and Fourth of July orations, are very much modified in the productions of well-instructed and candid American writers and public speakers. We observe on a late occasion in England, at the Wesleyan Conference, Bishop Simpson, the Massillon of American pulpit orators, said, "The triumph of America was England's triumph. Their object was the same, and they were engaged in the same work. There were more Englishmen who would go to America, than Americans who would come to England (laughter), and while they in England had the wealth, the power, and the elements of usefulness, they were bound to use it in the interests of religion."

On the same occasion, the Rev. Dr. Curry, editor of the New York *Christian Advocate,* the most widely circulated religious paper in America, uttered the following noble sentiments:

"He was proud," he said, "of England (as the Fatherland of his), and, as he had now gone up and down through that island, and had witnessed its signs of substantial wealth, and of social order, he felt that both the public institutions of the Government and the private virtues of the people were of the most valuable. He did not wonder that Englishmen were warmly attached to their own country, and he would say that were he not an American he should wish to be an Englishman. He rejoiced, too, that there now exists the most cordial good feeling between the two countries, and trusted that this would never be interrupted. They had very many interests in common, and should stand together in support of them."

On the last Fourth of July, the Rev. Dr. Newman, pastor of President Grant, who has finished a tour of the world, having been appointed to examine and report upon all the American Consulships of the globe, delivered a remarkable discourse on the progress of the nation, and also of the enlightened ideas and liberal institutions in Europe. In an allusion to the American Revolution, Dr. Newman says:

"Our forefathers were not slaves; they were English subjects—English freemen, and we misrepresent them and the struggle through which they fought, if we look upon them as bound with manacles. They had an appreciation of what belonged to an English subject. And because the mother country refused representation where she imposed taxation, therefore those forefathers arose in their English manhood, protested against the abuse of governmental power, and asserted that where there is taxation, there should be representation; and had Patrick Henry been admitted into the British Parliament to represent her American colonies, the United States of America to-day would have been the grandest portion of the empire of Great Britain."

In the same discourse the orator said:

"Behold England of to day, in her rule at home, as well as in her policy towards her colonies, pressing upon her colonial possessions practical independence. She demands that they shall be so far free as to legislate for themselves, and pay their own expenses. England is now gathering together her representatives from Africa, and proposes under her benign sway to form a republican government for long-despised and down-trodden Africa. Whatever may be said of the Old East India Company under British protection, let me say, from personal observation, that from the eternal snows of the Himalayas to the spicy groves of Ceylon, India of to-day has a wise and paternal government given her by Christian England."

CHAPTER LIX.

MISCELLANEOUS DOCUMENTS AND PAPERS, EXTRACTED FROM MANUSCRIPTS RESPECTING THE U. E. LOYALISTS IN THE DOMINION LIBRARY AT OTTAWA.

"CHARACTER OF THE MILITIA," ETC., ETC.

1. "Amongst the first settlers on the frontier of Upper Canada were those faithful and loyal men, the United Empire Loyalists, with the Six Nations of Indians, who, at the sacrifice of their all, were steadfast to the British Crown during the revolutionary struggle of the old British colonies, now the United States, for independence, and other United States citizens who had adopted Canada as a home for themselves and their children. That struggle ended by the treaty of 1783.

"Those faithful men, the U. E. Loyalists and their associates, sought an asylum under Britain's Crown in this, the then wilderness of Canada, which now stands as one of the most flourishing provinces of our beloved Sovereign. In that then wilderness the flag of England was unfurled, and after the lapse of one century, and on the commencement of another, that flag floats triumphantly over this loyal Canadian land. Those first settlers were our first militiamen, under our first and venerated Governor, Sir John Graves Simcoe, in the year 1791.

"The descendants of those faithful men, with some soldiers and sailors and others, the sons of Britain who had adopted Canada, were our first militiamen in the war of 1812; and those who are left of them are therefore the veteran soldiers of 1812. The war was declared by the United States Government against Great Britain, June 18th, 1812—involving Imperial interests alone, and not those of the colonies.* This declaration of war against Britain was the signal for the loyal inhabitants of Canada to rush *en masse* to the frontier of their country to repel invasion. In this momentous crisis we met our beloved Governor and Commander-in-Chief, the late Major-General Sir Isaac Brock, on the Niagara frontier, whose monument stands on the battle ground of Queenston Heights. That monument stands in remembrance of him who sacrificed his valuable life in duty to his King and in defence of our Canadian homes; in memory of him who caused the youthful part of the Militia of Upper Canada to be embodied in the Militia Flank Companies, to be trained for actual service in their country's defence; in remembrance of him in whom their entire confidence was placed—for where he led they were sure to follow."

II. The invasions of Canada by the Americans during the war were as follows:

	Men.
1. General Hull, at Sandwich	3,000
2. General Van Rensellaer, at Queenston	2,000
3. General Smyth, at Fort Erie	3,000
4. General Pike, Toronto	2,500
5. General Dearborn, Fort George	3,000
6. General Winchester, Chrystler's Farm, for Montreal	3,000
7. General Hampton, Chateauguay river, L. C., for Montreal	8,000
8. General Brown, Fort Erie	5,000
9. General Brown, Lundy's Lane	5,000
10. General Izzard, Fort Erie	8,000
11. General Wilkinson, Lacolle Mills, L. C	2,500
Total number of invaders	45,000

The foregoing is an aggregate of the United States forces employed in the attempt to invade and take Canada, when they

* Yet while the American Government professed to declare a *defensive* war—a war in defence of their rights at sea—the first act was *the invasion of Canada*, for which they had been collecting men and arms for several months before the declaration of the war; and thus the first acts of the Canadians were to provide for the defence of their country and their homes against the American invasions. The facts show that the real object of the American Government was to take Canada, and their invaded rights at sea was a mere pretext.

desired peace; and when peace was proclaimed, they did not find themselves in possession of an inch of Canadian territory.

"Thus it may be said as the opinion of all, that if the loyal inhabitants of Canada had not, in those days of trial and privation, stood to their arms under General Brock and other generals, Canada might not at this day be a continued appendage of the British Crown. In corroboration of this opinion, I here insert General Brock's answer to an address of the magistrates at Niagara after Hull's surrender of Detroit. General Brock said—

"That had not Western Canada rose in their might as one man, in defence of their rights, and in support of the constitution of Great Britain, his hands would have been as if tied, being without the aid of the regular British troops, who were all then engaged in the European war.

"Truly extracted from my book,
"JOHN CLARKE,
"Captain-Adjutant-General of Militia, 1812, '13, '14."

Colonel Clarke says of himself: "I was placed on duty by General Brock from the commencement of the war of 1812, as Lieutenant and Adjutant of the 4th Lincoln flank companies. In March I was promoted to the rank of Captain-Assistant-Adjutant-General of Militia by General Sir Roger H. Sheaffe, Administrator of the Government of Upper Canada; which place I retained until the peace of 1815."—"I served throughout the rebellion of 1837 and 1838—being invested with the command of an organized regiment of militia, the First Frontier Light Infantry."

Colonel Clarke's recollections and reminiscences are in every respect reliable, and are very valuable, extending to nearly 300 manuscript quarto pages, in the Parliamentary Library at Ottawa (entitled "U. E. Loyalists"). His own contributions are entitled, "Memoirs of Colonel John Clarke, of Port Dalhousie, C. W.; born in Canada in 1783: giving an account of the family's early arrival in the country in 1768; the progress of the settlers; the arrival of Governor Simcoe, his improvements and government; settlement of the Indians; the war of 1812—full particulars; the rebellion of 1837; the Welland Canal, and various other things connected with the progressive growth of Upper Canada."

TREATMENT OF CANADIANS BY THE AMERICANS WHO INVADED CANADA.

"In 1812 General Hull invaded the British province of Upper Canada, and took possession of the town of Sandwich. He threatened (by proclamation) to exterminate the inhabitants if they made any resistance. He plundered those with whom he had been on habits of intimacy for years before the war. Their plate and linen were found in his possession after his surrender to General Brock. He marked out the loyal subjects of the King as objects of his peculiar resentment, and consigned their property to pillage and conflagration.

"In the autumn of 1812, several houses and barns were burnt by the American forces near Fort Erie, Upper Canada.

"In 1813—April—the public buildings of York, the capital of Upper Canada, were burnt by the troops of the United States, contrary to the articles of capitulation. These public buildings consisted of two elegant halls, with convenient offices for the accommodation of the Legislature and the Courts of Justice. The library and all the papers and records belonging to these institutions were consumed at the same time. The Church was robbed, and the town library perfectly pillaged. Commodore Chauncey, who has generally behaved honourably, was so ashamed of this last transaction, that he endeavoured to collect the books belonging to the town and legislative library, and actually sent back two boxes filled with them; but hardly any were complete. Much private property was plundered, and several houses left in a state of ruin.

"In June, 1813, Newark, Niagara, came into possession of the army of the United States, and its inhabitants were repeatedly promised protection to themselves and property by Generals Dearborn and Boyd. In the midst of these professions, the most respectable of them, although non-combatants, were made prisoners and sent to the United States.

"Two churches were burnt to the ground. Detachments were sent under the direction of British traitors [of whom the traitor deserter Wilcox was the leader] to pillage the loyal inhabitants in the neighbourhood. Many farm-houses were burnt during the summer; and, at length, to fill up the measure of iniquity, the whole beautiful town of Newark, with a short previous intimation—so short as to amount to none, and in an intense cold day of the 10th of December—was consigned to the flames.

"The wretched inhabitants had scarcely time to save themselves, much less any of their property. More than 400 women and children were exposed without shelter, on the night of December the 10th, to the inclement cold of a Canadian winter. A great number must have perished, had not the flight of the American troops, after perpetrating their unfeeling act, enabled the inhabitants of the country to come to their relief.

"President Madison has attempted to justify this cruel act as necessary for the defence of Fort George. Nothing can be more false. The town was some distance from the fort; and instead of thinking to defend it, General McClure was actually retreating to his own shore when he caused Newark (Niagara) to be burnt. This officer says that he acted in conformity with the orders of his Government.

"The American Government, finding their defence useless, disavow the conduct of McClure, who appears to have been a fit agent for such a Government. He not only complied with his instructions; but he refined upon them, by choosing a day of intense severity, giving the inhabitants almost no warning until the fire began, and the conflagration in the night."

(The above facts relating to the burning, etc., are extracted from the proceedings of the Loyal Patriotic Society of Upper Canada, established at York for the relief of sufferers in the war; and of which Chief Justice Scott was President.)

The Royal and Patriotic Society of Upper Canada was established at Toronto, extended its branches to different parts of the Province, existed from 1812 to 1815, and did a great deal for the relief of sufferers by the war. On the destruction of the town of Niagara, large subscriptions were obtained and distributed for the relief of the sufferers. The following are extracts from its recorded proceedings:

"The inhabitants came forward in the most noble manner, as well as the gallant officers of his Majesty's troops.

Major-General Sheaffe	£200
Lieutenant-Colonel Bishop	100

with a vast number of liberal subscriptions, according to the means of the donors: so that in a short time upwards of £2,000 was raised to commence with.

City of Kingston sent		£500
Amherstburg	"	300
City of Montreal	"	3,000
Quebec	"	1,500

"The amount raised in the first year was £10,000.

"Eight hundred and sixty-four (864) families were relieved from starvation by this timely aid.

"The following summer a large meeting was held in London (England), at which the Duke of Kent, who had visited Canada twenty years before, presided. By his influence a very large sum was subscribed. The Bank of England graced the list with £1,000. This effort produced another £10,000.

Kingston in Jamaica sent		£2,000
Nova Scotia	"	2,500

"Indeed, the liberality evinced in all quarters was of the greatest service to the sufferers, and gladdened many bowed down by sorrow and indigence."

The whole of these interesting particulars may be seen in the Transactions of the Society, published in Toronto, 1814.

It may be interesting to the reader if I subjoin the address of the President, explanatory of the origin, character, and objects of this noble Society, the former existence of which is now scarcely known:

"AN ADDRESS

"*Copied from the Proceedings of the Loyal Patriotic Society of Upper Canada, who, by their funds, relieved much real distress to families in the war of 1812, '13, '14.*

"Gentlemen,—In the unprovoked war waged against us by the American Government, Providence hath evidently smiled on the justice of our cause.

"But our exertions have been attended with many privations and sacrifices hard to be borne, and should hostilities continue many more will be required.

"In order to mitigate some of these, the inhabitants of York came forward to contribute toward the comforts of the flank companies; and a large sum of money was raised for that purpose, of which the greater part is expended.

"But, on reflection, it appeared that something more might be done of a permanent nature, and that portion of the inhabitants who are not liable to military duty, eager to prove that their zeal in the cause is not inferior to that of those in actual service, formed themselves into a Society, named '*The Loyal Patriotic Society of Upper Canada,*' for the following distinct purposes:

"1st. To afford aid and relief to such families of the militia, in all parts of the Province, as shall be made to appear to experience particular distress, in consequence of the death or absence of some of their friends and relations.

"2nd. To afford like aid and relief to such militiamen as have been or shall be disabled from labour by their wounds or otherwise in course of the service aforesaid.

"3rd. To reward merit, excite and commemorate glorious events, by bestowing medals or other honorary marks of public approbation or distinction for extraordinary instances of personal courage or fidelity in defence of the Province by individuals, either of his Majesty's regular troops or militia forces.

"4th. Also the seamen on the lakes.

"This Society, so honourable in its nature, and which we hope will prove most important in its consequences, was first suggested by the Honourable Mr. Selby, and was received with acclamation.

"In a public meeting of the gentlemen of York and its vicinity, the Chief explained the great advantages likely to result from it, if generally supported; and, assisted by his most respectable colleagues, prepared views for its management. To these the meeting gave their cordial assent, and in a few minutes nearly $2,000 per annum was subscribed. There are some who have given during the continuance of the war one-tenth of their income.

"General Sheaffe, in a letter to the Chief Justice, our chairman, not only extols, in earnest language, the objects of the Society, but, far exceeding our expectations, presents us with £200. Colonel Bishop, a stranger [who was afterwards mortally wounded at Black Rock], and not an inhabitant of the Province, with a liberality above all praise, subscribes £100.

"Now, gentlemen, our object in addressing you is to procure your co-operation. Foremost in deeds of warlike glory, we desire that you should become sharers in the work of benevolence.

"Let your contributions be as small as you please—a halfpenny, a farthing per day—anything to show your good-will.

"It is not the value of what you give; it is your countenance that we mainly desire.

"We know that your means are narrow, but your example is inestimable; and we shall be proud of having you for our companions and supporters in mitigating the distress incident to the war.

"And when it is heard that the York Volunteers and their comrades, among the first in danger, have patronized this Society, the militia of other districts will be anxious to emulate the military glory of the conquerors of Detroit and Queenston, and will hasten to emulate you in contributing to the support of our benevolent design.

"Those that join will intimate to the captains what they are willing to give, while they are in active service, that it may be paid over monthly to the treasurer.

"And they will remember that they are soothing the sick and the wounded in war, protecting aged parents and helpless children, and doing all they can to comfort those whom they love and revere, who suffer during the horrors of war."

(Signed)   CHIEF JUSTICE SCOTT,
President.

ALEX. WOOD,
    Secretary.

The above excellent address is understood to have been written by the late Dr. Strachan, first Bishop of the Church of England of Toronto, and who acted the part of a true, a bold, and generous patriot during the war of 1812–15.

CHAPTER LX.

CLOSE OF THE WAR AND OF THE HISTORY OF THE U. E. LOYALISTS—
DEFEAT AND DISGRACE OF THE DEMOCRATIC INVADERS OF CANADA
—HONOUR AND SUCCESS OF ITS DEFENDERS—COMPARATIVE STATE
OF THE UNITED STATES AND CANADA AT THE CLOSE OF THE WAR—
MUTUAL RESPECT AND FRIENDSHIP BETWEEN AMERICANS AND CANA-
DIANS—CONCLUDING REMARKS.

THUS closed the war of the United States against Great Britain, in 1812-15—a war undertaken at the prompting of the scourge of Europe, Napoleon, but upon pretexts which were never so much as mentioned, much less reiterated, by the United States Commissioners when peace was proposed between Great Britain and America in 1815—a war in which the democratic rulers of the United States suffered both defeat and disgrace, while the loyal inhabitants of Canada maintained inviolate their honour and independence.

With the close of that war terminates the history of the United Empire Loyalists of Canada as a distinct and controlling class of the inhabitants; for their numbers had become so reduced by the ravages of time and war, and other classes of immigrants had become so numerous, between whom and the families of old Loyalists so many intermarriages had taken and were taking place, that the latter became merged in the mass of the popu-lation; and therefore my history of them as a distinct class comes to an end. All classes were Loyalists, and all had fought as one man in defence of their country during the recent war, although all had not fought for the life of the nation and the unity of the empire from 1776 to 1783, or been driven from their homes to Canada, to become the fathers of the inhabitants and founders of the institutions of our country. It would be out of place, and at variance with the title of my book, did I proceed to narrate and discuss the history of Upper Canada after the close of the war; but I may properly conclude my work by referring to a few facts leading to and arising out of the war, and the state of our country at its close.

The democratic party in the United States, which had confiscated the property of our forefathers, and exiled them from their homes, and compelled them to seek a home in the wilderness of Canada, had followed them with their enmities into their new place of refuge, and, by their emissaries, in conjunction with those of the French revolutionists, sought to insinuate a disturbing element into Canadian peace and safety from the commencement of the bloody French revolution to 1812, when it culminated, under the promptings of Napoleon and his obsequious tools, in the war of 1812-15, with a view to wrest Canada from Great Britain, and to divide the commerce of Europe between France and the United States. But how vain are the devices of men against the laws of God and of human society! The Gideon hundreds of loyal Canadians repelled and scattered, for more than two years, the Midian and Amalekite thousands of democratic invaders, until Great Britain, having chained the marauding tiger of Europe to the rock of St. Helena, despatched her thousands of soldiers to the aid of Canada, and sent her fleets across the Atlantic—sweeping the American coasts from Maine to Georgia—taking and burning their capital in retaliation for the American raid upon the capital of Upper Canada, and soon compelling the heretofore boasting Madison partizans to seek for peace without even the mention of their alleged causes of war with England. If the American armies were defeated and driven back in their repeated invasions of Canada, their commerce and commercial men suffered not less before the end of the war. Their annual exports declined, between 1811 and 1814, from £22,000,000 sterling to £1,500,000; their vessels to the number of 3,000 were captured; two-thirds of their commercial class were reduced to bankruptcy; an immense war tax was incurred; many thousands of lives had been sacrificed, and the Union itself imperilled by the threatened secession of the New England States.

On the other hand, Canada had felt deeply the calamities of war, it being the seat of the conflict, a large portion of its revenue and inhabitants having been diverted from their ordinary employments—having themselves chiefly to depend upon for their defence, while England was engaged in a twenty years' conflict for law and liberty in Europe. In the extremity of this contest, the democratic President of the United States combined with the tyrant despot of Europe to seduce and sever the Canadians from their British connection; but the Canadians nobly maintained their fidelity and triumphantly vindicated their honour and independence, though, in doing so, they suffered the desolation of many of their homes, shed many bitter tears for sires, and sons, and brothers, who had poured out their life's blood in defence of their country on the battle fields of both Upper and Lower Canada. Yet, upon the whole, the war did much good to Canada, apart from the success of its arms; it tended to cement the people together as one family; English, French, Scotch, Irish, and Americans had forgotten former distinctions and jealousies, and had all become Canadians, with increased devotion not only to the land of their nativity or adoption, but to the glorious mother country which had become the victorious champion of the liberties of Europe, and leader in the civilization of mankind.

Though, in the course of the war, Canada—especially Upper Canada, which had to bear the brunt of it—was greatly exhausted, emigration being checked, agriculture partially neglected, by the embodiments of militia and frequent mobilization of sedentary corps,—requiring some time after the war for the inhabitants to return to their old habits and resume their peaceful pursuits; yet Canada flourished financially during the war. Owing to England's supremacy on the ocean, Canadian trade and commerce were not seriously affected; taxes were light; not a few fortunes were made; money was plentiful, as the mother country paid most of the expenses of the war.

It is worthy of remark, as one of the notable features of the war, that no class of Canadians were more loyal, none more brave and devoted to the defence of the Government and institutions of the country, than were the Americans who had become settlers in Canada—not the United Empire Loyalists alone, but those who had from time to time emigrated from the United States of their own accord, and not on account of political persecution, as was the case with the old Loyalists.

The unfriendly feelings and even enmities which had been excited by the war between Canadians and Americans, soon changed into mutual respect and friendship; trade and commerce between the two countries were renewed and increased; intermarriages multiplied, with all the amenities and intimacies of social life. Though there has always been a democratic mob faction—latterly mostly Fenian—in the United States, which has seized every opportunity to invade and disturb the peace of Canada, yet it is well understood that this freebooting faction does not represent the sentiments or feelings of the industrious, business, commercial, intelligent, and Christian people of the United States, who, with few exceptions, are, as most of them were when Madison declared war against England in June, 1812, lovers of peace, law, and order, and friends of England and Canada, as well as of mankind; and we believe there are no more ardent well-wishers on the continent of America for the happiness and prosperity of the citizens of the American Republic than the loyal and patriotic inhabitants of Canada.

I may perhaps be expected to add a few words on the chief public occurrences which took place in Upper Canada after the war, but without discussing any of the questions which they involved.

From 1791 to the close of the war in 1815, and for some years afterwards, the Executive Government of the day commanded the votes of a majority of the House of Assembly. Public questions and measures were freely discussed; but no organized opposition appeared in the Assembly against the Administration. Shortly after the close of the war, however, the elements of discord began to be devoloped in the country. Many discharged officers of the British army, at the termination of the long European war, came to Canada with instructions from the Secretary of State for the Colonies to the Lieutenant-Governor of Upper Canada (himself an English officer), to provide for them; and they were appointed to all offices of emolument (with few exceptions), to the exclusion of the old Loyalists and their descendants and other inhabitants who had felled the wilderness, and made the country valuable, and had borne the burden and heat of the war in its defence. The administration of the Crown or Public Lands was sadly defective and partial, giving whole blocks to friends and speculators, while the applications of the legitimate settler were often rejected. It also began to be complained of that these large blocks of land given to individuals, and the one-seventh of the lands set apart as Clergy Reserves, greatly impeded the settlement and improvement of the country; that those who had occupied the Clergy Reserves on *leases* were required to pay higher rents on the renewal of their leases, or the purchase of the Reserves, on account of their increased value created by the labour of the tenants and their neighbours. A special Board of Management was appointed for these Reserves in the interest of the clerical claimants of them. The representatives of the Church of Scotland claimed to share in the proceeds of the Clergy Reserves, and a co-ordinate standing with the Church of England, as the endowed Church establishment of Upper Canada. The other religious persuasions had not the privilege of having matrimony solemnized by their own ministers, or the right of holding a bit of ground on which to worship God, or in which to bury their dead. It soon began to be claimed by the leaders of the Church of England that their Church had the sole right to the Clergy Reserves and to all the prerogatives of *the* Established Church, whose supremacy and endowments, it was now pretended, were essential to the loyalty of the people; notwithstanding, no people could have been more loyal than the Canadian people during the then recent war in defence of British supremacy, and who were as brave as they were loyal, though there were not then three settled Episcopal clergymen in all Upper Canada.

These, with various co-ordinate and minor causes, lost to the Lieutenant-Governor and his Executive Council the control and confidence of the representatives of the people, and in less than ten years after the war, the Governor and Council fell into a hopeless minority in the House of Assembly, but in opposition to it actually governed the country for fifteen years, until the dissatisfaction of the people became so general and strong that Commissions of Inquiry were sent out from England, which resulted in placing all religious persuasions on an equal footing before the law, in applying the proceeds of the Clergy Reserves to the general purposes of the education and improvement of the country, in making the heads of public departments (who were to be Executive Councillors) responsible to the House of Assembly, and holding their offices no longer than they enjoyed its confidence. From that time forward the Government became strong, the people contented, and the country prosperous and rapidly increasing in wealth, education, and intelligence—rendering, at this day, the inhabitants of the vast Dominion of Canada the lightest-taxed and the freest people on the American continent.

GENERAL INDEX.

Abercrombie (General)—Arrives in America with the troops, and forty German officers to drill and command regiments in America (which gives offence to the Colonists). i. 257.

Is disgracefully defeated by Montcalm (though commanding the largest force ever assembled in America). i. 258.

With General Loudoun, hesitates and delays at Albany, while the French generals are active and successful. i. 258.

Adams (John)—The prompter and adviser of hanging "Tories." ii. 127.

Address of Governor Winthrop and his company on leaving England, in 1630, to their "Fathers and Brethren of the Church of England," declaring their filial and undying love to the Church of England, as their "dear mother," from whose breasts they had derived their nourishment. i. 55.

Alliance between Congress and the Kings of France not productive of the effect anticipated, and deferred twelve months by France after it had been applied for by Congress. ii. 1.

American Affairs—Misrepresented in the English Parliament and by the English Press. i. 390.

American boastings groundless over the surrender of Cornwallis. ii. 46.

American Colonies—Their position in regard to England and other nations at the Peace of Paris, 1763. i. 274.

American Revolution—primary cause of it. i. 30.

American treatment of Canadians by Americans who invaded them. ii. 464.

Invasions of Canada, and their forces. ii. 262.

Amherst (Lord)—Supersedes Abercrombie as Commander-in-Chief, assisted by General Wolfe. i. 260.

Plans three expeditions, all of which are successful. i. 261.

His energetic movements. i. 262.

He receives all Canada for the King from the French. i. 267.

His parting address to the army. i. 268.

Anderson (Samuel). ii. 192.

Andros (Edmond)—Appointed local Governor of Massachusetts Bay, and Governor-General of New England; his tyranny; seized at Boston and sent prisoner to England. i. 215.

(Examined)—Acquitted by King William in Council, because he had acted according to his instructions. i. 215.

Articles of treaty and preamble. ii. 56.

Associations in the Colonies against the use of tea imported from England. i. 370.

Bancroft—Confirms the statement as to the aggressions and pretensions of the Massachusetts Bay Government. i. 200.

His interpretations against England. i. 247.

Baptists—The persecution of them instigated by the Rev. Messrs. Wilson and Newton, and justified by the Rev. Mr. Cotton. i. 120.

Barnard (Governor)—His reply to the Massachusetts Legislative Assembly. i. 357.
His recall and character. i. 359.

Bethune (Rev. John). ii. 192.

Boston and Massachusetts — Three Acts of Parliament against, all infringing and extinguishing the heretofore acknowledged constitutional rights of the people. i. 389.

Boston—In great distress; addresses of sympathy and contributions from other towns and provinces.
Fourth Act of Parliament, legalizing the quartering of troops in. i. 397.
General sympathy and liberality in its behalf. i. 404.

Boston Massacre—Soldiers acquitted by a Boston jury. i. 365.

Boyle (Hon. Robert)—In a letter in which he expostulates with the Massachusetts Bay rulers on the intolerance and unreasonableness of their conduct. i. 160.

Braddock's unfortunate expedition. i. 247.

Bradstreet (Colonel)—His brilliant achievement in taking and destroying Fort Frontenac. i. 261.

Bradstreet and Norton—Sent to England to answer complaints; favourably received; first thanked and then censured by the Massachusetts Bay rulers; Norton dies of grief. i. 142.

Brock (Sir Isaac)—His address to the Legislature of Upper Canada. ii. 341, 342.
Takes Detroit. ii. 352-354.
Proclamation to the inhabitants of Michigan. ii. 362, 363.
Killed at Queenston Heights. ii. 366.

Brown, Samuel and John—Their character and position. i. 35.

Banished from Massachusetts Bay for adhering to Episcopal worship. i. 35.
Misrepresented by Messrs. Palfrey and Bancroft. i. 37.
Their letters and papers seized, and their complaints successfully denied to the King by their persecutors. i. 46.
Their conduct unblamable. i. 42.

Bunker's Hill, Concord, and Lexington—Battles of, numbers engaged, with the accounts, on both sides. i. 460, 461.

Burke (the celebrated Edmund)—Reviews and denounces the persecuting laws and spirit of the Massachusetts Bay Puritans, during thirty years. i. 122.

Canadian Militia—Their character. ii. 461.

Canada—What had been claimed by old American colonies in regard to the payment of official salaries contended for by, and granted to Canada, to the satisfaction and progress of the country. i. 267.

Canada wholly surrendered to the King of Great Britain, through Lord Amherst. i. 267.

Canada—State of at the close of the war. ii. 471.

Carscallen (Luke). ii. 202.

Causes—Characteristics of early emigration to New England. i. 25.

Change of government in England and end of Lord North's administration. ii. 57.

Change of tone and professions at Massachusetts Bay on the confirmation of the King's restoration. i. 131.

The King's kind reply to their address —their joy at it, but they evade the six conditions on which the King proposes to forgive their past and continue their charter. i. 135—137, 139.

Characteristics of fifty-four years' government of Massachussetts Bay, under the first charter. 217.

Charles the First—Deceived by the misstatements of the Massachusetts Bay Puritans, to decide in their favour against the complaints made in 1632. i. 67.

His kind and indulgent conduct to the Massachusetts Bay Company, and how they deceived him. i. 67.

Charles the Second—His restoration; news of it received with joy in all the Colonies except in Massachusetts, where false rumours are circulated. i. 130.

Chateauguay, Battle of. ii. 413.

Chatham (Earl of)—Amendment; speech in the House of Lords (1774) against the coercive policy of the Ministry and defence of Colonial rights; his amendment opposed by Lord Suffolk, and supported by Lord Camden; negatived by a majority of 68 to 18. i. 423-429.

His bill "to settle the troubles in America" not allowed a first reading in the Lords. i. 425.

Chrysler's Farm, Battle of. ii. 419.

Clarendon (Earl of, Chancellor)—Reply to the address to the King, Charles II., of the Massachusetts Bay rulers, dated October 25, 1664, in which Lord Clarendon exposes the groundlessness of their pretensions, suspicions, and imputations. i. 160.

Clark (Colonel John), and his Manuscript contributions. ii.

Clinton (Sir Henry)—Succeeds General Howe as Commander-in-Chief. ii. 14.

Deceived as to the design of Washington and the French commander. ii. 42.

Fails to reinforce Lord Cornwallis. ii. 44.

Colonies—All resolve in favour of a general convention or congress and election of delegates to it, in 1774. i. 408.

How information on subjects of agitation was rapidly diffused throughout the Colonies. i. 405.

Colonial Assemblies—Their dissolutions. i. 356.

Colonists—Their agreements for the non-importation of British manufactured goods. i. 356.

Sons of Governors Barnard and Hutchinson refuse to enter into agreement, but are at length compelled to yield. i. 360.

Their effective services to England in the English and French war; their experience and skill thereby acquired in military affairs; their superiority as marksmen. i. 460.

Desire to provide as aforetime for their own defence and the support of their own local government, as is done in the provinces of the Dominion of Canada. i. 460.

Colonist—The writer a native. i. 1.

Colonies—Three causes of irritation in 1768. i. 348.

Unjust imputations in the British Parliament and Press against their loyalty. i. 353.

Their manly response to the imputations and assertion of British rights, led by the General Assembly of Virginia. i. 355.

Company of Massachusetts Bay—Write to Endicot and ministers sent by them against Church innovations. i. 49, 51.

Deny to the King and British public having made any Church innovations in Massachusetts. i. 53.

Complaints of banished Episcopalians, persecuted Presbyterians, Baptists, &c., to the King. i. 46, 137.

Complaints of the Massachussetts Bay Rulers—a pretext to perpetuate sectarian rule and persecution. i. 183.

Conduct and pretensions of Massachusetts Bay Rulers condemned and exposed by Loyalist inhabitants of Boston, Salem, Newbury, and Ipswich. i. 163.

Congregationalists—None other eligible for office, or allowed the elective franchise at Massachussetts Bay. i. 63.

Congress (First General Congress)—

Met at Philadelphia, September, 1774. i. 409.

The word defined. i. 409.

Each day's proceedings commenced with prayer. i. 410.

Its members and their constituents throughout the Colonies thoroughly loyal, while maintaining British constitutional rights. i. 410.

Its declaration of rights and grievances. i. 411.

Its loyal address to the King. i. 414.

Its manly and affectionate appeal to the British Nation. i. 416.

The address of its members to their constituents — a temperate and lucid exposition of their grievances and sentiments. i. 417.

Its proceedings reach England before the adjournment for the Christmas holidays in 1774, and produce an impression favourable to the Colonies. i. 420.

(Second Continental) meets in Philadelphia, September, 1775; number and character of its members. i. 442.

Its noble and affectionate petition to the King; the King denies an audience to its agent, Mr. Penn, and answers the petition by proclamation, declaring it "rebellion," and the petitioners "rebels." i. 443-445.

Its petition to the House of Commons rejected, and its agent, Mr. Penn, not asked a question. i. 444.

A large majority (Oct.1775) still opposed to independence, but unanimous in defence of British constitutional rights. i. 448.

Divided on the question of *Independence*, which is first moved in Congress in May, 1776—deferred, after long debates, for three weeks, by a vote of seven to five Colonies. i. 483, 484.

Manipulation and agitation to prepare the members of Congress and the Colonies for separation from England. i. 482-485.

Proceeds with closed doors, and its members sworn to secrecy.

Votes by Colonies, and decides that each vote be reported unanimous, though carried by only a bare majority. i. 486.

After three days' debate, the six Colonies for and seven Colonies against independence; how a majority of one was obtained in favour of it. i. 486, 487.

Refuses to confer with British Commissioners with a view to reconciliation. ii. 2.

Feelings of the people of England and America different from those of the leaders of Congress. ii. 14.

Sycophancy of its leaders to France. ii. 13.

Its degeneracy in 1778, as stated by General Washington. ii. 29.

The depression of its credit. ii. 30.

It confiscates and orders the sale of the property of "Tories." ii. 30.

Appeals to France for men and money as their only hope. ii. 40.

Fallacy of the plea or pretext that it had not power to grant compensation to the Loyalists. ii. 61.

Meets at Philadelphia, 10th May, 1776. i. 479.

Contests—Chiefly between the Colonists, the French, and the Indians, from 1648 to 1654. i. 250.

Colonies—their divided councils and isolated resources. i. 257.

Their alarming state of affairs at the close of the year 1757. i. 255.

Cornwallis—His antecedents, ii. 38; his severe policy injurious to the British cause, ii. 40; his defence of Yorktown, ii. 44; his surrender to the French and American armies, ii. 45; conditions of capitulation, ii. 46.

Count De Grasse—Sails from New York to the Chesapeake with a fleet of 28 ships and 7,000 French troops. ii. 43.

Crown Point taken from the French by the English. i. 263.

Debts—Incurred by the New England Colonies in the Indian wars; how Massachusetts was relieved by England, and made prosperous. i. 240.

Declaration of American Independence—How the vote of the majority of the Colonies for it was obtained, and how reported. i. 486, 487.
Copy of it. i. 488.
Homage of respect by the authors to the fathers of. i. 492-495.
Described. i. 492-495.
1. A renunciation of all the principles on which the General Congress, Provincial Legislatures, and Conventions professed to act from the beginning of the contest; proofs and illustrations. i. 496-499.
2. A violation of good faith to those statesmen and numerous other parties in Great Britain, who had, in and out of Parliament, defended and supported the rights and character of the Colonists during the whole contest; proofs and illustrations. i. 499-501.
A violation, not only of good faith, but of justice to the numerous Colonists who adhered to connection with the Mother Country; proofs and illustrations. i. 501-504.
4. The commencement of persecutions and proscriptions and confiscation of property against those who refused to renounce the oaths which they had taken, and the principles and traditions which had, until then, been professed by their persecutors and oppressors as well as by themselves; proofs and illustrations. i. 504-507.
The plea of tyranny. i. 504.
5. The commencement of weakness in the army of its authors, and of defeat in their battle-fields; proofs and illustrations. i. 508-513.
6. The announced expedient and prelude to an alliance with France and Spain against the Mother Country. i. 513-517.
New penal laws passed against the Loyalists after adopting it. ii. 5.

Detroit—Taken by the British under General Brock. ii. 354.

De Salaberry (General) — Defeats 10,000 Americans with 300 Canadians at Chateauguay. ii. 381.

D'Estaing—His doings and failures in America. ii. 17-27.

Diamond (John). ii. 202.

Doane. ii. 192.

Dudley (Joseph)—Appointed Governor of Massachusetts by King James II. i. 212.

Dunmore (Earl of)—Governor of Virginia, commits the same outrages upon the inhabitants of Virginia, and about the same time, as those committed by General Gage upon the inhabitants of Massachusetts. i. 462.
Assembles the House of Burgesses to deliberate and decide upon Lord North's so-called "conciliatory proposition" to the Colonies; the House rejects the proposition on a report prepared by Mr. Jefferson—a document eulogized in the strongest terms by the Earl of Shelburne. i. 464.

East India Company — Disastrous effect of its agreement with the British Government. i. 381.

East India Company's Tea—Causes of it being thrown into Boston Harbour, as stated on both sides. i. 377.

Elections in England hastened in the autumn of 1774; adverse to the Colonies. i. 419.

Emigrants to Massachusetts Bay—Two classes. i. 1.

Emigration to Massachusetts Bay stopped by a change of Government in England. i. 85.

Endicot—Leader of the first company of emigrants to Massachusetts Bay. i. 27.
His character. i. 27.
Becomes a Congregationalist. i. 29.
Abolishes the Church of England, and banishes its adherents. i. 29.
Cause of all the tyrannical proceedings against them. i. 42.

Finally condemned by the Company, but officially retained by them. i. 43-48.

England's best and only means of protecting the Colonies against French encroachments and invasion. i. 244.

Position in respect to other European Powers at the Peace of Paris in 1763. i. 273.

England—Its resources at the conclusion of the Revolutionary war. ii. 48, 49.

The war party, and corrupt Administration, is defeated. ii. 48, 49.

Change of Administration and of policy, both for England and the Colonies. ii. 53.

Names of new Ministers, &c. ii. 53.

English Generals and soldiers refuse to fight against the Colonists. i. 446.

English Government employs seventeen thousand German mercenaries to bring the Colonists to absolute submission. i. 446-479.

Its change of policy, and effect of it in regard to the Colonies after the Peace of Paris, 1763. i. 277.

Its first acts which caused dissatisfaction and alienation in the American Colonies. i. 279.

Falmouth (now Portland) bombarded and burnt, by Captain Mowat, of the British Navy. i. 446.

Five-sixths of the male population disfranchised by Puritan bigotry and intolerance at Massachusetts Bay. i. 63.

Fort de Quesne taken by the English and called Pittsburg. i. 263.

Fox (C. J.)—His amendment to Lord North's address to the King, 1775, rejected by a majority of 304 to 105. i. 430.

France and England at war; mutually restore, in 1748, places taken during the first war. i. 242.

Franklin (Dr.)—His evidence at the Bar of the House of Commons on the Stamp Act, etc. i. 308.

Dismissed from office the following day. i. 426.

His petition to the House of Commons rejected. i. 426.

Proposes to include Canada in the United States. ii. 54.

Counter scheme to defeat the proposition of the English Commissioners. ii. 58.

Outwits the English Commissioners. ii. 63.

His Indian scalp fictions. ii. 119.

French—Attempt to take Quebec. i. 266.

Bitter feeling between French and American officers and soldiers, at Rhode Island, Boston, Charleston, and Savannah. ii. 20-25.

Encroachments on the British Colonies, from 1748 to 1756. i. 243.

Evasions and disclaimers, while encroaching on the British Colonies and making preparations for war against England. i. 245.

Successes in 1755, 1756, and 1757, in the war with England. i. 252.

French Fleet—Its complete failure under Count D'Estaing. ii. 17.

French Officers and Soldiers—Their kindness to the English after the defeat of Lord Cornwallis. ii. 129.

Gage (General)—His arrival in Boston; courteous reception, as successor to Governor Hutchinson; his character. i. 398.

Summons a meeting of the Legislature, which adjourns to meet at Salem, and which replies respectfully but firmly to Governor Gage's speech; his bitter answer. i. 399.

His curious dissolution of the last Legislature held in Massachusetts Bay according to its first charter, which had proceeded with closed doors, and adopted by a majority of 92 to 12, declaring the necessity of a meeting of all the Colonies to meet and consult together on their present state. i. 401.

GENERAL INDEX.

Governor of Massachusetts, and Commander-in-chief of the British in America, commences the first attack upon the Colonists. i. 460.

Governments of the British Provinces. ii. 271-276.
 (1) Nova Scotia. ii. 274-277.
 (2) New Brunswick. ii. 277-280.
 (3) Prince Edward Island. ii. 280.
 (4) Lower Canada. ii. 281-306.
  (See table of contents, chapter xlv.)
 (5) Upper Canada. ii. 307-316.
  (See table of contents, chapter xlvi.)

Governor of Massachusetts Bay Puritans and a majority of the assistants or magistrates vote in favour of submitting to the decision of the King on the conditions of perpetuating the Charter; but Congregational Ministers advise, and the majority of the deputies vote against it. i. 208, 209.

Governors of South and North Carolina (Campbell and Martin), like Dunmore, Governor of Virginia, betake themselves to ships—the Colonists in each case being treated with like severity. i. 473.

Haight (Canniff). ii. 219.

Happiness and prosperity of Massachusetts during seventy years under the second Charter. i. 240.

Harris (Mrs. Amelia). ii. 228-256.

Hessian soldiers—Their unreliable and bad character. ii. 73.

Hildreth, the historian, on the gloomy state of American affairs at the close of 1780. ii. 41.

Hillsborough (Earl of)—Effects of his circular letter to Colonial Governors. i. 345.
 Joy in the Colonies at his despatch promising to repeal the obnoxious revenue Acts, and to impose no more taxes on the Colonists by acts of the British Parliament. i. 361.

Holland—Flight of Pilgrim Fathers to; trades there. i. 10.

Howe (Lord)—A monument erected to his memory in Westminster Abbey, at the expense of £250 sterling, by the Massachusetts Court. i. 260.

Hutchinson (Governor of Massachusetts) and his sons alone determine to land the East India Company tea in Boston. i. 376.
 His account of the transactions at Boston, and vindication of himself. i. 383.
 His conduct different from that of the Governors of other Colonies. i. 387.

Independence disclaimed by Franklin in 1773, by Washington and Jefferson and by leading New Englanders in July, 1775. i. 451-453.

Independents, origin of. i. 7.

Indians—Employed by both French and English in their wars. ii. 75.
 Their employment in the war with the Colonies, opposed by the English Generals. ii. 76.
 Their employment disadvantageous to England. ii. 76.
 Their alliance and co-operation sought for by Congress. ii. 77.
 Retaliations upon them by the Congress soldiers exceeded all that had been committed by the Indians upon the Americans—opinion of American writers. ii. 77.
 Much that was written against them during the Revolution, since shown by the letters and biographies of its actors to have been fictitious. ii. 78.
 Their employment against the English recommended by Washington, July 27th, 1776. ii. 80.
 Efforts of General Burgoyne to restrain them from all cruel acts and excesses. ii. 82.
 Their conduct injurious to the English cause and beneficial to the American. ii. 83.
 The unprovoked invasion of their country, destruction of their settlements, and desolation of their towns, orchards, and crops and farms, by order of Congress. ii. 84.

Further examples of "retaliation," so-called, upon the Indian settlements. ii. 106.

The "Tories" driven among them as their only refuge, and treated as "traitors;" their conduct and duty. ii. 107.

Indians (Six Nations) — Colonel Stone's account in detail of General Sullivan's expedition of extermination against the Six Nations of Indians. ii. 108.

Indians—Treatment of by the Puritans in New England. ii. 293.

Intolerance and persecution of Baptists, Presbyterians, etc., by the Massachusetts Bay Rulers, from 1643 to 1651. i. 112.

Invasions of Canada by Americans; numbers of invaders. ii. 462.

James II.— Succession to the throne; thanked by the Massachusetts Bay Rulers for his Proclamation which violated the rights of England, and cost him his crown. i. 216.

Jarvis (Stephen). ii. 193.
(William). ii. 193.

Johnson's (Sir William) victory over the French General Dieskau. i. 250.

Jones (David). ii. 193.
(Jonathan). ii. 193.

King Charles the Second—Enjoins to cease persecuting the Quakers; how answered. i. 135.

The King retains Puritan councillors, who are kindly disposed to the Massachussetts Bay Puritans. i. 138.

The King's pardon and oblivion of the past misdeeds of the Massachussetts Bay Rulers, and promised continuance of Charter joyfully proclaimed; but the part of the letter containing the conditions of pardon, and oblivion, and toleration withheld from the public; and when the publication of it was absolutely commanded, the Massachusetts Bay Rulers ordered that the conditions of toleration, etc., should be suspended until further orders from their Court. i. 139-141.

Royal Commissioners appointed by the King, to inquire into the matters complained of in the New England Colonies, and to remedy what was wrong. i. 145.

Royal Commission appointed; slanderous rumours circulated against the Royal Commissioners. i. 146.

Copy of it explaining the reason and object of it. i. 147.

Duly received by all the New England Colonies except Massachusetts, where slanderous rumours were circulated against the Commission and Commissioners. i. 146, 147.

King Charles the Second's reply to the long address or petition of the Massachusetts Bay Court, dated February 25, 1665, correcting their misstatements and showing the groundlessness of their pretended fears and actual pretensions. i. 166.

Kind letter without effect upon the Massachusetts Bay Rulers, who refuse to receive the Royal Commissioners; second and more decisive letter from the King, April, 1666. i. 169.

Grants Charters to Connecticut and Rhode Island in 1663, with remarks upon them by Judge Story. i. 172.

On receiving the report of his Commissioners, who had been rejected by the Massachusetts Bay Rulers, orders them to send agents to England to answer before the King in Council to the complaints made against the Government of the Colony. i. 179.

Entreated by the Massachusetts Bay Rulers, who try to vindicate their proceedings, and instead of sending agents, send two large masts and resolve to send £1000 sterling to propitiate the King. i. 180.

Desists for some time from further action in regard to the Massachusetts Bay Rulers, but is at length roused to decisive action by complaints from neighbouring Colonists and individual citizens of the invasions of their rights, and persecutions and proscriptions inflicted upon them by the Massachusetts Bay Rulers. i. 187.

Seven requirements of the Massachusetts Bay Rulers, in his letter to them, dated July, 1679, just and reasonable, and observed by all British Colonies at this day. i. 188.

King George III.—Alleged author of the scheme with the East India Company; his condemnation of the petitions and remonstrances from the Colonies. i. 382.

His speech at the opening of the New Parliament, March 30th, 1774; and answers of both Houses. i. 419.

Opposition to the Royal Speech in both Houses; protest in the Lords. i. 420.

Denounces the Earl of Chatham and others. i. 424.

La Fayette returns from France in 1778, with a loan of money and reinforcements of land and naval forces. ii. 33.

Liberty (civil and religious) established in Massachusetts, not by the Puritans, but by Royal Charter. i. 237.

Lippincott (Captain Richard). ii. 193.

ong Parliament—Its ordinances in regard to Massachusetts trade in 1642. i. 87.

Appoints Commissioners and Governor General to Massachusetts Bay in 1646, with large powers. i. 88.

Orders the surrender of the Massachusetts Bay Charter; and means employed to evade it. i. 99, 100.

Loudoun (Earl of)—Arrival of from England, with troops, as Commander-in-chief. i. 252.

Disputes between him and the Massachusetts Court, in regard to the Mutiny Act, and quartering the troops upon the citizens. i. 255.

His arbitrary conduct in quartering his officers in Albany and New York. i. 258.

Hesitates and delays at Albany; never fought a battle in America. i. 259.

Loyalists—Circumstances of, after the surrender of Charleston to the French and Americans. ii. 46.

Unprotected in the articles of peace. ii. 57.

Constituted a majority of the population of the Colonies at the beginning of the contest. ii. 57.

Sacrificed in the treaty, as stated by Dr. Ramsay and Mr. Hildreth. ii. 59-61.

What demanded had been sanctioned by all modern civilized nations, in like circumstances. ii. 61.

Their deplorable condition during the war; utter abandonment by the English commissioners. ii. 64.

Much of what was written against the Revolution, since shown by the biographies and letters of its actors to be fictitious. ii. 77.

Summary of their condition and treatment. ii. 123.

Changes of their relation and condition by the Declaration of Independence. ii. 124.

The elements of their affectionate attachment to England. ii. 125.

The largest part of the population of the Colonies after the Declaration of Independence. ii. 124.

Their claims to have their rights and liberties restored. ii. 125.

Their position and character, described by Mr. Hildreth, and abused by mobs and oppressed by new Acts, and authorities. ii. 125.

First scene of severity against them; new American maxim of forgiving "Tories." ii. 127.

Their treatment in New York, Philadelphia, Virginia, and other places. ii. 128.

Legislative and executive acts against them. ii. 130-136.

GENERAL INDEX.

Rhode Island, Connecticut. ii. 130.

Massachusetts. ii. 131.

New Hampshire, Virginia, New York. ii. 131.

New Jersey, Pennsylvania, Delaware. ii. 132.

Maryland, North Carolina, Georgia, ii. 132.

South Carolina. ii. 136.

Their treatment on their applications for compensation after the Revolution. ii. 139-144.

Their treatment by the British Government and Parliament after the Revolution. ii. 159-182.

Refused compensation by the States of America, as proposed in the Treaty of Peace, and contrary to the practice of civilized nations. ii. 159.

Their compensation advocated in both Houses of Parliament. ii. 160, 163.

Their agents in England ; proceedings of Parliamentary Commission ; results. ii. 166-182.

Driven from the United States to the British Provinces ; and sketches of twenty-three of them. ii. 191-204.

Dr. Canniff's account of their first settlement on the North shore of the St. Lawrence and in the country around and West of Kingston. ii. 203-208.

Their adventures, sufferings, and first settlement in Canada, privations and labours, as written by themselves and their descendants. ii. 206-270.

(See table of contents, chapter xli.)

Loyalists — New penal laws passed against them after the Declaration of Independence. ii. 5.

Loyalists, in Massachusetts, who maintain in the Court and among the people, the Royal authority. i. 162.

The true Liberals of that day. i. 152.

Lundy's Lane—Battle of. ii. 438.

Marsden (Rev. J. W.). i. 298.

Maryland General Assembly's reply to the message of the Lt. Governor on Lord Hillsborough's circular. i. 344.

Massachusetts and other Colonial grateful acknowledgments to England for deliverance from the French and Spaniards. i. 27.

Massachusetts Bay Rulers persecute the Baptists, etc. i. 87.

Prohibit writing or speaking in favour of the King as a capital offence, but authorize it in favour of the Parliament. i. 87.

Petition Parliament in 1651, and address Cromwell in 1651, 1654. i. 108.

Massachusetts Bay Rulers' treatment of Cromwell at his death, and their professions in regard to Cromwell and Charles the Second at his restoration. i. 124.

They evade the conditions on which the King promised to continue the Charter, and deny the King's jurisdiction. i. 149.

They present a long address to the King, and enclose copies of it, with letters to Lord Chancellor Clarendon, the Earl of Manchester, Lord Say, and the Hon. Robert Boyle. i. 152.

Massachusetts Bay Rulers aggressors throughout upon the rights of the Sovereign and of their fellow-subjects. i. 75.

They side with the Long Parliament and Cromwell ; their first address and commissioners to. i. 86.

They pass Acts for publication in England, and then adopt measures to prevent their execution in Massachusetts—such as the Navigation Act, Oath of Allegiance, the Franchise, Liberty of Worship, and Persecution of the Baptists and Quakers. i. 195.

They bribe Clerks in the Privy Council, and offer a bribe to the King. i. 205.

Their double game played out. i. 204.

Massachusetts circular displeasing to the British Ministry. i. 341.

Circular from Lord Hillsborough, Secretary of State for the Colonies. i. 341.

Massachusetts compensated by Parliament. i. 267.

Benefited by the English and French war. i. 270.

Massachusetts General Assembly refuse to legislate under the guns of a land and naval force. i. 357.

General Assembly—Its proceedings on the quartering of troops in Boston. i. 358.

Massachusetts never acknowledged the Act of Parliament changing its constitution without its consent. i. 407.

Its proceedings before the affairs of Lexington and Concord to enlist the Indians. ii. 79.

Massachusetts Legislative Assembly's noble circular to the Assemblies of other Colonies, on the unconstitutional and oppressive acts of the British Parliament. i. 338.

Massachusetts—Seed-plot of the American Revolution. i. 1.

First emigration to. i. 1.

Mahon (Lord)—His reflections on the American contest; apology for George III.; unhappiness of the Americans since the Revolution; unity of the Anglo-Saxon race. ii. 154.

Mather (Rev. Dr. Increase) makes a violent speech—appeals from man to God—decision against him. i. 209.

His proceedings in England. i. 226.

Fails to get the first Charter restored. i. 228.

First protests against the second Royal Charter, then thanks King William for it. i. 229.

Merritt (Thomas). ii. 196.

McDonald (Alexander). ii. 195.

McGill (John). 196.

McGillis (Donald). ii. 196.

McNab (Allan). ii. 202.

Moneys provided for the war, abstracted from England and expended in the Colonies. i. 270.

Montcalm, French General, captures Forts Oswego and William Henry. i. 253.

Morris (Roger). ii. 200.

Montreal besieged and taken from the French. i. 267.

Navigation Act passed by the Long Parliament in 1651, oppressive to the Southern Colonies, but regularly evaded in Massachusetts by collusion with Cromwell. i. 111.

Neal (the Puritan historian) deprecates the persecutions by the Massachusetts Bay Rulers. i. 120.

Newark (now Niagara)—Seat of Government of Upper Canada first established there. ii. 308.

Burned by the Americans. ii. 423.

New England—Two distinct emigrations to. i. 1.

Two separate Governments in for seventy years, and characteristics of each. i. 1.

New Plymouth—Original name of —first Sabbath in. i. 7.

First mild winter and early vegetation at. i. 8.

First "Harvest-home." i. 9.

Their government, toleration, oath of allegiance, loyalty. i. 15.

Their answers to the King's Commissioners. i. 18.

The melancholy end of their government. i. 22.

The loyalty and enterprise of their descendants. i. 23.

Ancestors of English Peers. i. 23.

New York—First Act of Parliament against. i. 329.

New York Legislature, which had not endorsed the first continental Congress, in 1774, now petitions Parliament on the subject of Colonial grievances; but its petition, presented by Mr. Burke, defended by Mr. Fox and others, is refused to be received, on motion of Lord North, by a majority of 186 to 67, and the Lords reject the same petition. i. 434-440.

Niagara (Newark) taken from the French by the English. i. 263.

Nineteen years' evasion by the Massachusetts Bay Rulers of the conditions on which King Charles II. promised to perpetuate their Charter. i. 193.

North (Lord)—His Bill to repeal the Colonial Revenue Acts, except the duty on tea. i. 368.
  His agreement with the East India Company rouses and intensifies opposition in America. i. 371.
  Combined opposition to it by English merchants and the Colonists. i. 372.
  Explains his American policy. i. 394.
  His resolution for address to the King, 1775, endorsing the coercive policy, and denouncing Colonial complaints as "rebellion;" debates on it. i. 426-429.
  Second great debate in the Commons on his warlike resolution. i. 430.
  His address made the joint address of both Houses of Parliament; the King's reply. i. 431.
  Lord North's proposed resignation and preparations for it. ii. 8.
  Defeat of his Administration. ii. 51.

Opinions of Lords Macaulay and Mahon on the success of a Commission recommended by the Earl of Chatham. ii. 8.

Origin of non-importation agreement in New York; sanctioned by persons in the highest stations. i. 360.

Origin of republicanism and hatred of monarchy in America. ii. 66.

Paine (Tom)—His appeal to the Colonists, called *Common Sense*, the first publication in America against monarchy. i. 450.
  Author of republicanism and hatred of monarchy in America; his character and writings, and their effects. ii. 66-72.

Palfrey's and other New England historians' unfair statements and unjust imputations against the British Government of that time. i. 190, 211.

Parliament—Its authority over the Colonies. i. 317.
  Three Bills passed by, to raise a revenue in the Colonies. i. 331.

Parliament passes an Act (1775) to punish the Colonies for countenancing Massachusetts. i. 433.

Parliament passes oppressive Acts in 1775 and 1776, with measures for employing foreign soldiers, Indians, and slaves against the complaining Colonists. i. 459.

Parliament passes no Act to authorize peace with America for three months after the accession of the new Ministry. ii. 54.

Parliament votes £115,000 sterling to compensate the Colonies for expenses incurred by them. i. 252.

Parties—Origin of political parties at Massachusetts Bay. i. 209.

Petitions and representations to the King from Episcopalians, Presbyterians, Baptists, etc., in Massachusetts Bay, on their persecutions and disfranchisement by the local Government. i. 137.

Petitions from various towns in England, Scotland, and Ireland against Lord North's coercive American policy. i. 425.

Pilgrim Fathers—who. i. 2.
  Their settlement, and residence of 12 years in Holland. i. 3.
  Long to be under the English Government. i. 3.
  Cross the Atlantic in the *Mayflower*. i. 3.
  Where intended to settle in America. i. 4.
  What known of Cape Cod before the Pilgrims landed. i. 4.
  Their agreement and constitution of government before landing. i. 5.
  Remarks upon it by Messrs. Bancroft and Young. i. 6.

GENERAL INDEX. 487

Inflated American accounts of their voyage. i. 7.

Their first "Harvest-home." i. 9.

Pitt (afterwards Earl of Chatham) changes the whole fortune of the war with the French in America in favour of England. i. 260.

Policy of the British Ministry in employing foreign soldiers and Indians, deprecated by all classes in Europe and America. ii. 72-74.

Pownall (Governor)—His speech and amendment in the House of Commons to repeal the duty on tea; rejected by a majority 242 to 204. i. 361.

Preface—The reason and objects of writing the history of the Loyalists of America. i. 3-5.

Protests and Loyal Petitions of the Colonists against English Parliamentary Acts to raise a rvenue in the Colonies. i. 337.

Puritan authorities alone adduced in this historical discussion. i. 59.

Puritan letters suppressed by the biographer of Governor Winthrop. i. 59.

Puritans of Massachusetts Bay Company. i. 24.
Their Charter and settlement in 1629. i. 23.
Their intolerance. i. 24.
Their wealth and trade. i. 25.
Their enterprise under two aspects. i. 26.
Professed members of the Church of England when they left England. i. 26.

Puritan treatment of the Indians. i. 298.

Puritan legal opinions in England on the constant violation of the first Charter by the Massachusetts Bay Rulers. i. 233.

Quebec taken by General Wolfe. i. 263.

Queenston Heights—Battle of. ii. 365-8.

Quo Warranto—Notice of sent to the Rulers of Massachusetts Bay in July, 1683, to answer to thirteen complaints against them for violating the Royal Charter; received in October, 1683; judgment given July, 1685, nearly two years afterwards. i. 208-211.

Remonstrances of the Rev. Drs. Owen, T. Goodwin, and other Nonconformist ministers in England against the persecutions by the Massachusetts Bay Puritans. i. 185.

Retrospect of the transactions between Charles I. and II. and the Massachusetts Bay Rulers from 1630 to 1666, with extracts of correspondence. i. 171.

Revolution—Principal characteristics of it, and the feeling which should now be cultivated by both of the former contending parties; by J. M. Ludlow. ii. 145.

Richardson (Rev. James)—Letter by. ii. 208.

Robinson (Beverley). ii. 196.

Robinson (Christopher). ii. 198.

Robinson (Sir J. B.). ii. 199.

Robinson (Sir C. K. P.). ii. 199.

Robinson (Morris). ii. 199.

Robinson (John). ii. 200.

Rockingham (Marquis of)—His death and its consequences. ii. 53.

Royal Charter (second) by William and Mary; nine principal provisions of it, establishing for the first time civil and religious liberty in Massachusetts. i. 229-233.

Royal Charter to Massachusetts Bay Puritans. i. 28.
Its provisions. i. 30.
Violated by the Massachusetts Bay Puritans. i. 33.
Transferred from England to Massachusetts Bay, and the fact concealed for four years. i. 69.

Royal Commission issued to examine into the complaints made against the Massachusetts Bay Rulers—conduct of parties. i. 72.

Royal Commissioners' Report on the Colony of Massachusetts Bay; twenty anomalies in its laws inconsistent with the Royal Charter; evades the conditions of the promised continuance of the Charter; denies the King's jurisdiction. i. 149.

Royal Patriotic Society of Upper Canada and its doings. ii. 464.

Royal Speech on meeting Parliament, October 26th, 1775, and discussions upon it. i. 474.

Ryerse (Rev. George)—Letter by. ii. 226.

Ryerse (Colonel Samuel). ii. 229.

Ryerson (Colonel Joseph). ii. 257.

Salaries of officials paid independent of the Colonies - cause of dissatisfaction. i. 366.

Saltonstall (Sir Richard) remonstrates against the persecutions by the Massachusetts Bay Rulers. i. 116.

Scadding (Rev. Dr.)—Sketch by. ii. 259.

Second Charter—Its happy influence upon toleration, loyalty, peace, and unity of society in Massachusetts. i. 237.

Seven years of war and bloodshed prevented, had Congress in 1776 adhered to its previous professions. ii. 56.

Shelburne (Earl of)—Correspondence with Dr. Franklin on negotiations for peace. ii. 54.

Simcoe (General Graves)—First Governor of Upper Canada. ii. 308.

Soldiers—The humiliating position of soldiers in Boston. i. 360.
   Insulted, abused, and collisions with the inhabitants. i. 365.

Spain joins France against England in 1779. ii. 28.

Spohn (Mrs. E. B.)—Paper by. ii. 264.

Stamp Act and its effects in America. i. 283.
   Virginia leads the opposition against it. i. 287.
   Riots in Boston against it. i. 288.
   Petitions in England against it. i. 291.
   Its repeal and rejoicings at it. i. 323.
   Extracts from speeches respecting it by Charles Townsend and Colonel Barré, and remarks upon them. i. 296.
   Extracts from the speeches of Lords Chatham and Camden on the passing and repeal of the Stamp Act. i. 302.
   Summary of events from its repeal, March, 1766, to the end of the year. i. 323-336.

Statements of the historians Hutchinson and Neal on the persecutions by the Massachusetts Bay Puritans. i. 185.

Story (Judge) on the happy influence of the second Charter, and improved legislation and progress of the Colony under it. i. 235.

Tea Duty Act virtually defeated in America. i. 370.
   Opposition to it represented in England as "rebellion," and the advocates of Colonial rights as "rebels" and "traitors." i. 388.

Tea—Duty of threepence per pound, to be paid in America into the British Treasury, continued. i. 363.

Three Acts of Parliament passed to remove all grounds of complaint on the part of the Colonists. ii. 6.

Ticonderago taken by the English. i. 263.

Treaty of Peace between Great Britain and the United States; rights and interests of the Loyalists sacrificed by it; omissions in it; protests against it in Parliament. ii. 164, 165.

Vane (Sir Henry) remonstrates against the persecutions by the Massachusetts Bay Rulers. i. 116.

Vice-Admiralty Courts and the Navy employed as custom-house offices in the Colonies. i. 331.

GENERAL INDEX. 489

Virginia House of Burgess's admirable answer to the Massachusetts Circular, 1668, and similar replies from other Colonies. i. 342, 343.
Rejects Lord North's so-called "conciliatory proposition" to the Colonies. i. 464.
Its traditional loyalty of Virginians, and their aversion to revolutions; but resolved to defend their rights. i. 464.
Remonstrate with Lord Dunmore for leaving the seat of his government and going on board of a vessel; assure him and his family of perfect safety by remaining at Williamsburg. i. 467.
Are horror-struck at Lord Dunmore's threat and proclamation to free the slaves. i. 465.
Moved by his fears, goes on board of ship, twelve miles from the seat of government. i. 466.
Attempts to destroy the town of Hampton; reduces to ashes the town of Norfolk, then the first commercial city in Virginia. i. 467, 471.
His conduct unlawful and inhuman; English accounts of his conduct. i. 470, 472.

War formally declared between England and France in 1756. i. 252.

War party and corrupt Administration defeated in the House of Commons, 1782. ii. 49.

War by the United States against Great Britain, 1812-1815. ii. 316-330.
(See table of contents, chapters xlvii., xlviii., xlix., l., li., lii., liii., liv., lv., lvi., lvii., lviii.)

War—Close of; remarks; conclusion. (See table of contents, chapter lx.)

Washington—Weakness of his army and depression of American finances in 1778. ii. 32.

His despondency without funds. ii. 41.
With the French commander plans an expedition to the South. ii. 42.
His skill and courage. ii. 47.
Washington recommended by Dunwiddie, Governor of Virginia, but his services are not recognised. i. 257.
Washington, under date of July 27th, 1776, recommends the employment of the Indians in the Revolutionary Cause. ii. 80.
Watts (Rev. Isaac)—A remarkable letter from him addressed to the Rev. Dr. Cotton Mather, explanatory of Neal's History of New England, on "the persecuting principles and practices of the first planters," and urging the formal repeal of the "cruel and sanguinary statutes" which had been passed by the Massachusetts Bay Court under the first Charter. i. 239.
White (Rev. John), projector and founder of the Massachusetts Bay Settlement. i. 26-28.
Wolfe (General)—His heroism at Louisburg. i. 262.
Takes Quebec. i. 263.
Wyoming—The massacre of, original inflated accounts of. ii. 85.
Four versions of it, by accredited American historians—Dr. Ramsay, Mr. Bancroft, Mr. Tucker, and Mr. Hildreth. ii. 85-90.
Discrepancies in four essential particulars of these four accounts. ii. 92.
Supplementary remarks upon, by the author of the Life of Joseph Brant, etc. ii. 94.
Massacre (alleged) of Wyoming—American retaliation for. ii. 99-106.
(See table of contents, chapter xxxv.)

ERRATA.

Vol. I.

Page 101, line 21, for "American" read "Armenian."
" 113, " 22, for "Pinchion" read "Pynchion."
" 113, " 16, for "some" read "years."
" 147, " 8, of note, the letter "r" is omitted in word "received."
" 147, " 30, " for "Road" read "Rhode."
" 243, " 12, for "Madras" read "Louisburg."
" 243, " 13, for "Louisburg" read "Madras."
" 250, " 1, for "man" read "war."
" 250, " 2, for "not" read "as."
" 298, " 10, of note, for "F. B. Marsden" read "J. B. Marsden."

Vol. II.

Page 57, line 13, for word "nearly" read "newly."
" 81, " 16, for word "retorted" read "reiterated."
" 197, " 36, for "Ragier" read "Roger."
" 205, " 2, for "Sherman" read "Sherwood."
" 235, " 17, for "Woodstock" read "London."
" 232-247, for "Proyer" read "Troyer."
" 240, line 6, for "mother" read "brother."
" 242, " 20, for "awkward" read "ill-natured."
" 245, " 38, for "stream" read "seine."
" 256, " 39, for "Ryerse" read "Ryerson."
" 308, " 36, for "burned" read "braved."

www.ingramcontent.com/pod-product-compliance
Lightning Source LLC
Chambersburg PA
CBHW051159300426
44116CB00006B/365